PARADISE AND PARADIGM

PARADISE AND PARADIGM

Key Symbols in Persian Christianity and the Bahā'ī Faith

Christopher Buck

State University of New York Press

Published by
State University of New York Press, Albany

Printed in the United States of America

For information, address State University of New York Press
State University Plaza, Albany, New York 12246

Production by Dana Foote
Marketing by Patrick Durocher
Cover illustration by Shiew-Yeu Loh

Library of Congress Cataloging-in-Publication Data

Buck, Christopher, 1950–
Paradise and paradigm : key symbols in Persian Christianity and the Baha'i Faith / Christopher Buck.
p. cm.
Includes bibliographical references and index.
ISBN 0-7914-4061-3 (hc : alk. paper)
ISBN 0-7914-4062-1 (pb : alk. paper)
1. Heaven—Baha'i Faith. 2. Baha'i Faith—Doctrines. 3. Heaven—Christianity—History of doctrines—Early church, ca. 30–600. 4. Syrian Church—Doctrines—History. 5. Heaven—Comparative studies. 6. Paradise—Comparative studies. I. Title.
BP388.H43 B83 1999
291.2'3—dc21
98-45882
CIP

10 9 8 7 6 5 4 3 2 1

For Nahzy Abadi Buck,
Takor, and Taraz

Icon of St. Ephrem in Theotokos Church in Diyarbakır, Turkey, 1218 C.E. Photograph courtesy of Gabriel Rabo.

'Abdu'l-Bahā, 1912. Photograph from the collection of Mr. Albert C. Killius. Courtesy of the Spiritual Assembly of the Bahā'īs of Springfield, Illinois.

From St. Ephrem the Syrian
An Ode on Noah and the Ark

O NOBLE NOAH!
Chorus: *Glory, Lord, to Thee!*
Afloat in the Flood, the All-
Ruler's Ark emerged
from the East; she winged to
the West,
wheeled South and then
sealed the North . . .
To her Saviour sing!
Her sequence sketched her
Defender's Device:
her course traced a cross!

With water and wood, Noah,
salt of the sea,
the Church did portray . . .
Myth and mystery,
Ark and Torah tell the self-same
story! . . .

Naves echo the Ark,
whose meaning they mark . . .
Faith (though I be frail) shall be,
Lord, my ship!
All those drown in doubt,
who would work Thee out!
To Thy Sire we shout!

Saint Ephrem the Syrian
(d. 373 C.E.)
An Ode on Noah and the Ark
(363–373)
(*Hymns on Faith* XLIX. 1; 3–6)
Translated by Andrew Palmer
(1993, 175).

From Bahā'u'llāh
"Song of the Holy Mariner"

O HOLY MARINER!
Refrain: *Glorified be my Lord, the*
All-Glorious!
Bid thine Ark of eternity appear
before the Celestial Concourse.
Launch it upon the ancient sea,
in His Name, the Most
Wondrous . . . .
Unmoor it, then, that it may sail
upon the ocean of glory . . .

O Mariner!
Teach them that are within the ark
that which We have taught thee
behind the mystic veil.

Perchance they may not tarry
in the sacred snow-white spot.
But may soar upon the wings of the
spirit
unto that station which the Lord
hath exalted
above all mention in the worlds
below . . .
May know the mysteries hidden in
the Seas of light.

Bahā'u'llāh (d. 1892 C.E.)
Song [or Tablet] of the Holy
Mariner (1863)
(Arabic section)
Translated by Shoghi Effendi
(1922).

Contents

Acknowledgments

This study was originally a dissertation researched at the Centre for the Study of Religion, University of Toronto (Canada's "Harvard of the North"), during Dr. Jane McAuliffe's tenure as director. It is therefore fitting that I acknowledge the members of my advisory committee: my Ph.D. supervisor, Dr. Willard G. Oxtoby (Trinity College), Dr. John Corbett (Scarborough College), and Dr. Maria Subtelny (University of Toronto), who replaced Dr. B. Todd Lawson (Institute of Islamic Studies, McGill University) as the third committee member.

As a dissertation, *Paradise and Paradigm* was successfully defended on 21 June 1996. Dr. Jonathan Z. Smith, Robert O. Anderson Distinguished Service Professor of the Humanities, University of Chicago, served as my external examiner. Dr. Smith's dissertation appraisal begins with this assessment: "Mr. Buck's thesis is a superior piece of work, one of the most sophisticated exercises on comparison that I have read, and, therefore, a work of historic importance with respect to the study of 'patristic' Christianity, a field that is notably 'primitive' with respect to comparative issues. Of the nearly one hundred dissertations I have served as director or reader for, in the fields of history of religions and early Christianities, this is, without question, one of the two or three best." Having closely followed the work of Jonathan Z. Smith over the years, to have had this brief personal and professional interaction with him has been profoundly inspirational.

All those who assisted me in researching Syriac and Bahā'ī primary and secondary sources contributed to the success of the project, as acclaimed by J. Z. Smith further in his appraisal: "The extraction of the central symbolic logic of both the Syriac and Bahā'ī materials is utterly convincing . . . This, then, contributes to a comparison across differences of the logics which richly illuminates both the specific symbols and the cultural matrix in which they are found." To Prof. Amir Harrak for his close reading of the manuscript, for the benefit of his linguistic expertise and for his uncanny acumen in making corrections and proposing revisions, I express my heartfelt appreciation. For their assistance with Syriac texts, I would like to thank His Grace Mar Emmanuel, Diocesan Bishop, Holy Apostolic Catholic Assyrian Church of the East, Diocese of Canada, and Bishop Mar Bawai Soro,

General Secretary of the Assyrian Church of the East in the United States. I would also like to thank Prof. Sidney Griffith of the Catholic University of America, and Prof. Edward G. Mathews, Jr., of Scranton University, for answering a number of questions of mine pertaining to both Ephrem and related Syriac texts. I am likewise indebted to Mr. Francis Sarguis, English language editor of the *Journal of the Assyrian Academic Society*, for having read and edited portions of this manuscript. For their research assistance in searching Baḥā'ī texts, I would like to thank Dr. Robert Stockman, Mr. Jonah Winters, and Mr. Sen McGlinn. My thanks to Dr. Juan R. I. Cole (University of Michigan) for his manuscript, *Modernity and the Millennium: The Genesis of the Bahā'ī Faith in the Nineteenth Century Middle East* (Columbia University Press, 1998), and for some important references.

For their support and encouragement, I acknowledge my colleagues at Millikin University: Provost Thomas Flynn, Dean Mauri Ditzler (Arts and Sciences), my current Chair, Dr. Edward Yonan (Religion), Dr. Kevin Murphy (History), Dr. Arvid Adell (Philosophy), Dr. Jo Ellen Jacobs (Philosophy), and to my newest colleague, my wife, Nahzy Abadi Buck (History). She has spent countless hours, late at night, supervising my laborious reading of Persian and Arabic texts. Her patience was surely tested by my complaints over irregularities in Persian orthography and printing, in the course of my becoming naturalized to the idiosyncrasies of another language and another, as it were, "soul." She has been gracious, staunch, and faithful in her support for my graduate work, as have my boys, Takor and Taraz. My thanks also to my colleagues at Carleton University, where I lectured from 1994 to 1996: Dr. Joseph Ramisch (former Chair of Religion), Ms. Maureen Sherman (administrator), and Carole Dence, Nestor Querido, and Dianne Tushingham (Teaching and Learning Resource Centre).

A special debt of gratitude is owed to my editor, Ms. Nancy Ellegate of State University of New York Press, who took an initial interest in the manuscript, acting on Jonathan Z. Smith's recommendation in his dissertation appraisal: "This is one of those rare theses in which the parts are so intricately and necessarily interrelated that one hopes for the rapid publication of the entire work rather than the separate publication of one or two chapters." Having first solicited peer reviews from two external readers, Ms. Ellegate guided me through the revision process, subsequent to and substantively based on the readers' reports. I wish to thank both external readers for their professionalism and valuable critiques. Dr. Robert Cummings Neville (Boston University), who opted to be named following the double-blind review, contributed greatly to the crystallization of my thinking on methodology, which, although eclectic, I have done my best to make explicit. I should also like to thank Ms. Dana Foote, freelance production editor for

State University of New York Press, who directed the production of this book.

To my new-found Assyrian friends in cyberspace and in print, I wish to express my gratitude for all of your encouragement and interest in my research, and for graciously welcoming an outsider into so rich and historic a Christian culture. It is my heartfelt wish that neither Christians (especially those of Assyrian, Chaldean, Syrian, and Aramaean heritages) nor Bahā'īs, will take offense at my work, as I have endeavored, to the utmost of my ability, to treat both Christian and Bahā'ī traditions with symmetry and a profound sense of respect, without privileging one tradition over another, as I aim for parity in the comparison.

Christopher Buck
Millikin University

Copyright Permissions

The author and publisher of this volume express appreciation to the following publishers and authors for permission to reprint excerpts from their respective copyrighted works:

1. **E. J. Brill:** Andrew Palmer. "The Merchant of Nisibis: Saint Ephrem and His Faithful Quest for Union in Numbers." In J. Den Boeft and A. Hilhorst, eds. *Early Christian Poetry: A Collection of Essays.* Supplements to *Vigiliae Christianae* 22. Leiden: E. J. Brill, 1993, pp. 167–233. Reprinted by permission of the publisher.
2. **Oxford University Press:** Ephrem the Syrian. *Saint Ephrem's Commentary: An English Translation of Chester Beatty MS 709 with Introduction and Notes.* Edited and translated by Carmel McCarthy. Journal of Semitic Studies Supplement, 2. Oxford University Press, 1993. Reprinted by permission of the publisher.
3. **Cambridge University Press** and **Robert P. R. Murray, S.J.:** Robert Murray. *Symbols of Church and Kingdom: A Study in Early Syriac Tradition.* Cambridge University Press, 1975. Reprinted by permission of the author. Reprinted with the permission of Cambridge University Press.
4. **Catholic University of America Press:** Ephrem the Syrian. *St. Ephrem the Syrian: Selected Prose Works.* Translated by Edward G. Mathews and Joseph P. Amar. Edited by Kathleen McVey. The Fathers of the Church, vol. 91. Washington, D.C.: Catholic University of America Press, 1994. Reprinted by permission of the publisher.
5. **Paulist Press:** Ephrem the Syrian. *Ephrem the Syrian: Hymns.* Kathleen McVey, trans. New York: Paulist Press, 1989. ©1989 by Kathleen E. McVey. Used by permission of Paulist Press.

6. **St. Vladimir's Seminary Press:** Ephrem the Syrian. *Hymns on Paradise.* Trans. by Sebastian Brock. Crestwood, N.Y.: St. Vladimir's Seminary Press, 1990. Reprinted by permission of St. Vladimir's Seminary Press, 575 Scarsdale Road, Crestwood, NY 10707, 1-800-204-2665.

7. **Bahā'ī Publications:** For excerpts from the following works of Bahā'u'llāh: *Gleanings from the Writings of Bahā'u'llāh; The Hidden Words; The Seven Valleys and the Four Valleys; Epistle to the Son of the Wolf; The Book of Certitude; Bahā'ī Prayers*; and for excerpts from the following works of 'Abdu'l-Bahā: *A Traveller's Narrative; Secret of Divine Civilization; Promulgation of Universal Peace.*

8. **Journal of Assyrian Academic Studies** (formerly, **Journal of the Assyrian Academic Society**): Christopher Buck. "Sapiential *Theōsis:* A New Reading of Ephrem the Syrian's *Hymns on Paradise.*" *Journal of the Assyrian Academic Society* 9.2 (1995), 80–125. Reprinted by permission of the publisher; and Christopher Buck. "The Universality of the Church of the East: How Persian Was Persian Christianity?" *Journal of the Assyrian Academic Society* 10.1 (1996), 54–95. Reprinted by permission of the publisher.

9. **Tryggve Kronholm:** Author of *Motifs from Genesis 1–11 in the Genuine Hymns of Ephrem the Syrian with Particular Reference to the Influence of Jewish Exegetical Tradition.* Coniectanea Biblica, Old Testament Series 11; Lund, Sweden: CWK Gleerup, 1978. Reprinted by permission of the author.

10. **Kalimát Press:** Moojan Momen, editor. *Studies in Honor of the Late Hasan M. Balyuzi.* Studies in the Bābī and Bahā'ī Religions, 5. Los Angeles: Kalimát Press, 1988. Steven Scholl, editor. *Waging Peace: Selections from the Bahā'ī Writings on Universal Peace.* Los Angeles: Kalimát Press, 1984. Excerpts from both titles reprinted by permission of the publisher.

11. **The Universal House of Justice, Bahā'ī World Centre:** For permission to publish the authorized translation of the Bahā'u'llāh's Tablets of the Hair. Bahā'u'llāh, *Tablets of Bahā'u'llāh Revealed after the Kitāb-i-Aqdas.* Haifa: Bahā'ī World Centre, 1978. Trans. by Habib Taherzadeh et al. Reprinted by permission of the publisher.

12. **George Ronald, Publisher:** Wendi Momen, ed. *A Basic Bahā'ī Dictionary*. Oxford: George Ronald, Publisher, 1988. Reprinted by permission of the publisher.

Prior Presentations and Publications

While a work-in-progress, portions of *Paradise and Paradigm* were originally presented as conferences papers and published as journal articles. These include:

- Highlights of chapters 1, 3, and 5 ("Comparing Symbol Profiles: Dimensional Models of the Bahā'ī Faith and Syriac Christianity") were presented as a paper read at the conference "Syriac Symposium II: Syria at the Crossroads: Cultural Interchange in Late Antiquity" (Washington, D.C.), 9 June 1995.
- Part of chapter 2 (section 2.3) was published as "The Universality of the Church of the East: How Persian was Persian Christianity?" *Journal of the Assyrian Academic Society* 10.1 (1996), 54–95.
- Part of chapter 4 (section 4.2) was presented as a paper, "Sacralizing the Secular: The Proclamatory Aqdas as a Response to Modernity." Read at the Fifth Scripture Studies Colloquium. Theme: The Kitāb-i-Aqdas. Institute for Bahā'ī Studies/Haj Mehdi Arjmand Memorial Fund (Wilmette, Illinois), 1 April 1995.
- With the kind permission of State University of New York Press, chapter 5, "A Symbolic Profile of the Bahā'ī Faith" is published in the *Journal of Bahā'ī Studies* 8.4 (1–48, 1998), original drafts of which were presented at three conferences: (1) 19th Annual Conference of the Association for Bahā'ī Studies North America (San Francisco), 10 Oct. 1995, (2) American Academy of Religion/Society of Biblical Literature Annual Meeting (Philadelphia), Bahā'ī Studies Colloquy (substitute paper), 19 Nov. 1995; (3) Texas Bahā'ī Studies Conference (Austin, Texas), 26 Nov. 1995.
- Part of chapter 7 (section 7.1) was published as "Sapiential *Theōsis:* A New Reading of Ephrem the Syrian's *Hymns on Paradise*." *Journal of the Assyrian Academic Society* 9.2 (1995), 80–125.
- The Syriac transliteration table on p. 438 is taken from my paper: "Computing Strategies for Transliterating Syriac." In SyrCOM-95: *Proceedings of the First International Forum on Syriac Computing* (in association with Syriac Symposium II), edited by G. A. Kiraz. Cambridge: Syriac Computing Institute, 1995. Postconference, on-demand proceeedings volume, pp. 113–26.

I

Comparing Paradises

Objective

Religions enshrine symbols, the stained glass windows of faith. Sacred symbols present an explorable treasury of religious thought—an information-rich, condensed language of spirituality. Symbols are the prisms of ideals and of other religious concerns. Symbols are susceptible to analysis and are proper objects of study. As symbols encode ideas, they require interpretation to be both understood and meaningfully compared. "We can see that an essential ingredient of the modern study of religion," writes Ninian Smart, "is *symbolic analysis*, which tries to throw light on the various themes which can be discovered cross-culturally through the exploration of various worldviews" (1985, 33). Symbolic analysis involves not only the exploration of religious worldviews intrinsically, but comparatively as well.

The scientific study of religion is said to have two levels of research: historical and comparative (Platvoet 1982, 3), as exemplified in the complementary research endeavors known as the History of Religion and the Phenomenology of Religion. Disciplined comparison, it has been said, is the central activity of the phenomenology of religion. Comparison creates perspective. By it, religions—systemically or aspectually—are mentally viewed together, with some kind of depth and sense of relationship. This study introduces a new comparative procedure in the academic study of religion: viz., the construction and comparison of multidimensional, symbolic profiles representing distinct religious worldviews—an experiment in comparative method. Correlating symbol and doctrine—the heart and soul of religion—this book attempts to resolve the similarity-difference paradox in two culturally related Abrahamic traditions in the Iranian context—early Persian Christianity and the Bahā'ī Faith—with special reference to Paradise imagery and its symbolic transformation, from Late Antiquity to modernity. While "Paradise" is originally a Persian loan word, modernity has revolutionized its meaning.

The preinterpretative justification for setting this investigative agenda should be made clear. In the interests of investigating religious transformations from the ancient to the modern world, the religion known as the Bahā'ī Faith affords a natural and obvious starting point for "working backwards." Born in the full light of modernity, the Bahā'ī Faith is an independent world religion, with Islamic origins. Charismatically established in 1863 in Baghdad by Mīrzā Ḥusayn-'Alī Nūrī Bahā' Allāh/official Bahā'ī spelling, Bahā'u'llāh ("Glory of God," 1817–92), a leader of the Persian Bābī movement out of which the Bahā'ī religion emerged, and constituted as a distinct faith-community in Adrianople in 1866, the Bahā'ī religion underwent transformations in ethos and organization throughout its three missionary phases, periods marked by the Islamic context (1844–92), international expansion to America and abroad (1892–1963), and global diffusion to nearly every country in the world (1963–present).

The Islamic context is coextensive with the ministries of both Bahā'u'llāh and his precursor, Sayyid 'Alī-Muḥammad Shīrāzī (1819–50), the prophet-martyr known as the Bāb ("Gate"). The Bāb had already effected an eschatological break from Islam by "revealing" what was universally regarded by Bābīs as a new Qur'ān (viz., the *Qayyūm al-Asmā'*) and law code (enacted in the *Bayān-i Fārsī*). While the Bāb's law code was formally distinct from the Islamic *sharī'a*, paradoxically the Bābī system was super-Islamic in the intensity of the piety it required, but supra-Islamic in ethos, having superseded the authority of both Qur'ān and *ḥadīth*.

Except for a two-year hiatus (1854–56) spent in solitude as a dervish, Bahā'u'llāh emerged as one of, if not the most effective leader of the Bābī exiles throughout the Baghdad period (1853–63), a period eschatologically charged with his own messianic secrecy. In his preeminent doctrinal work, the *Kitāb-i Īqān* ("Book of Certitude," 1861 [1974]), extemporaneously revealed in two days and two nights, Baha'u'llah advanced an extended quranic and biblical argument legitimizing the prophetic authenticity of the Bāb. This served as an oblique, advance legitimation for Bahā'u'llāh himself, who, in April 1863, announced his own role as "He Whom God Shall Manifest" (*man-Yuẓhiruhu'llāh*), the messianic theophany foretold by the Bāb. In public epistles to Queen Victoria, Napoleon III, Pope Pius IX, and other monarchs and religious leaders during the Adrianople period (1864–68) and in the early 'Akkā period (1868–92), Bahā'u'llāh announced his advent as the "World-Unifier" and "Promised One" of all religions. This was essentially a millenarian claim to multiple messiahship (viz., Ḥusayn *redivivus* for Shī'īs, the "Spirit of Truth" or *Parousia* of Christ for Christians, the "Everlasting Father" [Isaiah 9:6] for Jews, and Shāh Bahrām Varjāvand for Zoroastrians). The *kerygma*, or gospel, of this messianic claimant was a message that addressed modernity and, by extension, postmodernity.

In his proclamations to crown and mitre and universally to the "peoples of the world," Bahā'u'llāh advocated world peace, parliamentary democracy, disarmament, an international language, harmony of science and religion, interfaith concord, gender and racial equality, and other reforms, all of which were integrated by an overarching paradigm of world unity. Granting that these were modernist reforms, Baha'u'llah's response to modernity was to make peace sacred. In a precocious religious preparation for a global society, Bahā'u'llāh sacralized certain developments within the secular world (such as the abolition of slavery, governance modelled on the British parliamentary system, etc.), and promoted world reforms that went beyond the purview of Islamic reform advocated by contemporary Ottoman and Persian modernists.

Structurally precluding major schisms by designating successorship and the formation of democratically elected religious institutions, Bahā'u'llāh's Covenant (symbolized as "the Crimson Ark") became the organizing principle of the Bahā'ī community itself and the guarantor of its integrity as a community. In his Book of the Covenant (*Kitāb-i 'Ahd*), Baha'u'llah designated his eldest son 'Abdu'l-Bahā (d. 1921) as interpreter, exemplar, and successor, and who, in his *Will and Testament*, passed the torch of leadership to his Oxford-educated grandson, Shoghi Effendi (d. 1957), by designating the latter as the "Guardian" of the Bahā'ī Faith. Shoghi Effendi globalized and evolved Bahā'ī administration into a network of annually elected councils called National and Local Spiritual Assemblies, leading eventually to the election of the The Universal House of Justice in 1963, now established on Mount Carmel in Haifa, Israel.

The Bahā'ī Faith has been described as a derivative ("secondary") monotheism in the sense that it is the daughter religion of Islam. This genetic relationship is clearly illustrated in the typology of monotheisms developed by Alessandro Bausani, who proposed the following taxonomy in his classification of monotheistic religions, which include: (1) *Monotheisms proper*, in which Judaism and Islam are classed as primary monotheisms, with Christianity and the Bahā'ī Faith as respectively secondary (derivative, yet independent); (2) *Failed monotheisms*, which include Zoroastrianism as a primary monotheism, Manichaeism as a secondary monotheism, and Akhenaton's reform as an archaic monotheism; and (3) *Paramonotheisms*, which include Sikhism and various mysticisms (1963, 168). Thus Bahā'ī Faith stands in the same relationship to Islam as Christianity to Judaism. In my book, *Symbol and Secret* (1995a), I have discussed the relationship of Bahā'ī doctrine to Islam, the eschatological break of the former from the latter, and have identified some of the key symbols of the Qur'ān that exegetically and stylistically inform Bahā'ī texts.

With a following of only several million adherents at present, the population statistics of the Bahā'ī religion are not significant, but the growth statistics are remarkable. In its report on "World Religious Statistics" for the previous year, the 1988 Britannica *Book of the Year* names the Bahā'ī Faith alongside Christianity and Islam as the "most universal" of today's world religions. By a simple accounting of the number of sovereign and nonsovereign countries and territories in which it is formally established, the Bahā'ī Faith emerges as the most widely diffused religion in the world except for Christianity. As David Barrett observes: "Over 14 major religious systems are each now found in over 80 countries. Christianity, Islam, and the Baha'i World Faith are the most global" (1988, 303).

Working backwards from the Bahā'ī Faith's Islamic origins, I began to wonder if there were any specifically Christian antecedents to Bahā'ī symbolism. Of course, such an investigation had to be narrowed, because Christianity is really too broad a category and too sweeping a term for comparative purposes, considering that it adumbrates a veritable "family" of "Christianities." I therefore had to consider which *form* of Christianity should logically be selected for comparison, and why. The answer soon became evident: Persian Christianity was the tradition that was historically and culturally most proximate to Bahā'ī origins. Persian Christianity was attractive also because it tied into my broader research interests in "Persian" religions generally, from Zarathuštra to Bahā'u'llāh.

"Persian Christianity" refers to East Syriac Christianity under the Sasanian empire and beyond. The term *Persian Christianity* is used by A. V. Williams (1996), Stephen Gerö (1981; 1982) and others to refer to the "Church of the East"—the official name of the church—which was territorially coextensive with, yet surpassed, the orbit of the Sasanian empire. (Acknowledging that the term *Iranian* is technically more correct, both Syriac texts and the greater part of European scholarship employ the term *Persian* [Williams 1996, 38, n. 5].) This church is most commonly known as the "Nestorian" church, a "lamentable misnomer" (Brock 1996) that has, over time, become a scholarly term of convenience.

In Late Antiquity, Rome and Persia were the world's two superpowers. (The Sasanian Empire was in power from 224–651 C.E.) Except for short-lived armistices concluded under frangible treaties, both empires were constantly at war. Such "imperial warring" contributed to a more or less equal balance of power (Williams 1996, 37). Politically, as an imperative of survival when Persia was at war with Rome/Byzantium, Christians within the Persian Empire professed their loyalties to the Sasanian monarchy. On the feast of Epiphany (January 6) in 410 C.E., the Sasanian king Yazdegird I convened, by royal decree, the Synod of Isaac (Mār Isḥāq). Under imperial auspices as a sign of goodwill, the Church of Persia obliged the emperor in asserting its ecclesiastical independence. As a distinct hierarchical body, the Church of Persia took a further, more decisive step in establishing its doctrinal independence in 486 C.E., at the Synod of Seleucia-Ctesiphon, in total severance from the West. In due course, under Islamic rule, the East Syrian "Church of the East" would eventually have to coexist with West Syrian Jacobites, who were allowed to organize themselves into a separate *millet* distinct from that of the East Syrians, thus augmenting the Syriac Christian presence in Persia. In the medieval period, Syriac Christianity contributed to Islamic culture and religious life in Iran and Central Asia. (In chapter 2, the organization and diffusion of the Church of Persia will be reviewed in some detail.)

The Zoroastrian prelate, Kirdēr, in his well-known inscription on the Kaʿba-yi Zardušt, attests to the presence of both Syriac and Greek-speaking Christians (Williams 1996, 39). Wolfgang Hage puts this in a broader perspective: "Christianity, thus spreading over the Persian Empire, was mainly supported by the native Syrian and Iranian population, but to a lesser degree by those West Syrians and Greeks who had been deported as captives by the Persians from the temporarily occupied Roman border provinces into the East" (1988, 3). Although the majority of Persian Christians in the Sasanian empire must have been ethnic Syrians, the Church of the East was once a universal, multiethnic religion. It is probably true that ethnic Persians once formed the singlemost important ethnic minority of the Church of Persia. As historian Peter Brown has written: "The Christians within the Persian empire had begun to feel at home. In the fourth century, many had been foreigners, descended from the thousands of Syrians brought back as captives by Shapur I in the 260s. Times had changed. Christians now came from the Iranian population itself, through intermarriage and, occasionally, through conversion. Pehlevi (Middle Persian) joined Syriac as the other language of the Nestorian Church" (1997, 172).

The church within the Sasanian empire became increasingly "Persian" owing to the burgeoning number of native converts from Zoroastrianism, many of whom were, and still are, revered as martyrs. In the sixth century, the patriarch of the Persian church was Catholicós Mār Abā I (d. 552), a born Zoroastrian who was "educated in Persian literature" and who had once "scorned the Christians and despised the sons of the Covenant" (Williams 1996, 45, n. 36), and who himself became a martyr. We find unmistakable evidence of the importance of Zoroastrian converts to Persian Christianity in its principal historical sources: the official canons of synods; and the hagiographical acts of the Persian martyrs. Compiled under the direction of Catholicós

Timothy I (d. 823), the official documents of the Church of the East are recorded in the *Synodicon Orientale*, a record containing the acts of synods for the period 410–775 (Chabot 1902). In 544, at the Synod of Mār Abā, we discover that there were bishops of Iranian episcopates who had retained their Zoroastrian names, such as Ādur-Hormizd, Dādāfrīd, Hormizd, Mihr-bōzīd, Mihr-Narsēh, and Mihr-Hormizd (Williams 1996, 39). The Persian martyr Mār Giwargis, born with the Zoroastrian name Mihrām-Gušnasp, was, from youth, "thoroughly instructed in Persian literature and trained in the lore of the Magians," and was thus equal to his Zoroastrian persecutors in interrogations prior to his martyrdom (Williams 1996, 51–52).

Persian Christianity was, as stated, a historical development of East Syriac Christianity. As Christianity's most successful missionary church until decimated by the Mongols, the Church of the East sucessfully indigenized itself among local populations throughout the Persian Empire, Central Asia, India, and China. While it is true that Persian Christianity remained a predominantly Syriac tradition, with liturgy and instruction in Syriac, subsidiary Persian vernaculars were used to consolidate the influx of ethnic Iranian converts. Thus, there were imperial, ecclesiastical, ethnic, and vernacular elements that were distinctively Iranian.

Apart from the comparative agenda at hand, the study of Syriac Christianity provides an important corrective to a largely Eurocentric writing of Christian history. The Syriac language (Christian Aramaic) originated in Edessa—the "Athens of the East"—in the province of Osrhoëne (Mathews and Amar 1994a, 34). Syriac Christianity flourished in northern Mesopotamia (both Roman and Persian), in neighboring Adiabene (in 116 C.E., the Roman province of Assyria, reconquered by the Persians) and in points east. As its influence spread, Syriac emerged as the third international language of Christianity in Late Antiquity, thus ranking, alongside Greek and Latin, as one of the three great languages of Christian liturgy and missionary endeavor in the early centuries. As "the most important language of the Christian East" (Rilliet 1992c, 2: 809), Syriac was central to the diffusion of Christianity—in its concentric taxonomy—throughout the Persian Empire and along the Silk Road, through "Outer Iran," all the way to China. This linguistic and historical fact invests Syriac studies with an intrinsic importance. West to East, Christian identities shaped on the basis of Latin, Greek, and Syriac represent the three principal divisions of Christianity's first millennium, such that Syriac Christianity represents "a third cultural [Christian] tradition" (Brock, *apud* Drijvers 1996, 173).

What is so distinctive about pre-Persian, Syriac Christianity relative to other forms of the Christian faith (or "Christianities")? When one steps across the linguistic borders of the Latin West and the Greek

East into the spiritual frontier of the Syriac Orient, the Christian landscape suddenly becomes a Semitic hinterland, the inner landscape tinctured with a rich array of metaphors, expressions twinned with spiritual experience expressed in artistic enigmaticity. Largely absent here are the enormous debts to classical philosophy and its categories so pronounced in Hellenistic Christianity. In early Syriac Christianity, there was no effort to forge a synthesis between classical thought and Christian doctrine. Instead, native metaphors, rooted in vivid Semitisms, irradiate the literary horizon. Syriac Christianity was not propositionally controlled. More importantly, given its liturgical setting in Syriac worship, "theology" was popularly based, and was outside the province of the educated élite. Syriac liturgical theology bridges the typical gulf between so-called official and popular forms of religion.

Historically, it seemed obvious to me that "Persian" Christianity presented itself as the better candidate for comparison with the Bahā'ī tradition than mainstream Graeco-Latin "Roman" (later Byzantine) Christianity. Given the Islamic background of the Bahā'ī Faith, it is noteworthy that Tor Andrae had already conjectured a Syriac Christian source for the Qur'ān's description of Paradise (Andrae 1932, 71–72). Edmund Beck (1948 and 1961) disputed this suggestion. Whether mediated through its Islamic heritage or not, a preliminary comparison disclosed that Bahā'ī texts betray some intriguing affinities with Syriac texts.

As the formative period of Syriac spirituality, the fourth century was decisive in the development of all subsequent forms of Syriac spirituality. Because of this, it was not the trunk and the branches of the East Syrian ecclesiastical tree that most interested me, but rather the symbolic roots of Persian Christianity as exemplified in the hymns of St. Ephrem the Syrian (d. 373 C.E.) and the *Demonstrations* of Aphrahāṭ (d. c. 345 C.E.). Persian Christianity—and the early Syriac Christianity that predates it—actually begins with Aphrahāṭ, "the Persian Sage," who was the first Father of the Syrian church and "our first major Christian writer from outside the Roman Empire" (Brock 1994, 71). The earliest Syriac literature is said to have been of "clearly 'Persian'" origin (Rilliet 1992c, 2: 810), with respect to the twenty-three *Demonstrations* of Aphrahāṭ. He wrote during a period of intense persecution of Christians (Aph. Dem. XVI.1) and was understandably quite anti-Persian politically (V.1).

In addition to Aphrahāṭ, early Syriac Christianity is best exemplified in the hymns of Ephrem the Syrian, "the poet of the Christian paradox" (Brock 1983, 14), acclaimed to have been the greatest poet of Christianity in the patristic period. Not only is he the most important exemplar of early Syriac spirituality, Ephrem is as universal a representative of Christianity in Late Antiquity as any other single candidate. The early Syriac culture area, of which Ephrem was a part, was defined by coterminous "Roman" and "Persian" spheres of influence. This Christian milieu was a mosaic of Marcionites, Bardaiṣanites, and Manichaeans in which orthodox [Nicene] Christianity was originally a minority community known as Paluṭians, for whom "*enkrateia* [sexual holiness] was the religious ideal of almost all groups except the Bardesanites" (Drijvers 1996, 173). From his obscure origins among the Paluṭians, and within his own lifetime, Ephrem's reputation began to spread throughout the Christian world. He is the only Syrian Christian to have been canonized as a saint in the Catholic Church. As the more illustrious of the two, Ephrem will be privileged over Aphrahāṭ, while the latter will be adduced to supplement the former.

Although he lived on the Roman-Persian frontier, Ephrem was not a Persian; yet during his own lifetime, there was significant contact with Persian Christians, so much so that the theological school in Edessa (which Ephrem is traditionally said to have once headed) was known as "The School of the Persians" (Brock 1996, 33). In 489, the emperor Zeno closed the school, which then relocated to Ephrem's native city of Nisibis, which, in 363, had been ceded to the Persians. The fact remains that Ephrem was one of the principal spiritual forebears of the Church of Persia that formed less than forty years after his death. These two luminaries of Syriac spirituality—Aphrahāṭ and Ephrem—established the legacy on which the Church of Persia was later founded. In the present study, therefore, I shall explore these Syriac roots of Persian Christianity, for possible Christian antecedents of Bahā'ī symbolism.

The stamp of Syriac symbolism is visible throughout Syriac liturgy and imagery down to the present. Today, Syriac Christianity survives in Iraq and Iran (the heartland of the ancient Sasanian empire) as well as diasporally, in its several configurations: *Assyrian* (two Patriarchates, East Syriac ["Nestorian"] liturgy): (1) Assyrian Church of the East (New Calendarian—Tehran, Chicago); (2) Assyrian Church of the East (Old Calendarian—Baghdad). *Orthodox* ("Jacobite" with two Patriarchates, West Syriac liturgy): (3) Universal Syrian Orthodox Church of the Patriarchate of Antioch including its Church in India; (4) Syrian Orthodox of the Autocephalous Malankara Church of India. *Catholic* (Oriental Uniate): (5) Chaldean Patriarchate of Babylonia (Baghdad, East Syriac liturgy); (6) Syro-Malabar Church of India (East Syriac liturgy); (7) Syrian Catholic Patriarchate of Antioch (West Syriac liturgy); (8) Maronite Church (West Syriac liturgy); (9) Malankara Catholic Church (West Syriac liturgy). *Protestant:* (10) Mar-Thoma (Anglican); (11) Assyrian Evangelical Church (Tehran); (12) Assyrian Pentecostal Church; (13) "Philadelphia Church" (Iran); (14) various Assyrian Presbyterian congregations. Syrian converts to

Protestant denominations have been excluded from dialogue within the Syrian tradition.

In the first three of these four families, Ephrem has a distinct place of honor. Among these various Syriac Christian traditions, as a legacy, Aphrahāṭ's and Ephrem's imagery for Christ's incarnation is perhaps more faithfully preserved in the East Syrian tradition (Brock 1994, 82–83), as is evidenced in the liturgy known as the *Ḥudrā* ("Cycle"; Breviary). (See Appendix IV, "Fragments of a Lost Persian Christian Liturgy," at the end of this book.)

Collectively, these Syriac-oriented groups represent an attenuated, but living religion, contemporary with the Bahā'ī Faith. None of the present-day remnants of Syriac Christianity will, however, be selected for comparison. Instead, I have restricted my investigation to the formative period of Persian Christianity—before there was even an officially constituted "Church of Persia"—in order to study the most important and symbolically rich Syriac texts—particularly the hymns of Ephrem the Syrian and, to a lesser extent, the discourses of Aphrahāṭ, the Persian Sage—written during the golden age of Syriac literature.

While diachronically distant in respect of origins, bridged by the Islamic period, Persian Christianity is historically antecedent to the Bahā'ī religion by pedigree in the religious history of Iran. Comparison of Syriac Christianity and the Bahā'ī Faith is thus justified on grounds of common geographical, historical, ethnic and, to a lesser extent, linguistic contexts. Comparing the imagery of the two traditions should make it possible to demonstrate how symbolic transformation may be the reflex of an underlying paradigm shift of religious ideals.

As symbol systems, these two religions exhibit a wide range of expressive and ideological similarities, insufficiently classified as "parallels." The object of this study is to compare some of the dominant, world-defining Syriac symbols of early Persian Christianity with commensurate symbolism in the Bahā'ī Faith, with respect to the core paradigms (that is, the overarching and governing religious concerns) of each of the two religions. Obviously, Islam is presumed to have played an intermediary role in the transmission and transformation of Christian symbolism, as taken up in the Bahā'ī religion. While a suppressed genealogy is unavoidable in suggesting that symbolic transformations may occur as a result of paradigm shifts from one religion to another, I will be arguing analogically based on a coherence theory of truth.

The contribution I wish to make is primarily methodological. Through a systematic worldview analysis and disciplined comparison of worldviews, my objective is to interpret parallels by nuancing their differences—differences that correlate to the symbolic logics of the religions being compared. If successful, this project could suggest a model for synchronic comparisons of diachronically unrelated traditions. In the present study, however, there is at least a distant diachronic relationship between the Christian and Bahā'ī religions. If history looks at the causes, phenomenology can at least examine the effects.

Data selection typically excludes more than it includes, so that a decision governing data selection required justification. During preliminary research, this finding fell into focus: In both Syriac and Bahā'ī traditions, many dominant symbols related to notions of Paradise. Why? Because Paradise allegorizes ideals. Paradise imagery may be analyzed as the projection of religious ideals onto an eschatological canvas. Visions of Paradise are the stained-glass windows of worldviews, encompassing most of the imagery—or "key symbols"—to be analyzed in this study. Luxuriant gardens, fountains, flowing streams, succulent fruits, jewels, pearls, illumination—all of these images can be promoted within a religious community as a master allegory of all that is ideal. Paradise is demonstrably a reflex of prevailing standards of orthodoxy and orthopraxy. In the case of Persian Christianity, the path to Paradise seems to be sacramental. In the case of the Bahā'ī Faith, the path to Paradise appears to be sacrosocial.

Paradises and Paradigms

Ideals are "seen" in symbolic landscapes. Promotion of religious ideals, in Western religions, often takes the form of promises of Paradise. Visions of Paradise disclose an abundance of information relating to religious worldviews. As an afterlife, the existence of Paradise is not empirically demonstrable. Yet Paradise inspires hopes of reward for pious faith and for righteous works. In earthly terms, Paradise imagery contributes to "world building." Paradise has a social function, in addition to its traditional, eschatological role. As "realized eschatology," notions of Paradise influence faith-communities here on Earth.

Paradise images are certainly iconic. They can represent an ontological reality posited by scriptural authority with whatever propositional infallibility is ascribed to it. But such images may be reflexively symbolic as well. One man's paradise may not necessarily be another's. And so it is that there are different notions of Paradise across the religious spectrum. Within discrete religious systems, it may be observed that Paradise is confessionally referenced. It is keyed to a set of values and behaviors that embody beliefs about salvation and ideals of perfection. On an individual level, contemplation of Heaven is thought orienting and can supply strategies for action. For the faith-community, Paradise may function as a master symbol of a core religious paradigm, a controlling, conceptual model that governs ideal beliefs and behaviors.

Religions may share ideas in common about Paradise. This renders the comparison more interesting and challenging. Symbols may be "the same"—exhibiting formal affinity—but disclosing significantly divergent shades of meaning. Parallels may be seen as distorted mirror images. Visual nuances of one and the same image depend upon the mirrors themselves, which reflect that image, but perhaps in slightly different ways. Interpretations, after all, are forms of distortion.

Interpretations are governed by overarching paradigms. For the purposes of this study, the term *paradigm* is indebted to Thomas S. Kuhn's *The Structure of Scientific Revolutions* (1962). Kuhn's technical use of the term *paradigm* has recently been lexicalized in the 1993 *New Shorter Oxford English Dictionary*: "*Philos.* a mode of viewing the world which underlies the theories and methodology of science in a particular period of history" (2: 2093). This study extends that definition to a religious context, such that "paradigm" will now mean: "*Rel.* a model of viewing the world which underlies the beliefs and practices of religion and society in a particular period of history."

Paradigms can render parallels intelligible. As perspectival filters, paradigms provide a heuristic key for explaining parallels. To nuance formal similarities and to resolve conceptual differences, parallels need to be indexed to core paradigms, which are coefficients of anthropological and soteriological assumptions. The present investigation seeks to reference parallels to those controlling paradigms. As a contribution to what William Paden (1996a) has recently called the "new comparativism," this study proposes the following axiom for further research and refinement: *"Parallels" yield paradoxes of commensurability resolvable by paradigm "logics" within religious systems, resulting in symbolic transformation.* This is a testable statement, not on historical, but on thematic and typological grounds.

This investigation will explore how one religious paradigm may or may not compare to another, and, in so doing, attempts to render such comparisons schematically clear. Formally affine and distinctive symbols drawn from Syriac and Bahā'ī texts will be compared by an inventory of features, with respect to superordinating paradigms of each religion. As the main force of this research project is structural rather than historical, it is not within the scope of this study to prove historical influences. It prescinds from advancing claims of a genetic nature. While questions of historical transmission clearly fall outside of the province of this project, history will afford an anchor for the data, in relatively "thick" descriptions of both Syriac and Bahā'ī religious contexts.

Systems of Symbols

Symbolic analysis of religions proceeds from the fact that religions are systems of symbols. Anthropologist Clifford Geertz has privileged or highlighted the role of symbols in religion. In his 1965 essay, "Religion as a Cultural System," Geertz works out a definition of religion in terms of its symbols: "A religion is: (1) a system of symbols which acts to (2) establish powerful, pervasive, and long-lasting moods and motivations in men by (3) formulating conceptions of a general order of existence and (4) clothing these conceptions with such an aura of factuality that (5) the moods and motivations seem uniquely realistic" (1973, 90). This is a functional definition that has much tighter specifications than does a definition like "religion is a system of numinous symbols"—a definition that employs the same analogic model (Poole 1986, 440).

While favorably disposed towards Geertz's definition, Willard Oxtoby observes: "Many have found Geertz's article a useful mainstream representative of twentieth-century social theory of religion. This is so despite the evident elasticity of some of its wording. Just what, for instance, is an 'aura' of factuality? Just how, exactly, do symbols, rather than people, 'act'? But a strength of the definition is its parallel between clause 4 as intensification of clause 3, and clause 5 as intensification of clause 2" (1996c, 499). Note that it is not a requirement that the symbols themselves "seem uniquely realistic" but rather what they represent or evoke ought to seem realistic. Geertz defines a symbol as "any object, act, event, quality, or relation which serves as a vehicle for a conception—the conception is the symbol's meaning" (1973, 91). In the present study, scriptural symbols are "objects" as well as allegorical "acts" that metaphorically and narratively enshrine conceptions. Clearly, Geertz's definition intensifies the relation between religion and its symbols by defining religion in terms of its symbols.

Symbols are interesting, but why are they important for the Study of Religion? Sherry Ortner describes the importance of Geertz's own interest in symbols as methodological revolution of sorts: "Geertz's most radical theoretical move (1973b) was to argue that culture is not something locked inside people's heads, but rather is embodied in public symbols, symbols through which the members of a society communicate their worldview, value-orientations, ethos, and all the rest to one another, to future generations—and to anthropologists. With this formulation, Geertz gave the hitherto elusive concept of cultural symbols a relatively fixed locus, lending the study of such symbols a degree of objectivity previous lacking. The focus on symbols was for Geertz and many others heuristically liberating: it told them where to find what they wanted to study. Yet the point about symbols was that they were ultimately vehicles for meanings; the study of symbols as such was never an end in itself" (1984, 129). Religious symbols inform and structure religious consciousness.

Books are typically less interesting when devoid of illustrations. Perhaps the same could be said of scriptural texts as well. Symbols are the illustrations of sacred ideas and ideals. Symbols are more than illuminative. They have a focalizing function. The key to Ricoeur's theory of symbol is his formula (cited by C. Long 1986, 50): "*Le symbole donne à penser*" ("Symbol invites thought"). For Ricoeur, the symbol is a two-dimensional phenomenon, unifying dual universes of discourse: linguistically, symbols exhibit metaphoricity; and presemantically, symbols are rooted in the depths of human experience, from which derives their evocative power (see DeLoach 1983). "All texts," Dilworth writes, "convey meaning in assertive (propositional), active (morally and politically agential), and exhibitive (aesthetic, performative) modes of expression or judgment" (1989, 18). Symbols, by Dilworth's standards, are not assertive. But they are "active" and "exhibitive." Their agential role is stressed in the anthropology of religion.

Symbols are encoded metaphors. Behind symbolization, figuration will be assumed to exist. As Rice and Schofer state: "Extended over an entire text, the act of reading and interpretation is a complex interplay between symbolization and figuration. Although figures and tropes can be isolated for analysis, in reading there can be no figuration without symbolization and no symbolization without figuration" (1983, 37). Symbolism is a transformation of metaphoricity, with respect to its iconic function in representing nonphysical, or spiritual, reality. Apart from signs, which are explicit, symbols may possess what Royce calls "surplus meaning" (cited in Fawcett 1970, 28). A symbol is most commonly defined as "a material Object substituted for a moral or spiritual truth" (Bullinger 1968, 769). How does a symbol come to be? Bullinger states that a symbol is formed in three stages: (1) a metaphor or metonymy is used to *represent* something other; (2) the one is used to *imply* the other; and (3) finally, the one comes to permanently *substitute* for the other (ibid., 770). Wheelwright is simpler still. He suggests that a symbol is a "metaphor stabilized" (1960, 7).

To oversimplify, a symbol is a metaphor reified over time, being transformed, in the currency it acquires through recurrent usage, from a "unique flash of insight" to "a relatively stable element of perceptual experience, standing for some larger meaning or set of meanings which cannot be given, or not fully given, in perceptual experience itself" (Wheelwright 1962, 93, 92). Though Rice and Schofer do not give a definition of symbol as such, it is clear from their discussion of the symbolic process that a symbol is marked only by incompleteness, since there is no incompatibility between the text and context, as there is in figuration. Yet the reader detects the incompleteness and decodes the text symbolically (1983, 38).

Cain proposes what is one of the simpler approaches to symbol, in which the symbol mediates between subject and *numen*. By "numen" is meant the signified, perceived, extrarational, sacred reality of the believer's universe (1979, 340). (No ontological commitment is made in postulating this symbolic domain.) In this schema, the symbol evokes the presence of the *numen*. Typically, symbols find their "fulfillment" in numinously evocative ritual, dream, or vision. They may likewise be "realized" in the present through an act of identification, even if that be an exegetical one. If the Cross is the symbol of salvation, the object symbolized is Christ (the savior), the subject symbolized is man (the saved), while the *numen* is salvation (my example). Here, the symbol links subject and object, by linking the numinous with the evocative and sympathetic power of the symbolic. The symbol's referent is experientially, but not empirically, verifiable. The subjective apperception of the numinous through the symbolic is real enough. To the extent that symbols, as numinous archives of meaning, incorporate ideas, they may be said to hypostatize them. Ontological claims of a supramundane power may be studied as a psychological reification of that which is experienced or imagined. Not the ontology but, rather, the interpretive "reality" is of immediate hermeneutical concern.

One must determine how symbols concatenate. The symbol is an enigma. It is like an oracle; it needs to be deciphered. A symbol is not susceptible of interpretive closure, or "truth exhaustion," partly because of its recombinant possibilities in connection with other symbols. Charles Long observes that "religious symbols, precisely because of their intrinsic power, radiate and deploy meanings; the spread of these meanings creates an arena and field of power relationships" (1986, 2). Relationally, within a religious system, symbols possess what might be thought of as a kind of collective "dream logic." This process of decoding is not a purely mental operation. As an encoded metaphor, the symbol is not simply a code. It is a mode of expression. One might even speak of its emotional content. The symbol is the language of the heart.

As Oxtoby often says to his students, the methodological "proof of the pudding" is both in the pudding and in the eating of it. Which is to say that data selection is just as significant as the methodologies brought to bear on the data. To this end, selecting for the more important symbols becomes a methodological concern. Some symbols are more important than others in terms of their relative influence. There are dominant symbols and there are subsidiary symbols. Dominant symbols have been termed "key symbols" in the anthropology of religion. Constellations of subordinate symbols may cluster around key symbols, which are the affective and exhibitive poles of religious thought. Identification of preponderating symbols provides the necessary data for comparison. Interpretation of this data on comparative grounds derives from research design. In the next section, the concept of "key symbols" will be explained.

Key Symbols

In this study, Syriac Christianity and the Bahā'ī Faith are conceived of as constellations of information-rich key symbols, exhibiting a wealth of metaphorical language operating as concept indicators. In general terms, a religious symbol will be expected to significate "the knowledge by which self/society/action are joined" (Jensen 1992, 6). This is an integrative definition in its part-to-whole set of relations.

Given the existence of competing theories of the symbol, and its wide array of definitions, it is necessary either to invent or to adapt a paradigm, to the exclusion of others. This study will adapt Sherry Ortner's concept of the "key symbol." This technical term derives from symbolic anthropology. On the basis of her 1970 dissertation, Ortner (1973) developed a model of symbolism for "symbolic analysis"—a paradigm that will be adapted to the present study. Ortner wanted to show that cultures were not just clusters of symbols, but something more. Cultural symbols were more than even the ideologies they represent. A "key symbol"—a superordinating, dominant image of an idea or an ideal—is immediately cognizable. A key symbol commands respect, fixes attention on the intentional referent for which it stands, a silent yet evocative representation of something religious, present, ethereally imperial. Among the dominant "key symbols" of a given culture are "key scenarios" or schemas for enacting cultural behaviors. Ortner's paradigm will be employed independent of its original theoretical context and adapted to the discussion at hand.

Generally, key symbols are of two kinds: "summarizing" and "elaborating" (see schematic in Kippenberg 1985, 189; *apud* Goedendorp 1991, 117). "Summarizing" key symbols are iconic, sacred symbols, "objects of reverence and/or catalysts of emotion," such as the Cross for Christians, corresponding perhaps to the "Material" or "Artistic" (seventh) dimension of Smart's dimensional model of religion. What is the Bahā'ī counterpart of the Christian cross and spire? In the present-day Bahā'ī Faith, the continental Bahā'ī Houses of Worship come to mind, as does the Bahā'ī ringstone symbol. By its very nature, a summarizing key symbol is "clustered, condensed, relatively undifferentiated, 'thick'" (Ortner 1973, 1342). A summarizing symbol is characterized by "its focusing power, its drawing-together, intensifying, catalyzing impact upon the respondent" resulting in a "crystallization of commitment" (ibid.).

Summarizing symbols are said to "catalyze feeling." They speak to "a different level of response, the level of attitude and commitment." Such symbols "ground" a variety of "surface-level meanings to their deeper bases" (ibid., 1343). Ortner points to the American flag as a prime example: "The American flag, for example, for certain Americans, stands for something called 'the American way,' a conglomerate of ideas and feelings including (theoretically) democracy, free enterprise, hard work, competition, progress, national superiority, freedom, etc. And it stands for them all at once. It does not encourage reflection on the logical relations among these ideas, nor on the logical consequences of them as they are played out in social actuality, over time and history. On the contrary, the flag encourages a sort of all-or-nothing allegiance to the whole package, best summed up on a billboard I saw recently: 'Our flag, love it or leave.' And this is the point about summarizing symbols in general—they operate to compound and synthesize a complex system of ideas, to 'summarize' them under a unitary form which, in an old-fashioned way, 'stands for' the system as a whole" (ibid., 1340).

This study will take up Ortner's other category of "key symbols"—those which have an "elaborating" function. There are two primary modes in which key symbols operate: thought and action. "Root metaphors" and "key scenarios" respectively represent ideals of thought and action. In Ortner's "key symbols" paradigm, "root metaphors" serve to orient thought.

The term *root metaphor* was first developed as a key term and launched as a descriptive and analytic category by Stephen Pepper (1942). Pepper conceived of root metaphors as symbols imbued with tremendous elaborating power, in which the principal mechanism is the metaphor. Root metaphors were pivotal in the maintenance of *world hypotheses*—another term coined by Pepper—that roughly correspond to the notion of a worldview. Acting as a symbol, the root metaphor provides a set of categories for cognitive and affective conceptualizing of the world. Pepper linked his concept of root metaphors with Kuhn's notion of "paradigm": "According to his [Kuhn's] exposition," writes Pepper, "there is practically no difference between the function of a paradigm as a guiding pattern in scientific procedure and that of the root metaphor as a guiding conceptual pattern in world hypotheses except for the restricted scope of the former" (1984, 3: 200).

In Ortner's use of the term, a root metaphor is one in which "one can conceptualize the interrelationships among phenomena by analogy to the interrelations among the parts of the root metaphor (op. cit., 1341). Root metaphors serve to establish "a certain view of the world" (ibid.). A few words ought to be said about the term *metaphor* and how an understanding of metaphors in general might elucidate the role of root metaphors in particular. In her "key symbols" paradigm, Ortner seems unconcerned with linguistic distinctions between "symbol" and "metaphor." "Root metaphors" are simply a species of "key symbols." Nonetheless, it is important to bear in mind what a metaphor is and what a metaphor does, as this does relate to an appreciation of the dynamics of thought-orienting root metaphors.

Metaphor is arguably the ground of symbolism. Metaphor has been considered to be the most elaborate of tropes. Traditionally taking it to be the most fundamental form of figurative language, most theorists agree that a metaphor is based on association and, in its dynamic effect, triggers some kind of transference of meaning in the mind of the reader. Younger states: "The power of metaphor derives precisely from the interplay between the discordant meanings it symbolically coerces into a unitary conceptual framework and from the degree to which that coercion is successful in overcoming the psychic resistance such semantic tension inevitably generates in anyone in a position to perceive it" (1990, 164). Personification, for example, depends on verbal metaphors, metaphors of action (Dupriez 1991, 278). "Metaphorical thought," wrote Max Black, "is a distinctive mode of achieving insight, not to be construed as an ornamental substitute for plain thought" (1962, 237). A metaphor is aspectual. It may be thought of as the overlap of two meanings (Watson 1984, 263).

For example, in the verse, "Why, then, has Israel become a prey?" (Jer. 2:14), Israel is the "tenor" while the prey is the "vehicle" of the metaphor, in which the attribute of vulnerability is the "ground" or overlap of meaning between tenor and vehicle (Watson, op. cit.). This is very straightforward. The idea of Israel as prey implies vulnerability. In the metaphor, the transference of meaning is covert, whereas, in contrast, a simile literally "*proposes* the transference" (Hawkes 1972, 30). Negatively, Levin defines a metaphor as an expression evincing, in its composition, a degree of linguistic deviance, in which the meaning of a word swerves from its lexically codified usage. Due to their oddity, metaphors require first to be construed before being understood (Levin 1988, 1).

Positively, Ricoeur argues that metaphor, by virtue of its semantic innovation, "is the rhetorical process by which discourse unleashes the power that certain fictions have to redescribe reality" (1979, 7). Rice and Schofer define metaphor as follows: "Metaphor is characterized by a semantic and referential relationship made possible by the possession of one or more semantic features" (1983, 21). This definition, based as it is on resemblance or similarity, does not differ appreciably from traditional notions. Beyond mere juxtaposition, in highly encoded metaphors, there are condensed, numerous intersections of meanings, which are said to "contaminate" each other (ibid., 102).

In simpler terms, Thompson speaks of "metaphoric unity" in a text rich in figurative language, in which that unity interrelates symbolic elements of the text "vertically." "Metaphoric unity," writes Thompson, "occurs all at once; that is, a metaphor consists of simultaneous 'vertical' layers of language analogous to a musical chord" (1990, 354–55). Moreover, a metaphor "identifies rather than compares two elements" (ibid., 356), though Thompson does not pursue the implications of this contrast to simile. The use of such language does not merely illustrate and supplement demonstrative statements of doctrine. Metaphorical texts may in fact communicate more vividly and fully the experiential dimension of nondiscursive truth. A metaphor is more evocative than literal discourse. Figurative speech, from a cognitive perspective, requires a certain level of competence to decode. The same may be said of metaphorical and symbolic modes of discourse in religious texts (cf. Goodenough 1951). A certain competence is required to understand it.

"Key scenarios"—Ortner's other class of "key symbols"—serve to influence action. This is because "they are valued as implying mechanisms for successful social action." Key scenarios are endowed with "action elaborating power" that define "strategies" for "orderly social action in relation to culturally defined goals" (op. cit., 1340). Key scenarios "are culturally valued in that they formulate the culture's mean-ends relationships in actable forms" (ibid., 1341). The activity of symbols is seen, for instance, in cult and sacrament, where a symbol takes on a performative role in its creative or reconstitutive operations. Action instantiates its symbols. In the cultic domain, therefore, we can accept the Weberian notion that ideology influences behavior, such that key scenarios may have an ordering function. Just as root metaphors are thought orienting, key scenarios are action ordering. Ortner's concept of key scenarios is akin to Victor Turner's concept of "root paradigms," which have a persistent force in society. In Christianity, for example, Turner points to martyrdom as a root paradigm (Turner 1974).

To recapitulate, key symbols of the elaborating order subdivide along a thought/action axis, consisting of "root metaphors" (thought orientations) and "key scenarios" (action ordering). Root metaphors are "static formal images serving metaphor functions for thought" while key scenarios involve "dramatic, phased, action sequences serving scenario functions for action" (Ortner 1973, 1342).

Identification of key symbols within a single religious tradition constitutes internal analysis, as part of what one might call "worldview analysis," through employing what Ninian Smart has termed "*symbolic* analysis" (1985, 33). In Syriac and Bahā'ī sacred texts, particular attention will be given to two kinds of literary forms: (1) for analysis of root metaphors, genitive metaphors (the most complex type of noun metaphor and one that is frequently used to express Bahā'ī and Syriac root metaphors) will be used; and (2) for analysis of key scenarios, allegories, or symbolic narratives will be adduced. Although this paradigm is admittedly programmatic, the use of key symbols here should not be viewed as deterministic or overly constraining.

It is necessary to distinguish between the academic concept of "key symbols" and religious references to "symbols" within the Syriac and Bahā'ī traditions themselves. By using nearly identical terms—i.e., *key symbols* (symbolic anthropology) and *symbols* (Syriac and Bahā'ī terms)—the analysis runs the risk of being caught within a religious self-understanding that "entangles the analysis with the very discourse it seeks to interpret and explain" (Poole 1986, 413). The term *key symbols*—despite its terminological affinity to religious *symbols*—is conceptually independent. It is theoretically crucial to the performance of symbolic analysis that this distinction be maintained.

Dimensional Model

Analysis of data depends upon an adequate description of it. Adequate description is a requisite for explanation. Ninian Smart's "dimensional model" of religion assigns six "dimensions" to each religion (1985). For mnemonic purposes, I have coined the acronym DREEMS (Doctrinal, Ritual, Ethical, Experiential, Mythic, Social) to represent these dimensions. Defining religions as systems of symbols (Geertz), this study focuses on key symbols (Ortner), comprised of thought-orienting root metaphors and action-incentive key scenarios. Providing holistic descriptions of religions as symbol systems for worldview analysis, the invention of a "symbolic profile" orders an array of dominant, ideationally indexed images within respective "dimensions." These symbolic profiles are synoptic mappings of dominant key symbols within each tradition. Key symbols for the various dimensions of the DREEMS map are charted.

Clifford Geertz has defined religion as a "system of symbols." Sherry Ortner—Geertz's student—has classified and defined those symbols. Now that a paradigm for symbols has been adopted for the present study, we turn our attention to the religious "system" itself. What does it mean to say that a religion is a "system" of symbols? A cross-cultural, systemic model of religion is needed. Ninian Smart, a distinguished phenomenologist of religion, has offered such a model. It is an analytical apparatus, with a methodologically elegant, descriptive power. Whether or not this model gains widespread acceptance remains to be seen.

Smart has developed and refined what he calls a "dimensional" model of religion. It has the advantage of describing a given religion roundly, giving a picture of the religion in its totality. So long as phenomenologists are careful to surrender to the data and not to the model itself, the dimensional approach to religious systems can be quite useful. Although spirituality seems to be characterized by a certain depth of ineffability, Smart's six dimensions of religion provide superficial, yet necessary windows into the functioning of a faith community. Ideally, Smart's dimensional model is a simple taxonomy of religion.

In Smart's model of it, religion may be viewed from different angles, like turning a six-faceted jewel. Each facet is aspectual, representing one dimension. Each dimension also serves as a comparative frame for the focus of a comparison between two or more religions. Over the years, Smart has variously described these dimensions. In what probably has been his most important description of them, Smart's *Worldviews* introduces the following dimensions in this order: (1) the Experiential Dimension; (2) the Mythic Dimension; (3) the Doctrinal Dimension; (4) the Ethical Dimension; (5) the Ritual Dimension; (6) the Social Dimension (1985, ix).

In the 1995 reprint of *The World's Religions*, Smart has slightly revised these headings as follows: (1) The Practical and Ritual Dimension; (2) The Experiential and Emotional Dimension; (3) The Narrative or Mythic Dimension; (4) The Doctrinal and Philosophical Dimension; (5) The Ethical and Legal Dimension; (6) The Social and Institutional Dimension; (7) The Material Dimension. Under the last dimension, Smart subsumes the "Artistic" (Smart 1995, 10–21). In Ortner's terms of reference, it seems fairly obvious that the Material or Artistic Dimension is where the majority of "summarizing" symbols are to be found. The "Material" dimension adumbrates artistic and iconographic modalities of religion. In the Bahā'ī tradition, the ringstone symbol (designed by Bahā'u'llāh's son 'Abdu'l-Bahā [d. 1921]) and the distinct architecture of Bahā'ī Houses of Worship fit nicely here in the seventh dimension, but are excluded from the present study as they are not literary. For the purposes of the present study, the seventh dimension, concerned as it is with "summarizing" rather than "elaborating" key symbols, will be excluded from purview.

Smart's dimensional model is not without controversy. Recently, Michael Pye has argued that interculturally based theories of religion are in short supply and there is no single theory of religion that is sufficiently stabilized to command wide assent (1994, 52). Pye questions the utility of Smart's model with respect to Japanese religions, in which both "doctrinal" and "ethical" dimensions appear to be lacking (ibid., 59). Their absence leaves a gaping hole in Smart's paradigm. But is this an exception, existing in splendid isolation, that in effect "proves the rule"? Or has Pye exposed a weak link that will break Smart's theoretical concatenation of dimensions? I think that the lack of an ethical dimension in Japanese religions is perhaps taken up elsewhere, in a transconfessional way, from some other value system, religious or civil, lest we deduce from Pye's remarks that the Japanese who follow Japanese religions are altogether bereft of ethics. Smart's model seems to have withstood the scrutiny of other scholars over time, and to have enjoyed a certain popularity based on its utility. (It is probably too soon to speak of a near consensus.) Smart's dimensional model provides a powerful analytic framework that makes significant sense of complex religious, psychological, and social data by delimiting domains or "dimensions" of religion.

The present study will employ Smart's dimensional model of religion for descriptive purposes, presenting two datasets for comparison. In so doing, this project is by no means the "lengthened shadow" of Smart himself. The DREEMS scheme is an apparatus more for illustration than for analysis. Its utility is seen by the fact of its rather widespread acceptance in general texts on world religions. In the *Encyclopedia of World Faiths*, for example, "The Six Dimensions of Religion" are represented by a diagram, a graphic six-piece pie in which the dimensions, from the top going clockwise, are defined as follows: (1) *Ritual*: expressed in worship, sacrifice, and other sacred acts; (2) *Myth*: stories which encapsulate fundamental beliefs of a group; (3) *Doctrine*: systemization of beliefs and experiences; (4) *Ethics*: moral codes and guides to behavior; (5) *Social*: institutional forms of religion; (6) *Experiential*: personal spiritual experiences (Bishop and Darton 1990, 7).

Symbolic Profiles

The research design employed here is modular. It is constructed out of several models, of which Smart's is one, albeit a major one. The phenomena to be bracketed are key symbols, comprised of two classes: root metaphors and key scenarios. Although comparison of Syriac and Bahā'ī "key symbols" is abstract, the data is anchored in "local" traditions. This body of data has empirical force. Wedded to Ortner's key symbols paradigm, I have designed a schematic grid for descriptive and analytic purposes, which I call a "symbolic profile" of religion. A symbolic profile charts key symbols across the six-dimensional spectrum of religion. A twelve-symbol constellation is produced. Configurations of key symbols will thus be used for synoptic purposes. I have structured Syriac and Bahā'ī symbolic profiles using Smart's dimensional model of religion, but according to a different order. (See chapters 3 and 5 for symbolic profiles of Syriac Christianity and of the Bahā'ī Faith.)

This model is really a metaphor, a purely abstract but theoretically powerful instrument that in some sense "*constructs* the similarities in unexpected and insightful ways," as Poole explains: "The postulation of a metaphoric or analogical relation implicates a similarity-statement and thus, provides the possibility of a comparison-statement" (1986, 421). It should always be borne in mind that these categories (key symbols as well as dimensions) are extrinsic to the phenomena themselves. A caveat on typologies and taxonomies: Schemes are created by design. A certain amount of theoretical conniving goes into them. They are somewhat hazardous in that the data may serve to reinforce the typology rather than the other way around. A valid typology should exhibit predictive powers, but it must never be a determinant.

This model entails the analogic mapping of key symbols in a territory of dimensions of religion, as a theoretical lens to afford "'epistemic access' (Boyd, 1979) to two (or more) relatively similar—but also loosely distinguishable—entities before analysis draws and specifies the theoretically relevant distinctions between (or among) them" (Poole 1986, 420–21). Smart's model uses the analogy of dimensions to justify a classification system which itself filters and organizes the data (in the present study, of key symbols). The entire idea of dimensions is of heuristic value only. Care must be exercised against any temptation to reify the categories themselves. As we shall see, analysis of even a single key symbol discloses depth structures that transsect all of the categories. These categories of the sacred are not sacred categories.

Worldview Comparison

Smart holds that "the very heart of the comparative study of religion" is "the comparative analysis of worldviews" (1986a, 78). "Comparison," according to Jeppe Jensen, "is the basis of all communicable knowledge" (1992, 1). For specialists in the academic study of religion, comparison is the basis for generalizable principles on the nature of religion.

The enterprise of comparing religions has a history in the academy, in which Donald Wiebe has drawn attention to the problem of "motive and method" in the study of religion as an academic exercise (1988, cf. 1989). According to Henri Corbin (1981, 3), the allied concept of "comparative philosophy" was first explicitly formulated by Paul Masson-Oursel at the Sorbonne, who saw formal philosophical comparison not so much in terms of likenesses, which can be deceptive, but rather in analogies of relationships (of the type $a/b = c/d$). The problem of comparison is, in fact, bound up with the very origins of the Study of Religion as an academic field, and continues to challenge its foundations. The Study of Religion—which is properly a field of study rather than a discipline—was, in its inception, popularly known as "Comparative Religion." It originated out of comparative questions and endeavors. Sadly, the comparison of religions has lost much of its former respectability. As Jonathan Z. Smith observes: "Comparison has come to be, for many in the field, the sign of unscientific procedure" (1990, Preface).

The grander the comparative endeavor, the more susceptible it is to criticism. A good example of this kind of vulnerability is given by Talmon (1991), who has discussed the kinds of objections to comparatívism raised by specialists in biblical studies and the types of distortions that may result when data is abstracted out of context. It is, frankly, safer to be a specialist. The formal comparison of traditions may be less technically demanding than the work of specialists, but the methodological considerations are perhaps more challenging. By so saying, the assigning of degrees of difficulty is not intended; rather, "larger" philosophical considerations must be worked out before bodies of disparate data are to be "scientifically" compared with heightened methodological awareness. (Here, "scientifically" is used more in its verificatory sense apart from what has come to be known as the "scientific method" as religious data are typically not susceptible to quantification and must therefore be evaluated qualitatively.)

Ideally, comparison should explore for patterns, modalities, or relationships among disparate sources. This raises a fundamental question in the academic study of religion: What does it mean to compare? How does one interpret formal similarities between two traditions? What difference do differences make? Can formal differences be functionally analagous? Can formal similarities be functionally anomalous? Can differential explanations be formulated to interpret a complexity of similarities and differences? And how does one account for formal similarities that, over time, take on differences of meaning? Indeed, a process of symbolic transformation takes place when affine imagery takes on new shades of significance over time. If the present study succeeds in accounting for such symbolic transformation, it will have had explanatory power.

Comparison should attempt to explain why it sees what it sees, and why what it sees is significant. The larger issues, "the big picture," and whatever the "overwhelming question" might be, the research agenda, with its presenting problem—the mystery it wishes to solve—can only be framed rudely and abstractly. Indeed, comparison is a figment of the imagination, an "invention," as Jonathan Z. Smith notes: "Borrowing Edmundo O'Gorman's historiographic distinction between discovery as the finding of something one has set out to look for and invention as the subsequent realization of novelty one has not intended to find, we must label comparison an invention" (1982b, 21). Cynically, even the purpose of comparison is open to question, as Smith sums up well: "But the 'how' and the 'why' and, above all, 'so what' remain most refractory" (ibid., 35).

Methodology, the "logic of research" (Colpe 1979, 161), is not method *stricto sensu*; but the latter, as practical application, should arise from the former. In other words, a distinction obtains between methodology (as a philosophical orientation), and research technique (as applied methodology). Methodology is the watchdog of the Study of Religion. Its principal corrective value is that it is bias detecting and epistemologically aware. Methodology can tell us much about credibility, as well as the impingement of worldview on the research enterprise. The Study of Religion, in its purest disciplinary form, should not be value-oriented, although the discipline is oriented towards value systems.

Ideally, a "preliminary neutralization of the ideological factor" (Colpe 1979, 162) shall have taken place in the mind of the researcher. This need not preclude the bicameral life of the scholar as a holder of values, religious or humanist. C. J. Bleeker has been careful to unburden religious studies of its putative moral purpose without completely disengaging the discipline from having social impact in that direction purely as a by-product: "This judgment applies in the first place to the opinion of the people who think that the history of religions and the phenomenology of religion should mainly serve to foster world-peace and social harmony, by creating mutual understanding among the adherents of different religions. It is to be hoped that these high benefits for humanity may be the additional results of the studies which we have in view. . . . In fact, students of the history of religions and of the phenomenology of religion belong to different religious confessions and churches, or profess no religion; what unites them is the unbiased study of religion as a phenomenon of historical and current interest" (Bleeker 1979, 174–75; cf. idem 1972, 41–42).

As to research technique, the academic study of religion has yet not evolved any systematic rules for comparison. It lacks a methodological dogma; it has no canon of method. A formal comparison of religions that claims to be of native origin from within the Study of Religion is of prospective interest for the entire field. Such a comparative endeavor would constitute an "event" that, if compelling in its coherence, would command the attention of its professionals. A theoretically generic model is a candidate for generalization, even for export to other fields. Whether the present study will have any such methodologically generalizable potential, or not, is for others to judge.

"In no literature on comparison that I am familiar with," writes J. Z. Smith, "has there been any presentation of rules for the production of comparisons; what few rules have been proposed pertain to their *post facto* evaluation" (1982b, 21). From the vantage of the study of religion, one is obliged to look elsewhere for specific comparative strategies. Models of comparative methodology, in all practicality, are almost always imported from external disciplines: anthropology, sociology, and linguistics are prime examples of disciplines that have endeavored to formalize procedures for comparison. With regard to the study of religion, that discipline which has devoted the most attention to the problem of comparison at the methodological level appears to be anthropology of religion. A seminal article on the comparative method is that of Poole (1986).

Comparison has been defined as the attempt "to seek out affinities and oppositions" (Lonergan 1972, 250). J. Z. Smith stresses a functional dimension: "A comparison is a disciplined exaggeration in the service of knowledge. It lifts out and strongly marks certain features within difference as being of possible intellectual significance" (1990, 52). Smith has identified four primary modes of comparison: the *ethnographic*, the *encyclopaedic*, the *morphological*, and the *evolutionary*, to which he adds the *statistical*, the *structural*, and *"systematic description and comparison"* (1982b, 22–25). According to Jensen, the enterprise of comparison is said to encompass one or more of the following: (1) Forms; (2) Functions; (3) Structures; (4) Meanings (1992, 1).

The utility of the comparative method is that it serves as a phenomenological tool in the service of scholarship. In solving a "problem" in our understanding of religion in general, religions themselves are dissolved in the solution: "Comparison does not deal with phenomena *in toto* or in the round, but only with an aspectual characteristic of them. . . . The comparability of phenomena always depends both on the purpose of comparison and on a theoretically informed analysis. Neither phenomenologically whole entities nor their local meanings are preserved in comparison. What matters in comparison are certain variables that are posited by and cohere in theories and that are aligned with aspects of the phenomena to be compared through some set of correspondence rules" (Poole 1986, 414–15). Comparisons do not constrain religions. At best, they merely illuminate them.

Although comparison abstracts phenomena to extract variables for analysis, the researcher still comes back to the traditions under examination to test for coherence of the analytical result. Neither the adducing of parallels nor the adducing of dissimilarities must blur the respective contours of each tradition being compared. It is, after all, the contours that are to be compared—the shape of doctrine and the vision of experience—not the mass of details. Once this is done, underlying thought structures may be discerned, or at least hypothesized. Any comparison between two conceptual systems of spirituality has to be sensitive to differences, however overt or subtle. This having been said, it is likewise the enterprise of comparison to stake out similarities, and to comment on their significances. A hypothesis that tries to account for both similarities and differences is one that is at once "straining to identify the underlying pattern of stability of religious phenomena" while trying "to come to terms with the change factor: the moving, inconstant, spontaneous, irregular, discontinuous, non-forensic, once-only, explosive, surprise element" (Capps 1979, 185).

Under ideal circumstances, the quest of the comparative enterprise—to tease out underlying depth structures common to two or more traditions—may, on occasion, culminate in the scholar's peak experience, described by Jonathan Z. Smith as "the thrill of encountering a coincidence": "The discovery that two events, symbols, thoughts, or texts, while so utterly separated by time and space that they could not 'really' be connected, seem, nevertheless, to be the same or to be speaking directly to another raises the possibility of a secret interconnection of things that is the scholar's most cherished article of faith. The thought that the patterns and interrelationships that he has patiently and laboriously teased out of his data might, in fact, exist is the claim he makes when his work is completed as well as the claim that appears to be denied by the fact that he has had to labor so long. . . . And this is why coincidence is, at one and the same time, so exhilarating and so stunning. It is as if, unbidden and unearned by work and interpretation, a connection simply 'chose' to make itself manifest, to display its presence on our conceptual wall with a clear round hand" (1982c, 53). While comparison, in another Smithean sense, is "invention" in terms of the methodological artifice itself, successful comparison provides insight.

Discovery is its own reward. Not every study will repay the investigator in this way. The chances of a comparative study contributing significantly to the advancement of knowledge within the discipline of the Study of Religion is, on the one hand, limited by the lack of consensus on comparative methodology itself, yet, on the other hand, favored by the relatively open and uncanonized state of scholarship on matters comparative.

The "New Comparativism." Questions surrounding the role of comparison in the Study of Religion, as well as the methodology of comparison itself, have recently received renewed interest. In 1994, the North American Association for the Study of Religion organized two panels on what is being called the "New Comparativism." The first panel took place at the spring 1994 Midwest regional conference of the American Academy of Religion (AAR). The proceedings of this panel were revised and published in 1996. The follow-up symposium took place at the fall 1994 annual meeting of the AAR.

Martin commences the proceedings volume with a retrospective: "The study of religion in North America has been shaped by the work of Mircea Eliade more than by that of any other single scholar" (Martin 1996, 1). Much of Eliade's work has since been questioned. The validity of his methodology, together with the phenomenological/morphological tradition which Eliade so visibly represented, has often been rejected outright. "We thought it timely, therefore," Martin remarks, "to explore systematically the possible shapes of a post-Eliadean paradigm for the study of religion." This has everything to do with comparison, since "the field initially emerged from and around issues of comparison" (ibid.). Politically, in ways that directly affect funding, this is an issue that impinges on how one "justifies religious studies as a secular field" (Paden 1996a, 5).

These two symposia have largely been responses to the position paper given by William E. Paden, entitled, "Elements of a New Comparativism" (1996a). The paper begins with a cynical statement on the state of scholarship of comparison in the Study of Religion: there is precious little of it. Except for notable studies by J. Z. Smith and Poole (cited above), Paden wonders "how comparativist models have been advanced" (1996a, 5), if at all. "Classical comparativism" was marked by a relatively "contextless character" (ibid.). The older comparativist endeavors typically overleapt their emic contexts and, in so doing, obliterated local meanings and contexts. Comparativism to date has tended to be "laden with religious or anti-religious purpose," and has been problematic in university settings, owing to no small amount of "theological privileging, ahistoricism, and foundationalism" (ibid., 5–6).

The foundationalism to which Paden refers is characterized by discourse about "the sacred" or "the holy" that, without explicit bracketing, entails ontological commitments. The descriptor, "sacred," should demarcate a range of human behaviors that interact with objects deemed to be supernatural and sacred. Such objects of veneration are typically protected from profanization. But, whatever the "sacred" is to whomever, it must be "de-reified" (ibid., 6). To avoid foundationalism, the data must never be preinterpreted, or dogmatically privileged. This being said, Paden accepts the utility of a concept like "the Holy," so long as it is understood that this is a nonontological referent to "worldmaking" in the religious experience (ibid., 12).

Classical phenomenology privileges the generic, while anthropology foregrounds the culturally specific. Comparison must mediate between the two. To use an Eliadean term, the comparativist venture was, and still is, a quest for "patterns." Such a pattern is bilateral: it functions as a bridge, linking generic and culture-specific understanding. A pattern communicates dialectically between a "greater generalization (with its theoretic resonance) and narrower, more specific, local investigation (with its empirical constraints)" (ibid., 9). To this end, cross-cultural analysis must somehow strike a balance between morphological forms of analysis (phenomenology of religion) and anthropological studies. The former is generic, the latter is culture specific: "Comparative analysis," Paden maintains, "works a spectrum between macro-thematic patterns, which are trans-cultural, and micro-thematic patterns, which are intra-cultural" (ibid., 8). Paden adds this word of caution: "Comparative patterns are not fixed archetypes" but rather are "refineable concepts for uncovering, sorting out, and testing selected commonalities and differences between religious expressions." In an ideal investigation, such a pattern may become an "instrument of discovery" (ibid., 7).

Comparison should bring into bold relief differences as well as similarities. A balance between the two conserves a potential for deriving theoretical significance from the arbitrary juxtaposition of culturally embedded particulars. The more pronounced the contextuality, the greater the incomparability. Therein lies the paradox of comparison. But, Paden is quick to add: "By drawing attention to the selectively generic aspects of a religious practice, they provide a wider (and sometimes wider means 'human') context to the otherwise singular, opaque embeddedness of the object in the cultural horizon of its adherents" (ibid., 10). For Paden, comparativism is not simply typology or the description of the role of "the sacred" in human societies. "Rather," Paden concludes, "it is the central and proper endeavor of religious studies as a field of inquiry and the core part of the process of forming, testing, and applying generalizations about religion at any level" (ibid., 12). In other words, comparison forms the basis for theoretical analysis.

Marsha Hewitt responds to Paden's essay with some concerns of her own. This discussion stands in implicit dialogue with other critical discourses, notably current feminist theory. Paden's "New Comparativism" was not sufficiently developed. The "identification of patterns," which lies at the core of the comparative enterprise, was not "given the sustained theoretical attention required" (Hewitt 1996, 15). Moreover, Hewitt worries that such endeavors show "a greater preoccupation with establishing universal interpretive frameworks that sacrifice particularity rather than preserve it" (ibid., 16). She warns of "effacement or marginalization of particularity" if a proper dialectic is not maintained betweeen the two. Hewitt goes to the brink of openly opposing theory and fieldwork: "The relationship between theories and conceptualizations of religion and concrete human religious practice, in my view," Hewitt says, "represents one of the most significant challenges to the academic study of religion" (ibid.)

Furthermore, the academic study of religion "is political because it harbors a dimension of power" (ibid., 17) in the management of information. What concerns Hewitt most is "colonization or annexation of the other" (ibid., 15). This was the imperialism of the old comparativism. Without a proper relational theory of reciprocity, in which the researcher is understood within a process of interaction, there is a danger that "we end up imprisoned in an epistemological mirror where we see our own reflection, and little else" (ibid., 18). Of course, particularity without universality is also meaningless. For Hewitt, the new comparativism means a shift from the old view of *homo religiosus* to a concept of *homo faber*, or world builder (ibid., 19).

From a history-of-science perspective, Donald Wiebe tries to place comparativism within the history of *Religionswissenschaft*. He argues that the novel elements in Paden's "New Comparativism" lie in its departure from Eliade. Wiebe then embarks on a retrospective and shows that L. H. Jordan had articulated some of these very same concerns back in 1915. Wiebe extends the retrospective in reviewing some of the views of Andrew Lang, Edmund Leach, C. Scott Littleton, and Georges Dumézil. After standing once again on the shoulders of these giants, Wiebe concludes that "it is not clear from the history of the use of the so-called comparative method that it is really a method capable of any precise formulation." Simply going beyond Eliadeanism is not the same as advancing a new methodology. "It is a heuristic device of major importance," Wiebe concedes, "in coming to generalizations about things, events, and processes, and in that sense plays an important explanatory and theoretical role in those various fields of study in which it is used" (1996, 28). But it is not, as Paden would have us believe, the "central and proper endeavour" of the Study of Religion.

From the vantage of cognitive psychology, E. Thomas Lawson looks at the ways in which young children depend upon comparison to achieve crucial distinctions in their knowledge of the world. In this light, the "New Comparativism" is really not so new. It is, in fact, "a fundamental cognitive property" (1996, 32) and "*an essential ingredient in any approach that claims to advance our knowledge*" (ibid., 33). While comparison finds a firm footing in the quest for knowledge, comparison is only as good as the theory that supports it.

In Paden's responses to the panelists, he agrees with Hewitt's caveat against conceptual imperialism. Hewitt's interactive and moral strictures are simply protocols that are different from the methodologically refined and reflexive protocols that Paden has advocated. Notwithstanding, Paden claims that: "Comparativist understanding can also effect a kind of reverse colonization" through a process of demythologizing the constructs of the old comparativism, of maintaining a vigilant "suspicion of eurocentrisms and class values." (1996b, 39). (This came across as somewhat patronizing and unconvincing.) To his credit, Paden openly discloses some of the classic misuses which comparativism has served, to wit: "Christian apologetics using comparativism as an instrument of subordination, universalists using it to equalize religions, and romanticists and mystics using it to give prestige to religions of nature or of inner enlightenment over against historical, doctrinal religions" (ibid.). These are what the new comparativism must guard against.

Wiebe has acknowledged that Paden's program is "post-theological" and post-European. Paden argues that the New Comparativism is also post-Eliadean. Paden shares some of the same concerns as Wiebe over the legacy of Eliade. "The problematic nature of Eliade's phenomenology," Paden adjudges, "is his oscillation between these two vocabularies: the hermeneutics of symbols and the structuring activities of mythic and ritual behaviour." Nonetheless, Paden is not so dismissive of Eliade's contributions: "Much of Eliade's work on religious world building, minus his perennialist hermeneutical overlay, can thereby be converted into concepts of potential theoretic interest and testability" (ibid., 43).

While the new comparativism can salvage some good from the old, it must go beyond "the otherwise bankrupt intellectual capital of the history of religions tradition" (ibid.). Far from being a mere "extrapolation of patterns," Paden concurs with J. Z. Smith's call for "the integration of a complex notion of pattern and system with an equally complex notion of history" (1996b, 40, citing Smith 1982b, 29). Vigilant awareness of the dialectic shifts of perspective between cultural microscope and cross-cultural binoculars (my metaphor, not Paden's) is a self-regulating process not present in the old comparativism. Moreover, the new comparativism "is as interested in category critique as in category application" (1996b, 44).

Paden concedes Wiebe's criticism that the New Comparativism lacks a specific technique. This is rightly so, according to Paden, as comparative research does not follow a set procedure. Countering Wiebe's objection that comparison is not central to the Study of Religion, Paden argues: "Comparativism is the one activity without which there would be no field of religion" (ibid., 42). Concept formation necessarily derives from comparative work.

Paden politely rejects Lawson's cognitive psychology analogy, explaining that "the specific issue at hand is the transition from old to contemporary academic comparativism" (ibid., 44). What is new is the way in which similarities are nuanced. First of all, they are now considered aspectual, not essential. Similarity must attend to diverse local meanings and social functions. This does not implicate category ambiguity so much as a concept of "pattern reflexivity and differentiation," whereby similarity claims are nuanced by the subtleties of "graded judgments" (ibid., 45). A fundamental difference between the old and new comparativisms has to do with the overall research objectives: "Comparative work in this mode is not looking for ideological or ethical religious universals, but for determinative categories of human action and the intelligibility of those categories" (ibid.). Beyond the categories themselves, there is the problem of explanation. Comparativism, under certain circumstances, can explain what history cannot. "Thematic analysis," writes Paden, "can elucidate historical data and account for recurring patterns not explainable by historical diffusion" (ibid., 47). The problem is that there is lack of a "common theoretical matrix" as well as a common purpose.

Continued progress will most likely result from the ongoing interface among disciplines. In turn, this might bring closer the day when comparativism will come of age, and the Study of Religion might emerge as a "propaedeutic discipline" (ibid., 48).

Comparison in the present study. Scripturally based religions as well as oral wisdom traditions have contributed works of genius (whether "divinely inspired" or "revealed" or simply sagacious) that constitute vital ideological resources of civilization. In comparing Syriac Christianity with the Bahā'ī Faith, we are theoretically engaging two such vital ideological resources, two religious worlds. We are asking the sources for structures. This study will explore for patterning common to both Syriac Christian and Bahā'ī conceptual systems, through an analysis of their respective "key symbols." Although some sense of outcome is hypothetically anticipated, the results are not foreknown.

The object of the present study is to solve the problem of similarity in terms of difference. As an exercise in comparative method, it makes eminent sense to opt for a limited systematic comparison. This investigation therefore invokes Platvoet's (1982) research strategy of restrictive comparison, which is more amenable to investigative control (cf. Bloch 1970; Bock 1966; Eggan 1964; Goldschmidt 1966; Köbben 1970; Leach 1968; Marsh 1967; Sjöberg 1955). To a certain extent, method must be tailored to the data under study, yet any comparative study is implicitly a statement about comparative method. Conceived here is not a quantitative, but a qualitative method. It is case oriented rather than variable oriented. Method is a means to an end, but not the means to a predetermined end.

Terminological and philosophical comparisons (*intellectualist* theory), generally, represent the norm for formal comparisons of religious documents as primary sources. However, the present study is principally concerned with *symbolist* theory. According to Mircea Eliade, the historian of religions is, above all, a hermeneut, not a philologist (though philology remains a critical tool). Interpretation of the labyrinthine mass of religious data is what the history of religions is all about (1969, 91). "The historian of religions," explains Eliade, "is preoccupied uniquely with *religious* symbols" (ibid., 88). C. J. Bleeker adds that "philological and historical studies, brilliant as they may be, lead only halfways. The student of the history of religions should be more ambitious: he should never rest before he has clarified the religious significance of certain phenomena, however sphinxlike they may look" (1972, 44). Given that religious thinking is largely structured on prediscursive images or symbols, one contribution of this investigation is its emphasis on figurative language and symbolism as a complement to discursive religious thought.

The present study is interested in drawing a "comparison of comparisons," as it were, as an approach to traditions rich in metaphor. It is recognized that metaphorical commensurability is no guarantor of doctrinal affinity. Neither "truth" nor "logic" is of primary concern here. (According to Smart, the "logic" of religious studies entails the comparative analysis of religious doctrines, an operation of the philosophy of religion [Smart 1986b, 10].) In the present study, it is the metaphorical "lie" which is of principal interest, with respect to symbolism in general and Paradise imagery in particular.

The metaphorical expression of doctrine allows for both conceptual and expressive comparisons. With respect to religious paradigms, the soteriology of each system will also be compared, the social meaning of which in effect is community defining. Elements of social patterning, such as sacramental practices, modes of conduct, expressions of art and iconography, and other expressions of faith, lie beyond our purview here. Wherever appropriate, a discussion of key conceptual terms may prove illuminative.

In the dialogue between ideas and evidence, ideal-typic images will be compared synchronically instead of diachronically. This study is comparative-systematic (a generalized approach) and not philological-historical (the specifying approach). There is no need here to reduplicate the work of specialists except when the crux of an argument so depends. However, original sources will be consulted as a necessary control.

Phenomenology of religion necessarily draws from the history of religions. The outcome of the differences between Syriac and Bahā'ī symbol systems might provide some raw material for historical investigation, but the comparison at hand does not seek to implicate any historical theory. Of course, frequent reference to history is necessary for contextualizing the two symbol systems. Moreover, each symbol system will be analyzed in part in terms of a dialectic with history, which views each religion as a form of "response" to the challenges of the historical present.

In noting this debt to history, the present study makes no attempt to formulate a causal explanation in terms of history, in order to account for similarities and differences between early Syriac Christianity and the Bahā'ī Faith as symbol systems. Furthermore, this study will not address the genetic issue of diffusion (borrowing mechanisms) versus independent invention. Indeed, "genealogy and analogy must be distinguished" (Alderink 1992, 218). Rather, our focus is on questions of typological symmetry (and asymmetry), not on problems of historical relationships.

Whenever possible, without sacrifice to honest academic appraisal, Wilfred Cantwell Smith's canon of believer intelligibility will be kept under advisement. In its simplest form, Smith's canon holds: *"It is the business of comparative religion to construct statements about religion that are intelligible within at least two traditions simultaneously"* (1969, 52). This is really an open-ended variation on the "emic" approach of the phenomenologist of religion, who, exercising *epoché* or critical restraint, views the self-defining characteristics of any religion as validating (but not as the only verificatory criterion).

Notwithstanding, one of the implicative functions of the academic exercise is what Rudolph terms "the ideologically critical"—that is, "the dispute, from the point of view of historically gained insights, with the religions' own self-understanding, and the decisive demarcation of the differences from individual theologies (dogmatisms) and religious movements" (1979, 105).

Symbolic Transformation as Paradigm Shift

Operative hypothesis. Key symbols across Syriac and Bahā'ī traditions exhibit both similarities and differences, both partial and contrastive. Local differences may be "explained" in terms of systemic differences. Thus, this hypothesis: *"Parallels" yield paradoxes of commensurability resolvable by paradigm "logics" within religious systems.* This operating hypothesis requires that careful attention be given to both internal analysis (local) and external analysis (comparative).

Metaphors and symbols in the Bahā'ī Faith appear to compare closely with those in Syriac Christianity due to the operation of immanental, superordinating root metaphors and key scenarios common to each. Conceptual differences arising from these affective congruences may be explained by respective incommensurables of soteriology. To the extent that there is continuity between the two traditions, one may begin to speak, in dynamic terms, of a "paradigm shift" rather than a static paradigm difference. While the present study will not postulate a paradigm shift, it will explore for the possibility by undertaking the preliminary comparative work.

Specific hypothesis. Our specific hypothesis postulates: *Formal comparison of early Syriac Christianity and the Bahā'ī Faith is constrained by their paradigms (respectively, transformational purity and concentric unity), by which all phenomenological parallels must be interpreted.* Religions have systemic characteristics, which will be analyzed in terms of overarching "paradigms." Early Syriac Christianity appears to exhibit a paradigm of transformational purity, while the Bahā'ī Faith is modelled on a paradigm of concentric unity. The former is consonant with world-rejecting, vertical soteriologies of Late Antiquity. The latter is more of a "horizontal" soteriology. It resonates with modernity, to the extent of assimilating and rendering sacred certain aspects of modernity.

One fundamental difference between Christianity and the Bahā'ī Faith may be seen in Syriac Christianity's sacramental view of reality (purity paradigm) in contrast to the Bahā'ī Faith's universalist view of reality (unity paradigm). This similarity/distinctiveness paradox may be resolved historically in terms of a (theoretical) paradigm shift, partially mediated by Islam (community paradigm), from individual salvation to mutual salvation, the respective conditions for the realization of which are quite different in emphasis, though there is overlap in practice. Soteriologically, this contrast may be analyzed as an inverse relationship. Historical evidence will be referentially adduced as a warrant, but not as a proof for such a hypothesis.

Moreover, our specific hypothesis also holds that comparison of these two religions reveals an uneven distribution of expressively congruent root metaphors across several domains, but that key scenarios show fundamental divergences in the actualization of these root metaphors. One might say that demonstrable similarities are predictable due to a historically genetic relationship between the two faiths. We resist a temptation to posit a deeper relationship based on some kind of essentialist interpretation.

Interpretively, in terms of worldview analysis, what we predict will emerge from the comparative procedures outlined above is as follows: As religions of revelation in the Abrahamic tradition, early Syriac Christianity and the Bahā'ī Faith will most likely exhibit fundamental expressive affinities, but with local meanings indexed to their respective paradigms. Christ as "Physician," for example, dispenses immortality, while Bahā'u'llāh, as Physician, dispenses unity. Both dispense salvation in their respective conceptions of it.

Symbolic transformation is a coefficient of responses to changes in history. Early Syriac Christianity is based on a paradigm of purity. It is one response to Late Antiquity. In one respect, Ephrem rejected the "modernity" of his day by rejecting Hellenism. (On Ephrem's knowledge of Greek, see now Koonammakkal 1994). From another perspective, Ephrem rejected "archaic" religions as well. Bahā'u'llāh, however, embraced modernity by sacralizing it.

Contrastive comparison. Of intrinsic theoretical importance is contrastive analysis. Once expressive similarities are accounted for, fundamental differences between the two religions should become more apparent. Not lack of data, but lack of adequate theory characterizes the present state of most comparative endeavors in the Study of Religion. As J. Z. Smith observes: "The issue confronting the enterprise of religious comparison is not so much one of a lack of data, as one of inadequate theory ranging from matters of classification to more complex matters of interpretation and explanation" (1990, 118).

In *Drudgery Divine* (1990), Jonathan Z. Smith, in the words of one reviewer, "historicizes the comparative study of early Christianity and shows how it arises in the context of, and is used to sustain, various polemical positions, for example, blaming the corruption of Christianity on some opponent or other, whether it be Platonists, Jews, or Catholics." "In particular," the reviewer continues, "the comparative study of early Christianity was deeply entangled in Protestant anti-Catholic polemics that searched for and therefore created a pure and idealized early Christianity that had not been degraded through the absorption of practices and beliefs from other religions" (Eilberg-Schwartz 1993, 301). Smith's study gives pause for thought: Can any comparison of religions be value free?

It is necessary, therefore, to rely on method as a structural control. By delineating the research design which structures this study, a certain measure of falsification is made possible at the methodological level. There is likewise the need for interpretive control. Determination of key symbols discloses the metaphoric structures of a religious paradigm. If the underlying paradigm is not factored into a description and interpretation of these symbols, all control over their comparison is lost.

The present study is an operation of comparative method on mythopoeic thought. With respect to the hypotheses outlined above, the purpose of the worldview analysis undertaken in this study is to construct an integrated explanation to try to resolve the congruence/incongruence paradox in which Syriac Christianity and the Bahā'ī Faith are both alike and dissimilar. If valid, both the specific as well as operative hypotheses will qualitatively account for not only unexplained variance (contrast) but for unexplained consistency (correlation). Such an integrative method renders comparative phenomenology more precise.

II

A Historical Profile of Syriac Christianity

Syriac Christianity

The Christian world of the third and fourth centuries consisted of three major culture areas: (1) the Latin West (until its fall in 476 C.E.); (2) the Greek East (in 395, Byzantium); and (3) the Syriac Orient (northern Mesopotamia in the upper Tigris Euphrates valley; and the border province of Adiabene (see Neusner 1966), formerly known as "Assyria" under Trajan in 116 C.E., but reconquered by Persia). "The idea that the early Christian tradition was limited to its Greek and Latin expressions is still widespread," writes John Meyendorff. "This assumption distorts historical reality and weakens greatly our understanding of the roots of Christian theology and spirituality. In the third and fourth centuries Syriac was the third international language of the church" (1989, 1).

Introduction: Unlike Judaism and Islam, Christianity had no sacred language (Bausani 1971, 57). Nevertheless, Syriac comes very close to being a sacred Christian language, since Syriac is a dialect of Aramaic, the language Jesus spoke. There is a temptation to interpret early Syriac Christian texts as having reflexive value for reconstructing some type of quintessentially "pure" form of early Christianity—one that might have developed directly from the very structures of Jesus's own thought world. While such an enterprise is as romantic as it is problematic, Syriac studies is of intrinsic interest for its local color. It is a mosaic of images and symbols, an ornate cathedral of thought and spirit.

Spiritually as well as linguistically, Syriac Christianity is distinct from the Greek East and the Latin West. It is the least-studied stream of early Christianity, possibly the most challenging. "Whoever wishes to study the doctrine of the early Syriac Fathers will look in vain for formal treatments in clear propositions," warns Murray. "All is symbolic and figurative" (1964, 315). In its pre-schismatic period, early Syriac Christianity discloses the profoundly Semitic character of a comparatively less-hellenized form of Christian thought and praxis. Syriac Christianity is distinguished by its rich symbolism, its disdain of precise and reductionistic creedalism, its preponderantly liturgical expression of Christian truth in folk-level piety, and in its quest for purity of love and totality of religious commitment in anticipation of eschatological requital. The Syriac penchant for symbolism is pervasive. It suffuses the sanctuary, filling it with images of Paradise. Apart from its reality, Paradise certainly is imagined, and is a very "real" psychological presence.

Qualitatively, one significant difference between the mainstream Church of the Greco-Latin world and that of Oriental Christianity may lie in the realm of noëtics. The antithetical and substantial logic of Aristotle—introduced into Christian theology by medieval scholars—is said to have been rooted in the *haptic* (tactile) cognition of reality. The metaphoric way of expression in Oriental Christianity, on the other hand, is the manifestation of the logic of assimilations and identifications in the optical cognition of reality. This is really a carryover from Semitic spirituality, possibly mediated through some form of Jewish Christianity. (The Jewish-Christian hypothesis is the only one that, for Murray [1975a, 16], satisfies the number of significant coincidences attested in a wide range of early Syriac Christian documents.) In Syriac Christianity, therefore, one finds the perspectivist approach in which the proximal is synthesized with the distantial, giving rise to metaphoric expressions, parables, symbolic deeds, and visions (see Nandrásky 1980). This orientation expresses itself in Syriac Christian poetry as paradox and symbol, rather than by the definition and analysis one finds in Christian prose. (A symbolic form common to all Christian traditions was typology, the symbolic prefigurement of Christ in Christian reading of Jewish scriptures and in other texts as well.)

Although Syriac Christianity developed in both the Roman and Persian Empires and spread as far as China, for several centuries its legacy would predominate in Persia. In Late Antiquity, from the fifth century if not before, what was officially named the "Church of the East" (but more widely known as Nestorianism) became the most influential form of extra-Roman Christianity up to the Arab conquest and beyond, until the Mongol slaughter in the thirteenth century decimated the Syriac-speaking Church of Persia. The most pristine form of Syriac Christianity flourished in the period prior to the fateful Orthodox, Nestorian, and Monophysite schisms in which Greek Christological concepts were debated. These schisms took place in the fifth century. Notwithstanding, Syriac Christian imagery and typology were never in dispute (Murray 1975a, 36 and 347). Thus, early Syriac Christianity was a preschismatic, pre-Hellenized (with respect to later Christological debates) forerunner of the Church of Persia.

From its obscure origins, early Syriac Christianity slowly crystallized "as a sort of precipitate in a cloudy solution" (op. cit., 7). This was during a time when Rome and Persia were the "two shoulders of the world" as the Synod of 420 C.E. characterizes the two superpowers (Brock 1982a, 7). Between Rome and Persia was a border state caught in the middle, whose fortunes were tied to the spoils of war. The tiny principality of Osrhoëne was part of this power struggle, first between the Roman Empire and the Parthians, and later between the Byzantines and the Sasanian Persians. Osrhoëne was a small northern Mesopotamian kingdom around Edessa, from which Syriac is thought to have originated. In 132 C.E., Osrhoëne was established by a Seleucid governor of Persian ancestry named Osrhöes (Khusraw, Chosroes). Thereafter it was governed by rulers Arab ancestry until, in 211 C.E., the emperor Caracalla conquered Osrhoëne, turning it into a Roman province. It is said to have become a Christian state under the rule of Abgar VIII, known as Abgar the Great (177–212 C.E.). This oscillation of power had left Edessa relatively independent, until it came under Roman spear in 242 with the abdication of Abgar X.

Syriac Christianity thus developed from within the imperial domains of the Mediterranean world's two superpowers: the Roman Empire and the Persian Empire. Persian territory extended from Mesopotamia to the borders of India and from Armenia to Arabia (Rilliet 1992b, 2: 674). As a cultural interworld, Syriac Christianity straddled the frontiers of both empires. Its sphere of influence was an ellipse, with dual centers in Edessa (ancient Urhāy, capital of the Roman province of Osrhoëne in eastern Syria, now modern Urfa in southeastern Turkey) and in the frontier city of Nisibis (recaptured by Persia in 363 C.E.). Ancient Nisibis was an outpost of the eastern Roman Empire, now modern Nuseybin on the border between Turkey and Syria. Along the Silk Road, Osrhoëne and Adiabene met at Nisibis, on the boundary between East (the Persian empire) and West (the Roman Empire).

Ephrem the Syrian and Aphrahāṭ "the Persian Sage"

The two most important witnesses to early Syriac Christianity are Ephrem the Syrian (d. 373 C.E.) and Aphrahāṭ, "the Persian Sage" (d. c. 345 C.E.). These two writers established the grammar of images that became the core of Syriac spirituality during its formative period. Beyond the Syriac culture area, Ephrem is a truly universal representative of early Christianity by virtue of his widespread acclaim outside of his own immediate culture area. Although Ephrem wrote in Syriac, his fame spread across the Christian world, first to the Greek East, then the Latin West. Ephrem is arguably the greatest poet of the patristic age, and his "rediscovery" (Murray 1967) in recent years, as it were, has led to a revalorization of his reputation.

Aphrahāṭ the Persian Sage. The first major Christian writer in Syriac was Ephrem's older contemporary, Ya'qub Aphrahāṭ (Persian *Frahāṭ*, modern *Farhād*), known as "the Persian sage" (*ḥakkīma farsāyā*). Author of twenty-three theological *Demonstrations* or Treatises (*taḥwyāṯā*), little is known of Aphrahāṭ's life. Also known as Aphraates, he wrote his *Demonstrations* between 336 and 345 C.E. (the first ten were composed in 337; the next twelve [11–22] in 344; and the last in 345). Asmussen describes Aphrahāṭ as "the first historically distinct Iranian Christian of outstanding importance" (EIr 1: 570). Evidently, Aphrahāṭ was a Persian name (Justi 1895, 101–102, cited in McCullough 1982, 114, n. 4). "[H]is traditional surname 'the Persian sage,'" comments René Lavenant, "shows that he was a subject of the Persian empire" (1992, 1: 54). A fourteenth-century manuscript claims Aphrahāṭ to have been an abbot of the monastery of Mar Mattai near Mosul, which, although doubtful, still places him under Persian rule. There is no mention in Aphrahāṭ's writings of the Council of Nicea, as would be expected had he lived in the Roman empire. Nor does Aphrahāṭ mention Zoroastrianism, as would be expected of a Christian who lived in the Persian empire (McCullough 1982, 114–15). Yet there does appear to be a consensus on Aphrahāṭ's Persian context. This is reflected in a recent study, in which "Persian Mesopotamia" is established as Aphrahāṭ's historical setting (Koltun-Fromm 1996) Aphrahāṭ's fourteenth *Demonstration* was in fact addressed to the Christians of Seleucia-Ctesiphon, the capital of the Persian empire (Asmussen 1982), although the authorship of this text is in dispute (Pierre 1988, 1: 47–54).

In Aphrahāṭ's interpretations, primacy is given to spiritual truth over contemporary-historical truth, even though typological interpretation was itself considered "historical." The following piece of exegesis from Aphrahāṭ's *Demonstration* IV.5–6, *On Prayer*, is characteristic of the local Christianity in Persia to which Aphrahāṭ bears witness, and of Syriac spirituality in general: "Our father Jacob too prayed at Bethel and saw the gate of heaven opened, with a ladder going up on high (Gen. 28:12). . . . See, my beloved, how many symbols are hidden in that vision which Jacob saw: he saw the gate of heaven, which is the Messiah; he saw the ladder, symbol of the Cross; he anointed the stones, a type for the Peoples" (Brock 1987, 8–9). The narrative source material here is Jewish (cf. Brock 1979a, 225–26). In evidence is Aphrahāṭ's effective use of thematic parallelism, a traditionally Jewish literary form. Thematic parallelism runs throughout Aphrahāṭ. A good example of it is cited by Murray, who analyzes "The Grape in the Cluster" (Aph. Dem.

XXIII passim), an imaginative reflection on God's relationship with man, as inspired by Isaiah 65:8–9 (Murray 1975, 113–19). Not only did "the Persian Sage" employ simple parallelism, he extended parallelism as well. His use of Jewish themes, however, is not strictly exegetical. It is homiletic and creatively so. John Corbett (1987) has shown that many of Aphrahāṭ's themes are Pauline in nature.

The *Demonstrations* are stylistically vivified through rhythmic patterns within the prose discourse itself. Aphrahāṭ appears to have adapted a rhetorical device known as *syncrisis* (a figure of speech by which opposite things or persons are compared). Aphrahāṭ seems to have used syncrisis in a rhythmically formalized way. This special literary technique found in Aphrahāṭ is what Murray calls a "comparison-series" (SCK 42). Aphrahāṭ's exegesis safely remains within the limits of typology, with both ends of the exegetical process rooted in "history"—this being the definitive delimitation of *historia* and *theōria*. The prosaic prose of Aphrahāṭ, lapsing as it does into cadent thematic comparisons, anticipates the rich poetic and exegetical Syriac tradition to follow.

Ephrem the Syrian. The foremost Church Father of early Syriac Christianity, Ephrem the Syrian was born c. 306 C.E. in Nisibis (*Nṣībīn*; SCK 8), a strategic city along the Roman silk route. In 363 C.E., the Romans ceded Nisibis to the Persians. Ephrem made his new home in Edessa (the native Syriac name for which was Urhāy). Although Ephrem did not choose to remain in Nisibis, which was now a Persian outpost, his influence did. Syriac Christianity bridged the cultural divide along the Roman-Persian frontier, such that Ephrem's influence was coextensive with Persian Christianity. "In fact the doctor of Nisibis," writes one authority, referring to Ephrem, "is a privileged witness of the tradition of the primitive church of Persia, which lived at the margins of Greek culture" (Rilliet 1992a, 1: 276).

On the life of Saint Ephrem the Syrian (see Mathews 1989 and Lieu 1989), two hagiographic accounts are extant in Syriac. The most credible biographical details, however, are to be found in the *Encomium* pronounced on Ephrem by Gregory of Nyssa (d. 395). As a historian, Gregory assures us that his own account had derived from Ephrem's own writings and from no other source. As there is no evidence to suppose that Gregory knew Syriac, it is likely that the writings of Ephrem were translated at a very early date into Greek. Other Greek authorities on Ephrem include three fifth-century historians, Socrates, Sozomen, and Theodoret, as well as Jerome and Palladius. Details of these biographies have been presented and analyzed by J. Gwynn (1898).

What occasioned Gregory of Nyssa's biography was the fact that the early Church had annually commemorated Ephrem on the "Saint's

Day," normally observed on the anniversary of the death of the saint. In the East, the date was set at January 28. According to the *Chronicle of Edessa*, however, Ephrem died on 9 June 373 (Mathews 1994a, 36). This date continues to be observed as Ephrem's Feast Day in West Syrian tradition. Ephrem's tomb rests in the monastery of St. Sergius on the Mount of Edessa.

Evidently, Ephrem's parents were Christian (CH XXVI.10). At a youthful age, Ephrem experienced a personal conversion to Christianity (Virg. XXXVII.10) and was baptized (CH III.13). Ephrem mentions the first four bishops of Nisibis (CNis XIII–XXI). He grew up under the spiritual tutelage of Bishop Jacob of Nisibis, who was present at the Council of Nicea in 325 (Bundy 1991). Throughout his life in Nisibis, Ephrem had been a faithful deacon (*'allānā*) under three bishops: Jacob, Babu, and Vologeses (Mathews 1994a, 29). Having undertaken a vow of celibacy (HNis XV.9), Ephrem was one of the "Sons of the Covenant" (*bnay Qyāmā*). This is not Ephrem's turn of phrase here, but rather that of his biographer, Jacob of Sarug (d. 521). Because he had studied in Edessa and later became bishop of nearby Sarug, a town less than twenty-five miles south of Edessa, Jacob of Sarug's panegyrial *mēmrā* is of particular value.

Reflecting the native growth of an incipient Syrian asceticism, the concept of "Covenant" permeated Ephrem's thought world and structured the entire belief system of Syriac Christians. In *On Mār Ephrem the Teacher*, Jacob of Serug relates how Ephrem composed hymns and sung them to the harp, teaching lyrics and music to the "Daughters of the Covenant" as an antidote to the "poison" of the heretics (SCK 30). The expression "Daughters of the Covenant" for virgins deserves notice here. In speaking of the hagiography of the Edessan martyrs, Susan Ashbrook Harvey summarizes the meaning and importance of the concept: 'The simplicity of these narratives is belied by their strongly nuanced Syriac vocabulary, for the dialogues abound with the use of the terminology derived from the root *qwm*, 'to stand.' Christianity is repeatedly described here as a belief in which one 'stands'; and further, as a form of life and set of practices in which one 'stands.' The constant use of the root *qwm* for designating basic Christian life keeps us mindful of the place of asceticism in early Syriac Christianity. The term used here for the 'stance' of the Christian life is *qyāmā*, also carrying the sense of 'covenant,' as used for the *Bnay* and *Bnaṯ Qyāmā*. In the early fourth century, the Sons and Daughters of the Covenant were still an ambiguously defined part of the church, but the *Acts of Shmona and Guria* refer to the *Bnay* and *Bnat Qyāmā* as suffering particular abuse in these persecutions. The language of these *Acts* plays intentionally on *qyāmā*, 'covenant,' as another derivative from *qwm*: the 'covenant' of the consecrated life is not different from the 'stance' or covenant the lay

Christian has taken by the commitment of faith." (Harvey 1990, 199).

Another meaning of the term *qyāmā* that directly concerns the present study is that of "resurrection." Nagel (1966, 43f.) suggests that the term *qyāmā* means "standing" in the sense of *anastasis* ("resurrection"). The ascetics anticipated thus the *vita angelica* as "sons and daughters of the Resurrection." M. Williams, in reference to Nagel's study, states that "the Syrian *bnay qyāmā* / *bnāt qyāmā* tradition is another example of the development of the Jewish theme of 'standing before the Lord' (and assimilation to the condition of angels)" (1985, 90, n. 37; cf. Vööbus 1961 and Nedungatt 1973.)

Ephrem's life was tied to the vicissitudes of the Roman-Persian war. The Roman forces under Julian had suffered defeat in 363 C.E. at the gates of the Sasanid Persian capital of Seleucia-Ctesiphon (Middle Persian: *Tēspōn*). Julian's successor Jovian ceded to the Persian victor Shāpūr II (commonly written as Shapur) the northern Mesopotamian fortress-city of Nisibis, emptied of its Christian denizens. Attributing the fall of his native Nisibis to the apostasy of Julian, who was slain on the battlefield in the course of retreat, Ephrem relocated to Edessa, where he spent the final decade of his life. (There is some dispute as to whether or not Ephrem went directly to Edessa after Nisibis had been ceded to the Persians [see Mathews 1994a, 33].) Ephrem noted that the Persian king had evinced singular respect for the Christian churches by allowing the Roman Christians to depart in safety (a condition of surrender confirmed by the historian Ammianus Marcellinus), spared of the execution, enslavement, or forced exile into the eastern reaches of the Persian empire that had befallen other recalcitrant cities in Mesopotamia (McVey 1989, 22–23).

This was in stark contrast to the brutal state persecution of Persian Christians, who earlier had refused to pay the double head tax imposed on them, and whose open sympathies with Rome made them potentially traitorous to the Persian Empire. Christian relations with the Persian state were, to say the least, politically unenlightened. The exercise of royal clemency towards captured Roman Christians, which Ephrem witnessed, is not otherwise directly attested. As his relocation to Edessa attests, Ephrem chose to live in Roman territory rather than in Persia.

Syriac Christianity as a Mesopotamian Response to Late Antiquity

Competing forms of Christianity. From the time of Ephrem the Syrian and Aphrahāṭ "the Persian Sage," early Syriac Christianity had one foot in Rome, the other in Persia. Later Syriac Christianity would split into East Syrian and West Syrian divisions. The principal early centers of early Syriac Christianity were Edessa (Syriac: Orhay [*'wrhy*], modern Urfa, in southeastern Turkey) and Arbela (in northern Iraq).

Ephrem's purpose in writing liturgical hymns. Ephrem was a prolific author of a wide range of writings, including: (1) choral hymns (*madrāšē*) no fewer than five hundred in number, and a lesser number works of *sōgyātā* ("canticle"/ "song"); (2) verse homilies (*mēmrē*) composed in verses of seven syllables; (3) prose scriptural commentary (*puššāqā*) and controversial writings; and (4) works in artistic prose (Brock 1987, 31). The earliest extant manuscript of Ephrem's hymns is BL add. MS 14 571, copied by Julian of Edessa in the year 519 C.E. (Griffith 1987, 242). Unique as a universal figure in Late Antique Christianity, St. Ephrem was the only Syrian who was renowned and acclaimed among his Greek and Latin contemporaries.

In one sense, heterodoxy aside, Ephrem is decidedly preschismatic. Not long after Ephrem, Syriac Christianity split and hardened: Narsai (fl. 451–71) became the great consolidator of Nestorian Christianity, while Philoxenus of Mabbug (d. c. 522) was instrumental in the establishment of Monophysite Christianity. As a deacon, Ephrem had first served under James, Bishop of Nisibis. James was present at the Council of Nicea in 325 C.E., and had subscribed to the canons it promulgated. Although Ephrem is preschismatic as far as his church was concerned—a church that defined itself in accordance with the canons of Nicea—on the spiritual battlefront, one of Ephrem's major life objectives was to stem the influence of Marcionites, Manichaeans, and Bardaiṣanites. These were professed Christians whom Ephrem renounced as Christians.

Ephrem lived at a time when the Church felt it imperative to define what it held to be true against the threats of what it deemed untrue. In a pagan and Gnostic environment, it was necessary to defend the unity of God against, among others, the Marcionites, Bardaiṣanites, and Manichaeans (see *Motifs* 35–39). It then became necessary to define the unity of the Trinity. Only with the First Council of Constantinople (381) had a formula crystallized that confirmed the identity in nature between the Holy Spirit, and the Father and the Son. The Spirit emerged as a divine Person, the agent of man's sanctification. Špidlík states: "Such development can be seen, for example, in the works of Ephrem. In such early writings as *De paradiso* and the *Sermones de fide* the person of the Holy Spirit rarely appears. It is only in the hymns *De fide* that an ode is addressed to him" (1986, 30). Ephrem's own view of the Spirit appears to have reflected a development synchronous with that of the Church in its discussions leading up to the First Council of Constantinople.

In Edessa, Ephrem was clearly alarmed by the internal strife caused by the presence of Arians within the orthodox Christian community. The fledgling orthodoxy which Ephrem's Edessan congregation represented was clearly a minority. The dominant form of Christianity in Edessa at that time was that of the Bardaiṣanites, whereas the Christian community in which Ephrem found himself were known as "Palutians" after Paluṭ of Qona, bishop of Antioch. (Ephrem refers to Paluṭ by name in *Hymns Against Heresies*). Ephrem advocated a name change to that of "Christians." Orthodox "Christians" eventually prevailed in Edessa two or three decades after Ephrem's death. But victory would be won, not by faith but by force. Due in large measure to persecution of Bardaiṣanites by Bishop Rabbūla (d. 435) around 400 C.E., Edessa was purged of heretics. Prior to that, Ephrem triumphalistically alludes to what evidently had been Shāpūr's persecution of the Bardaiṣanites in Nisibis (CJ II.22; McV 240 and n. 100).

Evidently, the most important among these influences, positive and negative, was that of Bardaiṣanite Christianity. Added to these influences were certain ideas drawn from the fields of theology, philosophy, rhetoric, and the natural sciences, ideas which Ephrem had, in effect, hypostasized (SdF passim; Eccl. XLV.22; HdF XLVII.1, *Motifs* 24).

Christian heresies existed as the shadow of Christianity (Quispel 1951, unpublished p.c. to R. M. Grant). A shadow is both a contrast and a contour. The shadow may also be an accurate distortion of the real. In studying the so-called heresies of Ephrem's world, we get more than a picture in black and white. The variegated shades of heretical gray present striking nuances in our picture of Ephrem. As an arcane saying cannot be fathomed without knowledge of its allusions, so the hymns of Ephrem require information about the other Christians and sects of the day. These religions also supply some of the background necessary for a fuller appreciation of the subtleties of Ephrem's work.

Ephrem's battle against Marcionism. Prior to the advent of imperial Nicene Christianity and its coercive sanction, the religion of Marcion of Pontus and his followers, the Marcionites, was the dominant Christian spirituality in Syria (Bundy 1990, 111). In *Epistle* 41, the Emperor Julian states that entire Marcionite villages were wiped out by the imperial military (ibid., citing Wright 1923, III, Epistle 41). In the late second and early third centuries C.E., Bardaiṣan had fiercely opposed the influence of Marcion in Edessa. In his own way, Ephrem carried on the campaign. Ephrem wrote three discourses against Marcion in his *Prose Refutations* (Bevan and Burkitt 1921, Syriac text: 50–142 [Syriac text]; xxiii–lxv [trans.]). In his hymns, the most concentrated anti-Marcionite polemics are to be found in the cycle, *Hymns Against Heresies*. (Zenobius, a student of Ephrem, is reported also to have written against the Marcionites, but that work has been lost [Bundy 1988b, 31]. On Ephrem's disciples—whom Sozomen identifies as Zenobius, Abba, Abraham, Moses, Simeon, Paulonas, and Arad—see Outtier 1973, 20–21.)

As a Christian, Marcion was a radical interpreter of scripture in the extreme. Born in Sinope, on the Black Sea, Marcion was the son of a bishop. Around the year 140 C.E., Marcion journeyed to Rome, where he fell under the influence of a Gnostic teacher known as Cerdo, who taught that the God of the Old Testament was not the God of the New Testament. The Old Testament God was a god of justice. The God of the New Testament was a God of love and grace.

Developing the ideas of Cerdo to the point of the absurd, Marcion transformed the God of the Old Testament from a god of justice to a god of evil. In a work called the *Antitheses*, Marcion drove a wedge between the Law and the Gospel. In order to demonstrate this fundamental incompatibility between the two, Marcion contrasted passages from the Old and New Testaments in order to prove their essential incompatibility. Not only did Marcion reject the Old Testament completely, he pronounced the God of the Old Testament an evil deity, not to be confused with the God Jesus knew. According to Marcion, the universe was the design of the evil Deity of the Old Testament. An evil God created man.

By contrast, Christ was the Son of the Unknown God, the true God. Because the flesh is not good, Christ did not come in the flesh. Since there could be no such thing as a sinless body, a docetic Christ had to appear instead. Marcion frames his version of Christianity cosmologically, by separating salvation from creation.

Not only did Marcion reject the Old Testament, he rejected much of the New Testament as well. Among the four gospels, Marcion accepted only the Gospel of Luke as genuine. This he edited, by cutting out the genealogy, nativity, baptism, and temptation narratives, and the passage in the Nazareth pericope in which Jesus reads from a scroll of Isaiah. Marcion's Christology was docetic. Supernaturally, without mother, Jesus simply materializes in the synagogue at Capernaum in 29 C.E. as a fully grown man, according to Marcion's version of Luke. Marcion is believed to have published the first formal canon list around 140 C.E. Besides his expurgated Gospel of Luke, Marcion's canon also included ten epistles of Paul, which (leaving out the pastoral letters) he entitled the *Apostolicon*. For his views, Marcion was excommunicated in 144 C.E.

In *Hymns Against Heresies*, Ephrem takes the Marcionites to task for their assimilation of elements of Greek philosophy, for their elevation of matter to a quasi-divine state, and for their inconsistency in their interpretation of scripture. Furthermore, they deny the "one God" as well as the divinity and incarnation of Jesus. The Marcionites are said also to have denied corporeal resurrection (of body, soul, and spirit reunited), besides denying freedom of the will. Since they are not true Christians, they are bereft of salvation. Having rejected the "orthodox" consensus of Christianity, they are deemed schismatics (Bundy 1988b,

30). (Orthodoxy, in Ephrem's use of it, is obviously imperial Nicene orthodoxy.) In the course of his critique, Ephrem refutes Marcion's dichotomy between the Old and New Covenants, demonstrating that God's justice and grace are evident in both Testaments. Ephrem adduces the John the Baptist narratives of Luke to show continuity with the Old Testament, which is a positive testimony of God's activity in scriptures the authenticity of which Marcion contests (Bundy 1988b, 30). Throughout the entire range of Ephrem's hymns, allusions to Marcion, and to the error of his ways, are frequently encountered.

Bardaiṣan's countermove against Marcion was to let salvation begin with creation. Cosmology thus became a substructure of Bardaiṣan's soteriology (BarE 225). In Bardaiṣan's cosmos there is the triad *confusion*, *creation*, and *incarnation*. To *confusion* belongs the body, commingled as it is with an element of darkness. To *creation* belongs the soul, with all the fortunes of life destined to befall it. To *incarnation* relates the spirit, in which, through Christ, is offered the possibility of living in the will of God. Contrariwise, for the Marcionites, the God of the Old Testament was evil, and so was his creation, and so was man. Christ came as the son of "The Stranger"—a higher God—effecting a separation between creation and salvation. Salvation consisted of athletic ascesis, a transcendence of creation.

Ephrem contrasts Marcionites with Bardaiṣanites in the following verse: "He [the devil] adorns Bardaiṣan with fine clothes and precious stones. Marcion is clothed with the garb of a penitent. In the grottoes of Bardaiṣan are heard hymns and songs, amusements for the youth. Marcion fasts like a serpent" (Bundy 1988b, 31–32). This indicates that the practice of fasting was common to groups other than orthodox Christians. More importantly, we see in this jibe the contrast of two distinctive lifestyles, life embracing and life renouncing.

Ironically, it is quite likely that the "life-style and piety" of Marcionites and Manichaeans was "largely congruent" with that of Paluṭian Christians (Bundy 1988b, 30). According to David Bundy: "Finally one common element of early Syriac apologetic against Marcion and the Marcionites must be emphasized. One finds no critique, contrary to Western apologetic traditions, of Marcionite spirituality in extant texts. Marcionite asceticism was congruent with the Syriac cultural and religious heritage" (1988b, 31). As Bundy concludes: "Thus it would appear that Ephrem's goal was to preempt the metaphors of faith and establish the New and Old Testaments, nature and tradition as the exclusive province of Paluṭian 'orthodox' Christianity" (1988b, 31). For purposes of the present study, this is a very important observation, as not only lifestyle and piety, but metaphors as well, were held somewhat in common within the cultural sphere of northern Mesopotamian spirituality. The challenge facing Ephrem was to make distinctive use of this common stock of imagery.

Ephrem's battle against the Bardaiṣanites. Bardaiṣan (Syriac: Bar Dayṣān, 154–222 C.E.) was "the first and only person of importance in second-century Syriac Christianity" (Drijvers 1996, 162). He stood in an uncertain relationship to the church during his campaign against Marcionism, was a living literary presence and, from beyond the grave, a spiritual rival in Edessa during the final decade of Ephrem's life.

By his own hand, Bardaiṣan wrote the *Book of Mysteries*, and authored a *Book of Thunder* and a *Book of the Hosts*, according to Ephrem (CH I.14, LVI.9). Against Bardaiṣan's treatise, *Of Domnus*, Ephrem wrote a refutation. The predominance of Bardaiṣanite Christianity in Edessa, and its successful inroads in Nisibis, confronted Ephrem with one of his greatest missionary challenges. It is interesting to note that the *Book of the Laws of the Countries* (c. 200 C.E.), which represents a further development of the views of Bardaiṣan through one of his pupils, contains the earliest reference to Christians in Persia (SCK 26).

Bardaiṣan's pretense to "orthodoxy" is evident from the fact that he refuted the heretics of his day, notably Marcion (BarE 25–26). Bardaiṣan sought to reconcile astrology, Greek philosophy, and Christianity. His work therefore may be regarded as syncretistic and individualistic rather than intentionally heretical. Bardaiṣan's autochthonous religious syncretism, constructed with an orthodox veneer, fixes Christianity at the crossroads of cultures, in which Edessa, as Drijvers has observed, was in more than one respect a bordertown between East and West (BarE 213).

One irritant for Ephrem was the high social position of his dead opponent. Bardaiṣan was an aristocratic court scholar. "With [expensive] clothes and jewels," criticizes Ephrem, "[the Devil] adorned Bardaiṣan" (CH I.12; Bundy 1985, 606). In 195 C.E., Sextus Julius Africanus had personally met Bardaiṣan in Edessa. Julius Africanus reports that Bardaiṣan was a skilled archer at the court of King Abgar VII (ibid., 600, n. 16.) We learn from Aberkios—a great adversary against the Marcionites in the East—something of Bardaiṣan in person, as Aberkios chanced to meet the philosopher when the latter headed a delegation of Christians to greet the anti-Marcionite crusader. Aberkios describes Bardaiṣan as "distinguished from all others by his descent and wealth" (*Vita* of Aberkios, cited in BarE 170). Bardaiṣan's well-placed status as a "Parthian" courtier must have been an important factor in the spread of Bardaiṣanism among aristocrats. It is possible that the élite of Edessa for the most part were followers of Bardaiṣan (BarE 127).

Bardaiṣan's ideas are positively though unreliably represented by his disciple Philippus in *The Book of the Laws of the Countries*, which is a more developed and syncretistic exposition of Bardaiṣanite doctrine (Drijvers 1965). The author recounts the various customs and laws of the world to prove their diversity. This is used as an argument against determinism (BLC 40–59). Christians are presented as "the new people . . . that the Messiah has caused to arise in every place and in all climates by his coming" (BLC 58–60). Philippus refers to the conversion of King Abgar (BLC 58, 21–22), intimating the possibility of a governmentally recognized church (Bundy 1985, 601–602). Such good fortune was reversed when Bishop Rabbūla destroyed the Bardaiṣanite cult places in Edessa.

Cast in a Middle Platonist philosophical structure, Bardaiṣan's philosophy was basically that of "free will and consequently right conduct to eliminate evil" (Drijvers 1996, 172). Bardaiṣan preached a gospel of liberty, in which the spiritual potency of Freedom prevails over the forces of Fate and Nature. In Late Antiquity, there was a fear and dread of Fate. The gospel of Bardaiṣan was one of a liberation from the determinism of Fate. Bardaiṣan taught that the spirit joins the soul when the soul descends, through the spheres of the seven planets, to the human body at the moment of birth. Nature, Fate, and Freedom correspond to body, soul, and spirit, respectively formed by chaos, creation (individuation), and incarnation, of spirit (BarE 219–20). Liberty is a divine gift. It is dispensed through strength of spirit and the will to conquer temptations and to rise above immorality. Thus, Bardaiṣan's disciple Philippus wrote: "By its nature the lion eats flesh; . . . and the bee makes honey by which it sustains itself; and for this reason all bees are honeymakers. . . . But men are not governed in this manner; but in the things belonging to their bodies they maintain their nature like animals, and in the things which belong to their minds they do that which they wish, as being free and with power and as the likeness of God" (Segal 1970, 37). Endowed with soul, man can move beyond instinct. Bardaiṣan's teachings are structured by interlocking triads, the most important of which can be represented as follows: *Origin*: Chaos, Creation, Incarnation; *Anthropology*: Body, Soul, Spirit; *Destiny*: Nature, Fate, Freedom.

Man is at once natural, individual, and (potentially) spiritual. Bardaiṣan conceded that man is subject to the laws of Nature with regard to basic vital functions. And, to a considerable extent, events in life are determined by Fate. Liberty, however, is achieved through transcending the constraints of Fate. By the willed reflex of Freedom, man can navigate his own destiny through the interstices of Nature and Fate.

Salvation systems tended to depend on creation myths. Bardaiṣan's myth started from much different premises than the Genesis account. J. de Zwaan has aptly characterized Bardaiṣan's theology as an "evolutionist theodicy" (cited in BarE 54). According to Bardaiṣan, there originally existed five eternal elements (*'ityē*), each in its own region: water in the North, fire in the South, light in the East, wind in the West, darkness in the lower regions. Ephrem objected to this representation of the original state of the universe, as the coëxistence of the elements with God reduces God to a mere "arranger" rather than "the Creator" (CH XLVIII.2, Mathews SPW, 60–61). Chaos rose out of the commingling of these four pure elements with vile darkness. Eschatologically, Bardaiṣan denied resurrection of the body, presumably because "the nature of evil" inhered in the body's formation out of chaos.

Death is a necessary condition of mortality. It is not a consequence of the Fall. Physical death is a natural condition, not punishment for Adam's sin. Death is part of Nature. Spiritual death is another matter. Spirit only matters. Matter does not matter. Adam did bring about spiritual Death, just as Christ brought spiritual Life. It must be emphasized that these are spiritual conditions, not mortal. Immortality is not transformed mortality. Rather, it is the sinful condition of the soul itself that hinders the soul from entering Paradise at the "Crossing Place." As the soul empowers the body with consciousness, the spirit endows the soul with spirituality. The body is gross. The soul is subtle. It "wears" the body like a garment. The spirit is rarefied. The soul mediates between the two, between Darkness and Light. The spirit incorporates knowledge and free will, the image of God. It is Christ who brings deliverance of the soul. The body does not require redemption (BarE 154–57).

Bardaiṣan is the only early Syriac writer (besides Quq and the Quqites, a strange sect that will be introduced later) who wrote favorably about sexuality in its proper role in marriage. Sexual intercourse in marriage, taken beyond mere lust by a reflex of free will, deepens the interpersonal unity of husband and wife. Such a purposeful exercise of sexuality also entails responsible parenthood and the duty of parents to rear their children properly (Edakalathur 1994, 8–9).

According to Ephrem, the followers of Bardaiṣan were stolen from the Christian flock (CH XXII.3). They held concourse in caves (CH I.17), where songs and hymns were sung (CH I.18) and various writings explained, including works on astrology even to the exclusion of scripture (CH I.18). To certain passages of scripture Bardaiṣan gave a special interpretation (CH LI.13). To such forced exegesis Ephrem alludes: "How Error has erred in culling / bitterness from sweet flowers . . . / Even from fragrant scripture Error culls / poison for her lovers" (Nat. XXVIII.8, McV 216). To all appearances, the words of Bardaiṣan were perfectly reasonable and orthodox, but were secretly full of blasphemous mysteries (CH I.11, BarE 161–62).

The importance of Bardaiṣan is underscored by the fact that Ephrem wrote a prose refutation against Bardaiṣan attacking the latter's allegorism (Mitchell 1912). This treatise was written for the intellectual élite, of whom a certain Hypatius was one. There are other polemical works against Bardaiṣan ascribed to Ephrem, but these are of doubtful authenticity (Jones 1904 and other studies cited in BarE 129, nn. 1–5). Of his genuine works, Ephrem composed four hymns that were expressly anti-Bardaiṣanite, these being Hymns 53–56 of *Hymns Against Heresies*. Jensen has translated the entirety of Hymn 55 (Jensen 1994, 44–45; cf. Richardson 1990). These hymns are of interest, as heresies did, to some extent, determine Ephrem's agenda.

Bardaiṣan was evidently a well-meaning Christian, who had, after all, done his part to counter Marcion's radical critique of the scriptures. Enhancing his effectiveness as a philosopher and teacher, Bardaiṣan was a popularizer—some say the originator (which Brock 1985b, disputes)—of the lyric poem known as the *madrāšā*, a hymn composed in isosyllabic verse (stanzas constructed on a single syllabic pattern), employing literary devices of parallelism, word plays, alliteration, and rhyme (McV 26). His purpose in composing these songs, according to Ephrem, was his wish to appeal to young people (Skjaervo, EIr 3: 781). Like King David's number of Psalms, Ephrem notes that Bardaiṣan composed 150 such hymns (CH LIII.6). Occasionally Ephrem quotes from these hymns. Of the popular appeal and effectiveness of these songs, Ephrem laments: "[Bardaiṣan] created hymns and united them with musical accompaniment, and he composed psalms and introduced metres: with measure and weights he divided words. And the simple he corrupted with bitterness in sweetness, the sick who did not choose healing nourishment" (Segal 1970, 37).

To combat the effectiveness of these hymns, which enjoyed popular appeal, Ephrem himself became a master of the genre, composing over four hundred hymns. At Nisibis, according to Jacob of Serugh's homily on Ephrem, Ephrem is said to have founded choirs of women, which he personally directed (McV 28; cf. HyP 22–25, esp. 23 for portions of Jacob of Serug's verse panegyric on Ephrem). Thus, this form was mastered by Ephrem and survives as the most distinctive literary genre of early Syriac Christianity. Murray speaks of "Ephrem's stylistic and musical debt to Bardaiṣan," a debt "borne out by both literary-critical arguments and the very melody-titles of some hymns" (SCK 279). In other words, not only did Ephrem take over the *form* of Bardaiṣanite hymns, but even their very *melodies*. Given their popularity, these refrains must have been familiar to the Christian aristocrats in Edessa. There was also a common stock of *imagery* on which both Bardaiṣan and Ephrem drew. In so doing, Ephrem took over the tools of Bardaiṣan's own vehicle for propaganda—the strophic hymn—and turned it into a means of consolidating his own Christian communities.

Ephrem, moreover, addressed some of the salient *themes* of those hymns. He was, after all, engaged in at least an indirect dialogue with Bardaiṣanism, at the literary and liturgical levels certainly. In certain of the earlier hymns, the melody (*qālā*) was that of Bardaiṣan's son Harmonius, with Ephrem's lyrics substituted for those of Bardaiṣan! (Sprengling [1916] doubts the existence of Harmonius. On the possible Semitic provenance of his name, see Astour 1964, 199.) Ephrem fought fire with fire, so to speak, in composing hymns after the same fashion as Bardaiṣan, even to the extent of using the same music but changing the lyrics. Could it be possible that Ephrem took over any of the existing Bardaiṣanite *lyrics* as well, reworking them for his own purposes? But the question of Ephrem's literary dependence on Bardaiṣan (distinct from formal and thematic dependence) is beyond the scope of this study.

Ephrem's "Bardaiṣanite agenda" has a decidedly heuristic value for the study of his hymns, in which the ghost of Bardaiṣan looms. Ephrem's production of hymns after the fashion of Bardaiṣan leads the present writer to believe that there is much in the writings of Ephrem that bears inexplicit reference to Bardaiṣanite themes. For instance, liberty (*ḥerūtā*) is of great importance not only to Bardaiṣan, but to Ephrem as well, having devoted an entire hymn to the subject (CH XI, LumE 20). Over the soul's need for freedom Bardaiṣan and Ephrem are in implicit agreement: "Like ships, all things have their need: / the soul, of freedom" (CH V.20, SCK 252).

Ephrem seems content to characterize salvation in terms of liberty. He must, after all, speak in the religious language of the Bardaiṣanite aristocrats. According to Ephrem, Bardaiṣan "assigned too great a power to Nature and Fate" (BarE 160), thus restricting God's sovereign power. Anthropologically, Ephrem views free will—the human agent of liberation—as the quality by which Adam was fashioned in the image of God (Jansma 1973, 18). Of himself, Ephrem says: "Because you are a harp endowed of life and language, says he, your chords and words possess liberty. O harp, who of itself and according to its own will chants of its God" (HdF XXV, Beggiani 1983, 16). Ephrem speaks of "true freedom" (Virg. VI.12; McV 291) effected by Christ, in which exercise of the will on the part of the believer is a critical participatory factor: "Bound is the body by its nature for it cannot grow larger or smaller; / but powerful is the will for it may grow to all sizes" (Nat. I.98; McV 74).

According to Bardaiṣan, though good and evil enmesh humankind, a Christian is empowered to influence destiny through an act of will, since Christ countermands the force of the planets, or Fate (Norris 1990). Although God, through Christ, is more powerful than Fate, the notion that Fate somehow has its own domain of influence independent of God was unacceptable to Ephrem, who actually names

Bardaiṣan in the following criticism: "Bardaiṣan is cunning, who put that Fate under restraint / Through a Fate [God] that is greater, as it describes its course in liberty. / The thraldom of the lower, refutes him with the upper, / Their shadow refutes their body. / For that intent which restricted the lower, / Crippled the unrestricted freedom of the upper" (CH IV.9–10; BarE 160). The most powerful reflex of the will is through ethical rigor. Bardaiṣan effected a synthesis of disparate elements of Syrian paganism and recast them within a Judeo-Christian ethic.

Ephrem satisfies the Bardaiṣanite quest for liberty—a condition divested of astrological determinism—with the assurance that liberty is gained upon death (HdP XIV.2). The exercise of will can of course be positive or negative. The way in which the will should act as the master of its own destiny is clear. For both Bardaiṣan and Ephrem, the will's crowning achievement is to succeed in achieving liberty through the self-mastery of acting in accordance with divine commands, becoming righteous thereby: "Blessed is He Who wove the commandments / so that through them free will might be crowned; Blessed is He Who has multiplied the righteous, / (4) the witnesses who shout out concerning free will (CH XI.4; LumE 21).

In both Bardaisanite and orthodox systems, true liberty—for a soul possessing the will to attain purity—entails ethical rigor. But the ethics of the two religious systems differed not so much in principle as in practice, for Ephrem was inclined to the ascetic whereas Bardaiṣan was not. So great was Bardaiṣan's influence that Christians after the death of Ephrem resorted to a "final solution." Barbaric by modern standards, Bishop Rabbūla (d. 435 C.E.) persecuted the Bardaiṣanites and reconverted many Bardaiṣanites by force. Ephrem chose other means. In spite of his best efforts to discredit Bardaiṣan, Ephrem did compose a moving prayer for the soul of Bardaiṣan (CH LV.11; SCK 90, n. 2.).

Ephrem's battle against Manichaeism. The prophet Mānī (216–76 C.E.), a Persian born in Mesopotamia, was "perhaps the first person in human history ever to have consciously played the role of a world prophet" (Mojtabai 1978, 105). With a book in one hand and a staff in the other (he might have been lame), flamboyantly dressed in a blue cloak with red and green trousers (Yamauchi 1977, 48), the prophet Mānī established a religion that in fact crossed cultural divides. From its origin in Mesopotamia, within the prophet's own lifetime, the new religion spread far and wide throughout both the Roman and Persian Empires, and even into India. This is partly documented by known letters Mānī himself had written to communities of his followers in Babylon, Ctesiphon, Edessa, Armenia, Mesene, Susiana, India, and elsewhere (Bausani 1971, 55). Mānī owed much of his success to the patronage of Shāpūr ("King's Son") I, in whose retinue Mānī travelled for several years, throughout Persia and to the frontiers of the Roman Empire. Within the Roman Empire, Manichaeism was regarded by Romans as a Persian import. In 297 C.E., Diocletian issued an edict that condemned Manichaeans as enemy Persian agents who should be executed. Despite persecution, it flourished with an impressive degree of success.

As a young man, Mānī received visions of the "Twin-Spirit" (the *Syzygos*—his higher self). This was his heavenly brother, the Twin. This motif also appears in the *Acts of Judas Thomas* ("the Twin"—i.e., of Jesus). When the Twin appeared to him, Mānī beheld himself. The Twin-Spirit commissioned him with a message and empowered Mānī to fight the evil powers, Āz and Ahrmēn. The year of Mānī's first revelation was 228 C.E. Even from the age of four, Mānī had contact with the divine. At the age of twelve, Mānī experienced his first revelation. He kept it secret for twelve years, until he was twenty-four. In 240 C.E., Mānī began to preach. He proclaimed that he was the Spirit of Truth promised by Christ. Mānī was sent by Christ ("the heavenly Father")! Mānī's *The Book of the Giants* was translated into Persian (Henning 1946, 55). In this book, it is said: "But God, in each epoch, sends apostles: Šīt[īl, Zarathuštra,] Buddha, Christ" (ibid., 63). At the age of twenty-four, Mānī proclaimed himself to be a Prophet on the very same day Shāpūr I was crowned (12 April 240, cf. Haloun and Henning 1952, 201). In his *Šābuhragān*, Mānī proclaims: "Wisdom and deeds have always from time to time been brought to mankind by the messengers of God. So in one age they have been brought by the messenger called Buddha, to India, to another by Zaradust to Persia, in another by Jesus to the West. Thereupon this revelation has come down and this prophecy has appeared in the form of myself, Mānī, the envoy of the one true God in the Land of Babylon" (Lieu 1985, 60).

Mānī created his own canon, to ensure that he would bequeath the world's first fully authenticated scriptures to posterity. With variations, the Manichaean canon consists of seven books: (1) *The Living Gospel*; (2) *The Treasure of Life*; (3) The *Pragmateia*; (4) *The Book of Mysteries*; (5) *The Book of the Giants*; (6) The *Letters*; (7) *Psalms and Prayers*, together with the "Great Icon" that Mānī himself had painted. Moreover, precisely for the benefit of the Persian king Shāpūr I, Mānī summarized his teachings in (Middle) Persian, in a book known as the *Šābuhragān*. So important was this work that it is sometimes listed in place of *Psalms and Prayers* (ibid., 6). Mary Boyce (1975 and 1968) has conveniently assembled some of the extant Manichaean writings in Persian, including passages from the *Šābuhragān*. Scribes in constant attendance would record his sermons and words of wisdom. Some of these were compiled in a semicanonical book known as the *Kephalaia*.

"Persia," writes Arthur Vööbus, "formed a true meeting-place for various ascetically colored Christian trends." After mentioning Marcionites, the Valentinians, various kinds of Encratites, followers of Tatian and Bardaiṣan, Vööbus concludes: "Thus early Syrian Christianity in Persia was a melting-pot in which various rigorous influences were blended to become a particular mixture in mutual competition and cross-fertilization" (1958, 2: 10). In Edessa, Manichaeism had won great popularity. Preserved in the literary amber of the Cologne Mānī Codex (in Greek translation), Mānī's *Letter to Edessa* foreshadows the importance of the Manichaean community in the time of Ephrem: "The truth and the secrets which I speak about—and the laying on of hands which is in my possession—not from men have I received it nor from fleshly creatures, not even from studies in the Scriptures. But when [my] most blessed [Father], who called me into his grace, beheld me, since he did not [wish] me [and] the rest who are [in the] world to perish, he felt compassion, so that [he] might extend [his] well-being to those prepared to be chosen by him from the sects. Then, by his grace, he pulled me from the council of the many who do not recognize the truth and revealed to me his secrets and those of his undefiled Father and of all the cosmos. He disclosed to me how I was before the foundation of the world, and how the groundwork of all the works, both good and evil, was laid, and how everything of [this] aggregation was engendered [according to its] present boundaries and [times]" (Cameron and Dewey 1979, 51–53).

Not only in Edessa, but throughout the Roman and Persian Empires, Manichaeism became a popular contender against Christianity. Manichaeans in the West thought of themselves as genuine Christians. The new religion had a powerful and rational ethical appeal. The classic example of the attraction of Manichaeism is the case of Augustine, who, in the 360s, was a Manichaean for nine years. Augustine states from experience that Manichaeans taunted orthodox (Nicene) Christians as to "what the source of evil is, and whether God is bounded by a corporeal form and has hair and nails, and whether those men ought to be considered righteous who had many wives at the same time and killed men and made animal sacrifices" (Augustine, *Confessions*. 3.7.12, Starnes 1990, 129–30). Attracted by the apparent rationality of this method of argumentation, Augustine became a Manichaean for nine years, during which time he made his living by teaching the art of rhetoric (*Confessions* 4.2.2, ibid.).

As if recalling Manichaean critique, Augustine warns the exegete against taking figurative expressions literally (*De doctrina christiana* 3.5.9, ibid.). To Augustine, the Scriptures always seemed to him absurd whenever he "had taken them literally." The Scriptures finally made sense to him when they were expounded "spiritually." After listening to the sermons of Ambrose, Augustine discovered that the Christians in fact did not believe what the Manichaeans accused them of believing (*Confessions* 4.14.24, ibid.). By practicing the allegorical method of Alexandrine theologians, Augustine could counter Manichaean myths and theology.

Finally, as the *Chronicle of Séert* attests, the Catholicós Aḥay (d. 415) chose the final solution of burning Manichaean churches to eradicate the religion (Vööbus 1958, 7). One gets some idea of how thorough this eradication was by virtue of the fact that absolutely no Manichaean text survives in Syriac (Coyle 1979, 182).

Manichaeism is rich in myths. These myths are complex. At the heart of these myths, starting from the Primal Man, is a gospel of personal salvation, even though the eschatology is cosmic. Essentially, myths on the origin of man from the powers of evil constitute the most decisive element in Mānī's anthropology (Ort 1968, 203). Mānī's cosmic drama involves a contest between Two Principles in a sequence of Three Epochs in time:

1. *Past*: At this point in primordial time, Light and Darkness are separate. In preexistence, there was a primordial pair. This was the syzygy of Darkness and Light. Five elements belong to Light, five to Darkness. The five elements of light are sometimes called the "Maiden of Light" who is the soul of the Father. The five evil Archons—a demon, lion, eagle, fish, and dragon—are sometimes collectively referred to as the Prince of Darkness (Lieu 1985, 10).

2. *Present*: In this epoch, Light and Darkness intermingle. This is the battle of the Primal Man against the Prince of Darkness. Darkness invades Light. Light is trapped in darkness. Particles of light are trapped inside all living things, awaiting liberation. The body is Darkness. The soul is Light. Throughout history, the "King of Light" had sent prophets to reveal man's true nature. At the climax of history, God sent Mānī as the final bearer of the gospel of "knowledge and wisdom." One has to abstain from meat, wine, and marriage. A life of holiness prepares one for eschatological requital in the "Paradise of Light" (Lieu 1985, 8) where all freed light returns.

3. *Future*: In the eschaton to come, Light will separate from Darkness. Following the final battle, Jesus will return as the Great King on the Day of Judgement. The Elect will be transformed into angels, the sinners will be sent to hell. Then a Great Fire will blaze for 1,468 years. Light Particles will escape to Paradise to form a Pillar of Glory, while the Prince of Darkness will be cast into a deep pit.

Manichaeism has been called "a community of sanctification" (Ort 1968, 197). It was a *sancta ecclesia*. Gnosis was self-realization, followed by separation. Gnosis brought repentance. Repentance preceded asceticism. Asceticism was required for redemption. Very few sacramental rituals are known of. There were no rites of baptism. Mānī opposed external purification. Baptism was replaced by gnosis.

The spiritual "Living Water"—represented by gnosis—was contrasted with physical or "Turbid Water." Mānī had rejected Elchasaitism, the baptist religion in which he was raised from the age of four to twenty-four or twenty-five (cf. Koenen 1981).

There were two concentric circles of Manichaeans: monks (the "Elect") and the lay ("Auditors"). An initiatory cult may have existed that involved a kind of rite known as "sealing." Following a quarter of a century of research into Manichaean rituals, Puech speculates that the "Seal" required vows (the three moral seals) taken by the Elect to be ever mindful of their heart, mouth, and hands (Stroumsa 1986, 66, citing Puech 1979, 347–55). The "Elect" had to obey strict rules, perhaps the strictest of all religions (Ort 1968, 204). All sexuality was banned among the Elect, since pregnancy had to be avoided. For conception would trap the light of another soul within a body formed within the womb. Through vigilant self-denial, the Elect could attain perfection. Once perfected, at death the Elect return to the Paradise of Light.

Relative to his Elkasaite origins, Mānī effected a cultic shift from baptism to a curious food ritual. Mānī considered all living things to be ensouled with light. The Elect, observing the "Five Commandments" (laws of purity) along with the "Three Seals," were agents for the release of prisoned Light. Their purified bodies refined the food they consumed, as Light Particles were released through their belches. Such a meal was a sacrament, referred to as the Eucharist by Manichaeans in the West. Through what became known as the "Soul Service," Auditors gave alms to the Elect and prepared food for their redemptive meals. Daily gifts of fruit were given to the Elect. Melons and cucumbers were thought to possess a great deal of light that could be released through the eructions of the Elect. (Besides food rituals, it is also known that Manichaeans fasted.) In turn, the Elect, who wore white robes to symbolize their purity, imparted heavenly teachings to the Auditors. It also appears that confession of sins took on a cultic status. There were other rituals, too. Manichaeans celebrated Mānī's passion at the so-called Bēma-Feast ("Throne," "Tribunal," "Judge's Seat"), in which ceremony an empty throne represented the spiritual presence of Mānī himself (Bausani 1971, 55). Variously surviving Bēma-Psalms, including some in Middle Persian (Sundermann 1982a), attest to Mānī's exalted station in the eyes of his followers.

Unlike the Elect, Auditors could marry or have mistresses, but were discouraged from procreation. Moreover, they could possess property and wealth. They could lead ordinary lives. Not having attained the purity of the Elect, Auditors could hope to be reincarnated as a luminous fruit, to be consumed by the Elect and return, too, to the Paradise of Light. Auditors would return as humans. The profligate return to earth as beasts (Lieu 1985, 21). This special type of reincarnation is called *metaggismos* (rebirth in other forms of life—ibid., 56).

In sum, the fact that Ephrem wrote, in addition to his hymns, a prose refutation against the Manichaeans attests to their importance in fourth-century Nisibis and Edessa. Beyond Edessa, the only state to make Manichaeism its official religion was the Kingdom of the Western Uyghurs at Qočo in Central Asia, when its ruler was converted in the eighth century. Certain Manichaean imagery bears striking resemblance to Ephrem's own symbolic repertoire.

Ephrem's battle against Arianism. The unity of the Father, the unity of the Son with the Father, and the unity of the Trinity, the generation and procession of one from the other, the role of each in effecting salvation and sanctification, are all interrelated questions that constitute the problematics of any systematic theology. For the early Church, resolution of certain of these issues was seen as imperative for ecclesiastical reasons. Arianism alone, which had precipitated the Christological controversies of the fourth century, had irreparably split Church and empire and undermined its advances against paganism.

Ephrem establishes God as an experiential reality as one which at the same time poses a cognitive mystery (see Bundy 1986/1988a). Mystical discourses often qualify positive experience with negative theology. Thus Ephrem can sustain his paradox without lessening the intensity of either polarity: "However much, Lord, I would feel You, / it is still not You Yourself I touch. / For my mind can touch nothing of Your hiddenness: / it is just a visible, illumined, image / that I see in the symbol of You; / for all investigation into Your being is hidden" (CNis L.13, *Harp* 58). In the form of praise, this is a simple statement of the epistemological limits of human finitude. Ineffable experience defies explanation.

According to Ephrem, there are real epistemological limits to human experience, particularly with respect to human experience of the divine. For knowledge of something involves a comprehension of it, and that comprehension must be superior to the object of knowledge itself. This is impossible when it comes to the apprehension of either God or Christ: "Whoever is capable of investigating / becomes the container of what he investigates; / a knowledge which is capable of containing the Omniscient / is greater than Him, / for it has proved capable of measuring the whole of Him. / A person who investigates the Father and the Son / is thus greater than them! / Far be it, then, and something anathema, / that the Father and Son should be investigated, / while dust and ashes exalts itself!" (HdF IX.16, *LumE* 13).

Between Creator and creation yawns an ontological "chasm" (HdF LXIX.11). *Chasm* is the same Syriac term found in the Parable of Dives and Lazarus at Luke 16:26. The Divine Word is on the far side of the chasm, while the angelic host belong with humankind on the near side of the divide (*LumE* 12–13). In the passage below, Ephrem stresses the unfathomable mystery of God: "Thousands thousands stand, and ten thousand thousands haste. / The thousands and ten thousands, cannot search out the One: / for all of them stand, in silence to serve. / He has no heir of His Throne, save the Son Who is of Him. / In the midst of silence is the enquiry into Him, / when the Watchers [angels] come to search Him out. / They attain to silence and are stayed" (NPNF 13, 251–52; cf. McVey, 177–78, where Nat. XIV.20 = XXI.20).

Ten thousand is a symbolic figure for Ephrem (cf. CH XLII.9, SCK 75). As an exponent of ten, let us recall that in Syriac tradition as in other cultures, ten is the number of perfection. Both the numbers represented here and the scene itself recalls the Daniel's vision of the "Ancient of Days" (*ʿattīq yōmīn*): "A thousand thousands [*ʾelep ʾalepīm*; LXX *chiliai chiliades*] served him, and ten thousand times ten thousand [*weribbō ribwān*; LXX *muriai muriades*] stood [*yeqūmūn*; LXX *pareistēkeisan*] before him" (Spinks 1991, 24). The idea of standing has cultic significance (cf. Mullen 1980, 231). Ephrem's description of the heavenly host standing in immovable silence is thoroughly Semitic. "Standing" is, above all, steadfastness. The Christian monastic practice of standing was for the purpose of attaining transcendence (Williams 1985, 90).

The angelic "Watchers," later in this hymn, are said to have "seen Thee in the midst of the abyss"—a poetic description of beatific vision that can only be self-negating as well as self-affirming. There may also be an allusion here to the ancient Near Eastern motif of primeval chaos as the scene of theophany.

In any event, the Watchers, or angelic host, are myriad. The term *Watchers* (*ʿīrē*) represents "Angels" in both Jewish and Syriac traditions. The term may have had Akkadian (or Hebrew or Ugaritic) origins, though the influence of Persian divine beings has also been suggested (see Murray 1984 and 1990). If so, this favored the development of the idea of monasticism as a "*vita angelica*" on Earth, according to Murray (1975a 14, n. 1). Despite the near access to God they traditionally enjoy, their nearness to God is one of spiritual purity and not of epistemological knowing (i.e., not by "investigation" [*ʿuqqābā*] or "scrutiny" [*bṣātā*]), save in terms of a very positive negative theology, and in terms of experience rather than knowledge.

It is instructive to look at an alternative translation of Nat. XXI.20. McVey's is as follows: "A thousand thousands stood; ten thousand ten thousands ran. / Thousands and ten thousands were not able to investigate the One. / All of them in silence, therefore, stood to serve Him. / He has no consort except the Child that is from Him. / Seeking Him is in silence. When Watchers went to investigate, / They reached silence and were restrained" (Nat. XXI.20, McV 177–78). The context of this passage, as McVey points out, may not have resided within the original cycle of nativity hymns, but rather in the anti-Arian context more appropriate to the *Hymns on Faith*, from which the previous six strophes were drawn, perhaps inserted by a later hand (McV 177, n. 481).

Beck has shown that the entire cycle of *Hymns on Faith* was directed against the Arians. Ephrem's greatest sorrow and outrage with regard to the Arians was their disastrous effect on the Church, resulting in schism from within and undermining the very foundations of ecclesiastical authority (*Motifs* 27). The most pretentious Arian claim, in Ephrem's view, was not any particular line of interpretation as such, but rather the temerity to issue categorical statements about God in a way that was as epistemologically unsupportable as it was ecclesiastically divisive. Ephrem also criticized the same impulse among the orthodox.

In Syriac Christology, Christ's Sonship goes far beyond adoptive, elective, or other ideal relationships with God. Ephrem describes Christ as "the Son of the Hidden One, as He emerged into revelation" (Nat. II.9, McV 78). This is taken literally. Ephrem, the master of metaphor, knows the difference between metaphor and reality, and is well aware of the Christological consequences of both readings: Christ is truly God's Son, and for this reason God as "Father" is no metaphor but a reality: "And if His name 'Father' were a metaphor—which God forbid!—the names which go with it (*šmh' bny zwgh*) will lose their force under dispute" (HdF LII.2, Molenberg 1990, 139 and 141).

For Ephrem, God and Christ have been presented as mysteries beyond the reach of human ken. As if to reinforce such a notion in practical terms, Ephrem suggests that the soul is itself a mystery which man is powerless to unravel: "If, then, our knowledge cannot even achieve a knowledge of itself, / how does it dare investigate the birth of Him who knows all things? / How can the servant, who does not properly know himself, / pry into the nature of his Maker?" (HdF I.16, *Harp* 7). Again, this statement has Arianism in mind. From a fourth-century Syriac Christian perspective, the target could just as easily have been Greek philosophical theology. To resume, the unknowability of God apart, it is Ephrem's Christ who most fully reveals the mystery of God: "Who, Lord, can gaze on Your hiddenness / Which has come to revelation? Yes, Your obscurity / has come to manifestation and notification; / Your concealed Being / has come out into the open" (HdF LI.2, *LumE* 14).

Arianism was not extinguished by the Council of Nicaea. It continued to flourish (indeed, as the faith of some Roman emperors), as is evident in Edessa. Around the year 372, a *Life of Ephrem* relates that the Emperor Valens had visited Edessa with the intent of forcing

Arianism on the city. There, he threatened the orthodox Christians with a choice between apostasy and death. Protests ensued. Multitudes of Christians congregated at the Shrine of St. Thomas outside the city to await martyrdom, rendering the decree untenable at the time. Nevertheless, only three months after Ephrem's death, Bishop Narsai and some of the leading clerics (from Ephrem's church and others) were expelled from Edessa in September 373. Crowds of faithful followers followed them into exile (Segal 1970, 91). The *Chronicle of Edessa* asserts that in the year 373, Arians took over Ephrem's very church and held it for five years (HSC 57). With the death of Valens in 378, the Arian victory was fleeting, as orthodox clergy returned and regained possession of their churches.

Ephrem's battle against the Jews. "Particularly in Nisibis," Mathews writes, "Ephrem was engaged in heated debate with the Jews and it would be most unlikely that he had no more than a simple passing acquaintance with a Jewish tradition of exegesis" (SPW 62). The preponderant influence of Jewish exegesis upon Ephrem is pursuasively demonstrated by Tryggve Kronholm (1979).

In Persia, on the far side of Ephrem's Roman frontier, Aphrahāṭ speaks of his dialogue with a Jewish scholar (Aph. Dem. XXI). Over the course of their encounters, such debates intensified over the proper interpretation of the Old Testament. Ephrem's contact with Jews, however, was not amicable as was Aphrahāṭ's. Of this, Murray laments: "But it must be confessed with sorrow that Ephrem hated the Jews. It is sad that the man who could write the magisterial *Commentary on Genesis*, with the command it shows of the tradition which still to a great extent united Christians and Jews, could sink to writing *Carmina Nisibena* LXVII" (SCK 68). Local Jews are also the target of some of the *Hymns Against Heretics*, a collection of fifty-six hymns directed against the Marcionites, Bardaiṣanite, Manichaean, Arians, Quqites (see below), the Chaldeans, and other minor sects (*Motifs* 20).

Ephrem's battle against the Chaldeans. The pagans Ephrem most frequently attacks are the "Chaldeans" or astrologers. These are Babylonian stargazers of various stripes extending back to the days of Adam and reaching to the present in the paganism of the Emperor Julian. Of satanic inspiration, astrology constrains the sovereignty of God and consigns humanity to the whims of Fate, atrophying man's free will in the process. Sidney Griffith has devoted an excellent study to Ephrem's views on paganism as exemplified in the hymn cycle, *Against Julian* (Griffith 1987). Ridiculing how astrology failed Julian and led to his downfall, Ephrem writes: 'Who will ever again believe in / fate and the horoscope? / Who will ever again affirm / diviners and soothsayers? / Who will ever again go astray, / after auguries and

Zodiacal signs? / All of them have been wrong in everything. / So that the Just One will not have to instruct / each one who goes astray, / He broke the one who went astray, / so that in him those who have gone astray / might learn their lesson" (CJ IV.26, Griffith 1987, 260; cf. McV 257).

In *Hymns Against Julian*, Ephrem clearly distinguishes between Zoroastrianism and astrology. Julian the Apostate is ridiculed for having relied on the false prognostications of Chaldeans, while the Persian king, one of the Magi—symbolic of Christ's epiphany to the Gentiles (Nat. XXIV)—is praised by Ephrem for having destroyed the cultic centers of the Bardaiṣanites, something Ephrem felt that orthodox Christians themselves should have done (CJ II.22, McV 240).

Summary. In this section, an effort has been made to depict the religious world of Syriac Christianity in general, and of the localized setting in which Ephrem lived and of which he wrote. Fourth-century Mesopotamia displayed a rich and variegated religious landscape. In the midst of all this diversity, no single religion predominated. The world of Ephrem was characterized by a wealth of shared imagery and a web of religious syncretism. The various sects in Nisibis and Edessa turned these images like a kaleidoscope to produce different patterns using many of the same colors and shapes. In CH XXII.2, Ephrem names five heretics in the following order: Marcion, Valentius, Quq, Bardaiṣan, and Mānī. Evidently, they are named in chronological order—a fact that is confirmed by Jacob of Edessa (d. 708; Drijvers 1967, 107). As the Valentinians seem not to have figured prominently in Ephrem's day, no separate treatment was given to this Gnostic sect in the present study. In *Hymns Against Heresies*, Ephrem mentions Quq four times: "Quq also is a mystery to the Quqites by his name, / because he made them into pitchers, empty ones, by his doctrine" (CH II.6); "The Quqite has added and spoiled [viz. the Scriptures]" (CH XXII.2); "The Quqite named it [viz. the community] after his name" (CH XXII.3); "No more than the Audians are ashamed of the name 'owl,' / No more are the Arians and the Quqites ashamed" (CH XXIV.16, Drijvers 1967, 111–12).

The Syriac word *qūqā* means "pitcher," and Ephrem uses this to play on the name of Quq, the founder of the sect. In his *Prose Refutations*, Ephrem does not mention Quq at all, speaking only of Marcion, Bardaiṣan, and Mānī (Drijvers 1967, 108). These three figures had established rival Christian or semi-Christian communities in Nisibis and Edessa. Although Ephrem had vigorously contended against them, it was to little avail. Only persecution and forced conversions by Bishop Rabbula in the fifth century could eradicate their influence. And, of course, there were the Arians, who also were forcibly extirpated.

The Universality of the Church of the East: How Persian was Persian Christianity?

[This section previously appeared as a journal article (Buck 1996a). It is reprinted here by permission of the editors of the *Journal of the Assyrian Academic Society*.]

Persian Christianity was perhaps the first great non-Roman form of Christianity. The "Church of the East" was ecclesiastically "Persian" in that it was, with minor exceptions, the officially recognized Church of the Sasanian empire. The Church was politically "Persian" due to the role of Sasanian kings in the eleven Synods from 410 to 775 C.E. The Church was geographically "Persian" in that it was coextensive with but not limited to the orbit of the Sasanian empire. The Church of the East was only secondarily "Persian" in terms of ethnicity. Yet the presence of ethnic Persians vividly illustrates why the Church of the East became the world's most successful missionary church until modern times.

Although the majority of Christians in the church are assumed to have been ethnic Syrians, the Church of the East was once a universal, multiethnic religion. As a witness to the universality of the Church of the East in its heyday, it is probably the case that ethnic Persians formed the most visible and important ethnic minority of Christianity in Persia. This study will argue that the role of Iranian converts may have been far more significant than has so far been realized. Discoveries of Nestorian texts in Iranian languages (Middle Persian, Sogdian, New Persian) have proven conclusively that Syriac was not the exclusive language of liturgy and instruction in the Persian Church. In fact, part and parcel of the extraordinary missionary success of the Church of the East derived from its genius for adapting Christian worship to local vernaculars. Evidence of this gift for effective indigenization may be seen in the both the Assyrian and Chaldean services for the Feast of Epiphany, in which fragments from a lost Persian Christian liturgy are preserved and recited to this very day.

The importance of the Church of Persia has been diminished by the fact that mainstream church history has, to date, been primarily Eurocentric. This problem may be traced back to Eusebius of Caesarea (d. c. 339 C.E.), who has traditionally been acclaimed as "the Father of Church History" as it was he who wrote the very first *Ecclesiastical History*. As Sebastian Brock observes: "Eusebius passes over the history of the Church to the east of the Roman Empire in almost total silence" and that, as a result, "the legacy of Eusebius' model of a *Church History* has had an insidious influence on his successors, ancient and modern, encouraging the emergence of the excessively Eurocentric view of Church History that is generally current today"

(1996, 70). Consider the significance of the estimated size of West Syrian (Roman and Persian empires) and East Syrian (Persian) Christianity prior to and during the initial period of Islam. John Taylor, a historian of church history, notes: "For the first time since the seventh century, when there were large numbers of Nestorian and Syrian churches in parts of Asia, the majority of Christians in the world [today] are not of European origin" (1990, 635).

There is an implicit claim here that Syrian Christians and their converts outnumbered European Christians. The relative historical neglect of Syriac Christianity is all the more surprising, if Paulos Gregorios's estimate is correct. Speaking of the Syrians relative to other Christian populations, he states: "Before the sixth century they were probably the most numerous Christian group, larger than the Greeks, Latins, and Copts" (1987, 14: 227–28). So far-flung was the mission field, and so ethnically diverse was the Church of the East that it was possible, albeit under special historical circumstances, for a non-Syrian or non-Iranian to lead the entire church. This occurred in the year 1281 C.E., when Mār Yahballāhā III—a Turco-Mongol from the ecclesiastical province of China—was elected to the supreme office of Catholicós-Patriarch (see Hage 1988, 68–79). Yahballāhā's biography was originally written in Persian (not extant), and later translated into Syriac (ibid., 71, n. 9).

By "Persia" is meant something quite different from the territory of present-day Iran. Prior to the Sasanian empire, the Parthian empire (the Parthians were a people of northeastern Iran) extended from the Caspian Sea to the Persian Gulf and from Afghanistan to the Tigris. Broadly speaking, Persia in Sasanian times was a region lying both to the west and to the east of the Tigris River. Persia included what is now Iraq, part of Afghanistan, as well as Russian Azarbaijan.

According to Sasanian documents, Persians distinguished two kinds of land within their empire: Īrān proper, and non-Īrān ("Anīrān"). Although west of present-day Iran, Iraq was actually considered to be part of Iran. According to Wilhelm Eilers, the name al-'Irāq is actually a Persian word (*erāgh*), meaning, "lowlands" (Eilers 1983, 481). This etymology may not be absolutely certain. As Eilers observes: "For the Sasanians, too, the lowlands of Iraq constituted the heart of their dominions" (ibid.). This shows that Iraq was not simply part of the Persian Empire—it was the heart of Persia. Thus the Euphrates River formed the true western frontier of the Persian Empire (ibid.). There was a great overlap here with the linguistic territory of Syriac, a language based in northern Mesopotamia, the country stretching between the Tigris and Euphrates rivers and adjoining regions. Northern Mesopotamia consisted of the Syriac-speaking regions of Adiabene and Osrhoëne. This land formed much of present-day Iraq.

Bardaiṣan (Bardesanes, Bar Daiṣān, d. 222 C.E.) refers to the existence of Christians in the provinces of Pārs, Medea, Kāshān, and Parthia. Twice during his war against the Romans (viz., the two captures of Antioch in 256 and 260 C.E.), Shāpūr deported sizeable contingents of Greek-speaking Christian prisoners of war from Antioch and other cities and colonized these "spoils of war" in Persis, Parthia, Susiana, and Babylonia. According to the *Chronicle of Séert*, this resulted in there being two churches—Greek and Syriac—at Rēv-Ardashīr in Persis (Pārs) (Asmussen 1983, 929–30). Despite these ethnic boundaries, this was a fortuitous boon to Christianity in Persia.

The "Church of Persia" is principally an ecclesiastical term, designating the East Syrian Church, which flourished, albeit with episodic persecutions, in the Persian empire under the Sasanians. "Persian Christianity" is a more geographical or regional description term, adumbrating West Syrian Jacobites as well, who eventually sought refuge in the Sasanian kingdom. The term *Persian* by itself will be used to denote ethnic Iranian Christians, who were mostly converts from Zoroastrianism. Indeed, while the liturgy and instruction remained, for the most part, Syriac, a subsidiary Christian vernacular was Persian. During the Sasanian period, Brock notes that "Persian became an increasingly important literary vehicle for Christians" and that there was a "once extensive Christian literature in this language" (Brock 1982a, 18). So multiethnic was East Syrian Christianity that "Christians in the Sasanid empire employed a whole number of different languages for ecclesiastical use" (ibid., 17).

Aphrahāṭ "the Persian sage" is our earliest major witness to Christianity within the Persian empire. Likewise, F. Rilliet was quoted earlier as having stated that Ephrem "is a privileged witness of the tradition of the primitive church of Persia" (1992a, 1: 276). While developments that brought the Church of Persia into its own as a church independent of Rome were subsequent to both Aphrahāṭ and Ephrem, their legacy had a formative and abiding influence on Persian Christianity.

During the Parthian period (c. 141 B.C.E. to 224 C.E.), Rome replaced the Greeks as the arch-enemy of the East. While Christians were being persecuted within the Roman Empire, they were relatively free from persecution under the Parthians. Rome and Persia, superpowers of the early Christian world, were perpetually at war. This political conflict had a role in sparking religious conflict as well. In the fourth century, when Christianity became the state religion of the Roman Empire, Christianity became politicized. The superpower rivalry then took on overt religious overtones. Now, for non-Roman Christians, the pendulum between persecution and protection hinged on state religion as well as affairs of state. A rival religion competed with Christianity for power. This was the ancient Persian religion known as Zoroastrianism. This Persian monotheism, founded on an ethical dualism that, over the centuries, had degenerated into an ontological dualism, traditionally held to "good thoughts, good words, good deeds" as its sacred ideal. But in political reality, as the state religion of Persia, Zoroastrianism exercised quite the opposite in its treatment of Christians.

Zoroastrianism reached its zenith of power under the patronage of Shāpūr I (r. 241–272). Persian Christianity became the primary target of the intolerance with which the Magian religion became imbued. It was the chief priest Kartīr who had the Persian prophet Mānī tortured and executed. Social status or rank of nobility provided little protection from the widescale persecution of Christians at the hands of a fanatical Magian clergy. Not even the high-born Qandira (Candida) the Roman—who was the Christian consort of King Varahan II (r. 276–293)—was spared. It was Kartīr who probably instigated the first persecution of Christians in Persia. Persecutions continued throughout the rest of Shāpūr II's reign, and, sporadically, during the reigns of his successors, Ardashīr II (r. 379–383) and Vaharan IV (r. 388–399). Under the reign of Yazdagird I (r. 399–421), Christians were tolerated until the year 420 C.E. Christian sources, in fact, praise Yazdagird.

The discovery on Khārg Island in the Persian Gulf of no fewer than sixty Christian tombs indicates that by the year 250 C.E. there was already a strong Christian presence in Persia. These sixty tombs at Khārg, an island near Bushire and opposite Bahrain, were cut into a coral bank. Vestiges of Syriac inscriptions are still visible on the vertical columns of these Christian tombs (Bowman 1974). Stewart McCullough speculates that Christians on the mainland had selected the island as a place less vulnerable to disturbance by fanatical Zoroastrian priests. These sixty tombs may in fact have housed martyrs of persecutions instigated by the high priest, Kartīr (HSC 112), "who gave Zoroastrianism a new dimension by turning it into a religion that would brook no rivals in Iran" (HSC 102).

As a dual-authority polity, Christians within the Persian Empire had divided loyalties. During the reign of Shāpūr II (310–379 C.E.), Constantine (d. 337) converted to Christianity. In turn, Christianity was converted to the state religion of the Roman Empire. (Ephrem's native town of Nisibis was represented at the Council of Nicea in 325 C.E. by Bishop Jacob.) Unwittingly, after the transformation of the Roman Empire into a Christian state, Persian Christians became a political vanguard of Rome. This placed them in an even more precarious situation. Already vulnerable as a religious minority, Persian Christians were perceived as allied with the enemy, and not without justification. Three years after Constantine's death in 337 C.E., persecution against the Christians in Persia began.

In his *Life of Constantine*, Eusebius, the first historian of the Church, states that there were "many churches of God in Persia and that large numbers were gathered into the fold of Christ" (Brock 1982a, 1). Constantine's conversion to Christianity and the Christianizing of the Roman Empire cast a pall of suspicion over an estimated 35,000 Persian Christians, who fell victim to the Great Persecution that began in 339 C.E. and ended only with the death of Shāpūr II forty years later. (Large-scale persecution of Persian Christians was instigated mainly during times of war, when Christians were suspected of favoring the enemy [(ibid., 5].)

This situation was aggravated by overt pro-Roman sympathies held by some of the Persian Christians. Aphrahāṭ is a case in point. The Persian Sage writes: "The People of God have received prosperity, and success awaits the man who has been the instrument of that prosperity [i.e., Constantine]; but disaster threatens the army gathered together by the efforts of a wicked and proud man puffed up by vanity [Šāpūr]. . . . The [Roman] Empire will not be conquered, because the hero whose name is Jesus is coming with His power, and His army will uphold the whole army of the Empire" (Aph. Dem. 5.1.24, Russell, EIr 5: 524–25).

Survival necessitated an eventual break between Roman and Persian Christians. Eventually this break took place. The counterpart of Rome in the Persian Empire was Seleucia-Ctesiphon, the twin-city Sasanian capital where Persian Christianity officially constituted itself in the year 410 C.E. at the Synod of Mār Isḥāq, asserting its full independence in the Synod of Dādīšō' in 424 C.E. (See details in the section, "The Persian Synods," below.) The area encompassed by Persian Christianity included areas both within present-day Iran (such as the province of Pārs) as well as the frontier regions of Nisibis and Adiabene. Mār Isḥāq in fact proclaimed himself "bishop of Seleucia-Ctesiphon, Catholicós and Head (*rēšā*) over the bishops of all the Orient (*madneḥā*)" (Asmussen 1983, 931).

Ecclesiastical development within Persian Christianity has also been documented. Its anchor in orthodoxy seemed secure in its adherence to the Nicene Creed. Indeed, a certain "John of Persia" (Yohannan of Bēṯ Pārsāyē) is recorded as having represented Persia at the Council of Nicaea in 325 C.E. (Eusebius, in his *Life of Constantine*, remarked that "even a Persian bishop attended the Synod" [Asmussen 1983, 931, n. 6].) In 345 C.E., at the Synod of Seleucia, Bishop Pāpā bar Aggai sought to consolidate all of the churches in Persian territory under his rule. But the bishops of Persia proper thwarted this scheme. Particularly strong resistance came from Mīlēs of Susa.

Later, at the Synod of Mār Isḥāq (410), the Church of Persia was officially established in Seleucia-Ctesiphon, the royal capital of Persia. These were twin cities, situated on either side of the Tigris River.

This Synod commenced with a prayer for the king, Yazdagird I, who had granted tolerance and even favor to Christians and other minorities. The Synod officially adopted the Nicene Creed. Six "classical" provinces within the western regions of the Sasanian empire were represented in the official records of this synod. Geo Widengren has assembled a list of fifteen evangelized provinces in Sasanian Iran and in Central Asia (1984, 10–12). I have expanded Widengren's list to at least eighteen provinces, excluding "Outer Iran" (Central Asia). Some of these provinces were ecclesiastical provinces. The rest were bishoprics.

Shāpūr I's list of Sasanian provinces is given by Brunner (1983, 750), following a very useful and detailed map of "The provinces of early Sasanian Iran" (748–49). The following list gives all of twenty-five provinces of the Sasanian empire as enumerated in Shāpūr I's inscription on the Ka'ba-yi Zardusht. These provinces are represented in geographical order and by quadrant, according to the points of the compass (*kust*). Evangelized provinces are marked in bold: *South Quadrant*, southwest: (1) **Pārs**; (2) **Parthau**; (3) **Khuzistān**. *West Quadrant*: (4) **Maishān**; (5) **Āsūristān**; (6) **Nōdardashīragān**; (7) **Arbāyistān**. *North Quadrant*, north: 8. **Ādurbādagān**. Northwest: (9) Armin; (10) Wirōzān; (11) Sigān; (12) Ar(r)ān; (13) Balāsagān; **Parishkwārgar**; (14) **Māh**; (15) **Gurgān**. *East Quadrant*, east: (16) **Marv**; (17) **Harēw, Abaršahr**; (18) **Kushānshahr**. Southeast: (19) **Kirmān**; (20) **Sagistān**; (21) Turgistān; (22) Makurān; (23) Pārdān; (24) **Hind**; (25) **Mazōn**. **Outer Iran** [**Central Asia**]: (26) **Samarkand**; (27) Bactria; (28) **Sogdiana**.

Evangelized provinces of Sasanian Persia: The evidence. The first six ecclesiastical provinces of the Church of the East were formalized as hyparchies in the Synod of Mār Isḥāq (410 C.E.). These provinces did not represent all of the Christian districts within the frontiers of the Sasanian empire at that time. In Canon XXI, the assembled bishops express the hope that "the bishops from the far-away regions (*atrawātā raḥīqē*), from Pārs, the Islands, Bēṯ Mādāyē, Bēṯ R[az]īqāyē, indeed, even from the Abaršahr regions" would accept the decisions reached by the synod (Asmussen 1983, 932). All of these regions will be briefly discussed in the geographical-ecclesiastical overview that follows below.

South Quadrant, southwest: The concentrations of Syriac- and Greek-speaking captives lay in the western districts of the south quadrant (Brunner 1983, 751). (1) **Pārs:** This is the province in which John of Daylam established a monastery for Persian-speaking monks in the eighth century (Anon., EIr 7: 336). Pārs is mentioned as a bishopric in the Synod of 410. In the southwest province of Pārs (Fārs, Persia proper), the city of Ṣṭakhr (Iṣṭakhr)—summer capital of the Sasanians

—had become a diocese by 424 (Brunner 1983, 751). In its role as the spiritual centre of Zoroastrianism, in Ṣṭakhr was kept the dynasty's fire, the *Anāhīd-ardashīr*, described as the "ideological heart of the empire" (ibid.). Between 415 and 420 C.E., Pārs became an ecclesiastical province (Widengren 1984, 11). As of the Synod of Mār Bābay in 497, its metropolis was *Rēv-Ardashīr* (Rīshahr), from whence the Nestorian mission to India was directed. The province of Pārs included Qais Island, a distinct bishopric as of 544 C.E.; (2) **Parthau:** Aspadana (Spāhān, Ispāhān, Iṣfāhān) in the southwest province of Parthau is also mentioned in the Synod of Mār Dādīšō' (424); (3) **Khūzistān:** [Represented as an ecclesiastical province in the Synod of 410.] In the southwest quadrant of Sasanian Iran, the province of Khūzistān (Syriac: *Bēṯ Ḥūzāyē*) was also known as Parthian Susiana, Elymais, Elam. Its metropolis was the pre-Sasanian diocese of *Bēṯ Lāpāṭ* (later Gundē-Shāpūr). The ancient capital of *Shūsh* (Susa) became a diocese by 410, as was the case with *Karkā de Lādhan* (Ērānshahr-Shāpūr), and *Rāmhurmuz* (Rām-Ormazd-Ardashīr), the major city in the east of the province (Brunner 1983, 753). A bishopric was established in *Hormizd-Ardashīr* (Ahvāz), the later capital of Khūzistān (HSC 137). It was here that Mār 'Abda, a Persian Christian priest, was said to have destroyed a Zoroastrian fire temple adjacent to a Christian church, and who, as a result of this, suffered martyrdom (Williams 1996, 46, n. 37).

West Quadrant: (4) **Maishān:** [Represented as an ecclesiastical province in the Synod of 410.] In Lower Babylonia, the region around Baṣra in modern Iraq, the western province of Maišān (Mēšān, Mesene) had four bishoprics, with *Pherāt de Maišān* (later Vahman-Ardashīr) as its metropolis (cf. Streck, "Maisān" in *Encyclopaedia of Islam*, first edition); (5) **Āsūristān:** [Represented as an ecclesiastical province in the Synod of 410.] In what was known to antiquity as Babylonia, now Iraq, the western province (*shahr*) of Āsūristān (Syriac: *Bēṯ Arāmāyē*) was known as Assyria, although historical Assyria was actually to the north. In the Sasanian era, Iranians considered Āsūristān to be "the heart of Iran" (Brunner 1983, 757). The Catholicós of the Church of the East was the bishop of Seleucia-Ctesiphon, the Sasanian administrative capital and royal winter residence. The bishop of the district of Kashkar served as auxiliary (HSC 123); (6) **Nōdardashīragān:** [Represented as an ecclesiastical province in the Synod of 410.] The western province of Garamīg ud Nōdardashīragān (Syriac: *Bēṯ Garmay*) was north of Āsūristān between the Tigris and Little Khābūr rivers, and the mountains of Āzarbāyjān. Its metropolis was *Karkā de Bēṯ Selōk* (Kirkūk). This ecclesiastical province included the bishopric of Pērōz-Shāpūr (Faishābūr, HSC 137) and probably the diocese of Shahrazūr (Brunner 1983, 761). Garamīg used to be part of the province of Adiabene.

Evidently, Garamig was organized as a special province between 343 and 410 C.E. (Widengren 1984, 11); **Adiabene:** [Represented as an ecclesiastical province in the Synod of 410.] In what is now northern Iraq, the Sasanian buffer state Adiabene (Syriac: *Ḥedyab*, Ḥadyab) lay east of the Tigris, between the Greater and Lesser Zāb rivers. An organized Christian community since the late Parthian period, Adiabene's metropolis was *Arbela* (Irbīl); **Ḥulwān**: The ecclesiastical province of Ḥulwān (Syriac: *Bēṯ Mādāyē*, Māda) was established and organized by Catholicós Išoyabh Geddālāyā II between the years 628 and 643 (Widengren 1984, 12). It occupied the region of southern Media, now Albania (HSC 151); (7) **Arbāyistān:** [(Represented as an ecclesiastical province in the Synod of 410.] In Northern Mesopotamia, the western Sasanian province of Arbāyistān or Arabistān (Syriac: *Bēṯ 'Arbāyē*) had Ephrem's native city of Nisibis as its metropolis. Nearby, on Mount Īzlā, was the "Great Monastery"—the leading monastery in Christian Persia (HSC 170).

North Quadrant, north: (8) **Ādurbādagān:** The northern province of Ādurbādagān (Āzarbāyjān) had at least one bishop (HSC 151). Northwest: (9) Armin: No bishoprics attested; (10) Wirōzān: No bishoprics attested; (11) Sigān No bishoprics attested; (12) Ar(r)ān: No bishoprics attested; (13) Balāsagān: No bishoprics attested; **Parishkwārgar:** In the Caspian region of Dēlam (Dailam, Daylam) in the northern province of Parishkwārgar (Ṭabaristān), John of Daylam founded several monasteries. Later, John travelled to Arrajān (Argān) in Fārs, where he established two monasteries, one for Syriac-speaking monks and the other for Persian-speaking monks. In the *Book of the Laws of Countries*, Bar Daiṣān's pupil Philippus had already attested the presence of Christians in both nearby Gīlān and in Kushān: "Our sisters among the Geli and the Kushanians do not have intercourse with foreigners, and they who live in Persia do not marry their daughters" (Edakalathur 1994, 9, citing Drijvers 1965, 61). The Gēls, who were admired as valiant warriors, were the native inhabitants of Gīlān, which, along with Daylam, lay in the mountainous regions on the southern shores of the Caspian; (14) **Māh:** The northern province of Māh (central Media, the "core of Media" —Brunner 1983, 766) had a diocese in the city of Rayy (Syriac: *Bēṯ R*[az]*īqāyē*), otherwise known as 'Aqdā, Rhages. Mentioned in the the Synod of Mār Isḥāq (410); (15) **Gurgān:** According to the letter sent by Timotheos I (d. 823), Christianity had been established in Gurgān—the ancient Hyrcania (Widengren 1984, 11).

East Quadrant, east: As of the Synod of 424 C.E., it was evident that the Church of the East had expanded deep into central and eastern Persia, "into regions that were predominantly Zoroastrian" (HSC 126). (16) **Marv:** Between 415 and 420, Marv became an ecclesiastical province (Widengren 1984, 11). In the Synod of 554, the eastern province of Marv (Margiana), north of present-day Khurāsān, is mentioned as a hyparchy, although there appears to have been a Chistian bishop there as early as 334 C.E. From Marv, Christian missions proceeded on to Ṭukhāristān and to Transoxiana (Brunner 1983, 770); (17) **Harēw:** In the Synod of 585, the eastern province of Harēv (Herāt, Areia, i.e., modern Afghanistan) is mentioned as a hyparchy. (It had become a bishopric by 424.); **Abaršahr:** Also mentioned in the the Synod of Mār Isḥāq, the eastern province of Apar-šahr ("realm of the Aparni" clans) is also part of modern Khurāsān. The city of *Nēv-Shāpur* was its center; (18) **Kushānshahr:** The eastern province of Kushān (Ṭukhāristān), near the Upper Oxus in the northern part of what is now modern Afghanistan, had already been evangelized by the third century, if not by the second. On the coast in the district of Qaṭīf, a bishopric was established in the city of Paniyāt-Ardashīr by 576. The islands of Tārūt and Muḥarraq also became dioceses, along with Gerrha (Hajar—ibid., 757). Southeast: (19) **Kirmān:** In a letter to Simeon, metropolitan of Rev Ardashīr in Pārs (Fārs), Nestorian catholicós Isho'yahb III (647–659 C.E.), lamented that many Christians in Fārs and Kirmān, despite lack of persecution by Arabs, had converted to Islam to escape paying taxes (Morony 1990, 141); (20) **Sagistān:** In the Synod of Mār Dādīšō' (424), the southeastern province of Sagistān (Sēyānsa, Sijistān) was represented by two bishops (Widengren 1984, 5); (21) Turgistān: No bishoprics attested; (22) Makurān: No bishoprics attested; (23) Pārdān: No bishoprics attested; (24) **Hind:** By the sixth century, Iranian merchants dominated the Indian ports on the west coast of "India Interior." Christians there were under the authority of the church hyparchy of Fārs (Brunner 1983, 757). This fact was noted by the traveller Cosmas Indicopleustes, an Egyptian monk, who, during the first half of the sixth century, observed that "in the country which is called Male (Malabar), where pepper is growing, there is a bishop ordained in Persia" (Fiey 1996, 98). Cosmas also found "Persian" Christians on the islands of Ceylon and Socotra (King 1948, 2: 269). The office of the bishop of India was promoted to a metropolitan between the years 714 and 728 (Fiey 1996, 98); (25) **Mazōn:** The southeastern province of Mazōn included the territory referred to as "The Islands" (Syriac: *Bēṯ Qaṭrāyē*), i.e., eastern Arabia and Baḥrain, which had a monastery (HSC 167). Mazōn was transformed into a hyparchy as of the Synod of 676 C.E.

Outer Iran (Central Asia): (26) **Samarkand:** Samarkand (ancient Marakand) was a Nestorian province. The evidence for the establishment of Christianity there has been collected by Colless (1986); (27) Bactria: No bishoprics attested; (28) **Sogdiana:** The evangelization of the Sogdians represents the culmination of missionary efforts within the Sasanian empire, as Richard N. Frye observes: "In the east, too, Christian missionaries made converts among the Hephthalites and Sogdians, so one may infer everywhere a growing Christian influence at the end of the Sasanian empire" (1962, 224).

A total of some eighteen Sasanian provinces are thus known to have been evangelized. Nestorian missions extended far beyond the Sasanian borders, expanding east through Central Asia, and finally reaching to the end of the world as it was known, China. Numerically, this is 68 percent of the provinces of the Persian empire. By the fall of the Sasanian dynasty, before the Arab onslaught in the mid-seventh century, there were ten metropolitan sees (including the patriarchate) and ninety-six bishoprics (Brock 1982a, 3). Brock notes that "In what is today north Iraq, conversions to Christianity from paganism continued into the early Islamic period" (1982a, 3, n. 9; cf. Morony 1990, 1976, 1974). With the advent of Islam, the Church of Persia went into decline in terms of population, but certainly not intellectually nor in the prosecution of its missionary endeavors. It is estimated that the majority of the population of Iran was more or less fully converted to Islam between 850 and 950 C.E. (Morony 1990, 136–38). The Nestorian chronicler Mārī b. Sulaymān reported that "many" Christians in Iran had converted to Islam in the late tenth century due to persecution and to corruption of the clergy (Morony 1990, 143). However, in the mountain regions of the north, it took nearly two centuries for Islam to penetrate Daylam and Gīlān. Persia's conversion to Islam was nearly complete only with the establishment of the Seljuk empire (Schütz 1990, 219).

The Nestorian controversy and the independence of the Church of Persia. In the fifth century, from Narsai (d. c. 471) onward, the Church of Persia became, loosely speaking, "Nestorian," incorporating a dyophysite, "two-natures" (human-divine) position within its Christology. The term *Nestorian* is somewhat anachronistic here, since it is not attested in official documents of the East Syrian Church until the thirteenth century (McLeod 1979, 1). The anachronism is still descriptive in that it designates adherence to a diophysite Christology. The Assyrian Church of the East has a far greater doctrinal reliance on Theodore of Mopsuestia.

In 428 C.E., Nestorius had become the Patriarch of Byzantium. Nestorius taught that Christ was one person but had two distinct natures, divine and human. These natures remained separate, such that Mary was not, properly speaking, the "Mother of God" (*theotókos*). Nestorius rejected the divinity of the man Jesus. This was utter doom for Nestorius and his followers. Cyril of Alexandria, adamant in his belief that the two natures of Christ were united at birth, vigorously opposed Nestorius. He was anathematized at the Council of Ephesus (431 C.E.). Under Byzantine rule, Nestorians were forced to flee Edessa. They took refuge in Nisibis under Persian rule. This proved a blessing in disguise, as the Nestorian church, despite sporadic persecutions, flourished in Persia, steering as it did a steady course between alternate patronage and persecution.

Nestorius was held in high esteem by Narsai, the great consolidator of Nestorianism, popularly known as the "Harp of the Spirit" (*kinārā d-rūḥā*). (For a comparison between Narsai and Ephrem, see Jansma 1970.) The innocence of Nestorius is championed by Narsai in a homily in defense of the "Three Doctors"—Diodore of Tarsus, Theodore of Mopsuestia, and Nestorius. (See Martin 1899/1900 for Syriac text and translation.) "The Persian Christians, moreover, have never, with common consent, referred to themselves as 'Nestorians'; this was a derogatory title employed by the Monophysites for all dyophysite Christians" (Miller 1984, 528, n. 125). Rather, Persian Christians were Theodoran. Insofar as he followed Theodore of Mopsuestia, Nestorius was looked upon as orthodox and as one who was treated unjustly.

Generally, Persian Christians avoided referring to Nestorius by name. It was, after all, a lightning rod for criticisms of those errors traditionally ascribed to him. Yet the influence of Nestorius was undeniable. In its Syriac translation, Nestorius's *Book of Herakleides* exerted a powerful influence on Bābay the Great (d. 628—Brock 1985c, 128). However, Nestorius was by no means the major theologian of the Church of the East. That distinction rests with Bābay, who was the most important theologian of the Church of the East (Brock 1996, 33). "For the Persians," writes Geevarghese Chediath, "Babai's Christology was the Christology of their church" (1994, 165).

Bābay's major Christological treatise was *On the Union* (sc. of the two natures of Christ). In current scholarship, the term *Nestorian* is still a term of convenience, not of deprecation. This is not without precedent within the Church of the East itself. In the year 1609 C.E., for instance, Mār 'Abd Yeshua drew up the "orthodox creed of the Nestorians," having done so "in the blessed city of Khlāt in the church of the blessed Nestorians" (*apud* Adeney 1965, 484, n. 1). Centuries earlier, in the eighth century to be precise, Mar Shahdost of Tirhan (not Tehran) had composed a treatise entitled, *Why We Easterns Have Separated Ourselves from the Westerns, and Why We Are Called Nestorians*. In this text, the author refers to his faith-community as, "we, the Nestorians" (Davids 1994, 134–35).

Monarchs often took a vested and active interest in overseeing Persian Christianity. Sasanian kings took interest in various Synods. In 552, Kavādh's son Chosroes I (r. 531–579) imposed his own nominee as Catholicós for ratification at the Synod of 554. At the Synod of Mār Ezekiel (576), Chosroes I demanded that he be named in the litanies during the liturgy (Brock 1982a, 11). In 609 C.E., Chosroes II (r. 591–628) was outraged when his own candidate was passed over. So he forbade any subsequent election, which eventually left the Christian community temporarily without a head until the King's death nullified the ban. In the late sixth century, the Christian communities of Marv and Herat became prominent. In the year 651, the Bishop of Marv donated a sepulchre for the assassinated Yazdagird III (Russell, EIr 5: 524). But the relationship between Church and state was always tense and precarious. War-weary and overtaxed, many Persian Christians welcomed with palm fronds the Arab conquerors of Ctesiphon (ibid., 525–26).

The Persian synods. The Church of Persia held its own series of synods, the records of which have come down to us in the so-called *Synodicon Orientale* (edited, with French translation by Chabot [1902], German version by Braun [1900], unpublished English rendition by M. J. Birnie [Stirnemann and Wilflinger 1994, 88–89, and 119]). It is a record of the history of Christianity in Sasanian Iran.

This chronicle, however, is not contemporary. It was compiled by the Catholicós Timothy in the late eighth century. The first bishop of historical stature of the Persian capital of Seleucia-Ctesiphon was a certain Pāpā, who lived in the fourth century. Pāpā was opposed by Milēs, bishop of Susa, who deposed Pāpā from office when Pāpā tried to impose autocratic rule on Milēs's episcopal colleagues. Pāpā's effort to consolidate churches in Persia into a unified Church of Persia had failed.

The Church of Persia officially constituted itself in its first Synod of 410 C.E. According to Eilers (1983, 485), it was not until the year 409. C.E. that public Christian worship was first permitted within the Persian empire. This signal event occurred during the reign of Yazdagird (r. 399–422). Virtually isolated until the early fifth century, the Church of Persia—by virtue of its ancient autonomy—had no dependency on any western diocese, even in Antioch. (There was, however, a theory to the contrary, advanced by some medieval East Syriac writers, who maintained that the see of Seleucia-Ctesiphon had once been subordinate to the patriarchate of Antioch [Brock 1994, 75, n. 15, citing de Halleux 1978].) The patriarchal church structure in the Byzantine West had crystallized during the fourth and fifth centuries. And Byzantine influence can be seen in the first general synod of the Church of Persia, held in 410 C.E. This transpired when Mārūṯā, the Byzantine imperial envoy for peace negotiations between the Roman and Persian empires, set out to the Sasanian capital of Seleucia-Ctesiphon to align the Church of Persia with the norms of the Church of the West.

In this venture, Mārūṯā succeeded in enlisting the support of the Persian monarch, Yazdagird I. "It is significant," Brock remarks, "that the synod was convoked by the Shah himself" (1994, 73). By royal decree, the bishops of the realm were summoned to the capital. The Byzantine ecclesiastical envoy acted as co-president of the synod, along with the Catholicós [Archbishop], Mār Isḥāq. The synod promulgated a number of canons that regulated church doctrine, liturgy, and office in accordance with the prevailing practices of the West. A variation on the Nicene creed was also adopted. The rule of one bishop per city created problems in areas where there were multiple sees, due to the presence of sometimes Greek, Syriac, and Persian Christian populations. Several days after the initial session, Mārūṯā and Mar Isḥāq (Isaac) arranged for an official audience with the king, before whom all of the Persian bishops were assembled. This marked what was probably the very first time that the relationship between church and state was regularized (Brock 1994, 74).

Another synod was convoked in 420 C.E., under the presidency of the new Catholicós Yahballāhā and another Byzantine ambassador, Acacius of Amida. But in the Synod of 424, at which a Byzantine representative was not present, the full autonomy of the Church of Persia was espoused. Here, as in the three Petrine sees of Rome, Alexandria, and Antioch, the language of the Synod of 424 was couched in Petrine terms. In its canonical emancipation from Antioch, the Church of Persia placed itself outside the petrarchy of Rome, Constantinople, Alexandria, Antioch, and Jerusalem (Asmussen 1983, 941).

Vernacular Persian in Church of the East liturgy? What evidence is there to attest to the presence of an indigenous, ethno-linguistic Iranian presence in Persian Christianity, which was predominately East Syrian? Is it possible that ethnic Persians constituted the most important minority in the Church of the East, once a flourishing, multiethnic and thus "universal" Church? Gernot Wiessner (1971) has stressed the importance of the Iranian ethnic element in Nestorianism. Evidence suggests there was an appreciable ethnic Iranian representation in the Church of Persia. This is colorfully illustrated by an episode in the Syriac *Life of John of Dailam*. John of Daylam (variously spelled Dailam, Deylam) was an East Syrian saint of the seventh to eighth centuries, who lived in western Persia. The following narrative tells of a controversy that broke out among the monks in Arrajān over whether to conduct services in Syriac or in Persian: "Now the Persian and Syriac-speaking brethren quarrelled with each other over the services: the Persians said, 'We should all recite the services in our language, seeing that we live in Persian territory'; while the Syriac-speakers said, ['Our father is a Syriac-speaker, and so we should recite the services in our language, on account of the founder of the monastery; furthermore we do not know how to recite the services in Persian.' When Mār Yoḥannan saw the quarrel had arisen, he pacified the brethren and prayed to God with deep feeling. Thereupon he was told in a revelation from God: 'Build them another monastery the other side of the river, opposite this one, resembling it in every respect. Let the

Persian-speakers live in one, and the Syriac in the other.' So he built another monastery just like the first, and the Syriac-speaking brethren lived there. Thus the quarrel between the brethren was resolved" (Brock 1982c, 150–51).

This is plausible enough, especially in light of the resurgence of literary Persian in the ninth century. If this story has any basis in fact, it provides anecdotal evidence of a considerable segment of ethnic Iranians within the Church of Persia. A recent study pronounces the following verdict on the historicity of this account: "John traveled to Arrajān in Fārs, where he founded several monasteries: two of them were assigned to Persian- and Syriac-speaking monks respectively, so that neither community should be forced to celebrate services in a foreign language. Despite some chronological confusion and the legendary accretions typical of Syriac hagiographical literature, there is no reason to doubt the essential historicity of this biography" (Anon, EIr 7: 336). Indeed, there must have been a significant number of native Persians converting to Christianity. In the fifth century, imperial ambassadors from the Roman emperor Theodosius beseeched Yazdagird I (r. 399–421) to release from prison a deacon named Benjamin, to which the Shah replied: "Give me assurance in his own handwriting that he will not convert to his faith any more Magians in Persia. If so, at your request, I will free him from chains." This officially constituted one of the terms of the peace treaty of 561 (Brock 1982a, 10–11, n. 41) during the reign of Chosroes I (= Khosrow, r. 531–579) which established that there should be freedom of religion, but not to proselytize. Both Christians and Zoroastrians were forbidden to proselytize in their respective territories (Bausani 1971, 66–67).

According to Asmussen, "numerous" Christian converts in the fifth century had Zoroastrian names, attesting to the success of the Church of Persia in converting ethnic Iranians (Asmussen 1983, 942). By the fifth century, some of the chief Iranian festivals had already been turned into Christian feasts (Boyce 1983, 804). The influx of former Zoroastrians in the Church of Persia was of such magnitude that the Persian king Jāmāsp (r. 498–501) summoned a synod to deliberate on the problem of Zoroastrian marriage customs within the Christian community. That this was a topic of major concern in the sixth century is also attested by the earliest treatise of canon law by Catholicós Mār Abā I (d. 552), which was devoted to this subject (Brock 1982a, 4–5, n. 14). Further evidence of the conversion of ethnic Iranians is found in various other documents. In 595 C.E., the patriarch Sabrisho persuaded Chosroes II (r. 591–628) to grant Christians freedom of worship. According to the *Life of Sabrisho*, as a result many Persian noblemen converted (ibid., 6, n. 17). Prior to this, even a son of Chosroes I had become a Christian (ibid., 8–9, n. 34). This must have alarmed both the monarch and the Zoroastrian priests. Active proselytizing of Zoroastrians by the Nestorians was supposed to have ended as a matter of policy with the aforementioned truce of 561 C.E. concluded between Constantinople and Persia.

Christians in Persia constituted, in political scientific terms, a "dual authority polity" (a communal group having two sources of political authority—state and diasporal, the latter typically being ecclesiastical in the case of faith-communities). The Persian state was the political authority and (Imperial) Christianity the diasporal authority. Conversion to Christianity, for some, entailed spiritual fealty to Christianity in the West. Thus, Persian monarchs were, to a degree, rightly suspicious of Christians as sympathizers with the arch-enemy Rome, but were mistaken in their fear that this constituted any real threat. With one or two minor exceptions perhaps, Christian sympathy was hardly complicity. Yet, on the pretext of treason, many Christians paid with their lives for pro-Roman leanings. Over time, Christians tried to dispel this cloud of political suspicion and to enlist the support of the Persian monarchy.

Moreover, there is evidence that some Persian Christians were openly loyal to the Sasanian state. In the sixth century, a known convert from Zoroastrianism, named Grīgōr, was commissioned by Cawad [sic] as a general during a campaign against Rome (Brock 1982a, 11). Grīgōr is reputed to have in fact been the leader of the Persians in war against the Romans (Asmussen 1983, 934). During the large-scale persecution of Christians (339–379) that took place in the reign of Shāpūr II (r. 310–379), a Christian courtier named Gushtazad apostasized from Christianity but thereafter repented, to die a martyr's death. On being led off to his fate, Gushtazad insisted on sending a last message to Shāpūr II: "I have always been loyal to you and your father. Grant me one request: Let a herald proclaim that Gushtazad is being put to death, not for treason, but because he was a Christian who refused to renounce God" (Brock 1982a, 11). It should be added, however, that this loyalty to state did not constitute loyalty to a "nation" (ibid., 12).

The extent to which Persian Christians sought to curry favor with the state is seen in the *Synodicon*, in which Chosroes I is referred to as "the second Cyrus (*kwrš*)" (Asmussen 1983, 946) who is "preserved by divine grace." In Canon 14 of the Synod of 576, Persian Christians were told: "It is right that in all the churches of this exalted and glorious kingdom that our lord the victorious Chosroes, king of kings, be named in the litanies during the liturgy. No metropolitan or bishop has any authority to waive this canon in any of the churches of his diocese and jurisdiction" (Brock 1982a, 11). Even when Persian Christians went to such lengths to appease imperial suspicions as to Christian loyalties, religious persecution at the hands of fanatical and intolerant Magians posed a separate though related challenge to the Christian community.

Much of our information concerning the ethnic origins of Christian minorities in the Church of the East comes from martyrologies, in which indigenous converts—especially ethnic Iranian converts—figure prominently. The *Acts of Shīrīn* narrates the martyrdoms of its two heroines, Shīrīn and Gulindukht. Shīrīn of Karka de Beth Selokh was the daughter of Zoroastrian parents. For her Christian faith she was arrested and martyred in Seleucia in February 559. Gulindukht was related to Chosroes I and had been married to a Zoroastrian general. She was converted to Christianity by some Christian prisoners of war. Thrown into the Fortress of Oblivion (*Anūshbard*) after her refusal to revert to Zoroastrianism, she chose martyrdom, despite the intervention of Aristoboulos, a legate sent on a peace mission by the emperor Maurice (Brock 1982a, 10). She was martyred in 591. Himself a Zoroastrian convert, Jesusabran of Beṯ Garmay was another such martyr (HSC 158). In Iran, the royal martyr Shīndokht is remembered to this day.

Thus, there were, generally speaking, two types of persecution of Christian in Sasanian Persia. The first were large-scale persecutions perpetrated in times of war against Rome. An argument could be made that such persecutions were provoked by ill-disguised sympathies among many Persian Christians for Imperial Christianity and its Christian Emperor. Even in sporadic times of royal clemency and favor, the one grave danger Persian Christians had to face was the hostility of the Magi. This brought about the second type of persecution: persecution by Magians of prominent ex-Zoroastrian Christians, such as the martyrs Mār Abā and Giwargis. As Brock observes: "Other martyrs under the Sasanids were individuals, most of whom were converts of high-born Zoroastrian origin, whose prominence in society led to their denunciation by the Magian clergy and subsequent sentencing to death" (1982a, 5). Some of this persecution Christians had brought upon themselves, through isolated acts of vandalism that included the destruction of Zoroastrian fire temples (ibid., 6).

Despite the unrelenting pressure and threat to life and limb, former Zoroastrian converts to Nestorianism could aspire to Church leadership. One such convert was Catholicós Mār Abā I (d. 552), who became Catholicós in the year 540 C.E. (HSC 136). But he suffered considerably. Called before a council of the Magi in c. 541–542, he refused to alter the Church's canons on marriage, nor would he have Christians desist from their current practices of proselytization. For this he was detained in a village in Azarbaijan for seven years, from whence he exercised his leadership of the Church of Persia. Another type of leadership was that of the mystic, or "holy man." One such holy man was the renowned Nestorian mystic, Joseph Hazzāyā, who was from a high-born Zoroastrian family (Gerö 1987, 45, n. 22).

The pressures of a Zoroastrian environment were felt in all aspects of Christian life. Monasticism in Persia benefited from an influx of Monophysites, who were exiled to northwest Persia as a consequence of the anti-Monophysite policy of the emperor Justin (r. 518–527). (Ecclesiastically, the "Jacobites" as Monophysites continued to maintain ties with Antioch as late as the early seventh century [HSC 184]). At a debate he arranged at the royal court, Chosroes I was favorably impressed with the Monophysites who pleaded their cause in answer to Nestorian accusations. Chosroes decreed that the Nestorians henceforth leave the Monophysites free to build as many monasteries and churches as they pleased (HSC 153).

During the latter part of the fifth century, however, the character of Persian Christianity underwent a profound shift away from celibacy. Asmussen views this as a development resulting in part from the Persian predilection for Nestorianism: "There is scarcely any doubt that this special development of the history of the Church must be viewed against the growing contribution from Christian Iranians who, rooted from birth in Sasanian Zoroastrianism, quite naturally had to acknowledge Nestorianism as the most adequate expression for them of the new teaching to which they were attracted. This contribution from Iranians, perhaps particularly from the province of Fārs, the dynastic province, created at the same time the best conditions for the growth of a specifically Iranian, notably anti-ascetic, Christianity which replaced the original, clearly ascetic, Christianity, strongly dominated by Jewish-Christian elements" (Asmussen 1983, 943). In the Synod of Bēt Lāpāṭ, summoned and overseen by Barṣauma in 484 C.E., celibacy may have been abolished, but in the absence of any direct attestation of this, the Synod of Mār Aqāq in 486 became the effective instrument for the cessation of the practice of celibacy among the Nestorians (ibid., 944). Within the Church, this move was not without controversy, and there was much internal resistance against it. Notwithstanding, the Church of the East has always opposed the alleged Sasanian practice of consanguineous marriages.

Christian literature in Middle Persian. During the fifth century, the Christian church in Persia became independent of the patriarchate of Antioch. The reasons for this break appear to have been more political than religious. Not surprisingly, the fifth century saw the rise of a vernacular Christian literature in Middle Persian.

The first known Christian text in Persian (apart from scripture translations) was a summary of the Christian religion. Originally composed in Syriac by Elisha‘ bar Quzbāyē, it was translated into Persian by the Catholicós Aqāq (Acacius, bishop of Amida, d. 496) and presented to the Persian king, Kavāḏ I (r. 488–497, 499–531—Sims-Williams, EIr 5: 534). A parallel to this endeavor might be found in Mānī, whose only writing in Middle Persian was his *Shābuhragān*, "presumably in order to expound his teaching to Šāpūr," as Sundermann suggests (EIr 5: 537).

"At a very early date, particularly in the time of bishop Ma'nā at the end of the 5th century," writes Asmussen, efforts may be traced to create a Christian Persian literature. Judging from the dearth of extant Persian texts, such an assertion might appear hard to sustain. Nevertheless, within the Sasanian empire, Persian seems to have been a subsidiary Christian vernacular. For example, the most eminent of the Persian Christians in the generations prior to the Islamic conquest was Bābay (Babai) the Great (d. 628), who presided over the Nestorian church in Iran under Chosroes II. Bābay is said by Vööbus to have "received instruction in Persian and then started his medical studies at Nisibis" (EIr 3: 308). Jacob Kollaparambil argues that the East Syrian Christians must have taught and propagated the Christian message throughout Persia and within India as well. This, he claims, is attested in the *Chronicle of Séert* (citing the Syriac text in *Patrologia Orientalis* VII, 117) when it records that, around the year 470 C.E., Bishop Ma'nā of Rēv-Ardashīr wrote religious discourses, canticles, and hymns, in Persian and translated from Greek into Persian—i.e., Pahlavi, Middle Persian (Thomas and Vahman, EIr 4: 210)—the theological treatises of Diodore of Tarsus and Theodore of Mopsuestia and sent copies "to the islands of the sea" (Bēṯ Qaṭrāyē) and to India (1994, 28). (Some authors have confused Ma'nā of Shīrāz with the Catholicós Ma'nā, who lived in the first half of the fifth century.) Nicholas Sims-Williams is more precise in noting that Ma'nā of Shīrāz "composed various works in Persian, including hymns (*madrāšē*), 'discourses' (*mēmrē*), and responses (*'ūniātā*) for liturgical use" (*EIr* 5: 534). Vööbus refers to the same Ma'nā, "who is reported to have composed *madrāšē*, *mēmrē*, and *'ūniātā* in the Persian language" (1965, 161, n. 15). These compositions, of course, were based on Syriac models.

The royal city of Rēv-Ardashīr (Rīshahr) was a metropolitan province in Persia proper (Persis). It was the ecclesiastical capital of the province of Pārs. Over time, it had "grown into a superprovince having 18 suffragan eparchies" (Kollaparambil 1994, 27). Bruce Metzger believes that, on the basis of this information, it may be deduced that the scriptures had already been translated into Middle Persian. "Inasmuch as during the second half of the fifth century an eminent teacher Ma'nā of Shiraz, made translations of Diodorus, Theodore of Mopsuestia, and other ecclesiastical writers, from Syriac into his native Persian dialect," Metzger reasons, "we may be confident that the scriptures had already been translated" (1977, 276). Kollaparambil concludes: "Hence it is clear that, though the Persian Church used Syriac as the liturgical language, the medium of Christian instruction was the Persian language" (1994, 28).

This effort to create a body of Christian literature in the Persian vernacular was overshadowed by the ascendancy of Syriac, which reclaimed its place as the primary liturgical and literary language of the church in Persia. Syriac remained the language of the church in Persia, as seen in the *Acts of the Persian Martyrs*. Most of the martyrs were ethnic Persians. These Persians not only embraced the Christian faith, but also the Christian language as well (Syriac). Consequently, very little of this Christian Persian literature survived. Two legal works by the metropolitans Išoʿbokt and Simon provide a rare attestation of this Persian literary activity (Sims-Williams, EIr 5: 534).

Middle Persian translations of the Bible date from at least the fifth century C.E. There is both patristic and material evidence for this. In the fourth century, John Chrysostom (fl. 391), patriarch of Constantinople, affirmed that the teachings of Christ had been translated into the languages of the Syrians, the Egyptians, the Indians, the Persians, and the Ethiopians (Homily on John, in Migne, *Patrologia Graeca* LIX, col. 32). In the fifth century, Theodoret of Cyrrus wrote that Persians venerated the writings of the Christian apostles as having come down from Heaven. (*Graecarum affectionum curatio* IX. 936, in Migne, PG LXXXIII, col. 1045c).

The earliest Persian translations of scripture were probably undertaken for liturgical purposes. This is evidently the case with the Turfan Psalter, which is the only extant Middle Persian Bible version. It is represented by fragments of a translation of the Psalms, discovered at the ruins of the Nestorian monastery at Shuipang near Bulayïq in the Turfan oasis in northern Xinjiang (Chinese Turkestan). These Psalms were written in an archaic, cursive Book Pahlavi script, dating back to the fifth or fourth centuries, "though the manuscript may be younger," according to Kenneth Thomas and Fereydun Vahman (EIr 4: 210). The Turfan Psalter contains most of Psalms 94–99, 118, and 121–36. Its distinctively liturgical character is noted by Geo Widengren: "This manuscript was written for liturgical use, provided with antiphons, so-called *canons*, corresponding to the text now found in the breviary of the Nestorian church" (1984, 13).

Independent attestation of Middle Persian Bible translations is found in Zoroastrian polemical literature (Thomas, EIr 4:203), particularly in the ninth-century *Škand gumānīk vičār* ("The Doubt-Crushing Explanation"). "The Christians of Iran," comments Shaul Shaked, "were dependent largely on the Syriac versions of the Bible, but the activity of creating new versions in the current vernacular must have been part of the missionary effort of Christians" (EIr 4: 206). There is other evidence of such missionary endeavors, an essential component of which was the creation of a body of Christian scripture and literature in vernacular Persian. "From the late fifth century," Brock observes, "Persian became an increasingly important literary vehicle for

Christians" (1982a, 18). Brock further notes that "quite a number of extant Syriac hagiographic, legal and literary texts are in fact translations from lost Middle Persian originals" (ibid.).

Not only was there a Christian literature in Middle Persian, but inscriptions as well. Evidence of the very missionary endeavors that Shaked suggests are the Christian Pahlavi inscriptions of India. A cross bearing a Pahlavi inscription was found in the Syrian church in Kottayam, in the state of Kerala in India. Another such cross—the Cross of Travancore—is a replica of the famed cross from the church on Mount St. Thomas near Madras. This Cross of Travancore is inscribed in Book Pahlavi (Armajani, EIr 5: 544). Several post-Sasanian Christian seals inscribed in Arabic Kufic script bear the names of Persian owners (Lerner, EIr 5: 530 and idem 1977).

Christian Sogdian. Outside the Persian empire there were other Christian enclaves as well, such as the Nestorian center at Samarkand (Colless 1986). The Silk Road led to evangelization of Central Asia and the Far East. A number of Persians who settled along this trade route were Christians. Spreading the gospel required translation. Liturgical texts (including scripture translations) and some patristic writings were translated from Syriac into Pahlavi and also into Sogdian. This accords with Asmussen's position that use of Persian greatly augmented Nestorian missionary endeavors. "[N]o doubt," he states, speaking of the province of Pārs, "Christians there had a common language with the ruling dynasty, and by all accounts created a Christian literature in that language [Persian] that was to be of considerable importance for the later Nestorian mission in Central Asia" (1983, 931). In Outer Iran, in a region called Sogdiana (a province north of Bactria, between the Oxus and the Jaxartes rivers), the Nestorian church was well established by the early eighth century at the latest. Ironically, no Christian Sogdian texts have ever been found there.

In the Turfan oasis in Chinese Turkestan, a library of Christian manuscripts was unearthed at the ruins of a Nestorian monastery of Bulayïq. This library was quite extensive, and reflects the spiritual and intellectual interests of the monastic enclave there. The majority of these texts are in Syriac and Sogdian. Generally, Christian Sogdian is written in a Syriac Estrangela script, with three added characters to accommodate native Iranian sounds not found in Syriac. As to scripture, these texts included sixth-century Sogdian translations of the Gospels, Pauline epistles, and the Psalms. Among the abundant hagiographical literature in Sogdian is the life of John of Daylam (*vide supra*), the founder of two monasteries in Pārs, one Syriac and one Persian. Also found at Bulayïq was the *Acts of the Persian Martyrs* under Shāpūr II, and the life of Barshabbā, credited as the founder of Persian Christian communities as far east as Balkh (Sims-Williams,

EIr 5: 534). Martyrologies, though hagiographical, disclose much valuable religiocultural as well as biographical information.

Christian literature in New Persian. Close to the Turfan oasis, the second and third German Turfan expeditions discovered a very few Christian texts in nearby Toyoq, Qočo (Zieme), Astana, and Qurutqa. These texts were in Sogdian, Syriac, Turkish, and New Persian (ibid.). This, of course, has very clear liturgical implications. Sims-Williams states that "it is probable that the newly founded Christian communities initially employed Syriac and Middle Persian in their liturgy, the latter being gradually displaced by the successive local vernaculars, firstly Sogdian and ultimately New Persian" (EIr 4: 207). In the eleventh century or later, a New Persian-Syriac translation from the Syriac of Psalms 131, 132, 146, 147 was penned in Sogdian Syriac script. This is the earliest extant translation of Judeo-Christian scripture into New Persian (Thomas, EIr 4: 203).

Perhaps the most remarkable of all Christian manuscripts written in New Persian is the Persian *Diatessaron*. It survives in a unique manuscript: Dated 1547, it is housed in the Laurentian Library in Florence (Biblioteca Laurenziana Mediceo–Laurenziana, Cod. Orient. VII [81]). The Persian *Harmony* was translated from the Syriac by the Jacobite priest Īwannīs 'Izz al-Dīn Muḥammad b. Muẓaffar of Tabrīz, and was later copied by another Jacobite priest, Ibrāhīm b. Shammās 'Abd-Allāh, in Ḥisn Kayfā (a village on the Tigris in Iraq), 954 A.H./ 1547 C.E. (Thomas, EIr 4: 203). While it preserves many Diatessaronic readings, the Persian *Harmony* was composed in a different sequence than in the other Diatessaron exemplars. It is perhaps more accurate to speak of the Persian *Diatessaron* as a Gospel Harmony, independent of the *Diatessaron* itself and direct translations from it (Koester 1990, 409–10). Because of the fact that it is an illuminated manuscript, the Persian Diatessaron, in all likelihood, was intended for liturgical use (p.c., David G. K. Taylor, University of Birmingham, 31 August 1995).

A remarkable specimen of a Christian liturgy in New Persian is still in use today. Within the East Syrian "Assyrian" and Chaldean liturgies are the vestiges of a lost Persian Christian liturgy. These fragments are found in the Feast of Epiphany, midnight office. (See Appendix IV, "Fragments of a Lost Persian Christian Liturgy.")

From this all-too-brief survey, it is clear that Persian Christianity had successfully evangelized a number of ethnic Iranians. A recent doctoral dissertation has argued for a certain affinity between Persian Christianity and Zoroastrianism. In his *Narsai and the Persians: A Study in Cultural Contact and Conflict*, William Sunquist (1990) argues that this affinity may account for some of the missionary success of East Syrian Christianity in Persia. In addition to the East Syrians, Armenian Christians had also translated scripture into New Persian, evidently for missionary purposes (Stone 1979). There were, of course, a number of other significant mission fields, not the least of which was India, Tibet, Ceylon, as well as China. China was evangelized beginning in 635, according to the Syriac and Chinese stele of Xi'an (Hsi-an). (For a recent textual discovery, see Klein 1994).

Evidence shows that linguistic contact between Syriac and Middle and New Persian had been established. While Persian was not a Christian literary language as such, it was a Christian vernacular. It was instrumental in missionary endeavors in the Christian Orient. Added to this is the extensive literature in Christian Arabic during the Islamic period, providing the means and opportunity for the transmission and eventual transformation of Syriac Christian symbolism, as taken up in the post-Christian religions of Islam and the Bahā'ī Faith. Whether or not such lines of transmission were responsible for the diffusion of symbolism examined in this study, there was obviously a common fund of such symbols in the Abrahamic scriptural and oral traditions anyway. It is not necessary to answer the question of how symbolic transformations took place historically, but simply to establish that such transformations are phenomenologically best explained with reference to controlling paradigms.

III

A Symbolic Profile of Syriac Christianity

Syriac Symbol Theory

Syriac Christianity had a "genius for symbolic expression" (Murray 1982, 12). Spiritual truth was depicted in allegorical and homiletic narratives, illustrated with poetic images, as though Syriac authors wished to create an experience in the listener rather than impart truth merely discursively (Brock 1981, 70). Reliance on the symbol's surplus of meaning, employed in Syriac conceits, resulted in the transformation of Northern Mesopotamian mythological views of the cosmos (paganism/heresy) into a symbolic (Christological) universe. The exposition of a Christocentric world involved an imaginative, and often personified, use of natural images. Nowhere is this more vividly seen than in the hymns of Syriac Christianity's greatest writer, Ephrem the Syrian. Nature and Scripture are wedded, as Ephrem paints a rich landscape in vivid symbolic colors, animated by an array of dramatic biblical imagery. In a Christologically attuned cosmos, prophets and apostles come alive in the congregational minds of the pious.

Symbols abound in scripture and in nature. Indeed, everything in nature and in scripture is emblematic of Jesus. The Syriac term for "symbol" is *rāzā*. *Rāzā* has several dimensions of meaning. For instance, the "pearl"—which eloquently describes Christ and sexual holiness—is a "symbol" found in nature. In another context, *rāzā* embraces notions of Christ-bearing "types" secreted in the Hebrew scriptures. In its plural form, "symbols" (*rāzē*) is best translated as "mysteries." "Mysteries" is a euphemism for the sacraments in the Christian mystic initiations and devotions, including the waters of baptism. Thus, in Ephrem's theory of symbolism, there are three dimensions of symbols: Nature, Scripture, and Sacrament.

The triple domains of the symbolic become quite obvious from even a cursory reading of Ephrem. This three-fold categorization of

Ephrem's symbolism is noted by McVey (McV 84, n. 110). In Ephrem's hermeneutics, the presence of rhetorical alongside mystical terminology shows an appreciation for the figurative as well as prefigurative nature of scripture. In his comparatively literal works of prose exegesis, Ephrem distinguishes between the literal and figurative, as he interprets both "literally" (*sū'rāna'iṯ*) and "spiritually" (*rūḥāna'iṯ*, SCK 47).

The mystical basis for this lies in Ephrem's conceptual model of the interpenetration of spiritual and physical worlds, seen especially in the theme of baptism as reentry into Paradise (Brock 1987, xxiv–xxv). This somewhat corresponds to a triadic Syriac Christian anthropology—although far from uniform (see *Motifs* 58–59)—where man is tripartite psychosomatic unity, made up of physical body, animal soul, and divine spirit (cf. Gavin 1920). The idea of worlds of correspondence as a fundamental exegetical principle is succinctly expressed by Ephrem's dictum that the Garden of Paradise is "described in visibilities (*ktybt bglyt'*), praised for invisibilities (*šbyḥt bksyt'*)" (HdP I.1, *Motifs* 67). Ephrem's theory of symbolism may be explicated purely on the basis of his hermeneutical terminology:

Symbol (*rāzā*)

"Symbol"—or, better still, "mystery"—is arguably the key hermeneutical term in Ephrem's hymns, under which all of its equivalents are subsumed (On Ephrem's theory of symbol, see Murray 1976; idem, SCK; Beck 1958; idem, 1953; P. Yousif 1978b; idem 1976.) The English rendering of "symbol" for *rāzā* is terminologically but not conceptually equivalent. As Brock (*HyP* 42) is careful to point out, "symbol" in the works of the Fathers differs from the rather static significatory sense of "symbol" common in modern usage. In Ephrem's symbolic universe, the entire cosmos is suffused with symbolism pointing to a higher reality. But symbol is more than what it evokes. It participates in the reality of what it represents.

According to Yousif, the Syriac term *rāzā* had four senses in Ephrem's usage of it: (1) *Enigma*: In the original Persian loan word, which made its way into imperial Aramaic, "*rāzā*" originally denoted a royal "secret." Its Persian provenance is evident in its Aramaic occurrence at Dan. 6:4, where the term carries the sense of divine secrets; (2) *Mystery*: Beck has drawn a connection between Ephrem's use of *rāzā* and the Greek term *mystērion* (1958. 240). Significant is the fact that *mystērion* became the standard rendering of *rāzā*, rather than *symbolon*. The term doubles for sacramental rites and, when used in the plural, refers to the Eucharist (SCK 21). *Rāzā* could also refer to a spiritual reality surpassing human intelligence; (3) *A Simple Sign*: Nature affords many instances of symbols, which proclaim Christ;

(4) *Symbol-Mystery*: This sense of the term *rāzā* embraces notions of Christ-bearing "types" secreted in the Hebrew scriptures and, when used in the plural, "mysteries" (*rāzē*) denotes the "Sacraments." In the mystic Christian initiation, consisting of Chrism, Baptism (cf. Mitchell 1973), and the Eucharist, matter is dynamized by Spirit (*epiklesis*, Yousif 1978b, 48). In this respect, "symbols" are "mysteries" that transform and divinize the faithful Christian. Functionally, in Ephrem's hymns, there appear to be three basic symbol orientations: scriptural symbols, nature symbols, and sacramental symbols. As to symbols drawn from Nature, Ephrem, along with Syriac writers in general, makes use of a wide array of images from the various "kingdoms"—mineral, arboreal, animal, celestial, and so on.

Ephrem's vocabulary of symbolism involves a complex of more or less synonymous terms. In addition to *rāzā*, discussed above, there are some other important technical terms that inform Ephrem's theory of symbolism. Bou Mansour (1988) provides the most comprehensive and integrated treatment of these terms. First, let us take a look at Ephrem's typological use of scripture, a practice more familiar in mainstream Christianity.

Scripture

Syriac Christianity was caught in a bitter debate between two rival schools of early Christian exegesis, Alexandria and Antioch. The rival schools of Antioch and Alexandria locked antlers over allegorical exegesis, disputing whether or not it threatened the primary relevance of *historia*, the literal or "historical" integrity of scripture (Froehlich 1984, 18). The most powerful opponent of allegorical exegesis was Theodore of Mopsuestia (d. c. 428), later revered as the "Interpreter" *par excellence* of Eastern Christendom, who effectively dominated the exegetical tradition of the East for centuries. The Antiochene school did, however, admit a higher sense of scripture, a dimension of meaning termed *theōria*. Both allegory and *theōria* did employ an anagogical dynamic, the latter presumably retaining some connection with the literal text and its historical framework. (On patristic exegesis generally, see Torrance 1995 and Louth 1978).

Originally, allegorical interpretation arose from an impulse to rationalize the Homeric cycle. Thus myth turned into allegory. Christian exegetes were concerned that the process not reverse itself, lest allegory itself turn into myth. The danger of this happening was all too real. This would occur whenever a scripture susceptible to allegorical interpretation was used as a vehicle for Gnostic speculations that bore little, if any, relationship to the scriptural text itself. Gnostic readings, in effect, remythologized scripture. This became especially pernicious when foreign elements that were antithetical to received orthodox teachings were introduced, in the name of exegesis, thus "contaminating" the text.

Typical procedural devices of Alexandrian *allegoria*, as inherited from Hellenism, included the philological study of words and phrases, etymology, figuration, natural symbology, and numerology. Allegorization is forever associated with Origen (see Torjesen 1986), though his predecessors included the great mystic Clement of Alexandria and the Hellenistic Jewish aristocrat, Philo of Alexandria. Olsen (1977) argues that both "allegory" and "typology" are forms of the primordial category "symbol."

This controversy was coeval with the Arian controversy. Indeed it both predated it and extended far beyond it. In the fourth and fifth centuries, in some circles, it was imprudent to perform allegorical exegesis openly. In overt support for Antiochene repudiation of allegory, Syriac exegetes publicly espoused the literal, historical interpretation of the Bible, complemented by *theōria*, a process in which scripture is understood to have a higher symbolic value or meaning as well. Such interpretation was of course performed for the intellectual élite, with few literate enough to appreciate it.

The distinctively "deeper oriental colouring" of Ephrem's exegesis cannot fail to impress scholars such as Tryggve Kronholm, who, despite Ephrem's evident knowledge of Greek paganism, observes that in Ephrem "it is almost impossible to discover any definite traits betraying a direct knowledge of the leading Greek Christian exegetes of the time" (*Motifs* 25–26). Kronholm is categorical in his exegetical typification of Ephrem: "Commonly, though, Ephrem is seen as a representative of the θεωρία of the Antiochean School of Scriptural interpretation, and this is obviously true as far as his strikingly symbolical exposition on the basis of a *sensus simplex* exegesis is concerned. In this respect he clearly continues the anti-allegorizing, i.e., anti-Alexandrian strife of such exegetes as Theodore of Heraclea, Eusebius of Emesa, and Diodore of Tarsus" (ibid., 26). For the record, in his *Commentary on Genesis*, Ephrem is careful to disavow allegory: "Let no man say that the work of six days is an allegory; nor is it possible to say that in one moment took place what in reality took days to accomplish, nor that these are simply empty names or that something else is meant by these terms. On the contrary, let us be sure that, in truth, heaven and earth are as they were created in the beginning and that nothing else but Heaven and earth are meant by their names" (el-Khoury 1987, 95–96).

Ephrem's commentaries on scripture, in general, were primarily conditioned by the negative influence of rival religious communities, such as the Arians, Bardaiṣanites, Chaldeans (astrologers), the Jews, the Manicheans, and the Marcionites (*Motifs* 28–33). The perceived threat posed by these groups had steeled Christian resolve never to depart from the literal or "historical" sense of scripture. This has a pendant in the view that allegory is the servant of heresy. Allegory gave rise to myth, whereas *theōria* simply advances a symbolic understanding of scripture, one that reinforces what a Christian already knows, and desires to contemplate for spiritual edification. That Ephrem held to a *theōria* interpretation of scripture in poetry might require further nuancing owing to the fact that the Syriac equivalent of the term *theōria* is nowhere found in Ephrem's writings, according to R. Bondi (1985, 159).

Ephrem's hymns may be regarded as exegesis in the medium of poetry. His verse interpretations surpass the limits of his rather traditional prose exegesis. Remarkably, despite his strict adherence to the historic sense of scripture, Ephrem's creative symbolic use of Biblical allusions to enrich poetic imagery throughout his hymns is "definitely not admitted in exegesis" and evinces his independence in the handling of Biblical passages for homiletic purposes (el-Khoury 1987, 96, cf. Baarda 1962). El-Khoury is categorical in asserting that Ephrem "rejects all allegorizing." The author goes on to remark that Ephrem "is capable of breaking out of literalism into language rich in parallelism and symbols." This is supposedly for reasons of *persuasio*, not exegesis (1987, 96).

In fact, a "vast and rich web of exegesis" of scripture is found throughout Ephrem's poetry (*Harp* 12; cf. HSC 60 for opposing view) as his *Hymns on Paradise* amply attests. Syriac hymns exemplify a creative rather than narrow interpretation of sacred text. In defense of such exegetical license, Ephrem establishes the polyvalency of scripture: "If there only existed a single sense for the words of Scripture, then the first commentator who came along would discover it, and other hearers would experience neither the labour of searching, nor the joy of finding. Rather, each word of our Lord has its own form, and each form has its own members, and each member has its own character. Each individual understands according to his capacity and interprets it as it is granted him" (Comm. Diat. VII.22, *LumE* 34–35).

In a scholastic sense, hymnody was not a recognized exegetical genre. This fact gave Ephrem much freer exegetical license. When one compares Ephrem's exegetical writings with his liturgical hymns, there is basic conceptual congruence, but not an expressive parity. Scripture provided an abundance of images, inspiring a fund of interpretive material that went beyond the simple paraphrastic exegesis. In the sanctuary, therefore, where Ephrem's hymns were intoned, exegesis took on poetic license. The net effect is that Ephrem and other Syriac writers remythologized the universe, as part of one sustained Christological myth, as opposed to Gnostic speculations. There is the sense in which this freer interpretation was, for Ephrem's purposes, more accurate, as Mathews observes: "Ephrem had the particular genius to comprehend that the vehicle of poetry was the least inaccurate way to describe the Christian mystery which is, as the term suggests, essentially beyond human understanding" (SPW 46).

Whether or not Syriac interpretation was not substantially different from the allegorical interpretation it avowedly eschewed, the literature to date suggests that allegorical interpretation made its ostensible reentry into the Eastern Patristic tradition after Origen through the writings of Philoxenus of Mabbug (d. 523). In the final analysis, symbolic/allegorical exegesis was not an end unto itself, nor was it alone considered sufficient for spiritual progress, as Isaac of Nineveh (fl. c. 660–680) wrote: "What Scripture was not permitted to reveal, the pure mind is authorized to know—something that goes beyond what was entrusted to Scripture! Nevertheless the fountainhead for all these things is the reading of Scripture: from it comes the mind's beauty" (Brock 1987, 265).

Type (ṭūpsā) and reality (qnwm'). "Perhaps no other writer," observes Mathews, speaking of Ephrem, "has ever made such creative use of typology" (SPW 48). In Ephrem, "type" refers primarily to divine self-revelation in Scripture. A loan word from the Greek *typos*, it is clear that *ṭūpsā* for Ephrem is synonymous with *rāzā*, though the latter seems to have a broader application. There is evident synonymity between *ṭūpsā* and *rāzā*, but it is not coextensive (see Bou Mansour 1988, 26–35).

Typologically, practically all of the ancient biblical worthies were pointers to Christ, as Ephrem explains: "Adam saw in Enoch the typos of our Redeemer (*prwqn*), / . . . he [Enoch] is a symbol (*rz'*) of the Gardener (*gnn'*)" (*Motifs* 160). But typology is not limited to reading back Christ into ancient narratives. Exegetically, for example, Ephrem's practice of seeing pagans as "Christians by symbolic anticipation" accords with his finding a "symbol" (*rāzā*) of the Gentiles in the stone of Jacob (Gen. 26:3). Remarkably, Ephrem interprets the blessings of Jacob to refer, not to the tribes of Israel, but rather to the heathen nations (Darling 1987, 116–19). Yet *rāzā* must not be limited to its typological sense, as Murray cautions: "It is better not to limit the sense of *mystērion*/*rāz* to 'type' in the sense that, for example, Hebrews makes Melchizedek a symbolic prefiguration of Christ" (SCK 290). (For further on Ephrem's use of typology, see Schmidt 1989.)

Beyond Biblical "types," Ephrem's symbolic repertoire is drawn from the palette of Nature as well as that of Scripture. Speaking of Jesus as creator of the universe, Ephrem exclaims: "In every place, if you look, His symbol is there, / And when you read, you will find His types, / For by Him were created all creatures, / and He engraved His symbols upon His possessions. / When He created the world, / He gazed at it and adorned it with His images. / Streams of His symbols opened, flowed, and poured forth / His symbols on His members" (Virg. XX.12, McV 348–49).

McVey glosses this verse by observing that it was an ancient custom to mark one's belongings (McV 348, n. 278). All created things, as the handiwork of Christ, bear Christ's imprint. This is akin to the Syriac Christian notion of "sealing" (especially in relation to the sacrament of baptism), as in Ephrem's verse: "Today the Deity imprinted (*ṭbʿ*) itself on humanity, / so that humanity might also be cut into (*ṣbt*) the seal of Deity" (Nat. I.99, McV 74). Ephrem's theory of symbolism is thus an argument by Christological design. On the technical terms in this passage, McVey notes: "Here the 'types' (*ṭwps'*) are in scripture, while the 'symbols' (*r'z'*) and 'images' (*ywqn'*) are in nature, but Ephrem is not consistent in this usage" (McV 349, n. 279). However, exceptions appear to prove the rule that Ephrem's primary meaning for *ṭūpsā* is anything in scripture that might serve as a foreshadowing of the person and work of Christ. According to Mathews, Ephrem "recognized the symbolic nature of biblical discourse without having to turn to the allegorism of the Alexandrian school" (SPW 48).

Type points beyond itself to a "reality" (*qnwm'*, Eccl L.6). One exegetical technique deserves notice here. Speaking of Noah's Ark, Ephrem states: "If His type (*ṭwps'*) saved in this way, how much more will He save in his reality (*qnwm'*)." McVey notes that the phrase "how much more" is a typical interpretive device for Ephrem, analogous to the Rabbinic method of "*qal w homer*" (from light to heavy), an argument proceeding from a lesser to a greater example (Nat. I.58, McV 70, n. 50). In this strophe, "reality" is the equivalent of the Greek "hypostasis" (McV 70, n. 51). A pair of terms that functions in much the same way is "sign" (*nyš'/nīšā*) and "truth" (*šrr'/šrārā*, McV 71, n. 53). "'Truth'," according to Murray, is "the regular word for the fulfillment of a type" (SCK 47, n. 5). Biblical typology is "historical" in the sense that these symbols prefigure "reality" since they precede Christ in time and are fulfilled by his advent.

Shadow (ṭellālā) and Truth (šrārā). "Shadow" (*ṭellālā*) is another Ephremic technical term that conveys the sense of "type" (cf. Nat. V.16, McV 286, nn. 80, 82): "The wonder to see" says Ephrem in Virg. XIV.7, "the symbol and its prototype, the truth and its shadow (*r'z' w-tpnkh šrr' w-ṭllh*)" (McV 322 and n. 185). McVey states that the phrase is chiastic: As equivalencies, shadow is symbol, prototype is truth (McV 322, n. 185). This is confirmed by another verse: "Let us look upon the symbol as a shadow, / let us look upon the Truth as the fulfillment" (Azym. III.4, *Harp* 37). As type-antitype pairs, *symbol* and *shadow* are equivalent, while *prototype* and *truth* are likewise synonymous. These terms are also recombinant. If placed in the right relation to each other, the corresponding elements in these pairs are, in practice, interchangeable.

Metaphor (dmūtā). Often translated as "likeness," "metaphor" (*dmūtā*/ pl. *demwāṯā*) is generally considered equivalent to *rāzā* (*Motifs* 74, n. 93). In one hymn, Ephrem employs the striking image of a parrot being taught to speak from behind a mirror, to convey to what extent and how God chose to go in His effort to communicate with humankind: "Let us give thanks to God Who clothed Himself / in the names of the body's various parts: / Scripture refers to His "ears," to teach us that He listens to us; / It speaks of His "eyes," to show that He sees us, / and, although in His true Being there is no wrath or regret, / yet He put on these names too because of our weakness." The refrain, sung between stanzas, reinforces the theme of metaphoricity: "*Blessed is He Who has appeared to our human race under so many metaphors.*" Ephrem continues: "He clothed Himself in our language, so that He might clothe us / in His mode of life. He asked for our form and put this on, / and then, as a father with His children, He spoke with our childish state. / It is our metaphors that He put on—though He did not literally do so" (HdF XXXI.1–2, *LumE* 43–44).

What is surprising about the following metaphor is that it is a metaphor about metaphors, in which humanity is compared to a parrot, taught to comprehend what it can, on its own level and within its own limitations: "A person who is teaching a parrot to speak / hides behind a mirror and teaches it in this way: / When the bird turns in the direction of the voice which is speaking / it finds in front of its eyes its own resemblance reflected; / It imagines that it is another parrot, conversing with itself. / The man puts the bird's image in front of it, / so that thereby it might learn how to speak" (HdF XXXI.6, *LumE* 45). This is not mere poetry. It is a central, definitive, hermeneutical principle, for a popular laity to understand and take to heart. For their didactic content and edifying influence, Ephrem's hymns are far more effective than any diffuse effect from a scriptural commentary meant for the literate elite.

Not everything in scripture is a metaphor, however. Ephrem differentiates between metaphor and reality, aware of the Christological consequences of both ways of reading. Christ is truly God's Son, and for this reason God as "Father" is no metaphor but a reality, as seen in this passage previously cited: "And if His name 'Father' were a metaphor—which God forbid!—the names which go with it (*šmh' bny zwgh*) will lose their force under dispute" (HdF LII.2, Molenberg 1990, 139 and 141). In Syriac Christology, Christ's Sonship goes far beyond adoptive, elective, or other ideal relationships with God. Ephrem describes Christ as "the Son of the Hidden One, as He emerged into revelation" (Nat. II.9, McV 78). This is taken literally.

Allegory (peletā). "Allegory" appears to be the equivalent of "type." Ephrem calls the account of Jesus at the Wedding Feast at Cana a "mirror" (*mḥzyt' = maḥzītā*) in which "allegories" (sing.: *pl't' = peletā*) are expounded and traced" (Virg. XXXIII.1, McV 407 and n. 508). In a meditation upon Cain's murder of Abel, Ephrem presents Abel as the prototype of the crucified Messiah, in which Christ "spread out over him [Abel] the allegory (*pl't qṭlh*) of his death" (*Motifs* 146). Various explanations in the literature have been offered as to distinctions between type and allegory in Ephrem (on *peletā*, see Bou Mansour 1988, 52–57). Kronholm cites Schweizer, who hazarded this distinction: "La distinction entre Type et Allégoria (*Theōria et Allegoria*): se trouve chez Éphrem . . . qui par la première expression entend le sens mystique, au moyen duquel les mystères chrétiens sont déjà contenus dans l'A.T." (*Motifs* 145, n. 32).

Paradox. In the hymns of Ephrem, superadded to the use of *symbol* and *type* is *paradox*. Affirming the importance of the role paradox plays in Syriac spirituality in Seely Beggiani observes: "Perhaps the most striking form used by Ephrem and the Syriac fathers is paradox" (1983, 30). *Prdwksn* is the Syriac form of the Greek *paradoxon*. Edmund Beck differentiates Ephrem's use of *paradox* as a technical term from its use in rhetoric: "Ephrem uses the Greek word *paradoxon* not in its rhetorical sense but (like Justin, Origen and Theodoret of Ancyra) in the sense of divine mysteries revealed only to faith" (1977, 175 [English abstract]). In his polemic *Against Mānī*, Ephrem presents two *paradoxa*: One God exists; God created all else out of nothing. "This seems to be the only patristic passage," remarks Beck, "in which these two fundamental principles are presented exclusively as an object of faith" (ibid.).

"Paradox occurs, broadly speaking," according to El-Batanouny, "when two different levels of knowledge of the language, of communication, of reality, or of human behaviour are seen as one level, are mixed, or are superimposed" (1991, 129). "Paradoxical" method, according to Dilthey, is one which "obeys the logic of contending forces, or of contrasting concepts, which cannot be reconciled through some higher form of agreement. It is adversative in formal proposition" (1989, 29). Ephrem's paradoxes resolve themselves only at the level of the supernatural, particularly in regards to the Incarnation and the Virgin Birth: "Joseph caressed the Son / as a babe. He served Him / as God. He rejoiced in Him / as in a blessing, and he was attentive to Him / as to the Just One—a great paradox!" (Nat. V.16, McV 108). Christologically, the greatest of all paradoxes is Christ's *kenosis*: "Babe in the womb, since the seal (*ḥtm'*) of virginity / abides, the womb was for You / the royal palace, and the curtain. / Evidence of virginity upon it, evidence of virginity outside, / a fetus inside—a great paradox!" (Nat. XII.2, McV 134).

Through the technique of paradox, Ephrem conveys a sense of mystery leading to deeper faith. This contemplative dimension, in fact, is invited by the paraconsistent contradiction afforded by this literary device. Beggiani offers an interesting insight into the dynamism of the Syriac paradox: "In this approach, God's mysteriousness is preserved while events from human experience are juxtaposed antithetically as vehicles of meaning. Paradox is the imagination's counterpart to the intellect's use of analogy. It is one way in which human speech can embody divine realities" (1983, 30; cf. Ramsey 1969). MacGregor stresses why paradox need not deter logic: "What makes a paradox logically explorable is (1) that it is intended to make sense, and (2) that it is at least theoretically possible for an unprejudiced person to inquire whether it does or does not" (1973, 64). Though a challenge to the rational intellect, a paradox is supposed to make uncommon sense. Expressively, something is missing in its logical structure, on which paradox invites contemplation. This is an effective vehicle for nondiscursive truth; as so much of Ephrem's hymnic exegesis is the interpretation of one image by another.

Nature

Mirror. Ephrem was fascinated by mirrors. He speaks at length about the Gospel as a mirror in his *Letter to Publius* 1–2 (*LumE* 57–58). Mirrors appear everywhere in Ephrem's poetic world. "The Scriptures are laid out like a mirror," the poet writes, "and he whose eye is lucid sees therein the image of truth" (HdF LXVII.8, *LumE* 32 and 57, where Brock translates the same verse slightly differently: "The Scriptures are placed there like a mirror: / he whose eye is luminous beholds there the image of reality"). Note that the truth is not naked; it is clothed in an "image." This is an effective vehicle for nondiscursive truth, so much of Ephrem's hymnic exegesis is the interpretation of one image by another. This is often achieved through the technique of paradox. In another hymn, having exploited the symbolism of oil in procrustean fashion, Ephrem concludes: "The Anointed is all faces and the oil (*mešḥa*) is just like a mirror; / from wherever I look at the oil the Anointed (*Mešiḥa*) looks out at me from within" (Virg. VII.14, McV 296). This image of Christ appearing from the faces of believers anointed at baptism is as important as it is striking, for it establishes in the most graphic fashion possible the pervasive symbolic immanence of Christ. The contemplation of the mystery of Christ can never be exhausted. The tension between God's transcendence and immanence is not at issue here, since Christ becomes the agent of God's revelation.

Name. For Ephrem, there are two classes of names (*šmahē*) or "appellations" (*kunnayē*) in scripture, as established in CH XXXVI.9: divine attributes, or "literal reality" (*šrrh dptgm'*); and "likenesses of the Creator" (*dmwt' dbrwy'*), which is a metaphorical reality. The former are "perfect and accurate" while the latter are "putative and passing" (HdF XLIV.2, *Motifs* 174–75). As Brock translates: "God has names that are perfect and exact, / and He has names that are borrowed and transient; / these latter He quickly puts on and takes off" (HdF XLIV.2, *LumE* 45).

Recourse to metaphorical analysis of theophanic discourse is a common ploy in Judaism, Christianity, and Islam to deal with problems of scriptural anthropomorphism. So also in Ephrem, who affirms of God that "although in His true Being there is no wrath or regret, yet He put on these names because of our weakness" (HdF XXXI.6, *LumE* 43). The strength of Ephrem's conviction that scripture is inerrant does not blind him to the so-called metaphorical lie pressed into the service of truth. Summing up the distinction between Ephrem's major sources of symbolism—Scripture and Nature—Mathews states: "Symbols and types, from both nature and Scripture, now operate for Ephrem on two distinct planes: the horizontal, between the Old and New Testaments, and the vertical, between this world and Paradise" (Mathews, SPW, 53). These constitute the "Three Harps" that the Christian faithful play: "Blessed are you, O church, whose congregation / sings with three glorious harps. / Your finger plucks the harp of Moses / and [the harp] of our Savior and [the harp] of nature" (Virg. XXVII.4, McV 383).

Sacrament Mysteries (rāzē)

In Syriac Christian usage especially, "symbol" participates in that which it represents. A real symbol conjoins two realities. There is a certain dynamic power that resides in the sacramental "symbol." In the plural, *rāzē* comes to represent the "Mysteries" or Sacraments, in which the worshipper literally partakes of both symbol and its reality. There are many instances in Ephrem's hymns in which sacramental associations attach to Christological "types" in scripture. Sacramental "mysteries" seem to validate the symbolism of scripture and Nature in two ways: experientially, through contemplation of Christ; and through the mysterious and supernatural communication of divinity to Christians partaking of the sacraments. This will become quite evident in discussions of the "ritual" dimension of Ephrem's key symbols, to which we now turn.

The concept of a "Symbolic Profile". What are the most salient and dominant motifs in early Syriac Christianity? The determination of such root metaphors and key scenarios is admittedly selective, but it is based on a synopsis of the important literature on Ephrem. As an informal "control" for selecting Ephrem's most salient key symbols, the author has relied on occurrences of the word *favorite* in the scholarly literature. In a review of studies on Ephrem, whenever an authority like Robert Murray or Sebastian Brock uses the descriptor *favorite* in connection with Ephrem's choice of symbols, this is taken as a warrant for the salience of that key symbol. Wherever possible, the indicator *favorite* is cited at the beginning of each section below. For example, Mathews writes: "Perhaps Ephrem's favorite and best known image is that of the pearl" (SPW 54). This warrants privileging the pearl as a major Ephremic symbol.

The following table represents the key symbols privileged in this study:

A Symbolic Profile of Early Syriac Christianity in the Hymns of Ephrem

Dimension	**Key Scenario**	**Root Metaphor**
Doctrinal	The Way	Physician
Ritual	The Robe of Glory	Medicine of Life
Ethical	Sons/Daughters of Covenant	The Mirror
Experiential	The Wedding Banquet	The Pearl
Mythic	The Harrowing of Hell	Tree of Life
Social	Noah's Ark/Mariner	Paradise

Key Scenarios

Doctrinal: ***The Way***

"The Way" (*'ūrḥā*) is a doctrinal allegory, a drama of salvation-history, the context of the Christian *kerygma*, as poetically conceived by Ephrem. It is a common metaphor employed by the Church Fathers generally, but Ephrem's particular formulation of it bears the imprint of the poet's originality. "With the exception of limited parallels," Robert Murray remarks, "the allegorical figure of the Way seems to be entirely Ephrem's own invention" (SCK 249). Joseph Amar refers to the fact that "Beck [1965] has written extensively on the importance of the term *'ūrḥā* ('way') in Ephrem" (SPW 277, n. 24).

The figure of the Way—in Ephrem's usage—is neither a purely ethical concept nor an ecclesial appellation; neither is it the biblical "Way of the Lord" nor the primitive Church's self-designation. Rather, it stands for the pilgrimage of the human race through time (SCK 246). The key scenario of the Way is worked out in three entire hymns in CH XXV–XXVII. This key scenario will be described in all its important dimensions below. While the Way, as treated here, has primarily a doctrinal import, there are secondary dimensions of the Way that must also be taken into account, in order to do some justice to the complexity and the pervasiveness of the scenario throughout the other dimensions of Syriac spirituality.

The Christian message is predicated on a doctrinal view of salvation-history. Doctrinally, while the metaphor of the Way is not as prominent as some of the more salient Syriac motifs, it does seem to be a most expressive Syriac view of salvation history. The "Messengers of Peace" are the Prophets and Apostles. These epitomize the course of salvation history. After Adam, the Way back to Paradise lost was barred until the ancient worthies—Abel, Enoch, and Abraham—at last set out on the Way (CH XV.6). In Nat. XXII, after suggesting that fire-worshipping Magi (Zoroastrians, as distinct from the "Chaldeans") were secretly worshipping Christ, Ephrem says: "For the Compassionate One did not endure seeing the way closed. / Coming down in the conception, He opened the way a little. / Emerging in birth, He trod it out and set His milestones on it. / Blessed is the peace of Your way! / He chose the prophets; they made smooth the way for the People. / He sent the apostles; they cleared a path for the peoples. / . . . Blessed is He Who made straight our paths!" (Nat. XXII.20–21, McV 182–83).

It should be noted here that prophets and apostles are not synonymous. Prophets helped prepare the way for the coming of Jesus, through preaching repentance and righteousness and through prophecy as well. Prophecy, in its vaticinatory sense, is teleological. It charges history with eschatological tension. Hope for the advent of the Messiah was sustained on the basis of the prophets, whose vision of the future inculcated a sense of certitude in the promise of a divinely preordained destiny. Once the advent of Jesus had transpired, however, the cycle of prophecy was closed. Prophecy contained the seeds of its own demise. Once fulfilled, prophecy—along with the prophets who uttered prophecy—was no longer required. A new cycle had begun, in which apostles effectively took the place of prophets. Described as "Messengers of Peace" (CH XXV.1), clearing the Way and removing stumbling blocks (CH XXV.1), the Prophets and Apostles are "inns and milestones" along the Way (CH XXII.8, SCK 246), a veritable "chain of the Sons of Light" (CH XXV.6, SCK 248). Beck (1981) has published a study on the Prophets and Apostles as the "inns and milestones" along the Way.

"Milestones" also expresses the teleology of sacraments. In the first stage, the period of the uncircumcised, faith was obscure, animated by a vague hope in a Savior, with salvation dispensed only through prophetic and typological "mysteries"—a prefigurement of grace. The second stage, the period of the circumcised, was the Way "of the commandments" (CH XXVI.5), the dispensation of "the Law." The final stage began with John the Baptist, the "last and end of the

Prophets." From the dispensation of Law, emphasizing Justice, to the new dispensation of Grace, emphasizing Freedom (free will), the advent of Christ effected the transition from a cycle of prophecy to a cycle of fulfillment, in a shift from Prophets to Apostles as the primary instruments of God's will: "Mounted and reigned on Golgotha; / he [Jesus] ended the Way of the Prophets / and opened instead the Way of the Apostles" (CH XXV.2, SCK 248). The shift from prophecy to fulfillment is reflected elsewhere. In Virg. VIII.13, Ephrem is consistent in saying: "In John [the Baptist] He [Jesus] set a limit and restrained the prophets, / and he called and sent apostles. He dismissed and put to rest the former, / and put to work and wearied the latter" (McV 299).

The first stage—the Way of "Mysteries" (CH XXVI.5)—runs from Eden to Moses; the second—the Way of "Types"—extends from Moses to Christ; the third—the "Way of the Son" (CH XXV.3) or the "Royal Way" (CH XXV.1–2, 5)—is the age of the Church. The turning point in both historical time and in sacred time was when Christ broke the bars of the gates of Sheol, releasing the faithful dead, leading them back to the heavenly Paradise (CH XXVI.6). Along the Way, the "milestones" now take on a ritual dimension: "The sign of anointing [chrism] and of baptism / the breaking of bread and the cup of salvation, and the scriptures . . . / Blessed be the King, for the milestones of his Way / are mountains that cannot be hid!" (CH XXVII.3). Ever since, for over three centuries leading to the time of Ephrem, Christians continue to progress along the Way via the sacraments and baptism, in which the King's Son leads the way, following John the Baptist (CH XXV.5, SCK 248–49). The sacraments are more than milestones: they are mountains leading to the mountain of Paradise.

The "Right Way" represents commandments, leading the faithful along a righteous course of life. In his *Commentary on the Diatessaron*, Ephrem states that John the Baptist's mission was "preaching the remission of sins" through baptism, thereby "loosening the bonds of the Law, avenger of sins." The Baptist came "to inaugurate through grace that which was greater [than the Law]. Of salvation history, Ephrem concludes: "See how we are delivered from two sentences, one of nature and the other of legislation. . . . Moses led the people as far as the Jordan, while the Law led the human race as far as the baptism of John" (Comm. Diat. IX.12, SEC 159–60). Jesus came to replace the Law with grace and to compensate, with the gift of immortality, the sentence of "Nature"—death. Yet there are still ethical demands on the Christian, according to Ephrem. Although the advent of Jesus ushered in a dispensation of grace, justice is still served on a higher plane—that of free will. This liberty from the bonds of the Law is at the same time a commitment to righteousness, first expressed by a vow of purity in the form of sexual holiness, even in marriage.

The sacraments are a means to an end, but are neither ends unto themselves nor a sufficient means. The teachings of Jesus require an ethical consecration as the complement of ritual purification. The ethical demands of Jesus are therefore intensified, and not obviated by the efficacy of the sacraments. As Ephrem states: "The Son therefore is the thought of the Father" (Comm. Diat. X.15, SEC 173). The words of Jesus, in addition to his person and work, are ethical demands of Jesus that are binding on the Christian. As Ephrem explains in his Diatessaron commentary: "*Unless your righteousness exceeds that of the scribes and Pharisees* (Matt 5:20). The Law commands, *You shall not glean the gleanings of your plot, and you shall not shake the olive trees a second time, and you shall not glean your vineyard, but it shall be for the poor* (Lev 19:9–10). These are [addressed] to those under the Law. What, then, shall we say to those who are in Christ, to whom our Lord said, *If your righteousness does not exceed that of the scribes and Pharisees, you shall not enter the kingdom of heaven*?" (Comm. Diat. VI.4, SEC 112).

Once the Christian has achieved a state of virtue, he or she may attain the station of a prophet: "The wise person, by his counsels, is a prophet for those who need him" (Comm. Diat. XXII.4, SEC 335). The Christian leads a life of holiness along the Way, as part and parcel of the path of righteousness. In displaying moral virtue, but not in an ostentatious way, the Christian serves as a torch bearer, a reflection of the light of Christ, illuminating the darkness and leading the way for others to follow. The "holy man" or "holy woman" thus had a role to play in society. Expressed in terms of the image of the Way, the path of the saint has a goal, as Ephrem puts it: "The fruit is the goal of the right way that runs from this tree to the Cross" (CH XXVI.4, Mathews, SPW 116, n. 178). This "right way" is a form of orthopraxy, the ethical warrant of doctrine and the interiorized complement of the sacraments.

If the Way is to be followed, it follows that the Way is descriptive of Christian experience. In the Christian life, Ephrem likens Christians to merchants. These "merchants," as travellers along the Way, are heading towards a glorious destination. The Way leads to the Kingdom of Heaven, where the merchants will attain the presence of the King and receive his gifts (HdF LXVI.24). Thus they will live to behold the glory of the Father in beatific vision (CH XXV.2).

As merchants, Christians individually, and the Church as a whole, must beware of highwaymen. Still fraught with dangers along the Way, Christians must steer clear of the crooked ways of heretics (CH XXII.8; XXV.8–9; XXVI.10). Robbers lurk, to ambush merchants on their Way, having already stolen various milestones, being Scriptures and sacraments (CH XXVII.2–3). Thieves stalk to wrest sheep from Christ's fold (CH XXV.7). The "highwaymen" of whom Ephrem speaks obviously represent heretics, who pose a threat to the Christian Church and to individual salvation. The heretics were also Christians. But, from Ephrem's perspective, it would appear that an Arian Christian is accursed rather than saved. The ecclesiastical situation of Ephrem's orthodox Church was always a precarious one.

The Way is one way of describing the Christian "myth"—myth being the vehicle for Christian truth. "The Way" was necessitated by Adam's Fall and expulsion from Paradise (CH XXII.8; XXVI.6). Humanity was imprisoned in darkness, preferring to stay rather than set out on the Way (CH XXVI.7). For this reason, God sent prophets, to lead the way to Christ, who would then lead the way back to Paradise—a progression leading full circle, in which eschatological end-time and primordial event are united in sacred time outside of time itself. The Way epitomizes progress from primordial Paradise to eschatological Paradise, from origin to eschaton. Salvation extends, as Mathews translates CH XXVI.4, "from the Tree to the Cross, from one wood to the other, from Eden to Zion, from Zion to the holy Church and from the Church to the Kingdom" (1990, 103).

Ritual: ***Robe of Glory***

Sebastian Brock considers the Robe of Glory to be "Ephrem's favourite metaphor for the Incarnation" (*LumE* 68). "This simple image of clothing," Murray concurs, "is the Syriac Fathers' favourite way of describing the Incarnation" (SCK 69). It is, moreover, "perhaps the most frequent of all Ephrem's images" (*LumE* 25). Why? The "Stole of Glory" is a key scenario that dramatizes how primordial Paradise may be regained and immortality restored. This imagery is intimately bound up with the Christian rite of initiation, baptism. The Robe of Glory is a key scenario into which is compressed the whole of salvation-history. Like the Way, this picture of salvation-history has the same teleology, but with descriptively different "staging posts" along the way. Instead of a path, the image is that of a cloth.

The "Robe of Light" appears to have its roots in a midrash on Gen 3:21, in which Adam and Eve's "coats of skin" are glossed as Robes of Light. The essence of Ephrem's anthropology and soteriology are enshrined in this one image: "Our body became Your garment; Your spirit became our robe" (Nat. XXII.39, McV 185). The symbol of the Robe of Glory depicts stages of humanity's glory, fall, and redemption. These are bound up with "the three major events of Christ's life: the Nativity, the Baptism in the Jordan, and the descent to Sheol" (Harvey 1993, 120). The epitome of Syriac salvation history may be seen as an eschatological drama that could be meaningfully entitled, "Paradise Lost and Regained," with four acts: (1) Primordial Robes of Glory/Replaced by Fig Leaves; (2) Christ places Robe in Jordan;

(3) Robe regained at Baptism; (4) Robe as Wedding Garment in Paradise.

The Robe of Glory, which confers immortality by divinization (*theōsis*), depicts the drama of salvation: "All these are changes that the Compassionate One shed and put on / when He contrived to put on Adam the glory that he had shed. / He wrapped swaddling clothes with his leaves and put on garments instead of his skins. / He was baptized for [Adam's] wrongdoing and embalmed for his death. / He rose and raised him up in glory. Blessed is He Who came down, put on [a body] and ascended!" (Nat. XXXIII.13, McV 190; cf. *LumE* 65). The odyssey of the loss and recovery of the Robe of Glory has already been outlined above. But to do it justice, this saga deserves a rather "thick" description. the four basic acts in this drama of salvation-history may be retold as follows:

1. *Primordial Robes of Glory*: In Paradise, Adam and Eve were clothed in "Robes of Glory" or "Robes of Light." In the Jewish *Midrash Rabba on Genesis*, we learn that Rabbi Meir is reputed to have had in his possession a Hebrew manuscript of the Pentateuch, which at Gen. 3:21 read not "garments of skin" but "garments of light"; in the targumic tradition, the traditional "garments of skin" is rendered a "clothing of glory" (*LumE* 66). Such readings depend on two Hebrew homonyms: the reading of "light" (*'wr*) for the received reading of "skin" (*'wr—Motifs* 64–65, n. 59, and 217, 223). Brock has linked this robe tradition back to its ancient Near Eastern roots (1979a, 223). The garment of light, as Brock also points out, has a parallel, and possibly a precedent, in Zoroastrianism (cf. Widengren 1945, 5, 51). A world of sin was the consequence of the Fall, along with the loss of immortality. Sin, resulting from Adam's disobedience, effected the loss of Adam's perfection, with the consequence that he and his progeny became afflicted with the disease of mortality, which is fatal, leading to death with no possibility of eternal life. Probably Theodoret of Cyrrhus represents the Syriac view in maintaining that sin was passed on from generation to generation, but not by procreation. For Theodoret, marriage was a spiritual path equally as blessed as virginity (Ashby 1984, 133).

2. *Disrobed in disgrace*: After the Fall, Adam and Eve were stripped of their "robes of glory/light." Body and soul were alienated by the Fall. Given humanity's predicament, God saw fit to provide a special means of salvation. In mythical terms, the robe of glory, which houses the spirit, needed to be restored. Thus, as Brock puts it: "The entire purpose of the Incarnation is to reclothe Adam" (*LumE* 67).

3. *Christ places Robe in Jordan*: In effecting a plan for salvation of humanity, God "puts on Adam" or "a body" in order to "reclothe mankind in the robe of glory." Christ is born, not only as the perfect incarnation of God, but as the perfect man. Christ bears the primordial

Robe of Glory, forfeited by Adam. When John the Baptist baptizes Christ, Christ consecrates the water. In the course of his descent into the waters of the Jordan at baptism, Christ deposits the "robe of glory/ light" into the water, sanctifying for all time all baptismal water: "He [Jesus] put on the water of baptism, and rays flashed out from it" (Nat. XXIII.12, McV 190). The unfallen Adam places the Robe of Glory in the river Jordan.

4. *"Paradise Regained": Baptism as reinvestiture of Robe of Glory*: To recapitulate Ephrem's conception of salvation history, the Robe of Glory is lost but may be won back once more. The Robe of Glory which Adam lost in the Fall is recovered by the Christian at baptism (Brock 1982b, 12). The invocation of the Holy Spirit at baptism consecrates the baptismal font, effectively transforming that font into the waters of the Jordan in sacred time and space: "In baptism did Adam find / that glory that had been his among the trees of Paradise; / he went down and took it from the water, / put it on, went up and was held in honour in it" (Epiph. XII.1, *LumE* 7). Ephrem concludes: "Blessed are you whom they told among the trees, / 'We have found Him Who finds all, / Who came to find Adam who was lost, / and in the garment of light to return him to Eden'" (Virg. XVI.9, McV 331).

These four episodes—the Fall, the Incarnation, Christ's Baptism, and Resurrection—dramatically narrate the loss and recovery of this eschatological vestment. Because one thereby regains the lost stole of glory, baptism serves as a reentry into Paradise. With the proper attire, bestowed at baptism, the guest may attend the eschatological Wedding Banquet. The story of the Fall embeds some key assumptions that require a certain suspending of disbelief. The primary assumption is that sin precipitated mortality. Once this assumption is accepted, the key scenario is set. Adam was the fallen god; God descended from heaven, too, but through a different act of free will. Jesus, bearing the robe of immortality, was immersed in the River Jordan. This single act has consecrated the waters of baptism for all time. This sanctified water has mutliplied in countless baptisms for centuries. And so have the invisible Robes of Glory that are deposited in the waters. At least for this part of the scenario, the conferral of immortality did not require the death and resurrection of Christ.

The River Jordan symbolizes baptism and explains its significance as part of the drama of salvation. "He put on the water of baptism, and rays flashed out from it" (Nat. XXIII.12, McV 190). "Instead of with leaves from the trees," Ephrem writes, "He clothed them with glory in the water" (Epiph. XII.4, *HyP* 71).

This is the exoteric baptism. There is also an esoteric one, one that will be discussed in the next section. Of what value, one may ask, is the Robe of Glory if it is only to be sullied by the Christian receiving it? The answer to that is the notion of an ethical baptism.

To be truly worthy of the Robe of Glory, one should be "single." As the name implies, one of the meanings of the term *single* is the unmarried state. This is a state of sexual holiness, conceived of as a betrothal to Christ, in which the "Bride of Christ" remains chaste, until consummation at the eschatological "Wedding Banquet." A life of sexual self-denial involves a high degree of discipline. As in martyrdom, to be a Christian entails not only suppressing an instinctual biological need, it also involves possible persecution and related forms of "suffering" as a further witness to one's Christian faith. In his *Commentary on the Diatessaron*, Ephrem states that there are actually two baptisms required of the Christian: "There were two baptisms to be found in the case of our Lord, purifier of all. One was through water, and the other through the cross, so that he might teach about [baptism] of water through that of suffering. For, repentance for sinners is a crucifixion for them, which nails their members secretly, lest they yield to pleasures. This is what John had proclaimed before our Lord. Consequently, two baptisms are necessary for both just and sinners. If [only] one is present, it cannot vivify without its companion" (Comm. Diat. XXI.17, SEC 325).

Ethically, there is always a danger of forfeiting one's own eschatological standing. Metaphorically, one must be careful not to sully one's wedding garments. Guests at the royal festivities are admitted only if dressed for the occasion, with a stole of impeccable purity. This is like wearing a white wedding dress. One can ruin one's clothes, and so precautions must be taken against compromising one's standing as a guest at that banquet. Hence, Ephrem's warning: [To the melody: "The royal bride."] "O body, strip off the utterly hateful old man, / lest he wear out again the new [garment] you put on when you were baptized" (Virg. I.1, McV 261). The Robe of Glory was deposited in the River Jordan, and multiplied in every baptismal font, to be won by a Christian who knows its purpose and its worth. But the robe can be soiled and ruined by sin, its sanctification undone. The Robe of Glory is an emblem of holiness, not a guarantor of it.

The image of baptismal "Fire" symbolizes "Spirit." This expresses the spiritual aspect of the Christian initiatory rite. In baptism, the Christian is immersed in both water and fire, as Ephrem says: "O children of the baptismal font, / babes, who without spot, have put on Fire and Spirit, / preserve the glorious robe / that you have put on from the water. / Whosoever puts on the robe of glory / from the water and the Spirit, / will destroy with its burning / the thorny growth of his sins. (Epiph. IV.19–20, *LumE* 73).

The thought-provoking, mystery-inducing paradox of fire and water mixing together renders baptism all the more profound. What to all outward appearances is simple immersion in water, is psychologically an immersion into a symbolically powerful and dynamic vision of personal worth and purpose. Ephrem enriches a rather singular symbolic act of initiation with a constellation of images that connect with every aspect of Christian life and experience. In descent and ascent of immersion, baptism touches every current and movement in the initiate's life. This includes one most intimate form of expression, sexuality, in which the Christian suppresses one kind of fire for a spiritual "Fire" that can be mystically experienced.

Ethical: ***Sons/Daughters of the Covenant***

In Syriac Christianity, the "Covenant" usually refers to the celibate within the Church, who constituted its spiritual élite. Notwithstanding, a more general use of the term *Covenant* to designate the Church in its entirety evidently reflects the most primitive Syriac usage of that term. That this is clearly the case is demonstrated in Aphrahāṭ's interpretation of Daniel 7 in Aph. Dem. VII (SCK 61).

The "Sons and Daughters of the Covenant" is thus a collective name of the Church's core élite, who are considered to be the only full-fledged Christians. The term *bnay/bnaṯ Qyāmā* obviously served as a means of Christian self-identity. Covenanters were a continent and celibate circle within the Church. Given its importance in Aphrahāṭ, Ephrem must have known of this movement, which, if it had not established itself there already, evidently spread to his city of Edessa soon after his death in 373 C.E. (AbouZayd 1993, 105). Although never himself a monk, Ephrem advocated a life of chastity and continence. Only a few of Ephrem's hymns, those *Concerning Mār Jacob and His Companion* (CNis XIII–XVI, trans. Stopford NPNF 13: 180–86), may be said to be genuinely eremitic (ibid., 389), although it might be more fitting to describe these texts as preeremitic. Ephrem employs the term *Qyāmā* rather ambiguously. In one passage (CH XXII.21), the "Sons and Daughters of the Covenant" (the *bnay* and the *bnaṯ Qyāmā*) are idealized as those who lead lives of chastity and virginity. In another context (CH VI.19), Ephrem uses the term *Qyāmā* to refer generally to the Church (ibid., 105). Murray calls "the *Qyāmā*, the 'heart' of the Church" (SCK 16).

Membership in the *Qyāmā* obliged Christians so inclined to ascetic life. In his *Demonstrations*, Aphrahāṭ the Persian Sage—Ephrem's older contemporary—describes the discipline and spirituality of those known as Covenanters. "Covenanters" formed an inner circle among Christians within the Persian Empire and, evidently, in pre-Persian and Persian Nisibis as well. In Ephrem's time, these were not monks and nuns as such, as the Covenanters were premonastic, and were not isolated from the laity. As the "heart" of the Church, the Covenanters took up discipleship in Christ and ministered in various ways to the needs of the Church (SCK 13–16). Rather than taking vows of seclusion, these "Sons and Daughters of the Covenant" (*bnay/bnāṯ Qyāmā*) appear to have taken vows of inclusion, inasmuch as service to the Church was of far greater social consequence than hermitage or cloistered life. Ascetics, though shunners of society, play an important role in society, according to pseudo-Ephrem. Their intercessory prayer sustains the rest of the world, an idea which Vööbus depicts as "a favorite thought of 'Aphrēm" (HOA 3: 39).

The "Covenant" (*Qyāmā*) was a call to total sanctification, sacramentally sealed in baptism, following the taking of a vow of virginity or marital abstinence. *Qyāmā* hints at the angelic life, in ceaseless contemplation and praise of God, in company with the "Watchers" (*'īrē*) or angels in heaven. "Covenant" also implies steadfastness. These Christians are those who "took their stand" (*qāmw*) for Christ (SCK 15). In baptism and in sexual holiness, Ephrem describes the "single" Christian as a separate species, in contradistinction to the living dead: "See, our Lord's sword is in the waters, / which divides sons and fathers; / for it is a living sword, which (see!) / makes division of the living among the dead. / See! [people] being baptized and becoming / virgins and consecrated ones (*qaddīšē*), / for they have gone down, been baptized and have put on / that single Only One" (*l-haw ḥaḏ īḥīḏāyā*—HEpiph VIII.16, SCK 16, n. 1).

The image of the sword here suggests the idea of a holy war or contest (*agōnā*). One of the striking metaphors for the Covenanters was the "call to Battle." This is a call to holy war. Aphrahāṭ's use of this imagery draws on the Gideon narrative in Deut 20:1–8 (SCK 15, cf. Murray 1975a). This refers to a life of chastity and the discipline of focused contemplation of Christ.

This metaphor of holy war might have involved some transfers of martyr imagery. Asceticism, generally speaking, may be regarded as a movement which grew up in the aftermath of martyrdom. Asceticism, from this vantage, may be regarded as a continuation of the martyr tradition as well as the prophetic tradition. Certain key terms used to describe martryrs, such as *athlete, contest*, and the like, are transferred to ascetics, and as such are strong indicators of affinities with the martyr ideal (Brock 1973, 2). Ascetics are commonly referred to as "the victorious." Very likely this represents the phenomenon of non-sanguinary renunciation under new historical circumstances, when persecutions ceased. "The Angels," wrote Ephrem, "have received the gift of virginity without effort but you on the contrary on the basis of battle" (Virg. XV.4, HOA 3: 290; cf. McV 327).

Ephrem and his orthodox Christians were also engaged in another kind of holy war. Greek Christological controversies are hardly touched on in Ephrem's hymns, but heretical themes are. Continence and chastity were not ideals universally accepted in Syriac antiquity. Questioning Christ's virgin birth was one way to undermine Ephrem's paradigm of purity, grounded as it was in Mary and Jesus as supreme exemplars. In one hymn, Ephrem accuses Bardaiṣan of having denied the virgin birth of Jesus: "And because he said that it was completely impossible for a solitary one / To bring forth and to bear, he called our Lord the child / That was produced by two, through sexual union" (CH LV.2, BarE 145).

Not much has been recorded or alleged of Bardaiṣan's Christology, save that it was docetic, tinged with a Logos Christology, in which Christ as the "Word of Thought" or the "First Word" passed through Mary and sought lodging in the man Jesus (BarE 220–21). This is a docetic account of the Incarnation. According to CH LV.1, one of Bardaiṣan's Christological titles for Jesus was the "Son of Life." Bardaiṣan mythologized the familial metaphor for Christ. In this case Christ had both a celestial Father and Mother, from whose sexual union Paradise was also populated (LV.8). This doctrine formed a necessary adjunct to Bardaiṣan's system, in that he saw conception and birth as a natural process of purification, whereby evil is extruded (BarE 221).

Ephrem also had to explain Christ's origins, offering an alternative to the Bardaiṣanite Christology which then predominated in Edessa. In a sense, what Ephrem came up with was problematic for post-Chalcedonian Christology: viz., his use of the term *mixed* (*mzag*) with reference to the divine and human natures in Christ: "In Your revealed image / I saw Adam, but in the hidden one / I saw Your Father who is united [lit. "mixed"] with You" (Nat. XVI.3, McV 149). This explanation of the unity of divine and human natures in Christ was not sexual. It was not astral, nor elemental. It was not mythological, but rather ontological. It did not seek to achieve any synthesis with local pagan cults or mythology. Bardaiṣan's circle and its ideological system had effected a synthesis of traditional material with Christian teachings. Ephrem sought to check Bardaiṣan's influence by fighting fire with fire: Ephrem composed orthodox hymns to counter Bardaiṣan's heretical hymns.

We should expect Ephrem to have confronted Bardaiṣan and his followers head to head on the polemical front, and this he did. Throughout the rest of Ephrem's hymns one finds of course recurrent themes, and motifs for expressing those themes, and some of these may well have had in mind an antiheretical agenda. The need to stress the miraculousness of Christ's birth in other than a celebratory sense would hardly have been called for had Ephrem been preaching only to the converted. Because of the dominance in Edessa of Bardaiṣanite Christianity, as well as its strong presence in Nisibis, Ephrem's hymns had to address local points of controversy. Drijvers makes the point that Ephrem's hymns were composed for the ordinary congregation, "who with these Hymns were to attack the Bardesanites with their own weapons, for the making of hymns Ephrem had taken from Bardaiṣan" (BarE 128).

Sexual purity was thus an essential element in Syriac Christian spirituality. The importance of asceticism in early Syriac Christianity cannot be overrated. Passion for the ascetic ideal was part and parcel of a peculiarly Syrian "order of rapture" (HOA 3: 194). "The searing lava of mortification," writes Vööbus, "virtually scalds the works in which such accounts are recorded" (ibid., 195). Early Syriac Christian asceticism was at a primitive stage of development, which is why there was no Ephremic *Asceticon*, as it were. Rather, the "monastic witness" of Ephrem himself is "one of a pre-monastic life of evangelical chastity" (Mathews 1990, 101). The certitude of attracting the divine presence, the indwelling Deity, is exemplified by Ephrem's promise, cited above: "O body, if you have God live in your Temple, / you will also become His royal palace" (Virg. I.2, McV 262).

For Ephrem, the angelic life was a worthy goal of the true Christian. In HdP VI.12, Ephrem speaks of the wondrous fruits of Paradise, whose glory is surpassed by the "fruits of the victorious." "The flowers of Paradise took the victory / but then were vanquished / at the sight of the blossoms / of the celibate and chaste / at whose garlands / both creation and its Creator rejoice" (v.12). Indeed, the victorious are depicted as "the very likeness of Paradise" (v.14). In one hymn (CNis XIV), Ephrem seems to suggest that those who practice ascetic ideals can overcome the realm of Sheol (AbouZayd 1993, 266).

Experiential: ***The Wedding Feast***

The theme of the Wedding Feast recurs throughout Ephrem's hymns. Within the *Hymns on Paradise*, for example, this image is met with several times (HdP II.5; VII.15; IX.4–29; XI.14; XIV.8). The Wedding Feast is an end-time event, assuring the Christian of the glorious destiny of the chaste: "Assiduous fasts have stirred themselves / to become companions to guide the Bride of the King / so that she might be escorted and come / to the wedding feast all in white, / that she might be baptized there, and so shine out: / her crowns will come from her companions, / her adornment will come from her fasts. / She shall proceed amidst shouts of Hosanna, / before her shall shine a lamp with enduring oil. / Blessed is He who sent and escorted the Bride / of His First-Born Son, so that she might come / to the Bridal Chamber of His Light" (Ieiun. V.1, *LumE* 99). This is a triumphal description, alluding to Christ's entry into Jerusalem. There is also an allusion here to the Parable of the Virgins. Note the presence of the lamp and reference to its oil. The strategy for action in this key scenario is the practice of sexual holiness.

The Bridegroom is the central persona of this eschatological drama. "*Ḥatnā*, Bridegroom," according to Murray, "is one of the favourite titles by which the primitive Syrian ascetics expressed their passionate attachment to Christ, the 'Beloved' (*Ḥabbībā*). They looked forward to union with him in the eschatological wedding-feast (*meštūtā*; literally, 'drinking party') and thereafter in the heavenly bride-chamber (*gnōnā*)" (SCK 132). The Bridegroom (*Ḥatnā*) awaits the Bride Adorned (*kallta mṣabbattā*). The image of the Bridegroom orients the Christian to Christ, cultivating a sense of fidelity in spiritual love expressed in sexual purity.

Betrothal is a vow of celibacy that defines one's commitment to Christ. It would appear that betrothal involves something on the order of an arranged marriage, where certain conditions have to be met, for the marriage contract to be satisfied and consummated. But Ephrem's hymns are also permeated by a sense of love. Is there, in all this, an actual marriage proposal? Consider this text: "Blessed be you, Cana, for your bridegroom, / whose wine ran out, invited the Heavenly Bridegroom. / He invited the Inviter Who invited the Gentiles / to the new wedding feast and to life in Eden" (Virg. XVI.2, McV 329–30). This allusion to the Wedding at Cana described in the second chapter of the Gospel of John is faithful to the scriptural narrative (although Ephrem would probably have been more familiar with the text in the *Diatessaron*). But the faithful Christian, especially the chaste one, will be more than a guest at the Banquet. Such a person will be part of Christ's Bride, the Church. It is as if one were witnessing and participating in one's own marriage! Doctrinally, therefore, a Syriac Christian anticipates the eschatological Wedding Feast, and, in so doing, embraces his or her own betrothal to Christ as the Bridegroom.

The image of the Bridal Chamber impels one to self-sanctification, in which one's own body is seen as a locus of holiness, as both a temple and a palace. "The bridal chamber that passes away I have exchanged for You!" (Nat. VIII.21, McV 123) is the vow of the consecrated Christian. What is typically represented as an eschatological scenario can be inverted, so that the Christian sees his or her very life as an advance participation in the Banquet: "The soul is Your bride, the body Your bridal chamber, / Your guests are the senses and the thoughts. / And if a single body is a wedding feast for You, / how great is your banquet for the whole Church!" (HdF XIV.5, HyP 28; cf. *LumE* 100–101).

As stated, Christians envision themselves as betrothed to Christ. This requires total fidelity, something called "singleness." Singleness (*īḥīdāyūtā*) is celibacy, which defines total holiness. It is modelled on the life of Christ: There are three important dimensions of "singleness": (1) "singleness" as a religious lifestyle, leaving one's family and not marrying; (2) single-mindedness, in which one's entire focus in life is centered on Christ; and (3) belonging to a community of like-minded Christians who referred to their way of life as the "Covenant" (*qyāmā*), who formed an élite "Church within the Church" (SCK 13–16). Singleness preserves and prolongs the holiness conceived in baptism, frequently compared, in Syriac literature, to a womb.

In exchange for this fidelity is an experience in which the presence of Christ is felt in a most immediate way. The experiential potency of this metaphor can be cross-referenced with another metaphor, that of the sanctified body as the "Temple" or "Royal Palace" of Christ the King: "O body, if you have God live in your Temple, / you will also become His royal palace" (Virg. I.2, McV 262). There is a word play here, in which the Syriac term for "palace" (*hykl'*)—a cognate of the Hebrew *haykal* (McV 262, n. 6)—can also mean "temple" and "body." (These terms have both metaphorical as well as literal meanings). Christ dwells within the living palace of the "Royal Bride" (the name of the melody to which the first of the *Hymns on Virginity* is set [McV 261]) as she prepares to dwell in the heavenly palace of the King at the moment of requital, the *eschaton*.

The picture of the Royal Bride symbolizes an anticipated marriage to Christ in sacred time. The "Royal Bride" personalizes Christian holiness, which is based on both Christ's earthly and heavenly life. In his earthly life, Christ was unmarried. But in his eschatological existence in sacred time, Christ is betrothed to his bride, the Church, and to every Christian within it. If Christ is King (Messiah), then his betrothed becomes the Royal Bride. Thus, the Syriac Christian, whether individually as a man or woman, or corporately as the Church in its role as the Royal Bride, experiences all of the joy and anticipation that ideally characterizes a love relationship between a man and a woman about to enter into the sacred bond of marriage. This kind of visioning enables the Christian to forego short-term pleasures for long-term gains. Thus: "By a circumcised heart the uncircumcised becomes holy. / In the bridal chamber of his heart, dwells his Creator" (Virg. XLIV.20, McV 445; cf. *LumE* 104). Valuation of the body is reflected in the consecration it receives when the vow of chastity is taken. If the body is the Robe of Glory, it must be preserved as stainless, unsoiled by moral impurity.

As much as he exalts virginity, Ephrem is careful to point out that sexual holiness alone does not suffice for one to be invited to the Wedding Feast. In his *Letter to Publius*, a prose work, Ephrem narrates his vision of Paradise. One scene that he beheld has an element of surprise, of the unexpected: "I saw there pure virgins whose virginity, because it was not adorned with the precious ointment of desirable deeds, was rejected. . . . I drew near to the gate of the kingdom of heaven and I saw there those who did not bear the title 'virgin' who were crowned with victorious deeds, for their virtues filled the place of virginity. For just as those who had been espoused to Him only in their bodies had been rejected because they were naked of any garment of good deeds, so too those who had espoused their bodies in a chaste marriage while their spirit was bound to the love of their Lord were chosen, and they wore their love for Him like a robe with [their] desire for Him stretched over all their limbs. And when I saw those there, I said to myself, 'No one from henceforth should rely solely on the chaste name of virginity when it is lacking those deeds that are oil for the lamps'" (Mathews SPW, 350; cf. Brock 1976, 286). This, of course, refers to the Wise Virgins of the Gospel.

However powerful perfection is as an ideal, it is unlikely that the ordinary Christian, even after extraordinary diligence and effort, can present an absolutely stainless and morally pure wedding garment at the Banquet. Taking the frailties and foibles of human nature into account, Ephrem makes some provision for "whitening" one's robe: "The First-born wrapped himself in a body / as a veil to hide His glory. / The immortal Bridegroom shines out in that robe: / let the guests in their clothing resemble Him in His. / Let your bodies—which are your clothing— / shine out, for they bound in fetters / that man whose body was stained. / Lord, do You whiten my stains at Your banquet with Your radiance" (CNis XLIII.21, *LumE* 74). The "man whose body was stained" is an obvious reference to the rejected wedding guest in Matthew 22. Obviously, the guest had been given the appropriate clothing for the occasion, just as the Christian receives the Robe of Glory at baptism in anticipation of the Wedding Feast. One is required not only to have the proper attire, but to keep it unsullied as well.

As a corporate image, the Royal Bride personifies and transcendentalizes the faith-community's relationship to Christ. Of Christ the Bridegroom, Ephrem states: "[But] You are our bread, / and You are our bridal chamber and the robe of glory" (Nat. XVII.6, McV 155). Kronholm translates: "Thou [O Christ] art our bread; / thou art our bridal chamber, and the stole of our glory" (*Motifs* 115). And further, with reference to earthly marriage: "The bridal chamber that passes away have I exchanged for You" (Nat. VIII.21, McV 123). The sign for this is the "Seal": "Within the seal [of virginity] You dwell even now / within chaste women, and if anyone slanders / Your brides, the silent seal, / the curtain, rages out to meet him. / The seal cries out that our King is there" (Nat. XII.5, McV 134). McVey explains that a "seal" (*ḥtm'*) refers to the wax or molten metal which bore the imprint of a signet stamped upon it, this being a practice in antiquity, which served to identify letters and possession. In a previous stanza, Ephrem calls Christ "the Great Signet (*ṭb'*) of the King of Kings" (Nat. XII.3). Thus, Christ is the instrument used by God to identify those who belong to Him. So often one image evokes another, as with clothing imagery: "'May all evidences of virginity of Your brides / be preserved by You.

They are the purple [robes] / and no one may touch them / except our King. For virginity / is like a vestment for You, the High Priest'" (Nat. XVI.13, McV 151). Purple is of course the color and symbol of royalty. The status of the brides of Christ is such that not only is their chastity inviolate by virtue of their own choosing, but by dint of their status as part of the royal household.

Crowning may have been a part of the ritual of baptism as far back as the *Odes of Solomon*, which is probably the earliest extant work in Syriac (SCK 24): "Put on the crown in the true Covenant of the Lord" (Od. Sol. IX.11, trans. Charlesworth, *apud* SCK 14), had been adduced as evidence of this, although the baptismal reference of this passage has been disputed. A familiar marriage custom, "Crowning" during baptism signified the espousal of one's soul to Christ. According to Murray, this is evidenced in *Hymns on the Epiphany*: "Give thanks, O Daughter whose crowns are two! / Thy temples and thy children rejoice. / For see, the hallowing of thy temples in worship, / and the hallowing of thy children by anointing! / Blessed art thou, for at once there began in thee / the Shekina for thy inhabitants; / The Spirit descended on thy children" (Epiph. I.1, SCK 140). Reference in this stanza to "anointing" strengthens Murray's interpretation, who elsewhere describes the rite of baptism in some detail: "The rites of initiation begin with the 'signing' (*rušmā*), an anointing of the whole body, symbolizing the unction of the Holy Spirit, and certainly regarded as sacramental; baptism follows and then, immediately, reception of the Eucharist" (SCK 21).

There does not seem to be a consensus on the sacramental interpretation of "crowning," and so Murray's pronouncement on this invites more explicit textual validation. But the image is a familiar one. Another reference to crowning occurs in the *Hymns on Virginity*: "Let Cana thank You for her gladdening banquet! / The bridegroom's crown exalted You for exalting it, / and the bride's crown belonged to Your victory. / In her mirror allegories are expounded and traced, / for You portrayed Your church in the bride, / and in her guests, Yours are traced, / and in her magnificence she portrays Your advent. / Refrain: *Make even me worthy that by Your garments I may enter, / our Lord, Your glorious bridal chamber!*" (Virg. XXXIII.1, McV 407–408). McVey does not comment on the ritual element of crowning, but she does note "the hymn's emphasis on nuptial and royal imagery intensifies the triumphant eschatological tone" (McV 407). The image cluster in this passage alone is worth noting: Banquet, Bridegroom, Bride, Crown, Victory, Garments, Bridal Chamber.

Considering that this key scenario is modelled on the idea of marriage, a few words should be said concerning the earthly practice as it relates to its eschatological counterpart. Bardaiṣan held marriage in high regard. In the Syriac milieu, he was not alone in this view. I do not think there were any "tantric" elements in his system, such as we find with Quq and the Quqites (Drijvers 1967, 104–29). The lawfulness and sanctity of marriage is very Jewish. The Christian community associated with the Clementine *Homilies* XI.28–30 and XIII.13–19 (a partial Syriac translation of which is extant in the earliest dated Syriac manuscript, dated Edessa, 411 C.E.; SCK 26), affirmed the lawfulness of marriage, as did Aphrahāṭ and Ephrem, whom Murray characterizes as "non-encratite" (SCK 12 and n. 3).

Aphrahāṭ speaks of the option of marrying "before baptism" (Aph. Dem. VII, 345.12–13, SCK 15). Murray believes that Ephrem's description of the three "Cities of Refuge" for Christians indicates something along these same lines: The "Lower" City includes penitents not yet readmitted to full church life; the "Middle" City are righteous Christians, particularly those married believers not yet living in abstinence from conjugal relations; the "Perfect" City is reserved for the martyrs and ascetics (Eccl. XXIV.4, SCK 259).

Despite Ephrem's ascetic preferences, he accommodates the lawfulness and purity of marriage: "But intercourse is not defiled, / nor is marriage accursed. / Chastity's wings are greater and lighter / than [the wings of] marriage. / Intercourse, while pure, is lower (Nat. XXVIII.3, McV 215). This verse stands as a corrective to any notion that Ephrem's spirituality excluded the householder, and fully challenges Vööbus's conjecture that a vow of celibacy was required for baptismal rites in Ephrem's churches, notwithstanding that such vows were probably archaic by Aphrahāṭ's time (cf. SCK 11). The deeds of solitaries were to be appreciated but not always to be imitated. The lay life was also holy: "For to Him marriage is pure, / which is planted in the world like a vineshoot, / and children are like fruit hanging from it" (Virg. V.14, SCK 12, n. 4; cf. McV 285). After all, marriage was a metaphor for the Christian's ideal commitment to Christ. Celibacy was not a precondition for baptism in Ephrem's churches, even though it was considered the ideal path to "single-mindedness." The ascetic ideal notwithstanding, that school of love called marriage was considered lawful and holy, in the context of sanctioned praxis and vigil discipline.

Mythic: ***Harrowing of Hell***

In Syriac Christianity, there were three major events in Christ's life: the Nativity, the Baptism in the River Jordan, and the descent to Sheol (Harvey 1993, 120). The New Testament prophets Simeon and Anna are portrayed as recognizing, in the baby Jesus, the future Savior in terms of his conquest over Death: "Into the holy Temple Simeon carried Him / and sang a lullabye to Him, 'You have come, Compassionate One, / having pity on my old age, making my bones enter / into Sheol in peace. By You will I be raised / out of the grave into Paradise'" (Nat. VI.12, McV 112).

"One of the richest symbolic themes of early Syriac Christianity, which was passed on to the whole Christian world," according to Murray, "is the drama of Christ's descent to Sheol, or Hades, breaking open its doors, conquering death, and leading out the dead, from Adam on, who were awaiting redemption" (1982, 13). In antiquity, doors were barred as a kind of primitive deadbolt. Hence, the breaking of the "bars" of Sheol: "Bestow on yourselves, my brothers, the treasure of consolation / from the word our Lord spoke about His church, / 'The bars of Sheol cannot conquer her' [Matt. 16: 13–20, esp. 18]" (*On the Church* II, McV 222). On the basis of this New Testament imagery, the harrowing of Hell was developed into a full-blown, universal Christian myth.

In a sense, the resurrection of all righteous Christians has already taken place in sacred time, to be actualized physically on the Last Day: "By death the Living One emptied Sheol. / He tore it open and let entire throngs flee from it" (Nat. IV.38, McV 92). Ephrem makes it abundantly clear that Christ is the life force for life after death: "Without the breath of air no one can live; / without the power of the Son no one can rise" (Nat. IV.151, McV 100). In prefigurement of the Day of Judgment, it is as if Christians are envisioned as having been raised alongside Christ, at the very same time as Christ himself was resurrected! Of course, the dead are asleep until the eschaton, an eschatological fact to which Ephrem alludes: "Since by sins Adam let the sleep of death enter Creation, / the Awakener came down to awaken us from the slumber of sin" (Nat. I.62, McV 71; cf. *Motifs* 125).

In his many references to the harrowing of Hell, Ephrem weaves a rich tapestry of his favorite symbols. For instance, the Robe of Glory is related to Sheol imagery: "Death was amazed at You in Sheol, / that You sought Your garment and found [it]" (Virg. XXX.12, McV 397). Indeed, Christ's work is conceived as a series of "wombs": "The Womb of Sheol conceived Him and burst open" (Nat. IV.190, McV 103). This was clearly miraculous: "Against nature / the womb conceived and Sheol yielded" (Nat. X.7, McV 130). In another of his hymns, Ephrem personifies the Mount of Olives, who describes the evacuation of Sheol in terms of Christ's sovereign command: "'More than all who rejoice, I [Mount of Olives] rejoice to have seen Him / Who has made my lands rejoice and has been lifted up. I escorted Him / and I am going to hear His living voice / when He calls the dead, "Come out!" / They will all answer Him and emerge, / and not a bone will remain in Sheol / where [as yet] Lazarus alone has answered Him'" (Virg. XXXVI.10, McV 423; cf. SCK 78). The reference to bones here is important, as it was the popular belief that a person's essential personal identity resided in the bones, and that the hope of resurrection inhered in their preservation.

In one of Ephrem's dialogue poems, Christ's cosmic, salvific "work" performed in sacred time is vividly portrayed: "Death finished his taunting speech / and our Lord's voice rang out thunderously in Sheol, / tearing open each grave one by one. / Terrible pangs seized hold of Death in Sheol; where light / had never been seen, rays shone out from angels who had entered to bring out / the dead to meet the Dead One who has given life to all. / The dead went forth, and shame covered the living / who had hoped they had conquered Him who gives life to all" (CNis XXXVI.11, *Harp* 43). With the promise of deliverance from Sheol comes the promise of Paradise: "Adam's Lord came out to seek him; / He entered Sheol and found him there; / then led and brought him out / to set him once more in Paradise" (HdP VIII.10, *HyP* 135). This type of imagery seems to function almost as a vicarious near-death experience, in the modern, clinical sense of the term. The devout Christian who visualizes this scenario, practically at every liturgy, will live and relive a sense of what the future holds in store. Assurance of a glorious future vivifies and reinforces faith. Here, eschatology meets anthropogony.

Social: ***Noah's Ark/Mariner***

There is a New Testament basis for the image of Christ as a Mariner, in Christ's calming of "the storm-tossed sea," to use a lyric from the Christian hymn, "Peace: Be Still." Ephrem develops this image in several of his own hymns, of which this passage is an example: "O Master Mariner (*mallāḥā*), who hast conquered the raging sea, / thy glorious wood is a sign [or, 'has come']; / it has become the oar of salvation. / The wind of mercy blew, the ship set out on its course, / away from the raging sea to the haven of peace. / Blessed is he who has become the mariner of his own soul / and has preserved and unloaded his treasure!" (Virg. XXXI.15, SCK 251). This is evidently an allusion to Mark 6:45–52 and parallels.

A similar patristic theme is the ship coming to harbor, as the final destination for the tried and embattled Christian crew, captained by Christ: "Blessed is your harbor that received with love / the persecuted ship of disciples. / The sailor had seen your calm harbor / and enriched you with His discourses" (Virg. XX.1, McV 346). The harbor motif (i.e., "haven of peace") is well attested in the Syriac tradition (Hambye 1970). Widengren has shown the Mesopotamian antecedents to the Christian Syriac and Manichaean use of this imagery (1946, 96–103). But Ephrem's use of nautical imagery is not restricted to allusion to Christ's calming of the storm.

"Noah's Ark," Mathews observes, "was a favorite object of meditation for Ephrem" (1994b, 58, n. 57). The Syriac term for Noah's Ark is *kewēlā*, as distinct from *'arōnā*, the Ark of the Covenant (ibid.). The idea that the Ark was a protoype of the Church is commonly met with in Ephrem: "Even the type of the ark of animals envisages our Lord, / Who would build the holy church in which souls take refuge" (Nat. I.45, McV 69). "Instead of this distant Lord [Jesus]," writes Ephrem, speaking of Lamech who contemplates his son Noah, "the nearby symbol [Noah] consoled him" (Nat. I.56, McV 70). Over the deluge of evil that has plighted man throughout salvation history, Noah is the prototype, while Christ is the fulfillment: "His symbols are in the Torah, and his *typoi* in the ark; / the one testifies to the other: in the same way as they were emptied / [viz.] the inner parts of the ark, thus they were likewise emptied / [viz.] the symbols of the Scriptures; / for through his advent he has brought to an end / the symbols of the Law, and brought to fulfillment in his churches / the typoi of the ark. Praised be thy advent!" (HdF XLIX.5, *Motifs* 203).

At the helm is the Mariner, the Noachide prototype of Christ. The Manichaean Psalms, for instance, refer to Christ as the "Helmsman that is not drunken" (SCK 161). Ephrem treats both Noah and captaincy as typifying the role of Christ. "In Noah is thy Church depicted (*b-nwḥ ṣyr' 'dtk*)" (Virg. VIII.14, *Motifs* 184). McVey renders the same verse: "in Noah is portrayed Your church" (McV 299). As to captaincy, Kronholm glosses *mallāḥā* (literally, "seaman") as "Pilot" with *spnh'* ("boat-man") as a synonym, likewise translatable as "Mariner." Greer has devoted part of a study to the important picture of Christ as Mariner (Greer 1973, 65–128). This image appears elsewhere in Ephrem, as in one of his poetical homilies, *Memre on Nicomedia* V.11, where Christ is described as "the Pilot of that ark" (*mlḥh dhy kwyl'*—*Motifs* 194).

The Ark becomes even more Christological in the course of the voyage on which it embarks. In marking out all four cardinal points of the compass, the figure of the Cross is described, as Kronholm renders it: "The ship of the Lord of all flew upon the Deluge: / it went out from the east, and reached the west; / it circled over the south, and stretched out to the north. / Its flight over the water was a prophet unto the dry land, / and it proclaimed that its parturition was to become fruitful towards all sides / and spread towards all quarters. Praise be unto its Redeemer. / It drew through its course the ensign of its Guardian, / the cross of its Mariner, and the rudder of the Pilot, / who came to construct unto us the Church in the middle of the water, / and to redeem its inhabitants in the name of the Three Persons; / and the Holy Spirit performs its anointing instead of the dove, / even the symbol of its redemption. Praise be unto its Redeemer" (HdF XLIX.3–5, *Motifs* 194). Baptism "in the middle of the water" is initiatory; those in the ship have been baptized and saved through the sanctifying chrism of the Holy Spirit. The fact that baptism takes place in the engulfing deep of the Deluge relates baptism to the drowning of the earthly life, and the drawing up to a life of salvation. The threefold baptismal formula is attested only in post-Nicene manuscripts of Matthew 28:19 as the work of Shlomo Pinés has shown, and Ephrem's attention to the Holy Spirit shows this hymn to have been written late in Ephrem's life, if Śpidlík's assessment is correct.

The Mariner/Steersman (*spnh'*)—also referred to as the Pilot/Sailor (*mlḥ'*)—prefigures Christ, as the Ark foreshadows the Church. An early instance of Ephrem's use of Mariner as a metaphor for Christ is supplicatory. In a lamentation uttered by the city of Nisibis, personified by the poet as suffering under Persian siege in 350 C.E. when the Persian king Shapur II had dammed the local river in order to flood the outskirts of the town, Christ is invoked as "Helmsman" of the Ark of the Church: "The Flood bore the Ark, / while me the river threatens. / O Helmsman of the Ark, / be my pilot on dry land; / You rested the Ark on the haven of a mountain, / give rest to me too in the haven of my walls" (CNis I.3, *HyP* 10). On Christ as mariner, see Daniélou 1964, 58–79.

The Ark offered a "vision of peace" (*ḥzt' d-šyn'*; CNis I.7, *Motifs* 195–96) for the endangered Christians of Nisibis. But there was a greater danger. Ephrem had to live through war, yet it was internal warring within the Church that most troubled him. The *ecclesia pacis* was more of a wish-image than a reality. The Arians, after all, had fomented *bella ecclesiae*. Thus: "In the Church there is envy, [and] people bite, / whereas in the ark there was a covenant of peace (*qym' d-šyn'*), / [even] for the biting beasts" (HdF LXVI.8, *Motifs* 187). To the Ark that transformed the nature of the lion before the lamb, Ephrem draws a parallel with the ideal Church: "The concord (*'wywt'*), the mirror of peace (*mḥzyt' d-šyn'*), shines among us. / Blessed is the Calm One (*špy'*), who has depicted unto us beforehand / the symbols of calmness (*rz' špy'*) in the ark" (Eccl LI.3, *Motifs* 185–86). That the course of the Ark describes the figure of the Cross invests it as a symbol of universal salvation. Kronholm observes that "the voyage of this particular vessel, poetically conceived as the flight of a fowl, is regarded as typifying the universal reach of the Cross and the worldwide spread of the Church—a perspective delineated in an anti-Arian hymn" (*Motifs* 194). Ephrem also uses the image of the Ark to portray a hierarchy of holiness, or ranks, within the Church: "A symbol of the divisions / in that Garden of Life / did Moses trace out in the Ark / and on Mount Sinai too; / he depicted for us the types of Paradise / with all its arrangements: / Here is the harbor of all riches / whereby the Church is depicted" (HdP II.13, *HyP* 89; cf. *Motifs* 190).

In his analysis of Ephremic texts on Noah, Kronholm identifies nine phases of the Deluge narrative: (1) God's repentance of creation is figuratively interpreted to avert anthropomorphism; (2) Chastity and faith accent Noah's peerless righteousness; (3) The Ark is portrayed as a second Earth, spiritually as a figure of the Church—a Church of the Cross, of Chastity, of Peace; (4) The voyage of the Ark prefigures baptism and the global mission of the Church; (5) The dove which brings a leaf from the olive Tree of Life is glossed as messenger/ healer bearing a gospel/medicine; (6) The Ark's stranding on Mount Qardu signifies both banishment from Paradise and the birth of new life on Earth; (7) Noah's sacrifice and God's savoring of it receive a purely figurative interpretation; (8) Noah's drunkenness is seen in the context of his sobriety and sexual holiness; (9) The Tower of Babel is a work of Evil; the confusion of tongues is contrasted with the division of tongues at Pentecost (*Motifs* 173). The animals on the Ark do not engage in sexual intercourse, according to Ephrem: "Even the type of the ark of animals envisages our Lord,/ Who would build the holy church in which souls take refuge" (Nat. I.45, McV 69). Ephrem idealizes the Ark as a place in which bestial concupiscence is transformed into angelic chastity. For Ephrem, this is a type of Paradise.

Root Metaphors

*Doctrinal: **Physician***

"This is a major title of Christ," according to Robert Murray (SCK 199). "The common metaphor of Christ as physician," McVey observes, "is particularly prominent in Syriac Christian literature from the *Acts of Thomas* onward, and it also figures significantly in the Manichaean literature" (McV 229, n. 37). The importance of Physician imagery is already seen in Aphrahāṭ, the Persian Sage, in *Demonstrations* VII.2, 3, 6, 8: "There is a drug for every disease, and when a skilful physician hath found it, it [the disease] is cured. And for those that are wounded in our contest there is the drug of penance, which they may put on their sores and be healed. O ye physicians of our wise Physician, take you this drug, and with it shall ye heal the plagues of them that are sick. . . . So should not a man whom Satan has wounded blush to confess his sin and turn away from it and ask for the physic of penance. . . . But he also that hath shewn his sore and hath been cured, let him have a care of that place that was healed, that he be not smitten thereon a second time; for when one is smitten a second time his cure is hard, even to a skilful physician. . . . You again I would put in mind, ye physicians, that it is written in the books of our wise Physician that He did not withhold penance" (Jansma 1974, 30).

The image of the Physician is extensible in that it derives from an archetype of Christ, and is distributed among spiritual mentors on whom devolves the responsibility of pastoral "healing." Instancing Aphrahāṭ's rhythmic "artistic prose" (Aph. Dem. VII.4), Robert Murray transliterates and translates the following passage, in which the Persian Sage calls upon "physicians" (mentors) to treat spiritual battle "wounds" of Christian "soldiers" (ascetics): "You too, then, O physicians, / disciples of our glorious Physician, / ought not to withhold your medicine / from those who have need of healing (*W'af l-kon wale, 'asawata, / talmidaw d-'Asyan naṣṣiḥa, / d-la teklun 'asyuta / men man da-sniq d-net'asse*)" (1982, 10. [At Amir Harrak's suggestion, I have emended Murray's translation in the first line, "O Physician" (*sic*), to read: "O physicians."]).

All Syriacists agree on the importance of this symbol: "In Syriac *'āsyā* ('Physician') is a favorite Syriac title for Christ," states Joseph Amar (SPW 289, n. 96). Whenever a Syriacist writing on Ephrem uses the term *favorite*, that is an indication of the importance of the image under discussion and how prominently it figures in Ephrem's works. "'Physician'," according to Murray, "seems to be Ephrem's favourite title of all for Christ. It is a constant refrain in the *Diatessaron* commentary" (SCK 200). While this might be an overstatement, Ephrem's portrayal in prose of Christ as physician mirrors the same role depicted in poetry as well as in prose. In Ephrem's *Commentary on the Diatessaron* II.25, on the significance of the gifts of the Magi, the gifts of myrrh and frankincense symbolically "disclose the Physician who was to heal Adam's fracture" (Comm. Diat. II.25, SEC 73). "It became manifest," as Ephrem explains why earthly physicians were overawed by the Physician, "how much faith surpasses the [healing] art, and how much hidden power surpasses visible remedies" (Comm. Diat. VII.2, SEC 129). "So that the mind of the one who had been healed in her body might not be sick," comments Ephrem on the woman healed from a touch of Jesus' cloak, "he [Jesus] took care also with regard to the healing of her mind, since it was for the sake of the healing of minds that he also drew near to the healing of bodies" (Comm. Diat. VII.6, SEC 131). But Ephrem also stresses the importance of the Physician's spiritual healing: "When the crowds heard the splendid teachings of our Redeemer, they recognized that those of Moses were shadows, and that our Lord [was] *the Sun of Righteousness* [Mal 3:20]. For he gave health of body and soul to humanity" (Comm. Diat. VI.21b, SEC 124–25). "A little radiance from it [the Sun of Righteousness] is sufficient," Ephrem adds, "to remove sickness, as it does for the darkness" (Comm. Diat. VI.22b, SEC 125).

The hymn *Carmina Nisibena* XXXIV develops the theme of Christ as Physician most fully. In it, Ephrem regards the prophets and patriarchs (Abraham, Moses, Joseph, and Daniel) as "physicians" (stanzas 1–8). Yet the world still languished in sickness (XXXIV.9), and stands in need of restorative healing. Christ the Physician took pity, and restored us through the "Medicine of Life"—through the transfusion, as it were, of his own flesh and blood (XXXIV.10). So important is the Physician's "Medicine of Life" that one cannot really separate the two images, as will be seen in the next section.

Ritual: ***Medicine of Life***

"Jesus is our Physician," writes Ephrem, "and is our medicine" (CNis XXXIV.11). Jesus does what no earthly doctor is capable of (v.12, SCK 201). The treatment of the "disease" of mortality, brought on by Adam's sin, is beyond the doctor's ken. McVey observes that "Ephrem frequently characterizes Christ both as physician and as the medicine of life" (McV 87, n. 127). This is an important image of Christ in Aphrahāṭ as well (see Bruns 1990, ch. 6). Mathews concurs: "The term 'medicine of life,' Syriac, *samm ḥayyē*, is a favorite Syriac title of Christ" (1994b, 71, n. 122). This reflects a virtual consensus, as Amar reflects: "'Medicine of Life' (*samm ḥayyē*) is a particularly rich Syriac title for Christ" (SPW 279. n. 35).

The Medicine of Life effects divinization by transforming the believer's constitution, so that, in the end-time, bodies, having undergone a transformation making them impervious to mortality, will be paired with their souls to enjoy communion with Christ, at the Wedding Feast in Paradise. In trying to describe this heavenly elixir, Ephrem states: "There are various powers in the medicines of physicians. One, for instance, can totally purify; another can totally consume. One can strengthen, another can close [a wound], and yet another can burn, and another appease. But the heavenly medicine, which was sent from the Father, was everything to everyone. It opened [the eyes of] the blind, cleansed lepers, raised the dead to life, calmed the seas, and drove out demons" (Comm. Diat. X.7a, SEC 169). Of these powers which the Medicine of Life could effect, the most potent and decisive was the cure for death: "Blessed is the Physician who descended and cut painlessly / and healed the sores with a mild Medicine. / His Child was the Medicine that takes pity on sinners" (Nat. III.20, McV 87).

The Medicine of Life is not "the" (in the sense of a single medicine), but "three": Chrism, and the Wine and Bread of the Eucharist. Of the latter two, Brock states that "Ephrem envisages daily communion" (*LumE* 77). Ephrem reduces these sacraments to their natural components: "Wheat, the olive and grapes, created for our use— / The three of them serve You symbolically in three ways. / With three medicines You healed our disease. / Humankind had become weak and sorrowful and was failing. / You strengthened her with Your blessed bread, / and You consoled her with Your sober wine, / and You made her joyful with Your holy chrism" (Virg. XXXVII.3, McV 425; cf. SCK 77). The sense of triumph and jubilation here underscores confidence in the efficacy of the "Medicine of Life" to bring about the transformation of the

Christian, culminating in divinization. There is a certain logic to the notion of restored immortality. Immortality is seen as the "natural" or original state of man. The disease model points to the original state of man as somehow normative. The supernatural element in Christ's victory over death is that a "cure" for the "disease" of mortality promises restoration. While the cure is supernatural, it is also a return to the natural order of the universe as it once was. The believer is not required to accept a belief in the supernatural that did not already exist, as it were.

The promise of eschatological, physical transformation is a key concept. This involves an acceptance of the value of the body and of the integrity of the body-mind-spirit nexus. This is a different view of creation than rival forms of spirituality promulgated. Ephrem's view of matter was in stark opposition to Marcion's pessimistic view of creation, in which matter is the creation of a demiurge referred to as "the Stranger"—a Creator who is not the true Deity. In his *Commentary on the Diatessaron*, commenting on the wedding Feast of Cana (Jn. 2:1–11), Ephrem states: "He [Jesus] was not therefore introducing an alien creation, but was transforming the original creation, so that, through having transformed it, he would make it known that he was its Lord. Because he did not alienate it, we must know that it is not to be despised. Indeed these same created entities will be renewed at the end. For that will, which changed ordinary water effortlessly into wine, is capable of transforming all created entities to tastes which are beyond description, at the end of time" (Comm. Diat. V.12, SEC 99). As an antidote to death, Christ's own death was the decisive experiment in the efficacy of his own power to overcome death: "the Physician of His crucifiers. / With nails they fastened You, but You made them / like medicines for their pains. / They pierced You with a lance and water flowed forth, / as the blotting out of their sins' (Virg. XXX.9–10, McV 397).

A return to the sinless state is a precondition to the restoration of immortality, which is compromised by the nullifying contamination of sin. The decisive soteriological moment was when: "The Medicine of Life has entered Sheol/ and made its dead alive" (CNis XXXVI.14, SCK 235). Although patently "mythic" in terms of its personification, the Christ-event was decidedly real, and formed the basis of Syriac Christian eschatology which, after all, is simply a projection of its own soteriology.

Ethical: ***The Mirror***

The heart of spirituality is "the heart" itself. Ephrem compares the heart to a mirror. "Another favorite image of Ephrem," Mathews observes, "is the mirror" (SPW 55). In an overview of dominant Ephremic motifs, Murray observes: "He [Ephrem] is no less inspired by the olive tree, its properties and productions, by the sun, its light and warmth, and by mirrors—an important theme in his theology of symbols, as Dom Beck [1953] has well illustrated" (1976, 8). Amar reminds the reader that: "The mirror . . . is an image of great importance for Ephrem" (SPW 280, n. 43).

In one of his Nisibene hymns, Ephrem addresses the problem of the defective mirror: "One complains about a mirror if its luminosity is darkened, / because it has become spotted, or dirt has built up, / covering it over for those who look into it. / Beauty is no longer adorned in that mirror, / blemishes are no longer reproved in its reflection. / It is a cause for offence as far as anyone beautiful is concerned, / seeing that their beauty gets no advantage from it, / in the form of adornments as profit. / Blemishes can no longer be rooted out with its aid, / adornments can no longer be added with its help; / the blemish that now remains is a cause for offense, / that no embellishment has taken place is a further loss: / offence and loss have met together."

The Syriac term for *mirror* is *maḥzitā* (see Bou Mansour 1988, 61–70). Brock points out that, in Late Antiquity, mirrors were not made of mercury-coated glass, but were of bronze, and so required continual burnishing. Even if protected from dust, the mirror would still tarnish and thus require polishing (1982d, 138). Bearing this in mind, we see why Ephrem concludes: "If our mirror is darkened / this is altogether a source of joy to those morally ugly / in that their blemishes are no longer reproved; / whereas if our mirror is polished and illumined, / then it is our free will that has been adorned. / Refrain: Blessed is He who has polished our mirror" (CNis XVI.1–4, *LumE* 56; cf. NPNF 13:185). McVey speaks of "the image of the mirror as a means to self-knowledge and moral improvement" (McV 401, n. 490, citing Beck 1953).

Poetically, the image of the mirror might include any reflective surface. A prime example is that of oil. Speaking of the immanent spirit of Christ, Ephrem writes: "The Anointed is all faces and the oil (*mešḥa*) is just like a mirror; / from wherever I look at the oil the Anointed (*Mešiḥa*) / looks out at me from within" (McV 296). The simile, "the oil is just like a mirror," is more literal than metaphorical, considering that, in Late Antiquity, a bowl of oil was frequently used as a mirror. Word plays are a common feature in Ephrem's hymns. In this verse, the pun is somewhat predictable, as the latter is a cognate of the former. It is interesting to note that, although the image of Christ is mystically discernible wherever the poet turns his gaze, the Holy Spirit is not, for It "is too pure and invisible" (*km' kyt šp' wks'*) even "for a mirror" (*mnh d-mḥzyt'*—CH LV.4, *Motifs* 44).

In Ephrem's poetic use of the mirror, it is the image and not always the reflection that is important. The image in the mirror might or might not be a mirror image. "The Scriptures are laid out like a mirror," Ephrem states in a passage cited above, "and he whose eye is lucid sees therein the image of truth (HdF LVII.8, *LumE* 32). The "image of truth" referred to here is a spiritual ideal, not a human reality. The mirror is, in fact, often associated with the idea that humankind is created in the image of God, the most perfect reflection of which is to be seen in the person of Jesus Christ: In the following passage, Christ is described as a "Clear Mirror": "Clear Mirror constituted for the peoples. / They acquired a hidden eye, approached and contemplated it. / They saw their hatred; they reproached them[selves]. / Their faults they scoured in it; their ornaments they beautified in it. / Blessed is the one who confuted his hatred by Your beauty, / and Your resemblance was imprinted on him." (Virg. XXXI.12, McV 401).

The mirror is also an important Syriac image for self-purification. As stated above, Ephrem was fascinated by mirrors. Mirrors abound in Ephrem's symbolic world. The mirror is not always symbolic: "He polished a mirror [and] set it up for children to learn modesty" (Virg. XXV.16, McV 374). One example will suffice to instance symbolic usage: "In the mirror of the commandments / I will behold my interior face / so that I may wash off the dirt on my soul / and clean away the filth of my mind / lest the Holy One to whom I am betrothed sees me / and stands back from me in horror" (*Armenian hymns* 6, *LumE* 105). Ideally, when the heart is engaged in the contemplation of God, it is turned away from the self and turned toward God: "Let our prayer be a mirror, Lord, placed before Your face; / then Your fair beauty will be imprinted on its luminous surface. / O Lord, let not the Evil One, who is ugly, gaze on it, / lest his ugliness be impressed upon it. The mirror conceives the image of everyone who encounters it. / Let not all sorts of thoughts be imprinted on our prayer; / Let the movements of Your face, Lord, settle upon it, / so that, like a mirror, it may be filled with Your beauty" (Eccl. XXIX.9–10, *LumE* 56–57).

Whenever the mirror is turned to oneself, "beauty" or spirituality is what ought to be reflected. Self-reflection may or may not prove to be a rewarding experience. But the experience is always instructive. Naturally, what one does not wish to behold in a mirror is ugliness: "It is very difficult for the evil one to gaze at his ugliness. / Goodness, like a mirror, comes toward him / to refute by his ugliness one who thinks he is beautiful" (Virg. XI.1, McV 307). "Become his mirror," exhorts Ephrem, "that in your beauty she may see the beauty of the Word" (HdF LXXXIII.10, Mathews 1994b, 64).

"Using a favorite metaphor," writes McVey, Ephrem employs "the mirror as the instrument of divine ethical lessons" (McV 37). There is some evidence to suggest that the community of Ephrem was in ethical competition, so to speak, with their Christian rivals, the Bardaiṣanites. The Edessan native Bardaiṣan had high ethical standards for his followers. The exercise of free will was, in the views of both religious figures, of greatest importance. This ought to come as no surprise, as the metaphor of the heart as a mirror is a favorite patristic theme generally. "'Polish this interior mirror of yours'," Brock observes, "is the repeated exhortation of Syriac writers from St. Ephrem onwards" (1982d, 138).

Experiential: ***The Pearl***

True to the Christian Orient, the goal of existence is full and perfect deification, augmented through self-purification, a godly life of spiritual service, not of mere lip-service, culminating in the complete translation of body and soul into the realm of the spirit. Towards this end, the life of the celibate and of the continent was considered exemplary, a boon to the soul and to the world around it. Those who took a vow of sexual holiness formed the élite of the Church and served as models for less-disciplined Christians.

As a church within the Church, the sexually pure engendered a visible spirituality, which provided a leaven of enthusiasm for the upliftment of the entire Church (which metaphor Aphrahāṭ [Aph. Dem. XIV.680.25–26] applied to bishops; see SCK 87, n. 1). Taken together, the chaste and the virgins could be seen as "a peacock of the spirit." Virgins were deemed to be the very jewel of the Church, as in this verse: "Abounding in fasts / and in supplications / its bones are its treasures, / its tears are its talents; / its eye is its spring, / and its virginity / is its jewel within it, / a peacock of the spirit / which wears its adornments / upon its members!" (CH XLII.9–10, SCK 75). The term for "jewel" here is literally *beryl* (SCK 75, n. 2). Christians who kept themselves pure—that is, chaste—are thus compared by Ephrem to various types of ornaments, particularly gems and pearls. This type of imagery glorifies and ennobles the ascetic path.

More so than jewels, the pearl emerged as Ephrem's most important symbol of virginity. "Probably his most famous symbol," states Murray, "is the pearl" (1976, 8). "Perhaps Ephrem's favorite and best known image," Mathews concurs, "is that of the pearl" (SPW 54; cf. 1994b. 54). The image of the pearl (*marganītā*) is explored in Ephrem's *Hymns on the Pearl* (*Madrāšē 'al-Marganītā*), a collection of five hymns within the larger cycle known as the *Hymns on Faith*, an anti-Arian cycle of hymns. The *Hymns on the Pearl* begins: "One day, my brothers, / I picked up a pearl. I saw within it mysteries, / O sons of the kingdom, images and types / of that Majesty. It became a fountain / and from it I drank of the mysteries of the Son. / Refrain: Blessed is He who compared the kingdom on high to a pearl" (HdF LXXXI.1, Mathews 1994b, 57). Compare Brock's rendition: "One day, my brethren, I took a pearl into my hands; / in it I beheld symbols which told of the Kingdom, / images and figures of God's majesty. / It became a fountain from which I drank the mysteries of the Son" (HdF LXXXI.1).

Virginity, in Syriac spirituality, as well as sexual holiness in general, was essential for cultivating a purity of heart. Syriac Christianity's emphasis on virginity and chastity arose from a number of influences, not the least of which was the model of Mary, the virgin mother of Jesus, and Christ himself, who was also a virgin. Ephrem speaks devotionally of Mary, and of the Virgin Birth, of her "the womb" that "conceived You without intercourse" (Nat. XV.16, McV 146). It should also be noted that Ephrem's conception of virginity extends far beyond human sexuality, for Nature, in her pristine form, exemplifies virginity: "The virgin earth gave birth to that Adam, head of the earth; / the Virgin today gave birth to [second] Adam, head of heaven" (Nat. I.16, McV 65). For Ephrem, Nature imagery provides an important symbolic warrant for virginity.

His references to the Virgin Birth take on a slightly different complexion when advancing more strained and exotic analogies from nature, such as this one: "The Spirit spoke a parable in the worm, for it reproduces without sexual union" (Nat. I.10, McV 64). Here is a move beyond the confessional to the apologetic: "That which is by nature / mortal, gains life by chastity, / which is beyond nature" (Nat. XIV.18, McV 144). The symbol of the pearl functions in the same symbolic vein. The pearl, for Ephrem, was a perfect symbol of virginity, as the science of the day held that the pearl was formed by lightning striking the shell of the oyster (*LumE* 85). Thus, the "mother" of the pearl—a poetic allusion to the Virgin Mary—is referred to as "a virgin of the sea" (*Pearl* II.2).

The *Hymns on the Pearl* exhibit the polyvalency of Ephrem's key symbols. The term for "mysteries" that occurs in the opening verse is *rāzē*. In this context, Mathews glosses *rāzē* thus: "Ephrem uses this word, of Persian origin, most often to indicate those elements in nature that figure heavenly realities" (1994b, 57, n. 50). We see this in evidence throughout the five *Hymns on the Pearl*. An invidious comparison might be that of the pearl as a crystal ball, in which an array of images are said to appear. In contemplation of the pearl, Ephrem relates: "In its clarity I saw the Clear One (*šapyūtā*) / who is not clouded. In its purity / a great mystery: the body of our Lord / which is unsullied" (Pearl I.3). The word *šapyūtā* also means "lucid, luminous, pure, limpid" and often denotes the ideal vision of faith, the "luminous eye." This is also the ideal condition of a perfectly burnished mirror (*LumE* 85). God is pure and luminous, and for the eye of faith to be pure and luminous, purity of body and soul is required.

The *Hymns on the Pearl* are both timeless yet historically referenced. The symbol of the pearl is polyvalent, even to the point of being protean, yet it is definitely anti-Arian in Ephrem's use of it. The pearl arbitrates in matters of faith. Its integrity, its spherical indivisibility is to be admired rather than argued over, while its radiance is an eloquent witness to its recondite mystery. The pearl is an object of meditation to deepen one's faith. In this respect, the symbolic value of the pearl can never be exhausted. Its symbolism can, however, be frustrated or obscured. In permutating the manifold mysteries of the pearl, Ephrem draws a sharp distinction between contemplation and the Arian rationalism or "investigation": "Even the diver does not investigate (*bṣā*) / his pearl. In it all merchants / rejoice. They do not investigate (*bṣā*) / when it came to be. Nor does the king / who is crowned with it analyze (*ḥmas*) it" (HdF LXXXIV.3, Mathews 1994b, 67). "The pearl is a single substance (*qnōmā*) / that is full of light," Ephrem writes, while "Faith is an integral substance (*kyānā*) / that cannot be corrupted" (vv. 8 and 10, ibid., 68–69). It cannot be analyzed without fragmenting it (v. 9). What has been done to the pearl in such a case has been done to the Church. Its pristine unity is said to have been shattered by the Arian controversy.

In fine, the pearl's perfection, its luminosity and radiance defy any attempt to fathom its mystery. This does not mean that the pearl is without meaning. The significance of the pearl is reflective. When seen in the light of revelation, it is Christ. When viewed as a precious ornament for the pious Christian, it becomes, quite clearly, the "pearl of virginity."

Mythic: ***Tree of Life***

In the Persian *Diatessaron*, Jesus says: "I am the fruit-tree of truth (*man dirakht-i mīva-yi rāstī*)" (Messina 1951, 322, cited in SCK 96). This is an oblique biblical affirmation of what Christians would later say about Jesus Christ, viz., that he is the Tree of Life. "The Tree of Life is an important symbol for Ephrem," according to McVey (McV 64, n. 8). "The tree of life," Murray concurs, "[is] a rich and important theme in fourth-century authors" (1982, 13). "The cross as the 'Tree of Life' and source of the sacraments," writes Amar, "is a popular image among Syriac-speaking authors" (SPW 280, n. 40), as is "vine imagery" (278, n. 32). As Simo Parpola's recent study attests, the Tree of Life is a venerable symbol, attested as far back as fourth-millennium Mesopotamia (1993, 161).

Since the Tree of Life is both biblical and Mesopotamian, it is at once a native Syriac symbol as well as a familiar scriptural symbol. Linking the Tree of Life with Christ is a simple matter of typology. Typology often begins as analogy or parallelism. A good example is Enoch, who was translated into Paradise. Although immortality was conferred on him before the dispensation of Christ in historical time, the mechanism of immortality in sacred time in some way derived from the Tree of Life. This is why Ephrem says: "And, if Enoch, who got life, was unable to obtain life / without the Tree of Life—who is [then] able to obtain life / without the living Son, the fruit of him who gives life to everything" (Eccl. L.8, *Motifs* 160).

Transitionally, the Tree of Life reappears throughout salvation history, in both historic and sacred time. In the beginning, the Tree of Life resides in primordial Paradise. Personification is effectively employed by Ephrem to endow the Tree of Life with human as well as divine qualities: "Very sad was the Tree of Life / that saw Adam hidden from him. / Into the virgin earth he sank and was buried, / but he arose and shone forth from Golgotha" (Virg. XVI.10, McV 332; cf. *HyP* 60–61; *Motifs* 133). In a subsequent dispensation, the Tree of Life reappears in the episode of Noah: "In the beginning again upon the wood alighted the weary dove. / On You, the Tree of Life, came, took refuge [or, "symbolized," "typified"], and alighted the weary Testament; Revelations gazed at You; similes awaited You; / symbols expected You; likenesses longed for You; / parables took refuge in You" (Virg. VIII.5–6, McV 298; cf. *Motifs* 199).

Beyond parallelism is typology. Ephrem's use of typology is predominantly Christological. Beyond parallelism and typology is complete identification. Ephrem often equates the Tree of Life with Christ, and in so doing condenses salvation history into a single, polyvalent symbol. In his *Commentary on the Diatessaron*, Ephrem corroborates in prose what he does in verse. He explicitly identifies "the cross" with "the tree of life" (Comm. Diat. XXI.2, SEC 317). The two symbols merge into one.

Now, this one symbol can then bifurcate into two or more discretely distinctive myths. For instance, the Tree of Life, traditionally associated with Paradise, suddenly and dramatically makes its appearance in Hell: "The Blossom, troubled by / gloom and darkness and night / sprouted [into] a flower in Sheol. / It became the Tree of Life that saved creation" (Virg. LI.8, McV 463). Afterwards, and still in sacred time, the Tree of Life reappears in Paradise, where it stands supreme at the summit of Paradise. There, the Tree of Life ceases to be a symbol, except referentially, as Ephrem suggests: "As for that part of the Garden, my beloved, / which is situated so gloriously / at the summit of that height / where dwells the Glory, / not even its symbol / can be depicted in man's thought" (HdP III.1, *HyP* 90). Although technically the "Glory" or Shekinah denotes the presence of God and not the Tree of Life, Ephrem speaks of the Tree of Life in the verse following as if to conflate the two. In ancient Near Eastern imagery, "Glory" is a solar image. So when Ephrem describes the radiance of the Tree, conflation of Glory and Tree has taken place: "Perhaps that blessed tree, / the Tree of Life, / is, by its rays, / the sun of Paradise" (HdP III.2, *HyP* 91). Compare Kronholm's translation: "Certainly, the blessed tree, the tree of life (*'yln ḥy'*), / with its rays (*bzlyqwhy*), is the sun of Paradise (*šmšh dprdys'—Motifs* 73). This conclusion is original, although it seems anticipated by Kronholm, who comments: "The outstanding pre-eminence of the tree of life mirrors the foremost position of the divine Shekinah in the top/centre of Paradise (cf. Parad. II, 11, 6)" (*Motifs* 74).

In sum, in Ephrem's formally creative yet thematically consistent use of this symbol, the Tree of Life punctuates salvation history and sacred time. The Tree of Life appears in Eden, in the aftermath of the Deluge, in Sheol, and finally in eschatological Paradise. Complementing its decisive interventions in the unfolding of Ephrem's grand soteriological scheme, to the past and future Ephrem adds the present, in the Tree of Life's initiatory role in the sacrament of prebaptismal "signing" (chrism), and in the diurnal nourishment of the Christian in the form of daily communion.

The Tree of Life is the source of the sacraments, as Joseph Amar observes: "The cross as the 'Tree of Life' and source of the sacraments is a popular image among Syriac-speaking authors" (SPW 280, n. 40). Sacramentally, it provides the antidote to the "disease of mortality" that afflicts humankind: "'The Tree of Life brings hope' [Prov. 12:13 (Pes.)] to the dying," Ephrem writes, speaking of the immortality the Tree confers. Thus, typologically, "the hidden saying of Solomon found its explanation today" (Nat. I.8, McV 64). The essence of the Tree of Life is its oil, sacramentally used as a "white chrism," pressed from its fruit, the olive. "For oil became the key of the hidden treasure-house of symbols. / It propounds for us the similes of God Who became human. / The whole creation gave Him all the symbols hidden in it. / The scriptures also gave their parables, and they were explained in Him. / And the writings [gave] all their types and the Law also its shadows. / The olive tree stripped off and gave to the Anointed the comeliness of the symbols upon it" (Virg. V.16, McV 286; cf. *Motifs* 196). As to communion in relation to the Tree of Life, Ephrem writes: "The assembly of saints / bears resemblance to Paradise: / in it each day is plucked / the fruit of Him who gives life to all / in it, my brethren, is trodden / the cluster of grapes, to be the Medicine of Life" (HdP VI.8, *HyP* 111). Here we see a shift from olive imagery to vine imagery. On this dual imagery, Murray remarks: "The Tree of Life in it [Paradise] is the type of Christ as source of the Church's life, with reference both to the Eucharist and to the sacraments involving anointing, especially the pre-baptismal 'signing' (*rūšmā*). This means that the 'Tree of Life' is represented simultaneously as vine and as olive" (SCK 125).

In trying to solve the problem of consistency in this simultaneous symbolism of olive and vine, a text came to light that suggests that Ephrem has conceived of the grape vine as actually having been grafted onto the olive tree: "Blessed are you, O shoot that Truth cultivated; / He engrafted your medicine into the Tree of Life. / Your fruit exults and rejoices at all times / to drink the drink of the Book of Life" (Virg. XXIV.4, McV 366). As a result of the elixir of the sacraments, flowing from the Tree of Life, the Syriac Christian receives divinization, is transformed, and anticipates an eschatological life in Paradise.

Social: ***Paradise***

Susan Ashbrook Harvey characterizes the Syriac view of Paradise as restoration to a primordial state: "Salvation lies in humanity's return to its original state, as it was in Paradise before the Fall. The regaining of Paradise is a central concern for these Odes, as for much other literature of the time" (1993, 130). The following passage, from the *Hymns on Unleavened Bread*, corroborates this generalization: "The spiritual Bread of the Eucharist makes light and causes to fly: / the Peoples have been wafted up and have settled in Paradise. / Through the second Adam who entered Paradise everyone has entered it, / for through the first Adam who left it everyone left it. / By means of the Spiritual Bread, everyone becomes / an eagle who reaches as far as Paradise. / Whoever eats of the Living Bread of the Son / flies to meet Him in the very clouds" (Azym. XVII.9–12, *LumE* 79). The metaphor of the eagle is striking. Even more striking is the description of the sacraments in paradisal terms, not as an anticipated ascension, but as an experience of rapture in the here-and-now.

Recalling this verse, "The assembly of saints / bears resemblance to Paradise" (HdP VI.8, *HyP* 111), Ephrem states that the Church is a prototype of heaven. Yet it appears that what Ephrem is really doing is using Paradise as an extended metaphor for the Church! This conclusion is borne out by Murray's own observation: "Paradise is the type, as well as the eschatological goal, of the Church" (SCK 125). This theme will be explored in some detail in section 7.1 below. Indeed, Ephrem's eschatology is bound up with his view of Paradise, something Kronholm refers to as an "original/ultimate unity" (*Motifs* 61). With reference to HdP VI.8, Kronholm observes: "Paradise and Church are melted together into a unity" (*Motifs* 114).

Conclusion. The key symbols described in this "symbolic profile" neither exhaust nor fully elucidate Ephrem's complex symbol system. Perforce, this selection was to the exclusion of other key symbols. For this reason, the opinions of various Syriacists (or "Syriacisants") were adduced in order to provide some corroboration of the selection of the dozen or so symbols here represented. Given the constraints of space, it was not possible to flesh out the various constellations of subordinate symbols necessarily associated with each key symbol. However, some of the more important subsidiary symbols were treated. Most of these key symbols were found have some descriptive or thematic connection with Paradise. Upon reflection, this is quite natural to expect, as Paradise is the beatific vision of ideals.

The Syriac Paradigm of Purity

This study has situated Ephrem's hymns within the web of controversies among competing forms of Christianity. A complex of fourth-century influences must be borne in mind in the study of Ephrem's writings. Early in the fourth century, an Edessene could witness the vestiges of Marcionism, the influence of Manichaeism, the success of Bardaiṣanite Christianity, and the divisiveness of Arianism. The threat of Arianism served as a catalyst for orthodox self-definition in Christological and doxological terms. The Marcionites forced a reappraisal of what eventually became defined as the "canon" of scriptures. In the Syriac *Life of Ephrem*, it is said that nine heresies flourished in Edessa in the mid-fourth century. In this light, early Syriac Christianity may be analyzed as a response to a very localized form of Late Antiquity, as well as a further development in continuity with local tradition.

Ephrem lived on the border between Rome and Persia. On the other side of the border was the rival religion Zoroastrianism, but on his side of the political divide, Ephrem had to deal with divisions within his own religion: Marcionism, Bardaiṣanism, and Arianism. Manichaeism, a post-Christian religion, also posed a threat. Except for Arianism, these divisions were preschismatic in the sense that they represented more of a plurality of religions in Late Antique Syria rather than self-conscious schisms reacting against the authority of a council. Nevertheless, these "heresies" did, in a sense, set a thematic agenda, and establish categories and structures of discourse within which Ephrem's positive formulation of Christianity would be expressed.

A unique witness to the indigenously Syriac forms of spirituality of his time, Ephrem's hymns are particularly relevant to the study of early Syriac Christianity, for they bridge the divide between so-called official versus popular forms of religiosity, having been intoned in the pew as well as the pulpit. Syriac, a dialect of Aramaic, was the language spoken in Edessa and its province Osrhoëne in northern Mesopotamia. The composition of Ephrem's cycles of Hymns (*madrāšē*) may well have received an impetus from the use of such hymns in the dominant form of Syriac Christianity in his day, Bardaiṣanism, and possibly from the use of similar hymns in the successful local practice of Manichaeism, as attested in the Manichaean Psalm-Book, which survives in Coptic translation from the Syriac (cf. Säve-Söderbergh

1949). The Syriac provenance of the work is now generally accepted (SCK 27). Arius had originated similar techniques of propaganda in Alexandria. It was natural, therefore, that Ephrem would have seen the composition of hymns to be an effective antidote to the poison of heresy.

Orthodoxy (in Ephrem's view of it) had a precarious foothold in fourth-century Edessa. In Edessa, we recall that Ephrem's congregation was known as the "Paluṭians"—after Addai's disciple Paluṭ, an early bishop of Edessa (CH XXII.5). By Constantine's conversion, the advent of imperial Christianity greatly affected the situation in Edessa. The fortunes of the so-called Paluṭians were augmented by the fact that "orthodox" Christianity could now forcefully assert itself. So recent was this sudden turnaround for the Paluṭians in Edessa that the *Chronicle of Edessa* admits that the first orthodox church was not begun in Edessa until 313 C.E. It was completed in 324, after the Council of Nicea (Bundy 1985, 606). Around the same time, the orthodox church in Nisibis was built under Jacob of Nisibis, during the years 313–320 C.E. (Mathews SPW, 27). Of his own congregation, the Paluṭians, Ephrem wrote: "Their hands have let go [*plṭ*] of everything. There are no handles to grasp. They even called us Paluṭians, but we have spewed [*plṭ*] them out and cast away [the name]. May there be a curse on those who are called by the name of Paluṭ, and not by the name of Christ" (Segal 1970, 81). Note Ephrem's word play on two Syriac words that sound like Paluṭ.

The Paluṭians were but one of a welter of competing forms of Christianity. In both verse and prose, Ephrem refutes each of these rivals. All told, the presence of rival faith-communities in large measure determined Ephrem's literary agenda. To heretics of all ilks Ephrem alludes: "They receive the cup, in which the sons of the serpent / have mixed the dragon's gall" (Nat. XXVIII.8, McV 217; cf. CH I.11).

In fourth-century Nisibis and Edessa, the various forms of Christianity were, for the most part, communities of sanctification. Among all of these disparate and competing spiritual communities, there were interpenetrating influences. Asceticism was one such influence. Mesopotamia, moreover, was permeated by an ascetic fervor. Except for Bardaiṣan and Quq, enthusiasm for sexual holiness was "all but universal in the Syriac world" (SCK 11). Why is this? What was at stake? One reason for this is simple: If salvation is total, the body is included. In effect, the body became the pivot of salvation. Spirituality in early Syriac Christianity was based on competing notions of purity. Marcionite purity, to the extent that the religion was still practiced in the fourth century, was essentially ascetic and antimaterial. The practice of Syrian asceticism may have intensified under Manichaean influence.

Mānī's system was also antimaterial. It was anticosmic as well. For Manichaeans, purity meant freeing captive Light from the matter in which it was imprisoned. Mānī's system is based on a rather complex myth, which basically recounts the attack of darkness (evil) on the world of Light. (Bardaiṣan and Mānī relied heavily on pagan myths, whereas Ephrem's cosmogony is primarily scriptural.) A succinct characterization of Manichaean anthroprogony is given by Sundermann: "[M]an became a prison for Light under the rule of Lust" (EIr 6: 313). In terms of salvation, Ephrem refers to the Manichaean "Column of Glory" (*esṭūn šubḥa*), also called the Perfect Man (Mid. Pers. *mard īg ispurr*), through which Light trapped in matter is purified and transported to the moon, whence it ascends into the ship of the sun and thence to the Paradise of Light (ibid., 312). Knowledge (Gk. *gnōsis*, Mid. Per. *dānišn*) was a prerequisite for salvation, which was predicated on a rather speculative and highly mythical cosmogony that seems to have had more to do with notions of physicality rather than spirituality. Here, there is clearly an ontological dualism in view, rather than an ethical dualism.

Bardaiṣan's system presents a stark contrast. "The key word for Bardaiṣan's life and world view is liberty," writes Drijvers. "One could hardly expect otherwise of a man entertaining close ties with the Parthian feudal nobility, to which he may himself have belonged. We meet with the concept both in his anthropology and his cosmology, for the two are correlates" (BarE 219). True liberty was to be achieved by ethical rigor—a concomitant and guarantor of salvation—through the efficacy of personal will. Ephrem's own focus on spiritual freedom probably reflects the Bardaiṣanite agenda and offers an alternative to it. Whereas the key to salvation for Bardaiṣan was purification by righteousness through the exercise of free will, and Mānī's salvation was by knowledge and asceticism, Ephrem's system of salvation consisted of an exercise of righteousness and premendicant asceticism through the saving sanctification of Jesus Christ (cf. Bou Mansour 1984).

For Ephrem, and for Eastern and Oriental Christian traditions generally, salvation is typically not expressed in terms of forensic, juridical, or pecuniary metaphors so dominant in the Western patristic and especially Anselmian tradition. Sanctification may be defined as "the synergistic notion of interaction between the divine grace of God and the human will" (Fr. Andrew Morbey, Ottawa, p.c. 15 Feb. 1996). The goal is "divinization" (*theōsis*), a term that expresses communion with God. For Ephrem, there is no "Fall" in the sense of Original Sin. Rather, the "Fall" (a term he does not use) in Syriac Christian theology was the mortality that is the human condition, which came about when Adam forfeited immortality through the separation of his will from that of God's. It was not God's wrath that needed to be placated or appeased, but humanity's own imperilment that had to be addressed. It is deifying grace that transforms the true Christian, not vicarious atonement.

For Ephrem, Christ was "the Purifier of all" (Virg. XV.1, McV 326). The mystic investment of the "Robe of Glory" at baptism was a purification by grace. Ephrem epitomizes the work of Christ so: "His birth gives us purification, / His baptism gives us forgiveness, / His death is life to us, / His ascension is our exaltation" (Res. I.16, *Harp* 29). This practically reads like an "order of salvation." In Ephrem's thought, salvation is a means, not an ultimate goal. Salvation, by way of atonement, is the necessary precondition for sanctification. After baptism, a state of grace or purity required commitment and discipline. Sanctification was the path to some form of "union" or dynamic relationship with deity. But the effects of salvation could, in some respects, be forfeited or thwarted by the misuse of free will.

One proof of this is Ephrem's teachings on beatific vision. What are the conditions under which the soul may experience the presence of God? In a word, purity. Consider Ephrem's first hymn in his cycle, *Hymns on Fasting*: "Fasting secretly purifies the soul / So it can gaze on God and grow by the vision of Him. / For the weight that is from the earth, bends it back to the earth. / Blessed is he who gave us fasts,/ The sheer wings by which we fly to Him" (Ieiun. I.2). This idea of purification as a means to rarefication is a predominant theme in the HdP. Ephrem reiterates: "Fasting is bright and beautiful for any who bright enough / To gaze on God. The Turbid One, stirred up by anything / Cannot fix the eye on that Clear One. He who possesses a clear eye / He can gaze upon him; as much as it is given to him to gaze. / Instead of the clarifying wine, let us clarify our thought / So that we will be able to see the Clear One / Who overcame the Evil One by means of fasting, that Disturber of All" (Ieiun. I.3., translated by Gary A. Anderson, Sidney Griffith, and Robin Darling Young, "Saint Ephrem's *Hymns on Fasting*: An Annotated Translation and Concordance" (electronic document posted on the World Wide Web).

In these two stanzas, it is interesting to note, beatific vision does not seem to require the instrumentality of the senses, which is the standard Syriac rationale for a belief in corporeal resurrection, a belief that Ephrem accepts but radically spiritualizes. Assuming that beatific vision is the ultimate mystical experience, and the goal of the ascetic contemplative, the condition of purity that must be met overrides any other consideration. Purity, or sanctification, is the order of salvation beyond forgiveness. Purity is as much a reflex of will—as in the example of fasting—as it is of love. This exercise of will entails a state of freedom to choose, resulting in greater freedom from carnality and the bondage of sin. Through the efficacy of the sacraments, divine energies were communicated in a cultic life of sacramental transformation.

For Ephrem's Christians—those known as Paluṭians—purity meant total personal consecration. The most intimate condition of both mental and physical purity was virginity. Virginity was seen as a spiritual crown. Marital continence was ideal. For it was the life of angels. More importantly, sexual purity emulates the life of Christ. The great symbol of purity was the "pearl" of virginity. Virginity is total purity, not narrowly defined as asexuality. Ephrem likens virginity to beryls and pearls (Virg. II.5–6). Creation exemplifies virginity. Originally, God's creation was pure, virgin. The sin of Adam violated it. But baptism in Christ recovers it. Through Christ, original virginity is restored. The newly baptized Christian is thus a virgin (see SCK 12–18, which summarizes idem, 1975a).

Why was virginity so exalted? For the Christian, virginity was the seal of commitment to Christ, a vow taken to keep one's self pure for Christ, the Bridegroom, in anticipation of the eschatological wedding Feast, which was the pious hope of every Christian. Renunciation of marital intercourse was not based on a denigration of the "flesh" as inherently evil, as in some dualist models, but was positively founded on "three powerful conceptual models," according to Brock: (1) a betrothal to Christ as the mystical and eschatological Bridegroom; (2) the related notion of the believer's soul and the corporate Church being the "bride of Christ"—the sexually pure body consecrated as the "Bridal Chamber" of Christ; and (3) baptism as a reentry into Paradise, in which abstinence is practiced in imitation of the marital life of pre-Fallen Adam and Eve (*HyP* 25–33). Observes one author: "Ephraem considered the church to be the sacramental situation of paradise restored" (de Halleux 1983, cited by Griffith 1990, 28).

Thus, Syriac Christianity had its own model of sanctity—one of exemplary separation, of singleness, of inner unity, of adherence to a special "Covenant" (*Qyāmā*). Celibacy was consecrated, although the spirituality of Ephrem's time was still at a premonastic stage of development. "Ephrem's view of virginity," Murray observes, "like that of his Syriac predecessors, lacks an explicitly ecclesiological dimension; it is a matter of personal union with Christ" (SCK 156–57). Yet, those who took vows of celibacy formed a kind of "church within the Church"—a spiritual elite, who belonged to what was known as *benay* / *benat̲ Qyāmā*" (SCK 13).

While *Qyāmā* is typically rendered "Covenant," this term had rich and complex connotations, which included: (1) the act of "standing" (as indicated by the etymology of the word), indicative of such Christians who "took their stand" (*qāmū*) for Christ by joining the consecrated *Qyāmā* at baptism, and in vicariously participating with the angelic "Watchers" (*ʿīrē*) in unceasing praise of God; (2) a "pact" in respect of a promise or commitment to serve Christ unencumbered by sexual distractions; (3) expressing a commitment to celibacy, a call to "holy war," as in Aphrahāṭ's allegorical use of the Gideon story (Deut. 20:1–8) along with New Testament passages on spiritual warfare (SCK 13–15). A less attested connotation might have been the notion of resurrection.

The Covenant was a state of mind and lifestyle in which one devoted one's entire being for a spiritual purpose. "Holiness" (*qaddīšūṯā*) or consecrated "virginity" (*btūlūtā*) became the practice of the "single one" (*īḥīḏāyā*). The term *singleness* (*īḥīdāyūtā*) was the most basic concept in Syrian asceticism, connoting not only the sense of celibacy but of singlehearted devotion as well. In some ways, sexual holiness was liberating. For women, there were social advantages, according to Peter Brown (1988), in which the practice of ascetical ideals redounded to human dignity: (1) in social independence won by women; (2) in care for the poor; (3) in the significance of dress, affording decency and respect to those of low status vulnerable to the exploitations of nakedness.

Sexual holiness was not restricted to women. From a position of spiritual strength, male and female alike were encouraged to take vows of positive, socially involved celibacy. For married individuals, this meant a life of continence. But what of those who chose not to take vows of celibacy, as in the case of couples who raised families? Married Christians were also considered pure. Sexual intercourse performed within the marriage vow was pure. But it was not angelic. As Ephrem states: "For, in three ways that law is conveyed to us, since it gives family (*īqārā*), continence (*qūdšā*) and virginity (*btūlūtā*), possession (*qenyānā*), privation (*sūrāqā*), and perfection (*gmirūtā*)" (CH XLV.10, Edakalathur 1994, 47–48).

In Syriac hagiography, three key terms for spirituality stand out: "purity" (*dakyūtā*), modesty (*nakpūtā*), and holiness (*qaddīšūṯā*)" (Harvey 1996, 33–34). For the broadest representation, the Syriac concept of "purity" may be privileged as paradigmatic. Syriac spirituality, as represented by Ephrem, is based on a model of transformational purity. By "transformational purity" with regard to Syriac Christianity, I mean sacramental deification through the leading of an angelic life, a life that transcends sexuality, in a covenantal betrothal to Christ, in a positive embrace of the body, pressed into the service of Christ and Church, on the battlefield of free will. The life of purity was both the exercise of free will and the resulting freedom from carnality. In a word, purity was the paradigm of early Syriac Christianity, in which God, through Christ, would "teach [Adam/man] and bring him [back] to purity (*nlp nytywhy ṣyd dkyt'*)" (HdF XXXIV.7f., *Motifs* 122), leading to full participation in the energy and spirit of Christ's divinity.

IV

A Historical Profile of the Bahā'ī Faith

Introduction

Principles practically have a life of their own. They restructure consciousness. They act as social forces. They can revolutionize worldviews. They crystallize into symbols. They can become institutions. They are dynamics of world building. A system of principles wrestles the social monster of chaos, and the creation myth becomes a recreative reality. Social evolution is catalyzed. Perspectivally, a paradigm can function as a worldview. It patterns what we perceive. A paradigm shift, like the mirrors in a kaleidoscope, changes this pattern. Bahā'u'llāh has tried to effect a paradigm shift in the direction of world unity through a set of principles.

Ideas are anchored in history. This chapter introduces the Bahā'ī paradigm of unity in its historical context, providing a necessary background for understanding Bahā'ī ideals variously symbolized as images of paradise, without which the images themselves are seen as discarnate ghosts of a worldview, without a past to interpret the present.

Bahā'u'llāh

Despite a wealth of information about his teachings, as a historical figure, Bahā'u'llāh remains rather enigmatic and abstract. It is difficult to paint a picture of him. One Westerner has, fortunately, given a rare pen-portrait of Bahā'u'llāh, that not only gives an impression of his extraordinary charisma, but indicates the essence of his teaching as well. Cambridge Orientalist Edward Granville Browne, in his historic first interview with Bahā'u'llāh in 1890, records his first impressions when the former was granted an audience with the latter:

> The face of him [Bahā'u'llāh] on whom I gazed I can never forget, though I cannot describe it. Those piercing eyes seemed to read one's very soul; power and authority sat on that ample brow; while the deep lines on the forehead and face implied an age which the jet-black hair and beard flowing down in indistinguishable luxuriance almost to the waist seemed to belie. No need to ask in whose presence I stood, as I bowed myself before one who is the object of a devotion and love which kings might envy and emperors sigh for in vain!
>
> A mild dignified voice bade me be seated, and then continued: "Praise be to God that thou hast attained! . . . Thou hast come to see a prisoner and an exile. . . . We desire but the good of the world and the happiness of the nations; yet they deem us a stirrer up of strife and sedition worthy of bondage and banishment. . . . That all nations should become one in faith and all men as brothers; that the bonds of affection and unity between the sons of men should be strengthened; that diversity of religion should cease, and differences of race be annulled—what harm is there in this? . . .
>
> Yet so it shall be; these fruitless strifes, these ruinous wars shall pass away, and the 'Most Great Peace' shall come. . . . Do not you in Europe need this also? Is not this that which Christ foretold? . . . Yet do we see your kings and rulers lavishing their treasures more freely on means for the destruction of the human race than on that which would conduce to the happiness of mankind. . . . These strifes and this bloodshed and discord must cease, and all men be as one kindred and one family. . . . Let not a man glory in this, that he loves his country; let him rather glory in this, that he loves his kind. (Edward Granville Browne, Sir Thomas Adams Professor of Arabic, Cambridge University. Interview with Bahā'u'llāh, 'Akkā, Palestine, 15 April 1890. Browne 1891, 2: xxxix–xl)

The most complete biography of Bahā'u'llāh in English is Hasan Balyuzi (1980). Sources for the life of Bahā'u'llāh, for the most part, remain unpublished. Known primary sources for the life of Bahā'u'llāh include: (1) Nabīl's Narrative, especially part two; (2) *Mathnavī-i Nabīl-i Zarandī* (chronological poem published in Egypt); (3) the chronicle of Āqā Riḍā Qannad-i Shīrāzī; (4) the chronicle of Āqā Ḥusayn Ashchī; (5) the chronicle of Muḥammad-'Alī Salmānī; (6) notes of Mīrzā Ṭarāzu'llāh Samandarī; (7) the chronicle of Mīrzā Ḥabību'llāh Afnān; (8) The memoires of Zayn al-Muqarrabīn; (9/10) *Tarīkh-i Ẓuhūr al-Ḥaqq* (vols. 4 and 5) which contains many primary sources. Other narratives were commissioned by Shoghi Effendi, but there is as yet no public access to them (p.c. Dr. Ahang Rabbani, 2 Jan. 1996).

Bahā'u'llāh ("Splendor/Glory of God") was born Ḥusayn-'Alī on 2 Muḥarram 1233/12 November 1817 in Tehran. He is claimed to have been a descendant of the last Sasanian king, Yazdagird III (see "The Ancestry of Bahā'u'llāh," in Balyuzi 1980, 9–12). His father, Mīrzā Abbās, known as Mīrzā Buzurg-i Vazīr, served the court of Fatḥ-'Alī Shāh Qājār (1797–1834). As a high-ranking official, Mīrzā Buzurg belonged to a class of hereditary bureaucrats in Iran who dealt with administration, finance, and tax collection. The Nūrī family had extensive land holdings around its ancestral village of Tākur (as indicated by the name of Mīrzā Buzurg's father: Mīrzā Riżā-Qulī Big Tākurī) in Nūr, a district in the Persian province of Māzandarān.

In 1844, at the age of twenty-seven, Mīrzā Ḥusayn-'Alī Nūrī became a follower of the Bāb (d. 1850), whom he never met but with whom he corresponded. However, according to Amanat, it was only after 1847 that Ḥusayn-'Alī became openly active in the Tehran Bābī circle (Amanat 1989, 361–62). Partly by virtue of his prestige as a local notable, the charismatic Ḥusayn-'Alī became one of the leading figures of the Bābī movement. In the summer of 1848, at the Bābī conference at Badasht, in response to a call from the Bāb that the Bābīs ought to glorify God by adopting divine names, Bahā'u'llāh took on the spiritual title, Bahā' ("Splendor," "Glory").

In 1852, at the age of thirty-five, while incarcerated in an underground dungeon following a mass arrest of Bābīs triggered by an assassination attempt on the Shah, Bahā'u'llāh experienced his initial prophetic call, which took place through a series of dreams and visions. In one autobiographical statement, Bahā'u'llāh recalls: "By the righteousness of God! We were in no wise connected with that evil deed, and Our innocence was indisputably established by the tribunals. Nevertheless, they apprehended Us, and from Nīyāvarān, which was then the residence of His Majesty, conducted Us, on foot and in chains, with bared head and bare feet, to the dungeon of Ṭihrān. . . . We were consigned for four months to a place foul beyond comparison. . . . Upon Our arrival We were first conducted along a pitch-black corridor, from whence We descended three steep flights of stairs to the place of confinement assigned to Us."

"The dungeon was wrapped in thick darkness," Bahā'u'llāh continues, "and Our fellow prisoners numbered nearly a hundred and fifty souls: thieves, assassins and highwaymen. Though crowded, it had no other outlet than the passage by which We entered. No pen can depict that place, nor any tongue describe its loathsome smell. Most of these men had neither clothes nor bedding to lie on. God alone knoweth what befell Us in that most foul-smelling and gloomy place!" In such dire circumstances, an event transpired which would alter the course of Bahā'u'llāh's life, and give rise to a new world religion, which he would eventually establish later in the course of his ministry.

"One night in a dream," Bahā'u'llāh concludes, "these exalted words were heard on every side: 'Verily, We shall render Thee victorious by Thyself and by Thy pen. Grieve Thou not for that which hath befallen Thee, neither be Thou afraid, for Thou art in safety. Ere long will God raise up the treasures of the earth—men who will aid Thee through Thyself and through Thy Name, wherewith God hath revived the hearts of such as have recognized Him'" (ESW 20–21). This is a rare glimpse into the personality of messianic consciousness. This event precipitated within Bahā'u'llāh an acute sense of destiny and purpose. In another passage, Bahā'u'llāh recalls: "During the days I lay in the prison of Ṭihrān, though the galling weight of the chains and the stench-filled air allowed Me but little sleep, still in those infrequent moments of slumber I felt as if something flowed from the crown of My head over My breast, even as a mighty torrent that precipitateth itself upon the earth from the summit of a lofty mountain. Every limb of My body would, as a result, be set afire. At such moments My tongue recited what no man could bear to hear" (ESW 22).

In his Sūra of the Temple (*Sūrat al-Haykal*), Bahā'u'llāh describes a vision in which he beheld a celestial Maiden: "While engulfed in tribulations I heard a most wondrous, a most sweet voice, calling above My head. Turning My face, I beheld a Maiden—the embodiment of the remembrance of the name of My Lord—suspended in the air before Me. . . . Pointing with her finger unto My head, she addressed all who are in heaven and all who are on earth, saying: 'By God! This is the Best-Beloved of the worlds, and yet ye comprehend not. This is the Beauty of God amongst you, and the power of His sovereignty within you, could ye but understand. This is the Mystery of God and His Treasure, the Cause of God and His glory unto all who are in the kingdoms of Revelation and of creation, if ye be of them that perceive'" (GPB 101–102). This Maiden of Heaven is a salient Bahā'ī symbol. Briefly, the Maiden is taken by Bahā'īs to be a visionary personification of the Holy Spirit.

Bahā'u'llāh had intimations of his prophetic calling while still a youth. He recounts an experience in his early years that changed his life, when he had read Mullā Muḥammad Bāqir Majlisī's (d. 1111 A.H./ 1699 C.E.) traditional account of the treachery of the Jewish tribe of Banū Qurayẓa, whose betrayal had placed the earliest Muslim community in mortal danger. On grounds of treason, the prophet Muḥammad upheld a judge's order to punitively massacre all male members of that tribe (cf. Q. 33:26). MacEoin notes the impact of all this on the impressionable youth, writing that "the effect of this was to plunge him [Bahā'u'llāh] into a state of acute depression for some time, despite his recognition that 'what occurred had been the decree of God'" (MacEoin 1983, 223 on MA 7: 136; cf. ISH 34 and IQT 116ff). This characterization of the event truncates Bahā'u'llāh's own account of this psychological turning point.

Further in the narrative, Bahā'u'llāh discloses how he implored God to reveal to him the path to concord, amity, and unity among the peoples of the world. Bahā'u'llāh relates how, on his birthday (2 Muḥarram 1279 A.H. = 30 June 1862; Cole 1998, 115) in the year before the "Dawning" (Declaration in Baghdad, 22 April 1863), he experienced a transformation (*inqilāb*), a euphoria of ascendancy and exaltation, evidently a kind of transfiguration. This experience of inspiration and sense of mission lasted for twelve days, during which time he felt the full power of the revelation (*ẓuhūr*) given to him (MA 7: 136; RB 2: 348–49, citing AA 2: 17–18). However, there was a certain reluctance on the part of Bahā'u'llāh to accept his prophetic vocation: "Whenever I chose to hold My peace and be still, lo, the Voice of the Holy Spirit, standing on My right hand, aroused Me, and the Most Great Spirit appeared before My face, and Gabriel overshadowed Me, and the Spirit of Glory stirred within My bosom, bidding Me arise and break My silence" (GPB 102). Bahā'u'llāh began to "reveal" a number of "Tablets" for the edification of his Bābī compatriots. He effectively kept his messianic identity a secret, although intimations of it lent his writings an aura of eschatological tension and imminent disclosure.

After four months of captivity, Bahā'u'llāh was released from prison in Tehran, and spent the next decade in exile in Baghdad (1853 1863), where he maintained his messianic secrecy. Then, on 22 April 1863—on the eve of his departure to Constantinople (Istanbul)—Bahā'u'llāh broke his silence and privately, over a period of twelve days, declared his mission to a select few of his Bābī companions. (These twelve days of Riḍvān [Paradise], as Bahā'īs refer to the event, appear to mirror the twelve days of Bahā'u'llāh's transfiguration in 1862 [Cole 1998, 116].) At this time, Bahā'u'llāh made three major pronouncements: Bahā'u'llāh "(1) abrogated the Islamo-Bābī law . . . of offensive 'holy War' (*jihād*), advocating a pacifist attitude to the propagation of Babism; (2) asserted that no independent Messenger or Manifestation of God would appear (presumably after him) for at least a millennium (1,000 [presumably solar] years); and (3) claimed that through his declarative utterance, creation had been renewed" (Lambden 1991, 82, citing the Iran National Bahā'ī Archives [Private Printing] 44: 225). Bahā'u'llāh states that he, as commissioned by God, had abrogated whatever had been the source of suffering and disunity, having, in their place, promulgated principles that would ensure the unity of the human race (MA 7:136; RB 2: 348–49, citing AA 2: 17–18).

Bahā'u'llāh spent the next several months in exile in Constantinople, from which the Ottoman regime removed him to Adrianople. There, in 1866, Bahā'u'llāh commenced his public proclamation in a series of open letters addressed to political and religious leaders. Due to his growing influence, in 1868, Ottoman authorities finally banished Bahā'u'llāh to the fortress-city of 'Akkā in Palestine. From the prison at 'Akkā, Bahā'u'llāh continued to address open letters to the leaders of Europe and America. The majority of epistles Bahā'u'llāh sent to individual monarchs and religious leaders were, in fact, revealed shortly after his arrival in the prison of 'Akkā (AQA 1:341, Cole 1998, 60 and 207, n. 36).

Analysis discloses two sets of proclamations: (1) Tablets to kings and ecclesiastics, declaring Bahā'u'llāh's advent; and (2) Tablets universally addressed to the peoples of the world, announcing Bahā'u'llāh's world reforms. Of the summons to monarchs and pontiffs, the majority of these epistles were addressed to the leaders of the Great Powers, the leaders of the West. Apart from his collective apostrophes to world rulers, individual "Tablets" or epistles were sent to: (1) Queen Victoria, (2) Napoleon III, (3) Czar Nicolaevitch Alexander II, (4) Nāṣiri'd-Dīn Shāh, (5) Sulṭān 'Abdu'l-'Azīz, and (6) Pope Pius IX. In open letters woven into the text of the *Kitāb-i Aqdas*, Bahā'u'llāh also addressed Francis Joseph, Emperor of Austria and Hungary (K85), Kaiser Wilhelm I, King of Prussia (K86) and, collectively, Presidents of the Republics of the Americas (K88). Western sovereigns outnumbered Oriental rulers as recipients of this proclamation to royalty.

Actual delivery of such Tablets to their intended recipients must be verified on a case-by-case basis. For instance, successful dispatch of Bahā'u'llāh's Tablet to Queen Victoria remains unconfirmed. Bahā'u'llāh, in his last major work, *Epistle to the Son of the Wolf*, expresses the wish that: "Likewise, We mention some verses from the Tablet of Her Majesty, the Queen [Queen Victoria]—may God, exalted and glorified be He, assist her. Our purpose is that haply the breezes of Revelation may envelop thee, and cause thee to arise, wholly for the sake of God, and serve His Cause, and that thou mayest transmit any of the Tablets of the kings which might have remained undelivered. This mission is a great mission, and this service a great service" (ESW 59).

Independent attestation of this wish of Bahā'u'llāh is provided by "Count Cottrell" (Henry Edward Plantagenet), who was one of a very few Europeans who had actually met Bahā'u'llāh. Count Cottrell was in 'Akkā during the last year or two of Bahā'u'llāh's life, in connection with the 'Akkā-Damascus railway. Together with his wife and daughter, Count Cottrell had enjoyed Bahā'u'llāh's hospitality sometime between 1891 and 1892. On that occasion, the Count was given a copy of the Kitāb-i Aqdas in the hand of Mīrzā Āqā Jān, Bahā'u'llāh's amenuensis. Count Cottrell wrote:

> I have personal and intimate knowledge of the present leaders of the Babist movement in Persia, the four sons of the late Mirza Hussein, who are political prisoners in Akka, though the Shah within the last twelve months has repealed the penal laws

> against the sect, and is now very friendly. These princes have a large library of books written by their father on the peculiar doctrines of the sect, which aim at nothing less than the reconciliation of Buddhism, Christianity, and Mahomedanism. The father in his will directed his sons to transmit to all the sovereigns of Europe copies of certain of his works, accompanied by an autograph letter. The late Czar of Russia, since Mirza Hossein's decease, sent to the sons and obtained copies of several of the principal works and had them translated into Russian. The princes are very anxious to carry out the wish of their late father [Bahā'u'llāh], and to have copies of the works presented to Her Majesty the Queen; and also to obtain, unofficially, the countenance of the British Foreign Office to enable them to reach the other sovereigns with a similar object. They have furnished me with summaries of the principal works in Arabic and Persian, with the object of having them translated and published in Britain and in the United States of America. (Momen, 1981, 236)

The second set of proclamations concerns Bahā'u'llāh's announcement of his message. This is what is referred to by Cottrell when he says: "They have furnished me with summaries of the principal works in Arabic and Persian, with the object of having them translated and published in Britain and in the United States of America."

Bahā'u'llāh's writings were, and still are, considered sacred scripture. They constitute what is popularly characterized as the "creative Word of God" in respect of the text's motivating and integrating intention. "Creative" in this sense relates to the individual's response to the revelation. The charismatic leader's power to inspire his followers to meritorious deeds is summed up very nicely by Dilthey: "The creative principle emphasizes making a difference (the opposite of sameness), in which the new replaces the old. It generally functions as an assumption of volitional efficacy in the making of fact—of willpower, work, and effort, whether human or divine" (1989, 30). Bahā'u'llāh's extant works are the residue of his charisma, the source of inspiration and edification for Bahā'īs down to the present.

After a forty-year ministry, Bahā'u'llāh died in 1892. He had penned or dictated in excess of fifteen thousand "tablets" (*alwāḥ*; sing., *lawḥ*) in Persian and Arabic. In sheer volume, it is estimated that the entirety of Bahā'u'llāh's writings would, if bound together, comprise around one hundred volumes, or at least forty thousand manuscript pages. Actual counts and estimated total counts of the number of individual works written by Bahā'u'llāh, 'Abdu'l-Bahā, and Shoghi Effendi, which, together with the writings of the Bāb, constitute a vast corpus of authoritative texts: **Bahā'u'llāh**: *Unique Archival Items*: 7,160; *Estimated Total Items*: 15,000. **'Abdu'l-Bahā**: *Unique Archival*

Items: 15,549; *Estimated Total Items*: 30,800. **Shoghi Effendi**: *Unique Archival Items*: 16,370; *Estimated Total Items*: 30,100 (Anon. 1993, 48–49). Remarkably prolific, the preponderance of this primary source material is, nonetheless, correspondence.

The more formally universal writings of Bahā'u'llāh clearly form a class of their own, in view of their privileged status and their widespread use by Bahā'īs. These texts are programmatic expositions of Bahā'u'llāh's world reforms, such the Tablet of Glad-Tidings (*Lawḥ-i Bishārāt*). This exemplar of Bahā'u'llāh's major principles will be analyzed in the sections that follow.

The Bahā'ī Faith as a Response to Modernity

The preëminent Bahā'ī scripture is the Most Holy Book (*al-Kitāb al-Aqdas*, Persianized as *Kitāb-i Aqdas*), a text revealed (or compiled) in 1873, in which Bahā'u'llāh propounds his major laws and principles. Not all of these principles were for public proclamation. Obviously, some of them were, and it is evident that Bahā'u'llāh selected precisely which principles of the Aqdas to proclaim. In this selection process, it should be borne in mind that the Kitāb-i Aqdas exhibits a certain textual and ideological extensibility through the phenomenon of "re-revelation"—a term coined by Adib Taherzadeh (RB 4:372). By "re-revelation" is meant those works of Bahā'u'llāh that are excerpted and quoted (and thus, "re-revealed") within other works (also considered revelation). The best example of a text that contains a great wealth of previously revealed material is Bahā'u'llāh's last book, *Epistle to the Son of the Wolf* (1891). Another such text the Tablet of Glad-Tidings (*Lawḥ-i Bishārāt*), one of Bahā'u'llāh's more well-known works revealed in 1885 or later. Proposed reforms advocated in the Tablet of Glad-Tidings evidently derived from Bahā'u'llāh's Kitāb-i Aqdas, or from Tablets considered supplemental to it. In this light, the Tablet of Glad-Tidings may be seen as a programmatic summary of Bahā'u'llāh's world reforms. This work may be considered a distillation of the Aqdas for proclamation. The *Lawḥ-i Bishārāt* will thus be examined in three dimensions: (1) its function as a "Proclamatory Aqdas"; (2) its Aqdas and Aqdas-related content in the context of "re-revelation"; (3) the text as a response to modernity.

The Lawḥ-i Bishārāt as a "Proclamatory Aqdas" and its textual history. What larger purpose did the Tablet of Glad-Tidings serve? As an epitome of Bahā'ī principles, it appears that Bahā'u'llāh revealed the Glad-Tidings so that leaders in the West, and Westerners in general, might become familiarized with some of his world reforms, as enshrined in the Most Holy Book and in related texts. As such, this Tablet functioned in much the same way that a "press release" would today. Indeed, the Tablet of Glad-Tidings engaged the interest of two prominent Orientalists: Edward Granville Browne and Baron Rosen.

Oddly, in the copy of the Glad-Tidings that the Bahā'īs of Ishqabad sent to Baron Rosen in 1892, the fifteenth Glad-Tiding on constitutional monarchy was conspicuously absent (Rosen 1892a, 187). This occurrence was described by Browne as an "expedient" suppression (1893, xxv, n. 1.) Being the scholar that he was, Baron Rosen quickly found out about the fifteenth Glad-Tiding from his colleague at Cambridge. This discovery prompted a separate study, such that Baron Rosen actually published two journal articles on the Glad-Tidings. These are possibly the very first academic studies published on a single Bahā'ī text (1892a, 1892b). The first study was on the publication of the text itself, accompanied with a Russian translation of the Tablet in the form in which he had received it (1892a, 187). Soon after, Rosen found out about the missing section, and compared variants against another manuscript, presumably the Cambridge MS. Whether or not the omission was deliberate, or due to a scribal error, has not yet been determined. The second article therefore concerned the fifteenth Glad-Tiding and minor textual variants between the St. Petersburg and Cambridge manuscripts (1892b, 312–13). We do know from the testimony of Western missionaries and diplomats alike that Bahā'u'llāh took personal interest in the dissemination and delivery, the translation and even publication of such texts.

Bahā'u'llāh was also concerned about fair treatment by the press. In the "sixth Ṭarāz" [Ornament] of the *Ṭarāzāt*, Bahā'u'llāh writes: "In this Day the secrets of the earth are laid bare before the eyes of men. The pages of swiftly appearing newspapers are indeed the mirror of the world. They reflect the deeds and the pursuits of divers peoples and kindreds. They both reflect them and make them known. They are a mirror endowed with hearing, sight and speech. This is an amazing and potent phenomenon" (TB 39). He further states: "However, it behoveth the writers thereof to be purged from the promptings of evil passions and desires and to be attired with the raiment of justice and equity. They should enquire into situations as much as possible and ascertain the facts, then set them down in writing. Concerning this Wronged One, most of the things reported in the newspapers are devoid of truth. Fair speech and truthfulness, by reason of their lofty rank and position, are regarded as a sun shining above the horizon of knowledge" (TB 39–40).

Here, revelation has taken note of one of the salient features of modernity—the press. Indeed, the ubiquitousness of the press was destined to become one of the most profound influences on postmodernity. Newspapers are thus described as one of the marvels of the age. But the accuracy of journalists, in Bahā'u'llāh's estimation, left much to be desired. At one point in his ministry, Bahā'u'llāh addressed a Tablet to the London *Times*, exhorting the *Times* to remain true to principled journalistic standards. Because the press had not treated him or his movement fairly, this may be one of the reasons behind the way in which the Tablet of Glad-Tidings opens:

> *This is the Call of the All-Glorious*
> *which is proclaimed from the Supreme Horizon in the Prison of 'Akkā.*
> *He is the Expounder, the All-Knowing, the All-Informed.*
>
> God, the True One (*ḥaqq*), testifieth and the Revealers of His names and attributes bear witness that Our sole purpose in raising the Call and in proclaiming His sublime Word (*kawthar-i bayān*) is that the ear of the entire creation may, through the living waters of divine utterance, be purged from lying tales (*qiṣaṣ-i kāẕiba*) and become attuned to the holy, the glorious and exalted Word which hath issued forth from the repository of the knowledge (*'ilm*) of the Maker of the Heavens and the Creator of Names. Happy are they that judge with fairness. (TB 21/ MMM 116)

Steingass glosses *qiṣaṣ* as "histories, tales, stories, fables" (PED 973). The word itself is neutral—it may have either a positive or negative connotation, depending on the context. The negative context is supplied by the second element of the construct, *kāẕiba*, the feminine form of *kāẕib*, which means "a liar; false" (PED 1001). Since the outside world was laboring under false conceptions as to what Bahā'u'llāh's mission really was, the Tablet of Glad-Tidings was revealed as a kind of corrective counterpart to a press release, even though it was not, to my knowledge, specifically sent to a newspaper as such.

Aqdas content in the context of "re-revelation". One of the structural features of the Tablet of Glad-Tidings is what I shall refer to as its "Aqdas content." There is evidence for this. In the case of the copy intended for E. G. Browne, Bahā'u'llāh had authorized one of his sons, Mīrzā Badī'u'llāh, to personally send the document. On or prior to 22 January 1891, Bahā'u'llāh ordered the Tablet of Glad-Tidings be sent to Browne at Cambridge. (He also sent Browne a pair of spectacles as a gift!) Momen confirms that the *Lawḥ-i Bishārāt* "was sent to Browne from 'Akkā on Bahā'u'llāh's instructions" (1987, 485). This document is catalogued as F.25(9) of the Browne Manuscripts, Cambridge University Library.

Acting as Bahā'u'llāh's correspondent, Mīrzā Badī'u'llāh penned what in effect was a covering letter, in which the following statement is made. On folio 1a of the six-folio manuscript is a prefatory note, which says: "These Divine ordinances and commands formerly revealed in sundry epistles, in the Kitāb-i Aqdas, in the 'Illuminations,' 'Effulgences,' 'Ornaments,' etc., have, agreeably to the Supreme and

Most Holy Command, been collected, that all may become cognizant of the grace, mercy, and favour of God (great is His Glory!) in this Most Mighty Manifestation and this Great Announcement" (Browne 1892, 677).

This Tablet of Glad-Tidings, containing—as Cottrell himself has described—"summaries of the principal works in Arabic and Persian, with the object of having them translated and published in Britain and in the United States of America," was sent, accompanied by a covering letter, to Browne at Bahā'u'llāh's bidding by one of the latter's sons. This perfectly coincides with Cottrell's statement: "The father [Bahā'u'llāh] in his will directed his sons to transmit to all the sovereigns of Europe copies of certain of his works, accompanied by an autograph letter." In this "autograph letter," attention is drawn to what we can call the selection process.

Although copies of the Aqdas were sent to individuals, Count Cottrell and E. G. Browne being among them, one might speculate as to why the Aqdas itself was not delivered to "all the sovereigns of Europe," as Cottrell has said. Is it wise, one might ask, to present leaders of thought with the entirety of the text of the Aqdas? How could this possibly be interpretable to the uninitiated? The Aqdas, after all, is not systematically organised. As Shoghi Effendi observes: "All Divine Revelation seems to have been thrown out in flashes. The Prophets never composed treatises. That is why in the Qur'ān and our own Writings different subjects are so often included in one Tablet. It pulsates, so to speak. That is why it is 'Revelation'" (1981, 454).

In Bahā'u'llāh's Most Holy Book (*Kitāb-i Aqdas*), there is no express hierarchy of laws in terms of their relative weight or importance. For example, how could permission to wear sable or permission to use vessels of silver and gold be anything but subordinate to the Bahā'u'llāh's call for a universal language as the penultimate law of the Aqdas? Bahā'u'llāh, in any event, did not stress legalism, but rather virtue and principle. This seems to be indicated by a statement Bahā'u'llāh made to the effect that the Revelation had not been given for the sake of implementing outward laws as set forth in the *Bayān*, but rather for manifestating perfections and for attaining the stations of everlasting life (IQT 167, Cole 1998, 73 and 209, n. 83). This suggests that Bahā'u'llāh was inclined to attach greater importance to those social principles that might best accrue to the human advancement on a broad scale.

This hypothetical problem might have been a real consideration in the minds of Bahā'u'llāh and his sons and his followers. Evidently, the problem was resolved through a selection process, in which Tablets which represented, more or less, "summaries" (as Cottrell says) of the Aqdas, were chosen as those texts to be sent to royalty, to "all the sovereigns of Europe" as Cottrell has said. Indeed, all of the fifteen

Glad-Tidings—some twenty-one principles—are to be located in the Aqdas itself, directly or obliquely, and in related texts supplementary to the Aqdas, as collected and published in the authorized English translation, *Tablets of Bahā'u'llāh Revealed after the Kitāb-i Aqdas*. With its selection of principles primarily drawn from the Kitāb-i Aqdas and supplementary texts, the Tablet of Glad-Tidings might well be characterized as a "Proclamatory Aqdas." The *Lawḥ-i Bishārāt* was one important way in which Bahā'u'llāh himself highlighted, epitomized, and proclaimed the Kitāb-i Aqdas.

Internal evidence of the proclamatory intent of the Glad-Tidings is found in Bahā'u'llāh's address: "O people of the earth!" (TB 21). These principles were apparently privileged by Bahā'u'llāh over others in the Aqdas and supplemental texts. Not all of these principles receive the same emphasis today as when Bahā'u'llāh commended their proclamation. But they partially explain the structure of the Bahā'ī reformist agenda in its public form in the late nineteenth century.

The Tablet of Glad-Tidings as a response to modernity. For each Glad-Tiding, an endeavor will be made to demonstrate that twin processes of "sacralizing" and "desacralizing" may be seen at work in the Tablet of Glad-Tidings, as part of Bahā'u'llāh's dialectic with modernity. Desacralizing, on the one hand, is simply a process of abrogation, the rendering of certain Christian, Islamic, and Bābī practices as outdated, incommensurate with the exigencies of modernity, and thus no longer "sacred" with respect to divine authorization. On the other hand, the making sacred—or "sacralizing"—of certain secular values may be viewed as part of the Bahā'ī response to modernity. Secular European "civic virtues" appear to have been sacralized and constrained by Aqdas legislation, as well as the desacralization of certain Islamic and Christian excesses. Although much of the legislation in the Glad-Tidings concerns previous religious practices and attitudes, some of this is with reference to the West. Rather than trying to establish an intellectual pedigree for tracing directions of influence, a religious and political pedigree will suffice. Countries that served as positive models for the Bahā'ī reformist agenda will be indicated (from examples given in Bahā'ī primary sources). Questions regarding the nature of revelation are raised by such an analysis. Religious practices treated as negative models will be noted as well.

The eighteenth century in Europe was partly characterized by a break with divine-right monarchy and with established Church authority. Modernity grew out of decisive reactions against the religious and political absolutism of divine-right monarchy and established Church authority.

Modern Islam has responded in several ways to modernity. William Shepard has identified five: (1) Radical Islamism; (2) Traditionalism; (3) Neo-Traditionalism; (4) Modernism; and (5) Secularism, to which Rippin has added a sixth, (6) Post-Modernism. I propose adding a seventh response to modernity, taking up a less well-defined term from Rippin: (7) Post-Islamism. The Post-Islamic response to modernity, as manifested in the Bahā'ī Faith, exhibits two major dynamics: (a) the creation of a new source of authority; and (2) sacralizing of the secular. This pattern is evident throughout the "Proclamatory Aqdas."

Andrew Rippin (1993, 12–13) characterizes modernity as "that which renders the past problematic." Peter Berger's five "dilemmas of modernity" include Abstraction, Futurity, Individuation, Liberation, and Secularization. Similarly, Harvey Cox's "Five Pillars of Modernity" emphasize the roles of Nationalism, Technology, Bureaucracy, Profit Maximalization, and Secularization. The core values of modernity, now "global values," derive in part from the individual values of liberty, equality, and fraternity as espoused in the French Revolution, and social values of progress and science-based rationality characteristic of the Industrial Revolution (Beyer 1994, 99–101).

The religious reforms prosecuted in the Glad-Tidings are largely negative, such as the proscriptions against holy war, which Bahā'u'llāh evidently considered unholy. Bahā'u'llāh considered celibacy an unnatural state and the practice of confession an affront to human dignity. The process of desacralization in Bahā'u'llāh's religious reforms is complemented by positive reforms.

Sacralization is the complement of desacralization in Bahā'u'llāh's program of reform. Yet there is something asymmetrical here. Equality was extended to the sexes and fraternity globalized, while progress was assimilated to Bahā'u'llāh's theory of civilization (viz., an "ever-advancing civilization") and science and religion reconciled. In my analysis, the positive reforms, at least the social as distinct from individual reforms, are predominantly secular in nature. Let us consider Islam as an analogy. Certain of the identifiably pagan practices—stone worship, the annual pilgrimage to Mecca at the idol-filled Ka'ba, the kissing of the Black Stone, blood sacrifices to the gods, and so forth—were reconstituted in Islam, depaganized, and subordinated to the controlling principles of Islam's strict monotheism.

This process of Islamic reform might be described, as Bausani proposed, as the revolution of Monotheism, effected in the relocation of the sacred, the *Numinosum*. In an archaic worldview, the divine is immanent, not transcendent, and usually hostile rather than benign. The divine, moreover, is pluriform. There are nature spirits, idols, mobile demons capable of possession. Interaction with these spirits took the forms of placating wroth deities, surfeiting the olfactory senses of stone noses, appeasing the appetites of the gods, protecting against the Evil Eye. The monotheism of Islam effected a revolution in consciousness. Islam succeeded in disenchanting Nature of its sprites.

This revolution created an interspace between heaven and earth. Science replaced the occult, as Nature became objectivized rather than subjectivized. Astronomy replaced astrology, although not completely. Bahā'u'llāh's reforms were no less revolutionary. Bahā'u'llāh appeared in a polyreligious milieu. In the Tablet of Unity, he calls religious dogmatism a form of idolatry. By shattering the idols of dogma, of dysfunctional ritual, and exclusivism, Bahā'u'llāh reconfig-ures the sacred and recasts it in new universalisms.

World religions, as perceived by Bahā'u'llāh, act as both negative and positive social forces. They stand in need of realignment. Their dignitaries must shake hands, sign accords, deliberate together on social issues. And there are forces operating independently of religions. Secularism is outside the province of sacerdotal control, but well within Bahā'u'llāh's view of history, adumbrated by his theory of civilization. Prior to Bahā'u'llāh's attempts at integration, secularism stood and still stands as a rival to religion, brandishing its progressive but sometimes excessive humanism.

A hermeneutical principle that should be brought to bear in any responsible reading of the Glad-Tidings is the relationship between context and text. This approach seeks to anchor the text in its specific context, while at the same time attempting to extrapolate from the specific act of legislation any universal principle that may derive from it. For instance, of what possible consequence is the abrogation of a specifically Bābī, Islamic, or Christian practice, unless a universal principle inheres? How else could such particularized pieces of legislation have any significance for the people of the world as a whole? It is the generic principle that stands behind each of the specific reforms, rendering it interpretable in the context of world reform.

The pattern of these reforms is quite interesting. To oversimplify, Bahā'u'llāh's religious reforms are primarily negative (or, desacralizing) while his positive reforms are largely secular in the world's view of them. For example, author John Hatcher characterizes Bahā'u'llāh's Lesser Peace as essentially secular in nature. It is no less sacred a Bahā'ī value. The procedure of sacralizing the secular and desacralizing elements of the sacred may be analyzed as follows, with each Glad-Tiding analyzed in sequence, by text and context.

Abolition of Holy War

Text. The first Glad-Tiding is reminiscent of Bahā'u'llāh's first legislative act. On 22 April 1863, on the eve of his departure from Baghdad for exile to Constantinople, Bahā'u'llāh privately declared his prophetic mission to a select few of his Bābī companions, on an island in the Tigris River in a rose garden owned by Najīb Pāshā, one of the notables of the city. Bahā'u'llāh resided within the "Garden of Paradise" (Arabic: *Riḍwān*/Persian: *Riżvān*), as it became known, for twelve days (from sunset 20 April–sunset 2 May). This signal event is commemorated each year by Bahā'īs as the Festival of Riḍvan (sic). In the course of his Declaration, Bahā'u'llāh decreed that the religious law of holy war (*jihād*) was, once and for all, abrogated. This was immediately effective for the Bābī community. In principle, this decree was intended for Islam as well, and indeed for all religions.

A version of this legislation constitutes the first Glad-Tiding. It begins in Persian, and ends with an exclamation in Arabic—an eschatological flourish laden with paradise imagery. Here follows the text:

> O people of the earth (*yā ahl-i arż*)!
>
> ***The First Glad-Tidings***
>
> which the Mother Book (*umm al-kitāb*) hath, in this Most Great Revelation, imparted unto all the peoples of the world (*ahl-i 'ālam*) is that the law of holy war (*ḥukm-i jihād*) hath been blotted out (*maḥv*) from the Book (*kitāb*). Glorified be the All-Merciful, the Lord of grace abounding, through Whom the door of heavenly bounty hath been flung open in the face of all that are in heaven and on earth. (TB 21/ MMM 116–17)

The universal scope of its purview is quite evident. The abrogation of holy war, referenced to Babism and to Islam but extensible to all religions in principle, is expressed quite forcefully, for the verbal noun *maḥv* could sustain an even stronger translation, such as "obliterated" or "effaced" (PED 1191). The decree is universal, by authority of the revealer of God's will for humanity, Bahā'u'llāh, as his claim was understood. This truth claim, accepted as a matter of personal faith by Bahā'īs, carries with it Bahā'u'llāh's prerogative (as divinely inspired lawgiver) to enact legislation binding on the followers of all religions. In all practicality, however, such laws have only moral force at best and are binding only within Bahā'ī communities at present.

Aqdas content. Reference to the "Mother Book" (*umm al-kitāb*) brings Bahā'u'llāh's law code, the Most Holy Book, into relevance. The "Mother Book" is a synonym for the Aqdas itself (BBD 161). Originally a euphemism for the Qur'ān, since the Aqdas is now the Mother Book, either the Bāb's lawcode, the Bayān, or else the Qur'ān itself, is relegated to the status of a "Book" (*kitāb*), or scripture susceptible of abrogation. This law is obliquely related to the proscription against bearing firearms in the Aqdas proper (K159).

Response to modernity. Here is evidence of a process of desacralization. A distinction should be drawn between desacralization and secularization, even though both processes involve diminishing the dominance of religion as a source of policy. The desacralizing of holy war is aimed at both Islam and Babism and, in principle, at all religions. In some respects, the Bābī religion may be analyzed as an intensification of Islamic concepts, carried to a pious extreme. In the original Persian, the text behind the translation which reads "the law of holy war hath been blotted out from the Book" (*maḥv-i ḥukm-i jihād*) is considerably stronger in tone than a statement of abrogation pure and simple. As mentioned, a very explicit notion of obliteration is involved here, almost as if holy war is regarded as unholy war.

The specific kind of holy war in focus here is what Islamic tradition has tended, especially in modern times, to soften as being a "lesser *jihād*," subordinated to the "greater *jihād*" in the wider sense of "striving," by which spiritual mastery of self and passion is meant. The force of Bahā'u'llāh's legislation should not be lost on the reader, for *jihād* comes very close to being, and at times is actually defined as, the sixth Pillar of Islam. Holy war was also a prominent feature in the Bābī movement as well. Thus Bahā'u'llāh took pains to distance himself and his followers from this aspect of Bābī legacy, to begin anew with a fresh, comparatively pacifist ethos. According to Juan Cole, in *Modernity and the Millennium: The Genesis of the Bahā'ī Faith in the Nineteenth Century Middle East* (Columbia University Press, 1998), Bahā'u'llāh may be credited with having established the first indigenous peace movement in the modern Middle East—and one of only a few such peace movements to have matured into an organization, having been institutionalized as the Bahā'ī Faith (138).

Interfaith Amity

Text. The second Glad-Tiding is a positive formulation of the previous passage, in that interfaith amity—or transconfessional affinity—is the polar opposite of religious hatred and bigotry. Cole affirms this to be the case: In 1888 or 1889, Bahā'u'llāh forbade Bahā'īs from speaking ill of other religions (AQA 6:303–304, p.c. 21 April 1995). Cole also states that, in an epistle c. 1889, Bahā'u'llāh explicitly links his abolition of holy war and other forms of interreligious conflict to his exhortation that Bahā'īs should freely associate with adherents of other faiths, including Christians. To further interfaith amity, Bahā'u'llāh permitted the wearing of foreign clothes, and allowed Bahā'īs to read the sacred scriptures of other faiths (including the Bible), which, according to Bahā'u'llāh, were acts previously forbidden (either by Islam or Babism or both). In Bahā'u'llāh's revelation, "liberty" (*ḥurriyat*) has thus been granted to dispense with such restrictions (IQT 28–29, Cole 1998, 67 and 208, n. 66). Ideally, Bahā'u'llāh's fostering of concord among religions was calculated to reduce the incidence of intercommunal conflict, by stemming it at its spiritual source, so that there could no longer be any religious pretext for conflict. Formally a piece of Bahā'ī legislation, this text is supplemental to Bahā'u'llāh's lawcode, the Most Holy Book, but takes the form of an exhortation:

> ***The Second Glad-Tidings***
> It is permitted that the peoples and kindreds of the world associate with one another with joy and radiance (*bi-rawḥ va rayḥān*). O people! Consort with the followers of all religions in a spirit of friendliness and fellowship (*bi-al-rawḥ wa al-rayḥān*). Thus hath the day-star of His sanction and authority shone forth above the horizon of the decree of God, the Lord of the worlds. (TB 22/ MMM 117)

The first sentence is in Persian, the second in Arabic, evidently as a restatement of the first. In both occurrences, the text is often misread as as *rūḥ* (spirit) rather than *rawḥ* ("joy, friendliness," PED 591). This ambiguity in the text is resolved by the fact that Bahā'u'llāh is clearly using Qur'ānic language (Q. 56:89).

Aqdas content. The Arabic exhortation is almost certainly derivative from the Aqdas, or from a common source that stands behind the Aqdas text. In this Glad-Tiding, there are a few words added to the corresponding Arabic text of the Aqdas. There is a second occurrence in the Aqdas of this same teaching, this time with a call to interreligious fellowship for the purpose of teaching: "Consort ye then with the followers of all religions, and proclaim ye the Cause of your Lord, the Most Compassionate; this is the very crown of deeds, if ye be of them who understand" (K75/ MHB 47).

Throughout the history of Islam, contact by Muslims with followers of other religions was discouraged, because it involves contamination, rendering a pious Muslim polluted or ritually impure. Theoretically, Babism had a similar notion—one that seems hardly to have been practiced at all. In both Islamic and Bābī contexts, Bahā'u'llāh rendered interreligious fellowship morally desirable in abandoning the whole notion of ritual impurity, or "uncleanness." Once again, this is related to Bahā'u'llāh's Riḍvān Declaration: "God hath, likewise, as a bounty from His presence, abolished the concept of 'uncleanness', whereby divers things and peoples (*milal ukhrā*) have been held to be impure. He, of a certainty, is the Ever-Forgiving, the Most Generous. Verily, all created things were immersed in the sea of purification when, on that first day of Riḍvān, We shed upon the whole of creation the splendours of Our most excellent Names and Our most exalted Attributes. This, verily, is a token of My loving providence, which hath encompassed all the worlds" (K75/ MHB 47).

On this passage of the Aqdas, the pertinent note states that: "The concept of ritual 'uncleanness', as understood and practised in some tribal societies and in the religious communities of certain earlier Dispensations, has been abolished by Bahā'u'llāh" (K 212, Note 106, on K75). This is a roundabout and diplomatic way of referring principally to Shī'ī Islam, with its studied defenses against contamination (*najis*). Shī'a Muslims, unlike Sunnīs, developed an elaborate system for maintaining ritual purity in preparation for prayer. The *'ulamā'* had ruled that contact with a Westerner was ritually polluting, requiring a repeat of one's ablutions before praying.

Perhaps MacEoin's translation captures the specificity of the Arabic text that reads: "God has lifted the decree of uncleanness from all things and from other religions (*milal ukhrā*). . . . All things were immersed in the ocean of purity on the first [day] of Riḍwān" (1994, 59). Is *milal* here "divers things and peoples" (as in the official Bahā'ī translation) or "religions" (MacEoin's translation)? Typically, religions are concerned about ritual purity. Clearly, in this context and in its received meaning, *milal* refers to religious communities (PED 1310).

One of the more recondite of Bahā'u'llāh's stated achievements is his claim, in April 1863, to have "immersed" creation "in the sea of purification." It is enough to have effected such a transformation in religious worldview, to dispense entirely with notions of ritual impurity, especially with the idea that contact with unbelievers is undesirable. In any event, Bahā'u'llāh's call to interfaith amity was effectively blocked by the overwhelming contemporary insulations against interreligious social intercourse. Over time, whether or not it surmounted such ritual obstacles remains to be seen.

Response to modernity. Secularism had already integrated religious pluralism into society, by allowing freedom of religion. Obviously, the Islamic *dhimmī* system operated under religious rather than secular rules. In this Glad-Tiding, there is possibly an oblique European reference, as Westerners were generally considered unclean by Shī'a Muslims. In the Aqdas, the two consort passages were clearly directed to Bahā'īs. The rearticulation, or "re-revelation" of this legislation in the Glad-Tidings, effectively universalized interfaith affinity (in principle) as a goal to which all the peoples of the world should aspire. This law conduces to unity.

Universal Language

Text. Increased international conciliation involves an important matter of practicality: communication. Adoption of an international language as an adjunct to world unity was of paramount importance to Bahā'u'llāh. It was a proposal he advocated for nearly three decades of his life. This Glad-Tiding has its roots therefore in Bahā'u'llāh's early ministry, as far back as Constantinople in 1863. This is evidenced in Bahā'u'llāh's account of his meeting with Kemāl Pāshā (d. 1888), a European (geographically speaking), who was one of the Turkish dignitaries at the Court of Sulṭān 'Abdu'l-'Azīz. Although, by Bahā'u'llāh's account, Kemāl Pāshā had registered his support for the idea, the proposal went unimplemented (ESW 137–38). A minister of state having failed this expectation, it was only natural that Bahā'u'llāh would, later in his ministry, prevail upon royalty to carry out this noble undertaking:

> ***The Third Glad-Tidings***
> concerneth the study of divers languages. This decree (*ḥukm*) hath formerly streamed forth from the Pen of the Most High: It behoveth the sovereigns (*ḥażārāt-i mulūk*) of the world—may God assist them—or the ministers of the earth to take counsel together and to adopt one of the existing languages (*yak lisān*) or a new one (*va-yā lisān-i jadīdī*) to be taught to children in schools throughout the world, and likewise one script. Thus the whole earth (*ṣūrat-i arż*) will come to be regarded as one country. Well is it with him who hearkeneth unto His Call and observeth that whereunto he is bidden by God, the Lord of the Mighty Throne. (TB 22/ MMM117)

Aqdas content. This is the penultimate law of the Aqdas (K189). Indeed, it is the last piece of positive legislation in the Aqdas. Bahā'u'llāh foresaw the world's eventual adoption of such an auxiliary or universal language as the second sign of the "coming of age of the human race" (MHB 250). In the Most Holy Book, Bahā'u'llāh states: "O members of parliaments throughout the world! Select ye a single language for the use of all on earth, and adopt ye likewise a common script. God, verily, maketh plain for you that which shall profit you and enable you to be independent of others. He, of a truth, is the Most Bountiful, the All-Knowing, the All-Informed. This will be the cause of unity, could ye but comprehend it, and the greatest instrument for promoting harmony and civilization, would that ye might understand! We have appointed two signs for the coming of age of the human race: the first, which is the most firm foundation, We have set down in other of Our Tablets, while the second hath been revealed in this wondrous Book" (K189). The first sign of the "coming of age of the human race" referred to here is the emergence of a science capable of transmuting metals and other chemical elements, while the second sign is the adoption of a universal language (N194).

Response to modernity. While the biblical confusion of tongues is mythically accounted for in the Torah, overcoming linguistic anarchy—the reversing of Babel—is a clearly secular endeavor. Yet it is given religious merit by Bahā'u'llāh. In the Aqdas, members of parliaments are enjoined to effect such a convention, but elsewhere the responsibility devolves upon kings and even upon the Universal House of Justice itself. A two-stage process, Bahā'u'llāh sees first the adoption of a universal auxiliary language, followed in the more distant future by adoption of a primary rather than secondary international convention of communication.

Support of Patron King

Text. The nineteenth century was still an era in which sovereigns wielded absolute power. Their power was such that any proposal for furthering the public interest meant soliciting the king's support for such an undertaking. Bahā'u'llāh himself solicited such support for his cause. Unfortunately, it was not forthcoming. Two monarchs were later won over to the Bahā'ī Faith: Queen Marie of Rumania, who stated her Bahā'ī allegiance publicly in the *Toronto Daily Star* (28 October 1926) (Postlethwaite 1994 and Jasion 1994) and the reigning monarch of Western Samoa, His Highness Malietoa Tanumafili II, whose conversion to the Bahā'ī Faith was announced in 1973. But these conversions did not occur during Bahā'u'llāh's own lifetime. The fourth Glad-Tiding obliges public support for any monarch who embraces the Bahā'ī Faith or who otherwise champions noble ideals:

> **_The Fourth Glad-Tidings_**
> Should any of the kings (*ḥażrat-i mulūk*)—may God aid them—arise to protect and help this oppressed people (*īn ḥizb-i maẓlūm*), all must vie with one another in loving and in serving him. This matter is incumbent upon everyone. Well is it with them that act accordingly. (TB 22/ MMM 117–18)

Aqdas Content. This is really a restatement of a recurring theme sounded throughout Bahā'u'llāh's writings. In a more colorful version of this exhortation, the Aqdas text that stands behind this Glad-Tiding is as follows, beginning with a benediction upon any sympathetic king: "How great the blessedness that awaiteth the king who will arise to aid My Cause in My kingdom, who will detach himself from all else but Me! Such a king is numbered with the companions of the Crimson Ark—the Ark which God hath prepared for the people of Bahā. All must glorify his name, must reverence his station, and aid him to unlock the cities with the keys of My Name, the omnipotent Protector of all that inhabit the visible and invisible kingdoms. Such a king is the very eye of mankind, the luminous ornament on the brow of creation, the fountainhead of blessings unto the whole world. Offer up, O people of Bahā, your substance, nay your very lives, for his assistance" (K84; cf. K189). This is obliquely related to a third sign of the maturity of the world, according to Bahā'u'llāh. This has to do with the future reluctance of anyone to take on the role of monarch. The very gravity of kingship will be daunting, a responsibility so awesome that it will overwhelm anyone who might even contemplate it: "One of the signs of the maturity of the world is that no one will accept to bear the weight of kingship. Kingship will remain with none willing to bear alone its weight. That day will be the day whereon wisdom will be manifested among mankind" (K, Note 194, on K189 [p. 251]); BBD 132, s.v. "kingship, station of"; PDC 72).

Bahā'u'llāh had no designs for political power, either personally or for his religious system. He wrote that some individuals falsely imagined that he had designs on establishing a world government on earth (*irāda-yi ḥukūmat-i kullīya dar arż*)—even though he had, throughout his revelation (*dar jamī'-i alvāḥ*), forbidden the pursuit of political aspirations, except if a king were to accept the burden of office for assisting the Bahā'ī religion. Kings are the manifestations of divine Power (*mulūk maẓāhir-i qudrat-i ilāhīya and*) and Bahā'u'llāh's prime concern was that monarchs should be just. If their intent is the exercise of justice, then they are of God (IQT 261, Cole 1998, 35 and 203, n. 44).

Response to modernity. Considering the unbridled absolutism of nineteenth-century monarchy, this statement was certainly visionary. In Bahā'ī texts, there are no contemporary rulers who are singled out as paragons of just sovereignty, except for one: Queen Victoria. By extension, Great Britain's parliamentary system receives further recognition in that its framework of constitutional monarchy is singled out by Bahā'u'llāh as a model of good government. Bahā'u'llāh's eldest son and future successor, 'Abdu'l-Bahā, reiterates this preference: "The Constitutional Government, according to the irrefutable text of the Religion of God, is the cause of the glory and prosperity of the nation and the civilization and freedom of the people" (TAB 2:492). Speaking of England, in 1875 'Abdu'l-Bahā, wrote: "Where is this little island in the North Atlantic, and where the vast territory of the East Indies? Can such extension be obtained save by equal justice to all peoples and classes? At all events, by means of just laws, freedom of conscience, and uniform dealing and equity towards all nationalities and peoples, they have actually brought under their dominion nearly all of the inhabited quarter of the world, and by reason of these principles of freedom they have added day by day to the strength, power, and the extent of their empire, while most of the people on the face of the earth celebrate the name of this state for its justice" (TN 90).

This idealizing passage, farther on, alludes to medieval Europe and to its emancipation from the Inquisition with its lingering mentality. The author openly vaunts freedom of conscience, and credits a religiously secular state (Anglican secularism) with having made this possible. For rhetorical effect, 'Abdu'l-Bahā idealizes Great Britain for its achievements, in order to make the point that the East ought to take cognizance of certain of England's civic virtues. Granting this picture of an imperialist and colonialist power as adroitly romanticized, England's civilizing influence is acknowledged as a positive model worthy of emulation. Here, 'Abdu'l-Bahā suppresses any intention of dwelling on the dark side of colonialism.

On behalf of his followers, Bahā'u'llāh took a number of special measures to solicit protection from the Great Powers, but they were to little avail, save in the case of Queen Victoria. In a letter dated 14 May 1891, French Diplomat M. de Balloy speculates that Queen Victoria had evidently evinced sympathy towards the Bahā'īs: "The Queen of England has, it appears, recommended to the Shāh clemency and moderation in his own interest and in that of Persia" (Momen 1981, 356). This cannot be relied upon as solid evidence that the Queen had actually received Bahā'u'llāh's epistle and was favorably disposed thereto, Bahā'ī speculation notwithstanding. But it does seem to confirm Cottrell's statement that "the Shah within the last twelve months has repealed the penal laws against the sect" presumably due to Victoria's influence.

As background to Bahā'u'llāh's positive attitude towards kingship, Mangol Bayat has shown that Shī'ī thought is far more complex and innovative than that represented by the clerical scholars (*'ulamā'*) studied thus far. Moreover, from Safavid times onward, mystical Shi'ism, or theosophy, laid the foundation for contemporary socioreligious thought in Iran. A new breed of "lay, modernist intellectuals" appeared on the historical horizon in the latter half of the nineteenth century, who effectively adopted Western ideas and political models. The contribution of these lay activists lay in the realm of constitutionalism, liberal democracy, and secularism. The Constitutional Revolution of 1906 marked the ascendancy of the dissidents—lay and clerical alike—though the role of certain high-ranking *'ulamā'* has to be acknowledged as well. One result of constitutionalism was the transformation of calls for religious reforms into "demands for the secularization of important social institutions controlled by the ulama" (1982, xiv–xvi).

Yale professor Abbas Amanat sees Shi'ism in the Qājār period as a conflict between (1) scholastic Shi'ism—replete with a juristic system dominated by a clerical order—and (2) speculative Shi'ism, manifested in "recurring heterodoxies." Prior to the nineteenth century, the latter led a rather "subterranean" existence in Iran, but generated "a new momentum" in the nineteenth century in challenging the prevailing Islamic law code (*sharī'a*) and, to a certain extent, the political order of the day. In contrast to reform movements in Sunnī Islam, heterodox movements in Qājār Iran "inspired a conscious break with Islamic tenets" (Amanat 1984, 467). Bayat has observed that Bahā'u'llāh's policy of recognizing the legitimacy of the secular state has "embraced what no Muslim sect, no Muslim school of thought ever succeeded in or dared to try: the doctrinal acceptance of the *de facto* secularization of politics which had occurred in the Muslim world centuries earlier" (Bayat 1982, 130).

Loyalty to Government, Support of Bahā'ī Cause, Disarmament

Text. Bahā'u'llāh's call for active support for any monarch who champions the ideals of the Bahā'ī Faith does not detract from civic responsibility. Obedience to government is repeatedly enjoined by Bahā'u'llāh, as in this text:

> ***The Fifth Glad-Tidings***
>
> In every country where any of this people reside, they must behave towards the government of that country with loyalty, honesty and truthfulness (*bi-amānat va ṣidq va ṣafā bā ān dawlat*). This is that which hath been revealed at the behest of Him Who is the Ordainer, the Ancient of Days. It is binding and incumbent upon the peoples of the world (*ahl-i 'ālam*), one and all (*ṭurr*), to extend aid unto this momentous Cause (*amr-i a'ẓam*) which is come from the heaven of the Will of the ever-abiding God, that perchance the fire of animosity (*nār-i baghẓā'*) which blazeth in the hearts of some of the peoples of the earth may, through the living waters of divine wisdom (*āb-i ḥikmat-i ilāhī*) and by virtue of heavenly counsels and exhortations, be quenched, and the light of unity and concord (*nūr-i ittiḥād va ittifāq*) may shine forth and shed its radiance upon the world. We cherish the hope that through the earnest endeavours of such as are the exponents of the power of God (*qudrat-i ḥaqq*)—exalted be His glory—the weapons of war throughout the world (*silāḥ-i 'ālam*) may be converted (*tabdīl shavad*) into instruments of reconstruction (*ṣilāḥ*, rather than *silāḥ*) and that strife and conflict may be removed from the midst of men. (TB 22–23/ MMM 118)

Stylistically, Bahā'u'llāh engages the reader with a variety of literary techniques that invigorates the otherwise didactic content of the text. Opposition and word-play are in evidence here. Fire (*nār*) and light (*nūr*) are typically opposed in Bahā'u'llāh's writings. Note the word-play between "weapons of war" (*silāḥ*) and "instruments of reconciliation" (*ṣilāḥ*). Steingass defines *ṣilāḥ* as "reconciling, making peace" (PED 791) and glosses *silāḥ* as "arms, especially sword, mace, and stringless bow" (691).

Loyalty to Government. This legislation is very early, dating back to Bahā'u'llāh's reform of the Bābī community in the aftermath of the Bābī uprisings and the bloody persecution that followed the attempt on the life of the Shah. This legislation is repeated in the Most Holy Book, to wit: "O people of the world! . . . Take heed not to stir up mischief in the land after it hath been set in order. Whoso acteth in this way is not of Us, and We are quit of him. Such is the command which hath, through the power of truth, been made manifest from the heaven of Revelation" (K64). And further: "No one must contend with those who wield authority over the people; leave unto them that which is theirs, and direct your attention to men's hearts" (K95).

Support of Bahā'ī Cause. Several passages of the Aqdas (K1, K102, K132) invite or even oblige support from the peoples of the world (as well as kings). As a consequence of such support, "the light of unity and concord (*nūr-i ittiḥād va ittifāq*) may shine forth and shed its radiance upon the world."

Disarmament. Disarmament is a necessary precondition of international security. National interests must be preserved, but not at the imperilment of the planet. In the authorized translation of the Kitāb-i Aqdas, note 173 explicitly links K159 with this Glad-Tiding (MHB 241). This teaching is related to the proscription against bearing firearms in K159.

Beyond his progressivist theophanology, Bahā'u'llāh formulated a theology of civilization. The Book of Certitude had served to consolidate Bahā'u'llāh's spiritual authority in the missionary process. The expression of this divine prerogative is worked into the very language of practically every major act of legislation. Typical of this kind of reformist articulation predicated on divine authority is the passage below, which sets the tone for Bahā'u'llāh's laws: "The word of God which the Supreme Pen hath recorded on the ninth leaf of the Most Exalted Paradise is this: In all matters moderation is desirable. If a thing be carried to excess, it will prove a source of evil. Consider the civilization of the West, how it hath agitated and alarmed the peoples of the world. An infernal weapon hath been devised, and hath proved so cruel a weapon of destruction that its like none hath ever witnessed or heard. The purging of such deeply rooted and overwhelming corruptions cannot be effected unless the peoples of the world unite in pursuit of one common aim and embrace one universal faith. Incline your ears unto the call of this Wronged One and adhere firmly to the Lesser Peace." Bahā'u'llāh concludes this passage with a prophecy: "Strange and astonishing things exist in the earth but they are hidden from the minds and the understanding of men. These things are capable of changing the whole atmosphere of the earth and their contamination would prove lethal" (TB 69). Given the explicit context of lethal weapons, Bahā'īs detect in these words a chilling foreboding of the invention of nuclear weapons.

Response to modernity

Loyalty to Government. In an age of revolutions, Bahā'u'llāh's reforms were considered revolutionary, but not his means for change. He advocated transformation within society, not a revolution against any regime.

Support of Bahā'ī Cause. This has already been commented on (*vide supra*).

Disarmament. Bahā'u'llāh's principle of collective security has a Qur'ānic precedent, yet its internationalist formulation represents a transformation of that principle. I am not aware of any contemporary Islamic reformer—or at least of any Persian reformer—who had advocated something similar to the disarmament strategy proposed by Bahā'u'llāh below:

> The Great Being, wishing to reveal the prerequisites of the peace and tranquillity of the world and the advancement of its peoples, hath written: The time must come when the imperative necessity for the holding of a vast, an all-embracing assemblage of men will be universally realized. The rulers and kings of the earth must needs attend it, and, participating in its deliberations, must consider such ways and means as will lay the foundations of the world's Great Peace amongst men. Such a peace demandeth that the Great Powers should resolve, for the sake of the tranquillity of the peoples of the earth, to be fully reconciled among themselves.
>
> Should any king take up arms against another, all should unitedly arise and prevent him. If this be done, the nations of the world will no longer require any armaments, except for the purpose of preserving the security of their realms and maintaining internal order within their territories. This will ensure the peace and composure of every people, government and nation. We fain would hope that the kings and rulers of the earth, the mirrors of the gracious and almighty name of God, may attain unto this station, and shield mankind from the onslaught of tyranny. (*Lawḥ-i Maqṣūd* [Tablet of Maqṣūd], in TB 165)

That such a teaching was articulated within a religious rather than secular context is significant. One might say that Bahā'u'llāh anticipated the need for world order through the normalization of international relations and its regulation under international law. Another strategy against war advocated in Bahā'ī sources comes from the bottom up, rather than the top down. The following passage is a relatively obscure text, not widely published, but the message is of sufficient relevance and interest as to warrant citing it in full. In this text, 'Abdu'l-Bahā advocates certain practical measures be taken to bring pressure to bear on countries either contemplating or actually engaged in waging war without just cause. One such measure is disinvestment. Another is arms control. A third is the demand for justification:

> The ideals of Peace must be nurtured and spread among the inhabitants of the world; they must be instructed in the school of Peace and the evils of war. First: The financiers and bankers must desist from lending money to any government contemplating to wage an unjust war upon an innocent nation. Second: The presidents and managers of the railroads and steamship companies must refrain from transporting war ammunition, infernal engines, guns, cannons and powder from one country into another. Third: The soldiers must petition, through their representatives, the Ministers of War, the politicians, the Congressmen and the generals to put forth in a clear, intelligible language the reasons and causes which have brought them to the brink of such a national calamity. The soldiers must demand this as one of the prerogatives.

The next passage gives a hypothetical example of what the soldiers might wish to say. I believe this to be one of the most rhetorically striking instances of eloquence in 'Abdu'l-Bahā's overall skills in discourse:

> "Demonstrate to us," they must say, "that this is a just war, and we will then enter into the battlefield otherwise we will not take one step. O ye kings and rulers, politicians and warmongers; ye who spend your lives in most exquisite palaces of Italian architecture; ye who sleep in airy, well-ventilated apartments; ye who decorate your reception halls with lovely pictures, sculptures, hangings and frescoes; ye who walk in perfect elysiums, wreathed in orange and myrtle groves, the air redolent with delicious perfumes and vocal with the sweet songs of a thousand birds, the earth like a luxuriant carpet of emerald grass, bright flowers dotting the meadows and trees clothed in verdure; ye who are dressed in costly silk and finely woven textures; ye who lie down on soft, feathery couches; ye who partake of the most delicious and savoury dishes; ye who enjoy the utmost ease and comfort in your wondrous mansions; ye who attend rare musical concerts whenever you feel a little disconcerted and sad; ye who

adorn your large halls with green festoons and cut flowers, fresh garlands and verdant wreaths, illumining them with thousands of electric lights, while the exquisite fragrance of the flowers, the soft, ravishing music, the fairy-like illumination, lends enchantment; ye who are in such environment: Come forth from your hiding-places, enter into the battlefield if you like to attack each other and tear each other to pieces if you desire to air your so-called contentions. The discord and feud are between you; why do you make us, innocent people, a party to it? If fighting and bloodshed are good things, then lead us into the fray by your presence!" (*Star of the West* 5.8 [1 Aug. 1914]: 116–17; Scholl 1984, 66–67)

This passage illustrates how focused Bahā'ī texts are on the cessation of war. While the Bahā'ī Faith is not strictly pacifist—as it does have a theory of just war—war is predicated as an option to be taken only when all other attempts at conflict resolution have been exhausted. Just war is restricted to defense against invasion, in which all other countries of the world (viz., the international community) are obliged to unite in order to thwart the aggressor.

The Great Peace

Text. At the level of global reform, Bahā'u'llāh is not specifically concerned with the rehabilitation of the fortunes of Islam. There is no harking back to lost glory, no appeal to Qur'ānic foreshadowing of modern times. The tide of influence turns in Bahā'u'llāh's efforts to work outside the pale of Islam. The West becomes the new mission field, the grand social experiment for the implementation of the Bahā'ī peace initiative.

The pursuit of world order characterizes a major social thrust in Bahā'u'llāh's program of reform. The global reform Bahā'u'llāh had envisioned is largely up to world leaders to execute. The fortunes of Islam are not central to this vision, nor is it even a nominal concern. Bahā'u'llāh's reforms are decidedly post-Islamic. Legislatively, his point of departure for his global peace initiative was his abrogation of Islamic holy war (see the first Glad-Tiding). The following text is brief because it is purely referential. (The first sentence is in Persian, followed by a benediction in Arabic.):

The Sixth Glad-Tidings

is the establishment of the Lesser Peace (*ṣulḥ-i akbar*), details of which have formerly been revealed from Our Most Exalted Pen (*qalam-i a'lá*). Great is the blessedness of him who upholdeth it and observeth whatsoever hath been ordained by God, the All-Knowing, the All-Wise. (TB 23/ MMM 118)

Aqdas content. This is not commented on in the Aqdas proper, but it is a recurrent theme in texts supplementary to the Aqdas. The term used in the Persian original literally means the "Great Peace" (*sulḥ-i akbar*), but, in order to distinguish this stage of social evolution from the Most Great Peace (a future Golden Age predicted by Bahā'u'llāh), "Lesser Peace" is used instead. Thus, *ṣulḥ-i akbar* is "Lesser" in relation to the Most Great Peace (*ṣulḥ-i a'ẓam*).

Response to modernity. Sacralizing international relations seems to be the intent of this text. In prosecuting his global peace initiative, Bahā'u'llāh addressed public epistles to various world leaders. The program for reform advocated by these principles was expressed in religious terms; but, as John Hatcher observes, "such a peace" is "essentially secular in nature" (1994, 252).

Freedom of Dress

Text. This is not an issue with which Westerners are familiar. In the nineteenth-century Muslim world, conformity was expected in habits of dress and other customs. One's clothing was the book cover by which one was meant to be judged. Moreover, Shī'a Islam frowned upon the lax and immoral nature of Western dress. This created further social barriers between East and West. Bahā'u'llāh rescinded such restrictions as unwarranted and divisive:

> ***The Seventh Glad-Tidings***
>
> The choice of clothing (*zimām-i albisa*) and the cut of the beard and its dressing are left to the discretion of men (*'ibād*). But beware, O people, lest ye make yourselves the playthings of the ignorant (*mal'ab al-jāhilīn*). (TB 23/ MMM 118–19)

The term used here for "freedom of dress" is *zimām-i albisa*. Literally, *zimām* is defined as "a halter fastened to the ring of a camel's nose, a rein, a bridle." Thus, the expression, *zimām-i ikhtiyār* becomes "the reins of self-control" (PED 620). The translation is somewhat misleading with respect to gender. Since women do not normally have beards, the obvious reference is to men with respect to the freedom to dress one's beard. But this context-dependent gender referencing does not apply to the rest of this Glad-Tiding. The term *'ibād* (pl. of *'abd*, "servant," "slave") refers to the generality of humankind (PED 833).

Aqdas content. The relevant Aqdas passage is as follows: "It hath been forbidden you to carry arms unless essential, and permitted you to attire yourselves in silk. The Lord hath relieved you, as a bounty on His part, of restrictions that formerly applied to clothing and to the trim of the beard. He, verily, is the Ordainer, the Omniscient. Let there be naught in your demeanour of which sound and upright minds would disapprove, and make not yourselves playthings of the ignorant. Well is it with him who hath adorned himself with the vesture of seemly conduct and a praiseworthy character" (K159; cf. K9).

Response to modernity. This Glad-Tiding contains an oblique reference to the West, in that, at one time, Shī'ī Islam forbade the adoption of European apparel. In liberating men from the restrictions imposed by religion with respect to the trim of the moustache and length of the beard (N175; cf. N12), it appears that Bahā'u'llāh has implicitly extended freedom of dress to women as well, moderated by a personal sense of modesty. In principle, this Glad-Tiding permits Western dress while not stating any preference for it, allowing women as well as men choice of apparel. The practicality of this ruling is seen, not in the lifting of any previous restriction *per se*, but in removing one of the religious and cultural barriers to unity between East and West.

Monasticism Prohibited

Text. Evidently, Bahā'u'llāh had the Christian West in mind when he ruled on those Christian practices he deemed of little societal benefit. These criticisms are cast in the form of legislation, for it is presumably the prerogative of a lawgiving prophet to abrogate prior religious laws and traditions. Unlike stock Muslim writings of the period, Bahā'u'llāh does not resort to ridicule of Christians, who were always easy targets of Muslim anti-Christian polemics. Besides his innate sense of grandeur, Bahā'u'llāh obviously intended the Tablet of Glad-Tidings to be read by Christians. The text reads as follows:

> **_The Eighth Glad-Tidings_**
>
> The pious deeds (*a'māl*) of the monks and priests among the followers of the Spirit (*ḥaẓarāt-i rahaba va khūrīhā-yi millat-i ḥażrat-i rūḥ*) [Jesus]—upon Him be the peace of God—are remembered in His presence. In this Day, however, let them give up the life of seclusion (*inzivā'*) and direct their steps towards the open world (*qaṣd-i fażā namāyand*) and busy themselves with that which will profit themselves and others. We have granted them leave to enter into wedlock (*tazwīj*) that they may bring forth one who will make mention of God, the Lord of the seen and the unseen, the Lord of the Exalted Throne. (TB 24/ MMM 119)

The tone, as mentioned, is conscientiously respectful. There is not a hint of condescension. A "life of seclusion"—referring to monasticism—is expressed by the word, *inzivā'*, a standard Persian term for seclusion, retirement (PED 110).

Aqdas content. In the Aqdas, asceticism is criticized: "How many a man hath secluded himself in the climes of India, denied himself the things that God hath decreed as lawful, imposed upon himself austerities and mortifications, and hath not been remembered by God, the revealer of Verses" (K 36). In this Glad-Tiding, however, Bahā'u'llāh is kinder in his criticism, saying: "The pious deeds of the monks and priests among the followers of the Spirit [Jesus]—upon Him be the peace of God—are remembered in His presence" (TB 24). Note 61 in the authorized Aqdas translation explicitly links this Glad-Tiding with the Aqdas verse just cited (MHB 195).

Response to modernity. Summing up Bahā'u'llāh's legislation with respect to Christianity, Shoghi Effendi states that the Kitāb-i Aqdas "abolishes the institution of priesthood; prohibits slavery, asceticism, mendicancy, monasticism, penance, the use of pulpits and the kissing of hands; prescribes monogamy" (MHB 14). Note that, in this cluster of proscriptions, Shoghi Effendi has brought together diverse elements from the Aqdas to paint a composite picture of the negative practices of nineteenth-century Christianity that Bahā'u'llāh wished to change.

Prohibition of Confession

Text. In 1875, during his own lifetime, Bahā'u'llāh commissioned his eldest son and future successor, 'Abdu'l-Bahā, to compose a treatise on statecraft for the benefit of the Shāh of Iran, on the order of a "Mirrors for Princes" genre (such as the *Qābūs-nāma*). The resulting *Treatise on Civilization* (*Risāla-yi Madanīya*)—published in English as *The Secret of Divine Civilization*—provides contemporary evidence of Bahā'ī thinking on monasticism and certain other "accretional" practices of Catholicism. In his praise of Luther, 'Abdu'l-Bahā writes: "Luther's position as regards the freedom of religious leaders to marry, the abstention from worshipping and making prostrations before images and representations hung in the churches, and the abrogation of ceremonials which had been added on to the Gospel, was demonstrably correct" (SDC 42). As with other desacralizing patterns, this Glad-Tiding seeks to restore dignity to the repentant, who needs no intercessor in the forgiveness of sins, which is the prerogative of God in any case. Wishing to spare Catholic and Eastern Orthodox Christians from the unwarranted humiliation resulting from auricular confession, Bahā'u'llāh ordains:

The Ninth Glad-Tidings

> When the sinner (*'āṣī*) findeth himself wholly detached and freed from all save God, he should beg forgiveness and pardon (*ṭalab-i maghfarat va āmurzish*) from Him. Confession of sins and

> transgressions (*iẓhār-i khaṭāyā va ma'āṣī*) before human beings (*nazd-i 'ibād*) is not permissible, as it hath never been nor will ever be conducive to divine forgiveness (*sabab va 'illat-i āmurzish va afv-i ilāhī nabūda va nīst*). Moreover such confession before people results in one's humiliation and abasement (*ḥaqārat va ẕillat*), and God—exalted be His glory—wisheth not the humiliation of His servants. Verily He is the Compassionate, the Merciful. The sinner should, between himself and God, implore mercy from the Ocean of mercy, beg forgiveness from the Heaven of generosity and say: [A prayer follows here.] (TB 24–25/ MMM 119–20)

Aqdas content. "To none is it permitted to seek absolution from another soul" (K34) is the concise formulation that stands behind this Glad-Tiding (cf. Note 58 in MHB 193–94). In this Glad-Tiding, Bahā'u'llāh reveals a prayer for the forgiveness of sins, functioning analogously to the Lord's Prayer, which asks God to dispense forgiveness.

Response to modernity. In desacralizing the Catholic Sacrament of Penance, Bahā'u'llāh has implicitly endorsed Luther's reform, which 'Abdu'l-Bahā explicitly praised. This kind of legislation may have been intended as some form of "liberation" for the Christian, by the disencumbrance of practices seen as man-made rather than divinely ordained.

Abrogation of Book Burning

Text. Without context, this Glad-Tiding is a bit curious. The legislation is quite specific, and one would have to know the circumstances of the practice to which Bahā'u'llāh is referring, in order to understand why there is a mention of it in the first place. The text states:

> **_The Tenth Glad-Tidings_**
>
> As a token of grace from God (*faḍl min lidā Allāh*), the Revealer of this Most Great Announcement, We have removed from the Holy Scriptures and Tablets (*zabūr va alvāḥ*) the law prescribing the destruction of books (*ḥukm-i maḥv-i kutub*). (TB 25/ MMM 121)

Aqdas content. I refer to this Glad-Tiding as the abrogation of "book burning" as the term is more familiar than "the destruction of books" (*maḥv-i kutub*). In the Tablet of the World, Bahā'u'llāh also refers to "the burning of books" (TB 91). In the Aqdas, Bahā'u'llāh declares: "God hath relieved you of the ordinance laid down in the Bayān concerning the destruction of books" (K77). Note 109 likewise refers to this Bayānic prescription. From the specificity of this law, a general principle may be inferred to fend against any such repression.

Response to modernity. The specific abrogation here has to do with a law in the Persian Bayān VI.6 (Browne 1987, 377–78). Inherent in this repeal of specific legislation is a general principle which applies to a wider, more historic religious practice, as the Bābī law was never implemented.

In the Dark Ages, censorship was used by church authorities to stamp out heresy. The Fourth Lateran Council in the year 1215 proscribed the works of Aristotle. Later, in 1564, the Council of Trent established the Index of Forbidden Books, in force for centuries. And, in 1633, Galileo was forced by the Inquisition to recant his Copernican belief that the earth was not the center of the universe. Three and a half centuries later, the Church herself recanted. The positive principle complementing the abrogation of book burning is arguably freedom of the press. Freedom of the press was enshrined in the Constitution of the United States in 1791 by adoption of the First Amendment, which states: "Congress shall make no law . . . abridging freedom of speech or of the press." This, too, is respected in the Bahā'ī teachings.

Sciences and Arts

Text. The Muslim religious establishment in Persia were generally opposed to the acquisition of European sciences. The Bāb had also discouraged the study of European sciences. The following text presents a marked contrast:

> ***The Eleventh Glad-Tidings***
>
> It is permissible to study sciences and arts (*taḥṣīl-i 'ulūm va funūn*), but such sciences as are useful (*'ulūmī ka nāfi' ast*) and would redound to the progress and advancement of the people (*va sabab va 'illat-i taraqqī-yi 'ibād ast*). Thus hath it been decreed by Him Who is the Ordainer, the All-Wise. (TB 26/ MMM 121)

Aqdas content. The Aqdas passage that stands behind this Glad-Tiding reads simply: "We have permitted you to read such sciences as are profitable unto you, not such as end in idle disputation; better is this for you, if ye be of them that comprehend" (K77). While expressed as permission by Bahā'u'llāh, 'Abdu'l-Bahā actively promoted the study of Western science.

Response to modernity. In this Glad-Tiding, Bahā'u'llāh is clearly sacralizing education, the model of which is Western education. Udo Schaefer has already drawn attention to affinities between the Bahā'ī doctrine of education and the philosophy of the Enlightenment (1983, 161).

This doctrine is developed in 'Abdu'l-Bahā's *Treatise on Civilization*, already referred to above, a work which Browne considered to be primarily secular (Browne 1987, 250). Lithographed in 1882, it is, in fact, the earliest dated Bahā'ī publication, although it is thought to have been preceded by an undated lithograph of the *Kitāb-i Īqān* (Buck 1995). I believe it is methodologically sound to use the *Treatise on Civilization* as indirect attestation of Bahā'u'llāh's thinking circa 1873, as the treatise was written just two years later.

The author remarks: "Today throughout the five continents of the globe it is Europe and most sections of America that are renowned for law and order, government and commerce, art and industry, science, philosophy and education" (SDC 10). Later in this treatise, 'Abdu'l-Bahā singles out the island of Japan as a model of development and progress, that Persia might do well to emulate. After praising Japan's adoption of "techniques of contemporary progress and civilization, promoting sciences and industries of use to the public, and striving to the utmost of their power and competence until public opinion was focused on reform" (SDC 111), 'Abdu'l-Bahā concludes: "Observe carefully how education and the arts of civilization bring honor, prosperity, independence and freedom to a government and its people. . . . If necessary, education should even be made compulsory" (ibid.). It would appear that Japan as well as England and France (SDC 110–11) are regarded as models of that secular virtue, "progress."

Work as Worship

Text. The following exhortation stresses the importance of a work ethic. It is expressed as a personal obligation, but with societal consequences. There is obviously a relationship between individual moral values and social ethics. The following statement is traditional in the sense that Islam provides a precedent for it: The celebrated mystic of Islam, Ibn al-'Arabī (1992), had already accorded the status of worship to work performed in the absence of worship: "Most people complain that this world, their work to secure their sustenance, and their work as householders for their families, take time away from their worship. Know that work done heedfully, with consideration for others, in accordance with proper behavior, for the pleasure of Allah, is also worship."

Bahā'u'llāh has expanded on this concept somewhat. Ibn al-'Arabī answers the problem of time taken away from worship, while Bahā'u'llāh adds work to the time of worship. The former is a substitute, the latter an extension of worship. The gravity Bahā'u'llāh attaches to work represents an emphasis of a higher magnitude. While the work ethic was never enshrined as a pillar of Islam, this ethic was taught as a fundamental Bahā'ī principle:

The Twelfth Glad-Tidings

It is enjoined upon every one of you to engage in some form of occupation, such as crafts, trades and the like (*bi-amr min al-umūr min al-ṣanāyiʿ wa al-iqtarāf wa amthālihā*). We have graciously exalted your engagement in such work to the rank of worship (*nafs al-ʿibādat*) unto God, the True One (*al-ḥaqq*). Ponder ye in your hearts the grace and the blessings of God and render thanks unto Him at eventide and at dawn. Waste not your time in idleness and sloth. Occupy yourselves with that which profiteth yourselves and others. Thus hath it been decreed in this Tablet from whose horizon the day-star of wisdom and utterance shineth resplendent.

The most despised of men in the sight of God are those who sit idly and beg. Hold ye fast unto the cord of material means, placing your whole trust in God, the Provider of all means. When anyone (*har nafsī*) occupieth himself in a craft or trade, such occupation itself is regarded in the estimation of God as an act of worship (*ʿibādat*); and this is naught but a token of His infinite and all-pervasive bounty. (TB26/ MMM 121)

Aqdas content. Except for the penultimate sentence, which is in Persian, this predominantly Arabic passage is taken verbatim from the Kitāb-i Aqdas (K33; Arabic text, KA 29–30). Missing, however, is the initial address: "O people of Bahā'!" (*Yā ahl al-Bahā'!*)" as if to universalize this passage, rendering it applicable to all the peoples of the world rather than to Bahā'īs alone. The enshrinement of the work ethic as a precept in the Bahā'ī lawcode serves to ward off any natural inclination to indigence in a Bahā'ī society.

Response to modernity. In sacralizing work, we see here the articulation of a work ethic that has some affinities with the Protestant work ethic, although a relationship between the two cannot be historically argued. That the Christian must prove his moral worth to the glory of God through proficient and reliable industry in commerce, craft, or profession, as propounded by Calvin, is the Puritan way, contributing, as Max Weber (1950 [1904–1905]) has shown, to the birth of the "spirit of capitalism" and the rise of the industrial West. Elsewhere, Bahā'u'llāh speaks of the work ethic as "the secret of wealth (*asbāb-i ghanā* [*sic*])" (HWP #80, ET: HW 53; Persian text: KM 67 reading *ghanā* instead of *ghanā'*; cf. PED 896).

House of Justice

Text. This is one of the foundational texts for the creation of a democratically elected consultative body, known as the Universal House of Justice, first elected in 1963, on the centenary of Bahā'u'llāh's declaration. As Bahā'u'llāh envisioned it, this institution would eventually be invested with legislative authority, for the progressive application to human society of Bahā'u'llāh's laws and principles for the new age. Although Bahā'u'llāh's teachings require various practical applications of his unity-based peace plan, the overarching responsibility of the Universal House of Justice is to ensure that the emerging world civilization evolves infrastructures and policies that are based on justice and conduce to peace:

> ***The Thirteenth Glad-Tidings***
> The men of God's House of Justice (*rijāl-i bayt-i 'adl-i ilāhī*) have been charged with the affairs of the people (*umūr-i millat*). They, in truth, are the Trustees of God among His servants and the daysprings of authority in His countries.
>
> O people of God! That which traineth the world is Justice (*'adl*), for it is upheld by two pillars (*du rukn*), reward and punishment (*mujāzāt va mukāfāt*). These two pillars are the sources of life (*ḥayāt*) to the world. Inasmuch as for each day there is a new problem and for every problem an expedient solution, such affairs should be referred to the Ministers of the House of Justice that they may act according to the needs and requirements of the time. They that, for the sake of God, arise to serve His Cause, are the recipients of divine inspiration from the unseen Kingdom. It is incumbent upon all to be obedient unto them. All matters of State (*umūr-i sīyāsīyat-i kull*) should be referred to the House of Justice, but acts of worship (*'ibādāt*) must be observed according to that which God hath revealed in His Book.
>
> O people of Bahā (*yā ahl-i bahā'*)! Ye are the dawning-places of the love of God and the daysprings of His loving-kindness. Defile not your tongues with the cursing and reviling of any soul, and guard your eyes against that which is not seemly. Set forth that which ye possess. If it be favourably received, your end is attained; if not, to protest is vain. Leave that soul to himself and turn unto the Lord, the Protector, the Self-Subsisting. Be not the cause of grief, much less of discord and strife. The hope is cherished that ye may obtain true education in the shelter of the tree of His tender mercies and act in accordance with that which God desireth. Ye are all the leaves of one tree and the drops of one ocean. (TB 26–27/ MMM 122–23)

Aqdas content. This Glad-Tiding, in its entirety, is a re-revelation from the Tablet of Effulgences (*Ishrāqāt*). The eighth "Effulgence," from which the thirteenth Glad-Tiding is taken, is prefaced by the statement: "This passage, now written by the Pen of Glory, is accounted as part of the Most Holy Book" (MHB 91–92). The eighth *Ishrāq* is thus regarded as an extension of the Aqdas, which is why it is included in the authorized English translation of the Aqdas. For related Aqdas texts, cf. K42, K52, K29, K147.

House of Justice. There is, in this text, a certain measure of separation of church and state. Religious obligations are left inviolate. Although the institution itself is based on social values informed by Bahā'u'llāh's revelation, the kinds of decisions the Universal House of Justice is mandated to legislate are of a practical, one might say secular, nature. Just as the Judaeo-Christian ethic informs North American and European court systems, so does the Bahā'ī ethic provide normative standards for the exercise of justice within a Bahā'ī system. Thus, the Universal House of Justice is given the authority to act on matters on a case-by-case basis, "according to the needs and requirements of the time." For related Aqdas texts, cf. K88, K 187, K158.

Reward and Punishment. The authority to execute justice requires setting boundaries on acceptable and unacceptable behavior. Force is the servant of justice, although the use of force must be constrained by specific measures justifying its application.

Bahā'ī Virtues. The purpose of a Bahā'ī's life is to acquire virtues, and to carry forward an ever-advancing civilization. The development and proper functioning of the Universal House of Justice greatly depends on the character of individuals that make up a society. For society to become a just society, the prevailing standards of justice within any system of government require the support of responsible citizens. Otherwise, justice is vitiated.

Response to modernity.

House of Justice. For a global society, certain universal standards can alone ensure the uniform application of justice. The Marxist critique of structured economic injustice, for example, identifies market hegemonies and various forms of exploitation. Adoption of measures that regulate free markets and, at the same time mobilize the world's resources for the benefit of those countries most in need at any given time, requires a situational, needs-based deliberation on actions to be taken, constrained by overarching principles of justice. This is possible only when international consensus is achieved on such standards. The emergence of an international community of nations, along with the reification, legislation, and implementation of international law, advances the world towards a global civilization predicted by the majority of futurists. Bahā'u'llāh's own vision of an emerging world civilization was, to say the least, precocious enough for any thinker of the nineteenth century. The concept of a world religion as providing a universal system of personal and social values is one of the unique features of Bahā'u'llāh's system. Principles, in order to be effective, require a certain measure of institutionalization, and for this purpose, Bahā'u'llāh conceived of the Universal House of Justice, which eventually was brought into being in 1963.

Reward and Punishment. Reward and punishment (*mujāzāt va mukāfāt*), in Bahā'ī thought, fall within the province of justice. In sacralizing justice, Bahā'u'llāh seems to have secular models in view. Reflexive evidence of this comes from Bahā'u'llāh's interpreter, 'Abdu'l-Bahā, who writes: "Freedom of conscience and tranquility of heart and soul is one of the duties and functions of government, and is in all ages the cause of progress in development and ascendancy over other lands. Other civilized countries acquired not this preeminence, nor attained unto these high degrees of influence and power, till such time as they put away the strife of sects out of their midst, and dealt with all classes according to one standard. All are one people, one nation, one species, one kind. The common interest is complete equality; justice and equality amongst mankind are amongst the chief promoters of empire." 'Abdu'l-Bahā concludes this passage by remarking: "Interference with creed and faith in every country causes manifest detriment, while justice and equal dealing towards all peoples on the face of the earth are the means whereby progress is effected" (TN 87).

Bahā'ī Virtues. The last section of this Glad-Tiding is an apostrophe to Bahā'īs to maintain the lofty ideals they profess by corresponding standards of conduct. Bahā'īs are counselled to be united. By authenticating civic virtues with personal integrity reinforced by group solidarity, Bahā'u'llāh bids his followers to promulgate his teachings, to thereby become agents of transformation in bringing a message of hope and unity to a fractured world.

Visitation

Text. Regarding a widespread practice, the following text has to do with saint veneration. While such a practice is not condemned, it is constrained by the countervailing principle of moderation, as set forth below:

> ***The Fourteenth Glad-Tidings***
>
> It is not necessary to undertake special journeys (*ziyārat*) to visit the resting-places of the dead. If people of substance and affluence (*ṣāḥibān-i qudrat va vus'at*) offer the cost of such journeys to

> the House of Justice (*bayt-i 'adl*), it will be pleasing and acceptable (*maqbūl va maḥbūb*) in the presence of God. Happy are they that observe His precepts. (TB 27–28/ MMM 123)

Aqdas content.

Visitation. No corresponding Aqdas or supplemental text was found, a minor exception to the thesis that the content of the Tablet of Glad-Tidings is primarily based on the Bahā'u'llāh's previous legislation. The outward concern of this Glad-Tiding is to unburden the religiously minded of their sense of obligation in undertaking arduous journeys for the purpose of "visitation" of the shrine of a saint. A widespread practice in his world at the time, Bahā'u'llāh must have seen the expenditures required for such journeys as being beyond the means of many, and, for those who could afford it, a less than optimal use of financial resources.

House of Justice. That same religious impulse can just as readily be satisfied through contributing the expense of such journeys to the Universal House of Justice, as a living shrine, as it were. Presumably, the same measure of personal blessing would accrue from such an action. The Aqdas refers to the House of Justice in several places in the text (K42, K52, K29 and K147).

Response to modernity.

Visitation. This not exactly a case of the desacralizing of a religious practice, but rather its modification. In the Muslim world, tombs of the Shī'ī Imāms, Ṣūfī mystics, warriors, martyrs, and patriarchs represent rich options for expression of personal piety and the seeking of intercession by the saints for personal forgiveness and blessing. Various reform movements in the past have turned a critical eye on the practice of saint veneration, which Bahā'u'llāh is here moderating. Bahā'īs have their own shrines, and "pilgrimage" to the Bahā'ī shrines in Haifa is not constrained by this Glad-Tiding.

House of Justice. Contributions of personal wealth to this institution is not charity, but rather a philanthropic act. Other kinds of expenditures considered to be excessive or extravagant are also disapproved of in Bahā'ī texts.

Constitutional Monarchy

Text. Cole characterizes Bahā'u'llāh's thought as representing a "precocious advocacy of democracy" invigorated by his "millenarian ideas"

(1992, 3). The fifteenth and final Glad-Tiding makes explicit the kind of democracy Bahā'u'llāh publicly endorsed:

> **The Fifteenth Glad-Tidings**
>
> Although a republican form of government (*jumhūriyat*) profiteth all the peoples of the world, yet the majesty of kingship (*shawkat-i salṭanat*) is one of the signs of God. We do not wish that the countries of the world should remain deprived thereof. If the sagacious combine the two forms into one, great will be their reward in the presence of God. (TB 28/ MMM 123)

Aqdas content. Bahā'u'llāh respected the institution of monarchy. The expression, "majesty of kingship" (*shawkat-i salṭanat*) is akin to the Persian expression *shawkati shāhāna*, which Steingass glosses as "imperial majesty" (PED 767). Although kings are individually and collectively addressed in the Aqdas, the issue of constitutional monarchy is not. For such precedents, we look to texts supplementary to the Aqdas. Bahā'u'llāh made public his preference for constitutional monarchy, on the order of the British model. In the Tablet of the World (*Lawḥ-i Dunyā*), Bahā'u'llāh writes: "The system of government which the British people have adopted in London appears to be good, for it is adorned with the light of both kingship and of the consultation of the people" (TB 93/MMM 53). His advocacy of constitutional monarchy notwithstanding, political realities dictated the exercise of discretion. As previously mentioned, in the copy of the *Lawḥ-i Bishārāt* which the Bahā'īs sent Baron Rosen sometime prior to 1893, Browne observes that "the Bahā'īs appear to have thought it expedient to suppress . . . the 15th and last clause, recommending constitutional government" (Browne 1893, xxv, n. 1).

Response to modernity. Sacral kingship has had a long history—venerable and not so venerable—in the Orient. Its 2,500-year legacy was a proud heritage of Persia until the 1979 revolution in Iran. Bahā'u'llāh conserves the notion of sacral kingship while desacralizing absolutism. In sacralizing the parliamentary system, England is held up as a model. In this regard, Bahā'u'llāh has singled out for recognition one specific act of British legislation along with the democratic structure of British governance. In his Tablet to Queen Victoria (*Lawḥ-i malikah wiktūriya*), Bahā'u'llāh states: "We have been informed that thou hast forbidden the trading in slaves, both men and women. This, verily, is what God hath enjoined in this wondrous Revelation. . . . We have also heard that thou hast entrusted the reins of counsel into the hands of the representatives of the people (*zimām al-mushāwara bi-ayādī al-jumhūr*). Thou, indeed, hast done well" (PB 33–34, Arabic text in AMR 133, cf. Cole 1992, 7–8).

There is a question of legislative priority here. Did Bahā'u'llāh forbid slavery prior to Queen Victoria's decree? Historically, the answer has to be negative. The British Parliament had already outlawed the slave trade itself in 1807, authorizing search and seizure of suspect ships and payment for the liberation of slaves. This secular reform was in large part due to the antislavery movement led by abolitionists William Wilberforce and Thomas Clarkson. In 1833, Britain outlawed slavery entirely. This was in advance of President Lincoln's "Emancipation Proclamation" of January 1, 1863. Such reforms were taking place in the secular world prior to Bahā'u'llāh's declaration in that same year. However, Bahā'u'llāh is the first founder of a world religion to explicitly abolish slavery by divine decree.

For the purposes of this discussion, Queen Victoria clearly acted on her own in the context of her own enlightened policies. Bahā'u'llāh endorses England's nineteenth-century democratic reforms, particularly as enacted in the Reform Act of 1867, which greatly extended parliamentary suffrage. What is relevant to the discussion at hand is that Bahā'u'llāh clearly has the British model in mind, and has sacralized this essentially secular form of governance. Again, possibly for the first time in the history of religions, the founder of a world religion has legislated or endorsed a system of governance. Islam had no such system holistically speaking, for much that we find in the historic Muslim empires was the result of Arab conquerors assimilating and adapting elements of the art of governance from culturally superior civilizations.

Bahā'u'llāh's Summary

Text. The Bahā'ī Faith has its immediate roots in the Bābī movement, on Islamic soil, growing far beyond the bounds of Islam itself. At the same time, Babism might, in a certain sense, also be thought of as a "reform" of Islam, parallel to one reformer's project of an "Islamic renaissance." Nonetheless, one scholar has noted that Babism, like Malkum's reform, entailed the use of specifically Islamic terminology, but for purposes fundamentally alien to the Islamic faith (Algar 1973, 59). This is all the more true with respect to Bahā'ī reforms. In the following text, Bahā'u'llāh distances his reforms from both Islam and Babism, and, in principle of course, from any religious practice that foments discord:

> In former religions (*maẕāhib-i qabl*) such ordinances as holy war (*ḥukm-i jihād*), destruction of books (*maḥv-i kutub*), the ban on association and companionship with other peoples or on reading certain books had been laid down and affirmed according to the exigencies of the time (*bi-muqtaẕīyāt-i vaqt*); however, in this

> mighty Revelation (*dar īn ẓuhūr-i a'ẓam*), in this momentous Announcement, the manifold bestowals and favours of God have overshadowed all men, and from the horizon of the Will of the ever-Abiding Lord, His infallible decree hath prescribed that which We have set forth above. . . . We earnestly beseech God—exalted be His glory—to aid the rulers and sovereigns, who are the exponents of power and the daysprings of glory, to enforce His laws and ordinances. He is in truth the Omnipotent, the All-Powerful, He Who is wont to answer the call of men. (TB 28–29/ MMM 123–24).

Aqdas content. The paragraph following the fifteenth Glad-Tiding is similar to a passage from the Tablet of the World, which states: "The unbelievers and the faithless have set their minds on four things: first, the shedding of blood; second, the burning of books; third, the shunning of the followers of other religions; fourth, the extermination of other communities and groups" (TB 91). In the Tablet of Glad-Tidings, the first three social evils are the same, with the fourth being "the ban . . . on reading certain books" (TB 28).

Beyond ideological genetics, there is some direct textual dependence on the Aqdas as well: All of the Arabic text of GT12 (except for the final sentence) is taken verbatim from K33, cited in its entirety except for the address to Bahā'īs (thus universalizing the Bahā'ī work ethic). GT2 seems to derive from K144 with several words added. GT13 is dependent on the Eighth Splendour (*Ishrāq*).

Response to modernity. The Islamic background of the Bahā'ī Faith largely accounts for much of the tenor of Bahā'ī thought, but does not wholly explain its post-Islamic content and worldview. This interplay of Islamic and non-Islamic elements is difficult to sort out, but the result of this ideological transformation was, in any event, the emergence of an independent world religion. Scholarship has naturally come to identify the obvious Islamic components of Bahā'ī thought, but scholarship has yet to describe adequately the historical and religious metamorphosis of Bahā'ī ideology from its ideological chrysalis.

A progressive distancing from Islam became an important element in the emergent Bahā'ī self-identity. Amanat, summing up the successive stages of Bābī/Bahā'ī reform, states: "In the aftermath of the Babi persecutions of 1852 and the exile to Iraq, Bahā'ullāh gradually transformed the messianic militancy of the Bābīs into a pacifist, largely nonpolitical current. . . . The social message of the new faith spilled over the bounds of the Babi religion and implied in its universalism a greater reconciliation with the needs of the modern secular world. Increasingly in the closing decades of the nineteenth century, Bahā'ī social doctrine tended to distance itself from its own Shi'ite origin and move in the direction of modern morality and ethics. The Babi legacy was no doubt crucial in the way the Bahā'īs were able to adopt this essentially non-Islamic outlook" (Amanat 1989, 414).

It is interesting to note that Bahā'u'llāh sought to reverse the direction of influence, by addressing epistles (individual and collective)—in a rather forceful, theophanic voice—to the reigning potentates of his day, in Europe and West Asia. As 'Abdu'l-Bahā had characterized the relation between East and West: "Even as education and progress travel from West to East, so does the spiritual fire travel from East to West" (ABL 49). Bahā'u'llāh's global reformist agenda surpasses the Islamic mind-set in scope, and may, from a certain point of view, represent the sacralization of typically secular concerns.

Conclusion. In a metaphysical realm of discourse, beyond praise or blame of the West, Bahā'u'llāh goes so far as to account for the ascendancy of the West. In the Tablet of Wisdom (*Lawḥ-i Ḥikmat*), Bahā'u'llāh states: "When the eyes of the people of the East were captivated by the arts and wonders of the West, they roved distraught in the wilderness of material causes, oblivious of the One Who is the Causer of Causes, and the Sustainer thereof, while such men as were the source and the wellspring of Wisdom never denied the moving Impulse behind these causes, nor the Creator or the Origin thereof. Thy Lord knoweth, yet most of the people know not" (TB 144). This is a truth claim, pure and simple. It is beyond verification or falsification.

The Tablet of Glad-Tidings seems to have been a call for world reforms, both religious and political. Generally, Bahā'u'llāh endorsed certain secular reforms (constitutional monarchy, adoption of Western sciences by the Muslim Middle East) and proposed others (peace negotiations and a global summit for disarmament, universal language), while stipulating that religions—principally Christianity, Islam, and the Bābī movement—should abandon such practices such as confession, celibacy, mendicancy, and so forth. In a word, Bahā'u'llāh wanted to sacralize that which was conducive to world peace and the unity of humanity, and to end religious practices that were militant, ascetic, and fundamentalist in nature. In terms of the relative weight of each Glad-Tiding, there seems to have been a certain unevenness to the proposed reforms. Nonetheless, the *Lawḥ-i Bishārāt* comes close to being the most programmatic and representative epitome of Bahā'u'llāh's world reforms to be found in a single work.

Bahā'u'llāh's response to modernity is at the same time his response to the West. At the end of the *Lawḥ-i Bishārāt*, Bahā'u'llāh actually characterizes the Glad-Tidings as divine legislation ("laws and ordinances"). These principles—some representing European civic virtues—are sacralized. Through the agency of the "Proclamatory Aqdas," Bahā'u'llāh set in motion this sacralization process through spiritualization of "civil religion" at its finest. In fine, Bahā'u'llāh refined and systematized certain emergent "global values" and the sacralized secular power in the interests of world-reform.

The Tablet of Glad-Tidings was addressed to the peoples of the world, delivered to scholars, hand-copied, lithographed, printed, translated, and presented to various individuals as representing the basic Bahā'ī agenda for world reform. Although all of Bahā'u'llāh's estimated 15,000 individual works—the bulk of it correspondence—is considered revelation, the universal Tablets, especially those which I call representations of the "Proclamatory Aqdas," form a class of their own.

Bahā'u'llāh himself is reported to have said: "Had this Cause been revealed in the West, had Our verses been sent from the West to Persia and other countries of the East, it would have become evident how the people of the Occident would have embraced Our Cause" (GPB 253). Hand of the Cause of God (a Bahā'ī dignitary), George Townshend mades the following observation (evidently with Shoghi Effendi's assent): "Bahā'u'llāh from the beginning seems to have realized the special capacity of the progressive and enterprising West. He took the most vigorous steps possible to bring the Truth of the Age to the knowledge of the West and its leaders. Debarred from delivering His message to Europe in person, He wrote from a Turkish prison a general Tablet to the Christians, and another Tablet to the Sovereigns and leading men of the world but especially to the rulers of Christendom" (GPB vi).

For Bahā'īs, the *Lawḥ-i Bishārāt* enjoys a certain preeminence, along with several other texts, among the writings of Bahā'u'llāh. In the words of 'Abdu'l-Bahā: "Direct thine attention to the holy Tablets; read thou the *Ishrāqāt*, *Tajallīyāt*, the Words of Paradise, the Glad Tidings, the *Ṭarāzāt*, the Most Holy Book. Then wilt thou see that today these heavenly Teachings are the remedy for a sick and suffering world, and a healing balm for the sores on the body of mankind. They are the spirit of life, the ark of salvation, the magnet to draw down eternal glory, the dynamic power to motivate the inner self of man" (SWAB 61). This is, of course, based on a diagnosis of disunity as the source of the world's societal travail.

Once the world sees itself as one homeland, according to a Bahā'ī perspective, international cooperation can proceed apace, to address the physical crises humanity faces, such as overpopulation, hunger, disease, and civil war, to name a few. The Tablet of Glad-Tidings, as an epitome of Bahā'u'llāh's revelation, was intended to be read by political leaders and leaders of thought as well, in order to plant the seeds of world peace and world unity in the minds of those in the nineteenth century who had the power to effect change, and, in some cases, had the power to effect changes rather decisively. Bahā'u'llāh's efforts, as history records, went unheeded. His influence on the world would, at best, be considerably delayed and only gradually felt.

There is some historical regret in all this. In a little-known Tablet, 'Abdu'l-Bahā laments a lost historical opportunity, in which Europe's potential receptivity to Bahā'u'llāh's program of world reform was unrealized. As though born out of time as well as out of place, oppression in Bahā'u'llāh's native land is contrasted with the climate of openness in Europe: "A thousand years must elapse before Persia can, by the aid of material power, rise to the height of the peoples and governments of Europe. . . . But for his chains and prison, Bahā'u'llāh by this time would have gained absolute ascendancy over the minds and thoughts of the peoples of Europe. . . . Ponder then in your heart, what the coming of Bahā'u'llāh would have achieved! Had he appeared in Europe, its people would have seized their opportunity, and his Cause, by virtue of the freedom of thought, would by this time have encompassed the earth" (Shoghi Effendi 1926, 30–31). This Tablet of Abdu'l-Baha was translated by Shoghi Effendi in a letter dated 12 January 1923 to the National Spiritual Assembly of the United States. Note that pronomial references to Bahā'u'llāh are not capitalized by Shoghi Effendi here.

The evidently sacralized secularisms of some of the Glad-Tidings possibly finds its analogue in the Turkish *'urfī* theory of the Sulṭān's powers (Levy, EI[1] 4:1031), in which the basis for secular lawmaking arises when the Islamic lawcode does not provide a solution for a given social problem. In such cases, the standards of "necessity" and "reason" may be invoked to enact legislation with the force of law (Mardin 1962, 102). In the Tablet of Glad-Tidings, necessity and reason are invoked as adjuncts to revelation, the authority needed to balance the secular with the spiritual.

In his sociology of the Bābī and Bahā'ī religions, Peter Smith identifies social reformism, modernization, and millennial perspective as a major motif in Bahā'ī consciousness during the formative period: "The second major motif which permeated the Baha'i Faith in the 1866–1921 period represented a complex of religious and social concerns centring [sic] on the idea of the transformation of the world. These concerns involved both a clear millennial vision and a programme of more 'secular' social reformism. Both elements were strongly imbued with a religious ethos, however, and both formed part of what was regarded as the latest stage of God's plan for mankind" (1987, 74).

The Glad-Tidings may be analyzed in the context of modernity, arguably as a response to it. This is proposed as a framework of analysis, and is not meant to detract from the intrinsic originality of Bahā'u'llāh's reforms, nor to reduce them to mere reactions to modernity. Modernity simply provides a context for the text. The response is a creative, religious solution, in which the perceived values of modernity are sacralized, integrated into a unifying paradigm, and placed under the moral and social ethical constraints of religion. The history of the future will alone determine whether or not Bahā'u'llāh's response to modernity has in any way acted as a catalyst for an emerging global self-consciousness, one that reintegrates secular and sacred domains.

V

A Symbolic Profile of the Bahā'ī Faith

Abstract

Advanced study of the Bahā'ī Faith must still deal with basics. While considerable progress has been made in historical research on Bābī and Bahā'ī origins, much foundational work in Bahā'ī studies remains to be done at the level of text. Based on primary sources, this study will present a "symbolic profile" of Bahā'ī consciousness, to the extent that it is shaped by the writings of Bahā'u'llāh and ancillary texts. To order and classify the symbols, this profile will employ Ninian Smart's dimensional model of religion, using the present writer's acronym, DREEMS (Doctrinal, Ritual, Ethical, Experiential, Mythic, Social). Sherry Ortner's key symbols paradigm, consisting of thought-orienting "root metaphors" and action-inciting "key scenarios," completes the profile, while John Wansbrough provides insight into the formation of a new religious ethos through a process of symbolic transformation. This study will highlight some of the predominant Bahā'ī symbols, to which others may surely be added.

Bahā'ī Symbol Theory

What makes a religion distinctive? Islam affords an analogy. In *The Sectarian Milieu*, John Wansbrough discusses the emergence and formation of the early Muslim community. Islam arose from within a pre-existing "sectarian milieu"—a welter of "hardly distinguishable confessional groups" (SM 98). Contemporary historical sources disclose "the fact of Arab hegemony in the Fertile Crescent but virtually nothing of the confessional community called Islam" (SM 118). What, then, led to the emergence of "Islam" as a distinct ethos, beyond the Arab

Note: This chapter was published in the *Journal of Bahā'ī Studies* 8.4 (1998): 1–48, by permission of the State University of New York Press.

ethnos? It was not the Arab conquests in which the self-definition of Islam inhered: "The elaboration of Islam was not contemporary with, but posterior to the Arab occupation of the Fertile Crescent and beyond" (SM 99). Islam, as a religion, was not coeval with conquest. The political force of the early Arab expansion of the first two Islamic centuries did little to advance the ethos of the religion itself. A religious ethos requires interpretation and development.

Imagery reifies the abstract. The ethos of Islam was shaped, in part, by a constellation of powerful, thought-orienting symbols. "Fundamental to the documentation of confessional identity," Wansbrough asserts, "was selection of appropriate insignia from the monotheist compendium of symbols, *topoi*, and theologoumena" (SM 99). When these took shape and crystallized into their final form, they became "schemata of revelation" which "eventually generated a kind of subsidiary imagery," fixed within an "initial range of symbols" (SM 100). Rather than the military and political fact of conquest by Arabs who professed Islam, it was "the collection of confessional insignia which," according to Wansbrough, "eventually crystallized as 'Islam'" (SM 128). "Similarly," Wansbrough continues, "the ecclesiological imagery of Aphrahat and Ephrem exhibits the successful, if occasionally strained, adaptation of a quite extraordinary range of motifs whose original symbolic value for the authority of the Church was anything but obvious" (SM 102–103). Whether in Islam or in early Syriac Christianity, symbols serve to orient the thoughts of the believer, inspiring and modelling strategies for action. An emergent symbol canon plays an emblematic role in communal self-definition.

Symbols migrate. They can be taken up or assimilated from one tradition by another. This phenomenon involves a process of "symbolic transfer" (SM 102), resulting in a "transmission history of symbols" (SM 103). "The migration of symbols," Wansbrough observes, "may be either productive or reductive" but "the crucial process is after all one of assimilation." "It is hardly surprising," as Wansbrough points out, "to find that those descriptions of community origins associated with the monotheistic confessions exhibit more similarities than differences" (SM ix). While there are certainly formal similarities among the Western religions, this study will argue that the differences are paradigmatic. While symbols may be quarried from prior traditions and taken up in a new tradition, the symbols are reinterpreted in their new setting. How does this relate to the formation of a distinctive Bahā'ī ethos?

The Persian roots of the Bahā'ī Faith are well known. Classical Persian poetry—particularly Perso-Islamic mysticoerotic poetry—is the source of much of Bahā'u'llāh's imagery. Much of Bahā'ī symbolism may in fact be of pre-Islamic. Some symbols are ancient, and are inherited, like an ancestral gene pool, from one historically contiguous tradition to the next. Symbols of Christian, Jewish, and Mesopotamian origin were doubtless mediated through both Islam and Persian cultural traditions. In the Persian symbolic landscape, it stands to reason that, while prescinding from arguing any direct symbolic genealogy, the pre-Islamic stratum would certainly include elements from the symbolic constellation underlying Persian Christianity.

Originality must still be factored into analysis of these images. "However derivative the components, however disparate their original symbolic values and underlying mythologies," Wansbrough states, "their retention in a fresh configuration entails a successful semantic shift" (SM 102). This "fresh configuration" of symbols also involves a successful paradigm shift. The emergence and crystallization of Bahā'ī identity derives from its universal impulse, not from its ethnic origins, and resides in its symbolic insignia, its grammar of images—images that are derivative, but reconfigured by a dynamic originality.

Crucial to the crystallization of a distinctive Bahā'ī paradigm, and to an elaboration of the Bahā'ī ethos, were several factors, not the least of which was 'Abdu'l-Bahā's role in formulating and furthering a core set of Bahā'ī "principles" and Shoghi Effendi's privileging of Bahā'ī texts in what texts he chose to render into English. While acknowledging these elaborative developments, this study will focus primarily on some of the predominant and formative key symbols in Bahā'u'llāh's writings. Such a project may be considered an exercise in what Ninian Smart terms "worldview analysis" (1985, 2).

In his analysis of the Bahā'ī symbolic vision, Alessandro Bausani writes: "An expression like: 'the dove of eternity sings on the branches of the Ṭūbā tree' (the name of a tree symbolic of Muslim paradise) is susceptible of three levels of interpretation: (a) *realistic level*: in a pretty garden on a verdant tree a dove sings fascinating melodies; (b) *mystic-symbolic level*: in the Gardens of Paradise, outside of this lowly world, saints and blessed ones sing the praises of God; (c) *realistic-symbolic level*: Bahā'u'llāh at an exact moment in our time sends forth into the world a renewing spirit that will recreate it and give it form again in unitary visible forms, revealing his Writings in a definite place on the earth (the vicinity of Mt. Carmel). The spatial and temporal concreteness, therefore, remains but makes itself translucent with eternity" (Bausani 1979, 43).

This expression, "*translucent with eternity*," is instructive, particularly with respect to the symbol's opacity. A symbol is opaque until it is understood. It need not even be explicable. It is sufficient for it to be intuited. For the one to whom the symbol makes inspirational sense, the symbol is translucent, at once a way of looking at present reality, and at the same time affording a glimpse of the potential future, of a possible collective scenario, of the ideal real, the translucent shadows of the spiritual world to which a Bahā'ī is ontologically and morally committed.

These symbols take on a life of their own. In the inner world of spiritual consciousness, Bahā'u'llāh speaks of "subtle mysteries." These are described as the "fruits of communion" with God in the garden of the heart. "By My life, O friend," Bahā'u'llāh writes, "wert thou to taste of these fruits, from the green garden of these blossoms which grow in the lands of knowledge, beside the orient lights of the Essence in the mirrors of names and attributes—yearning would seize the reins of patience and reserve from out thy hand, and make thy soul to shake with the flashing light, and draw thee from the earthly homeland to the first, heavenly abode in the Center of Realities, and lift thee to a plane wherein thou wouldst soar in the air even as thou walkest upon the earth, and move over the water as thou runnest on the land" (SV 3–4). A series of potent images impels the believer to recreate waking life. Like dream-logic, Bahā'ī symbolism is the logic of a vision of the world at peace, given its initial moral and spiritual impetus by Bahā'u'llāh. This poetic vision is a resource. It instills faith. If such faith is ceative, it expresses itself in action. In this way, faith shapes social reality.

An exhaustive survey of symbols that occur, for example, in Bahā'u'llāh's correspondence, is not required for determining dominant motifs. A frequency inventory of motifs in Bahā'u'llāh's writings would simply amount to a statistical, academic exercise, with an uncertain validity in the Bahā'ī experience of Bahā'u'llāh's writings, given its selective and limited exposure to them. Although the corpus of this Bahā'ī scripture is enormous—it is estimated that Bahā'u'llāh "revealed" around 15,000 "Tablets" of which some 7,000 are extant—those texts which exerted the most profound influence on Bahā'ī communal consciousness are a relatively small and select number of the best-known and widely circulated works of Bahā'u'llāh. It is methodologically sound, therefore, to restrict data selection to the most renown and influential writings of this charismatic, messianic founder.

Bahā'u'llāh's acknowledged masterpieces include, among other works, the following: *The Most Holy Book* (1873), Bahā'u'llāh's weightiest work; *The Book of Certitude* (1861–62), Bahā'u'llāh's foremost doctrinal work; *The Hidden Words* (1858), Bahā'u'llāh's principal ethical work; *The Seven Valleys* (1856), Bahā'u'llāh's greatest mystical work; *The Essence of the Mysteries*, with its "Seven Cities"; *The Four Valleys*, complement of the *The Seven Valleys*; *The Tablet of Tajallīyāt*, with its four Effulgences; the *Tablet of the World* (1891), with its "five fundamental principles for the administration of the affairs of men"; the celebrated *Sura of the Temple* (1869), inscribed in the form of a pentacle, with Bahā'u'llāh's epistles to Pope Pius IX (1869), Napoleon III (1869), Czar Alexander II, Queen Victoria (1869) and Nāṣiru'd-Dīn Shāh (1868) inscribed within each of the five radial points of the star; the *Tablet of Ṭarāzāt*, with its six "Ornaments"; *The Tablet of Ishrāqāt*

(1885), with its the nine "Splendours"; the *Kalimāt-i Firdawsīya* (1889), with its eleven "Leaves of Paradise"; the *Tablet of Bishārāt* (1885 or later), with its fifteen "Glad-Tidings"; the *Words of Wisdom*, with its twenty-two aphorisms; the *Epistle to the Son of the Wolf* (1891), with excerpts from most of these Tablets.

On the basis of these representative texts, it is possible to create a "symbolic profile" of the Bahā'ī Faith. Twelve "key symbols" are divided into two classes: key scenarios (action-inspiring narratives or mythic/cosmic events) and root metaphors (thought-orienting images). Each key symbol has three facets: Personal, Proclamatory, and Global. "Personal" refers to individual spirituality. "Proclamatory" relates to Bahā'u'llāh's eschatological role and authority as "World Reformer." "Global" emphasizes the actual content of Bahā'u'llāh's world reforms. Thirty-six texts have been selected. Unless otherwise noted, all transliteration supplied in these texts is based on my own reading of the Persian and Arabic originals.

A Symbolic Profile of the Bahā'ī Faith as Represented in the Writings of Bahā'u'llāh

Dimension	Key Scenario	Root Metaphor
Doctrinal	The Promised One	Physician
Ritual	The Covenant	Wine / Water of Life
Ethical	Illumination	Mirrors / Gems
Experiential	Lover and Beloved	Journey / Path
Mythic	The Maid of Heaven	Lote-Tree / Sinai
Social	Crimson Ark / Holy Mariner	Paradise

Key Scenarios

*Doctrinal: **The Promised One***

The symbol of the "Promised One" may be conceived of as a "prophetic/apocalyptic scenario." Its strategy of action is recognition of Bahā'u'llāh's prophetic credentials, leading to the embrace of faith in his revelatory authority, followed by a transformation in the believer's own life, as he/she seeks to translate belief into action. The prominence of this key symbol is self-evident. For the nonspecialist in Bahā'ī studies, one validating warrant for the privileging of this key symbol might well be the fact of its lexicalization in Wendi Momen's *A Basic Bahā'ī Dictionary*. (Focused encyclopedias are useful in sketching consensus.) There, the entry "Promised One, the" is glossed: "The Promised One of the Bayān, 'Him Whom God Shall Make Manifest': Bahā'u'llāh. The

Promised One of Islam, the Qā'im: the Bāb. Generally, the Promised One of all religions: Bahā'u'llāh" (BBD 188). Although this term is conceptually shared with Bahā'u'llāh's forerunner, the Bāb, and, to a lesser extent, with Christ and Muḥammad in their respective roles as fulfiller figures, Bahā'u'llāh is the primary referent.

In Bahā'ī texts one finds a certain dialectic between theology and history, embodied in the concept of "Progressive Revelation." Progressive Revelation may be thought of as the theophoric movement in history achieving its most definitive, though not final, expression in the advent of Bahā'u'llāh. Like Einstein's advancement of a theory of relativity in the physical universe, Bahā'u'llāh advanced a theory of religious relativity in the spiritual and moral universe—a theory that explains differences among religions in light of their similarity of purpose. In Christian terms, this is the Bahā'ī counterpart to "salvation-history," the religious "message" of history (SM 1). The poetic depiction of this view of history is symbolically concentrated in the figure of the "Promised One" within the context of Progressive Revelation (the Bahā'ī technical term for successive prophetic dispensations). Some typical texts in which the Promised One is mentioned are as follows:

> *Personal*: The Sūra of Vafā: "Say, God is my witness! The Promised One Himself (lit., *haykal al-maw'ūd*) hath come down [from heaven], seated upon the crimson cloud (*ghamām al-ḥamrā'*) with the hosts of revelation (*junūd al-waḥy*) on His right, and the angels of inspiration (*malā'ikat al-ilhām*) on His left, and the Decree hath been fulfilled at the behest of God, the Omnipotent, the Almighty. . . . Hearken thou (*isma'*) unto the Words of thy Lord (*kalimāt rabbika*) and purify thy heart (*ṭāhir ṣadraka*) from every illusion (*kull al-ishārāt*) so that the effulgent light of the remembrance of thy Lord may shed its radiance upon it, and it may attain the station of certitude (*al-mūqinīn*)." (TB 182–83/ AKA 172)

Analysis. Key to personal salvation is recognition of Bahā'u'llāh as the "Promised One." The conviction that prophecy fulfillment has transpired, that the eschaton has been consummated, characterizes what scholars call a "realized eschatology." Once decoded, the messianic dignity of the "Promised One" plays on traditional millenarian tensions, brought to life historically by the nineteenth-century chiliastic movements of Shaykhism and Bābism. If Bahā'u'llāh's prophetic credentials are true, it follows that Bahā'ī doctrine has the same warrant of authenticity.

> *Proclamatory*: Tablet to Czar Alexander II: "O peoples of the earth! . . . Say: This is an Announcement (*naba'*) whereat the

> hearts of the Prophets and Messengers (*afidāt al-nabīyīn wa al-mursalīn*) have rejoiced. This is the One Whom the heart of the world (*qalb al-'ālam*) remembereth and is promised in the Books of God, the Mighty, the Glorified (*al-maw'ūd fī ṣaḥā'if Allāh al-'azīz al-ḥakīm*). . . . Say: I verily have not sought (*mā aradtu*) to extol Mine Own Self (*vaṣf nafsī*), but rather God Himself (*nafs Allāh*) were ye to judge fairly." (PB 29/AMR 54)

Analysis. The "Promised One" expresses a key scenario of prophecy and fulfillment. The symbol of the Promised One presupposes messianic expectations in the world's major religions. This is phenomenologically borne out by a comparative study of apocalyptic texts. But the idea that messianic visions are universal and convergent is entirely a Bābī concept modelled on Islamic thought, taken up in Bahā'u'llāh's proclamations. Thus, Bahā'u'llāh announces himself as the "Promised One" foretold by the prophets of old. According to Wansbrough, this kind of symbolism "reveals a concept of authority based on precedent" (SM 130).

> *Global*: Tablet to Janāb-i Mīrzā Ṣādiq: "Verily I say, this is the Day in which mankind can behold the Face, and hear the Voice, of the Promised One (*āfāq-i ẓuhūr*). The Call of God (*nidā-yi ilāhī*) hath been raised, and the light of His countenance (*anvār-i vajh*) hath been lifted up upon men. . . . Great indeed is this Day! The allusions made to it in all the sacred Scriptures as the Day of God attest its greatness. The soul of every Prophet of God, of every Divine Messenger, hath thirsted for this wondrous Day (*yawm-i badī'*). . . . God grant that the light of unity (*nūr-i ittifāq*) may envelop the whole earth, and that the seal, 'the Kingdom is God's,' may be stamped on the brow of all its peoples." (GWB 10–11 [VII]/MHB 15)

Analysis. This last passage illustrates a problem in translation, where the idea of "the Promised One" is supplied by the context of the text rather than as a technical term. What is rendered "the Promised One" is literally "Horizons (plural!) of Revelation" (*āfāq-i ẓuhūr*; sing. *ufuq*). The precise technical term for "Promised One" in Bahā'ī texts is the rather colorless word, *maw'ūd* (PED 1346). Recognition of the Promised One is linked with a mission—on the part of both the Promised One and his followers—of unity (*ittifāq*). The term used here may also be rendered "harmony" or "concord" (PED 15).

The "Promised One" is a symbol of world-historical proportions. Bahā'u'llāh foretells the will of God for humanity in this age, Bahā'īs believe, and forecasts the future on the basis of his messianic role in shaping it. As Bahā'u'llāh states: "Even as He [Jesus] saith: 'But ye cannot bear them now.' That Dawning-Place of Revelation saith that on that Day He Who is the Promised One will reveal the things which are to come. Accordingly in the Kitāb-i Aqdas, and in the Tablets to the Kings, and in the Lawḥ-i Ra'īs, and in the Lawḥ-i Fu'ād, most of the things which have come to pass on this earth have been announced and prophesied by the Most Sublime Pen" (ESW 148). When the promises of the Promised One come to pass, they validate his prophetic credentials.

Ritual: ***The Covenant***

In the context of Bahā'ī studies, certain problems arise in the use of the term *ritual* as a classification of Bahā'ī practices. This problem has been discussed elsewhere (Buck 1996b).

The Covenant is a Bahā'ī key scenario, the importance of which is empirically indicated by the fact that it is lexicalized and explicated in four distinct entries in *A Basic Bahā'ī Dictionary* (s.v. Day of the Covenant; Covenant, Greater and Lesser; Covenant of Bahā'u'llāh; Covenant-breaker, BBD 64 and 60–62). The Covenant obliges Bahā'īs to not only recognize the counsels and laws of Bahā'u'llāh, which are binding on every Bahā'ī, but to recognize the authority of the elected, legislative Bahā'ī councils as well. One might conceive of the "Covenant" motif as an "authority scenario"—concerned with spiritual authority in general and with successorship in particular. Ortner's requirement that a key scenario function as a "strategy for action" is satisfied here, in that the Covenant is a symbol stressing obedience.

In Weberian terms, the "Covenant of Bahā'u'llāh" accentuates Bahā'u'llāh's charisma, its devolution upon his successors ('Abdu'l-Bahā, Shoghi Effendi), and its routinization in Bahā'ī administrative institutions (the Universal House of Justice, National and Local Spiritual Assemblies). In the words of Shoghi Effendi, the Covenant is a divinely ordained "instrument" ordained by Bahā'u'llāh "to direct and canalize these forces let loose by this Heaven-sent process [the Revelation of Bahā'u'llāh], and to ensure their harmonious and continuous operation after His ascension" (GPB 237). The following passage has to do with what is generally referred to as the "Primordial Covenant" (*mithāq*), referring to a famous verse in the Qur'ān in which God asks His creatures, "Am I not your Lord?" (*alastu bi-rabbikum*—Q. 7:172):

> *Personal*: Persian Hidden Word #19: "O My Friends (*ay dūstān-i man*)! Have ye forgotten that true and radiant morn (*ṣubḥ-i ṣādiq-i rawshānī-rā*), when in those hallowed and blessed surroundings ye were all gathered in My presence beneath the shade of the tree of life (*shajara-yi anīsa*), which is planted in the all-glorious paradise (*firdaws-i a'ẓam*)? Awe-struck ye listened as I

> gave utterance to these three most holy words: O friends! Prefer not your will to Mine, never desire (*hargiz ma-khwāhīd*) that which I have not desired for you, and approach Me (*nazd-i man*) not with lifeless hearts (*dil-hā-yi murda*), defiled with worldly desires and cravings. Would ye but sanctify your souls (*ṣadr-rā*), ye would at this present hour (*ḥāl ān*) recall that place and those surroundings, and the truth of My utterance (*bayān-i man*) should be made evident unto all of you." (HWP #19; ET: HW 29) (Note: In the Persian text, HWP #19 is actually numbered #19 and #20. This affects the subsequent numbering, so that the Persian and English numbers are off by one (but occasionally not, which is very confusing. Thus there are eighty-two Persian *Hidden Words* in English, and eighty-three in Persian. Persian text of HWP #19 [and #20]: KM 32–33.)

Analysis. The Primordial Covenant of preeternity is a paradigm for all time, especially the present. In Islam, the Primordial Covenant (Q. 7:172) is, in the words of Annemarie Schimmel, "the metahistorical foundation between God and humankind" (Schimmel 1994, 253). In religious epistemology, the confessional community itself is a cognitive category: the *ecclesia* (SM 130–31). In Wansbrough's terms, Islam's privileging of the Primordial Covenant may be understood as "legitimation of communal membership" which involves "the introduction of a theophany" in a process of docrinal development that is historically "posterior to the social formulation" (ibid.) of the community. The Primordial Covenant is transferred from preëxistence to the present:

> *Proclamatory*: Tablet of Splendours: "Say: 'Yea, by Him that rideth upon the clouds!' Paradise is decked with mystic roses (*jinnat bi-awrād al-ma'ānī*), and hell (*al-sa'īr*) hath been made to blaze with the fire of the impious (*nār al-fujjār*). Say: The light hath shone forth from the horizon of Revelation, and the whole earth hath been illumined at the coming of Him Who is the Lord of the Day of the Covenant!'" (TB 119/ AKA 69)

Analysis. "Reference to the past," as Wansbrough notes, "is paradigmatic and retroflexive, again an expression of nostalgia" (SM 132). To this *Hidden Word* (Persian #19) we may usefully apply Wansbrough's description of *numen*, in which legitimation is subsumed "as the product of a private vision" (SM 131). Bahā'u'llāh employs a numinous form of legitimation for ecclesiastical purposes. "There is no question here of historical location," Wansbrough comments, "the achievement—in this case the recollection of the primordial event—is personal, timeless in the sense that the precise circumstances of the epiphany do not really matter." "In this context, the eternity of divine utterance,"

Wansbrough adds, "being always and anywhere available, does not conflict with the alleged historicity of its public manifestation" (SM 131).

In Bahā'ī salvation-history, the Covenant of God entails prophetic successorship from age to age, attested by the covert terms of prophecy. It is generally accepted that the individual believer has an obligation to embrace eschatological fulfillment when the advent of a true prophet occurs, constituting a fresh locus of authority.

> *Global*: Book of the Covenant: "O ye that dwell on earth (*ay ahl-i 'ālam*)! The religion of God is for love and unity (*muḥabbat va ittiḥād*); make it not the cause of enmity or dissension. . . . We fain would hope that the people of Bahā may be guided by the blessed words: 'Say: All things are of God.' This exalted utterance (*kalima-yi 'ulyā*) is like unto water for quenching the fire of hate and enmity (*nār-i żaghīna va baghżā'*) which smouldereth within the hearts and breasts of men. By this single utterance contending peoples and kindreds will attain the light of true unity (*nūr-i ittiḥād-i ḥaqīqī*). . . . That which is conducive to the regeneration of the world (*ḥayāt-i 'ālam*) and the salvation of the peoples and kindreds of the earth (*nijāt-i umam*) hath been sent down from the heaven of the utterance of Him Who is the Desire of the world." (TB 220, 222, 223/ MMM 400, 403)

Analysis. "Within the monotheist tradition," Wansbrough writes, "the organizing principle of a confessional community may be located in its definition of authority" (SM 50). Bahā'u'llāh's authority may be viewed as the organizing principle of the Bahā'ī community. "The concepts of legitimation and redemption, familiar to every student of comparative religion," he elsewhere states, "are sociologically archetypal and more or less constant in the analysis of monotheist faiths" (SM 130–31). Wansbrough speaks of Islam, and by extension any of the monotheistic faiths, as "theodicy based upon a public epiphany deposited as the document of revelation" (SM 130). Under these terms of reference, Bahā'u'llāh is the epiphany and his writings the record of revelation. That revelation serves as the founding document, the constitution of the community.

The Covenant of Bahā'u'llāh has both external and internal dimensions. The external covenant concerns world unity. The internal covenant is focused on internal unity within the Bahā'ī community. The Covenant governs and guarantees the integrity of the community, as it models unity in a grand social experiment. While the Bahā'ī Faith has little or no "ritual" in the performative sense of the term, its "ritual" elements are expressed in communal and individual worship. The Covenant, while subscribed to at the level of the individual, functions as the collective agreement to abide by the leadership provided by elected Bahā'ī institutions (Local Spritual Assemblies, National Spiritual Assemblies, The Universal House of Justice). To merit moral authority in the eyes of the world as a model of global unity, the integrity of the Bahā'ī community must be maintained, free of schism, while allowing for mature and constructive freedom of expression.

Ethical: ***Illumination***

"Illumination" covers a range of Bahā'ī metaphors that are obviously luciferous in nature. This is an ethically charged key scenario. Its strategy for action is to orient the believer in the direction of spiritual enlightenment, resulting in a transformation of thought and action. Various entries in *A Basic Bahā'ī Dictionary* attest the symbolic importance of illumination. These entries include specific metaphors and names of Tablets that are constructed on models of illumination, to wit: century of light; Day of God; Dayspring of Revelation; Daystar; *Ishrāqāt*, Splendours; *Tajallīyāt*, Effulgences; *Ṭarāzāt*, Ornaments; Seven Candles of Unity. These have one image in common: enlightenment. Three representative texts are as follows:

> *Personal*: Persian *Hidden Words* #73: "O My Friend (*ay dūst-i man*)! Thou (*tu*) art the day-star (*shams*) of the heavens of My holiness (*samā'-i quds-i manī khud-rā*), let not the defilement of the world (*kusūf-i dunyā*) eclipse thy splendor. Rend (*kharq kun*) asunder the veil of heedlessness (*ḥijāb-i ghaflat-rā*), that [untranslated text: "free of covering or veil" (*bī-parda va ḥijāb*)] from behind the clouds (*khalf-i saḥāb*) thou mayest emerge resplendent and array all things (*jamī'-i mujūdāt-rā*) with the apparel of life (*bi-khil'at-i hastī*)." (HW 50, Persian text, KM 62)

Analysis. Radiance, metaphorically, is typically the property of spirituality. But sometimes it can be its opposite, as in some instances of fire imagery. Thus, light imagery has its "dark" side as well. In HWP #57, Bahā'u'llāh warns that association with the ungodly "turneth the radiance of the heart into infernal fire." Light is capable of being either eternal or infernal, visible or eclipsed. Either way, the power to influence is potent and potentially omnipresent, like the spiritual sun dawning on the symbolic landscape, constrained mainly by the obstructing resistance of individual willpower. Here, the individual is urged to overcome self and passion, in order to radiate spirituality.

> *Proclamatory*: Tablet of Maqṣūd: "The Great Being saith (*ḥaẓrat-i mawjūdāt mī-farmāyad*): The Tongue of Wisdom (*zabān-i khirad*) proclaimeth: He that hath Me not is bereft of all things. Turn ye

away from all that is on earth and seek none else but Me. I am the Sun of Wisdom and the Ocean of Knowledge (*manam āftāb-i bīnish va daryā-yi dānish*). I cheer the faint (*pazhmurdigān-rā*) and revive the dead (*murdigān-rā*). I am the guiding Light that illumineth the way (*manam ān rushanāyī ka rāh-i dīda binamāyam*). I am the royal falcon on the arm of the Almighty (*manam shāh-bāz-i dast-i bī-nīyāz*). I unfold the drooping wings of every broken bird (*par-i bastigān-rā bigushāyam*) and start it on its flight (*va parvāz biyāmūzam*)." (TB 169/ AKA 103)

Analysis. Illumination requires a source of illumination. Here, Bahā'u'llāh is represented as an illuminator, not a redeemer. The "Sun of Wisdom and the Ocean of Knowledge" evokes a panoramic image in which the entire landscape is suffused with the power and animus of God, focused through Bahā'u'llāh. By means of this pantheistic symbolism, the revelation of God is represented as the ground of spiritual being. The wisdom/knowledge complex serves as a mental and moral beacon along the spiritual path. In this use of extended, but mixed, metaphors, the bird-souls are animated by the royal falcon, a figure of phoenixlike powers. The grandeur of such a scene serves as a proclamation of the greatness of the Bahā'ī revelation.

Global: Epistle to the Son of the Wolf: "The utterance of God is a lamp (*mishkāt-i bayān*), whose light (*miṣbāh*) is these words (*īn kalima*): ['O peoples of the world! (*ay ahl-i 'ālam*)—missing in translation.] Ye are the fruits of one tree, and the leaves of one branch (*hama bār-i yak dārīd va barg-i yak shākhsār*). Deal ye one with another with the utmost love (*bi-kamāl-i maḥabbat*) and harmony (*ittiḥād*), with friendliness (*maviddat*) and fellowship (*ittifāq*). He Who is the Day-Star of Truth beareth Me witness! So powerful is the light of unity (*nūr-i ittifāq*) that it can illuminate the whole earth (*āfāq-rā*). . . . This goal excelleth every other goal (*īn qaṣd sulṭān-i maqāṣid*), and this aspiration is the monarch of all aspirations (*īn amal malik-i āmāl*)." (GWB 288 [CXXXII]/ MHB 184/ ESW 14)

Analysis. Individual enlightenment is internal. But society is external. By his enlightenment, Bahā'u'llāh provides the means for not only individual, spiritual advancement, but for the progress of society as well. In Bahā'ī soteriology, personal salvation is dynamically linked to the needs of humanity. Systematic theologians may refer to this as mutual salvation. Belief in Bahā'u'llāh is a commitment to mutual salvation. As the sun (the Day-Star) is the source of all daylight, the power of unity to illumine the entire world is logically entailed. This image also suggests its opposite: disunity—or darkness—the Bahā'ī counterpart of "chaos" in its own Genesis myth of a world socially recreated. Bahā'u'llāh has globalized light imagery to express his gospel of unity. (As a textual note, the sentence from this last passage, "Ye are the fruits of one tree, and the leaves of one branch" appears to be a citation from the Tablet to Mānakchī [DD 7–8].) Bahā'ī ethics are predicated on unity.

Experiential: ***Lover and the Beloved***

The strategy for action in this key scenario is to deepen the identification of the believer with God, as "revealed" or personified in Bahā'u'llāh. In Bahā'ī terms, the "heart" is defined as: "The symbolic centre of an individual's spirituality" (BBD, s.v. "heart," 101). Similarly, the heart of Bahā'ī spirituality is God, who is revealed through Bahā'u'llāh, the perfect mirror of the attributes and will of an otherweise inscrutable Deity. As the symbol of God, Bahā'īs relate to Bahā'u'llāh as the Beloved. A carryover from Islamic mysticism (Ṣufism), this may be thought of as a "mystical scenario." Poetically, this relationship is expressed in a variety of motifs:

> *Personal*. [Untitled Tablet]. "Hear Me, ye mortal birds! (*ay bulbulān-i fānī*). In the Rose Garden of changeless splendor (*dar gulzār-i bāqī*), a Flower (*gulī*) hath begun to bloom (*shikufta*), compared to which every other flower is but a thorn (*khār*), and before the brightness of Whose glory the very essence of beauty (*jawhar-i jamāl*) must pale and wither (lit., *bī miqdār*). Arise, therefore (*pas*), and, with the whole enthusiasm of your hearts (*az dil*), with all the eagerness of your souls (*az jān*), the full fervor of your will (*ravān*), and the concentrated efforts of your entire being (*az tan*), strive to attain the paradise of His presence (lit., *liqā-yi bī-zavāl*), and endeavor to inhale the fragrance of the incorruptible Flower (lit., *gul-i bī mathāl*), to breathe the sweet savors of holiness (*rāyiḥa-yi quds-i ruḥānī*), and to obtain a portion (*ḥiṣṣa*) of this perfume of celestial glory (lit., *nasīm-i khwush-i ṣabā-yi ma'navī*). Whoso followeth this counsel will break his chains asunder, will taste the abandonment of enraptured love (*īn pand band-hā bigusilad va silsila-yi junūn-i 'ishq-rā bijunbānad*), will attain unto his heart's desire (*dil-hā-rā bi-dil-dār rasānad*), and will surrender his soul into the hands of his Beloved (lit., *jān-hā-rā bi-jānān sipārad*)." (GWB 320–21/ MHB 206/DD 30)

Analysis. In one of his Words of Wisdom, Bahā'u'llāh says: "The essence of love is for man to turn his heart to the Beloved One, and sever himself from all else but Him, and desire naught save that which is the desire of his Lord" (TB 155). Here, "rose and nightingale" imagery, suffused with Ṣūfī symbolism, vivifies and intensifies the experience of believer identification with the Theophany, Bahā'u'llāh, pictured here as a celestial rose. The Lover/Beloved relationship is expressed in the relationship of birds to the exquisite setting of a rose garden, in which a rose of surpassing beauty enthralls the bird-souls. Just as the quest for the Beloved is the paramount goal of Islamic mysticism, so, too, the mystical scenario in Bahā'ī texts is the quest for the Beloved as the revelation ("glory" or "splendor") of God, implicit in the name, Bahā'u'llāh.

> *Proclamatory*: [Untitled Tablet]: "Behold how the manifold grace of God, which is being showered from the clouds of Divine glory (*faḍl-i subḥānī az ghamām-i raḥmānī*), hath, in this day (*dar īn ayyām*), encompassed the world (*iḥātik*). For whereas in days past (lit., *agar-cha tā hāl*) every lover (*'āshiqān*) besought and searched after his Beloved (*ma'shūq and maḥbūb*), it is the Beloved Himself Who now is calling His lovers (*ma'shūq ṭālib-i 'ushshāq mī-namāyad*) and is inviting them to attain His presence (*va maḥbūb jūyā-yi aḥbāb gashta*). Take heed lest ye forfeit so precious a favor (*īn faḍl-rā ghanīmat shamrīd*); beware lest ye belittle so remarkable a token of His grace (*va īn ni'mat-rā kam nashmurīd*)." (GWB 320/ MHB 206/DD 29–30)

Analysis. This is a proclamation that the Beloved has arrived, but with a dramatic twist. A background in the Persian mystical tradition is essential in grasping the full impact of this poignant passage. In traditional Persian poetry, it is always the lover who seeks after the Beloved. In this scene, however, Bahā'u'llāh evokes a sudden reversal of roles: It is now the Beloved who beckons the lover. The "grace" of such a turnaround cannot be lost on the reader: a real, reciprocal relationship between the lover and the Beloved is now possible. This imagery speaks to the rapport between believer and Theophany.

> *Global*: Tablet of Maqṣūd: "The Word of God is the king of words (*sulṭān-i kalimāt*) and its pervasive influence is incalculable. It hath ever dominated and will continue to dominate the realm of being. The Great Being saith: The Word is the master key for the whole world (*miftāḥ-i a'ẓam*), inasmuch as through its potency the doors of the hearts of men (*abvāb-i qulūb*), which in reality are the doors of heaven (*abvāb-i samā'*), are unlocked (*maftūḥ*). No sooner had but a glimmer of its effulgent splendour shone forth upon the mirror of love (*mir'āt-i ḥubb*) than the blessed word 'I am the Best-Beloved' was reflected therein. It is an ocean (*bahr*) inexhaustible in riches, comprehending all things (lit.,

> *dārā va jāmi'*). Every thing which can be perceived (*har-cha idrāk shavad*) is but an emanation therefrom (*ẓāhir gardad*)." (TB 173/ AKA 107)

Analysis. In this text, the Beloved is incarnated in scripture. Scripture mirrors the wishes of the Beloved. This mystical scenario helps the believer cultivate more deeply a love of God, personified in Bahā'u'llāh as the "Best-Beloved"—orienting the believer, as a strategy for action, to reliance on the "Word of God" as the "king of words." The universal ramifications of this passage are obvious: Bahā'ī scripture is placed on a par with sacred scripture, surpassing even the Bible or the Qur'ān in revelatory immediacy. Note how Paradise (the "doors of heaven") is equated with the "doors of men's hearts." The image of the Beloved focalizes and intensifies the experiential dimension of Bahā'ī life.

Mythic: ***The Maiden of Heaven***

"Scripture," as Wansbrough defines it, "is understood to record a single historical act: the transfer by angelic mediation of God's decree from a celestial to a terrestrial register" (QS 131). In Bahā'ī terms, the "angelic mediation" to which Wansbrough refers is the celestial "Maiden of Heaven" (*ḥūrī*). She is a singular houri, understood by Bahā'īs to symbolize the Holy Spirit and the source of Bahā'u'llāh's revelation. Not to be trite, but the celestial Maiden is Bahā'u'llāh's muse, as it were. Her symbolic importance is indicated by the lexical entry in *A Basic Bahā'ī Dictionary* (s.v. "Maiden of Heaven," 142–43). Although the idea of otherwordly, black-eyed damsels is quranic, Bahā'u'llāh's specific maiden imagery originated with the Bāb, who wrote in the "Sūra of the Maiden" (*Sūrat al-Ḥūrīya*): "O people of the earth! By the righteousness of the One true God, I am the Maid of Heaven (*al-ḥūrīya*) begotten by the Spirit of Bahā (*waladtanī al-bahā'*), abiding within the Mansion hewn out of a mass of ruby, tender and vibrant; and in this mighty Paradise naught have I ever witnessed save that which proclaimeth the Remembrance of God by extolling the virtues of this Arabian Youth." (*Qayyūm al-Asmā'* 29, tr. SWB 54; cited in Lambden 1997–1998, 34). To the extent that the Maiden of Heaven is symbolic, she is mythic. This does not, however, diminish her reality.

Bahā'u'llāh has described the Maiden of Heaven in a number of works. She appears to function as his alter ego or celestial twin, as it were, almost in a Manichaean sense. She also has a corporate (symbolic of faith-community) function in that she is the litmus test of spiritual perspicuity and faithfulness, in her mythic search for the faithful believer. This is what one might consider an emotively intensifying "identification scenario" in which the believer's faith in Bahā'u'llāh is deepened through contemplation on the Maiden of

Heaven's fidelity to her beloved. This figure will be explicated later, in the concluding section dealing with what is termed "the core Bahā'ī myth."

More traditionally Islamic is the pairing of houris with believers in Paradise. Here, the identification scenario predicates "admittance into Paradise" with fulfilling the will of God:

> *Personal*: Sūra of Vafā (=Wafā—titles of Arabic tablets are Persianized in Bahā'ī usage): "As to Paradise (*al-jannat*): It is a reality (*ḥaqq*) and there can be no doubt about it, and now (*al-yawm*) in this world it is realized through love of Me and My good-pleasure (*ḥubbī wa riḍā'ī*). Whosoever attaineth unto it God will aid him in this world below, and after death (*ba'd al-mawt*) He will enable him to gain admittance into Paradise (*fī jannat*) whose vastness (*arḍ*) is as that of heaven and earth. Therein the Maids of glory and holiness (*ḥūrīyāt al-'izzat wa al-taqdīs*) will wait upon him in the daytime and in the night season, while the day-star (*shams*) of the unfading beauty of his Lord will at all times (*fī kull ḥīn*) shed its radiance (*yastaḍī'*) upon him and he will shine so brightly that no one shall bear to gaze at him." (TB 189 / AKA 117–18)

Analysis. Paradise is pictured anthropomorphically on purpose. Maidens of Heaven, as inhabitants of paradise, take on a variety of symbolic functions in Bahā'u'llāh's writings. In a departure from Bahā'u'llāh's primary use of Maiden symbolism, the Qur'ān's promise of dark-eyed damsels requiting the true believer is preserved in this passage, as a traditional Islamic warrant of the reality of Paradise. Thus, the Maidens retain their eschatological function in tending to the faithful soul in heaven. On one level, this provides assurance of the afterlife—described in ideal but nevertheless earthly terms—creating a romantic expectation the sensuality of which is decoded at a higher level of discourse. While the maidens are real, they are not literal. They are actually symbolic embodiments of spiritual perfections, which have become the alter egos of faithful believers. Bahā'u'llāh disenchants Paradise of a certain amorous sensuality which too literal a reading of quranic texts entails. The Qur'ān's mysticoerotic descriptions are held to be purely symbolic. This does not disinvest Paradise of its reality, but rarefies the believer's understanding of it. The Maidens are personifications of the pearls of insight, the intimate companions of the pious soul. Individual enlightenment may be thought of as a lesser form of revelation: viz., inspiration, dependent upon Bahā'u'llāh's revelation, with which a singular Maiden par exellence is associated.

> *Proclamatory*: Tablet of Riḍvān: "Within this Paradise, and from the heights of its loftiest chambers, the Maids of Heaven (*fī hā*

> *ḥūrīyāt min a'lá al-ghurafāt*) have cried out and shouted: 'Rejoice, ye dwellers of the realms above (*ahl al-jinān*), for the fingers of Him Who is the Ancient of Days are ringing, in the name of the All-Glorious, the Most Great Bell (*nāqūs al-a'ẓam*), in the midmost heart of the heavens (*quṭb al-samā'*). The hands of bounty have borne round the cup of everlasting life (lit., *kawthar* [a river of Paradise] *al-baqā'*). Approach, and quaff your fill." (GWB 32/ MHB 29)

Analysis. In Bahā'ī understanding, the Maiden of Heaven is intimately linked with the agency of revelation. Her role eludes precise formulation. It is safest to say that the Maiden of Heaven is coincident with the act of revelation. The Maiden's first role is that of annunciator. In this respect, she is the counterpart of the archangel Gabriel in Islam. The Maiden's first appearance to Bahā'u'llāh was during his imprisonment in the "Black Pit" (Sīyāh-Chāl) in 1852, where, in a vision, she assured Bahā'u'llāh of God's protection and, moreover, of God's revelation to him. In Christian terms, this may be thought of as Annunciation. In this passage, the Annunciation becomes proclamation, a public announcement of Bahā'u'llāḥ's advent, not *the* Maiden, but by the houris of paradise generally. This heavenly acclaim compensates for the relative lack of earthly recognition, as only a small proportion of the world's population professes to be Bahā'īs.

> *Global*: [Untitled Tablet]: "Through the might of God and His power (*bi-quva-yi yazdānī va qudrat-i ruḥānī*), and out of the treasury of His knowledge and wisdom (*kanz-i 'ilm va ḥikmat-i rabbānī*), I have brought forth and revealed unto you the pearls that lay concealed in the depths of His everlasting ocean (*la'ālī-yi ṣadaf-i bahr-i ṣamadānī*). I have summoned the Maids of Heaven (lit., *ḥūrīyāt-i ghuraf-i sitr va ḥijāb-ra*) to emerge from behind the veil of concealment, and have clothed them with these words of Mine—words of consummate power and wisdom (*dar maẓāhir-i īn kalimāt-i muḥkamāt maḥshūr nimūdam*). I have, moreover, with the hand of divine power, unsealed the choice wine of My Revelation (lit., *inā'-i musk-i aḥadīya-rā*), and have wafted its holy, its hidden, and musk-laden fragrance (*ravā'iḥ-i quds-i maknūna*) upon all created things. Who else but yourselves is to be blamed if ye choose to remain unendowed with so great an outpouring of God's transcendent and all-encompassing grace, with so bright a revelation of His resplendent mercy?" (GWB 327–28/MHB 210–11)

Analysis. Beyond the Qur'ān, in Bahā'ī texts, the Maiden imagery focuses attention on Bahā'u'llāh, the earthly locus of Paradise. This Bahā'ī "myth" even extends beyond Bahā'u'llāh: the Maiden also has an apocalyptic function, orienting Bahā'īs to the advent of another Manifestation of God a millennium or so (future timing unspecified, but understood as 1,000 or more years later, based on other Bahā'ī texts) in the future, as indicated in Persian Hidden Words #77.

In this passage, the dark-eyed damsels are "clothed" in scripture. The implication being that the reading of scripture actuates an encounter with the maidens, who, in mystic transport, unveil to the believer the divine "wisdom and power" that reside in the text. Bahā'ī scripture is thus transcendentalized, but universalized at the same time. While paradise is typically thought of in transcendent, "vertical" terms, scripture potentializes paradise in mundane, "horizontal" terms. If its function is to orient humanity to the will of God, then sacred scripture potentially has global, world-historical influence. It is premature to assess the present or eventual impact of the Bahā'ī revelation, which is seen as having covert as well as overt influences on globalization.

Social: ***The Crimson Ark and the Holy Mariner***

The Crimsom Ark forms part of what one might refer to as a faith-affirming "scenario of assurance and solidarity," which conduces to social cohesion. The "Holy Mariner" is modelled on the patriarch Noah, an archetypal savior figure. While the specific imagery of the Ark traces back to the Bāb, I have not yet found a Bābī text in which the Mariner himself actually figures in a key scenario or dramatic scene. Indicative of their twinned, symbolic importance, both Crimson Ark and Holy Mariner are found as entries in *A Basic Bahā'ī Dictionary* (s.v. "Ark, Crimson" [24] and "Holy Mariner, Tablet of the" [105]). The Crimson Ark, much like Noah's ark, is a symbol of salvation. The Ark is a corporate symbol. It suggests that individual salvation cannot be dissociated from the community of the saved. The following texts are representative of such imagery:

> *Personal*: Words of Paradise: "Blessed (*ṭūbá*) is he who preferreth (*akhtāra*) his brother before himself. Verily, such a man is reckoned, by virtue of the Will of God, the All-Knowing, the All-Wise, with the people of Bahā who dwell in the Crimson Ark (*ahl al-Bahā' fī al-safīnat al-ḥamrā'*)." (TB 71/ AKA 39)

Analysis. In this beatitude from the "Tenth Leaf of the Most Exalted Paradise," admittance into the Crimson Ark is conditioned not only on belief, but on altruism. If the purpose of faith is to effect a spiritual transformation of the individual, it follows that belief must be actualized and amplified in moral behavior. In this "scenario of assurance and solidarity," there is, indeed, assurance of salvation, but only if one who professes to be a Bahā'ī actually becomes a Bahā'ī in character. This is not a matter of faith versus works, as in St. Paul or Luther, because faith and works cannot be opposed in Bahā'ī thought. One is the complement of the other. Faith is the catalyst of personal transformation. Perfection (whether by faith or works) is not required, but rather a personal transformation effected by certitude of faith (belief in Bahā'u'llāh), moral rectitude (in following the Bahā'ī laws and Covenant) and sanctification (internalized holiness) which may be said to constitute a Bahā'ī "order of salvation"—to borrow a Christian concept expressed in systematic theology. When moral behavior is socially referenced, each individual's actions are seen as having communal significance. The ark-dwellers, as the biblical narrative suggests, must live together in harmony. The Ark saves not only from without, but from within.

> *Proclamatory*: Kitāb-i Aqdas (*al-Kitāb al-Aqdas*): "How great the blessedness that awaiteth the king who will arise to aid My Cause in My Kingdom, who will detach himself from all else but Me! Such a king is numbered with the companions of the Crimson Ark—the Ark which God hath prepared for the people of Bahā. All must glorify his name, must reverence his station, and aid him to unlock the cities with the keys of My Name, the omnipotent Protector of all that inhabit the visible and invisible kingdoms. Such a king is the very eye of mankind, the luminous ornament on the brow of creation, the fountainhead of blessings unto the whole world." (K84, 50)

Analysis. As with the first selection, this second text identifies the inmates of the Crimson Ark as the "people of Bahā"—the Bahā'īs. While Bahā'īs hail from every background, a Bahā'ī member of royalty, as a public figure, has a position of considerable importance. The monarch who professes to be a Bahā'ī, as had Queen Marie of Rumania who stated her Bahā'ī allegiance publicly in the Toronto *Daily Star* (28 October 1926) and now His Highness Malietoa Tanumafili II of Western Samoa, whose conversion to the Bahā'ī Faith was announced in 1973, has a distinct place of honor within the Ark. In the miasma of social chaos, the enlightened ruler is described as "the very eye of mankind," a moral beacon. A member of royalty can add greatly to the prestige of the Faith, aiding in its proclamation.

> *Global*: Tablet of Carmel: "Ere long will God sail His Ark (*safīnat Allāh*) upon thee, and will manifest the people of Bahā (*ahl al-Bahā'*) who have been mentioned in the Book of Names (*Kitāb al-Asmā'* = *Qayyūm al-Asmā'*?)." (TB 5/ GWB 16/ AKA 19; Lambden 1997–1998, 35, n. 33)

Analysis. This final passage is construed as a prophecy foretelling completion of the Seat of the Universal House of Justice on the sacred slopes of Mt. Carmel (BBD, s.v. "Ark," 23). Thus, the Ark is launched by the Holy Mariner (Bahā'u'llāh) from Baghdad, and comes to rest on Mt. Carmel. Over both land and sea, the Crimson Ark rises above the flood of social chaos. On the sacred mountain, the Ark symbolizes the Bahā'ī institutions, especially the Universal House of Justice, the elected, international Bahā'ī council that oversees the Bahā'ī world. Religion must be institutionalized before it can be truly effective in promoting reform, so long as institutions canalize spiritual energy and activity for the welfare of others. Administering the affairs of the Faith requires proficiency in the art of consultation. Its efficacy is predicated on the integrity of individual members who, collectively, function as institutions. Now that the Universal House of Justice is the helm of the Bahā'ī ship of state, it functions as the proverbial Mariner.

Root Metaphors

Doctrinal: ***Physician***

While key scenarios inspire ideal behavior, root metaphors orient thoughts. Of course, thoughts typically precede action, so the result is much the same. It may be said that root metaphors complement key scenarios.

As salvation systems, world religions have something to offer. Each religion's offer of salvation is referenced to a particular human predicament, whether that be sin, as in the case of Christianity, or suffering, as in the case of Buddhism. A religion cannot dispense salvation unless there is a presenting problem to be overcome. In the Bahā'ī worldview, the root of all social evil is disunity, from injustice to war. This is a disease model, certainly. It follows, therefore, that where there is a disease, there ought to be a cure. As the diagnosis and treatment of a disease requires a physician, spiritual disorders require the intervention of a "divine physician":

> *Personal*: Tablet to Mānakchī Ṣāḥib: "The All-Knowing Physician (*pizishk-i dānā*) hath His finger on the pulse of mankind (*rag-i jahān* [lit., pulse of the world]). He perceiveth the disease (lit., *dard*, pain), and prescribeth, in His unerring wisdom, the remedy (*darmān*). Every age (*har rūz-rā*) hath its own problem (*rāzī* [lit., secret]), and every soul (*har sar-rā*) its particular aspiration (*āvāzī*). The remedy the world needeth in its present-day afflictions can never be the same as that which a subsequent age may

require. Be anxiously concerned with the needs of the age ye live in (*imrūz-rā nigarān bāshīd*), and center your deliberations on its exigencies and requirements. . . . Say (*bigū*): O ye who are as dead (*ay murdigān*)! The hand of Divine bounty proferreth unto you the Water of Life (*āb-i zindigānī*). Hasten and drink your fill. Whoso hath been reborn in this Day, shall never die; whoso remaineth dead, shall never live." (GWB 213/MHB 138–39).

Analysis. While the remedy in this passage is not specified, the authority of the divine physician is stressed. The "All-Knowing Physician" is Bahā'u'llāh. He prescribes the cure for the world's social ills, but the remedy cannot be forced on people. While it may give the impression of being too facile, the cure offered by Bahā'u'llāh, in his capacity as the divine physician, is unity. This unity is really a complex of interlocking interventions, addressing social reforms as well as individual transformation. Still, despite its multifarious applications, the organizing principle, the healing force, is unity. Unity is not a hard pill to swallow, but it does involve a regimen. So long as humanity (the corporate patient) does not place itself under the care of the Physician, it will fail to avail itself of the cure. In the next passage, the socioreligious "cure" is proclaimed, in an open letter to Queen Victoria:

Proclamatory: Tablet to Queen Victoria: "O ye elected representatives (*aṣḥāb al-majlis*) of the peoples in every land! Take ye counsel together, and let your concern be only for that which profiteth mankind, and bettereth the condition thereof, if ye be of them that scan heedfully. Regard the world as the human body (*ka haykal insān*) which, though at its creation whole and perfect (*ṣaḥīḥ wa kāmil*), hath been afflicted, through various causes, with grave disorders and maladies. . . . That which the Lord hath ordained as the sovereign remedy (*al-daryāq al-a'ẓam*) and mightiest instrument for the healing of all the world is the union (*ittiḥād*) of all its peoples in one universal Cause (*amr wāḥid*), one common Faith (*sharī'a wāḥida*). This can in no wise be achieved except through the power of a skilled, an all-powerful and inspired Physician (*ṭabīb ḥādhiq kāmil mu'ayid*)." (GWB 254–55/MHB 164)

Analysis. From 1866–1870, in open letters to the world's most powerful rulers and religious leaders of his day, Bahā'u'llāh proclaimed his mission and the essential elements of his teachings. In his epistle to Queen Victoria (c. 1869), a solution to the world's ills is offered, in the form of a universal value system, a moral code to which all nations and peoples might subscribe. Such a proposal was intrinsically momentous and sudden, ahead of its time. At that time, however, Bahā'u'llāh did not have the status and thus the perceived authority to warrant serious consideration of his world reforms by world leaders. Apart from the veracity of the truth-claims it entails, this Hippocratic root metaphor suggests that the entire planet should recognize the prescriptive authority of Bahā'u'llāh as "a skilled, an all-powerful and inspired Physician." Time will tell whether or not the Bahā'ī religion will succeed in its utopian aims to bring about world unity.

> *Global*: Tablet to Fatḥ-i A'ẓam: "The Prophets of God should be regarded as physicians (*payāmbarān* [sic] *chun pizishkān-and*) whose task is to foster the well-being of the world and its peoples, that, through the spirit of oneness (*bi-darmān-i yigānigī*), they may heal the sickness of a divided humanity (*bīmārī-yi bīgānigī*). . . . The whole of mankind (*mardumān-ra*) is in the grip of manifold ills (*bīmārī*). Strive, therefore, to save its life through the wholesome medicine (*darmān*) which the almighty hand of the unerring Physician (*pizishk-i yazdān*) hath prepared." (GWB 80–81/MHB 59)

Analysis. As a faith-community, Bahā'īs are known for their ideological commitment to making the earth as one homeland. Whether in the realm of the secular or of the sacred, implementation of Bahā'ī ideals is effected through a variety of instrumentalities. However, most of the actual progress towards world unity to date has taken place in the secular sphere. This fact has been acknowledged in certain Bahā'ī texts, in which non-Bahā'īs have been recognized for their contributions to the advancement of peace, justice, and world order. Bahā'u'llāh praised Queen Victoria for having abolished slavery in her kingdom, especially at a time when the slave-trade continued to be practiced in the Muslim world. President Woodrow Wilson is another prime example of this kind of recognition. 'Abdu'l-Bahā once commented that Wilson and his ideals signalized the dawn of the Most Great Peace (ADJ 85). The cure was already being partially administered by enlightened leaders, as though it were the spirit of the age. This powerful root metaphor inclines Bahā'īs to interpret events that promote global unity, in both secular and sacred spheres, as evidence of a divine Physician at work, behind the scenes.

Ritual: ***Wine/Water of Life***

Sacred beverages, as portrayed in Bahā'ī texts, are elixirs of immortality, knowledge, and ecstasy. The Water of Life, for instance, was introduced by the first of three physician texts cited above. Wine is a salient motif. Its relative importance is indicated by its selection as a separate entry in *A Basic Bahā'ī Dictionary* (s.v. "Wine," 236). A recent journal article on the Bahā'ī symbolism of wine underscores its importance (Hatcher 1994b; cf. McAuliffe 1984):

> *Personal*: Persian *Hidden Word* #62: "O Son of Dust (*ay pisar-i khāk*)! Turn not away thine eyes (*chashm mapūsh*) from the matchless wine of the immortal Beloved (*az khamr bī mithāl-i maḥbūb-i lāyazāl*), and open them not (*chashm magushā*) to foul and mortal dregs (*bi-khamr-i kadra-yi fānīya*). Take (*bar gīr*) from the hands of the divine Cup-bearer (*az dast-i sāqī-yi ahadīya*) the chalice of immortal life (*ku'ūs-i bāqīya*), that all wisdom may be thine (*tā hūsh shavī*), and that thou mayest hearken (*shinavī*) unto the mystic voice calling from the realm of the invisible (*az surūsh-i ghayb-i ma'navī*). Cry aloud (*bigū*), ye that are of low aim (*ay past fitrat-an*)! Wherefore (*chirā*) have ye turned away from My holy and immortal wine (*sharāb-i bāqī-yi qudsam*) unto evanescent water (*āb-i fānī*)?" (ET: HW 46, Persian text, KM 56)

Analysis. Wine is most frequently used as a metaphor for God-intoxication induced by the revelation of Bahā'u'llāh. As the earthly locus of divinity, Bahā'u'llāh is seen as the powered presence of the sacred, the nimbus of the numinous, the incarnation of divine attributes, as God revealed. This discovery, for those who embrace it, gives cause for celebration. The celestial champagne is unsealed, so to speak, upon reunion with the Beloved (recognition of Bahā'u'llāh), but the real reward, in Bahā'ī terms, is the satisfaction gained in fidelity to Bahā'u'llāh's laws, to which wine is symbolically compared. In the preamble to the Most Holy Book, Bahā'u'llāh characterizes his law-code as "choice Wine":

> *Proclamatory*: Kitāb-i Aqdas: "By My life! He who hath drunk the choice wine of fairness from the hands of My bountiful favour will circle around My commandments that shine above the Dayspring of My creation. Think not that We have revealed unto you a mere code of laws. Nay, rather, We have unsealed the choice Wine (*raḥīq makhtūm*) with the fingers of might and power. To this beareth witness that which the Pen of Revelation hath revealed. Meditate upon this, O men of insight!" (K5–K6/KA 21)

Analysis. Wine is a heavenly beverage, symbolic of ecstasy. As a key symbol, it can never be literalized. Bahā'u'llāh has distinguished alcoholic wine from symbolic wine: "We meant by this Wine, the River of God, and His favour, the fountain of his living waters, and the Mystic Wine and its divine grace, even as it was revealed in the Qur'ān, if ye are of those who understand" (cited in Hatcher 1997, 223). The intoxication of the spirit must be earned, while the intoxication of earthly wine is simply a reflex of the nervous system to a low-level poison.

The intoxicant is outlawed, not the intoxication. The believer who abstains from wine is one who is likely to comply with other religious requirements. In the application of the Bahā'ī proscription of wine, a principle of gradualism is followed, especially in traditional cultures where wine drinking is accepted and is part of the prevalent lifestyle. As a root metaphor, wine speaks to the ritual dimension of the Bahā'ī religion (by which its legal dimension is meant), in symbolically expressing obedience to Bahā'ī law while literally forbidding, in principle and wherever practicable, the consumption of wine itself.

Bahā'u'llāh invites scrutiny of his laws and precepts, to inspire confidence in their wisdom and potential efficacy. The laws are rooted in principles—principles worthy of recognition, whose merit deserves to be celebrated. Engendering enthusiam for the Bahā'ī agenda, this passage sets a tone for the rest of the Most Holy Book and its supplementary texts.

> *Global*: Kitāb-i Aqdas: "This day, it behoveth whoso hath quaffed the Mystic Wine of Everlasting Life from the Hands of the loving-kindness of the Lord his God, the Merciful, to pulsate even as the throbbing artery in the body of mankind, that through him may be quickened the world and every crumbling bone." (K173/KA 82)

Analysis. While wine is a corporate symbol for Bahā'ī laws, these laws are intended for the world to follow. Observing Bahā'ī laws aids in the individual's spiritual progress and transformation, and has an edifying impact on society. That impact may be small, but it is cumulative.

Ethical: ***Mirror/Gems***

Reflective, radiant, and lustrous, mirrors and precious stones and pearls are often clustered together in Bahā'ī texts, with more or less equivalent symbolism. Mirrors need burnishing, gems require polishing, pearls must be lustrous rather than dull. It is not the fact of being a jewel that counts; rather, it is the quality of refinement that proves the jewel's worth. So it is that refinement of mind and heart is what counts most, yet these are not ends unto themselves. The true test of refinement is the impact of spiritual attainments on society.

Most of Bahā'u'llāh's symbolism is purely Perso-Islamic, but the immediate background of Bahā'ī symbolism is Bābī. The Bāb made extensive use of mirror imagery, to wit: "The One true God may be compared unto the sun and the believer unto a mirror. No sooner is the mirror placed before the sun than it reflects its light. The unbeliever may be likened unto a stone. . . . Indeed, if God willeth, He is potent to turn the stone into a mirror. . . . Had he wished to become a crystal, God would have made him assume crystal form" (SWB 103). As the most perfect reflective surface, the mirror of the heart is said to reflect supernal light. But the mirror must first be polished, and oriented towards the source of light, before it can reflect light. This self-refinement is expressive of ethical intent and assiduous application:

> *Personal*: The Seven Valleys: "O My Brother! (*ay barādar-i man*) A pure heart is as a mirror (*qalb-i laṭīf bi-manzala-yi ā'yīna ast*); cleanse it with the burnish of love and severance (*bi-ṣayqal-i ḥubb va inqiṭā'*) from all save God, that the true sun (*āftāb-i ḥaqīqī*) may shine within it and the eternal morning (*ṣubḥ-i azalī*) dawn. . . . Yea, these mentionings that have been made of the grades of knowledge (*marātib-i 'irfān*) relate to the knowledge of the Manifestations of that Sun of Reality (*ma'rifat-i tajallīyāt-i ān shams-i ḥaqīqat*), which casteth Its light (*nūr*) upon the Mirrors (*marāyā*). And the splendor of that light is in the hearts (*tajallī-yi ān nūr dar qulūb*), yet it is hidden under the veilings of sense (*ḥujabāt-i nafsānīya*) and the conditions of this earth (lit. *va shu'ūnāt-i 'araḍīya*—[text misread as *arḍīya*]), even as a candle within a lantern of iron (*chun sham' zīr-i fānūs-i ḥadīd*), and only when the lantern is removed (literally, *murtafa'*, "raised") doth the light of the candle shine out. In like manner, when thou strippest the wrappings of illusion (*ḥujabāt-i afkīya*) from off thine heart, the lights of oneness (*anvār-i aḥadīya*) will be made manifest." (SV 21, 23–24/AQA III: 113, 116)

Analysis. Mirrors are perfect reflectors only under perfect conditions. Bahā'u'llāh's image of the mirror is that of a brass mirror, not the mercury-coated glass we now think of as mirrors. Mirrors reflect whatever is in front of them, but cannot reflect unless polished. The burnishing of mirrors spoken of in Bahā'ī texts assumes an essential orientation of the heart's mirror towards the realm of spirit, so that what is required is not reorienting the mirror so much as refining it.

> *Proclamatory*: The Book of Certitude: "The door (*abvāb*, lit. "doors") of the knowledge (*'irfān*) of the Ancient of Days (*dhāt-i azal*) being thus closed in the face of all beings, the Source of infinite grace, according to His saying, "His grace hath transcended all things; My grace hath encompassed them all," hath caused those luminous Gems of Holiness (*javāhir-i quds-i nūrānī*) to appear out of the realm of the spirit (*'avālim-i ruḥ-i ruḥānī*), in the noble form of the human temple, and be made manifest unto all men, that they may impart unto the world the mysteries of the

unchangeable Being, and tell of the subtleties of His imperishable Essence.

These sanctified Mirrors (*īn mārāyā-yi qudsīya*), these Day Springs of ancient glory, are, one and all, the Exponents on earth of Him Who is the central Orb of the universe (*shams-i vujūd*), its Essence and ultimate Purpose (*jawhar-i maqṣūd*). . . . These Tabernacles of Holiness (*hayākil-i qudsīya*), these Primal Mirrors (*mārāyā-yi avalīya-yi azalīya*) which reflect the light of unfading glory, are but expressions of Him Who is the Invisible of the Invisibles (*ghayb al-ghuyūb*). By the revelation of these Gems of Divine virtue all the names and attributes of God, such as knowledge and power, sovereignty and dominion, mercy and wisdom, glory, bounty, and grace, are made manifest." (BC 99–100, 103/KI 74–75, 77)

Analysis. Images frequently associated with mirrors in Bahā'ī texts are gems and pearls. All three are metaphorically synonymous. In this passage, there is a shift in focus from imperfect to perfect mirrors, from imperfect to perfect gems. The perfect mirrors are the "Primal Mirrors"—the Prophets or Manifestations of God—from which all secondary mirrors borrow their light. Unique to the Primal Mirrors is their ability to translate invisible light to visible light. This, of course, is supernal light, defined as the attributes of God. Reflection of godly radiance at the human level are spiritual attributes, nearly all of which have ethical associations. Whatever the symbolism, Bahā'u'llāh's proclamations draw a dynamic connection between the prophets or "Manifestations of God" and the installation or personal discovery of the higher self.

Global: Words of Paradise: "O people of Bahā! The source of crafts, sciences and arts is the power of reflection. Make ye every effort that out of this ideal mine (*ma'dan-i ḥaqīqī*) there may gleam forth such pearls of wisdom and utterance (*la'ālī-yi ḥikmat va bayān*) as will promote the well-being and harmony (*āsāyish va ittiḥād*) of all the kindreds of the earth." (TB 72/ AKA 40)

Analysis. Development of human potential, if it fails to make the world a better place, is seen as fruitless. In the American Tibetan Buddhist tradition, this has been called "spiritual materialism." Society without religion is ill equipped to cultivate human virtues and nobility of character. Without the positive influence of religion, society can promote humanism and materialistic idealism, but this is unlikely to produce qualities of compassion and altruism, at least to the degree that religion can in its ideal form. In the Bahā'ī worldview, the measure of a person's worth is the degree to which he or she has made a positive contribution to human welfare. The alleviation of suffering, the moral and scientific education of society, and the general betterment of the human condition is integral to the Bahā'ī theology of mutual salvation. Pearls and gems are typically semiprecious or rare, as are saints, great artists, or renowned scientists. This "Word of Paradise" therefore concerns trades, professions, and scientific research, establishing a linkage between individual and social ethics.

Experiential: ***The Journey***

In her phenomenology of mysticism, Evelyn Underhill (1961, ch. 6) speaks of three motifs universally used to narrate mystical experience in forms of allegory. These are: the journey, alchemy, and love (cited by Schimmel 1982, 64). In Ṣūfī literature, the salience of these motifs cannot fail to impress the reader. The interior "journey" (*safar*) symbolizes the "wandering" (*sulūk*) of the "wayfarer" (*sālik*) on the path to God. "Alchemy" (*al-kīmiyā'*) is the soul's transformation along the way. Platonically passionate "love" (*'ishq*) leads to union with the Divine. The first and third motifs are easily intertwined in stories of the quest for the Beloved.

At the heart of Persian Ṣūfī poetry is love mysticism. Earthly love, or "metaphorical love" (*'ishq-i majāzī*), is emblematic of heavenly love. The nightingale and the rose—the lover and the beloved—is a salient motif. Allegorically, spiritual love is richly symbolized by the longing of the nightingale (*bulbul*) for the rose (*gul*, cf. Schimmel 1958). 'Aṭṭār has the nightingale exclaim: "The nightingale has no strength to love the Sīmurgh— / for the nightingale the love of the rose is enough" (Schimmel 1992a, 179).

Ṣūfī mysticism was a major stream that fed into Bahā'u'llāh's expressive style and evolving program of reform. According to Amanat, Bahā'u'llāh's early works composed in the Ṣūfī tradition "reveal a mystical outlook pivotal to his later messianic claims and his sociomoral reforms" (1989, 364). Foremost among the mystical works of Bahā'u'llāh is *The Seven Valleys* (*Haft Vādī*). Unofficially, Bahā'u'llāh's *The Seven Valleys* was the first Bahā'ī book ever published, lithographed in India by Jamal Effendi. (Because the work was published anonymously, many thought Jamal Effendi was himself the author.) The revelation of *The Seven Valleys* was occasioned by the questions of Shaykh Muḥyi al-Dīn, the Qāḍī of Khāniqayn, a village northeast of Baghdad near the Persian border. Based on 'Aṭṭār's celebrated fable, *Manṭiq al-Ṭayr* (commonly known in English as *The Conference of the Birds*), Bahā'u'llāh draws heavily on the symbolism of the mystical quest. Both Farīd al-Dīn 'Aṭṭār (d. 1220) and Bahā'u'llāh employ the symbolizing strategy of allegory to engage others in mystical experience. The *Manṭiq al-Ṭayr* is the journey of thirty birds (*sī murgh*) in quest of the King of Birds, the *Sīmurgh*. The title comes from Q. 27:16, "O men, we have been taught the speech of birds [*manṭiq al-ṭayr*]" (Rodwell). This legendary Phoenix is said to live on "Mount Qāf" at the end of the world.

A philosophical bird allegory—the *Risālat al-Ṭayr* (Treatise of the Bird) by Ibn Sīnā (d. 1037)—had set a literary precedent over a century prior to 'Aṭṭār. As a philosophical work, the protagonist of this story is the rational soul, on its path to the realm of pure Intellect. Such a conjunction (*ittiṣāl*) with celestial Intelligence was antithetical to the Ṣūfī quest, however. The tale is about a bird which, after freeing itself from the nets in which it was ensnared, joins its companions in a journey across eight mountain peaks, in quest of the lofty palace of the King beyond the eighth mountain. It is this allegory in form, though not in content, that set a literary precedent for 'Aṭṭār (Schimmel 1992a, 178). (For English translation, see Heath 1992a; cf. idem 1992b and 1994. A manuscript of Ibn Sīnā's Arabic prose treatise is archived in the Istanbul University Library [A. Y. 1458].)

Other possible sources for 'Aṭṭār's allegory include an Arabic *Risālat al-Ṭayr* (Treatise of the Bird) by Muḥammad al-Ghazzālī (d. 1111—Schimmel 1992, 178); the Persian *Risālat al-Ṭayr* (Treatise of the Bird) by Aḥmad al-Ghazzālī (d. 1126; cf. Ritter, EI^2 1: 753); and a long *qaṣīda*, the *Tasbīḥ al-Ṭuyūr* (Rosary of the Birds) by Sanā'ī (d. 1131—cited in Schimmel 1992, 178). Sanā'ī was a master of the *mathnavī*, poetry composed in rhyming hemistiches for epic purposes (ibid., 301). The masterwork on 'Aṭṭār is still that of Helmut Ritter, *Das Meer der Seele* ("The Ocean of the Soul," 1955/1976), although the space devoted to *Manṭiq al-Ṭayr* is limited.

'Aṭṭār's *Manṭiq al-Ṭayr* contains a section narrating the actual journey through seven valleys. This piece is sometimes published independently under the title *Haft Vādī* (Nurbakhsh 1990, 167–68). Once the allegory is decoded, it is clear that the flight of these birds is modelled on the Night Journey of the Prophet Muḥammad, as 'Aṭṭār (MṬ) himself intimates: "A hundred thousand hearts and souls were destroyed / Until Muḥammad one night reached ascension to heaven" (Schimmel 1982, 65). The Prophet's steed, *Burāq* (Lightning), is mentioned in 'Aṭṭār's Seventh Valley: "First put aside the Self, and then prepare / To mount Boraq and journey through the air" (CB1 205/MṬ 257). As Peter Awn observes: "The internal structure of the work resembles an ascending spiral staircase" (1987, 14: 114). Carl Ernst has already treated the symbolism of soul-birds (1992, 353–66). The Sīmurgh is a symbol of the Godhead.

Gaining insight into the structure of early Bahā'ī thought is possible by studying Bahā'u'llāh in light of 'Aṭṭār. Except for the inversion of the fourth and fifth valleys, the sequence of the valleys is identical. The Ṣūfī al-Sulamī (d. 1021 C.E.) once wrote: "Sufism has a starting point, an end, and stages in between" (Schimmel 1994, 85, n. 56). The term *maqām* (stages or station) is quranic, in the verse which reads: "None of us but hath a certain station (*maqām*)" (Q. 37:164, Nicholson 1967, 370–71).

"Stations" are attainments. They mark progress in the path of discipline. "States" are gifts of grace, flashes of experience. In the *Gulistān*, the Persian poet Sa'dī has Jacob, biblical father of Joseph, say: "My state [*ḥāl*] is that of leaping lightning" (lit., worldly lightning [*barq-i jahān*]—Sa'dī 1964; cited in Nasr 1972, 75, Persian text, n. 15). Bahā'u'llāh speaks of a condition in which one's soul is made "to shake with the flashing light" (SV 4). Rumi has expressed the distinction between the two: "The *ḥāl* [state] is like the unveiling of the beauteous bride, / While the *maqām* [station] is the [king's] being alone with the bride" (*Mathnavī* 1: 1435, Schimmel 1975, 99). Progress in reaching any or all of the "stations" was considered cumulative and thus permanent. "States," however, were experienced as states of grace—transitory, like "flashes of lightning," according to al-Junayd (Nicholson 1967, 181). One might say that, on the Ṣūfī "path" (*ṭarīqa*), there was an interplay between what in Christian terms might be referred to as works and grace.

In one of the first classic Sufi manuals—*Kitāb al-Luma' fī al-Taṣawwuf* (Book of the Flashes on Sufism)—Abū Naṣr al-Sarrāj (d. 988) enumerates seven stages along the mystical path (1914, 42–54; cited in Sells 1994, 103): (1) repentance (*tawba*), (2) abstinence (*wara'*), (3) renunciation (*zuhd*), (4) poverty (*faqr*; cf. Q. 35:16), (5) patience (*ṣabr*; cf. Q. 2:103), (6) trust in God (*tawakkul*), and (7) acceptance (*riḍā*). These are followed by ten "states" (*aḥwāl*) of the soul: watchfulness (*murāqaba*), nearness (*qurb*), love (*maḥabba*), fear (*khawf*), hope (*rajā'*), longing (*shawq*), intimacy (*uns*), tranquillity (*iṭmi'nān*), contemplation (*mushāhada*), and finally, certainty (*yaqīn*; cf. Q. 102 and 56:95), which is both the beginning and end of all of the "states." Sarrāj later adds two other states: intoxication and evanescence (Baldick 1989, 55). Al-Sarrāj's "stations" reflect a Qur'ān-based, moral psychology characteristic of Sufism's ascetic origins. Subtelny (1994) mentions Anṣārī's *Manāzil al-sā'irīn* (Stages of the Mystics), the most famous Ḥanbalite treatise on Sufism. 'Aṭṭār's sequence represents a love-centered paradigm. This shift probably occurred due to the influence of the woman mystic, Rabi'a al-'Adawīya (d. 801), who established the primacy of altruistic Love (*maḥabba*) for mystical intimacy (*uns*—see Smith 1928).

The present writer's comparison of the two *Haft Vādī* texts in Persian found that the theme of pain (*dard*) was a salient motif throughout all of Aṭṭār's seven valleys, whereas an atmosphere of ecstasy pervades Bahā'u'llāh's portrayal of the same quest. To illustrate this relationship, the translated names of each of the valleys will be paired with their corresponding technical terms in Persian. Illustrative phrases drawn from the English translations of these two texts are cited, as evidence of the recurrence of pain as 'Aṭṭār's *leitmotiv* and ecstasy as Bahā'u'llah's own innovation on 'Aṭṭār:

> 'Aṭṭār's *Haft Vādī*: (1) Quest (*ṭalab*): *By pain and grief* (CB1:170); (2) Love (*'ishq*): *Paths of misery* (CB1:173); (3) Gnosis/Insight (*ma'rifa*): *Path brings sorrow* (CB1:181); (4) Detachment (*istighnā'*): *This journey's pain* (CB1:190); (5) Unity (*tawḥīd*): *Lonely, long austerity* (CB1:191); (6) Bewilderment (*ḥayrat*): *A place of pain* (CB1:196); (7) Nothingness (*fanā'*): *This painful place* (CB1: 204). A technical discussion of each of these valleys is given by W. Skalmowski. (1992)
>
> Bahā'u'llāh's *Haft Vādī*: (1) Search (*ṭalab*): *Nor downhearted* (SV 5); (2) Love (*'ishq*): *Heaven of ecstasy* (SV 8); (3) Knowledge (*ma'rifa*): *Content with decree* (SV 12); (4) Unity (*tawḥīd*): *Ascend to heaven* (SV 17); (5) Contentment (*istghnā'*): *From anguish to joy* (SV 29); (6) Wonderment (*ḥayrat*): *Oceans of grandeur* (SV 31); (7) True Poverty and Absolute Nothingness (*faqr-i ḥaqīqī va fanā'*): *Ecstasy alone*. (SV 39)

Bahā'u'llāh does not strictly follow this sequence of valleys. Elsewhere, in his *Essence* (lit., 'Gems') *of the Mysteries* (*Jawāhir al-Asrār*)—another mystical work revealed in Baghdad—there is a section in which the mystic quest takes the form of a journey through seven cities. A comparison of the two sets of valleys/ cities is as follows:

> *Jawāhir al-Asrār*: (1) Search (*ṭalab*); (2) Love/Yearning (*'ishq wa jadhb*); (3) Unity (*tawḥīd*); (4) Wonderment (*ḥayrat*); (5) Nothingness (*fanā'*); (6) Subsistence (*baqā'*); (7) City of No Name: (a) Acquiescence (*taslīm*); (b) Contentment (*riḍa*).
>
> *Haft Vādī*: (1) Search (*ṭalab*); (2) Love (*'ishq*); (3) Knowledge (*ma'rifat*); (4) Unity (*tawḥīd*); (5) Contentment (*istighnā'*); (6) Bewilderment (*ḥayrat*); (7) True Poverty/Nothingness (*faqr-i ḥaqīqī va fanā'*).

The final valley of the *Seven Valleys* is "The Valley of True Poverty and Absolute Nothingness" (*faqr-i ḥaqīqī va fanā'*). Schimmel notes that "poverty" (*faqr*) "can become almost a coterminous synonym of *fanā'*, ('annihilation')" (1992b, 103). *Fanā'* is transcendence of the self, and *baqā'* is absorption in God. Traditionally associated with the doctrine of *fanā'* is Bāyizīd Bisṭāmī (d. 874), but Julian Baldick cautions that there is no early source for this (1989, 37). The positive notion of *baqā'* (literally, "survival" or "abiding") as well as *fanā'* has also been ascribed to al-Kharrāz of Baghdad (d. 899—Baldick 1989,

40). By the imagery of the journey, the reader is oriented towards the goal: recognition of Bahā'u'llāh as eschatological requital (cf. Fāḍil-i Māzandarānī 1923). At the end of the Valley of Knowledge, on the verge of Unity, Bahā'u'llāh states: "At this hour the morn of knowledge hath arisen and the lamps of wayfaring and wandering are quenched" (SV 16). The Persian text reads: "*Dar īn vaqt ṣubḥ-i ma'rifat ṭāl' shud va chirāgh-hā-yi sayr-i sulūk khāmūsh gasht*" (HV 108). The following three texts suggest some of the imagery associated with the key symbol of the journey, which, in context, involves a constellation of symbols:

> *Personal*: Persian *Hidden Words* #1: "O Ye People that have Minds to Know and Ears to Hear! The first call of the Beloved (*avval surūsh-i dūst*) is this: O mystic nightingale (*ay bulbul-i ma'navī*)! Abide not but in the rose-garden of the spirit. O messenger of the Solomon of love (*ay hudhud-i sulaymān-i 'ishq*)! Seek no shelter except in the Sheba of the well-beloved (*ṣabā-yi jānān*), and O immortal phoenix (*ay 'anqā-yi bāqī*)! dwell not save on the mount of faithfulness (*qāf-i vafā*). Therein is thy habitation, if on the wings of thy soul thou soarest to the realm of the infinite and seekest to attain thy goal." (ET: HW 23; Persian text: KM 21)

Analysis. An equation is drawn between the Beloved, Sheba, and the Phoenix, invoking different symbolisms, but with the same message. Ultimately God is meant. Some Ṣūfīs believed that direct beatific vision of God was possible, while others did not. Bahā'ī theology rejects the possibility that God can be seen by human eye. No ziggurat can reach that high. Mortal man cannot bridge the chasm between the finite and the infinite. But God can bridge that gap by means of revelation. Because knowledge of the will and attributes of God is relative to the degree that these are revealed, the mystic quest is best served by a pilgrimage to God's place of revelation. This, according to Bahā'ī theophanology, changes from age to age. The latest revelation of God to humanity is in the person of Bahā'u'llāh, Bahā'īs hold. This is why the Phoenix is interpreted as quintessentially God, but manifested in God as revealed in Bahā'u'llāh. For this reason, a distinction obtains between Bahā'u'llāh as an historical figure and Bahā'u'llāh's spiritual reality. Allegorically, God takes the form of the Phoenix, is revealed by the Phoenix, but both is and is not the Phoenix.

> *Proclamatory*: [Untitled Tablet]: "We have revealed Ourself unto men, have unveiled the Cause, guided all mankind towards God's Straight Path, promulgated the laws and have enjoined upon everyone that which shall truly profit them both in this world and in the next; yet they have pronounced judgement to shed My blood,

whereat the Maid of Heaven hath wept sore, Sinai hath lamented and the Faithful Spirit was made to sigh with grief." (TB 251)

Analysis. The journey is interior, but progress along the Path requires external piety and righteousness. In *The Seven Valleys*, Bahā'u'llāh makes the requirements of this journey explicit with respect to religious law: "In all these journeys the traveler must stray not the breadth of a hair from the 'Law,' for this is indeed the secret of the 'Path' and the fruit of the Tree of 'Truth'; and in all these stages he must cling to the robe of obedience to the commandments, and hold fast to the cord of shunning all forbidden things, that he may be nourished from the cup of the Law and informed of the mysteries of Truth" (SV 39–40). Holiness and mystical attainments are thus inseparable: "Be swift in the path of holiness, and enter the heaven of communion with Me. Cleanse thy heart with the burnish of the spirit, and hasten to the court of the Most High" (HWP #8, ET: HW 25–26; Persian text: KM 27).

> *Global*: Tablet of Maqṣūd: "The Great Being saith: O ye children of men! The fundamental purpose animating the Faith of God and His Religion is to safeguard the interests (*ḥifẓ*) and promote the unity (*ittiḥād*) of the human race, and to foster the spirit of love (*maḥabbat*) and fellowship (*ittifāq*) amongst men. Suffer it not to become a source of dissension and discord, of hate and enmity. This is the straight Path (*sirāṭ-i mustaqīm*), the fixed and immovable foundation." (GWB 215 [CX]/MHB 140/TB 168)

Analysis. Here, the mystic "journey" and the "Straight Path" are considered inextricable complements. This relationship between adherence to religious law and mystical striving was not always a happy one. Especially in the nineteenth century, many Ṣūfīs were antinomian, and would consider themselves above Islamic law. In many cases, this led to indulgence in wine and even addiction to opium (both are forbidden by Islam). Despite the rich legacy of classical Ṣūfism—a legacy that is extended in Bahā'u'llāh's mystical writings—the proliferation of various Ṣūfī orders not only had a demoralizing but also a divisive effect in Islam, which was not given to modern notions of pluralism. Bahā'u'llāh reintegrates the exterior and interior dimensions of religion and predicates authentic mystical attainments on the performance of both.

Mythic: ***Lote Tree/Sinai***

Sinai imagery in Bābī and Bahā'ī symbolism has both biblical and quranic roots. Bahā'u'llāh's designated successor and interpreter,

'Abdu'l-Bahā (d. 1921), clusters the image of the "Promised One" with traditional Sinai imagery: "the Blessed Beauty [Bahā'u'llāh] is the One promised by the sacred Books of the past, the revelation of the Source of light that shone upon Mount Sinai, Whose fire glowed in the midst of the Burning Bush" (WOB 127). Here, the image of Bahā'u'llāh is that of the source of revelation, rather than the recipent of it. The Sinaitic "Fire" is colored crimson.

Assimilation of Sinai imagery in Bahā'ī sources is purely typological, a process Wansbrough observes as occurring within Islam: "Exempla preserved and transmitted from the 'past' (whether or not fictive) may be the deposit of an antiquarian impulse, but also witness to a concern for present and future" (SM 130). The adducing of such exemplars is said to be "paradigmatic" in a way that is "ahistorical, formally though not substantively" (SM 130). The paradigmatic function of Lote Tree/Sinai imagery is to present Bahā'u'llāh as the classic revelator with a new twist: Instead of simply being the channel of revelation as have been previous messengers, Bahā'u'llāh claims to have been the source of revelation for those messengers. Some representative texts are as follows:

> *Personal*: Arabic *Hidden Words* #63: "O Son of Man! The light (*al-nūr*) hath shone on thee from the horizon of the sacred Mount (*al-ṭūr*) and the spirit of enlightenment (*rūḥ al-sanā'*) hath breathed in the Sinai of thy heart. Wherefore, free thyself from the veils of idle fancies and enter into My court, that thou mayest be fit for everlasting life (*al-baqā'*) and worthy to meet Me (*al-liqā'*)." (HW 18–19, Arabic text, KM 19–20; cf. Lambden 1988, 121)

Analysis. The language of revelation, usually reserved for prophets, is metaphorically applied here to the individual. There is a sense in which the knowledge of God comes about as a personal disclosure or "revelation." If the heart is likened to Mt. Sinai, the individual's higher self becomes a Moses personified, leading one in an Exodus out of slavery into the Egypt of one's baser passions. The Promised Land is Paradise which, in this case, is attainment to the "Presence" (*al-liqā'*) of God, by which the Manifestation of God (Bahā'u'llāh) is meant. Here the mythic imagery shifts from Sinai in the wilderness to a palace throne, as both symbolize the revelation of God's law and of divine command ethics.

> *Proclamatory*: Sūrat al-Bayān: "Say: The Revelation sent down by God [lit., the latter turn: *karrat al-ukhrā*] hath most surely been repeated, and the outstretched Hand of Our Power hath overshadowed all that are in the heavens and all that are on the earth. We have, through the power of truth, the very truth,

manifested an infinitesimal glimmer of Our impenetrable Mystery, and lo, they that have recognized the radiance of the Sinaitic splendor (lit., the denizens of the Mount: *al-ṭūrīyūn*) expired, as they caught a lightning glimpse of this Crimson Light (*al-nūr al-ḥamrā'*) enveloping the Sinai of Our Revelation (lit., the Sinaic locale: *buq'at al-sīnā'*). Thus hath He Who is the Beauty of the All-Merciful (*jamāl al-raḥmān*) come down in the clouds of His testimony, and the decree accomplished by virtue of the Will of God, the All-Glorious, the All-Wise." (GWB 282/AQA IV: 110, Lambden 1988, 134)

Analysis. Considering that the Bābīs were from a predominantly Muslim background, a word should be said about the literary form: "Say!" In his form-criticism of the Qur'ān, Islamicist Richard Bell theorized that the "Say!" passages of the Qur'ān were intended for Muslims to commit to memory, for reciting to nonbelievers when the authenticity of the Qur'ān or the veracity of Islam was being challenged. Bahā'u'llāh employs this quranic rhetorical device as a form of revelation recognizable by Muslims/Bābīs, while recontextualizing it within a new revelatory context. While the quranic "Say"-passages are somewhat creedal in nature, Bahā'u'llāh's say-passages tended to be more poetic or metaphorical.

This passage is an obvious allusion to the twenty-eighth chapter of the *Qayyūm al-Asmā'* (=QA), in which the Bāb, through a creative and dramatic use of Sinai imagery, foretells the advent of a messiah. The wealth of imagery used here can all too easily be glossed over as ornate, when it is, in fact, condensed and highly allusive. A certain measure of metaphorical competency, not to mention biblical and quranic literacy, is required to "decode" such a panoply of metaphors. Even so, there is innovation on some time-honored biblical and quranic imagery. For instance, rarely, if ever, in the Torah or Qur'ān is "Crimson Light" to be found. However, in *Qayyūm al-Asmā'* 28 and elsewhere, the Bāb references "crimson Light" to the Sinaitic "Fire" or epiphany (*tajallī*) at Q. 7:143 (Lambden 1988, 102, citing SWB 53). The Bāb (QA 28; cf. QA 60) speaks of himself as "this Blessed Tree (*al-shajara al-mubāraka*) dyed crimson with the oil of servitude" (Lambden 1988, 96; cf. 98), and as "the Crimson Tree (*shajarat al-ḥamrā'*)" (ibid., 105). Subtle creativity is a feature of the Bāb's own originality, which, while distinctive, is quranically "familiar."

The preponderating influence on Bahā'u'llāh's imagery is, in fact, that of the Bāb. As Lambden points out, Bahā'u'llāh's imagery of the "Crimson Light" emanating from the Sinaitic "Fire" harks directly back to *Qayyūm al-Asmā'* 28, which contains a prophetic passage heralding a messianic advent described as "the fierce and crimson Light," understood to refer to Bahā'u'llāh (ibid., 134; cf. 138, 142). In mythic resonance with Moses/Sinai imagery, this passage is no doubt a proclamation of Bahā'u'llāh's messianic role for Bābīs.

In our third example of Lote Tree/Sinai imagery, the following passages were once thought to belong to Bahā'u'llāh's "Tablet of the Hair" (*sic*), when it first appeared in the December 1938 issue of *Bahā'ī News*, in a translation published by permission of Shoghi Effendi. The contents of this "Tablet" have since been determined to have derived from several sources. These are documented in the citations below:

> *Global*: "Tablets" of the Hair:
>
> [1] He is the Almighty! My hair is My Messenger. It is calling aloud at all times upon the branch of Fire within the hallowed and luminous Garden of Paradise, that perchance the inmates of the realm of creation may detach themselves from the world of dust and ascend unto the retreats of nearness—the Spot where the Fire seeketh illumination from the light of the Countenance of God, the Glorious, the Powerful.
>
> O ye that have consecrated yourselves to this Fire! Sing ye melodies, pour out sweet tones, rejoice with exceeding gladness and make haste to attain the presence of Him Who is the Object of adoration, bearing witness that no God is there besides God, the All-Knowing, the All-Wise, the All-Compelling. (UHJ 1981; Arabic: Behmardi 1986–90, number 39)
>
> [2] He is the God of Wisdom! My hair is My Phoenix. Therefore hath it set itself upon the blazing fire of My Face and receiveth sustenance from the garden of My Countenance. This is the station wherein the Son of Imran [Moses] removed from the feet of selfish desire the coverings of attachment to all else but Him and was illumined by the splendours of the Light of holiness in the undying Fire kindled by God, the Potent, the Gracious, the Ever-Forgiving. (Lambden 1988, 129; UHJ 1981; Arabic: Behmardi 1986–1990, number 40)
>
> [3] He is the Most Excellent, the Best Beloved! A lock of My hair is My Cord. He who layeth fast hold on it shall never to all eternity go astray, for therein is his guidance to the splendours of the Light of His Beauty. (UHJ 1981; Arabic: Behmardi 1986–1990, number 41)
>
> [4] He is God! My hair is My Veil whereby I conceal My Beauty, that haply the eyes of the non-believers among My servants may not fall upon it. Thus do We conceal from the sight of the ungodly the glorious and sublime beauty of Our Countenance. (UHJ 1981; Arabic: Behmardi 1986–1990, number 38)
>
> [5] He is the Eternal! My hair beareth witness for My Beauty that verily I am God and that there is none other God but Me. In

> My ancient eternity I have ever been God, the One, the Peerless, the Everlasting, the Ever-Living, the Ever-Abiding, the Self-Subsistent.
>
> O denizens of the everlasting Realm! Let your ears be attentive to the stirrings of this restless and agitated hair, as it moveth upon the Sinai of Fire, within the precincts of Light, this celestial Seat of divine Revelation. Indeed there is no God besides Me. In My most ancient pre-existence I have ever been the King, the Sovereign, the Incomparable, the Eternal, the Single, the Everlasting, the Most Exalted.
>
> O peoples of the heavens and of the earth! Were ye to sanctify your ears ye would hear My hair proclaim that there is none other God except Him, and that He is One in His Essence and in everything that beareth relationship unto Him. And yet how fiercely have you cavilled at this Beauty, notwithstanding that the outpourings of His grace have encompassed all that dwell in the billowing oceans of His Revelation and Creation. Be ye fair therefore in your judgement concerning His upright Religion, for the love of this Youth Who is riding high upon the snow-white She-Camel betwixt earth and heaven; and be ye firm and steadfast in the path of Truth. (UHJ 1981; Arabic: Behmardi 1986–1990, number 33)

Analysis. This is a truly mythic cluster of images. While the image that unifies these texts is Bahā'u'llāh's hair, Moses/Sinai imagery features prominently, especially in recurring references to the Sinaitic "Fire," which, as stated above, is associated with crimson as a consistent feature of Bābī/Bahā'ī color symbolism. The final selection has global import in that it is addressed to the "peoples of the heavens and of the earth." Especially dramatic is the use of referential "voice" in the narrative. Note how God is represented as speaking in the first person, following which the text suddenly shifts to use of the third person. This is consistent with the image of Moses as the "Interlocutor of God"—an epithet for Moses taken up in Bahā'ī texts. Such Islamic images as the She-Camel contribute to this rich mix of metaphors. The overall impact of these five passages is to effectively convey the spiritual authority of Bahā'u'llāh.

In Bābī/Bahā'ī symbolism, the importance of the symbol of the Lote Tree is indicated by its inclusion as a separate entry in *A Basic Bahā'ī Dictionary*, defined as follows: "The 'Tree beyond which there is no passing.' Originally, the tree which, in ancient times, the Arabs planted to mark the end of a road. In the Bahā'ī Writings, a symbol of the Manifestation of God, the 'Tree beyond which neither men nor angels can pass'; specifically, Bahā'u'llāh. Sometimes called the Divine or Sacred Lote Tree" (s.v. "Sadratu'l-Muntahā," 200). Bahā'u'llāh himself has explicated the symbolic significance of the "Lote Tree" (*sidra*): "The Holy Tree (*sidra*) is, in a sense, the Manifestation of the One True God, exalted be He. The Blessed Tree in the Land of Saffron (*za'farān*) referreth to the land which is flourishing, blessed, holy and all-perfumed, where that Tree hath been planted" ("Errata" to TB 137, cited in Lambden 1988, 145). The Lote Tree is associated with the "Blessed Tree" mentioned in the celebrated "Light Verse" of the Qur'ān (Q. 24:35). In Bābī and Bahā'ī imagery, the Burning Bush and the Lote Tree are equivalent, interchangeable, conflated (Lambden 1988, 146).

Social: ***Paradise***

Paradise unifies Bahā'ī imagery. Paradise evokes all that is ideal on earth. In this respect, Bahā'ī formulations of Paradise are far more utopian than eschatological, insofar as a distinct social agenda and a discreet set of individual behaviors are rhetorically encouraged. Among the informal canon of other key terms, Paradise is given an entry in *A Basic Bahā'ī Dictionary* (s.v. "Paradise" [173] and "Heaven and Hell" [101]). As anthropologically referenced symbols, heaven and hell refer to spiritual (and unspiritual) conditions.

Paradise can be literal or symbolic, or both. In Bahā'ī sacred texts, a conscious effort is made to draw correspondences between Earth and Heaven. In this way, celestial Paradise is emblematic of the ideal society on Earth. Thus, the "vertical" or otherwordly dimension of paradise intersects with the "horizontal" or realized paradise on Earth, from transcendence to immanence. To the extent that images of heaven are associated with the expression of human spirituality at its finest, a true believer can strive to experience paradise on Earth.

> *Personal*: Untitled Tablet: "Whoso (*va har nafsī*) hath recognized the Day Spring of Divine guidance and entered His holy court (*ṣubḥ-i hidāyat va fajr-i aḥadīyat fā'iz shud*) hath drawn nigh unto God and attained His Presence (*bi-maqām-i qurb va vaṣl*), a Presence which is the real Paradise, and of which the loftiest mansions of heaven are but a symbol. Such a man hath attained the knowledge of the station of Him Who is 'at the distance of two bows,' Who standeth beyond the Sadratu'l-Muntahā." (GWB XXIX, 70/MHB 53)

Analysis. Quranic imagery is used in this passage as an allusion to the archangel Gabriel, who was the source of the revelation given to the Prophet Muḥammad in the form of the Qur'ān. Rather than association with Muḥammad himself, Bahā'u'llāh is typologically identified with Gabriel. As such, a related epithet of Bahā'u'llāh, used as a prophetic circumlocution, is "Sender of the Messengers" (*mursil-i rusul*), while the Bāb has been called, in the Arabic Tablet of Aḥmad, the "King of the Messengers" (*sulṭān al-rusul*), while Muḥammad has been named by Baha'u'llah as the "Seal of Thy Prophets and of Thy Messengers" (BP 30, based on Q. 33:40), where the term for "Messengers" is *sufarā'* (sing., *safīr*, "ambassador"). This progression—"Seal of the Messengers" (Muḥammad), "King of the Messengers" (the Bāb), "Sender of the Messengers" (Bahā'u'llāh)—illustrates the explicit teleology of Bahā'ī salvation-history.

Earth–Paradise correspondences are reciprocal. In the passage cited, Heaven becomes a symbol of ideal society. Whatever the "loftiest mansions of Paradise" are, it is not Bahā'u'llāh's purpose to disclose or speculate. Rather, the imagery of celestial habitations is employed to symbolize the potential for unity on Earth. This is the manifestation or fullness of the Kingdom of God on Earth, if one may be allowed to invoke the Lord's Prayer as an analogy. The intent is to foster improved social relations, as personal welfare of the few cannot be morally divorced from the welfare of the many.

> *Proclamatory*: Tablet to Czar Alexander II: "O Czar of Russia! Incline thine ear unto the voice of God, the King, the Holy, and turn thou unto Paradise, the Spot wherein abideth He Who, among the Concourse on high, beareth the most excellent titles, and Who, in the kingdom of creation, is called by the name of God, the Effulgent, the All-Glorious. Beware that nothing deter thee from setting thy face towards thy Lord, the Compassionate, the Most Merciful." (ESW 57)

Analysis. In this proclamation to the Czar of Russia, which is still the world's geographically largest country, Bahā'u'llāh alludes to his own vocation as the revealer of God's will for humanity in the modern era. In rhetorically trying to enlist the support of the Czar, however, it is those who are struck by the claims made in this passage who may be impelled to investigate Bahā'u'llāh, rather than the Czar, and to decide individually on the veracity and authenticity of Bahā'u'llāh's truth-claims.

The prophet (called the "Manifestation of God" in Bahā'ī theophanology) is an extension and effulgence of the divine glory. Bahā'u'llāh, like Jesus Christ in Trinitarian terms, is nominally and functionally "God" for all revelatory intents and purposes. However, Bahā'ī doctrine categorically rejects incarnation, a feature of Trinitarian belief, in which Christ is equated with God by virtue of sharing the same "essence." Bahā'ī doctrine excludes consubstantiality. The Manifestation of God is said to be God in nature, not in essence. This distinction contextualizes Bahā'u'llāh's proclamation to the Czar.

Paradise presupposes the presence of God. It also presupposes the presence of people. Entrance into Paradise is based in part on finding it. Because of its mythic proportions, Paradise has been popularly understood as primordial, otherworldly, and eschatological, but rarely in societal terms of reference, as a paradigm of the ideal faith-community.

> *Global*: Persian *Hidden Words* #18: "O Ye Dwellers in the Highest Paradise! (*ay ahl-i firdaus-i bar-īn*). Proclaim unto the children of assurance (*ahl-i yaqīn-rā*) that, within the realms of holiness, nigh unto the celestial paradise, a new garden hath appeared, round which circle the denizens of the realm on high and the immortal dwellers of the exalted paradise. Strive, then, that ye may attain that station, that ye may unravel the mysteries of love from its wind-flowers and learn the secret of divine and consummate wisdom from its eternal fruits." (HW 27, Persian text, KM 31–32)

Analysis. Some ancient imagery is being recycled in this announcement of a new paradise. The thought orientation is clear: One is asked to conceive of the revelation of Bahā'u'llāh as the proximate locus of Paradise. To become Paradise-worthy, after finding out about the new paradise, one must potentialize the spiritual qualities inherent in every human being. This is not a matter of "meriting" paradise in the faith-vs.-works debates within primitive Christianity, a debate that resurfaced in the Reformation. In Bahā'ī anthropological terms, each human being is already a spiritual creature. The goal of human existence, therefore, is to know and love God, to acquire virtues, and carry forward an ever-advancing civilization. In making the world a better place to live, consecrating one's time and talent in the path of service to humanity contributes to social evolution, which, in utopian terms, is the bringing about of Paradise on Earth.

A Core Bahā'ī Myth? The unity of the preceding imagery is evident throughout Bahā'u'llāh's writings, most particularly in the allegorical texts. Most of the key symbols described above are constituent elements in the *Tablet of the Holy Mariner*, which is probably Bahā'u'llāh's most well-known allegory (see epigraph opposite page 1). It was on March 26, 1863, that Bahā'u'llāh revealed the *Tablet of the Holy Mariner* (Walbridge 1996, 163), in a field known as Mazra'a-yi Vashshāsh, on the outskirts of Baghdad (Gail 1982, 19).

There are two parts to the Tablet of the Holy Mariner—one Arabic, the other Persian. John Walbridge has provided a useful description of this celebrated tablet (1996, 163–65). The Arabic section is independent of, though related to, the Persian, such that each may be considered a distinct Tablet in its own right. Only the Arabic version has been translated. There may be a certain significance in the fact that the Arabic *Tablet of the Holy Mariner* was the first complete work of Bahā'u'llāh's to be translated by Shoghi Effendi in his capacity as the Guardian of the Bahā'ī Faith. When originally published in the *Star of the West* magazine on 17 May 1922, it bore the title, "The Song of the Holy Mariner." This was later renamed "The Tablet of the Holy Mariner," and is included as an appendix in various editions of Bahā'ī prayer books:

Tablet of the Holy Mariner

He is the Gracious, the Well-Beloved!

Refrain: Glorified be my Lord, the All-Glorious!

* O Holy Mariner! Bid thine Ark of eternity appear before the Celestial Concourse. * Launch it upon the ancient sea, in His Name, the Most Wondrous. * And let the angelic spirits enter, in the Name of God, the Most High. * Unmoor it, then, that it may sail upon the ocean of glory, * Haply the dwellers therein may attain the retreats of nearness in the everlasting realm. *

Having reached the sacred strand, the shore of the crimson seas, * Bid them issue forth and attain this ethereal, invisible station, * A station wherein the Lord hath, in the Flame of His Beauty, appeared within the deathless tree; * Wherein the embodiments of His Cause cleansed themselves of self and passion; * Around which the Glory of Moses doth circle with the everlasting hosts; * Wherein the Hand of God was drawn forth from His bosom of Grandeur; * Wherein the Ark of the Cause remaineth motionless even though to its dwellers be declared all divine attributes. *

O Mariner! Teach them that are within the Ark that which We have taught thee behind the mystic veil, * Perchance they may not tarry in the sacred snow-white spot, * But may soar upon the wings of the spirit unto that station which the Lord hath exalted above all mention in the worlds below, * May wing through space even as the favoured birds in the realm of eternal reunion; * May know the mysteries hidden in the Seas of light. *

They passed the grades of worldly limitations and reached that of the divine unity, the center of heavenly guidance. * They have desired to ascend unto that state which the Lord hath ordained to be above their stations. * Whereupon the burning meteor cast them out from them that abide in the Kingdom of His Presence. * And they heard the Voice of Grandeur raised from behind the unseen pavilion upon the Height of Glory: * "O guardian angels! Return them to their abode in the world below," * "Inasmuch as they have purposed to rise to that sphere which the wings of the celestial dove have never attained." * Whereupon the ship of fancy standeth still, which the minds of them that comprehend cannot grasp. *

Whereupon the Maid of Heaven looked out from her exalted chamber. * And, with her brow, signed to the Celestial Concourse, * Flooding with the light of her countenance the heaven and the earth. * And as the radiance of her beauty shone upon the people of dust, * All beings were shaken in their mortal graves. * She then raised the call which no ear through all eternity hath ever heard, * And thus proclaimed: "By the Lord! He whose heart hath not the fragrance of the love of the exalted and glorious Arabian Youth," * "Can in no wise ascend unto the glory of the highest heaven." *

Thereupon she summoned unto herself one maiden from her handmaidens, * And commanded her: "Descend into space from the mansions of eternity," * "And turn thou unto that which they have concealed in the inmost of their hearts." * "Shouldst thou inhale the perfume of the robe from the Youth that hath been hidden within the tabernacle of light by reason of that which the hands of the wicked have wrought," * "Raise a cry within thyself, that all the inmates of the chambers of Paradise, that are the embodiments of the eternal wealth, may understand and hearken"; * "That they may all come down from their everlasting chambers and tremble," * "And kiss their hands and feet for having soared to the heights of faithfulness;" * "Perchance they may find from their robes the fragrance of the Beloved One." *

Thereupon the countenance of the favoured damsel beamed above the celestial chambers, even as the light that shineth from the face of the Youth above His mortal temple; * She then descended with such an adorning as to illumine the heavens and all that is therein. * She bestirred herself and perfumed all things in the lands of holiness and grandeur. * When she reached that place, she rose to her full height in the midmost heart of creation, * And sought to inhale their fragrance at a time that knoweth neither beginning nor end. * She found not in them that which she did desire, and this, verily, is but one of His wondrous tales. *

She then cried aloud, wailed and repaired to her own station within her most lofty mansion, * And then gave utterance to one mystic word, whispered privily by her honeyed tongue, * And raised the call amidst the Celestial Concourse and the immortal maids of heaven: * "By the Lord! I found not from these idle claimants the breeze of Faithfulness!" * "By the Lord! The Youth hath remained lone and forlorn in the land of exile in the hands of the ungodly." * She then uttered within herself such a cry that the Celestial Concourse did shriek and tremble, * And she fell upon the dust and gave up the spirit.

> It seemeth she was called and hearkened unto Him that summoned her unto the Realm on High. Glorified be He that created her out of the essence of love in the midmost heart of His exalted paradise! * Thereupon the maids of heaven hastened forth from their chambers, upon whose countenances the eye of no dweller in the highest paradise had ever gazed. * Glorified be our Lord, the Most High! * They all gathered around her, and lo! they found her body fallen upon the dust. * Glorified be our Lord, the Most High! * And as they beheld her state and comprehended a word of the tale told by the Youth, they bared their heads, rent their garments asunder, beat upon their faces, forgot their joy, shed tears and smote with their hands upon their cheeks, and this is verily one of the mysterious grievous afflictions. * Glorified be our Lord, the Most High!

This Tablet is filled with Paradise imagery, the original focus of which was the Bābī community, out of which the inchoate Bahā'ī community emerged. This narrative constitutes the core Bahā'ī myth, of the soul's journey to the presence of God in the person of Bahā'u'llāh, and in fidelity to his Covenant. Scenes of paradise, in heaven above, are used allusively in Bahā'ī texts as an imagistic ideal of an idea faith-community, on earth below. The *Tablet of the Holy Mariner* concludes with a section in Persian. Based on my own reading of the original text, while consulting Walbridge (1996, 164–65), the following narrative highlights significant words from the Persian.

Bahā'u'llāh, the narrator, introduces himself as "the Persian 'Irāqī" (*al-fārsī al-'irāqī*). The story resumes. By order of the Holy Mariner (*mallāḥ-i qudsī*), the passengers embark on the divine ship (*ahl-i fulk-i ilāhī*), the ancient Ark (*safīna-yi qidamī*), to sail upon the Ocean of Names (*baḥr-i asmā'*). The purpose of the voyage was to transverse the stages of human limitations so that, by the leave of God, the travellers could reach the shores of Unity (*shāṭī'-i tawḥīd*), where they might quaff the chalice of Oneness (*tajrīd*). With the aid of God, the divine Ark voyaged across the Ocean of Wisdom (*āb-i ḥikmat*), until it reached a station in which the Stagnant Name (*ism-i sākin*)—probably an allusion to Bahā'u'llāh's arch-rival, Mīrzā Yaḥyā Ṣubḥ-i Azal)—seized control (*sabaqat girift*) and diverted its course (*majrá*). As a result, the Ark of the Spirit became motionless, prevented from further travel.

At this moment, there came a decree from Heaven. The eternal Mariner (*mallāḥ-i baqā'*) disclosed to the shipmates (*ahl-i fulk*) one single letter from the mystic, arcane word (*ḥarfī kalima-yi ikhfā'*), so that, with assistance from the invisible realm, they might pass through the Valley of Bewilderment of their lower natures (*vādī-yi ḥayrat-i nafsānī*), enter into the joyous atmosphere of spiritual oneness (*vaḥdat-i ruḥānī*), and reach the summit of the divine Qāf of Immortality (*qāf-i baqā'-yi jān*) [mystic mountain thought to be in Qafqāz], to attain the presence of the Beloved (*liqā'-i hażrat-i jānān*).

As the passengers of the vessel (*ahl-i kashtī*) received word from the celestial Friend, they opened their mystic wings (*par-i ma'ná*) at once (*fī al-fawr*) and soared into the holy atmosphere (*havā-yi qudsī*). By the grace of God (*fażl-i ilāhī*) and divine mercy (*raḥmat-i subḥānī*), they passed over the perilous ravines of self and passion (*'aqabāt-i nafs va havá*), and over the deepest pits of the hells of ignorance and blindness (*darakāt-i ghaflat va 'amá*).

At this time (*dar īn vaqt*), from God's holy realm there blew the breezes of Paradise (*nasā'im-i riżvān*), wafting over their bodies. And after winging their way through the atmosphere of nearness to God (*qurb-i ilāhī*), having traversed the spiritual stages (*sayr-i maqāmat-i ma'navī*) along the way, the birds (*ṭayr-ān*), safe and sound, reached their final destination and alighted (*nuzūl nimūdand*) in the homeland of the lovers (*vaṭan-i 'āshigān*).

Whereupon the dwellers of this station (*sakkān īn maqām*) arose to serve their guests. The immortal Youths (*ghulām-ān-i bāqī*) and the holy Cupbearer (*sāqī-yi qudsī*) proceeded to serve ruby-red wine (*khamr-i yāqūtī*). The guests became so intoxicated with the wine of divine knowledge (*khamr-i maḥrūf*) and goblet of divine wisdom (*kās-i ḥikmat*) that they were freed from their own existence (*hastī-yi khud*) and everything in the universe. Attaching their hearts (*dil bastand*) to the beauty of the Friend (*dust*), they remained for centuries (*qarn-hā*) in that privileged spiritual station (*ān maqām-i khwush-i rūḥānī*) and that holy, divine rose garden (*gulzār-i quds-i raḥmānī*).

With the utmost bliss did they remain and tarry, until the gales of the divine Test (*nasā'im-i imtiḥān-i subḥānī*) and the winds of the ordeal of the Sovereign (*aryāḥ-i iftatān-i sulṭānī*) gusted from the Sheba of the command (*amr*) of the Eternal, such that they were attracted to the beauty of the Cupbearer (*jamāl-i sāqī*) and forgot the Immortal Visage (*vajh-i bāqī*). They thus imagined the shadow (*ẓill*) as the sun (*shams*), and mistook black specks (*ashbāḥ*) for light (*nūr*). Whence they pursued (*qaṣd namūdand*) mere mirages of the Greatest Name (*mi'ārij-i ism-i a'ẓam*). The birds desired to fly in that atmosphere (*ān havā'*), and to enter that Seat and Palace (*maḥall*). And as they flew, the divine assayers (*ṣarrāfān-i ilāhī*), with the divine touchstone (*bi-miḥakk-i qudsī*) and by the decree (*amr*) of God, descended (*īshān nāzil shudand*) upon them. And because the assayers did not scent the fragrance of the spiritual Youth (*aryāḥ-i ghulām-i ma'navī*) from the bird-souls, all (*jamī'-rā*) were barred from further progress. And there transpired what had been recorded in the Preserved Tablet (*lawḥ-i maḥfūẓ*).

Bahā'u'llāh then warns his followers not to become enamored of the mystic Cupbearer, and not to become so inebriated with the wine of knowledge and wisdom. The wayfarer should seek guidance from him and not from the manifestations of Satan. Those who quest the mystic path should first unite their outward and inward beings.

This Tablet and its interpretation should be referenced to a later revelation known as the *Lawḥ-i Hawdaj* or the *Lawḥ-i Sāmṣūn*, in which Bahā'u'llāh makes explicit reference to the *Lawḥ-i Mallāḥ al-Quds*. Bahā'u'llāh had been living in exile in Baghdad from 1853 to 1863. He left Baghdad on 3 May, 1863 for Constantinople, capital of the Ottoman empire. En route, there was a port on the shore of the Black Sea, known as Sāmṣūn, to which Bahā'u'llāh and his entourage arrived in early August 1863. There, the *Lawḥ-i Sāmṣūn* was revealed. Its circumstances of revelation have been recounted in an unpublished narrative of Āqā Muḥammad Riḍā-yi Qannād-i Shīrāzī (Balyuzi 1980, 195; cf. RB 2: 6, 16; Gail 1982, 35; GPB 157). Stephen Lambden (1985) has published the previously unpublished Arabic text, to which he has attached a provisional translation and helpful commentary.

In contrast to the *Tablet of the Holy Mariner*, in which the Mariner himself is said to have been addressed with a "secret, sorrowful Call" (Lambden 1985, 94), the *Tablet of Sāmṣūn* is celebratory and joyous in tone. Both these texts narrate what might be thought of as a mystical pilgrimage to the sacred presence of Bahā'u'llāh, the locus of divine revelation, defined as the presence of God. In the *Tablet of the Holy Mariner*, Bahā'u'llāh is ordered by God to take command of his ship, the Ark of Eternity. This is a metaphorical description of Bahā'u'llāh's assumption of leadership of the Bābī community, of which the Ark is a corporate symbol. The doleful tones of this tablet indicate the opposition that Bahā'u'llāh would inevitably face from those Bābīs who were partisans of Bahā'u'llāh's half-brother and arch-rival, Mīrzā Yaḥyā Ṣubḥ-i Azal. In the *Tablet of Sāmṣūn*, Bahā'u'llāh's status as leader of the Bābīs has consolidated considerably, even though the final rupture with Ṣubḥ-i Azal would not take place until 1866 in Adrianople. On the shore of the Black Sea, the ocean voyage, described previously in the *Tablet of the Holy Mariner*, becomes a concrete eventuality, even though the Black Sea itself is "transcendentalized" (Lambden 1985, 88).

These two works stress the relationship between the integrity of personal faith and the integrity of the spiritual community. Allegories typically involve corporate or collective imagery. Clearly, the "Ark of Eternity" (referred to in later texts as "the Crimson Ark") is the Bahā'ī community. The use of this image is anchored in the Bābī constellation of images. Bahā'u'llāh appropriates and enlarges upon the same imagery found in the *Qayyūm al-Asmā'*, in which the Bāb is understood as prophesying the advent of Bahā'u'llāh and his community of followers. The *Tablet of the Holy Mariner* literally describes the "maiden voyage" of the Ark, in the sense that the Maiden of Heaven is sent to assay the fidelity of those who would embark on the Ark, at a time when Bahā'u'llāh was about to make his momentous declaration on the eve of his exile to Istanbul. The loyalty of the passengers (who were among Bahā'u'llāh's fellow exiles) was tested every step of the way. Such Ark/ Mariner imagery recurs throughout Bahā'u'llāh's writings, of which the following text is representative: "Verily, the sea of calamity hath surged, and gales have overtaken the Ark of God, the All-Encompassing, the Self-Subsistent. O Mariner! Be not daunted by gales, for He Who is the Breaker of Dawns is with Thee in this darkness which hath enveloped the worlds" (Balyuzi 1980, 326; cf. 185).

One can appreciate why Shoghi Effendi, in his new capacity as Guardian of the Bahā'ī Faith following the death of 'Abdu'l-Bahā in 1921, chose this tablet to be the first complete work of Bahā'u'llāh to offer, in translation, to the Bahā'ī community. It is as though the entire allegory was reenacted when Shoghi Effendi took the helm and, as the new Mariner, steered the course of the Bahā'ī world from 1921 to 1957. The *Tablet of the Holy Mariner* is an archetypal allegory replayed in transitions of leadership in Bahā'ī history. These transitions precipitated tests of loyalty among Bahā'īs. The so-called Covenant-Breakers—those who challenged the designated leadership prerogatives, in succession, of Bahā'u'llāh, 'Abdu'l-Bahā, Shoghi Effendi, and now, the Universal House of Justice—seriously threatened the integrity of the community. Thus, the import of the Mariner allegory is never lost on Bahā'īs, even though the rest of the imagery is difficult, complex, and recondite. This is why this particular allegory arguably constitutes the core Bahā'ī myth, in the voyage of an Ark that is launched in Baghdad and finally comes to rest on the slopes of Mount Carmel.

The Bahā'ī paradigm of unity. Bahā'ī portrayals of Paradise are typically reflexive. Paradise is seen as a reality in the afterlife, but the angelic life begins in this life. Metaphors and scenarios of Paradise function to inspire lofty thought and to model ideal behavior in the present. Virtually all of the imagery used to portray ideal-typic scenes has, in a sense, been "recycled" from previously familiar paradise imagery. This grammar of images rehearses a stock repertoire of that which is heavenly. The specifically Bahā'ī use of these key symbols is organized and structured around ideals of unity, ranging from a heart-to-world nexus to unity of thought and purpose in world undertakings. This integrative worldview is the controlling force behind all of the passages cited above, and amply illustrates the Bahā'ī paradigm of concentric unity, which is the organizing principle behind almost every glimpse of paradise Bahā'u'llāh inspires.

VI

Paradise Similarities and Paradigm Differences

Procedure for Dimensional Analysis

In this chapter, formal comparisons of Syriac and Bahā'ī symbols will be undertaken. In chapters 3 and 5, key symbols have been explicated within each of the two traditions being investigated. These images will now be cross-traditionally compared and referenced to the Syriac Christian and Bahā'ī paradigms which furnish a synchronic framework of analysis for comparison.

Doctrinal

Dogmatics, as a rule, treats first of the Person of Christ, then of the Work of Christ. Throughout the history of Christianity, the Church had never articulated or enforced a definitive and binding formula of the Atonement, nor was there ever a universally held theory of redemption. Winslow gives a fair assessment of this unresolved problem in early Christianity: "It has often been stated—too often perhaps—that it was the Fathers' experience and understanding of salvation which was the primary and determinative influence upon the development of their christologies. If this is true (as I am persuaded that it is), there is a significant irony in the fact that so-called orthodoxy finds its fundamental terminological and credal articulation in a 'doctrine' which attempts to elucidate who Christ *was*, and not in a 'doctrine' which sought to express what he *did*. . . . Students of the period are all familiar with the great variety of 'atonement theories' which proliferated in the second through fifth centuries" (1984, 393).

In Christian antiquity, there were several such theories of the Atonement, such as martyr theology, *theōsis*, recapitulation, ransom paid to the devil, or reconciliation through sacrifice. (On early Christian atonement theories, see Slusser 1983, and on *theōsis* in particular, cf. Strange 1985.) However, there did emerge a fundamental rivalry between two opposing notions of salvation, erupting in the Arian controversy. Tension developed between ethical and ontological views of salvation, that is, between (1) conformity to the divine will and (2) man's sharing in God's being (cf. Gregg and Groh. 1981, 161–83). The former is an existentialist approach, the latter an essentialist paradigm. Ephrem himself was disinclined to rigidly define Christ, as had the Arians. A curious consequence of this is noted by Botha: "In light of the well-known formulation of Chalcedon a century later, namely that Christ was 'in two natures, inconfusedly, unchangeably, indivisibly, inseparably,' Ephrem's statements that he 'changed himself against his nature' and that 'the divinity imprinted itself in humanity' sound patently heretical" (1989, 26). Although Ephrem prescinded from rationalizing about Christ, he vehemently attacked Arians because they did.

On the use of language employed by the Church Fathers to speak of the work of Christ, Winslow makes a telling observation: "And what one immediately discovers is that the soteriological language of the Fathers makes considerably greater use of mythic concepts than does their christological language. It is less precise; it is more patient of paradox and contradiction; it is more experientially oriented; it has a dramatic flavor of joy, enthusiasm and risk which ignores nice metaphysical distinctions and, remarkably, avoids polemical argumentation. Basically, when the Fathers spoke of the *person* of Christ, they attempted to stay within the boundaries of logical and rational categories (although this was of course ultimately impossible). But, when the Fathers spoke of the *work* of Christ, their words exploded the careful limitations imposed by logic and entered happily into the area of mystery, expressed through fluid imagery and ever-changing and ever-changeable concepts" (1984, 393). Winslow's remarks on patristic meditations on the saving work of Christ seem a very appropriate prolegomenon to the soteriology of Ephrem. Bahā'u'llāh's imagery is no less metaphorical or poetic.

A careful comparison of both formal parallels and idiosyncratic images promises to disclose much about the symbolic codes of each tradition. We commence with our comparison of Syriac and Bahā'ī imagery.

The Way *(Syriac Doctrinal Key Scenario)*

Ephrem's allegory of "The Way" (*'ūrḥā*) is a depiction of salvation-history. In Murray's translation of a passage cited in section 3.1 above (where Matthews' translation was given), we find this recapitulation of the myth of the Way: "For the sake of the fruit he [God] laid the Way

/ which [runs] from the Tree right to the Cross; / it extended from the Wood to the Wood / and from Eden to Zion, / from Zion to Holy Church / and from the Church to the Kingdom" (CH XXVI.4, SCK 247). The Way was trailblazed by a succession of Prophets, who paved the way for Jesus. Ephrem states that Jesus "chose the prophets; they made smooth the Way for the people; / He sent the apostles; they cleared a path for the People" (Nat XXII.20–21, McV 182). The Apostles replaced the Prophets, for there was no longer any need of them once Jesus Christ had advented himself. When prophecy is fulfilled, the office of the prophet is obviated. "Let us worship the One," Ephrem urges, "Who walked within the way, and He was the Way on the way" (Nat. III.14, McV 86).

Setting aside the question of salvation itself and its mechanisms, this image of prophetic history is perfectively compatible with the Bahā'ī concept of "Progressive Revelation." Just as the vocation of the prophets was completed at the appearance of Jesus—because their prophecies were fulfilled by him—so the "Cycle of Prophecy" or the "Adamic Cycle" (*kur-i Ādam*)—in the Bahā'ī scheme of salvation-history—was followed by the "Cycle of Fulfillment" or the "Bahā'ī Cycle" (*kur-i Bahā'ī*).

But in Ephrem's epitome of salvation history, the succession of prophets, culminating in the advent of Christ, is actuated by God for an overarching, if not sole purpose: viz., "for the sake of the fruit"—meaning the Eucharist, with the sanctification and salvific immortality it provides. As the Bahā'ī system has little in the way of ritual, and, like Islam, is entirely lacking in sacraments, what would otherwise appear to be mutually commensurate imagery is distinguished by the presence of a sacramental dimension in Christian salvation-history that is absent in the Bahā'ī view of prophetic history.

The Promised One *(Bahā'ī Doctrinal Key Scenario)*

In his epistles to the reigning monarchs and rulers of his day, Bahā'u'llāh announced himself as the Promised One. This purports to be the voice of revelation, its own self-validating epistemic warrant. Bahā'u'llāh's proclamation is, in a sense, the "authorizing voice of a world-text"—the Bahā'ī revelation. As David Dilworth states: "This is the standard voice of religious texts. It bears witness to a higher wisdom or the revelation of an absolute knowledge, of which the text constitutes a transparent, self-transcending medium. This is the authorizing perspective of all sacred scriptures and their theological traditions, and also of various philosophers who speak of or for God" (1989, 27).

In the key scenario of the Promised One, a Bahā'ī perspective on Jesus is gained. In effect, it is a post-Christian Christology. It is to be expected that a post-Christian claimant to revelation (such as Mānī,

Muḥammad, the Bāb, or Bahā'u'llāh) within the Western religious tradition should have something to say regarding his predecessor, Jesus Christ.

The text which follows is perhaps Bahā'u'llāh's most important statement as to the station of Jesus Christ. Expressed as a eulogy, written in response to several questions posed to Bahā'u'llāh by a Christian priest in Constantinople, the death of Christ, in Bahā'u'llāh's perspective, takes on a significance that surpasses the traditional Christian understanding of it. For Christ's sacrifice is presented within the context not only of sin and salvation, but of civilization as well. The passage is an Arabic excerpt from an otherwise lost Tablet (which might be referred to as a *Lawḥ-i Qassīs*), quoted in Bahā'u'llāh's lengthiest Tablet to Fatḥ-i A'ẓam (in Persian). Adib Taherzadeh (RB 3: 244) states that the recipient of this Tablet was a Christian bishop. The identity of this bishop is not known.

In this surviving fragment, Bahā'u'llāh states: "Know thou that when the Son of Man (lit., *al-ibn*, 'the Son') yielded up His breath (*al-rūḥ*) to God, the whole creation wept with a great weeping. By sacrificing Himself, however, a fresh capacity was infused (*ista'adda*) into all created things (*kullu shay'*). Its evidences, as witnessed in all the peoples of the earth, are now manifest before thee. The deepest wisdom (*ḥikmat*) which the sages have uttered, the profoundest learning (*al-'ulūm*) which any mind hath unfolded, the arts (*al-ṣanāyi'*) which the ablest hands have produced, the influence (*qudrat*) exerted by the most potent of rulers, are but manifestations of the quickening power (*ta'yīd*) released by His transcendent, His all-pervasive, and resplendent Spirit. We testify that when He came into the world, He shed the splendor of His glory (*tajallá*) upon all created things. Through Him the leper recovered from the leprosy of perversity and ignorance. Through Him, the unchaste and wayward were healed. Through His power, borne of Almighty God, the eyes of the blind were opened, and the soul of the sinner sanctified (*tazakkat*). Leprosy may be interpreted as any veil that interveneth between man and the recognition of the Lord, his God. Whoso alloweth himself to be shut out from Him is indeed a leper, who shall not be remembered in the Kingdom of God (*fī malakūt Allāh*), the Mighty, the All-Praised. We bear witness that through the power of the Word of God (*min kalimat Allāh*) every leper was cleansed (*ṭuhhira*), every sickness was healed, every human infirmity was banished. He it is Who purified the world (*wa-innā-hu la-muṭahhir al-'ālam*). Blessed is the man who, with a face beaming with light, hath turned towards Him" (GWB 85–88/MMM 62 and IQT 93).

Given its Islamic milieu, this passage is remarkable for its superlative glorification of Christ. In orthodox Christianity, the "Work of Christ" is bound up with man's relationship to God, and this aspect of "functional Christology" is by no means passed over by Bahā'u'llāh.

Abandoning the speculative, ontological "substance Christology" of the classical period, Bahā'u'llāh describes the "quickening power" (*ta'yīd*) unleashed by Christ's sacrifice and its impact on civilization, bears witness that "the soul of the sinner" has been "sanctified" (*tazakkat*—PED 299, s.v. *tazakkī*) and acknowledges that the world has been purified by Christ, the Purifier of the world (*muṭahhir al-'ālam*—PED 1259, s.v. *muṭahhir*). Three aspects of salvation effected by Christ are singled out in Bahā'u'llāh's Tablet to the priest of Constantinople: quickening, sanctifying, purifying. The healing motif is associated with the last two. It is tempting to try to read into the text what theology calls the "order of salvation" (a doctrine of Lutheran orthodoxy, but the meaningful aspects of the idea are quite widespread [Weber 1981, 2: 193–209]). But there appears to be no sequential progression of spiritual states developed in this Tablet. However, as this text focuses on what systematic theology terms the "effects" of the work of Jesus Christ, it appears to extend the "order of salvation" as it were, to civilization itself.

Bahā'u'llāh sees Christ's sacrifice as having an impact not only on the human soul but on the whole panorama of human events. Not only has the individual sinner been saved, but civilization has been quickened as well (on v.n. *isti'dād* "fresh capacity"—cf. AED 595 and PED 53). To salvation therefore is added a dimension of the work of Christ which Bahā'u'llāh identifies as "quickening power" (*ta'yīd*)—often rendered in the Bahā'ī writings as "divine assistance." Steingass glosses *ta'yīd* as "strengthening, infusing fresh vigour" with the attendant notion of "divine assistance" (PED 278; cf. Wehr 1973, 37). In one of Bahā'u'llāh's prayers, Jesus is described as having been sent "for the edification of Thy people, infusing thereby the spirit of life into the hearts of the sincere among Thy servants and the faithful among Thy creatures" (PM 37).

Bahā'u'llāh seems to be saying that the pervasive power of Christ's influence lent a cultural vigor to the West, contributing to its masterpieces of art, its discoveries of science, its human values and even its temporal power, resulting in the ascendancy of the "Great Powers" of nineteenth-century Europe. Thus it is clear that, in Bahā'ī doctrine, the work of Christ is extended to civilization itself, spiritually contributing to its social evolution. Identifying Christ with civilization was, historically, a gradual process, in which secular time was merged with sacred time. Weber (1981, 2: 166, n. 2) notes that the first Christian calendar, which saw events in history as tied to the Christ event, originated with Dionysius Exiguus (c. 500–550 C.E.)—a practice permanently established by the Venerable Bede (c. 673–735 C.E.).

There is a decidedly "Christian" dimension in the symbol of the Promised One. Christology reaches its fulfillment in the Parousia, the return of Christ, and Bahā'u'llāh makes that claim. One Bahā'ī "proof" of Christ's "return" has a kind of Syrian Christian logic. In his *Commentary on the Diatessaron* 3:10, Ephrem glosses John the Baptist's denial of being Elijah *redivivus* (John 1:19–21) and Jesus' affirmation that indeed he was (Matt. 11:14; 17:12–13): "*The Jews sent to John and said to him, Who are you? He confessed and said, I am not the Messiah. They said to him, Are you Elijah? He said,* But our Lord called him Elijah, as Scripture attests. However, when they interrogated him, he said, 'I am not Elijah.' But Scripture does not say that John came in the body of Elijah, but, *In the power and the spirit of Elijah*" [Luke 1:17] (SEC 78–79).

In a similar fashion, in *Some Answered Questions*, 'Abdu'l-Bahā resolves this apparent contradiction of scripture on a higher plane of understanding. He does so in order to elucidate the biblical meaning of "return"—specifically in regard to the "return of Christ" as a feature of traditional Christian eschatology, and as a warrant of the plausibility of Bahā'u'llāh's claim. 'Abdu'l-Bahā states: "Therefore, when Christ said, 'This is Elias,' He meant: this person is a manifestation of the bounty, the perfections, the character, the qualities and the virtues of Elias. John the Baptist said, 'I am not Elias.' Christ considered the qualities, the perfections, the character and the virtues of both, and John regarded his substance and individuality" (SAQ 134). Suffice it to say that the Syriac symbol of the Way points to Christ as the penultimate event of salvation-history. Bahā'u'llāh's symbol of the Promised One points to the ultimate event of salvation-history, seen as the advent of Bahā'u'llāh himself.

Physician—I *(Syriac Doctrinal Root Metaphor)*

It has been established that the key symbol of the Physician is an important one in both Syriac and Bahā'ī traditions. According to Brock and others, this symbol is of Mesopotamian origin. Be that as it may, the vocation of healer and the healing arts is a universal feature of human society. The role of the physician in human societies is so visible and so important that it stands as an attractive, even predictable metaphor of choice for the spiritual teacher. Historically, a number of distinguished Syrian Christians had a visible presence in the Sasanian courts as royal physicians.

It is fairly obvious what a physician does, and what the role of a physician is. The physician is a healer, and, in situations in where death is imminent and one's very life hangs in the balance, the physician plays a decisive role as the instrument of salvation. The Physician is an ideal image of one who saves peoples' lives, without whose intervention there would be no hope of recovery or even of life. In *Carmina Nisibena* XXXIV, Ephrem regards the prophets and patriarchs (Abraham, Moses, Joseph, and Daniel) as "physicians" (stanzas 1–8).

Yet the world still languished in sickness (v.9), and still stood in need of restorative healing. Christ the Physician took pity, and restored humanity through the "Medicine of Life"—through the transfusion, as it were, of his own flesh and blood (v. 10). "Jesus is our Physician," writes Ephrem, and "he is our medicine" (v. 11). Jesus does what no earthly doctor is capable of (v. 12, SCK 201).

As there is thought to be a spiritual existence above and beyond carnality, a body/soul/spirit trichotomy reinforces a belief in two levels of life—physical and spiritual. In both Syriac and Bahā'ī traditions, the soul is in some sense the animus of the body, while the spirit is the life-principle of the soul. The question remains: If the primary function of a divine Physician is to save, then how is this parallel imagery in the two traditions to be properly understood?

At the root of Syriac and Bahā'ī conceptual systems are their respective soteriologies. Therein lies the difference in meaning of their expressive similarities. In the Syriac symbol system, the body/soul requires salvation along with that of the soul/spirit. In Syriac eschatology, this is because, in the afterlife, the soul requires the instrumentality of the senses for its powers of perception. In Syriac belief generally, death is a coma, a cryogenic state of suspended animation awaiting the eschaton for the restoration of the original spiritual/psychic/somatic unity of the individual. In contrast, not unlike the Bardaiṣanite scheme, the Bahā'ī system dispenses with the body for afterlife purposes. Notwithstanding, Bahā'ī doctrine maintains that there still exists a afterlife "form" (*haykal*), in which the soul subsists.

A disease model supplies much in the way of an extended metaphor. The sinner is the patient, suffering the vicissitudes of a condition of sin and separation from God. In the Syriac paradigm, the patient is afflicted with the "disease of mortality." Salvation, at its most elemental level, requires physical resurrection, made possible by Christ, who conquered Death. In the Bahā'ī system, physicality is viewed as temporal and as unworthy of salvation. Bahā'ī anthropology rests on quite different assumptions about man and the universe. This is not to diminish the importance of the body. But it simply has no soteriological role. The body is indispensable to physical life, but not so for spiritual existence. In Bahā'ī terms, the disease that plights humankind is disunity, not mortality. Physical death is accepted as inevitable.

For Ephrem a transformation of divinity into humanity (Incarnation) takes place so that the reverse process may become possible (salvation as divinization/immortality). In Bahā'ī doctrine, the human predicament is ignorance resulting in the social chaos of disunity, not loss of immortality. The human predicament is not just individual, it is also corporate. In the Bahā'ī worldview, it is *unity*, not *immortality*, which is the Paradise that needs to be regained. This is primarily a difference in emphasis.

Physician—II *(Bahā'ī Doctrinal Root Metaphor)*

Bahā'u'llāh is fond of the same pastoral imagery of healing. In his Tablet to Janāb-i Muḥammad (MHB 57–60), Bahā'u'llāh writes: "The Prophets of God should be regarded as physicians whose task is to foster the well-being of the world and its peoples, that, through the spirit of oneness, they may heal the sickness of a divided humanity" (GWB 80). This sickness is diagnosed as disunity, seen as the source of all social ills. The modern world requires a precise diagnosis and a specific prescription: "No man, however acute his perception, can ever hope to reach the heights which the wisdom and understanding of the Divine Physician have attained. Little wonder, then, if the treatment prescribed by the physician in this day should not be found to be identical with that which he prescribed before. How could it be otherwise when the ills affecting the sufferer necessitate at every stage of his sickness a special remedy? In like manner, every time the Prophets of God have illumined the world with the resplendent radiance of the Day Star of Divine knowledge, they have invariably summoned its peoples to embrace the light of God through such means as best befitted the exigencies of the age in which they appeared" (GWB 80). This statement suggests that there were supposed to be religious differences, considering that societies had fluctuating priorities over the course of history.

Christ and Bahā'u'llāh are both divine Physicians in their respective traditions, but each seems to have had a particular specialization. In the divine scheme of things, it happens that each patient (as defined in Christian and Bahā'ī traditions) requires a different specialist. In a word, as divine physicians, the Syriac Christ proffers the cure of *theōsis*, or divinization, while Bahā'u'llāh, as Christ returned, prescribes unity as the cure. These cures are somewhat inverse in relation to one another: In the former, the cure is primarily focused on the individual, while in the latter, the cure is a reflex of societal transformation. The presenting problem of the corporate patient—humanity as a body—is different in Syriac and Bahā'ī systems. In the Syriac diagnosis of the world's ills, humanity is ravaged by the "disease of mortality" transmitted by Adam after the Fall. The Bahā'ī diagnosis of disunity is at a considerable remove from the Syriac view of humanity's predicament, so it should come as no surprise that the panaceas are also different. However, the secondary symptoms of the patient, in both traditions, exhibit considerable overlap.

Therefore it is clear that the metaphor of Physician (and its pendant, healing) is common to both Faiths. Humanity stands in dire need of intervention in order to be relieved of the afflictions that beset it. The diagnoses differ, and so do the medicines, as well as the way in which they are administered. In each case, the Physician comes up with the proper diagnosis. The Physician then prescribes the right medicine. But the medicine is really a cure that has not yet been invented, at least with the potency needed, so the Physician develops the cure before administering the medicine. This makes the Physician all the more indispensable. The Physician, in a sense, has a monopoly on the cure, which makes the cure so crucial. The pharmacology of salvation requires the prescription of the wise Physician.

In certain respects, the end result is similar. Both cures call upon the willingness of the patient to undergo a regimen of spiritual and, to a certain extent, physical discipline in order to become a worthy and effective agent of transformation in healing of the world. The call to such a ministry demands a commitment on the part of the active believer. Many of the same spiritual values and virtues are evident in both ethical systems. But the ritual elements are distinctively at variance with one another.

Ritual

One cannot escape the impression that death represented the gravest fear for Christians in Syria in the fourth century. Fear of death, after all, is a very human dread. The drama of salvation from start to finish has as its theme the contest with death. Even in terms of images used in Greco-Roman Christian traditions, Susan Ashbrook Harvey observes: "The imagery most popular in the Greco-Latin churches was that of resurrection, of baptism as a dying and rising, and the baptismal water as the grave, following on the Pauline teachings of Rom 6:4–6 especially. In early Syriac tradition, baptism was above all a rebirth, following John 3:3–7, and the baptismal water was the 'womb' that bore true sons and daughters for the heavenly kingdom" (1993, 119). Referring to the apparent "ignoring [of] the role of His [Christ's] death and resurrection" in connection with Syriac Christian baptism, Brock observes: "The same sort of problem might be seen to apply to the early Syriac emphasis on Christ's baptism in the Jordan as the source of Christian baptism, apparently ignoring the role of His death and resurrection" (*LumE* 71).

From a Western Christian perspective, approaching Syriac texts for the first time, the unexpected absence of resurrection imagery in Syrian Christian baptism is indeed surprising. But, in a broader perspective, one might conclude that, while baptism confers the Robe of Glory, Christ's resurrection empowers *theōsis*, through the sacraments taken together—Chrism, Baptism, and Eucharist. The promise of immortality is embodied in this Athanasian-like verse: "The Most High knew that Adam had wanted to become a god, / so He sent His Son who put him on in order to grant him his desire" (CNis LXIX.2, *LumE* 126).

Robe of Glory *(Syriac Ritual Key Scenario)*

The Robe of Glory was Ephrem's favorite image of the Incarnation. With Adam's disobedience of God came the loss of godliness, one aspect of which is immortality. Adam was stripped of his radiance, the "Robe of Glory," less frequently referred to as his "Robe of Light." The Bible intimately links sin with death. It was to be expected that Ephrem understood Paradise Lost in the very same terms. Salvation makes it possible for the Fall to be reversed.

To recapitulate, the four dramatic episodes of salvation history involving the Robe of Glory are: (1) the Fall (loss of the Robe); (2) the Incarnation; (3) Christ's Baptism (depositing the Robe in the river Jordan); (4) Resurrection (when the Robe of Glory will be worn at the Wedding Feast). In order to understand Ephrem's doctrine of Incarnation, intimately bound up as it is with his soteriology, we must first review the human predicament, as it is portrayed in primordial terms. Again, robes figure prominently in the picture. The robe of immortality is a key element in this drama. Apparently, the robe of light transforms its bearer. It is no mere ornament. It is not worn for its symbolic form; it is worn in order to divinize the one who wears it.

The piece of cloth called the "Robe of Glory" is a sort of sacramental Shroud of Turin. This is because Christ, or at least his saving power, is imprinted on this mystical fabric. The Incarnation, after all, had a distinct purpose: "Today the Deity imprinted itself on humanity, / so that humanity might also be cut into the seal of Deity" (Nat. I.99, McV 74). Somehow, Deity or its power to deify is what is so distinctive about the Robe of Glory.

Even the Nicene Creed says nothing about the mode of union of God in Christ. Curiously, an unnamed Nestorian (a Christian holding to two persons/*parsopa* Christology in which divine and human indwell in Christ) opponent of Philoxenus (d. 523) had maintained: "Just as a king puts on purple clothes which remain in their own hypostasis, outside the hypostasis of the king, so did God put on the different hypostasis of a man who served him as his purple robes" (cited by Philoxenus, in Brock 1982b, 18). For Philoxenus's Nestorian, there is more than one robe. If the plurality of robes had any significance, perhaps they represented successive prophets in the course of salvation history. In this kind of imagery, which is static rather than dynamic, the king is unaffected by the royal vestment; the robe simply renders God "visible." This type of imagery, though unacceptable to Philoxenus, is closer to Bahā'ī metaphoricity.

To be sure, Bahā'u'llāh, like Ephrem, is fond of robe imagery. Unlike Ephrem, Bahā'u'llāh states that man has already been invested with the robe of immortality. Bahā'ī soteriology thus concerns itself with other matters entirely, as in HWA #14: "O Son of Man! Thou art

My dominion and My dominion perisheth not, wherefore fearest thou thy perishing? Thou art My light and My light shall never be extinguished, why dost thou dread extinction? Thou art My glory and My glory fadeth not; thou art My robe and My robe shall never be outworn. Abide then in thy love for Me, that thou mayest find Me in the realm of glory" (ET: HW 7; Persian text: KM 5–6).

If immortality is a given in Bahā'ī anthropology, what then is Bahā'ī salvation? There are numerous pronouncements on this question in the Bahā'ī writings. To sustain the metaphorical comparisons already drawn, a soteriological formula involving enrobement is to the point. In his Tablet to Janāb-i Muḥammad, Bahā'u'llāh writes: "And now concerning thy question regarding the nature of religion. Know that they who are truly wise have likened the world unto the human temple. As the body of man needeth a garment to clothe it, so the body of mankind must needs be adorned with the mantle of justice and wisdom. Its robe is the Revelation vouchsafed unto it by God. Whenever this robe hath fulfilled its purpose, the Almighty will assuredly renew it" (GWB 81).

A robe is worn. So is a ring. Although not frequently, the idea of clothing is also used Bahā'ī texts to describe the modality of "Manifestation" as opposed to Incarnation. In his *Tablet of the Manifestation*, Bahā'u'llāh gives this illustration: "Consider a goldsmith: verily, he makes a ring, and although he is its maker, yet he adorns his finger with it. Likewise God the Exalted appears in the clothing of the creatures" (Holley 1928, 206). This runs counter to Ephrem in doctrine but not necessarily in image. In the passage below, Ephrem speaks of transformation of divine nature, an impossibility in Bahā'ī thinking. But the image has some interesting affinities with that of Bahā'u'llāh's goldsmith: "That Lord of the natures today / changed himself against his nature / so that it should not be difficult for us / to change our wicked will. . . . / Today the divinity / imprinted (*ṭeb'at*) itself in humanity / so that humanity should also decorate (*tesṭabat*) itself / in the signet-ring (*ṭab'a'*) of divinity (Nat. I.97, 99, Botha 1989, 26). In Syriac studies, this passage from Ephrem's *Hymns on the Nativity* is typically compared to Athanasius's formula to the effect that God became man that man might become God (*On the Incarnation* LIV.3). In another translation of Nat. I.97, 99, we read: "The Lord of natures today was transformed contrary to His nature; / . . . Today the Deity imprinted Itself on humanity, / so that humanity might also be cut into the seal of Deity" (McV 74, where, in n. 66, the parallel to Athanasius is adduced).

This problem apart, for purposes of comparison, we may observe that Bahā'u'llāh's goldsmith fashions a ring out of humanity; in Ephrem, saved man may wear the signet ring of divinity. The ring in the former is visible, the wearer invisible; the ring in the latter is invisible, the wearer visible. The fundamental difference between the Syriac and Bahā'ī conceptual systems is that the former is based on a model of Incarnation whereas the latter is based on a model of Manifestation. This difference has a direct impact on the ritual dimension of each religion.

The Covenant *(Bahā'ī Ritual Key Scenario)*

This leads to the Bahā'ī conception of the Covenant. To the Christian who sees in Bahā'u'llāh the reality of Christ and the eschatological realization of Christ's return in the person of Bahā'u'llāh, the following beatitude applies: "Blessed is he who hath remained faithful to My Covenant" (TB 17). "Every receptive soul," Bahā'u'llāh proclaims, "who hath in this Day inhaled the fragrance of His garment and hath, with a pure heart, set his face towards the all-glorious Horizon is reckoned among the people of Bahā in the Crimson Book" (TB 220). The "Crimson Book" refers to Bahā'u'llāh's Book of the Covenant.

The most potent image of the Covenant that Bahā'īs have is that of a man: 'Abdu'l-Bahā. Bahā'īs consider him to be the "Perfect Exemplar" of Bahā'u'llāh's teachings. Designated by Bahā'u'llāh himself to be his successor and the infallible interpreter of his teachings, 'Abdu'l-Bahā bears the distinction of being the "Centre of the Covenant" of Bahā'u'llāh. There is no exact counterpart to this in Syriac Christianity, except for the notion of apostolic succession.

One major difference between Bahā'i and Syriac Christian church organizations is that there is no clergy in the Bahā'ī Faith, which is another consequence of its nonsacramental character. A bishop administers the sacraments, but if there are no sacraments to administer, then there is no need of a bishop, except for pastoral work. It is this pastoral ministry that is conserved in the Bahā'ī system of annually elected Local and National Spiritual Assemblies. (The international governing body of the Bahā'ī world is called the Universal House of Justice, elected once every five years by the National Spiritual Assemblies who convene in Haifa, Israel, for that purpose.) This question of the necessity and efficacy of the sacraments brings us to a consideration of the Syriac Medicine of Life.

Medicine of Life *(Syriac Ritual Root Metaphor)*

Christian views on the nature of the soul and its immortality were by no means uniform. Wolfson (1956, 72–74) points to three Fathers (Tertullian, Origen, and Augustine) who held that the soul is immortal, a tenet that has profound implications for soteriology. Tertullian (*De Resur. Carn.* 25) appealed directly to Plato (d. 347 B.C.E.), who is said to have declared in no uncertain terms: "Every soul is immortal."

It is the "safety" of the soul that is at stake. The soul, though immortal by nature (*immortalis natura*) is lost. Christ came to rescue the soul from divine retribution. For Origen, the soul is immortal by virtue of its essence (*substantia*) and is said to "partake" of divine nature. Augustine ascribes absolute immortality to God alone, yet the soul is said to possess an immortality peculiar to itself.

Philosophically, the position that the soul is immortal is decidely Platonic, whereas its denial is Aristotelian. (Wolfson [1956, 102–103] points out how Aristotle, originally a disciple of Plato, started out believing the soul to be immortal, but later concluded that this was not so.) There is no classical philosophical justification for resurrection, only scripture. The only philosophical analogues to which the Fathers could appeal were distant: (1) the Stoic doctrine of palingenesis; and (2) transmigration of souls—doctrines ascribed to Pythagoras, Empedocles, and Plato (Wolfson 1956, 75–76).

The most metaphorical modern treatment of early Christian paradigms of death and resurrection appears to be that of Jaroslav Pelikan (1961), who presents the views of five church Fathers in terms of shapes: Tatian (*arc*: sharp beginning and end); Clement of Alexandria (*circle*: cyclical platonic views); Cyprian (*triangle*: realized and anticipated life in God); Origen: (*parabola*: preexistence and afterlife); Irenaeus (*spiral*: obedience to death in this life). Differences in resurrection beliefs correlate directly to anthropology, regarding the nature of the soul (whether immortal or not) and the constitution of the resurrection body (whether gross, subtle, or formal). Another indicator is the status of the special dead: Elijah, Lazarus, the crucified thief, martyrs, the righteous.

Christians throughout the Roman Empire practiced banqueting for the special dead (family and martyrs). This was a practice that had to be outlawed by Christians themselves, and by the fourth century, it appears that this practice finally ceased. The Christian cult of the dead raises a significant question as to the status of the presently dead. On the basis of archaeological evidence, the popular scene of the Resurrection of Lazarus has to be understood from a different perspective: "It depicts the present reality of resurrection rather than belief in another world. . . . [The early Christians] ate with the dead, asked for their assistance. . . . The resurrection motif supports neither a view of otherworldly immortality nor a view of end-time judgement and resurrection. The presence of the dead [within the community] was made possible through the redeeming act of the wonder worker Jesus. These resurrected dead then were part of the extended Christian family" (Snyder 1985, 61, cited by Smith 1990, 131). In the Christian catacombs, banqueting for the dead assumed the presence of the dead, though, with the relics of the dead still interred, they could hardly be said to have resurrected. Yet afterlife did not depend on resurrection.

It did, as did all other Christian paradigms, predicate liberation from death on the victory of Christ over death.

Behind belief in physical resurrection, the body is not malefic, but is to be loved. Two forms of this belief prevailed, depending on the distinction made between body (*sōma*) and flesh (*sarx*). The resurrection body constituted of flesh is presumably reconstituted of the same original atoms. This, of course, was philosophically difficult to maintain, given the organic nature of the body, which was always in flux. The concept of bodily resurrection was more believable, as the resurrection body would be "glorified"—that is, its gross substance would be transformed in some way into something subtle. The problem with this view surrounded the instrumentality of the senses. The body-soul unity was necessary to maintain due to the inability of the soul, not to subsist, but to perceive if deprived of the senses. If the nature of Paradise renders the senses obsolete, however, the justification for corporeal resurrection is logically contradicted (cf. Wolfson 1961, 83).

There was also a belief, current in early Christianity, in spiritual resurrection. The pejorative view of this belief was its allegedly "docetic" nature. This view is closely linked with spirit/matter dualism. Matter, in which the spark of light (the soul) is entrapped, is depreciated as dark and evil. Gnostics who held to this view sought escape from mortality, not a restoration or prolongation of it.

Bardaiṣan is said to have altogether denied physical resurrection. Against this doctrine Ephrem's Hymns XLVI and LI of the cycle known as *Carmina Nisibena* are directed. For Bardaiṣan, the body has no need to be redeemed. Christ brought deliverance to the soul through the spirit. The body is of little consequence. Freedom is gained through harmony with God's order. The soul cannot do it alone. The spirit of man or "Reason" (*madd'ā*)—the third component in Bardaiṣan's anthropological triad—is, by contrast, is wholly spiritual (Skjaervo, EIr 3: 782). It is what relates man to God, through transcendence above nature and fate.

Adam wrongly used this divine trust, thereby barring the soul—to which the spirit is connected—from returning to its celestial origin, the "Bridal Chamber of Light." With this trichotomous concept Ephrem tacitly agrees: "Far more glorious than the body is the soul, / and more glorious still than the soul is the spirit, / but more hidden than the spirit is the Godhead" (HdP IX.20, *HyP* 143). These transformations establish the *loci* of salvation. Exercise of the will becomes the agent of salvation.

In contrast to Bardaiṣan, Ephrem held that the soul, while in the body, resembles an embryo, and cannot enter Paradise unaided. Only when the soul is reunited with the bodily senses in the *eschaton* can it fully function in Paradise (HdP VIII.5–7, *HyP* 133). As Ephrem states in another verse: "At the end / the body will put on / the beauty of the soul, / the soul will put on that of the spirit, / while the spirit shall put on / the very likeness of God's majesty" (HdP IX.20, *HyP* 143). To the level of the soul will the body be transported, Ephrem explains, while the soul ascends to the level of spirit, the spirit in turn attaining God's presence or "majesty" (HdP IX.21).

With this explanation couched in mystic vision, Ephrem has ideologically rescued the body from its snatcher, the heretic Bardaiṣan. At the same time, Ephrem reminds us that his description of Paradise is entirely metaphorical (HdP XI.7, *HyP* 156). The eschatological "Bridal Chamber of Light" (Ieiun. V.1), of which Bardaiṣan also spoke, is, in its realized form, "the bridal chamber of such a person's heart" (Virg. XLIV.20, *LumE* 99 and 104). "Even though it [Paradise] may appear terrestrial because of the terms used," Ephrem explains, "it is in its reality spiritual and pure" (HdP XI.4, *HyP* 155). Clearly, a local Edessan controversy over the immortality of the soul had its impact on Ephrem's soteriology of *theōsis*.

If it is conceded that the soul is immortal, there is then no need for divinization. The power of baptism and the sacraments to confer immortality is seriously undermined. Soteriology, as Ephrem knew it, would have to be redefined. But it seems that Ephrem's soteriology was not entirely predicated on *theōsis*. Divinization in terms of "substance" is one thing, but becoming godly is quite another. As argued below in section 7.1, Ephrem's soteriology stands midway between the underdeveloped Jewish afterlife picture of the abyss of Sheol and the speculative Middle-Platonist doctrine of *asōmata* and Bardaiṣan's refutation of bodily resurrection. (For a diagrammatic picture of Sheol, see McDannell and Lang 1988, 4.) Ephrem's Paradise resurrects the form of the body but not its substance, and predicates Paradise-worthiness on ethical advancement that would rival that of any Bardaiṣanite.

The poetic artistry of Ephrem is wide ranging. It includes a panoply of literary devices, not the least of which is word-play. This is an example of it: "In Bethlehem the slayers mowed down the fair flowers so that with them / would perish the fair Seed in which was hidden the Living Bread. / The Staff of life had fled so that it might come to the sheaf in the harvest. / The Cluster that fled while young, gave Himself in the trampling / to revive souls with His wine. Glory to You, the Medicine of Life!" (Nat. XXIV.17, McV 196). In this verse, as in Nat. XXV.6, Ephrem puns Christ's title as "the Living Bread" with "Bethlehem" which means, "house of bread" (McV 201, n. 561). This is all part of Ephrem's vast repertoire of sacramental imagery.

The "Medicine of Life" is distinctively Syriac, although it has a wider patristic background. Medicine of Life imagery might well have been based on Eccl. 6:16. The Medicine of Life is the antidote to the mortality brought on by Adam's sin. Through the Syriac sacrament of communion, the Medicine of Life confers immortality. "A treasure of medicines is Your great day / on which the Medicine of Life shone forth for the severely wounded" (Nat. IV.24, McV 91).

The Eucharist is a mystery, and the Syriac "Medicine of Life" is singular. It is prescriptively specific. It is communicated in the sacrament of the Eucharist, which is literally wine, but invested with a rich symbolism. In this sacramental cup, the restorative elixir of divinity begins its work of divinization. This brings us to the Bahā'ī symbolism of wine.

Wine/Water of Life *(Bahā'ī Ritual Root Metaphor)*

In both systems, the dispensation of spiritual elements is typically represented as nourishment. The symbolism of this nourishment is necessarily physical. It will not do to represent this medium in terms of anything that by human standards is gross. The symbolism of divine sustenance is not well served by the image, for example, of a steak. To argue from absurdity, the steak metaphor is problematic in a number of ways. Meat has sometimes been used to represent advanced spiritual teachings (because it is substantive but hard to digest), as contrasted with milk (which is easily assimilated, as by infants and neophytes). But when the sustenance under consideration is the direct influx of divinity, or the immediate experience of the divine, it is mead and not meat. In such a context, only the most refined symbolism, as the archaism goes, is "meet and seemly." Symbolically, a pure beverage is a far more appropriate image for the assimilation of divinity (Syriac), or for the assimilation of divine teachings (Bahā'ī).

Pure beverages—Wine, and the Water of Life—are more or less common to both traditions. In the Bahā'ī tradition, the "water of life" represents nourishment in the form of divine teachings, and the divine influence those teachings impart. Wine is the happiest of the beverage images, being the closest example of a true parallel in both religious systems. While, sacramentally, wine is a symbol of the blood of Christ, in Syriac tradition wine still retains its association with feasting, merriment, and mirth (even though Ephrem is traditionally represented as one who cautions against laughter). Wine is a cause of joy. The presence of divinity is mystically rapturous, to the point of being inebriating. But inebriation is the wrong word to use with respect to the Syriac tradition, which McVey refers to as "sober inebriation," in her gloss on Nat. IV.110: "by the wine that maddened us, we became modest" (McV 98 and n. 169). This appears to be a contrastive allusion to the drunkenness of Noah, that resulted in his immodesty.

Wine is also more personal. It is typically portrayed in a festive setting. In the imbibing of wine at the eschaton, one does not serve one's self. One is served, usually by the savior figure or by a celestial being. Reunion with the Beloved is a cause for celebration. How this union is to be achieved—and by what modality—does not alter the symbolism of wine, eschatologically speaking. When Syriac texts refer to the actual practice of drinking wine, which is forbidden in Bahā'ī law, the sacraments are meant. Eschatologically, although not sacramentally, the Bahā'ī symbolism of wine is not only an affine metaphor with respect to the Syriac symbolism of wine, it is also comparable in content.

Ethical

There are degrees of perfection and glory far beyond the state of incipient salvation. Moral development, in both Syriac and Bahā'ī perspectives, is crucial to the progress of the soul. There is some evidence to suggest that the community of Ephrem was in ethical competition, so to speak, with its Christian rivals, the Bardaiṣanites. The Edessan native Bardaiṣan had high ethical standards for his followers. The exercise of free will was, to both Syrian figures, of greatest importance. We now proceed to a comparison of four selected key symbols of distinctively ethical import.

Sons/Daughters of the Covenant *(Syriac Ethical Key Scenario)*

Ephrem held virginity in high regard as a charism which, embodying renunciation, faith, and love, offered a path to perfection. The Sons and Daughters of the Covenant were conceived as having entered into the angelic life. In the practice of virginity, one has the potential to become superior to angels through the reflex and power of the will, which is seen as a uniquely human endowment. Notwithstanding, virginity alone was no guarantor of spiritual purity, though for Ephrem it represented an ideal kind of mortification. As to the Robe of Glory mentioned in the previous section, only a virtuous raiment befits so august an occasion as the eschatological Wedding Banquet. The Robe cannot be soiled by sin. One such sin may be the sin of omission.

The religious population of Edessa was very purification oriented. Ephrem and Bardaiṣan and Mānī unwittingly concur that purification was necessary for salvation, but their followers pursued this end through various means. Bardaiṣan effected a synthesis of disparate elements of Syrian paganism and recast them within a Judeo-Christian ethic. To achieve purification, his rival Mānī chose asceticism; Bardaiṣan opted for ethical rigor, in which knowledge and faith are requisite. Ephrem seems close to Bardaiṣan on this count, while at the same time incorporating elements of ascesis into his system, evidently lacking in Bardaiṣan's: "He Who gave hope in baptism / gave repentance lest hope be cut off by Him. / But harsher is the work after you have been baptized / than that work before you have been baptized. / Sins before baptism / by simple work are able to be atoned. / And if the imprint of scars sullies [the Christian], / baptism whitens and wipes them clean. / But sins after baptism / with double works are able to be overturned. / When works and mercy have truly healed, / the imprint of scars will call for a miracle" (Virg. XLVI.22–27, McV 450–51). This view of salvation is a far cry from justification "by faith alone." Apt here is that curious expression found in the pseudo-Clementines, "the faith of works" which comes to the present writer's mind, with all of the spiritual dangers of salvific complacency of which Hebrews 10:26–29 warns. In his meditation on the Day of Judgment so graphically portrayed in the *Letter to Publius* (cited above in chapter 3), Ephrem is careful to secure the necessity of works in terms not of salvation but of merit. Virginity alone does not assure a place in the Wedding Banquet.

The symbol of the Sons and Daughters of the Covenant has no exact counterpart in Bahā'ī texts. As important—indeed, as central—as the symbol of the Covenant is in Bahā'ī symbolism, the relative emphasis on sexual holiness as the defining criterion of fidelity to a spiritual ideal is not met with in the Bahā'ī tradition. Premarital chastity and sexual fidelity in marriage are stressed in Bahā'ī teachings. In fact, paradigm differences between the two religions become apparent even here. In Syriac Christianity, sexual holiness conserves union with Christ, whereas sexual holiness, as defined in Bahā'ī teachings, functions as a basis for a unified society, founded on the integrity of the family as the essential foundation of community.

Illumination *(Bahā'ī Ethical Key Scenario)*

More commonality is to be met with in the symbolism of light. The Bahā'ī key scenario of illumination pervades Bahā'ī texts. Take, for instance, Bahā'ī teachings on philanthropy. Bahā'u'llāh says of the spiritually minded man of wealth: "By the Most Great Name! The splendor of such a wealthy man shall illuminate the dwellers of heaven even as the sun enlightens the people of the earth!" (HWP #53). Various other forms of righteousness are given similar descriptions. The imagery of illumination is intended to ennoble. It intensifies the expression of Bahā'ī ethics. Bahā'u'llāh speaks of the righteous person as one who "even as the true morn doth quicken and illumine the hearts of the dead" (HWP #58). Light is not simply diurnal, it is eternal: "Thou art My light and My light shall never be extinguished, why dost thou dread extinction?" (HWA #14). The source of this light is said to be God Himself, who reveals that "within thee I have placed the essence of My light" (HWA #12). Light in these and similar passages is supernal. Its effects in invisible realms are comparable to the enlightening and lifegiving properties of physical light in the visible world.

Light imagery abounds in Syriac texts. It is predominantly used of Christ, particularly with respect to Christ as the "Sun of Righteousness" foretold by Malachi. Another Ephremic use of light imagery has to do with symbolizing the Godhead, especially in relation to the Holy Spirit: "Take as symbols of the Father the sun, of the Son the light, and of the Holy Spirit the warmth. / Being one, yet therein is to be seen a trinity; who can explain what lies beyond comprehension? / The one is multiple: the one consists of three, and the three constitute one, a great astonishment, a manifest wonder. / The sun is distinct from its radiance, yet mingled with it, for its radiance is also the sun. / Yet none speak of two suns, though its radiance is also a sun to those down below. / Nor do we speak of two Gods, our Lord being also God over creation" (HdF LXXIII.1–6, *Harp* 83–84). In this particular instance, this metaphor has striking affinities with Bahā'ī imagery (cf. TAB 117).

In the Bahā'ī context, there is a certain utility to the symbolism of resplendence, for the promotion of unity is served by it. Here, the relative differences in emphasis between the two conceptual systems follows a paradigmatic pattern, but there does appear to be considerable substantive as well as ethical overlap between the two systems.

The Mirror *(Syriac Ethical Root Metaphor)*

The bronze mirrors of Syriac antiquity required burnishing and polishing, to remove rust and dust. Analogously, although God is the source of spiritual illumination, the self is the agent of its own purification. When, through spiritual discipline, the mirror is perfected, God is reflected in heart of the self. If the mirror is external to the self, then the self-reflection operates in much the same way, with an effort by the individual to better one's appearance.

Perfect mirrors are flawless reflective surfaces. The most perfect mirror is that of the Gospel. In his *Letter to Publius*, Ephrem writes: "You would do well not to let fall from your hands the polished mirror of the holy Gospel of your Lord, which reproduces the image of everyone who gazes at it and the likeness of everyone who peers into it. . . . It paints every detail on itself. It rebukes the ugly ones for their defects so that they might heal themselves and remove the foulness from their faces. It exhorts the beautiful to be watchful over their beauty and even to increase their natural beauty with whatever ornaments they wish, lest they become sullied with dirt" (Mathews, SPW 338–39).

The mirror is a source of reflection. This reflection is of two kinds. The first is the communication of divine attributes and teachings (the Gospel mirror, and Jesus as Mirror). The second is self-knowledge, or self-realization, in which the heart is the mirror of the self. In Syriac culture, the heart was thought to be the seat of both the emotions and the intellect. Whether the mirror is internal or external, in Syriac and Bahā'ī traditions the mirror is the eye of the soul. In it, the soul beholds its own being. If enlightened, the soul beholds itself in the light of divinity.

In Syriac Christianity, the symbol of the mirror appears to have little specific sacramental referent. Ethical (or moral, as distinct from ritual) and not elemental considerations are paramount here. The mirror is an ideal symbol of the ethical dimension of both Syriac Christianity and the Bahā'ī Faith, and of religion generally.

Mirror/Gems *(Bahā'ī Ethical Root Metaphor)*

Bahā'u'llāh adduces the symbolism of the mirror in much the same way: "Upon the inmost reality of each and every created thing He hath shed the light of one of His names, and made it a recipient of the glory of one of His attributes." "Upon the reality of man, however," he continues, "He hath focused the radiance of all of His names and attributes, and made it a mirror of His own Self. Alone of all created things man hath been singled out for so great a favor, so enduring a bounty." "These energies with which the Day Star of Divine bounty and Source of heavenly guidance hath endowed the reality of man," he states, "lie, however, latent within him, even as the flame is hidden within the candle and the rays of light are potentially present in the lamp." Bahā'u'llāh concludes: "The radiance of these energies may be obscured by worldly desires even as the light of the sun can be concealed beneath the dust and dross which cover the mirror. Neither the candle nor the lamp can be lighted through their own unaided efforts, nor can it ever be possible for the mirror to free itself from its dross. It is clear and evident that until a fire is kindled the lamp will never be ignited, and unless the dross is blotted out from the face of the mirror it can never represent the image of the sun nor reflect its light and glory" (GWB 65–66). The symbolism of the mirror in Syriac and Bahā'ī traditions is nearly a mirror image, one of the other.

This is also true for the imagery of precious stones and gems in both traditions. For example, Ephrem equates "the precious stones of the ephod" with "knowledge and truth" (HdP XV.7, *HyP* 184). As we have already seen, Ephrem compares virgins to precious beryls. In a similar vein, Bahā'u'llāh writes: "Be an ornament to the countenance of truth, a crown to the brow of fidelity, a pillar of the temple of righteousness, a breath of life to the body of mankind, an ensign of the hosts of justice, a luminary above the horizon of virtue, a dew to the soil of the human heart, an ark on the ocean of knowledge, a sun in the heaven of bounty, a gem on the diadem of wisdom, a shining light in the firmament of thy generation, a fruit upon the tree of humility" (GWB 285).

Experiential

The spiritual path is said to have its own intrinsic value. The integrity of a truly spiritual Christian or Bahā'ī is such that neither will swerve from the path whether from temptation or by ordeal. The path has a destination. It leads to Paradise, to the environs of the divine presence. In eschatological terms, when the Lover has attained Paradise and is reunited with the Beloved, a banquet ensues. While union with the divine transpires eschatologically, it may be anticipated and experienced mystically. In Western traditions, this is the so-called peak mystical experience—the ineffable "beatific vision."

There are mystics who have claimed to have beheld God. But in Syriac and Bahā'ī traditions, God is inscrutable. Whatever beatific vision is in store for the Syrian Christian or for the Bahā'ī, God will not be seen. Rather, it is the savior-figure, be it Christ or Bahā'u'llāh, with whom the believer unites. Direct beatific vision is an impossibility in that both Syriac and Bahā'ī doctrines proceed from the confession of God's occultation from human ken. There would be no need for a doctrine of revelation if a natural theology were sufficient, had humankind direct epistemological access to the Creator.

As in the Latin West and in the Greek East, Syriac tradition generally acknowledges the incomprehensibility of God (Graffin and Malingrey 1972). One patristic concept involves the idea of a divine Reality existing as a causal force, efficiently prior to any form of divine fiat or theophany. This causal preëxistence of pretemporal preëxistence is described by the notion of silence. Of God's hiddenness (*kasyūtā*), Ephrem avers: "His aspect cannot be discerned, / that it should be portrayed by our understanding: / He hears without ears; He speaks without mouth; / He works without hands; He sees without eyes. [Refrain: *Praise to the One Being, that is to us unsearchable!*]" (CNis III.2, trans. Stopford, NPNF 13: 171). By implication, this passage suggests that anthropomorphisms are purely referential and have no literal truth value. The paradox of a God Who "speaks without mouth" is resolved when Christ's role as God's "Voice" enters into the picture.

There are those who are persuaded that the unmanifest God might well represent a reality that transcends the Christian notion of the Trinity. In this sense, the unmanifest Deity is a kind of "hidden Fourth" (Weber 1981, 1: 365–70), the principle of cosmic unity in the extradivine universe, the "superessential Unity" spoken of by pseudo-Dionysius (*De oratione* X.2, Špidlík 1986, 45). Bahā'ī and Syriac

Christian doctrines of the mystery of God have served as points of departure for theologies of revelation. Doctrines of God's presence counterbalance acknowledgments of God's epistemological absence. Though God is in some sense revealed, the revelation itself is a veil. The light reveals the orb of the sun but conceals its core. There is fundamental agreement between Ephrem and Bahā'u'llāh on the mystery of God and the extension of that mystery in the person of God's revealer. The act of revelation is never full disclosure. The sun is both revealed and concealed by the radiation of its light. The mystery is revealed to be a mystery.

Yet circumstances at the eschaton permit God to be "seen" insofar as God is revealed in Christ or in the reality of Bahā'u'llāh. Reunion with Christ for the Christian, and reunion with Bahā'u'llāh for the Bahā'ī are events that, in both traditions, are depicted in very personal, even endearing terms. The Wedding Feast, for instance, is a kind of beatific vision—a vision of God as Christ, pictured in the most intimate and vivid of human terms, love.

The Wedding Feast *(Syriac Experiential Key Scenario)*

Sexual holiness, the celibate ideal, is a state of total sanctification. The early Syriac Christian model of one's ideal relationship to Christ is that of marriage. Except perhaps for the love of a parent for his or her child, there is no stronger metaphor for the love of Divinity than in the bond of human marriage. If the truest test of love is fidelity, then love for Christ requires the same commitment to fidelity as would be expected of a marriage partner. This is akin to the common Greco-Roman ideal of chastity as loyalty to the absent spouse. A Syrian Christian betrothal to Christ requires not only psychological fidelity, but physical chastity.

For Ephrem, the ideal was virginity, and in marriage, continence. However, neither Aphrahāṭ nor Ephrem condemned marriage. Marriage is holy and pure, and so is conjugal love: "For to Him marriage is pure, / which is planted in the world like a vineshoot, / and children are like the fruit hanging from it" (Virg. V.14, SCK 12, n. 4).

References to the Wedding Feast abound in Ephrem's hymns. At the Wedding Feast, a picture of the Bride as adorned with ornaments occurs in the *Hymn on Resurrection* III, in which hymn nuptial imagery receives its "fullest treatment" at the hands of Ephrem, who writes: "See, she sits in the King's palace, / dressed in the ornaments of the King" (Res. III.7, SCK 138–39). This type of imagery is similar to that of the Lover and the Beloved. While there is certainly a sense of betrothal in the Bahā'ī texts, that love does not express itself in ascetic commitments, even though chastity is highly prized. The main purpose of Bahā'ī chastity is probably to strengthen the family. When the sexual impulse finds its fulfillment within marriage rather than outside of it, the marriage bond is strengthened and the children are more protected from the trauma of divorce.

Lover and the Beloved *(Bahā'ī Experiential Key Scenario)*

Through a similar use of the present as a tense metaphor, Bahā'ī texts portray the eschaton with certitude. In Bahā'ī texts, the eschaton is consummated in the advent of Bahā'u'llāh in the form of a realized eschatology. Thus, it is said: "The mystic and wondrous Bride, hidden ere this beneath the veiling of utterance, hath now, by the grace of God and His divine favour, been made manifest even as the resplendent light shed by the beauty of the Beloved" (HWP end, ET: HW 55; Persian text: 68–69). This is the concluding passage of the Persian Hidden Words.

There is a certain sense in which the Christian has realized such a fulfillment in the advent of Christ. The paradigmatic difference has to do with preparation for such an event. While the Wedding Feast is the dominant scenario in Syriac eschatology, presupposing, of course, the Christian's recovery of the Robe of Glory and the rescue from Sheol, Bahā'ī texts tend to emphasize the banqueting rather than a marriage as such, even though nuptial imagery is a feature of the Bahā'ī eschaton as well.

The Pearl *(Syriac Experiential Root Metaphor)*

For Syriac Christianity and the Bahā'ī Faith alike, Nature also is an object of spiritual contemplation. According to Mathews, "the entire aim of Ephrem's poetry is not to explain the system of the universe nor to impose his own ideas of the Christian message on others, but rather to give birth in God's creatures to that true worship of the Creator of all, and to instill a desire to live the mystery of God's love toward humanity" (1994b, 51). This is clearly the case in Ephrem's symbolism of the pearl.

In the *Hymns on the Pearl*, the pearl invites contemplation, but defies investigation (HdF LXXXI.2, 10–11, 15; LXXXIV.2–3). This is a parry against Arian overrationalism. The pearl is a mirror, inviting meditation on the magnificence of the Word (LXXXIII.10). The pearl is a fountain of mysteries (LXXXV.2). Like Christ, the pearl is a symbol of purity (LXXXI.3). The pearl represents Christ's pure conception in the womb of the virgin Mary (v. 4), just as the pearl is formed in a virginal way within the oyster shell (LXXXII.4). (The pearl was thought to have been formed by lightning striking the shell.) The pearl, moreover, symbolizes a woman's virginity, a precious asset to be safeguarded (LXXXIII.14). The pearl is singular among all other gems.

While precious stones represent angelic beings, the pearl alone is a worthy symbol of Christ (LXXXII.3). The pearl, when pierced by an awl to be fashioned into jewelry, exemplies the crucifixion (LXXXII.12; LXXXIV.15). The pearl is perfection in every way (LXXXIV.8). Finally, the pearl symbolizes spiritual victory, as it is set in gold to form a royal crown (LXXXV.13). Throughout these hymns, there appears to be only a single explicit reference to the sacraments (i.e., the Medicine of Life at LXXXV.8). When one reads the *Hymns on the Pearl*, one is impressed by the experiential profundity of the pearl as an object of contemplation.

The Christological and ascetic specificity of Syriac pearl imagery precludes any equivalence with Bahā'ī imagery, although the image of the pearl is occasionally associated with chastity in the latter. Pearl imagery is also used in nonascetic contexts, particularly with reference to wisdom or insight.

The Journey *(Bahā'ī Experiential Root Metaphor)*

While Bahā'ī texts have no direct counterpart to the Ephrem's allegory of the pearl, the symbol of the journey offers the widest possible range of contemplation. In Bahā'u'llāh's foremost mystical work, *The Seven Valleys*, the object of the mystic's search is the elusive but ever-present Beloved. In the Valley of Search, the wayfarer embarks on a journey leading to "the realm of the spirit, which is the City of God" (SV 7). In the final stage, the Valley of True Poverty and Absolute Nothingness, "this city" is glossed as "the station of life in God" (SV 41). All seven progressions are considered "grades of contemplation" (SV 34).

There appears to be a functional parity of both the pearl and the journey, as they are mystical paths to a more profound contemplation of the Beloved, be it Christ or Bahā'u'llāh. From a Bahā'ī perspective, both savior-figures manifest the same reality. Both key symbols are primarily experiential. They invite mystical transport into spiritual worlds.

Mythic

Myth is a fiction, in relation to real time, yet serves as a vehicle of truth. Myth, in its Syriac and Bahā'ī contexts, is properly understood as operating in sacred time. More precisely, the most dramatic events of myth typically take place in eschatological time.

Harrowing of Hell *(Syriac Mythic Key Scenario)*

The Harrowing of Hell represents Christ's victory over Death. This event is a key scenario that provides assurance of salvation. It is not so much punishment of Hell that was feared, but extinction. Christ overcame the powers of the natural world, mythically represented by the principalities of the underworld. No greater victory could possibly be imagined. No more wondrous a gift could be conceived.

In a Syriac setting, Christ's victory over death promised the release of souls from the slumber, or coma, of Sheol. Although this salvation is freely available, it is not freely dispensed. One has to discover it on one's own. The gift of eternal life is miraculous, but not instantaneous. Spiritual transformation is required, effected through partaking of the sacraments combined with a progressive sanctification of one's spiritual being through a life of holiness. Only the holy inherit Paradise, the eschatological Eden: "Let us give thanks to the Son / Who entered Sheol on foot, / plundered it, and emerged. Blessed be Your resurrection!" (Nat. XVIII.31, McV 164).

There is simply no Bahā'ī counterpart to this myth, which ties into a sacramental theology, and its attendant belief in physical resurrection—something that is entirely absent in Bahā'ī doctrine. There is no Bahā'ī analogue to the disgorgement of Sheol, to the breaking of its bars, or to the image of Sheol as a womb, even though Bahā'ī texts treat life in this world as a womb for the afterlife. In a Bahā'ī context, one's reality is already assumed to be spiritual. Extinction is not to be feared, but rather the pangs of regret and the lingering obsessions of carnality that can never be fattened or appeased upon death. Hell is a spiritual condition, in the Bahā'ī conception of it. It psychospiritual, rather than psychosomatic.

The Maid of Heaven *(Bahā'ī Mythic Key Scenario)*

Almost in a Manichaean way, the Maiden of Heaven appears to be Bahā'u'llāh's alter ego. Or, as Lambden has expressed it, the Maiden of Heaven is Bahā'u'llāh's "transcendent Self" (p.c., 17 March 1996). Typical of such texts is this: "Say: Step out of Thy holy chamber, O Maid of Heaven, inmate of the Exalted Paradise! Drape thyself in whatever manner pleaseth Thee in the silken Vesture of Immortality, and put on, in the name of the All-Glorious, the broidered Robe of Light. . . . Unveil Thy face, and manifest the beauty of the black-eyed Damsel, and suffer not the servants of God to be deprived of the light of Thy shining countenance" (GWB 282–83). This is a mythic proclamation of Bahā'u'llāh's advent, in which sacred time is merged with real time. It has no real counterpart in Syriac texts, except in the sense of dialogue as a literary device. Ephrem has a number of dialogue poems, in which such things as Love and Reason, Death, the Cana Wedding, and so forth are personified and given a voice for didactic purposes.

Tree of Life *(Syriac Mythic Root Metaphor)*

The Tree of Life is an ancient Mesopotamian symbol that is intimately bound up with sacral kingship. The quintessentially Syriac development of this symbolism is its sacramental dimension. The Tree of Life is the source of the sacraments, and is represented simultaneously as a grape-bearing vine and as an olive tree (SCK 125). While the Tree of Life is typically depicted as an olive tree, cluster-bearing branches have been grafted onto it. From the Tree of Life, the Medicine of Life may be obtained. Although Adam, in his pre-Fall state, was perfect, he was not immortal. Neither was he mortal. But he certainly became mortal after he partook of the forbidden fruit. By contrast, the Christian may become immortal by partaking of the fruit of the Tree of Life, from whence comes the Medicine of Life, the properties of which have already been outlined.

Bahā'ī texts also speak of the Tree of Life, which is more or less interchangeable with the divine Lote Tree—an Islamic symbol appropriated by Bahā'u'llāh to symbolize the Manifestation of God (see next section). In both Syriac and Bahā'ī traditions, the Tree of Life represents the savior-figure. But the respective emphases in the secondary symbolisms of the Tree of Life diverge, and follow the paradigmatic differences that inhere in the two religions: In Syriac Christianity, the Tree of Life is predominantly sacramental in its life-giving capacity, while in the Bahā'ī Faith, the Tree of Life—and the Lote Tree—are primarily revelatory. The revelation of Bahā'u'llāh is a gospel of unity. Hence, tree imagery is equally as expressive of the message of unity: "The utterance of God is a lamp, whose light is these words: Ye are the fruits of one tree, and the leaves of one branch. Deal ye one with another with the utmost love and harmony, with friendliness and fellowship" (GWB 288).

Lote Tree/Sinai *(Bahā'ī Mythic Root Metaphor)*

Like so much of Bahā'u'llāh's other imagery, the symbol of the divine Lote Tree goes back to the Bāb, who declared: "This Tree of Holiness, dyed crimson with the oil of servitude, hath verily sprung forth out of your own soil in the midst of the Burning Bush" (SWB 52). Bahā'u'llāh advances a similar declaration, employing much the same symbolism: "O Kings of the earth!" Bahā'u'llāh proclaims: "Give ear unto the Voice of God, calling from this sublime, this fruit-laden Tree, that hath sprung out of the Crimson Hill, upon the holy Plain" (PB 7). Like the Crimson Ark and the Crimson Book and the Crimson Spot, the Lote Tree is crimson also: "Kindle then in the hearts the blazing fire which this crimson Tree hath ignited, that they may arise to extol and magnify His name amidst the adherents of all Faiths" (TB 196).

Both the Tree of Life and the Lote Tree are frequently encountered in Bahā'ī texts—the difference being that the former is associated with Eden while the latter is associated with Sinai. Sacramental imagery is totally absent in Bahā'ī Lote Tree/Tree of Life imagery, again reflecting the paradigmatic difference between Syriac Christianity and the Bahā'ī Faith.

Social

There are some striking symbolic resonances in this dimension, for the Noachide and Edenic imagery in Syriac and Bahā'ī texts alike may be read as allegories of the ideal Church/faith-community.

Noah's Ark/Mariner *(Syriac Social Key Scenario)*

The patriarch Noah is a soteriological prototype of Christ: "Noah anticipated Him [Christ]—Noah who surmised that by Him the ark stood still; / if His type (*ṭwps'*) saved in this way, how much more will He save in His reality (*qnwym'*)" (Nat. I.58, McV 70). Mount Ararat now becomes a heavenly destination: "Blessed is that person who has steered his boat straight into Paradise" (HdP XIV.5, *HyP* 177). The Ark is a metaphor for Paradise, and is thus a double metaphor for the ideal Church: "Noah's Ark marked out by its course the sign of its Preserver, / the Cross of its Steersman and the Wood of its Sailor / who has come to fashion the Church in the waters of baptism: / with the three-fold name He rescues those who reside in her, / and in the place of the dove, the Spirit administers her anointing / and the mystery of her salvation. Praise to her Saviour" (HdF XLIX.3–5, *LumE* 43; cf. Kronholm's translation cited in chapter 3). As Noah is the model of Christ, Christ is the exemplar of the Christian: "Skilled Sailor Who has conquered the raging sea, / Your glorious wood is a standard; it has become the rudder of life. / Your wind of mercy blew; the ships set straight out / from the raging sea to the harbor of peace. / Blessed is he who has become a sailor for himself, / has preserved and brought forth his treasure [on dry land]" (Virg. XXXI.15, McV 401; cf. Murray's translation cited in chapter 3). This suggests both personal and mutual salvation—the salvation of others.

Noah's Ark carried animals, who are typologically likened unto orthodox Christians, especially those who practice sexual holiness. This has already been described in some detail in chapter 3. It is noteworthy that "Mariner" (*mallāḥā*) as applied to Christ is absent in Aphrahāṭ, although there is considerable precedent for it in primitive Christianity (SCK 87, n. 4). There is a difference in emphasis here, since Bahā'u'llāh requires fidelity to the full range of his laws, which include chastity, but not continence in marriage. Both Ephrem and Bahā'u'llāh use ark imagery to symbolize the saved—and saving—faith-community, in the Ark of which the animals transcend their feral and carnal nature.

The Crimson Ark and the Holy Mariner (*Bahā'ī Social Key Scenario*)

In the Bahā'ī tradition, the Crimson Ark bears Bahā'īs. The captains of each of the Arks—Christ and Bahā'u'llāh—steer their vessels to safety. To the extent that these are ecclesiastical symbols, they compare quite favorably. In the respective descriptions of each, both of these Arks represent assurance of salvation, ultimacy of purpose, and certainty of destination. The passengers on board both ships must be of high moral fiber, although sexual holiness is more narrowly defined and rigorous in the Syrian Ark. Noah's Ark has a hierarchy, while no such divisions exist in the Crimson Ark. But both Mariners—Christ and Bahā'u'llāh—have roughly the same vocation.

The utility of this image for comparative purposes is optimized by the fact that the Arabic *mallāḥ* is virtually the exact counterpart to *mallāḥā* in Syriac. The Holy Mariner is Bahā'u'llāh himself. God addresses the Mariner, commanding him to embark on a voyage, to fulfill his destiny. The significance of God's bidding is this: *The Tablet of the Holy Mariner* was written on the eve of Bahā'u'llāh's imminent assumption of leadership of the Bābī community in the face of almost certain opposition by certain factions. The Ark represents the religion of Bahā'u'llāh and what is referred to in Bahā'ī terminology as the Covenant. The dwellers within the Ark are the faithful believers. God bids the Mariner—the captain of the Ark of salvation—to embark on his voyage in the face of impending adversity. This narrative, of which the epigraph on page vii of this book is an excerpt, is at the heart of what might be considered the core Bahā'ī myth: the soul's journey to the Manifestation of God (= Bahā'u'llāh, the Holy Mariner) and steadfastness in the Covenant (= the Crimson Ark).

Paradise—I (*Syriac Social Root Metaphor*)

Although Syriac and Bahā'ī metaphors of Paradise are formally affine, they differ in kind. However, as the study of Ephrem's *Hymns on Paradise* in chapter 7 might suggest, there appears to be some convergence of the two relatively disparate portrayals of Paradise, as Ephrem's depiction of Paradise may, at one level, be read as an allegory of the Church here on Earth. Nevertheless, there is a certain physicality, for lack of a better word, that is present in Ephrem's descriptions of Paradise, that is singularly absent in Bahā'u'llāh's own portrayal of it. As will be shown, upon close examination, the presumed physicality of Ephrem's vision of Paradise is called into question by his radical spiritualizing of it. It would appear that Ephrem's vision could be read on two levels—a "physical" and a supraphysical description that transcendentalizes traditional Syriac categories.

Paradise—II *(Bahā'ī Social Root Metaphor)*

See chapter 7, below.

Summary of Results

Doctrinal. Ephrem's allegory of the **Way** compares favorably to Bahā'u'llāh's image of **Promised One**, in that there is a succession of prophets that prepares the way for a savior-figure. When that savior-figure appears, the cycle of prophecy is ended. The advent of the promised Savior ushers in an era of fulfillment. However, there is a difference in the respective purposes of the Syriac and Bahā'ī saviors. The former conquers death, while the latter overcomes disunity. This is seen in the respective Syriac and Bahā'ī imagery of the **Physician**: While the imagery is affine in the sense that humanity is ill and requires the intervention of a divine physician, both the diagnosis and the cure differ in the two traditions. In the Syriac tradition, the patient is afflicted with the disease of mortality, while the presenting problem of the patient in the Bahā'ī system is the disease of disunity. While the doctrinal imagery is surprisingly commensurate, the fundamental difference is sacramental.

Ritual. The **Robe of Glory** reinforces the Syriac sacramental theology. Comparable robe imagery was found in the Bahā'ī writings, but this represented a metaphorical affinity rather than a conceptual one. This is because the Syriac and Bahā'ī robes are different. This difference is met with in the scenario of the Wedding Feast (see below), the preparation for which is both sacramental and ethical. By contrast, the Bahā'ī image of the **Covenant** has an overarching interest in unity, particularly in preserving the communal integrity of the Bahā'ī administrative system. The symbol of the Covenant is personified in the life of Bahā'u'llāh's eldest son and designated successor, 'Abdu'l-Bahā, who was appointed by his father as the "Centre of the Covenant" and the infallible "Interpreter" and perfect "Exemplar" of Bahā'u'llāh's teachings. Thus there is a considerable overlap in the ethical dimension as well. If ethics represent the soul of ritual, then the practice of both plays a determinative role in the spiritual progress of the individual Bahā'ī. In maintaining the ritual centrality of the sacraments in the Syriac tradition, the **Medicine of Life** functions as a kind of elixir of immortality, mystically dispensed by Christ; whereas the descriptively comparable Bahā'ī image of the **Wine/Water of Life** achieves a different end. Wine is a more heavenly image, often appearing in eschatological descriptions of the believer's "reunion" with Bahā'u'llāh, while the Water of Life is more descriptive of the teachings of Bahā'u'llāh. Although the latter has some curative properties, the Water of Life emphasizes nourishment, while Wine represents the intoxication of mystical ecstasy. In this respect, the Syriac tradition has a very similar use of the imagery of Wine as "sober inebriation" (McV 98). However, the Syriac imagery of Wine is literal as well as figurative, wine being part of the Eucharist.

Ethical. **The Sons and Daughters of the Covenant** represent an "athletic" and "military" order in the Christian ranks. One might think of the "Covenant" as an open convent. Like Catholic monks and nuns, the Sons and Daughters of the Covenant are betrothed to Christ. (Of course, every Christian is.) Taking this engagement literally, the Syrian Christian practices abstinent "singleness" in fidelity to that betrothal, in anticipation of the heavenly requital. There is a comparable splendor in the Bahā'ī imagery of **Illumination**. While refinement of character is common to both traditions, and while both traditions employ an abundance of light imagery generally, there is a more defined social emphasis on various forms of unity in the Bahā'ī tradition. The Syriac image of the **Mirror** is extensive, and is certainly not limited to ethical illustration. The Gospels and Nature herself are represented as mirrors. Indeed, for Ephrem, anything and everything is potentially a mirror, because the universe is one, vast Christological mirror. In the Bahā'ī tradition, **Mirror/Gems/Robes** fit into a broader category of ornamental finery, as the truly ethical person is seen to have a beauty of heart and a splendor of character that can best be represented through the accoutrements of wealth as emblems of one's spiritual nobility and stature.

Experiential. The **Wedding Feast** in Syriac tradition is narrowly seen as the eschatological reward for sexual holiness. But the Robe of Glory, which is the wedding garment, is still in danger of being stained. Therefore the Christian has to be vigilant against temptation and sin. On the mystical path in the Bahā'ī tradition, the **Lover/Beloved** imagery is certainly comparable to Syriac bridal imagery. But the fidelity the Bahā'ī is expected to practice is being "faithful to the Covenant," which is more comprehensive than sexual holiness. While high standards of chastity are demanded by Bahā'ī law, such fidelity covers a broader range of behavior. The **Pearl** is a multivalent symbol in Syriac tradition, but it never loses its primary reference to virginity, which Christ refers to a the "Pearl of Great Price." At least this is the Syriac understanding of it. Ephrem's imagery of the Pearl is so vast that it has a decidely contemplative importance, and that is why it is classed here as having a primarily "experiential" function. The **Journey** is also experiential, being indicative of the soul's quest for God, in the person of God's Theophany, Bahā'u'llāh.

Mythic. The **Harrowing of Hell** is clearly mythic, and is a key scenario in the Syriac tradition. The Christian partakes of the sacraments as an antidote to the "drug of death," in preparation for release from Sheol on the Resurrection Day. The Bahā'ī image of the **Maid of Heaven** is equally as mythic, and is seen as the personification of the Holy Spirit. She is perhaps the alter ego of Bahā'u'llāḥ himself, in a sort of Manichaean sense. The Syriac **Tree of Life** is a very old image that can be traced back to ancient Mesopotamia, and is frequently met with in the Bahā'ī writings as well. As expected, the main difference behind Syriac and Bahā'ī uses of this stock Abrahamic imagery is that the Syriac tradition sees the trees as having a sacramental symbolism through the Eucharistic "fruit" it produces, such as the grape for the Wine of communion. In the writings of Bahā'u'llāh, **Lote Tree/Sinai** imagery is primarily proclamatory and eschatological in Bahā'u'llāh's use of it.

Social. In the Syriac tradition, **Noah's Ark/Mariner** imagery has ascetic overtones. The animals on the Ark are chaste. When the wolf lies down with the lamb, this is because the bestial nature has been transformed into an angelic one. In the Bahā'ī writings, the **Crimson Ark/Mariner** imagery is of an equally salvific nature, but without the sexual—or rather, asexual—overtones. Syriac **Paradise** imagery exalts sexual holiness above all else, while Bahā'ī **Paradise** imagery idealizes unitive behavior.

Results of Comparison

Syriac Christian symbolism is predominantly sacramental, while Bahā'ī symbolism is unitive. Both symbolisms exalt the role of ethical behavior and pastoral outreach in the service of salvation. The Syriac and Bahā'ī traditions are marked by a high degree of metaphorical commensurability, with substantive commonalities in the Doctrinal, Ethical, Experiential and Social dimensions—albeit with their respective sacramental/nonsacramental differences—while in the Ritual and Mythic dimensions are seen the greatest divergences, which are readily explained by their respective idiosyncratic, paradigmatic agendas.

VII

Paradise and Paradigm

Introduction

In this chapter, both of the religions under study will be reviewed holistically, as syntheses of their respective key symbols. Portraits of Paradise will be sketched out for each religion. Each picture of Paradise will offer insights into the respective paradigms of early Syriac Christianity and the Bahā'ī Faith. From these vantages, a unity of symbolism will emerge in the dynamic interplay of images and ideas. The first half of this chapter is a study of Ephrem's *Hymns on Paradise*, in which Syriac eschatology is correlated with Christian ideals, with special reference to paradise and the ideal Church. The last half of this chapter correlates Bahā'ī ideals with conceptions of Paradise, with special reference to paradise and ideal society.

Sapiential *Theōsis*: A New Reading of Ephrem the Syrian's *Hymns on Paradise*

[This section was previously published as a journal article (Buck 1995b), and is reprinted here with the kind permission of the editors of the *Journal of the Assyrian Academic Society*.]

Précis

A fresh reading of the *Hymns on Paradise* (HdP) discloses how Ephrem the Syrian reworked soteriological presuppositions and thought-forms current in fourth-century Syria to effect a transformation of the doctrine of *theōsis* (deification), freeing it from its substantive categories, to lay emphasis on divinization at the sapiential level. See, for instance, HdP XII.15, where Ephrem states that "the human person can become / the likeness of God, / endowed with immortal life [i.e. *theōsis*] / and wisdom [i.e. sapience] that does not err" (HdP XII.15, *HyP* 166). While the form of the doctrine with its anthropological considerations was kept intact, the manner of Ephrem's affirmation of *theōsis* was tantamount to its sophistication, in what amounted to a reformulation of the doctrine itself. In Ephrem's eschatological scheme—which exalts form over substance—body, soul, and spirit are rarefied beyond physicality, while corporeality is maintained. Even the argument for the body's afterlife existence—the instrumentality of the senses being required for the soul's ability to perceive—is effectively undermined by the obviation or precluding of the senses in the soul's immediate cognition of the delights of Paradise. This innovation lent Ephrem's doctrine of *theōsis* a greater potential for realization, in which eschatological Paradise came to enjoy a more edifying immediacy among the faithful. Ephrem's poetic articulation of sapiential *theōsis* struck a balance between the Bardaiṣanite rejection of corporeal resurrection and the more earthbound, Irano-Semitic notions of disgorgement of the dead and the pairing of bodies with disincarnate souls for requital at the *eschaton*. (For possible Persian influences on Syriac afterlife concepts, see Morton Smith, EIr 4: 200–203 and Widengren 1960.) At the same time, Ephrem's symbolic transformation of Paradise reflexively served as an allegory for the Church. An unanticipated consequence for modern Christianity, according to Brock, is that "precisely because he locates Paradise outside geographical space," Ephrem's "views are left unaffected by modern advances in scientific knowledge" (*HyP* 55).

Introduction

Called "the greatest poet of the patristic era" (Rilliet 1992a, 1: 276), Ephrem the Syrian composed the *Hymns on Paradise* (Syriac: *mdrš' d-prdys'*) in his native Nisibis (modern Nusaybin in Turkey) before his twilight years in Edessa (363–373). (On the historical context of Ephrem's life, with a critical review of the primary sources, see Mathews, SPW, 12–45.) These hymns, considered by Mathews to have been "perhaps Ephrem's most beautiful hymns" (1994b, 47, n. 10), are of the genre called *madrāšē*, composed in syllabic metres. Clearly, as the name implies, such odes often performed *midrash*, or commentary, on scripture, for the edification of the faithful. An original and imaginative commentary on the account of Eden in the Book of Genesis (chapters 2 and 3), the *Hymns on Paradise* is a liturgical cycle of fifteen hymns, depicting the primordial Paradise of Adam to be the future (and possibly the present, with respect to an ante-Paradise) abode of the righteous. Documenting Ephrem's cosmogony, anthropology, and soteriology, these hymns penetrate deep within the ethos of early Syriac Christianity.

Ephrem has painted a visionary landscape from a palette of symbols of immanent transcendence. That the Paradise depicted in the

Hymns is clothed in metaphor, as Ephrem tells us, raises some questions as to how transcendent these symbols are and how immanent they may be at the same time. In other words, if Paradise is described in metaphor, could Paradise itself be a metaphor?

Ephrem's poetry was not recited, but sung. Choirs of virgins intoned these hymns in melodies already familiar to the congregation. Under such circumstances, we could easily picture how these lyrics, drawing on the Genesis narrative, could be so effective in performing exegesis for the benefit of lay Christians. This liturgical medium did not diminish or detract from the subtlety and allusive depth of Ephrem's interpretations, but some metaphorical competence on the part of the listener was surely required to follow such a hymn in all its interpretive details. Perhaps some of the finer points of Ephrem's exegesis might have been lost on the listener, but his hymns were popular just the same. Far more effective than any tome of theology, the *Hymns* had a formative impact in structuring the religious consciousness of those singing and of those who listened. The scriptures were expounded in a most memorable way. These hymns are rich and vivid; they must have inspired contemplation. The *Hymns on Paradise* must have captured the imagination of Ephrem's congregation, whom he served as deacon. The theme of Paradise must of been of especial interest.

Visionary texts purport to give us a glimpse of the afterworld, of Heaven and Hell, and of intermediate states, if any, in between. Ephrem tells us that in a vision, induced while reading scripture, he was suddenly transported to Paradise, a place which he begins to describe in some detail. Typically, in apocalyptic texts, such a mystic transport or rapture involves a "heavenly journey"—usually made possible by the assistance of a celestial being. Not so in the case of Ephrem, who hardly exceeds scripture in his own portrayal of Paradise. This seems to be the case with other Syriac Christian texts as well, in that "no Syriac apocalypse belongs to the type identified [. . . as . . .] apocalypses with a heavenly journey (with or without interest in history). The heavenly journey motif seems to be foreign to Syriac apocalyptic" (Martinez 1987, 339). Not through a purely mystical vision, but rather on the basis of scripture enhanced by poetic licence, the heavenly scenes Ephrem paints are for pastoral purposes.

The *Hymns on Paradise* are edifying in their dramatization and vivifying of details disclosed or implied by scripture. Though the hymns ostensibly focus on the afterlife (both prior to and after Resurrection), much of the imagery idealizes Christian life and community here on Earth. The moral truths of these hymns are not merely couched in the metaphorical "lie" for poetic effect. There was something real about Paradise that Ephrem had to explain in a surreal way. Could Ephrem's portrayal of Paradise have served as an allegory for a realized eschatology here on Earth? In reading Ephrem, we must bear in mind that Syriac Christianity expressed its truths in a symbolic rather than philosophical fashion (cf. Brock 1981, 70). Ephrem's hymns are not systematic expositions. Despite modern literary notions of the authorial fallacy, Ephrem's intentions are not difficult to divine. In composing the *Hymns*, Ephrem had Christians in mind. When the hymns were sung, thoughts turned heavenward. In his own Church, Paradise was the mirror on the intellectual ceiling. It reflected back.

The poet was poetically transported to Paradise, so that Paradise might be transported to the reader. This study argues that Ephrem has inverted worlds of correspondences. In an arc of descent, Paradise is a metaphor for the ideal Christian community. The "victorious" martyrs, for instance, are said to sometimes reside in this world: "From their abodes / the children of light descend, / they rejoice in the midst of the world / where they had been persecuted; / . . . Blessed is he who has seen / together with them, his beloved ones, / below in their bands of disciples, and on high in their bridal chambers" (HdP I.6, *HyP* 79–80). Which means, for Ephrem's listeners, that the souls of the beloved martyrs descend to local Nisibis; and, also, to Edessa. One might argue that the martyrs, as depicted here, descend to an *eschatological* Earth, the inheritance of the leonine meek. But Ephrem does not exclude the present time frame, and so this event has a potential immediacy.

It is as if the souls of the martyrs themselves, from the realm of sacred time to the sundial shadows of Roman and Persian Syria, had a charismatic role to play in this world as well. If read in this light, such a stanza must certainly have inspired and consolidated the emerging Paluṭian congregation in which Ephrem ministered as deacon. In an arc of ascent, Paradise is the symbol of a reality to which the faithful aspire and in the reality of which they already mystically participate. Here, the active principle of mystical experience is divinization at the level of sacrament, and good works at the level of praxis.

The Hymns on Paradise as liturgy. The manuscript tradition of Ephrem's hymns has been conveniently summarized by Kronholm (*Motifs* 17–19). The *Hymns on Paradise* are genuinely Ephremic, of uncontested authenticity. Ephrem's hymns were orders of public worship. As mentioned earlier, the hymns were performed liturgically. They were sung by choirs of virgins, affectionately known as the "Daughters of the Covenant" (*bnaṯ Qyāmā*), according to a Syriac *Life of Ephrem* (SCK 30, n. 1). As *madrāšē*, the *Hymns on Paradise* were meant to be sung, as distinct from the *mēmrē*, poetic homilies composed in verses of seven syllables, intended for reading. The *Hymns* consist of unrhymed stanzas comprised by a stanzaic pattern of syllables in the following pattern: 5 + 5 / 5 + 5 / 5 + 5 / 7 / 5 + 5 / 5 + 5.

More than worship, these litanies lit candles of doctrine in the minds of the faithful, within the stained glass and gathered silence of contemplation beneath the angelic galaxy of fourth-century Christian Syria. Jerome (*De viris illustribus* 115) informs us that, in certain churches, Ephrem's hymns were sung, following the scripture lections (Palmer 1993, 181, n. 10). Accessible to the illiterate, not restricted to the intellectual élite, these *Hymns* valorized religious truths and so became a shaping influence on local Christians. For the modern study of early Christianity, these hymns tell us much about the form and content of popular and not just of official religiosity, where the act of praise became part of the text. Thus, in any study of Syriac Christianity in Late Antiquity, liturgy cannot be marginalized. Of Ephrem's hymns, as liturgical rites, it could rightly be said: "A demand is made on actors enacting the rite to preserve a tacit management of paradox and ambiguity to realize its theological basis in a credible manner" (Flanagan 1991, 13).

Were the *Hymns on Paradise* meant to induce a realized eschatology? This is a question of the relationship between content and intent. Just what was being realized, if anything, in the *Hymns*, and what were the probability structures that could sustain such a realization? This much may be hazarded: these hymns, as mirror of the holy, were rites of contemplative passage into Paradise, mystic transports to the empyrean realms on high, visions of the celestial to inspire those on Earth treading the spiritual path leading to heaven.

In a realized state, Paradise is where the heart is: "In the bridal chamber of such a person's heart, the Creator resides" (Virg. XLIV.20, *LumE* 104). According to Semitic anthropology, the heart is the seat of the intellect as well as that of the emotions (*HyP* 192). Of the immanence of Paradise in this world, Ephrem assures: "The breath that wafts / from some blessed corner of Paradise / gives sweetness / to the bitterness of this region, / it tempers the curse / on this earth of ours" (HdP XI.10, *HyP* 157). Paradise is a presence, a fragrance that wafts from the realm above to the sanctuary below. But can it be realized? To approach such a question, Ephrem begins by teaching the Christian what Paradise is not. In Ephrem's *Hymns*, Paradise is real, but not always literally so.

The mirror of scripture. Ephrem's *Letter to Publius* may be said to be the prosaic counterpart of *Hymns on Paradise*, the former attesting the eschatology of the latter in several important respects. Ephrem speaks of the Gospel as "a figure" for the beauty of the Kingdom of Heaven. Through the Gospel looking-glass, this realm is visible to "the luminous eye." "There," Ephrem writes, "Paradise is visible, joyous with its flowers" (*Letter to Publius* 2, *LumE* 58). "The Scriptures are placed there like a mirror," the poet explains, "and he whose eye is luminous beholds there the image of reality" (HdF LXVII.8, *LumE* 57 and 32 [alternate trans.]).

Ephrem uses a metaphorical visionary form to express an eschatological reality (Yousif 1984). Gazing into "the mirror of the Gospel," Ephrem writes: "I saw there beautiful people, and I was desirous of their beauty; and I saw the place of the good where they were standing, and I was eager for their position. I saw their bridal chamber, which no one who has not a lamp may enter; I saw their joy, and I myself sat down in mourning, not possessing works worthy of that bridal chamber. I saw them clothed with the 'robe of light,' and I was grieved that I had prepared no virtuous raiment" (Brock 1982b, 19).

Metaphors of the incomparable. Tensions exist between literal and metaphorical descriptions of Paradise. It is an unusual move for a poet to explicate his own poetry, but Ephrem took preceptive measures against any temptation on the part of audience to take his metaphors literally. Ephrem is quite clear about the figurative nature of his descriptions: "If someone concentrates his attention solely / on the metaphors used of God's majesty, / he abuses and misrepresents that majesty / and thus errs / by means of those metaphors . . . / Do not let your intellect/ be disturbed by mere names, / for Paradise has simply clothed itself / in terms that are akin to you" (HdP XI.6–7, *HyP* 156). Brock characterizes Ephrem's idea of God's "putting on metaphors" as a virtual reality, a second form of incarnation (*HyP* 48). In fact, Ephrem uses several technical terms to highlight divine metaphoricity in Scripture and in Nature as well: symbol (*rāzā*); metaphor (*dmūtā*); allegory (*pelētā*); and type (*ṭupsā*), are among some of them.

The anthropology of the Hymns on Paradise. Ephrem plays on the ambiguity of metaphor and exploits the polyvalency of symbol so as to present Paradise in ecclesial as well as in otherworldly terms. In this sense, the hymns, once intoned, may be considered conceptually theurgic, in what Brock terms an "engagement" (*LumE* 29) with the metaphors. In this tension between the metaphoric and the realized, realization is achieved through accepting some of Ephrem's metaphorical correspondences between Paradise and parish. Brock resolves the tension through making a crucial distinction between "historical" and "sacred" time. He writes: "Because the paradisiacal life of the *eschaton* belongs to sacred time, it is possible for it to be experienced, in varying degrees, by individuals already in historical time on earth" (*LumE* 17). If Paradise may be partly realized on Earth, how is it experienced in heaven? With physical or spiritual senses? With body or mind, or both? To understand the modality of being a dweller in Paradise, a description of Ephrem's anthropology is required.

Trichotomy vs. dichotomy. One must beware of relying too heavily on any single analysis of Ephrem's thought. A case in point surrounds the issue of anthropological trichotomy vs. dichotomy. In his effort to situate Ephrem within the School of Antioch, el-Khoury opted for the latter: "Ephrem, typically Antiochene, espouses a dichotomous idea of man as the only created being capable of reconciling that old dualistic pair, matter and spirit" (1982, 1361). This association suggests, in the present writer's opinion, an urban Ephrem tinged with Hellenism, though this is incommensurable with the fact that Syrians rarely spoke Greek. Vööbus cites the instance of Ephrem's contemporary John Chrysostom, who complains that folk from the countryside could not understand his preaching in Greek since they knew only Syriac as their mother tongue (HOA 3: 196 and n.7). For Brock, Murray and Kronholm, Ephrem is more Semitic than he is Antiochene (see *Motifs* 25–28).

Spirit, according to el-Khoury, is not problematic for maintaining an Ephremic body-soul duality. Spirit (*rūḥā*) is "the spiritual principle of the body" (1982, 1364) which Ephrem describes as grains on a stalk of wheat (HdF XLII.10). Unfortunately, el-Khoury does not elaborate on the relationship of spirit to soul, or whether the two are synonymous or not. Kronholm reminds us that Ephrem's views on the soul, as with his anthropology in general, are not uniform. "It is, however, indisputable" concludes Kronholm, "that Ephrem's anthropological conception is *fundamentally* trichotomic" (*Motifs* 58). Yousif feels that trichotomy is "perhaps too strong a term" (1978, 55, n. 7). Notwithstanding, Ephrem's triune conception of man is explicitly set forth in the *Hymns*: "Far more glorious than the body (*gūšmā*) / is the soul (*nāfšā*), / and more glorious (*šebīḥ*) still than the soul / is the spirit (*tar'īṯā*), / but more hidden than the spirit / is the Godhead" (HdP IX.20, *HyP* 143 and 53). This may have some basis in Bardaiṣan's trichotomy (cf. Skjaervo, EIr 3: 782).

"Man," states Ephrem, "is perfected as triune: spirit, and soul, and the body as the third" (Ieiun. App. II.9, *Motifs* 59). Elsewhere, Ephrem speaks of "the three shapes of man" and that "man was constructed triunely" (CH LII.1). Technical terms for this trichotomy greatly vary (ibid.). "The three Names are sown in three ways," states Ephrem in another hymn, "in the spirit, the soul, and the body, mysteriously." Further: "If the spirit suffers, it is entirely imprinted by the Father; / if the soul suffers, it is wholly mingled with the Son; / and if the body is burnt in martyrdom, / then its communion with the Holy Spirit is complete." (HdF XVIII.5, Yousif 1978a, 53). Stewart offers this translation of the same passage: "If the spirit suffers, then it is entirely sealed with the Father; if the soul suffers, it is entirely united (*mzīgā*) with the Son; and if the body confesses and burns, it communes entirely with the Holy Spirit" (1991, 195, n. 124). This same idea is compressed in one line in *Hymns on Faith* XIII.3: "though our spirit suffer, our soul be separated, our body burnt" (op. cit., 56).

The "imprinted" spirit refers to its being divinized. The Syriac verb for "imprinted" is *ṭb'*, which belongs to the context of coinage, seals, and signets (McV 74, n. 66). It is in the nature of the spirit to be imprinted, that is, to take on the nature of that to which it aspires. In this passage is seen a total divinization of the complete, triadic person. In a distinction maintained to this day by Persian Christians, "spirit" refers to the spiritual principle in man, just as the "body" represents the physical being. The spirit can incline either way, in recrudescence to a feral state or in heliotropic inclination towards the spiritual sky.

The uniquely individual "soul" is mediate; it exists in both "worlds." Like the Father, one's own "spirit" transcends the physical world which it is crudely said to inhabit. Like the Son, one's "soul" is spirit incarnate, so to speak. Like the Holy Spirit, one's "body" is the locus on Earth of the divinizing effects of the Holy Spirit. (The latter had scarcely crystallized in Ephrem's writings as a divine Person until the Arian crisis, which prompted the beleagured poet to compose his *Hymns on Faith*, when Arianism had insinuated itself in Edessa [cf. Bruns 1989].) Since the spiritual realm corresponds only to the physical realm in form if not then in metaphor, the internal logic of such a view would dictate that, at some eschatological point, the body must transcend its own physicality in order to "live" in the spiritual realm of Paradise. According to Kronholm, el-Khoury is "mistaken in regarding the dichotomy as fundamental" (*Motifs* 162 n. 24, and 58, n. 33). Yet Kronholm does not state what role the spirit plays in Ephrem. It is clear from the passage above, however, that the spirit is more instinct with power, more rarefied, more subtle than the soul.

Scripture may have been determinative of these categories. St. Paul speaks of the Christian's "spirit, soul, and body" (1 Thess 5:25). According to Śpidlík, this trichotomic formula became traditional in the East (1986, 29). Ephrem drew an explicit analogy between the Trinity and the constituent elements in man. The analogy is more than poetic—it is noetic. The spirit links man to God through the Holy Spirit. There is a sympathetic connection between the Holy Spirit and the human spirit. This charismatism is crucial to salvation, the transcendence of the animal condition, the transition from feral anarchism to true freedom. The vehicle of the spirit is the soul, just as the vehicle of the soul is the body. Without soul, the body is lifeless; without spirit, the soul is lifeless. As intermediary, the soul can incline either way.

The dichotomy of trichotomy. The substances of man are two: spirit and matter. What really matters is the "gray matter," so to speak, in between! The soul can incline in either direction. This much has been said: if the soul gravitates towards the mundane, it becomes carnal, taking on the amoral properties of carnality in the moral sense. It may also be that the soul, in so doing, retains, as it were, the physicality of carnality itself, in plastic commensurability with the low estate of its consciousness. The soul that turns towards spirit, becomes spiritual not only in a moral sense, but takes on the properties of the spirit, and is physically translated in the process. The soul, nonetheless, stands in need of a vehicle, according to all formulas of *theōsis*.

The resurrection body is not the body of the Fall. The resurrection body is the primordial body in which the potential for immortality resided. The earthly body must therefore be transformed into a resurrection body adapted to a spiritual state. After death, the earthly body does not persist in substance at least in its original density, but rather in form and function. One thing is for certain: in the body/soul dualism, the soul has preëminence (Eccl. XXX.2). In forcing Ephrem's texts to conform to an Antiochene body/soul paradigm, el-Khoury appeals to HdP IX.20 to assert the priority of the soul over the body, yet makes no reference whatsoever to the priority of the spirit over the soul (1982, 1362).

Spirit. The immortality of the soul depends on the spirit, the divine principle in the soul. The soul was not born by choice; it is *reborn* by choice. Its rebirth consists of its union with a spiritual family of Father (God), Mother (the Holy Spirit), and Brother (Christ), the latter identification conceptually implicit in the idea of adoptive sonship. Ephrem states: "Let us learn about God from God himself: Just as he can be apprehended by means of his names as being God and the Righteous (One) and also the Good (One), so his (other) name 'Father' shows that he is a genitor. For the very name of fatherhood bears witness to (the existence of) his Son. And although he is the Father of one, through his love he is (the Father) of many" (HdF LII.1, Molenberg 1990, 139). Brock terms this new kinship with Christ as "brother" a dispensation of *parrhesia*, variously translated as "freedom" (to address God as "Father"), "confidence," and the like (1979b, 54).

Explicit mention of Christ as Brother is found in Mary's song to her infant: "Be God to the one who confesses You, and be Lord / to the one who serves You, and be brother / to the one who loves You so that You might save all" (Nat. XVI.1, McV 149). Jacob of Serug is more forthright in asserting: "Baptism makes us children so that we become brothers of the Only Begotten" (Brock 1979b, 55).

This assimilation of divinity was considered re-creative. Immortality is one thing; level of consciousness quite another. Even the wicked had an afterlife. Their afterlife consciousness-bound to carnality, such souls could scarcely be said to have "eternal" life in the strict etymological sense of the word: life "outside of time." The spirit in them is part of their essential anthropology; its dormancy is death in a relative sense. Even in primordial time there was what Ephrem refers to as a "hidden death" (Cruc. VIII.13, *LumE* 20).

The soul. The soul is "invisible." Ephrem is careful to distinguish the soul from the body's shadow, though idea of soul and shade seem to be antitypically analogous. The soul, moreover, is "great and perfect," yet is "altogether dependent on the Body" (Eph. Hypat., Mitchell 1912, 1: civ). Ephrem describes the soul, Syriac *nafšā*, as the "bride of man" (Eccl. XXXVIII.8, HdF XVIII.10, el-Khoury 1982, 1363). The soul is likewise the bride of Christ: "The soul is Your bride, the body Your bridal chamber. / Your guests are the senses and the thoughts. / And if a single body is a wedding feast for You, / how great is Your banquet for the whole Church!" (HdF XIV.5, *HyP* 28; cf. *Harp* 19).

The soul has three qualities: reason, (potential) immortality, and invisibility (el-Khoury 1982, 1363). Though invisible, the works of the soul are quite visible and indicate its spiritual state. Though death is necessarily the separation of the soul from the body, it seems that the body physically dies but not the soul. The soul of course can be spiritually "dead," that is, carnal and thus inert. It can, so to speak, "die"—through spiritual insensitivity—prior to physical death. Though the soul is not existentially dead in the afterlife, it is not fully alive. The soul in some sense is self-existent, but when deprived of the instrumentality of the bodily senses, "it lacks true existence" (HdP VIII.5, *HyP* 133). It seems that Ephrem's teachings on the soul stand midway between Tatian's categorical denial of the immortality of the (unsaved) soul (*Oratio ad Graecos* XIII.1) and Bardaiṣan's affirmation to the contrary.

The "soul of our soul". As reflexive evidence, an expression found in a post-Ephremic Syriac writer might prove illustrative. In his homily on the indwelling of the Holy Spirit, Philoxenus speaks of the Holy Spirit whom we receive from God" at baptism as "the soul of our soul" (Brock 1979b, 47). Unless purely metaphorical or an innovative post-Ephremic development, such an expression might suggest that, as the soul gives life to the body, the Spirit gives life to the soul. The Holy Spirit, in the first order of the trichotomic mingling, energizes the human spirit through the spirit of faith. The spirit is intimately bound up with the soul, more intimately than the soul is bound up with the body. As there is no separation imaginable in the spirit/soul fusion, the soteriological challenge is to eschatologically place the head back on the fabled headless horseman. It appears that, for Ephrem, the soul can subsist without the body, but it cannot subsist without the spirit. It is as if the relationship of spirit to soul to body is like that of a spark to flame to wick.

The body as vehicle for the soul. Ephrem's world is a hierarchy of mirrors within a kaleidoscope of symbols. Even if el-Khoury were right in holding Ephrem to a body-soul dichotomy, it would still be truer to speak in terms of a body-soul unity, for "they are a mirror of one another" (Eph. Hypat., Mitchell 1912, 1: cv). For Ephrem, the body is personalized, of value to the soul. The body is the soul's organ of perception and expression. The wholeness of a human being is predicated on it. Death, by definition, is the separation of body and soul. Life, conversely, is the uniting of body and soul. They need to be, as it were, remarried. But the conditions of their remarriage should be looked at very closely, as use of the word *body* may prove more context dependent than a surface reading of Ephrem might otherwise suggest.

Christ, in overcoming death, brings life. The death of the righteous is overcome by the divinization effected through uncompromised salvation. The dying process is reversed, as the body is reunited with the soul at the Last Judgment. During the interval between, Syriac Christianity paints a picture of the soul as a sleeping ghost (Gavin 1920), though Ephrem limns out a more positive picture in that the righteous wait their rewards in mansions reserved for them in the foothills just outside the Paradise (HdP VIII.11). No gnostic liberation from the body is conceived by Ephrem, though the body of the righteous in Paradise will be liberated from the disease of mortality. Rather than the soul being a spark of light trapped in the darkness of materiality, the soul is a spark of light shining in a lamp. The body is the lamp. At death, the lamp is broken. At the *eschaton*, the lamp is not merely reassembled; rather, it is recreated. Its once-opaque glass is recast as pure crystal.

There is some evidence to suggest that an individual is not in all respects materially equatable with his/her physical body. Were this to be so, the body would be resurrected in its gross state. We know that Ephrem held the resurrection body to be of a different, higher order than the material body. The former is incorruptible, the latter is not. Paradise is comprised of a spiritual substance, as Kronholm points out: "The Paradisiacal world is to him [Ephrem] neither earthly/ corporeally material, nor spiritually immaterial, but of a particular spiritual substance" (*Motifs* 69). If the substance of Paradise is spiritual, so must be the substance of the glorified body. For purposes of edification, it should be noted, this distinction was not pressed very hard. Otherwise, Ephrem would had to have accounted more for the discontinuity rather than the continuity envisaged in the somatic moment of the *eschaton*.

Ostensibly, the purpose of salvation in the fourth century was a purity worthy of immortality. This statement is perhaps too wooden, but it does broadly reflect a contemporary Christian yearning. Augustine himself goes so far as to say that "there was no other reason for the coming of Christ" apart from the resurrection of the body. "Take away death, the last enemy," Augustine preached, "and my own flesh will be my dear friend throughout eternity" (cited by G. Lawless 1990, 184). This goal of immortality is effected by an alchemy of the body, soul, and spirit into a new alloy, with the divinity of Christ as the elixir or potency.

Not viewed as the origin of sin, the body is rather the victim of sin. The mystery of the Eucharist is that a transubstantiation of body and soul is effected through a special immanence of the divine. Through the sacraments, divinity is said to "mingle" (*mzag*) with the believer's physical being in a kind of transformative fusion. Sanctification of the body and not just the soul is the work of a divine Physician, administering the medicines of salvation, sacramentally communicated in the "wheat, olive and grape" (Virg. XXXVII.3, SCK 77). Flesh, however, is not coterminous with the body, as examination of the following anthropological terms will bear out:

> *'Afrā*: "Dust" here is used in a purely earthly context, in regard to the material composition of the body. *Qaumā*, or *qaumtā*: "Height" or "size" in the sense of "stature" can refer to the human form and the humanness predicated of its upright posture. *Besrā*: "Flesh" can signify a human being, composed of flesh and blood. Some sense of "sinfulness" is attached to its Christian usage. As in the Hebrew, *besrā* can also mean "anyone" or "everyone" (el-Khoury 1982, 1362). *Pagrā*: There is a conflict among leading scholars of Syriac over the Greek equivalent of this term. Beck equates *pagrā* with *sōma* (1986, 8), while el-Khoury holds that the term generally corresponds to the Pauline usage of sarx (1982, 1362). Used as an anatomical term or for any corporate entity, *pagrā* anthropologically means "body" in contradistinction to the mind. *Gūšmā*: It is evident that *pagrā* and *gušmā* are synonyms, as Ephrem suggests in this parallelism: "Glory to that Voice (*qālā*) that became a body (*gušmā*) / and to the lofty Word (*melltā*) that became flesh (*pagrā*)" (Nat. IV.14, McV 100). According to el-Khoury, the former is generally considered to be the Syriac counterpart to the Pauline concept of *sōma*. The term *gušmā* indeed refers to a corporeal "body," but "emphasizes its role as the vessel of the soul." Matter, in this sense, is that which was formed by the spirit. The spirit, in turn, is informed by the senses. (1982, 1362–63)

Asceticism and the transformation of the body. The importance of asceticism in early Syriac Christianity cannot be overrated. Passion for the ascetic ideal was part and parcel of a peculiarly Syrian "order of rapture" (HOA 3: 194). "The searing lava of mortification," writes Vööbus, "virtually scalds the works in which such accounts are recorded" (ibid., 195). There is no Ephremic *Asceticon*, as it were. Rather, the "monastic witness" of Ephrem himself is "one of a pre-monastic life of evangelical chastity" (Mathews 1990, 101).

In the absence of contemporary sources, a document from the school of Ephrem may have some reflexive value in reconstructing the ascetical dimension of Ephrem's teachings in terms of principles though not of practices. Though Vööbus is incorrect as to its authenticity (Mathews 1990, 91–92), the first part of pseudo-Ephrem's "Letter to the Mountaineers" (Vööbus 1947) is a valuable post-Ephremic source for our knowledge of Syrian asceticism in Late Antiquity. (Vööbus pronounced the second part as an "alien body" or interpolation [HOA 3: 35].) This document describes monasticism in its primitive form, which Vööbus terms "eremitism"—a kind of premonasticism (HOA 3: 31).

The "mountaineers" (*ṭūrāyē*) are ascetics of whom pseudo-Ephrem speaks highly: "You see, my brothers, how great an army (lies) on the mountain" (ibid., 35). Also spoken of as *pārūšā* ("prudent")—employed in the monastic meaning of "separated ones"—pseudo-Ephrem addresses these anchorites with veneration as "brother mountaineers" (ibid.) situating them thereby on the mountains of either Nisibis or Edessa or both.

Suffering (*'ūlṣānā / ḥaššā*), according to pseudo-Ephrem, is the force that transforms the spiritual being. It is the hallmark of the ascetic ideal. Through mortification, the body is crucified. It is for this purpose Christ came, as an exemplar, that mendicants might experience his passion and its transformative effects: "Jesus died to the world in order that no one should walk sensuously by it. He died to our world in his body in order that he might make (us) alive by his body to his world. And he mortified the life of the body in order that we may not live carnally by the flesh. He was made the master, a teacher not in tribulations of others but by his own suffering. And he himself first tasted bitterness and (thereby) showed us that no one could become his disciple by name but only through suffering" (HOA 3: 32).

In this context, pseudo-Ephrem expresses the teleology of asceticism in a new way: ascetics, in the context of their contests of faith against the beasts of instinct urged on by the gladiators of demonic temptation, are represented as true martyrs, "martyrs of hiddenness" (*Mēmrā on the Solitaries and Mourners*, HOA 3: 45–46). This is akin to Origen's "martyrdom of conscience" (*Exhortation to Martyrdom* XXI, Špidlík 1986, 76).

Asceticism, generally speaking, may be regarded as a movement which grew up in the aftermath of martyrdom. From this vantage, asceticism may be regarded as a continuation of the martyr tradition. Certain key terms used to describe martyrs, such as *athlete*, *contest*, and the like, are transferred to ascetics, and as such a strong indicators of affinities with the martyr ideal (see Brock 1973, 2). Very likely this represents the phenomenon of nonsanguinary renunciation under new historical circumstances, when persecutions ceased. Ascetics, though shunners of society, play an important role in society, according to pseudo-Ephrem. Their intercessory prayer sustains the rest of the world, a idea which Vööbus depicts as "a favorite thought of 'Aphrēm" (HOA 3: 39).

Relevant to the present study is the concept of the gradual *theōsis* of the body of the ascetic, exemplifying a theology of activity. Suffering, in the *Letter to the Mountaineers*, transforms the physical being into that of an angel and produces God's image in man (HOA 3:45). Have angels, then, bodies? Earth angels in the Syrian desert did. Ascetics came to be regarded as incarnating, so to speak, an *angelikos bios*. The difference is of course subtle.

Paradise Lost. The story of the Fall is so familiar that its retelling may seem superfluous. There are, however, certain elements and motifs in Syriac lore that are not Occidental commonplaces. One might think of the Paradise narrative in its Syriac reading as something like the fable of the Emperor's new clothes. Pre-Fall Adam was King of Paradise. Both in the fable and in the Genesis account, the King is robed in splendor, but through vanity (in Adam's case, the wish to become a god) both ended up shamefully naked. Ephrem symbolically condensed the primordial episode of the Fall in the idea of the stole of glory, the "robe of light." This garment is the golden fleece of Syriac Christian soteriology. Its recovery was the odyssey of Christ. Its investiture was the cherished hope of every Christian. Indeed, the very idea of clothing is the most frequently recurring imagery found throughout the various hymn cycles (see *LumE* 25).

As in early Zoroastrianism, the key concept in Ephrem's anthropology is choice. In the interplay between free will and the will of God, Adam's Fall was the result of his own volition and miscalculation. The serpent is not to blame, but is culpable as an accomplice. Adam mirrors the human predicament. His free will is the crux of spiritual capacity. Its optative exercise alone is determinative. As such, God predetermined neither Adam's mortality or immortality. With Adam's disobedience of God came the loss of godliness, one aspect of which is immortality. Adam was stripped of his radiance, the "Robe of Glory," less frequently referred to as his "Robe of Light." The Bible intimately links sin with death. It was to be expected that Ephrem understood Paradise Lost in the very same terms. Salvation makes it possible for the Fall to be reversed. It is up to every true Christian to reverse the Fall.

The pre-Fall figure of Adam serves as an inverse eschatological paradigm of what it is possible for the righteous to become. Adam's investiture as King of Paradise, Priest, and Prophet (the so-called *tria munera* which becomes the triple office of Christ)—heightens the extent of the Fall and sharpens the contrast between saved and unsaved. It was Christ, strictly speaking, as the agent of creation, who fashioned Adam of dust, breathed into Adam his soul (is the soul therefore the breath of God?), and invested him with glory (*šwbḥ'*). The "Glory" of the Robe may have something to do with the charisma of God's presence, the Hebrew notion of *kabod ha-shem*, the "Glory of God" which Ezekiel beheld, but this must remain only a suggestion as a review of the literature discloses very little in this connection. In any event, Adam was in every respect the "image of God," and it is this original-image relation that Christ restored. The vaunted "Robe of Glory"—invisible to the naked eye—may be restored through baptism. Ephrem reminds us in the opening verse of *Hymns on Paradise* that Paradise itself is invisible to the mortal eye. Thus, in scripture, Paradise is "described in visibilities, praised for invisibilities" (HdP I.1, *Motifs* 67). The robe, presumably, is visible in Paradise.

Paradise regained—baptism as reentry into Paradise. Brock invokes Dante here in describing this final stage as "Paradise regained" (1979b, 51). To recapitulate Ephrem's conception of salvation history, the Robe of Glory is lost but may be won back once more. The mythology surrounding the Robe rationalizes the efficacy of the Sacraments according to the following drama of salvation: Act One: *Primordial Robes of Glory*: In Paradise, Adam and Eve were clothed in "Robes of Glory" or "Robes of Light." Act Two: *Disrobed in disgrace*: After the Fall, Adam and Eve were stripped of their "robes of glory/light." Act Three: *Christ places Robe in Jordan*: God "puts on Adam" or "a body" in order to "reclothe mankind in the robe of glory." In the course of his descent into the waters of the Jordan at baptism, Christ deposits the "robe of glory/ light" into the water, sanctifying for all time all baptismal water. Act Four: *Robe regained at Baptism*: The invocation of the Holy Spirit at baptism consecrates the baptismal font, effectively transforming it, in sacred time and space, into the waters of the Jordan. The "robe of glory" which Adam lost in the Fall is recovered by the Christian at baptism (Brock 1982b, 12).

Paradise to come. In CNis XXXVI.7, Death is personified. In one of its speeches, Death confesses: "There are two men—I must not deceive—whose names are missing for me in Sheol: Enoch and Elijah did not come to me; . . . they might have entered Paradise and escaped [from Sheol]" (HdP V.9, *HyP* 105). The figure of unsaved Eve provided a typological exemplar. Eve resides not in Paradise but in Sheol (Nat. XIII.2, McV 137). This picture of all deceased humanity in Sheol partly conflicts with another scenario described by Ephrem in the *Hymns on*

Paradise, that of the resting-place for the righteous, awaiting the Resurrection. Furthermore, Paradise "is full of spiritual beings" (HdP V.9, *HyP* 105), who banquet, in what appears to be a reference to the present and not to future bliss: "There, manifest and fair / to the eye of the mind, / are coveted banquets of the just / who summon us / to be their companions and brothers" (HdP VI.16, *HyP* 114).

The bones of the righteous remain in Sheol while the souls of the righteous tarry in the outskirts or environs of Paradise. This is partly indicated by Ephrem's eschatological vision, in which "no bone will remain in Sheol" (Virg. XXXVI.10, SCK 78). As in the passage above, Ephrem drops some hints to the effect that the souls of the righteous are not really asleep after all. Apart from the Semitic question of the bones, Ephrem depicts a resort for the righteous deceased until the time of the Resurrection: "Thus in the delightful mansions / on the borders of Paradise / do the souls of the just / and righteous reside, / awaiting there / the bodies they love" (HdP VIII.11, *HyP* 135).

This ante-Paradise is definitely not Sheol. The problem is that, though the soul is self-existent (HdP VIII.5, *HyP* 133), the disincarnate righteous are in a state of deficient sensation and consciousness (HdP VIII.7, *HyP* 133) since the body is instrumental to perception, without which the soul "lacks true existence" (HdP VIII.7, *HyP* 133). The soul cannot die at death; for otherwise the sacraments would be devoid of efficacy. Nor does its preservation seem to be entirely insentient. Ephrem speaks of death, but not of the death of souls in terms of subsistence.

At death, the soul takes flight (HdP IX.16). The body remains interred until trumpets summon. The Resurrection, however conceived, is a definite event in the writings of Ephrem. This climax of salvation history cannot be spiritualized away. It is open to conceptual reconsideration. Elsewhere, Ephrem does speak of the disgorgement of the dead by Sheol at Christ's harrowing (Darling 1987, 119), though whether or not this was understood at a purely literal level is perhaps open to question.

Paradise realized: Heaven on Earth. According to Brock, though Ephrem is "at a considerable remove from his contemporaries St. Athanasius, St. Basil and the two Sts. Gregory" in thought pattern and expression, yet they are "essentially at one" in their conceptions of the mystery of the Trinity and the Incarnation (*LumE* 3). "The Syriac Fathers, no less than the Greek," concludes Brock, "see the *theōsis* or divinization of man as the end purpose of the inhominization of God" (1982, 20).

Earthly body and the resurrected body. There is a fundamental problem of identity and difference between the earthly body and the resurrected body. There had been a long-standing debate within and without early Christianity over the vexed question of the resurrection of the body. The pagan philosopher Porphyry (d. *c*. 301) had attacked Christianity for its monstrous and ridiculous belief in physical resurrection. Around the year 177 C.E., Celsus summarized pagan objections to Christianity, calling it "the hope of worms." After all, who in his right mind would desire a body that had rotted? "The resurrection is both revolting and impossible," Celsus concluded (Barnard 1984, 44). This problem will repay a moment's consideration.

Virginity and the angelic life. For Ephrem, true to the Christian Orient and East alike, the goal of existence is full and perfect deification, the life of lived dogma, the translation of body and soul into the realm of the spirit. Does teleology condition views of salvation or does the reverse? Towards this end, the life of the ascetics was considered exemplary, useful to the soul. As a church within a church, the ascetics enriched a sense of spirituality generally, like a spiritual leaven. Virgins were the jewel or "beryl" of the Church. Taken together, the solitaries and virgins could be seen as "a peacock of the spirit" (CH XLII.10, SCK 75). The deeds of solitaries were to be appreciated but not always to be imitated. The lay life was also holy. Celibacy was not a precondition for baptism in Ephrem's churches, even though it optimized "single-mindedness." The ascetic ideal notwithstanding, that school of love called marriage was considered lawful and holy, in the context of praxis and contemplation.

"The Angels," wrote Ephrem, "have received the gift of virginity without effort but you on the contrary on the basis of battle" (Virg. XV.4, HOA 3: 29). The idea here, to put it crudely, is that since there was no sex in primordial Paradise nor is there marriage in heaven, angels are virgins in a world in which sex has no place. Angels are undifferentiated as to gender. In a world in which sex is instinct with power to tempt, virginity represents the ascetic ideal to become angelic. (For a critique of this ideal from a feminist perspective, see Castelli 1986.) In the process, one has the potential to become superior to angels.

Realized Paradise. The Robe of Glory originates in primordial time. It is reinvested in eschatological time. It is acquired in historical time, in its coincidence with what Brock calls "sacred time," drawing the inevitable conclusion: "The life of the baptized Christian should accordingly be that of a realized eschatology" (1982, 19). In a hymn attributed to Ephrem, but of doubtful authenticity, the "eschatology is certainly 're-alized'," according to Murray: "See, you are reclining at the wedding-feast / which is the Holy Church, / and you are eating the living body / and drinking His pure blood" (SCK 257).

The Problem of postbaptismal sin. Salvation notwithstanding, it is possible to forfeit one's lot in Paradise: "Sins before baptism / by simple work are able to be atoned. / And if the imprint of scars sullies [the Christian], / baptism whitens and wipes them clean. / But sins after baptism / with double works are able to be overturned." (Virg. XLVI.24–26, McV 450–51). Brock renders this passage so: "Sin committed before baptism / can be absolved easily, in baptism, / And even if the mark of the sin's wounds is deep, / yet baptism will whiten and wipe them away; / But post-baptismal sins can only / be reversed by means of double labours." (1976b, 63). Does this indicate loss of immortality at the substantial level or at the sapiential level? Here, soteriology stands or falls on its supporting anthropology.

The substances of man's creation. The Syriac term for "substance" is *qnūmā*, which varies according to the nature (*kyānā*) of a thing. Ephrem states that the Creator "infused into the powdered dust a manifold spring (*m'yn' dpwršn' nsk bh bdḥyḥ'*)" (CNis XLIX.3, *Motifs* 57). This spring, a metaphor for the soul, gives life to the dust. Conversely, in Paradise, "springs of wisdom" are said to burst forth from the mouths of its dwellers (HdP IX.8). This indicates that the substance of Paradise is considerably different from that of Earth; the constitution of Paradise is of a separate order altogether. In both earthly and celestial realms the soul is said to abide. The body, however, will have to undergo such transformation at the *eschaton* that the differences in many respects likely outweigh the similarities.

The substance of Paradise. Paradise, in Ephrem's vision of it, is, to a great extent, informed by Jewish concepts (cf. Séd 1968). But it is not wholly informed by them. Paradise is mountain, towering above all earthly mountains, its underside said to be circular, overarching land and sea (HdP I.8) like a dome. Paradise is, above all, a cosmic mountain, a nonphysical yet nonetheless a sarcous environ, at a metaphorical level at least. One of the challenges of reading Ephrem is having the metaphorical competence to decode Ephrem wherever this may be warranted, and to accept the rest at face value.

Kronholm notes on the basis of Beck's analysis that "Paradise in Ephrem's view is not 'eine rein geistige Grösse' . . . nor is it corporeally/terrestrially material, as is seen in HdP XI" (*Motifs* 69, n. 78). Elsewhere, the Swedish scholar states categorically: "The Paradisiacal world is neither corporeally material, nor spiritually immaterial, but it is constituted of a spiritual substance, in Ephrem's view" (*Motifs* 163 n. 27, citing Beck 1951 and Ortiz de Urbina 1955). This is obvious from HdP XI.4: "Let not this description of it [Paradise] / be judged by one who hears it, / for descriptions of it / are not at all subject to judgment, / since, even though it might appear terrestrial / because of the terms used, / it is in reality / spiritual and pure. / Even though the name of "spirit" / is applied to two kinds of beings, / yet the unclean spirit is quite separate / from the one that is sanctified" (*HyP* 155). This passage is interesting in that it is quite clear that some kind of translation of the physical being must take place, for Paradise is too rarefied for gross matter. Elsewhere, Ephrem likens Paradise to the wind, which has "no outer array or substance at all" (HdP XV.1, *HyP* 182).

What is the Robe of Glory and its substance? Mary, in effect, was the first to be baptized by Christ, to receive the transforming touch of divinity: "The Son of the Most High came and dwelt in me, / and I became His mother. As I gave birth to Him/ —His second birth—so too He gave birth to me / a second time. He put on His mother's robe / — His body; I put on His glory" (Nat. XVI.11, *Harp* 15). What is "glory"? Of what substance is it? Glory is light; this is a metaphorical tautology, of course. The Robe of Glory is often called the Robe of Light. Both are references to divinity. Glory and light represent the Holy Spirit. Hence: "John whitened the stain of sins with ordinary water, so that the bodies might be rendered suitable for the robe of the Spirit that is given through our Lord. Because the Spirit was with the Son, the Son came to John in order to receive baptism from him, so that He [Jesus] might mix with the visible water the Spirit who cannot be seen, so that those whose bodies perceive the wetness of the water might perceive in their minds the gift of the Holy Spirit" (de Dom nos. 55, *LumE* 72). The Robe of Glory thus is bestowed in the waters of baptism. It is the equivalent of the Pauline metaphor of "putting on Christ" (*LumE* 72–73). What effects, then, does this Robe of Glory have?

Problems inherent in Ephrem's soteriology. Often compared to Athanasius's formula that God became man that man might become God (*On the Incarnation* LIV.3), Ephrem gives an epitome of salvation in *Hymns on the Nativity* I.97, 99: "The Lord of natures today was transformed contrary to His nature; / . . . Today the Deity imprinted Itself on humanity, / so that humanity might also be cut into the seal of Deity" (McV 74; cf. n. 66, where McVey suggests a parallel with Athanasius). Patristic doctrines of *theōsis* taken together, Maurice Wiles explains that when speaking in terms of divinization, "the Fathers did not intend the parallelism to be taken with full seriousness." "The Word," moreover, "who was fully God, did not become fully man that he might make us full men becoming fully God. In speaking of man's divinization the Fathers intended to convey that men should become gods only in a secondary sense—'gods by grace' (ϑεοι κατα χαριν) . . . ; it was never believed that they would become what the Word was—namely, 'God by nature' (ϑεος κατα φυσιν)." (1967, 107–108, cited by Strange 1985, 342–43). Strange states that Wiles has "questioned the need for a fully divine saviour when the salvation men receive is of grace and not of nature. As he observed, men become gods only in a secondary sense; they do not become what the Word is. Why should the saviour have to possess a divinity any different from the one he bestows?" (ibid., 343). Wiles's criticism does not seem to have occurred to the ancient critics of Christianity, such as Celsus and Porphyry, as the question is Christian and not pagan.

In any event, the Eucharist is an elixir performing an alchemy of body and soul. The wafer is, as it were, the alchemist's "orange egg" and immortality is won. In the ancient concept of the soul being handicapped if left, literally, senseless, the spiritualization of the inner man was coterminous with that of the outer man through a spiritual agency. If spirit has the power to form matter, by the very same logic, spirit has the power to transform matter.

In this respect, the transformation is complete. Matter is no longer matter, for matter no longer matters. As Ephrem states: "And if these things which are to come are more subtle than the Body in accordance with the places (in which they are), so it (i.e., the Body) will undergo change. For that Will which made it gross for the gross purpose which is here present, made it for that Spiritual abode which is yonder" (Eph. Hypat., Mitchell 1912, 1: cv). At best, its form and functions persist, and even that may in some sense be metaphorical, bound by the constraints of our language to explain the ineffable. The following examples will suffice to show that Ephrem, contrary to his assertion that the soul's perceptions are tied to the instrumentality of the body, is able to speak of its relative irrelevance:

Obviating taste. The *Hymns on Paradise* possess their own "grammar of images," so to speak, with gridded ambiguities of images that interlock, giving rise to different levels of interpretation (Maguire 1987, 42; cf. Farrugia 1990). In Paradise, for instance, the body has no other function than to act as an instrument of perception, as the locus of the senses. Even so, we can eliminate taste from the necessary instruments of perception, as the rarefied body in Paradise does not eat: "but yonder it is souls, instead of bodies, that crave food" (HdP IX.20, *HyP* 142). Rather, the soul is sustained by "joy" (HdP IX.23). One of the senses, therefore, is no longer needed: that of taste. In Paradise, there is neither material food nor drink (IX.9), as the repast, of an utterly different order, is spiritual and sapiential. "The teeth do not weary," (HdP IX.9, *HyP* 139), presumably because they do not chew! Of Paradise, Ephrem states that "the senses were no longer able / to contain its treasures / so magnificent they were— / or to discern its savors" (HdP VI.2, *HyP* 109).

Obviating the olfactory sense. What, then, of the sense of smell? Paradise is perfumed with fragrances, to be sure, "its scents most wonderful" (HdP IV.7, *HyP* 100). It may be that it is "adapted" to perceive "wisdom": "That Garden is / the life-breath / of this diseased world" (HdP XI.10, *HyP* 157). Like Divinity perhaps, Paradise is both transcendent and immanent. Paradise transcends the senses, but its vivifying breezes waft into the congregations of the faithful here on Earth. By simple elimination, if the sense of smell cannot perceive these breezes, a spiritual organ is the only faculty of perception that can.

Obviating physical sight. To achieve beatific vision, physical sight is not necessary. Not sight *per se*, but insight is required. Hence Ephrem says: "With the eye of my mind (*b-'aynā d-re'yānā*) / I gazed upon Paradise" (HdP I.4, *HyP* 78 and 38–39). And, further: "the sight of Paradise / is far removed, / and the eye's range / cannot attain to it" (HdP I.8, *HyP* 80). The premillennial denizens of Sheol, who presumably live in a discarnate state, are able to gaze on Paradise from across the "Abyss" (HdP II.12), as was the case with the rich man and Lazarus at Luke 16:26, as Ephrem is careful to point out. Presumably this visual acuity has nothing to do with a carnal cornea and retina, as this state is prior to the Resurrection. At best, the organs of the senses may be transformed into organs of the soul at the *eschaton*.

There are doubts about even this, if we take into consideration the various descriptions of perception in the afterworld that Ephrem paints. Physical organs of perception, certainly, cannot enjoy the beatitude of Paradise, as there "carnal desires no longer exist" (HdP II.3, HyP 85), not due to resistance to temptation but rather to its irrelevance to a nonphysical domain of satiety. "For what mind," avers Ephrem, gazing on Paradise from without, "has . . . the faculties to explore it?" (HdP III.1, *HyP* 90). "For feeble eyes," continues Ephrem in the same vein, "cannot gaze upon / the dazzling sight / of its celestial beauties" (HdP XI.8, *HyP* 156). And yet, it was with the mind's eye, and not the physical eye, that Ephrem was able to gaze on Paradise, in the wake of his mystic transport while reading Scripture: "The eye and the mind / traveled over the lines / as over a bridge, and entered together / the story of Paradise. / The eye as it read / transported the mind; / in return the mind, too, / gave the eye rest / from its reading, / for when the book had been read / the eye had rest, / but the mind was engaged" (HdP V.4, *HyP* 103). Ephrem's rationale for the resurrection of the body is that the soul depends upon the body, as the locus of the senses, for perception. Yet the physical senses of ocular vision, taste, and smell are, as demonstrated above, eschatologically obviated. The afterlife relevance of the senses, on the one hand, is affirmed by Ephrem but, on the other hand, such senses are circumscribed: "My eye indeed remained outside, but my mind entered within" (HdP V.5, *HyP* 104).

One does not see in Ephrem any dependence upon his elder contemporary Aphrahāṭ. Otherwise, we might have seen in Ephrem a more pronounced concept of what the Persian Sage had variously referred to as "spiritual senses": "spiritual senses of the mind" (*regšay hawnā rūḥānē*); "senses of the mind" (*regšay hawnā*); "senses of thought" (*regšay maḥšabṯā*); "senses of the intelligence" (*regšay tarʿīṯā*); "senses of the intellect" (*regšay reʿyānā*); "senses of meditations" (*regšay hemsayhōn*); "eyes of the senses" (*ʿaynay regšē*); [invisible] "organs within" (*hadāmē d-lgaw*); "organs of the soul" (*hadāmē d-nafšā*); "senses of the soul" (*regšay d-nafšā*) (adapted from Stewart 1991, 165–66).

Aphrahāṭ, in *Demonstrations* XIV, in describing the wonders of creation, speaks of what can be accepted as the Syriac counterpart to the Greek idea of the spiritual senses: "The wings of understanding are spread out, / and the wings of thought are unfolded, / and the senses of the intellect are exploring, / and the eyes of the conscience are contemplating / and the pupils [of its eyes] roam to and fro / so that the investigation may be known to sight and to knowledge / while not comprehending their limits" (Stewart 1991, 165). This concept contextualizes the Syriac *Liber Graduum* when it speaks of the "organs within" or of the "organs of the soul" and thus we find Ephrem speaking of the "inner senses of thoughts" in HdF IV.6 (ibid., 166, n. 234). If Ephrem concedes the existence and functionality of such senses, why not their relative autonomy? This is a problem that arises in any attempt to systematize Ephrem's anthropology and the eschatology upon which it is predicated. The present study proposes one solution: The *Hymns on Paradise* are crafted in such a way as to appeal to the more mundane conceptions of afterlife requital more readily accessible to the common lay Christian, whereas, at a more abstract level of reading, the hymns may be read as professedly metaphorical, both in terms of Paradise itself and in its allegorical inversion to describe the status and profundity of the Christian communal life on Earth.

It should come as no surprise therefore when Kronholm concludes that Ephrem's views on the soul "are not uniform" (*Motifs* 58). The soul, in contradistinction to the beast, is endowed with speech (CNis XLIV.1). The soul, moreover, has the ability, through the agency of speech, "to express wisdom" (HdP VIII.8, *Motifs* 58). It is this sapiential ability that is of such anthropological importance in the process of *theōsis*.

Bodily, not physical, resurrection. Hymn VIII of the *Paradise* cycle makes it abundantly clear that the soul cannot function adequately without its companion, the body. Ephrem's Paradise is not incorporeal. (That may, however, be immaterial.) There is reason to believe, however, that the resurrection body and its disports in Paradise are rather of a different order altogether. One clue is the nature of Paradise itself. Assuming the resurrection body will be adapted to its celestial environs, we may infer that it would not differ fundamentally from the constitution of the leaves of Paradise. The leaves of Paradise, we are told, "are spiritual" yet "have taken on bodily form" (HdP XI.8, *HyP* 156). This indicates that the Resurrection is corporeal in form, but not so in terms of flesh.

If this is an inaccurate assessment, it could at least be said that the bodily resurrection that Ephrem envisions is substantially different from physical resurrection. Not only is the sight of Paradise achieved by insight, the mind's eye, but the entire resurrection body itself is likened by Ephrem to the mind: "A hundred times finer / and more subtle / are the bodies of the righteous / when they are risen, at the Resurrection: / they resemble the mind" (HdP V.8, *HyP* 105). The rarefication of which Ephrem speaks is of such subtlety that the "spiritual beings" (*rūḥānē*, Beck 1986, 21). are described as "so refined in substance that even thoughts cannot touch them!" (HdP V.10, *HyP* 106). Elsewhere Ephrem relates: "Bodies, / with their flow of blood, / receive refinement there / after the manner of souls; / the soul that is heavy / has its wings refined/ so that they resemble/ resplendent thought . . . / For bodies shall be raised / to the level of souls, / and the soul / to that of the spirit, / while the spirit will be raised / to the height of God's majesty" (HdP IX.19, 21, *HyP* 143).

The Resurrection, therefore, in Ephrem's conception of it, is not simply an "arising" in the sense of revivification. It is an "arising" in the sense of a spiritual ascent, in which the whole tripartite being of man is "raised" to new life and to new heights. In what manner may we conceive of this? In this present life, in what really amounts to a realized eschatology for Ephrem, "the mind . . . is spiritual" (HdP VI.2, *HyP* 109) and it is the mind in mystic transport, and, at the *eschaton*, something like the mind into which the resurrection body is transformed, that can attain the environs of Paradise and, by the blessing of its Creator, enter into its Garden. There is in fact the suggestion that the metaphors Ephrem employs for his portrayal of Paradise may be decoded. From HdP VI.6 and elsewhere, we may thus infer: *Symbols of Paradise* (Symbol = Referent): Bud = Heart; Produce = Rational Speech; Fruit = Words (Deeds, VI.11); Plants = Truth; Sweet Scents = Love; Blossoms = Chastity (VI.12); Beauty = Mind (VI.13); Flowers = Virtuous Life (VI.13); Garden = Free Will (VI.13); Earth = Human Thought (VI.13); Trees = "Victors" (VI.14); Treasure Store = Hidden Mysteries (VI.25).

Asōmata, eidic vision, and "mixing". Evidently, Ephrem's anthropology shares certain features with that of Bardaiṣan, the "Aramean philosopher" as Ephrem calls him (BarE 165). In one respect, there may be this affinity: body and soul are separable, but not soul and spirit, which is hidden in the soul. The levels of Paradise correspond with degrees of spiritual development and perfection. There, the human encounter with things divine is vivid and immediate. One gets the impression, *inter alia*, that although the necessity of the body is formally recognized by Ephrem, in practice the body is an appendage that must be radically rehabilitated to adapt itself to the clime of the sublime. In the heights of Paradise, the soul is sustained, as it were, intravenously. Its apprehension is direct, in what can best be metaphorically understood as an implicit, Origenistic duplication of the external senses to describe the operation of faculties of cognition in the inner recesses of the soul. These faculties may be arrested in an aborted embryonic state in the unsaved person. With no debt to Origen intended, Ephrem's eschatological anthropology may be described as eidetic and transfigural.

"The assembly of saints," writes Ephrem, "bears resemblance to Paradise" (HdP VI.8, *HyP* 111). Of greater moment, by contrast, is the resemblance of Paradise to the Church, where the metaphors of Paradise are inverted, serving as an allegory for the Church. Ecclesiastically, the zigguratic ascents of the cosmic Mountain refer primarily not to the terraced levels the Paradise itself, but rather to the Church: "The mystery of the levels / of that Garden of Life / He prefigured in the Ark / and at Mount Sinai. / Symbols of Paradise / and its disposition he has depicted for us; / established, fair and desirable in every way, / in its height and its beauty, / in its fragrance and variety. / It is the haven of all riches; / in it the Church is symbolized" (HdP II.13, SCK 258).

Conclusions. The *Hymns on Paradise* purport to give an otherworldly glimpse into the afterlife. Theses hymns, however, belong more properly to exegesis than to the genre of apocalypse. No supernatural agency for this vision served as intermediary. Rather, Ephrem was mystically "transported" to Paradise during his reading of Scripture.

Nature, of course, everywhere spoke to Ephrem of the hidden God, the revealed Christ, and of the sanctifying Spirit; but Scripture informed him of eschatological matters more directly. Ephrem's paradise is informed by his views on human nature, and this is where anthropology may be seen to structure eschatology. The edifying intent of the hymns is quite apart from these concerns: it is Ephrem's ecclesiological vision which the *Hymns on Paradise* was meant to inspire.

The trichotomy fundamental to Ephrem's anthropology allowed for Syriac mysticism to speak of progress along somatic, psychic, and pneumatic stages (HOA 3: 329). The doctrine of *theōsis* may be seen as a controlling principle here. Indeed, this soteriology—so prevalent in the fourth century—clearly structures, but does not control, Ephrem's teachings on the work of Christ.

Deification was effected through chrism, baptism, and the Eucharist. The poet wrote extensively on the efficacy of these mysteries.

But salvation was no guarantor of spirituality. For this, free will took precedence, as it was possible to forfeit one's place in Paradise as a consequence of postbaptismal sin. The eschatological wedding garment stood in danger of being stained. It was ethical vigilance that maintained eschatological preparedness.

As we would expect, Christ's divinity did not minimize his humanity in Ephrem's view. This is an important consideration in conserving the ethical teachings which came to characterize Ephrem's system which was in ethical competition with that of Bardaiṣan. To do so would be so weaken the effective basis of the divine "economy"—the effective means of salvation.

It has been the purpose of this study to argue for a shift in emphasis in Ephrem's *Hymns on Paradise* from the belief in physical resurrection to a doctrine of what might be termed sapiential *theōsis*. The argument presented in this study was difficult and methodologically involved, and had to be unpacked in a cumulative way. The concept of sapiential *theōsis* is not an attempt to split cumin seeds, as the Romans would say, but rather an effort to demonstrate the subtle ways in which Ephrem speaks in a traditionally Semitic vein, yet innovates on the tradition of "the sleep of the soul" in which the body and soul repose in Sheol until the Resurrection Day. Ephrem pays lip service to this doctrine, but does not consistently support it.

Ephrem departs from the Syriac tradition of the Sleep of the Soul in two significant respects: In the hymns, Ephrem indulges in speculation in which the righteous, awaiting the Resurrection, reside in mansions outside the environs of Paradise (HdP VIII.11; cf. V.15). A further innovation by Ephrem is the idea that sinners (presumably, those who are repentant) may receive chastisement and forgiveness in a kind of purgatory situate between the Fire and the Garden (HdP X.14; cf. I.16–17).

Controversy over the immortality of the soul impacts on the soteriology of *theōsis*. If it is conceded that the soul is immortal, there is then no need for divinization. The power of baptism and the sacraments to confer immortality is seriously undermined if divested of their elixiric effect in the alchemy of body and soul. But it seems that Ephrem's soteriology was not entirely predicated on *theōsis*. He does not set out to prove it, nor is he at pains to defend it, though he refers to it frequently. In so doing, Ephrem simply elaborates on its eschatological consequences.

Divinization in terms of "substance" is one thing, but becoming godly is quite another. The doctrine of *theōsis* was a fourth-century given. For Ephrem, immortality was not so much at issue. Christ had assured the rewards of Paradise. Ephrem was concerned to present Paradise in a homiletic light. Rather than drawing on Nature as a point of departure for homily, as so often happens in medieval preaching, Paradise serves as the natural setting of matters spiritual, upon which a homily may be constructed. Aphrahāṭ's description of the wise man, in *Demonstrations* XIV, the realized eschatology of which is patent, could easily fit the scheme of Ephrem's *Hymns on Paradise*: "He is a great palace for his Maker: / the King of the heights comes and dwells in him, / raises his mind to the heights / and makes his thoughts soar to the sanctuary, / revealing to him treasures of all kinds . . . / The Watchers hasten to serve him / and the Seraphs cry 'holy' to his glory, / flying with their swift wings, / their garments white and resplendent, / veiling their faces from his splendour, / rushing swifter than the wind . . . / His form and appearance are on earth / but his mental senses are above and below. / His thought is swifter than the sun, / his insights flash faster than the wind, / swift as on wings in every direction." (Murray 1990, 150 and 151). On this passage, Murray concludes that Aphrahāṭ "does not spell out what his words imply" and that "it is only towards the end of the passage that its relevance becomes clear": to wit, "Aphrahāṭ is holding up cosmic order as a model for order in the Church" (ibid., 151). The same thing may be said of Ephrem's intent in the *Hymns on Paradise*.

Ephrem's teachings on the afterlife stand midway between the underdeveloped Jewish concept of Sheol and Bardaiṣan's refutation of bodily resurrection. Against Gavin's dichotomous picture of soul-sleep and resurrection with only suspended animation in between, Ephrem has created a hiatus in eschatological time where in the souls of the righteous enjoy proximity to Paradise and are, evidently, conscious. As said before, this appears to be an Ephremic innovation, indicated by Ephrem's reservations over indulgence in such speculation: "As I reflected I was fearful again / to suppose that there might be / between the Garden and the fire / a place where those who have found mercy / can receive chastisement and forgiveness" (HdP X.14, *HyP* 153).

External witness for this concept may be found in Theodoret of Cyrrhus, in his description of the ascetic who was a namesake of Aphrahāṭ: "May I enjoy it even now, since I believe him to be alive, to belong to the choir of angels, and to possess familiar access to God even more than before; . . . now that he has shed the burden of the passions, he enjoys, as a victorious athlete, familiar access to the Umpire" (1985, 79).

To free this single witness from its splendid isolation, the testimony of the pilgrim nun Egeria may also be adduced. In the course of her pilgrimage itinerary, just a few years after Ephrem's death, Egeria visited Edessa in 381 C.E. and was shown a portrait of King Abgar, a presumed mosaic portrait of whom has recently been discovered (Drijvers 1982; cf. Segal 1983 who doubts the king's identity). Of this monarch who embraced the Christian faith, the bishop of Edessa is recorded by Egeria as saying: "The look on Abgar's face showed me, as

I looked straight at it, what a wise and noble man he had been, and the holy bishop told me, 'That is King Abgar. *Before he saw the Lord*, he believed in him as the true Son of God'" (Wilkinson 1971, 115–16). If this statement accurately reflects the Christian Orient in the fourth century, we see that between soul sleep and body rising is the conscious spirit enjoying beatific vision.

The consequences of this testimony are far-reaching. Prior afterlife concepts and Christian preoccupation with *theōsis* largely determined the form and overt content of Ephrem's soteriology. While basically faithful to the soul sleep/resurrection scenario, Ephrem does not deprive the righteous of Paradise of even a single eschatological moment, be it realized or actual. By means of this apparent innovation, the shift in emphasis in Ephrem's towards more ethical and sapiential considerations is seen. Christianity can then be presented as progressive sanctification within a traditional scheme of *theōsis*. The body, literally, becomes lost in thought!

Ephrem is conditioned but not constrained by a propositionally controlled system of belief. A distinction obtains between theological and mystical formulas of faith. Church policy was established by successive synods of bishops. To be sure, Nicea held sway over Ephrem, the council which he refers to as the "excellent synod" (CH XXII, Stewart 1991, 17). In terms of Christology, McVey shares the observations of several of her peers in noting that Ephrem's language of "mixing" of divine and human natures in Christ "would be problematic for post-Chalcedonian Christology" (McV 149, n. 356).

Paradise shares the same role as Nature for homiletic purposes. The Syrian poet deftly transferred Paradise imagery to Earth and set up the Church as a rival to Paradise! The comparison is explicit; conceptually, nothing is lost in translation here: "More fitting to be told / than the glorious account / of Paradise / are the exploits of the victorious / who adorned themselves / with the very likeness of Paradise; / in them is depicted / the beauty of the Garden. / Let us take leave of the trees / and tell of the victors, / instead of the inheritance / let us celebrate the inheritors" (HdP VI.14; *HyP* 113–14). This is more than homily; it is realized eschatology. Ephrem's very vision of Paradise attests to its realizability, to which "both worlds" (refrain, HdP XV) are invited. For Ephrem, the irreducible physicality of the body is not its bones, but rather its *form*. Ephrem's Paradise resurrects the form of the body but not its gross substance, and predicates Paradise-worthiness on an ethical advancement that would rival that of any Bardaiṣanite. In this respect, Ephrem recalls Origen who, in affirming the Resurrection, states that the "initial substratum [of the body] will not rise" (Origen, *Commentary on Psalm* I.5, Dechow 1975, 347), and that the continuity of the body is to be seen in its essence, considered to be its form (ειδος). The fact that "not a bone will remain in

Sheol" (Virg. XXXVI.10, McVey 423) need not present a problem here. Where bone turns into stone, fossilization preserves the skeletal form. Resurrection, in Ephrem's portrayal of it, is not committed to recalcification.

The *Hymns on Paradise* cycle is, in effect, a double allegory. "Allegory," according to Frank Kermode, "is the patristic way of dealing with inexhaustible hermeneutic potential" (1979, 44). Nothing could be more true for Ephrem. Like the Qur'ān, as Beck's earlier studies have shown (1948 and 1961), Ephrem paints Paradise in vivid earthly terms, where the most delectable delights of the natural world provide all the elements for an extended metaphorical transference to the celestial realm. In turn, the delights of Paradise are transformed by Ephrem into an allegory for the spiritual life on Earth such that the holy life, and not Paradise itself, becomes the most cherished reward of the saint. "Paradise," writes Ephrem, "lauded the intellect" and "the flowers [of Paradise] gave praise to virtuous life," while the "fruits of the righteous were more pleasing to the Knower of all" (HdP VI.13, *HyP* 113). The atmosphere, as one ascends the mountain of Paradise, becomes more and more rarefied, such that: "Bodies, / with their flow of blood, / receive refinement there / after the manner of souls; / the soul that is heavy / has its wings refined / so that they resemble / resplendent thought" (HdP IX.19, *HyP* 143). And, further: "but if it be joy / which inebriates and sustains, / how greatly will the soul be sustained / on the waves of this joy / as its faculties suck / the breast of all wisdom" (HdP IX.23, *HyP* 144).

In the Banquet of Paradise, which is the subject of Hymn IX, the "breast of all wisdom" sustains the "faculties of the soul"—this is sapiential *theōsis*. If "we are what we eat"—as the adage goes—when Ephrem tells us that God shall impart "His wisdom to our tongue" (HdP IX.27, *HyP* 146), on which "gift" the inhabitants of Paradise are said to "ruminate," the whole being is here pictured in sapiential terms. "From their mouths," says Ephrem of the denizens of heaven, "there burst forth . . . springs of wisdom" (HdP IX.28, *HyP* 146). Here, in language which Ephrem in Hymn XI stresses is metaphorical, "springs" is the image. "Wisdom" is the reality.

In Hymn VIII, Ephrem reaffirms the eschatology of Resurrection. The body is said to be necessary for the soul's perception. But the more Paradise is described further on in the hymn cycle, the more it becomes clear that the body is increasingly irrelevant, even to the point of being marginalized. The "faculties of the soul" begin to take over, as the bodily senses are in every way obviated. It is as if the doctrine of corporeal resurrection was itself transitional, beyond which a higher reality obtains. Body is rarefied to the level of soul; the body becomes sapiential. The body is, when all is said and done, a chrysalis. The butterfly emerges in the last half of the *Hymns on Paradise*.

A distinction obtains between form and reality. Consider the leaf of Paradise, as a "bodily" object. Its essence is "spiritual" though it has assumed "bodily form." These celestial leaves "have been changed," Ephrem continues, "so that their vesture may resemble ours" (HdP XI.8, *HyP* 156–57). Where "yonder it is souls, / instead of bodies, that crave food" (IX.18), where "the soul receives sustenance / appropriate to its needs" (IX.18), where soul food, as it were, "is the very fragrance of Paradise" (IX.17), in which, in any event, "bodies shall be raised / to the level of souls" (IX.21, *HyP* 142–43). The pinnacle of spiritual experience is beatific vision, imparted "with flashes of light" for "the small" and "with rays more intense" for "the perfect" (IX.25, *HyP* 145). In Ephrem's *Hymns on Paradise* is found a hierarchy of mirrors, metaphors turned heavenward but refracting earthward. One must be careful not to confuse the image with the reality which, in any event, inspires a picture with a thousand edifying Syriac words.

Ecclesial Exegesis. To the extent that Ephrem's interpretation of Paradise was directed towards the Church, the HdP as exegesis seem to follow, in an unspoken way, a view if interpretation akin to the Rules of Tyconius. The *Rules of Tyconius*, which was the first hermeneutical treatise in the Latin West, professedly served as "pathways of light" guiding one through "vast forest of prophecy" (Tyconius 1989, 3; cf. Bright 1988). This treatise impressed Augustine deeply. In adopting the *Rules of Tyconius* as a model and standard for Christian interpretation, Augustine said of the seven rules: "All of these rules except one, which is called 'Of Promises and Law,' cause one thing to be understood from another, a situation proper to figurative locutions" (*On Christian Doctrine* III.37, ibid.). Though written by a Donatist who wrote in North Africa during the second half of the fourth century, the text stands on its own merits as an ingenious interpretive system which kept the church at the heart of all exegetical activity under its influence. Remarkably, the *Rules of Tyconius* is not primarily Christological. Rather, it is ecclesiological.

Ephrem's *Hymns on Paradise* is a mystical midrash on the Eden narrative in Genesis. It was read in an ecclesial light. Soteriologically, Ephrem exalts form over substance in his descriptions of the glorified, resurrected body. Bardaiṣan had denied the resurrection of the body, but not of the soul. Perhaps in response to Bardaiṣan, and the philosophical speculation which he so successfully popularized, Ephrem's *Hymns on Paradise* struck a compromise between incorporeal and corporeal doctrines of resurrection. For Ephrem, the irreducible physicality of the body was not so much its bones, but rather its form. Each in his own way, both Bardaiṣan and Ephrem rejected the impurity of gross physicality. Bardaiṣan denied the resurrection of the body; Ephrem transforms the resurrection body and practically divests it of its physicality.

In treating Paradise as an allegory of the Church, Ephrem has, in effect, created a "paratext." The idea that, in certain cases, "exegesis becomes part of the text itself" (Kugel 1986, 100) lies behind the neologism, "paratext." Here, use of the modern formative "para" should be fairly self-evident: the "paratext" of exegesis is the paraphrasable interpretation mentally read alongside or with the text. In an overarching way, in Ephrem's meditations on the Eden narrative, the major paratext of Paradise is the Church.

Paradise and paradigm. Images and ideas are the twin hemispheres of the religious mind. The bicameral interaction of the imaginal and the abstract focus the believer on the archetypes of belief. To give a more complete description of any religious worldview, concepts should be complemented by conceits. In Ephrem, the Church is imagistically conceived of as Paradise. Since it is an extended metaphor, its imagery is extensible. Individually and collectively, paradise imagery can represent different facets of church life and experience. The phrase from the Lord's Prayer—"on earth, as it is in Heaven"—perfectly expresses both imagistically and ideologically the Ephrem's artifice at work in the HdP.

Ephrem's Paradise is at once ecclesiastical and eschatological. Its imagery expresses a paradigm of purity. This is a purity that "cures." It cleanses the soul of the "disease" of mortality. It restores primordial immortality. Life in Paradise, in both worlds, is for the pure. The pure in heart are Christians who are sexually pure and morally stainless. On this point, perhaps Ephrem and Bardaiṣan might agree. In a quote from Theodore bar Koni, Bardaiṣan, in one of his lost songs, taught: "And lo, the natures, all of them—with created things they hastened, to purify themselves and remove what was mingled with the nature of evil" (Segal 1970, 38). Although Ephrem rejects Bardaiṣan's creation myth, the pursuit of ethical purity in both systems is, in nonascetic terms, comparable. In fine, Syriac Christianity's response to Late Antiquity is the quest for purity, in which chrism, baptism, and the Eucharist become the ointment, fountain, and elixir of immortality, while the imagery of Paradise ennobles the sanctified soul.

Paradise and World Unity in the Bahā'ī Writings

Religious portrayals of the ideal society are the counterpart of the utopias of secular visionaries. In Bahā'ī texts, the ideal society is given a symbolic depth that adds a dimension largely absent in secular reformist rhetoric. Paradise is the ideal of perfection. This imagery has the power to inspire. In Bābī and Bahā'ī texts, Paradise is frequently associated with the heart within the individual, and, in the case of

Bahā'ī texts, with an ideal society that has achieved concentric levels of unity.

The Bāb, Bahā'u'llāh's herald, strikes an image in which Spirit is personified, giving a voice to Paradise: "O people of the earth! By the righteousness of the One true God, I am the Maid of Heaven (*al-ḥūrīya*) begotten by the Spirit of Bahā, abiding within the Mansion hewn out of a mass of ruby, tender and vibrant; and in this mighty Paradise naught have I ever witnessed save that which proclaimeth the Remembrance of God by extolling the virtues of this Arabian Youth. Verily there is none other God but your Lord, the All-Merciful" (SWB 54; *Qayyūm al-Asmā'* 29; Lambden 1997–1998, 34). Bahā'u'llāh has taken up this imagery in portraying the Maiden of Heaven as the personification of the Bahā'ī revelation.

In his own writings, Bahā'u'llāh has taken up a wealth of Bābī imagery. The "Arabian Youth" here refers to the Persian founder of the Bābī religion, known as the Bāb, who is seen as the precursor of Bahā'u'llāh and therefore the co-founder of the Bahā'ī Faith. This same image of an "Arabian Youth" will be employed by Bahā'u'llāh himself, as a circumlocution. The other figure in this scene is the celestial Maiden. Ruby is obviously an image of the heart, by virtue not only of its color, but also its worth. The location of Paradise is important here, for Paradise resides in the heart (consciousness). Although it is the heart that matters, so does society. Paradise is both esoteric and exoteric. Its external form is the ideal society, based on concentric unities radiating from the heart. We shall now explore these types of unity in Bahā'ī teachings, in order to demonstrate that paradise imagery is used to reinforce Bahā'ī ideology by vivifying it with the most potent of teleological symbols available in religious discourse.

Bahā'īs often speak of unity without differentiating among various kinds of unity, apart from the so-called three onenesses popularized in "fireside" teaching. These three onenesses are the oneness of God, the oneness of religion, and the oneness of humankind. ("Oneness" is popularly equated with unity, although the unity of the third category is hardly of the same order as the first.) For academic purposes at least, a more precise typology of the kinds of unity discussed in the writings of Bahā'u'llāh and in the discourses of his eldest son and designated interpreter, 'Abdu'l-Bahā, is in order. The following inventory is original in that a systematization of Bahā'ī concepts of unity finds its only precedent in an old and obscure article entitled, "Ways to Wholeness," by Raymond Frank Piper (1944). Piper's typology is as follows: I. **Foundational Unities:** A. *Spiritual*: divine, prophetic, religious, historic, universal unities. B. *Human*: biological or racial unity; psychological, mental or selfic unity. II. **Aids to Unity:** C. *Social Aids to Unity*: political, juridical, economic, educational, linguistic, social-organic unities. D. *Spiritual Aids to Unity*: scientific, aesthetic, ethical unities (ibid., 776). Piper's typology is a surprisingly original and sophisticated approach. It is unusual in that Baha'ı apologists, as a rule, were not given to systematizing Bahā'ī teachings, apart from expatiating on stock lists of core Bahā'ī principles, typically enumerated as twelve, with variations.

The following types of unity have a textual basis in the Bahā'ī writings. Other Bahā'ī teachings may be extrapolated from the Bahā'ī principles of unity, but are clearly subordinate to Bahā'u'llāh's overarching unity paradigm. Discreet principles of unity include, but are probably not limited to, the following ideological taxonomy of the Baha'i unity paradigm:

Spiritual Unity: (1) Unity of God; (2) Unity of Revelation; (3) Unity of Religion; (4) Unity of Humankind; (5) Unity of Gender (Equality of Men & Women).

World Unity (from the *Seven Lights of Unity*): (6) *First Candle*: Unity in the Political Realm; (7) *Second Candle*: Unity of Thought in World Undertakings; (8) *Third Candle*: Unity in Freedom; (9) *Fourth Candle*: Unity in Religion; (10) *Fifth Candle*: Unity of Nations; (11) *Sixth Candle*: Unity of Races; (12) *Seventh Candle*: Unity of Language.

Moral Unity (from the *Tablet of Unity*): (13) Unity in Religion (*ittiḥād dar dīn*); (14) Unity in Speech (*ittiḥād dar qawl*); (15) Unity of Deeds (*ittiḥād-i a'māl*); 16. Unity of Station (*ittiḥād-i maqām*); (17) Unity of Wealth (*ittiḥād-i amvāl*); (18) Unity in Society (*ittiḥād-i nufūs*).

Other Forms of Unity: (19) Unity (Equality) of Rights; (20) Unity of Knowledge (Harmony of Science and Religion): (21) Unity (Universality) in Education; (22) Unity of Bahā'īs; (23) Unity in Marriage/Family Unity.

This inventory of the various types of unity as described in Bahā'ī texts is not exhaustive. It is proposed as a framework of analysis for a systematic description of basic Bahā'ī teachings. This systematization invites further refinement.

Since Bahā'ī teachings are modelled on a paradigm of unity, it is useful to ask Bahā'īs what they mean by it. Some of the relevant texts will now be interrogated. It will be shown that such texts tend, as a rule, to illustrate unity through various kinds of Paradise imagery. It should be noted that Paradise imagery in the Bahā'ī writings is both metaphorical and actual. Paradise is metaphorically realized in leading an exemplary Bahā'ī life and in helping to build a more just and virtuous society. Actual Paradise is seen as a reality. It is the afterworld of the pious, as in all traditional religious teachings. Paradise, it should be noted, is not exclusively reserved for pious Bahā'īs, as

'Abdu'l-Bahā explains: "Then as to what thou hast asked me for pious people who died before they heard the Voice of this Manifestation. Listen: Those who have mounted to God before hearing the Voice, if they followed the rules of conduct as laid down by Jesus and always walked in the straight path, they have obtained this Dazzling Light after their rising to the Kingdom of God" (TAB 2: 478). The point here is that afterlife paradise is the consequence of one's having first tried to create paradise on Earth.

I. Spiritual Unity

Unity of God *(tawḥīd-i ilāhī)*

Belief in the unity of God, in Bahā'ī theology, goes beyond any notion of numerical unity or singularity. Such belief entails viewing God as an apophatic Mystery, while at the same time recognizing the revelations of God as interventions in human history. Bahā'u'llāh defines "the true meaning of Divine unity" as recognition of "the one Power Who exerciseth undisputed sovereignty over the world of being, Whose image is reflected in the mirror of the entire creation." (GWB 166; cf. RB 1: 100). The unity of God is also manifested in the unity of God's revelation (see below). This unity goes beyond a mere philosophical disposition, a doctrinal orthodoxy or a contemplative correctness. Although, strictly speaking, the acknowledgment of divine unity entails a strictly apophatic theology at a conceptual level, the practical implications of such an acknowledgment have everything to do with recognizing God's revelation, God's "presence" as it is manifested to history by way of revelation.

Paradise imagery. The promise of Paradise is offered to those who embrace "the Day Spring of the Unity of God," to that soul "who hath quaffed . . . the sealed wine of His Revelation" and who "shall be numbered with the inmates of Paradise" (GWB 340–41). This is an eschatological promise, a future reward. Mystically, the spiritually awakened are said to inhabit both worlds at once, such that, "Whilst walking amongst mortals, they soar in the heaven of the divine presence" and who "without wings . . . rise unto the exalted heights of divine unity" (KI 67). Divine unity is experienced in moments of mystical rapture. Lest such ecsatic transports be pure flights of phantasy, they should be grounded in revelation, defined in the next section.

Unity of Revelation

Revelation, in the Bahā'ī conception of it, is a message from God, universally addressed to the human world, even if that social "world" was merely tribal at an early developmental stage in the earth's social evolution. Revelation is mediated by the revolutionary spiritual geniuses of human history, such as Abraham, Moses, Zoroaster, Kṛṣṇa, the Buddha, Jesus Christ, Muḥammad, the Bāb, and Bahā'u'llāh, who represent, respectively, the founders of the great world religions of Judaism, Zoroastrianism, Neo-Hinduism, Buddhism, Christianity, Islam, the Bābī religion and the Bahā'ī Faith. In oral cultures, from a Bahā'ī perspective, it is certain that there were "Manifestations of God"—the Bahā'ī technical term for prophets—sent to indigenous peoples, but there are problems of historical attestation. For instance, in popular, though not official, Bahā'ī belief, there has been a growing recognition of the spiritual greatness of the historic Iroquois "Peacemaker" Deganawida, a "native son" of what is now Canada and who, according to the Iroquois influence hypothesis, may have provided the basic model for American democracy (see Buck 1996c).

Inscribed over one of the nine arched entrances to the Bahā'ī House of Worship in Wilmette (north Chicago) are the words of Bahā'u'llāh: "All the Prophets of God proclaim the same Faith." Speaking of the fraternity of all of the Prophets or "Manifestations of God" who have successively influenced the course of human history, Bahā'u'llāh writes: "If thou wilt observe with discriminating eyes, thou wilt behold Them all abiding in the same tabernacle, soaring in the same heaven, seated upon the same throne, uttering the same speech, and proclaiming the same Faith. Such is the unity of those Essences of Being, those Luminaries of infinite and immeasurable splendor! Wherefore, should one of these Manifestations of Holiness proclaim saying: 'I am the return of all the Prophets,' He, verily, speaketh the truth" (KI 153–54/GWB 52). This unity implies that each world religion, in its pure form, compares favorably with other world religions.

Ideally, in Bahā'ī belief, world religions are quintessentially "divine in origin, identical in their aims, complementary in their functions, continuous in their purpose, indispensable in their value to mankind" (Shoghi Effendi, WOB 58). This Bahā'ī universalism needs to be historically contextualized. Bahā'u'llāh's theory of civilization embodies a teaching known as "Progressive Revelation." In this view of salvation history, while there is unity among all of the historic founders of world religions, there is a hierarchy among them relative to their respective roles in human history. Although Jesus is the equal of Muḥammad, the revelation of Muḥammad supersedes that of Jesus, having been revealed at a more advanced stage of human history. In our historical present, at this juncture in history, Bahā'u'llāh is seen as the latest (but not the last) of God's Messengers, having revealed the teachings required for this day and age. According to Bahā'ī thought, the will of God for humanity today is unity. Bahā'u'llāh's mission is to bring about this unity.

Paradise imagery. In Bahā'ī theophanology, the Manifestation of God is an extension of the presence of God. It is the transcendent become immanent, without diminishing the beyondness of God. Throughout Bahā'u'llāh's writings, the connection between Paradise and divine "Presence" is dynamic. Recognition of Bahā'u'llāh is tantamount to beatific vision, in that such a believer mystically "gaineth admittance into the most exalted Paradise and attaineth the station of revelation and vision before the throne of Thy majesty" (TB 116).

The advent of Paradise has traditionally been an eschatological concern. Bahā'u'llāh's claim to prophecy fulfillment at first raises more questions than it answers. Hence Bahā'u'llāh's answers to such questions as: "They say: 'Where is Paradise, and where is Hell?' Say: 'The one is reunion with Me; the other thine own self, O thou who dost associate a partner with God and doubtest'" (TB 118). While warning of Hell, Bahā'u'llāh extends an invitation to humanity to enter into Paradise: "Witness its devouring flame. Haste ye to enter into Paradise, as a token of Our mercy unto you, and drink ye from the hands of the All-Merciful the Wine that is life indeed" (PB 99).

Bahā'u'llāh's proclamations are suffused with Paradise motifs: "On His right hand," writes Bahā'u'llāh, speaking reflexively, "flow the living waters of grace, and on His left the choice Wine of justice, whilst before Him march the angels of Paradise" (PB 83). An invisible Paradise—the spiritual state of faith—is expressed in visible terms: "Paradise is decked with mystic roses, and hell hath been made to blaze with the fire of the impious. Say: 'The light hath shone forth from the horizon of Revelation, and the whole earth hath been illumined at the coming of Him Who is the Lord of the Day of the Covenant!'" (TB 118/ESW 133–34). The advent of Bahā'u'llāh is associated with a realized eschatology in which Paradise may be mystically gained.

Unity of Religion

Religion is both idealized and criticized in Bahā'ī texts. The excesses of religion are barriers to unity. The religious proposals one finds in Bahā'ī texts are thus a mixture of positive and negative reforms. The negative reforms are not expressed as simple criticisms. Rather, the worst of the perceived evils of religion are categorically "abrogated," in a legislative sense, through Bahā'u'llāh's rulings.

Among the positive teachings of Bahā'u'llāh with respect to religion is the call to interfaith concord. Interfaith amity has already been discussed as the second Glad-Tiding. Some of Bahā'u'llāh's positive teachings represent the obverse of the same coin, being the criticism of a religious evil. Thus, peace among religions (positive teaching) is not simply the abolishing of holy war (religious evil). It is a reversal of holy war—the call to an active interfaith diplomacy. In the Tablet of Ornaments (*Lawḥ-i Ṭarāzāt*), Bahā'u'llāh writes: "The second Ṭarāz [Ornament] is to consort with the followers of all religions in a spirit of friendliness and fellowship" and to "associate with all the peoples and kindreds of the earth with joy and radiance" in order "to promote unity and concord" (TB 35–36).

According to Bahā'ī thought, religions in their pristine form are each inspired by God. They do not significantly differ in their core teachings, each having been revealed by the same Deity. Bahā'u'llāh explains: "That the divers communions of the earth, and the manifold systems of religious belief, should never be allowed to foster the feelings of animosity among men, is, in this Day, of the essence of the Faith of God and His Religion. These principles and laws, these firmly established and mighty systems, have proceeded from one Source, and are rays of one Light. That they differ one from another is to be attributed to the varying requirements of the ages in which they were promulgated" (ESW 13).

One implication of this teaching is that once the nonessentials of religion have been identified and forsaken over time, religions will begin to make profound discoveries about how much they share in common. This realization could result in more sweeping ecumenical impulses, such that interfaith encounters might begin to reshape global thinking about the need to unify people of all confessions. Dogmas will gradually be harmonized with universal principles. Tertullian's credo of absurdity will be overturned, as belief in the incredible will give way to belief constrained by reason. This is more properly dealt with in under the heading, "Unity in Religion"—the integration of religion as distinct from the cooperative, pluralistic Unity of Religion—treated in a section below.

Paradise imagery. Unity of religion and the unity of humankind are intertwined in Bahā'u'llāh's system. Nature imagery as well as Paradise imagery form part of the ideal picture of a world free of the "hell" of religious teachings that condone violence as an perverse path to paradise. The primary purpose for religion throughout history has been to ennoble and to unify humanity. The Bahā'ī model for world unity is based on certain core precepts, such as Bahā'u'llāh exhortation: "O contending peoples and kindreds of the earth! Set your faces towards unity. . . . This wronged One hath, ever since the early days of His life, cherished none other desire but this, and will continue to entertain no wish except this wish. . . . To this beareth witness the Tongue of Grandeur from His habitation of glory" (GWB 217–18). Note Bahā'u'llāh's autobiographical reference to his resolve to dedicate his life to unity "ever since the early days of His life." The Paradise imagery used here is referential, and has to do with the authority of this pronouncement. The "Tongue of Grandeur" is Bahā'u'llāh, who claims divine authority in revealing the word of God, and "His habitation of glory" is his exalted station, pictured as an abode of Paradise. This sentiment of interfaith harmony naturally leads to the next principle, the oneness of humankind, considered the cornerstone of Bahā'ī consciousness.

Unity of Humankind

Ideally, religion ought to be conducive to human unity. If religion is the cause of strife, particularly of bloodshed and of war, then religion becomes the source of the very evil it was intended to combat. According to Bahā'ī teachings, the nonexistence of such a religion is preferable to its existence. One of the principal ways to counter religious discord is to demonstrate how unity can be achieved through a simple adjustment in perspective. "Ye are the fruits of one tree, and the leaves of one branch" is one of the most well-known Bahā'ī proverbs. "So powerful is the light of unity that it can illuminate the whole earth" is another such maxim, both of which are inscribed over arched entrances to the Bahā'ī House of Worship in Wilmette. (There are nine aphorisms inside and nine outside. These two are on the outside.) Note the effective use of metaphor here. These statements are pithy. They are emotive. They inspire. To some, they are profound. They are certainly Bahā'ī, although such sentiments could legitimately have meaning in other religious traditions. The Bahā'ī paradigm of unity simply privileges these sentiments over any other kerygma one might find in Bahā'ī texts, such as personal salvation. Bahā'u'llāh calls the quest for unity "the monarch of all aspirations" (ESW 14), suggesting that all other spiritual aspirations are subordinate to the overarching vision of unity.

Paradise imagery. Numerous passages in the writings of Bahā'u'llāh and in other Bahā'ī texts exhort humanity to unity. This is one: "The word of God which the Supreme Pen hath recorded on the seventh leaf of the Most Exalted Paradise is this: O ye men of wisdom among nations! Shut your eyes to estrangement, then fix your gaze upon unity. . . . It behoveth you to . . . set your hearts on whatever will ensure harmony. . . . O people of the earth! Appreciate the value of this heavenly word. Indeed it may be likened unto a ship for the ocean of knowledge and a shining luminary for the realm of perception" (TB 67–68). Metaphorically, this teaching is a "leaf" that had floated down from a tree in Paradise—not from just a generic Paradise, but from "the Most Exalted Paradise," which suggests that this teaching is supremely heavenly. Imbuing such an exhortation with an aura of sanctity underscores the loftiness of this ideal. Other metaphors are used just as effectively: unity is described as an Ark crossing the ocean of knowledge. Illumination and resplendence, as from a star of high magnitude, are said to from unity as well. This type of discourse vivifies the teaching, reinforcing the self-valuation of conscience.

Unity of Gender (Equality of Men and Women)

The equality of men and women is a fundamental Bahā'ī principle. To a certain extent, the explicitness and importance of this teaching in Bahā'ī texts lends a certain credence to the claim that the Bahā'ī Faith is the first religion to proclaim, from its very inception, gender equality. Such a teaching did not require interpretation, nor did it need to be deduced from another, perhaps more general, principle. This teaching is very explicit, particularly in the writings and discourses of 'Abdu'l-Bahā. (Bahā'u'llāh's style of discourse is more poetic, while 'Abdu'l-Bahā—Bahā'u'llāh's successor as interpreter and moral exemplar—is typically more direct.) In practice, the equality of men and women is implemented at a practical level, though not always as systematically as one might expect. The teaching, and the vision of community expressed in it, is absolutely central to Bahā'ī community life and plays a key role in its vitality.

Bahā'u'llāh has established the principle of gender equality in various texts. A representative statement is as follows: "Exalted, immensely exalted is He Who hath removed differences and established harmony. . . . [T]he Pen of the Most High hath lifted distinctions from between His servants and handmaidens and . . . hath conferred upon all a station and rank on the same plane. He hath broken the back of vain imaginings with the sword of utterance and hath obliterated the perils of idle fancies through the pervasive power of His might" (*Women* 1; RB 4: 200). This passage explicitly associates unity with equality.

Hyperbole does not exceed reality in this case, as many would agree that gender equality certainly qualifies as being among God's "consummate favours and all-encompassing mercy." Where there is not equality of the sexes, women are at the mercy of men rather than the mercy of God. Gender inequality, historically, has been the norm until the twentieth century, when reformers have campaigned vigorously for such changes as women's suffrage and rights and income parity. Traditionally, religions have tended to sanction gender inequality. Finding a religion that predicates its very identity on a body of principles of which gender equality is integral is nothing short of a personal discovery for most Bahā'īs.

'Abdu'l-Bahā has extended his father's teaching in certain ways. For instance, he identified equality of the sexes as a peace issue, and, in so doing, has prophesied: "War and its ravages have blighted the world; the education of woman will be a mighty step toward its abolition and ending, for she will use her whole influence against war. She will refuse to give her sons for sacrifice upon the field of battle. In truth, she will be the greatest factor in establishing universal peace and international arbitration. Assuredly, woman will abolish warfare among mankind" (PUP 109). Precisely by what means will woman collectively bring about this change? "Another fact of equal importance in bringing about International Peace is Woman's Suffrage," 'Abdu'l-Bahā explains. "When they [women] shall have a vote, they will oppose any cause of warfare" (*Star of the West* 3.10 [8 Sept. 1912]: 27).

Paradise imagery. In the Bahā'ī compilation, *Women*, there are several passages in which the superiority of woman is spoken of as both potential and actual realities: "Bahā'u'llāh has greatly strengthened the cause of women," according to 'Abdu'l-Bahā, who predicts that, in the future, men will recognize the accomplishments of women, and will exclaim: "Verily ye deserve to adorn your heads with the crown of everlasting glory, because in sciences and arts, in virtues and perfections ye shall become equal to man, and as regards tenderness of heart and the abundance of mercy and sympathy ye are superior" (PT 182–84). Woman is spoken of here in expectant as well as ideal terms, assured of winning her rightfully deserved "crown of everlasting glory" in reaching her full potential. 'Abdu'l-Bahā was emphatic in saying that "the greatness of this Wondrous Age will be manifested as a result of progress in the world of women" (*Women* 8). A world without war is halfway to paradise.

II. World Unity

In this section, seven types of unity will be examined. These are enumerated in a Tablet dated 1906 in response to a letter from a Bahā'ī woman in Scotland. 'Abdu'l-Bahā speaks of these seven unities prophetically. Certain of these prophecies are expected to come to pass before the close of the twentieth century. The text is of such importance in Bahā'ī thought, that it is cited, at length, as follows:

> O honoured lady! For a single purpose were the Prophets, each and all, sent down to earth; for this was Christ made manifest, for this did Baha'u'llah raise up the call of the Lord: that the world of man should become the world of God, this nether realm the Kingdom, this darkness light, this satanic wickedness all the virtues of heaven—and unity, fellowship and love be won for the whole human race, that the organic unity should reappear and the bases of discord be destroyed and life everlasting and grace everlasting become the harvest of mankind . . .
>
> In cycles gone by, though harmony was established, yet, owing to the absence of means, the unity of all mankind could not have

been achieved. Continents remained widely divided, nay even among the peoples of one and the same continent association and interchange of thought were well-nigh impossible. Consequently intercourse, understanding and unity amongst all the peoples and kindreds of the earth were unattainable. In this day, however, means of communication have multiplied, and the five continents of the earth have virtually merged into one. And for everyone it is now easy to travel to any land, to associate and exchange views with its peoples, and to become familiar, through publications, with the conditions, the religious beliefs and the thoughts of all men.

In like manner all the members of the human family, whether peoples or governments, cities or villages, have become increasingly interdependent. For none is self-sufficiency any longer possible, inasmuch as political ties unite all peoples and nations, and the bonds of trade and industry, of agriculture and education, are being strengthened every day. Hence the unity of all mankind can in this day be achieved. Verily this is none other but one of the wonders of this wondrous age, this glorious century. Of this past ages have been deprived, for this century—the century of light—hath been endowed with unique and unprecedented glory, power and illumination. Hence the miraculous unfolding of a fresh marvel every day. Eventually it will be seen how bright its candles will burn in the assemblage of man.

Behold how its light is now dawning upon the world's darkened horizon. The first candle is unity in the political realm, the early glimmerings of which can now be discerned. The second candle is unity of thought in world undertakings, the consummation of which will ere long be witnessed. The third candle is unity in freedom which will surely come to pass. The fourth candle is unity in religion which is the cornerstone of the foundation itself, and which, by the power of God, will be revealed in all its splendour. The fifth candle is the unity of nations—a unity which in this century will be securely established, causing all the peoples of the world to regard themselves as citizens of one common fatherland. The sixth candle is unity of races, making of all that dwell on earth peoples and kindreds of one race. The seventh candle is unity of language, i.e., the choice of a universal tongue in which all peoples will be instructed and converse. Each and every one of these will inevitably come to pass, inasmuch as the power of the Kingdom of God will aid and assist in their realization. (SWAB 30–32)

Each of these various kinds of unity will be highlighted below. The first quotation cited under each of these headings will be drawn from the text above. Following a description of each of the seven candles of unity, some remarks on attendant paradise imagery will be made.

Unity in the Political Realm

"The first candle is unity in the political realm, the early glimmerings of which can now be discerned." Political unity is typically based on political realism. Treaties and other international protocols are like inventions: necessity is their proverbial "mother." Global international consensus helps reify international law, such as the United Nations covenants and declarations. Once reified and accorded a certain measure of conferred authority, these have become of source for a burgeoning body of international law. This has been viewed by some Bahā'ī thinkers as a process of social evolution leading to eventual world self-government (as distinct from a unitary world government). The process of disarmament is clearly foreseen in the Bahā'ī writings as one important series of developments in the political realm, which may superficially, but legally, qualify as "unity."

Unity of Thought in World Undertakings

"The second candle is unity of thought in world undertakings, the consummation of which will ere long be witnessed." This form of unity envisions international cooperation in pursuit of pragmatic objectives. Here, 'Abdu'l-Bahā foretells what Bahā'u'llāh forthtells, in calling for various global undertakings. In the *Lawḥ-i Maqṣūd* (1881), Bahā'u'llāh refers to God as "the Great Being," who, in several passages, addresses humanity on issues of universal import. These "divine sayings" in some ways recall the *ḥadīth qudsī* of Islamic tradition, except that the pronouncements of the Great Being are not articulated in the first person: "The Great Being saith: O ye children of men! The fundamental purpose animating the Faith of God and His Religion is to safeguard the interests and promote the unity of the human race, and to foster the spirit of love and fellowship amongst men. . . . Our hope is that the world's religious leaders and the rulers thereof will unitedly arise for the reformation of this age and the rehabilitation of its fortunes. Let them, after meditating on its needs, take counsel together and, through anxious and full deliberation, administer to a diseased and sorely afflicted world the remedy it requireth" (TB 168).

A number of twentieth-century international convenants and protocols suggest that there has already been a *"unity of thought in world undertakings"* in some areas, such as world health and, more recently, in matters of ecology and international trade. Other kinds of undertakings adumbrated by this passage might include economic and social development projects sponsored by the international community, as well as joint space ventures and other forms of international scientific endeavor.

Unity in Freedom

"The third candle is unity in freedom which will surely come to pass." One example of unity in freedom is freedom of conscience. Recounting Qājār Iran's persecution of the Bābīs and Bahā'īs for crimes of conscience, decrying the savagery of it all, 'Abdu'l-Bahā, in 1888, stated: "Freedom of conscience (*āzādigī-yi vujdān*) and tranquility of heart and soul is one of the duties and functions of government (*vaẓā'if va savāliḥ-i ḥukūmat*), and is in all ages the cause of progress in development and ascendancy over other lands. Other civilized countries acquired not this preeminence, nor attained unto these high degrees of influence and power, till such time as they put away the strife of sects out of their midst, and dealt with all classes according to one standard" (TN 87; TN 158 [Cambridge edition]. Persian text in Browne [ed.], *Maqāla-yi Shakhs-i Sayyāḥ*, I. 193—cf.Cole 1998, 36-37 and 203, n. 50).

Unity in Religion

"The fourth candle is unity in religion which is the cornerstone of the foundation itself, and which, by the power of God, will be revealed in all its splendor." Unity in Religion is explained under the same heading in the next section (Moral Unity).

Unity of Nations

"The fifth candle is the unity of nations—a unity which in this century will be securely established, causing all the peoples of the world to regard themselves as citizens of one common fatherland." There is one signal event which, according to 'Abdu'l-Bahā, would be the hallmark of the unity of nations: "True civilization will unfurl its banner in the midmost heart of the world whenever a certain number of its distinguished and high-minded sovereigns—the shining exemplars of devotion and determination—shall, for the good and happiness of all mankind, arise, with firm resolve and clear vision, to establish the Cause of Universal Peace. They must make the Cause of Peace the object of general consultation, and seek by every means in their power to establish a Union of the nations of the world. They must conclude a binding treaty and establish a covenant, the provisions of which shall be sound, inviolable and definite. They must proclaim it to all the world and obtain for it the sanction of all the human race. This supreme and noble undertaking—the real source of the peace and well-being of all

the world—should be regarded as sacred by all that dwell on earth. All the forces of humanity must be mobilized to ensure the stability and permanence of this Most Great Covenant" (SDC 64). This text seems to foreshadow the emergence of the United Nations. 'Abdu'l-Bahā was deeply impressed with Woodrow Wilson's creation of the League of Nations: "As to President Wilson, the fourteen principles which he hath enunciated are mostly found in the teachings of Bahā'u'llāh and I therefore hope that he will be confirmed and assisted. Now is the dawn of universal peace; my hope is that its morn will fully break, converting the gloom of war, of strife and of wrangling among men into the light of union, of harmony and of affection" (SWAB 311–12).

Unity of Races

"The sixth candle is unity of races, making of all that dwell on earth peoples and kindreds of one race." Reference has already been made to Cambridge Orientalist E. G. Browne and his historic interview with Bahā'u'llāh in 'Akkā in 1890. In the course of that interview, Bahā'u'llāh spoke of a future society in which differences of race will be annulled. "O ye discerning ones!" Bahā'u'llāh exclaims in a Tablet, "Verily, the words which have descended from the heaven of the Will of God are the source of unity and harmony for the world. Close your eyes to racial differences, and welcome all with the light of oneness" (ADJ 31).

Unity of Language

"The seventh candle is unity of language, i.e., the choice of a universal tongue in which all peoples will be instructed and converse." This teaching was discussed above as the third Glad-Tiding.

Paradise imagery for the seven lights of unity. Many of the Bahā'ī counsels and principles are described as having come down from Paradise. For instance, the idea of an international language, cited above, is described by Bahā'u'llāh as one of the teachings of Paradise: "The word of God which the Supreme Pen hath recorded on the eighth leaf of the Most Exalted Paradise is the following: We have formerly ordained that people should converse in two languages, yet efforts must be made to reduce them to one, likewise the scripts of the world, that men's lives may not be dissipated and wasted in learning divers languages. Thus the whole earth would come to be regarded as one city and one land" (TB 68).

During the last quarter-century of his ministry, Bahā'u'llāh repeatedly called upon world leaders to exercise leadership in bringing about peace and prosperity among nations. Of particular interest here is Bahā'u'llāh's call upon the world's religious leaders to exercise collective wisdom in addressing global issues. His call for a reconciliation of religions provides a basis for common cause. Of far greater moment is political unity. One aspect of political unity, as mentioned, is disarmament. On this crucial security and peace issue facing the world today, Bahā'u'llāh has advocated the convening of a global summit of world leaders in order to draw up and enact international protocols guarding disarmament (see text cited above under the fifth Glad-Tiding). "It would be preferable and more fitting," Bahā'u'llāh states elsewhere, "that the highly honored kings themselves should attend such an assembly, and proclaim their edicts. Any king who will arise and carry out this task, he, verily will, in the sight of God, become the cynosure of all kings. Happy is he, and great is his blessedness!" (ESW 31). This beautitude does not directly invoke Paradise imagery. Of course, if "War is hell," as the saying goes, then disarmament may be its own paradise.

In Bahā'ī thought, a number of other concerns not ordinarily associated with peace are explicitly identified as peace issues. One of the important issues on the Bahā'ī agenda for peace is racial tolerance and, beyond that, racial amity. "The accomplishment of unity between the colored and the white," 'Abdu'l-Bahā writes, "will be an assurance of the world's peace" (ADJ 33). He explicitly describes racial harmony as a kind of Paradise: "This is a new cycle of human power. All the horizons of the world are luminous, and the world will become indeed as a garden and a paradise. It is the hour of unity of the sons of men and of the drawing together of all races and all classes" (*London* 19.)

There is the assurance that the consequence of putting all of the Bahā'ī principles into practice will be Paradise on Earth: "The principles of the Teachings of Bahā'u'llāh should be carefully studied, one by one, until they are realized and understood by mind and heart—so will you become strong followers of the light, truly spiritual, heavenly soldiers of God, acquiring and spreading the true civilization in Persia, in Europe, and in the whole world. This will be the paradise which is to come on earth, when all mankind will be gathered together under the tent of unity in the Kingdom of Glory" (PT 22–23).

III. Moral Unity
(from the Tablet of Unity)

Unity in Religion *(ittiḥād dar dīn)*

In Bahā'u'llāh's "Tablet of Unity" (*Lawḥ-i ittiḥād*)—one of at least two such Tablets—"unity in religion" (*ittiḥād dar dīn*) is described as the instrument for the triumph of the Cause of God. Religious assemblage (*ijtimā'*) is portrayed as the mystic sword of God (Monjazeb 1995). Religious unity can prove to be a powerful social model. If the Bahā'īs establish such a model, governments would take an interest in trying to apply the Bahā'ī model to society at large. Distinct from the plurality of "Unity of Religion" (item 3, above), "Unity in Religion" is a singularity. When a country becomes predominantly Bahā'ī, it follows that the citizens might democratically adopt the Bahā'ī Faith as a "state religion." In such an eventuality, minorities would be given equal rights (see item 19, below). Formal or *de facto* adoption of a state religion typically follows a long history of individual conversions. In the Bahā'ī Faith, conversions are always voluntary, and are the result of an individual's quest for truth.

Paradise imagery. Unity remains an abstract notion, a wish-image, unless internalized and exemplified. The achievement of unity is elusive. The authenticity and legitimacy of the Bahā'ī social gospel requires unity. Unity does not come easy. The Bahā'ī experience has shown that unity requires vision, volition, and vigor, if it is ever to be a viable model for others. A part-to-whole relationship is seen between Bahā'ī unity (see item 22, below) and world unity. 'Abdu'l Bahā writes: "If once the beauty of the unity of the friends—this Divine Beloved—be decked in the adornments of the Abhā Kingdom, it is certain that within a very short time those countries will become the Paradise of the All-Glorious, and that out of the West the splendours of unity will cast their bright rays over all the earth. We are striving with heart and soul, resting neither day nor night, seeking not a moment's ease, to make this world of man the mirror of the unity of God." (SWAB 84). Once achieved, whenever sustained, Bahā'ī unity is assured a role to play in the world-at-large. Once united, according to this text, the world itself will become the "Paradise of the All-Glorious."

Unity in Speech *(ittiḥād dar qawl)*

This unity has three dimensions: (1) harmony of discourse, which is the first meaning of "unity in speech"; (2) harmony of word and deed; and (3) the exercise of wisdom in speech. Here, Bahā'u'llāh speaks also of altruism and of personal virtue. Leading such a life conduces to "victory."

In the Bahā'ī writings, "mere" words are the self-indictment of irrelevance and even hypocrisy. When words are authenticated by deeds, a unity of one's inward and outward being is achieved. In the opening lines of the Words of Paradise (*Kalimāt-i Firdawsīya*), Bahā'u'llāh writes: "It behoveth the people of Bahā to render the Lord victorious through the power of their utterance and to admonish the people by their goodly deeds and character, inasmuch as deeds exert greater influence than words" (TB 57). Although deeds do exert a greater influence than words, words can be deeds. Such is the case in effective teaching of the Bahā'ī Faith, seen as the most meritorious of deeds.

Paradise imagery. "O Children of Adam!" Bahā'u'llāh proclaims, "Holy words and pure and goodly deeds ascend unto the heaven of celestial glory. Strive that your deeds may be cleansed from the dust of self and hypocrisy and find favor at the court of glory; for ere long the assayers of mankind shall, in the holy presence of the Adored One, accept naught but absolute virtue and deeds of stainless purity. This is the day-star of wisdom and of divine mystery that hath shone above the horizon of the divine will. Blessed are they that turn thereunto" (HWP #69).

Unity of Deeds *(ittiḥād-i a'māl)*

As the philosophy of education presses a distinction between declarative knowledge and procedural knowledge, Bahā'ī writings differentiate between declarative and internalized forms of spirituality. Once internalized, spirituality is considered authenticated when acted upon. Goodly deeds are the residue of faith. In the Tablet of Unity, Bahā'u'llāh speaks of the collective "unity of deeds" (*ittiḥād-i a'māl*) that results from a high level of personal commitments to translating vision into volition and action.

Paradise imagery. "As to Paradise," Bahā'u'llāh assures, "it is a reality and there can be no doubt about it, and now in this world it is realized through love of Me and My good-pleasure. Whosoever attaineth unto it God will aid him in this world below, and after death He will enable him to gain admittance into Paradise whose vastness is as that of heaven and earth. Therein the Maids of glory and holiness will wait upon him in the daytime and in the night season, while the day-star of the unfading beauty of his Lord will at all times shed its radiance upon him and he will shine so brightly that no one shall bear to gaze at him. Such is the dispensation of Providence, yet the people are shut out by a grievous veil" (TB 189). The expression, "My good-pleasure," typically refers to acceptance of believer's moral striving, having performed goodly deeds in the path of God's commandments as revealed by Bahā'u'llāh.

Hence, this prayer for the believer: "Empower me, then, O my God, to be reckoned among them that have clung to Thy laws and precepts for the sake of Thee alone, their eyes fixed on Thy face. These, indeed, are they whose wine is all that hath proceeded out of the mouth of Thy primal will, whose pure beverage is Thine enthralling call, whose heavenly River is Thy love, whose Paradise is entrance into Thy presence and reunion with Thee. For Thou hast been their Beginning and their End, and their Highest Hope, and their Supreme Desire" (PM 299).

Unity of Station *(ittiḥād-i maqām)*

The ideal demeanor of Bahā'īs is to see one's own self in relation to others, such that all people might ideally be on the same "plane" (*suq'*) and station (*maqām*). If these words are accepted and established through God's power and might, the world would, truly, become the most effulgent Paradise, according to Bahā'u'llāh (Monjazeb 1995; RB 4: 193).

Paradise imagery. In his Tablet known as the *Words of Paradise*, Bahā'u'llāh refers to the principle of equality and reciprocity as one of the leaves of Paradise: "The word of God which the Supreme Pen hath recorded on the third leaf of the Most Exalted Paradise is this: O son of man! If thine eyes be turned towards mercy, forsake the things that profit thee and cleave unto that which will profit mankind. And if thine eyes be turned towards justice, choose thou for thy neighbour that which thou choosest for thyself. Humility exalteth man to the heaven of glory and power, whilst pride abaseth him to the depths of wretchedness and degradation" (TB 64).

Unity of Wealth *(ittiḥād-i amvāl)*

Towards the end of his Tablet of Unity, Bahā'u'llāh states that unity of wealth (*ittiḥād-i amvāl*) is the source of cheer and joy and exultation and that, from it, the attribute of altruism (*muvāsāt*) is manifested. Bahā'u'llāh goes on to explain that altruism ranks higher than equality (*musāvāt*). Thus, the philanthropy of *muvāsāt* exceeds the equitable distribution of wealth that is the reflex of *musāvāt* (RB 4: 195). In a similar vein, 'Abdu'l-Bahā states that "the Teachings of Bahā'u'llāh advocate voluntary sharing, and this is a greater thing than the equalization of wealth. For equalization must be imposed from without, while sharing is a matter of free choice" (SWAB 114–15). This is philanthropic altruism, and is constrained by the expenditure of expendable wealth in a way that is noninjurious to the security of self or family.

Paradise imagery. Philanthropy, or "charity," is considered a celestial virtue. One of Bahā'u'llāh's exhortations to philanthropy and lesser forms of charity is described as the "tenth leaf of the Most Exalted Paradise." After briefly commenting on Q. 59:9, Bahā'u'llāh concludes: "Blessed is he who preferreth his brother before himself. Verily, such a man is reckoned, by virtue of the Will of God, the All-Knowing, the All-Wise, with the people of Bahā who dwell in the Crimson Ark" (TB 71). Bahā'u'llāh paradise imagery is used to encourage the practice of philanthropy: "By the Most Great Name! The splendor of such a wealthy man shall illuminate the dwellers of heaven even as the sun enlightens the people of the earth!" (HWP #53). Similarly, Abdu'l-Bahā speaks of the noble philanthropist as "one of the people of paradise" (SDC 25).

Unity in Society *(ittiḥād-i nufūs)*

Unity of humankind is the pivotal Bahā'ī social teaching. Bahā'u'llāh writes: "He Who is the Day-Star of Truth beareth Me witness! So powerful is the light of unity that it can illuminate the whole earth. The One true God, He Who knoweth all things, Himself testifieth to the truth of these words" (GWB 288/ESW 14).

Paradise imagery. In an extensively idealized vision of unity in society, 'Abdu'l-Bahā uses celestial imagery. A brief passage will suffice to convey an impression of the language being used: "The sight and insight of some were illumined by the light of grace, and there were some who, hearing the anthems of unity, leapt for joy. There were birds that began to carol in the gardens of holiness, there were nightingales in the branches of the rose tree of heaven that raised their plaintive cries. Then were decked and adorned both the Kingdom on high and the earth below, and this world became the envy of high heaven" (SWAB 8).

IV. Other Forms of Unity

Unity (Equality) of Rights

On the evening of 9 June 1912, at a Unitarian Church in Philadelphia, 'Abdu'l-Bahā said: "Seventh, Bahā'u'llāh taught that an equal standard of human rights (*musāvāt-i ḥuqūq*) must be recognized and adopted. In the estimation of God, all men are equal; there is no distinction (*ḥuqūq-i vāḥid*) or preferment for any soul in the dominion of His justice and equity" (PUP 183; *Khiṭābāt* 440). This principle is imaged in several texts, particularly in relation to metaphors of justice.

Paradise imagery. Equality of rights is best dispensed through justice. "Exalted is the Lord of Wisdom, the Possessor of Great Bounty. The word of God which the Supreme Pen hath recorded on the sixth leaf of the Most Exalted Paradise is the following: The light of men is Justice. Quench it not with the contrary winds of oppression and tyranny" (TB 66–67). If this teaching metaphorically came down from Paradise, the consequences of following it cannot be far removed from some notion or experience of Paradise.

Unity of Knowledge (Harmony of Science and Religion)

In Bahā'ī thought, complementarity of science and religion constitutes the unity of knowledge. From Haifa, on 21 September 1921, 'Abdu'l-Bahā wrote to an eminent Swiss scientist, Dr. Auguste Forel (d. 1931): "We regard knowledge and wisdom as the foundation of the progress of mankind, and extol philosophers who are endowed with broad vision" (BR 220). It certainly appears that Bahā'ī texts go so far as to relinquish to science authority over its own domain, withdrawing religious claims to superior knowledge about the material world. A recent anecdote proves this point: When the editors of *Encyclopaedia Iranica* asked Bahā'ī scholar Moojan Momen to write an article on Bahā'ī cosmology, he contributed a short article saying that Bahā'īs accepted the cosmological findings of contemporary scientists! (Cole, p.c. 1 May 1995).

Paradise imagery. "Put all your beliefs into harmony with science; there can be no opposition, for truth is one," 'Abdu'l-Bahā has stated. "When religion, shorn of its superstitions, traditions, and unintelligent dogmas, shows its conformity with science, then will there be a great unifying, cleansing force in the world which will sweep before it all wars, disagreements, discords and struggles—and then will mankind be united in the power of the Love of God" (PT 146).

Unity (Universality) in Education

This category is taken from Piper. Bahā'u'llāh links education with unity: "Bend your minds and wills to the education of the peoples and kindreds of the earth, that haply the dissensions that divide it may, through the power of the Most Great Name, be blotted out from its face, and all mankind become the upholders of one Order, and the inhabitants of one City" (GWB 333–34). 'Abdu'l-Bahā speaks of the need for a universal curriculum: "Eighth, education is essential, and all standards of training and teaching (*vaḥdat-i uṣūl va qavānīn-i tarbīyat*) throughout the world of mankind should be brought into conformity and agreement; a universal curriculum (*tarbīyat-i vāḥida*) should be established, and the basis of ethics be the same (*yak uṣūl va ādāb*)" (PUP 183; *Khiṭābāt* 440, cf. 438; Persian text adds: "unity of humankind" [*vaḥdat-i ā'lam-i bashar*]).

Paradise imagery. One aspect of the universal curriculum which 'Abdu'l-Bahā advocates is its spiritual dimension, in which "unity in education" partly consists of a morals education. A child who has benefitted from such an education "will become a peerless plant in the gardens of the Abhā Paradise" (SWAB 124). Speaking of the education of children, in which spiritual refinement is combined with academic achievement, 'Abdu'l-Bahā idealizes the outcome, stating that "this lowly earth will become the Abhā Kingdom [Paradise], and this netherworld the world above. Then will this fleck of dust be as the vast circle of the skies, this human place the palace-court of God, this spot of clay the dayspring of the endless favours of the Lord of Lords" (SWAB 128–29).

And further: "Then will this darksome place grow luminous, and this abode of earth turn into Heaven. The very demons will change to angels then, and wolves to shepherds of the flock, and the wild-dog pack to gazelles that pasture on the plains of oneness, and ravening beasts to peaceful herds, and birds of prey, with talons sharp as knives, to songsters warbling their sweet native notes." "For the inner reality of man," 'Abdu'l-Bahā explains, "is a demarcation line between the shadow and the light, a place where the two seas meet; it is the lowest point on the arc of descent, and therefore is it capable of gaining all the grades above. With education it can achieve all excellence; devoid of education it will stay on, at the lowest point of imperfection. (SWAB 130–31). It is interesting how the Ṣūfī cosmology of the Arc of Descent (worlds of emanations) and the Arc of Ascent (spiritual progress) is here brought into relation with education.

Unity of Bahā'īs

"If any differences arise amongst you," counsels Bahā'u'llāh, "behold Me standing before your face." Such unity is a form of paradise as it mirrors forth God's will: "We love to see you at all times consorting in amity and concord within the paradise of My good-pleasure, and to inhale from your acts the fragrance of friendliness and unity, of loving-kindness and fellowship. Thus counselleth you the All-Knowing, the Faithful" (GWB 315–16).

Paradise imagery. The heart of Bahā'ī communal life is the Nineteen-Day Feast. On the ideal gathering of Bahā'īs, 'Abdu'l-Bahā idealizes the Nineteen-Day Feast as "a rose-garden of the Kingdom" in which "those enraptured beings [Bahā'īs] may be gathered together in the heaven of His mercifulness, that they may chant the verses of divine unity amidst the celestial concourse, sing the melody of His praise and glorification in the Abhā Kingdom, raise the voice of jubilation in the realm on high and the cry of exultation and ecstasy in the Abhā Paradise" (*Deepening* 195).

Unity in Marriage/Family Unity

Family unity, the basis for which is a united marriage, is seen as the bedrock of societal well-being. Marriage has an exalted station in Bahā'ī teachings. In the hierarchy of unity, it is expected that partners in marriage strive to deepen their union over the years. Divorces do occur in Bahā'ī communities. Provision is made for divorce in Bahā'ī law. But divorce is frequently a source of some embarassment to Bahā'īs who, after all, profess the importance of unity, the crown jewel of the treasury of Bahā'ī idealisms. As Shoghi Effendi aptly puts it: "If we Bahā'īs cannot attain to cordial unity among ourselves, then we fail to realize the main purpose for which the Bāb, Bahā'u'llāh, and the Beloved Master lived and suffered" (14 October 1928; *Family* 32 [#100]).

Ideally, marriage deepens one's capacity for love. This human quality can enhance the unitive potential of married individuals in society. Bahā'īs view marriage as the fundamental unit of society. This has a basis in Bahā'ī texts. For instance, 'Abdu'l-Bahā indicates that the marriage bond is a kind of "primal oneness": "And above all other unions is that between human beings, especially when it cometh to pass in the love of God. Thus is the primal oneness made to appear; thus is laid the foundation of love in the spirit. It is certain that such a marriage as yours will cause the bestowals of God to be revealed. Wherefore do we offer you felicitations and call down blessings upon you and beg of the Blessed Beauty, through His aid and favour, to make that wedding feast a joy to all and adorn it with the harmony of Heaven" (SWAB 119–20). If society is to be more unified, so must relationships based on a commitment of love.

Paradise imagery. A typical Bahā'ī text encouraging unity in marriage is this one: "It is highly important for man to raise a family. So long as he is young, because of youthful self-complacency, he does not realize its significance, but this will be a source of regret when he grows old. . . . In this glorious Cause the life of a married couple should resemble the life of the angels in heaven—a life full of joy and spiritual delight, a life of unity and concord, a friendship both mental and physical. . . . Their ideas and thoughts should be like the rays of the sun of truth and the radiance of the brilliant stars in the heavens" (*Family* 30 [#93]). Bahā'ī prayers for children are suffused with paradise imagery.

Summary. 'Abdu'l-Bahā expanded on the various kinds of unity propounded by Bahā'u'llāh, and has thus enriched Bahā'ī conceptions of unity. In a talk given in the morning of 9 June 1912 at the Unitarian Church, Fifteenth Street and Girard Avenue, in Philadelphia, 'Abdu'l-Bahā ends his speech with this prediction: "All will become as one family, one people, and the same susceptibility to the divine bounty and education will be witnessed among mankind" (PUP 176). This statement is not a word-for-word translation, but is based on notes taken by Edna McKinney, who was present. Fortunately, a Persian transcription for this speech exists. In the Persian original, in the space of a single sentence, 'Abdu'l-Bahā enumerates seven types of unity: [1] One Family (*'ā'ila-yi vāḥida*); [2] One Nation (*millat-i vāḥida*); [3] One People (*jins-i vāḥid*); [4] One Nation/Homeland (*vaṭan-i vāḥid*); [5] One Political System (*siyāsat-i vāḥid*); [6] Oneness of Emotions (*iḥsāsāt-i vaḥida*); [7] Oneness of Education (*tarbiyat-i vāḥida*) (*Khiṭābāt* 440). But the sum total result of unity is to effect unity concentrically, on every level and in all spheres of human endeavor, so that the world will be transformed from its animal condition into an angelic disposition: "Perchance will the lovers of God succeed in upraising the banner of human unity, so that the one-coloured tabernacle of the Kingdom of Heaven will cast its sheltering shadow over all the earth" (SWAB 90).

One distinction between the Bahā'ī model of unity and the call to harmony found in older scriptures, according to 'Abdu'l-Bahā, is one of transcending the boundaries of communal insularity. Bahā'īs should endeavor to foster unity in whatever society they find themselves, without regard to religious affiliation: "In every dispensation, there hath been the commandment of fellowship and love, but it was a commandment limited to the community of those in mutual agreement, not to the dissident foe. In this wondrous age, however, praised be God, the commandments of God are not delimited, not restricted to any one group of people, rather have all the friends been commanded to show forth fellowship and love, consideration and generosity and loving-kindness to every community on earth" (SWAB 20–21). In other words, what should distinguish Bahā'īs is their commitment to unity for all humanity, without distinction as to religious affiliation. Perhaps 'Abdu'l-Bahā was obliquely referring to the Islamic distinction between the "Abode of Islam (*dār al-Islām*) and the "Abode of War" (*dār al-ḥarb*). What perhaps distinguishes the Bahā'ī Faith from this Islamic dichotomy and from other religions in general is the Bahā'ī hierarchy of values, in which world unity is at the top of the agenda. This is indicated by Bahā'u'llāh himself: "After man's recognition of God, and becoming steadfast in His Cause, the station of affection, of harmony, of concord and of unity is superior to that of most other goodly deeds" (*Family* 28 [#86]).

Of his own authority to advance and promulgate his religion of unity, Bahā'u'llāh wrote: "Be ye fair therefore in your judgement concerning His upright Religion, for the love of this Youth who is riding high upon the snow-white She-Camel betwixt earth and heaven; and be ye firm and steadfast in the path of Truth" (Lambden 1988, 129). All of Bahā'u'llāh's teachings on unity may be summed up in this single statement: "The well-being of mankind, its peace and security, are unattainable unless and until its unity is firmly established. This unity can never be achieved so long as the counsels of the Pen of the Most High are suffered to pass unheeded" (GWB 286).

In fine, a number of representative texts have been adduced to illustrate the centrality of Bahā'u'llāh's unity paradigm in Bahā'ī teachings, and how such texts employ Paradise imagery as a rhetorical device, to impress upon the reader the importance of unity in its various forms: "Strive ye with all your hearts . . . until this dark world be filled with light . . . and this dust heap of a fleeting moment be changed into a mirror for the eternal gardens of heaven, and this globe of earth receive its portion of celestial grace. Then will . . . earth bring forth the roses and sweet herbs of blessings without end, and become from pole to pole the Abhā Paradise" (SWAB 36–37). Like this text, Bahā'ī contemplative life is filled with paradise imagery. Pictures of Paradise, in the Bahā'ī experience, provide a mental anchorage for personal development and productive socialization. Paradise is sought, not for afterlife recompense and eschatological requital, but for a present reality.

Perhaps the simplest expression of unity as paradise may be found in this straightforward equivalence: "[C]onsider love and union as a delectable paradise, and count annoyance and hostility as the torment of hell-fire" (TAB I, 37). Taken individually, each of these "unities" outlined above has probably been conceived of by other philosophers and thinkers. But what may be unique about these Bahā'ī principles is the fact that they have been integrated into a single value system, and made sacred. As 'Abdu'l-Bahā has concluded: "These precepts were proclaimed by Bahā'o'llāh [*sic*] many years ago. He was the first to create them in the hearts as moral laws. Writing to the sovereigns of the world, he summoned them to universal brotherhood, proclaiming that the hour for unity had struck—unity between countries, unity between religions" (DP 85). Paradise imagery does not exhaust Bahā'ī symbolism, but it is the heart of the Bahā'ī conception of unity, concentrically conceived of as widening circles of unity, from self to society, and from one's very soul to the Deity beyond unity.

VIII

Conclusions

Interpretation of Results

Paradise and Paradigm is an experiment in comparison. Since the present writer had already undertaken a study of the Islamic background of the Bahā'ī religion in his monograph, *Symbol and Secret* (1995a), the possibility of even older interreligious resonances made for an attractive and original research project. To conduct a nonapologetic comparison between Christianity and the Bahā'ī Faith on common historical grounds, it was necessary to determine which specific Christian tradition had the closest ties to "Persia."

It was determined that East Syrian Christianity was the most commensurate Christian tradition for comparative purposes. This selection is somewhat contradicted by the fact that, in present-day Iran, Armenian Christians now outnumber "Assyrian" Christians two to one. But historically, until the Mongol debacle, East Syrian Christianity was the dominant form of Christianity throughout Sasanian Iran. (The Persian empire was territorially much greater than present-day Iran, and included what is now modern Iraq.) Northern Mesopotamia, where Syriac Christianity originated, was of particular interest, for in the Sasanian period, Mesopotamia was considered "the central region of Iran" (Bausani 1971, 146).

How "Persian" was Persian Christianity? Based on the outcomes of this reseach project, the following conclusions may be drawn with respect to the so-called Persian dimensions of East Syrian Christianity: (1) Ecclesiastically (by virtue of its autocephalous independence), (2) politically (insofar as Persian synods were under imperial Sasanian patronage), (3) geographically (the Church of Persia having spread throughout the Sasanian empire and well beyond), (4) ethnically (by virtue of numerous Iranian converts from Zoroastrianism), and (5) linguistically (due to the presence of local Persian vernaculars), it could be said that the Church of the East was far more "Persian" than "Roman"—even though the Church of Persia had subscribed to the Council of Nicea and had adopted the Western model of church organization. Although East Syrians formed the majority of the Church of the East, it has been argued, on the strength of the evidence adduced, that ethnic Persians had formed the most important ethnic minority of the Persian "Church of the East." Once a universal, multiethnic religion, the Church of Persia was Christianity's most successful missionary church until modern times, and was arguably the most important form of non-Roman Christianity in Late Antiquity.

While early Syriac Christianity predates the official establishment of the Church of Persia, Ephrem the Syrian and Aphrahāṭ the Persian Sage were formative influences. Indeed, the Nestorian liturgy known as the *Ḥuḏrā* (which contains fragments of a lost liturgy in vernacular Persian, as shown in Appendix IV below), is traditionally ascribed to Ephrem. Although the material is drawn from a variety of sources and authors, the stamp of Ephrem is indelible.

Method and interpretation require evaluation to assess validity, with a view to refinement. This section, *Interpretation of Results*, will be followed by four more sections: *Evaluation of Research Design*; *Counterindications*; *Suggestions for Further Study*; and *Relevance to the Study of Religion*.

Symbols and significations. Symbols ensoul religion. Chariot thrones, wheels of fire, jewels, crystal seas, vaulted empyreans, multitudes of voices, fire and brimstone, reward and punishment, eschatons and apocalypses—these are the focal, imagistic epitomes of religious worldviews. Symbols are invested with a numinous, psychological presence. They express religious beliefs and aspirations with an ideological economy, and elicit a profusion of sentiments. Some symbols disclose much about the structure of belief. Such encoded, imagistic "projections" may have heuristic value for the discovery of unifying paradigms, or complexes of ideals and beliefs that structure worldviews.

The key symbols treated in this study were, for the most part, symbols of Paradise. Indeed, the constellations of "key symbols" selected for comparison were determined to be dominant within their respective traditions.

Syriac Christian and Bahā'ī traditions appear to share a common ontological commitment. In their "noumenal" sense of reality, both religions point to a "transphenomenal, supersensible, and eternally perfect realm or activity" (Dilworth 1989, 28). This "eternally perfect" realm is Paradise. Paradise imagery may be explored as a mythic form of discourse. Visions of Paradise disclose much about particular religious worldviews in cosmic, heavenly terms. Within the sanctuary of visionary texts, under the spire of aspirations, in the inner sanctum of images, it is possible to peer into the very heart and soul of religion. In

Paradise texts, the phenomenologist of religion can discover some of the richest treasures of religious contemplation: creeds beyond words.

Descriptions of Paradise may embody major theory formulations about spirituality that bear a direct relationship to controlling, religious paradigms. Once decoded, exhibitive statements about "the other world" can have a referentially this-worldly meaning. The symbolic "method" of early Syriac Christian and the modern Bahā'ī texts is one in which "one observes a logic of higher agreement, which presupposes and accomplishes a synthetic unity of opposites, contrasts, or multiplicities. Partial, abstract views are subsumed and reconciled—whether aesthetically, actively, or propositionally—in an emerging whole" (ibid., 29). As such, the "emerging whole" constitutes a paradigm. At its most basic level of operation, that paradigm is soteriological in nature. Its logic and purpose is to save.

Soteriology and paradigm differences. The single most important heuristic key for comparing early Syrian Christian and Bahā'ī systems is soteriology, which is typically at the core of religious paradigms (cf. Oxtoby 1973).

Christianity is at heart a message of salvation. Christianity is typically defined as a post-Easter, Resurrection faith. (There is a cynical but compelling view that resurrection belief was augmented by a compensatory wish-image: "The expectation of resurrection and the establishment of a divine kingdom provided one answer to the question of why God did not intervene on behalf of his people" [McDannell and Lang 1988, 13].)

Christian soteriology is intimately bound up with Christology. In turn, Christology is bound up with notions of the Trinity. This is why the Trinitarian controversies that erupted in the fourth century were followed by the Christological controversies in the fifth. The Trinity has been a major obstacle to rapprochement between Islam and Christianity, due to the strict monotheism of the former.

The relationship of the one, monarchial God to the Trinity has troubled Christian theologians as far back as the Church Fathers. A major difficulty in any patristic formulation of the Trinity is the concept of "Primal Cause." Gregory of Nazianzus is a case in point. In attempting to defend the doctrine of the Trinity from the charge of tritheism, the Cappadocian Father wrote: "But when we look at the three in whom the Godhead exists, who derive their timeless and equally glorious being from the primal cause, we have three objects of worship" (*Oration* XXXI.14, tr. L. Wickham and F. Williams in Norris et al. 1991, 198 and 286). On this statement, Norris comments: "One difficulty for any Trinitarian theology that uses the concept of a 'primal cause' is the placement of that cause within the scheme. The conundrum seems impossible to solve. If the primal cause is the Father, then the Father is different from the Son and the Spirit. But if that cause is outside or before the three, then part of the definition of God does not reside within the three. No matter which approach Gregory chooses, a puzzle remains. . . . It is a Biblical puzzle that remains unsolved" (1991, 198–99).

No Christological dogma ever stood revealed. To conserve what unity it could, the Church perforce had to work out its creedal and confessional standards during periods of Christological controversy. Thus, the doctrines of the Incarnation and Trinity were hammered out in the Councils of Nicaea (325 C.E.), Ephesus (431 C.E.), Chalcedon (451 C.E.), Constantinople II and III (553 and 681 C.E.), and the Redemption in the councils of Orange (529 C.E.) and Trent, sessions V and VI (1546 and 1547 C.E.). The ecumenical councils, starting from the canons of Nicaea to which both Ephrem's church and the Church of Persia subscribed, were intended to unify the Church doctrinally, even if this meant expulsion or coercion of Christian dissidents. But imperial Christian rulings did not resolve all of the problems they were intended to solve. Pelikan observes that "the trinitarian developments had not really prepared the church for the problematics of the christological issue" (1974, 1: 228–29). Christology and Trinitarian doctrine were so interrelated that the formulation of one impacted the other. Ephrem did not try to solve the Christological puzzle. The Syrian saint embraced the bewildering and enriching ambiguites of the mystery of the Godhead, and condemned the Arians for their sophistic overrationalizations that undermined Christian faith and savaged Christian unity.

At the root of the Christological debates in the fifth century lay the fundamental issue of the relation between body and soul (Cooke 1990, 73). In Christian consciousness, forgiveness of sins and the death of Christ and his victory over death are interrelated. In the theology of the Greek-speaking Church, Christ as Redeemer liberated us not so much from guilt as from our mortality, our "sickness unto death." Though the Latin West began to move away from the doctrine of *theōsis* (deification) prevalent in the Greek East, no explicit doctrine of reconciliation was settled upon in the period of the early Church. There is one point of departure from which all Christian theories of redemption proceed: the sinful human plight. The Syriac Orient at the time of Ephrem exhibits a telling concern for the "sickness" into which humankind had fallen. Notwithstanding, Winslow rightly points out that "there was no such thing, among the Fathers, as *soteriological* orthodoxy" (1984, 394).

In the case of early Syriac Christianity, soteriology and symbolism have a much more dynamic relationship than in other forms of Christianity. For Ephrem, God is revealed in two modes: in Nature (*kyānā*) and in Scripture (*ktābā*). But far more efficacious than revelation is God's Incarnation, and the dispensation of Christ's own deity through the sacraments. A cultic interpretation of Christianity came to predominate Ephrem's thinking. Divinity was communicated and came to be experienced through the "mysteries" or sacraments, constituting the soteriologically efficacious presence of God. (For a biblical perspective on divine presence, see Terrien 1978; on sacrament and presence, cf. Schoonenberg 1967.) The link of sacramentality to Christological issues is absolutely basic to Ephrem.

The absence of sacramental imagery in the Bahā'ī writings reflects one difference of fundamental importance between the two religious systems: the Bahā'ī Faith does not hold to a sacramental worldview. In this study's theoretical treatment of the Bahā'ī Faith, reference to "the unity paradigm" as its major descriptor actually reflects a Bahā'ī self-understanding, thus satisfying Wilfred Cantwell Smith's canon of believer intelligibility. While the term *unity paradigm* was independently conceived during the writing of the first draft of this dissertation, it has come to the author's attention that this term had already been coined by the German Bahā'ī author Udo Schaefer, who explains what he meant by the expression: "In selecting the term 'unity paradigm' the author intends to convey the new understanding of religion: the new image of religious phenomena and of religious history; and its inherent concept of divine salvation (*Heilsgeschichte*). This concept of unity is central to the teachings of Bahā'u'llāh" (1992, 55). It should be added, however, that the use of the technical term *paradigm* is external to the Bahā'ī texts themselves.

Perhaps the fundamental difference between Bahā'ī and Syriac Christian paradigms reflects the tenor of their times. Ninian Smart writes perceptively of the emergence of the Bahā'ī Faith and of the basis of its appeal: "It is an example of a spiritual revolution which intuitively recognized the global state of world culture before its time and gave religious preparation for this unified world" (1995, 480). The most Ephrem could have been expected to say in this regard concerned the unity of the Church (HdF. LII, SCK 150; cf. Murray 1963). By means of the thick historical descriptions presented in this study, Syriac/Persian Christianity was analyzed as a response to Late Antiquity, while the Bahā'ī Faith was seen as a reponse to modernity. This determination rendered paradigm analysis all the more meaningful, as each of the two religions was viewed as being anchored to history. This historical dimension has added a verificatory power to the paradigm analysis.

In the case of Syriac Christianity, the paradigm of purity—referenced to the core soteriological myth of the Robe of Glory—reflects an overarching interest in Paradise-worthiness, in preparation for which a state of sanctification is achieved through sacramental divinization, the angelic life of sexual holiness (the Covenant), and the pastoral extension of Christ's ministry through ethical refinement in the form of good deeds. The Bahā'ī paradigm of unity—referenced to the core myth of the Noachide and Sufistic journey to the Paradise of the Beloved and fidelity to the Covenant of Bahā'u'llāh—places emphasis on justice and integration as a form of societal sanctification, achieved through widening circles of unity from Heart to Earth, as a refraction of Paradise in the prism of unity.

Evaluation of Research Design

As a self-inventory of the research performed, the author will attempt to assess the strengths and weaknesses of the research project. To put a slight twist on the expression, "the best defense is a good offense," the present writer will try to anticipate criticisms of the project in advance of others' reviews of it. The following questions need to be asked and deserve honest answers.

Are the comparisons limitative? Comparative projects run greater risks if the scope is too broad, the range of data too variable, and the amount of data too much to cope with. There is also the problem of uncritical and hypercritical selection of parallels. Two extremes must be avoided. The first is uncritical "parallelomania"—untested conclusions drawn from superficial resemblances. The other extreme is hypercritical reductionism, in which all similarities are "deconstructed" into culturally indexed solipsisms. As a corrective, the present study interprets similarities by means of differences, to arrive at meaningful, limited comparisons the methodology of which may contribute to a general phenomenology of religion. Constraints on comparison claims will serve to rehabilitate comparison from its tarnished image as a largely "unscientific" procedure.

Are the comparisons accurate? Since a formal comparison involves at least two religions, the researcher has a professional responsibility to achieve some mastery of the present state of scholarship on each tradition being compared. The integrity of the comparative enterprise depends upon the accuracy and perspicuity of the researcher, and on some facility with the original texts. If the researcher's knowledge of the traditions is deficient or otherwise suspect, the whole exercise risks collapse into a caricature.

In a comparative research endeavor, one must establish a rationale for the synchronic juxtaposition of diachronically distant religions. Moreover, a diachronic dimension in such a study is necessary to anchor the data in history, and to provide context. That context suggests much in the way of interpretation, and constrains it. Without a thick description of the historical setting of each religion, the comparison may become too abstracted from those webs of relationships that symbiotically instantiate fields of meaning for each of the religions being compared. A purely synchronic comparative exercise makes the mistake of atomizing the texts. History affords the surest control of the integrity of worldview analysis.

With respect to the texts themselves, there is certainly a massive literature in Syriac, with many manuscript treasures yet to be studied. These are predominantly Semitic in thought as well as in language. Although Aphrahāṭ, "the Persian Sage"—our first major witness to Syriac Christianity—is thought to have been an ethnic Iranian, Ephrem was not. Notwithstanding this fact, Ephrem's influence is both foundational to and coextensive with Persian Christianity, officially known as the Church of the East. Whether or not liturgical texts attributed to Ephrem in post-Ephremic liturgical reforms are genuine, Ephrem's traditional association with the liturgy of both West and East Syrian Christianity is explicit, thus according him an honorific presence in Syrian worship down to the present. In fact, so pervasive is early Syriac symbolism throughout the Syriac hymn cycle known as the *Ḥuḏrā* and other Syriac liturgies that Ephrem's legacy need only be recognized, rather than proven.

Some difficulty arises over the question of to what extent the Church of Persia was ethnically Iranian. This study has determined that Persian (Middle Persian, and New Persian, Sogdian) was a subsidiary Christian vernacular. The discovery of a lost Persian Christian liturgy preserved in the *Ḥuḏrā* was of particular importance in this regard. Extant Nestorian texts in Iranian languages are actually very few, but formed part of what is thought to have been a once extensive literature (Brock 1982a, 18).

The "revelation" of Bahā'u'llāh was analyzed as a response to modernity, in which Bahā'u'llāh was shown to have "sacralized" some of the more salubrious developments of the modern world (i.e., Europe), just as he had "desacralized" some of the excesses of prior religions, notably of Babism and Shi'ism. Such an approach will not endear many Bahā'īs, who might misconstrue this kind of analysis as reductionism, when a dialectical relationship between Bahā'u'llāh and his historical context is what is actually being argued. In this regard, it is worth noting a similar conclusion drawn by B. Todd Lawson: "His [Bahā'u'llāh's] religion can be seen as a response to the challenges posed to the Islamic world; the manner in which his teachings both arose from within the parent religion and acquired their own distinct identity is unique in the history of modern Islam" (1995, 176).

Is this study "axiomatically posited"? A comparison must have a purpose, a point. The most utilitarian comparisons are those that demonstrate some kind of genetic nexus. Utilitarian comparisons are most supportive of historical arguments. Then there are also "larger" comparisons, supportive of the high theories of phenomenology. This latter purpose represents the research aims of the present study, which have been clearly articulated in chapter 1.

Are analogical and differential relationships equitably balanced? A methodologically self-conscious comparison should result in positive and/or negative outcomes. A negative outcome is reached when apparent similarities are overruled by differences of more fundamental import. Thus, superficial adducing of parallels for comparative purposes may be invalidated on the basis of systemic differences, which may yet exhibit some phenomenological similarities. These similarities can never be wholly abstracted from the systems that produce them. Wholly abstracted similarities are modern mythologies.

Was there analytical control? This study compared key symbols across two traditions. Synchronic analysis of these symbols was constrained by fairly "thick" descriptions of Syriac and Bahā'ī contexts and belief structures. Such diachronic considerations provided some necessary constraints, as previously stated.

Ninian Smart's dimensional model of religion provided an admittedly Procrustean, taxonomic atlas of Syriac and Bahā'ī traditions. An "anatomy" of each religion could then be objectivized and a "comparative anatomy," as it were, facilitated. The symbolic profiles that were then built on the structure of Smart's dimensions enfleshed, with imagistic thew and ideological sinew, the paradigmatic skeleton of each tradition. Insights emerged as to the distinctive characteristics of the two worldviews being compared. The technique of worldview analysis performed here by means of symbolic profiles is one attempt at model building. Equitable comparability between early Syriac Christianity and the Bahā'ī Faith has provided a framework for analysis of differences.

Are the hypothetical patterns testable? The general hypothesis was this: *"Parallels" yield paradoxes of commensurability resolvable by paradigm "logics" within religious systems.* In the abstract, this hypothesis is extended to include . . . *resulting in symbolic transformation.* This final clause is implicated by the findings of this study, but it does not form a part of the phenomenological argument. A phenomenological finding ought to have its historical exemplars to support it. But the finding itself does not constitute a historical argument as such. The specific hypothesis states: *Formal comparison of early Syriac Christianity and the Bahā'ī Faith is constrained by their paradigms (respectively, transformational purity and concentric unity), by which all phenomenological parallels must be interpreted.* The exemplar adduced in section 1.7 still holds: *"Christ as "Physician," for example, dispenses immortality, while Bahā'u'llāh, as Physician, dispenses unity. Both dispense salvation in their respective conceptions of it.* Here is a clear phenomenological "parallel," in which the similarity is interpreted in terms of difference.

Counterindications

The integrity of this study requires that it take inventory of some of the classic pitfalls of comparison. Paden warns of three dangers of "the comparative enterprise in academic settings." These are: "theological privileging, ahistoricism, and foundationalism" (1996a, 6). Other counterindications arise from the particularities of the present study. These include scalar bias, data selection, and false parallels.

Theological Privileging. The Study of Religion is a secular undertaking. The integrity of any study is diminished if tainted by covert theological privileging, at which point the research becomes self-serving—apologetic, circular, and denominational. Moreover, one must be vigilant against any unconscious impingement on a research enterprise, particularly of one's own worldview, value system, assumptions, vested research interests, pet theories, and possible prejudices. This cannot be avoided in absolute terms, but it can be monitored and disciplined. As one control, Syriac and Bahā'ī traditions have received equal treatment as a consequence of a carefully crafted, structural symmetry incorporated in the research design and implemented accordingly.

Ahistoricism. It is necessary to avoid what Paden calls "the contextless character of classical comparison" (1996a, 5). While comparison of key symbols selected from two traditions that are historically distant in time can only be characterized as synchronic, it was neither ahistorical nor transhistorical. As a counterbalance to the synchronic dimension of the comparison, the basic descriptions of early Syriac Christianity and Bahā'ī Faith undertaken in chapters 2 and 4 were diachronically focused. That is to say, the abstract profile of each religion was grounded in history.

This study suggests, but does not prove, that some of the key symbols within Bahā'ī tradition may represent transformations of Syriac Christian parallels which, historically, preceded the Bahā'ī Faith by well over a millennium. However, the following objection has to be addressed: *The influence of Islam must have been a key factor in any such transformation.* This is undoubtedly true for most of the key symbols treated in this study. However, as the historical hypothesis—which is undeveloped and undefended—is nevertheless implicated by the results of this study, such an undertaking is left to a future research project. A tested theoretical model for the mechanism of symbolic assimilation and adaptation are singularly lacking, such that even the proof of contact does little more that state provenance. Provenance may account for—but does not explain—the process of adaptation. A case in point is the figure of Jesus in the Qur'ān, where antecedence may show derivation, but not idiosyncratic amplification.

To be sure, Islamic symbolism informs Bahā'ī symbolism. But the extent to which Islam took up Syriac Christian symbolism is largely unknown. Annemarie Schimmel has provided some much-needed descriptions of Islamic symbolism. Her work is primarily phenomenological. Her most comprehensive phenomenological investigations were presented in her 1992 Gifford Lectures (Schimmel 1994). Of those key symbols that were later taken up in the Bahā'ī Faith, Schimmel has touched upon the primordial Covenant (109, 114, 174, n. 85, 253), Illumination (on light symbolism: 12, 13, 16–17), the Lover and the Beloved (on the Beloved: 105–109), the Maiden of Heaven (on houris: 105–106, 236), the Ark (on Noah's Ark: 25 and 57), Wine (on wine symbolism: 16, 108–109, 111, n. 54)/Water of Life (7 and 182), Mirror (31–32, 45, n. 78 and 81)/Gems (on the symbolism of precious stones: 4–5), the Journey (27 and 64–66), the Lote Tree (on the Lote Tree, the Tree of Life, and other symbolic trees: 15–20), and Paradise (passim). Absent in Schimmel's phenomenology was any background information on the "Promised One" or the Physician as key symbols, which figure so prominently in Bahā'ī texts. Phenomenological investigations such as Schimmel's are primarily descriptive. No strict typology was attempted, and no historical argument adduced.

To have analyzed the Bahā'ī religion simply as a projection of universalized Islam would neither have done justice to the contemporary Bahā'ī worldview nor to the substance and ethos of the Bahā'ī scriptures themselves. The texts have their own voice. Moreover, the Bahā'ī paradigm is an obvious departure from that of Islam. As pervasively as the latter informs the former, the Bahā'ī kerygma and its supporting imagery has its own symbolic constellations and ideological configurations. The idiosyncrasies of Bahā'ī texts still await basic descriptions in the scholarly literature.

Foundationalism. Comparison is seen by many in the field as a relic of nineteenth-century quests for a unified theory to "explain" religion. Except for the primary methodological hypothesis of this study (viz., *"Parallels" yield paradoxes of commensurability resolvable by paradigm "logics" within religious systems*), theoretical universals remain uninvestigated for fear of committing, once again, the original methodological sin of foundationalism.

While the determination of key symbols was rather straightforward, defining a governing paradigm for Syriac Christianity was not so easy, and the paradigm advanced in this study may be controversial. A crucial factor was the central importance in Syriac spirituality of the notion of *theōsis*, or divinization. This process of sacramental and social Paradise-worthiness justifies use of the term *transformational* in reference to the hypothesized Syriac paradigm of "transformational purity." Selection of the term *purity* was heavily influenced by broader notions of sanctification, in which asceticism and sexual purity played a major role. The pervasive imagery of "bridal mysticism" accentuated the role of purity, which has more profound connotations than righteousness. While the sacraments—which are at the cultic heart of Syriac spirituality—are the decisive factor in the "transformational" component of the Syriac paradigm, "purity" itself is effected by the full exercise of the Syriac Christian, "angelic" lifestyle.

Scalar Bias. Every investigator needs to factor into the interpretation of his or her results the well-known dictum: "The scale creates the phenomenon." This axiom is a caveat attributed to the scientist, Henri Poincaré (1854–1912) and was often cited by Mircea Eliade (Paden 1992, 4). Its application to the present study might suggest that key symbols have a predominantly rhetorical function, and that the correspondence between worldview and mode of expression is not necessarily symmetrical. To adduce an example from the Qur'ān, a very inaccurate picture of Islam would be generated if only the early Meccan suras were studied, because the salient imagery in those revelations is apocalyptic, whereas later portions of the Qur'ān are much more narrative and prescriptive. The "scale" in this research project was qualitative, subject to the biases of the author's own subjectivity. The cogency and validity of similarity assessments in this study are basically a question of interpretation. Constraints on data selection are addressed in the next section.

Data Selection. While the state-sanctioned form of Christianity in Sasanian Iran was Nestorianism (less commonly, but more properly referred to as the "Church of the East"), the West Syrian Jacobites, or Monophysites, also had a presence in Persia. In point of fact, the Christian presence in Iran had local fluctuations. The most obvious instance is that of the Armenians, who were clearly the most prominent group of Christians in Safavid Iṣfahān. In the sixteenth century, Shāh 'Abbās had relocated a large sector of the Armenian population of Julfa on the Araxes and colonized them in Iṣfahān ("New Julfa"), in order to divert the Silk Route to Iran. Whatever historical argument may be advanced in the direction of Christian influence in Iran will have to take the Armenian community into account.

The selection of key symbols for this study was to the exclusion of a number of other significant symbols. Wherever leading Syriac specialists had identified any particular image as a "favorite" symbol of Ephrem, this was interpreted as a warrant for the privileging of the said symbol for research purposes. Thus, in the case of Syriac Christianity, the selection of key symbols reflected something of a unpolled consensus. The selection of key symbols for the Bahā'ī section had a similar sort of informal control—prior encyclopedic selection—which was the privileging of certain Bahā'ī symbols for inclusion in Wendi Momen's *A Basic Bahā'ī Dictionary*. As comparativist, the present writer could simply attend to such prior determinations.

False Parallels. An image common to two traditions may have divergent conceptual linkages. A case in point is Syriac and Bahā'ī notions of the soul, supported by references to the phenomenon of the dream. This example involves the basic anthropological question surrounding the soul and its presumed or conditional immortality. Here, use of an analogy common to both traditions produces diametrically opposed results. One example will be given here: the image of the dream. Syriac and Bahā'ī texts use the phenomenon of the dream to support differing notions of the soul. To quip the folk lyric, both Ephrem and Bahā'u'llāh in effect say that "[after]life is like a dream."

Ephrem relates the traditional Syriac idea of the postmortem "sleep of the soul" to the phenomenon of the dream: "And even the dream which it (i.e., the Soul) sees apart from it (i.e., the Body) when it (i.e., the Body) is asleep, when it awakens and . . . *[the Soul requires the Body to tell of the dream it has seen; the dream really comes from both of them].* The dream, therefore, which it sees apart from the Body the Soul does not (really) see apart from it; by it (*i.e.*, the Body) and with it and in the midst of it . . . *[the Soul has its dream] . . . [they depend upon each other, in slumber and in sleep they are not separated from one another]* since they are mingled with each other. But in death . . . they are separated, and . . . from one another—as they were mixed together *[in hope . . . on their Resurrection—since they have their Resurrection as a dream so that just after their sleep Recollection (?) comes to both, so after death]*" (*Fifth Discourse to Hypatius*, in Mitchell 1912, 1: cvi). In this difficult and convoluted passage, Ephrem fails to explain how the soul processes and stores sensory input, the experience of which is deferred until such time as the body is reunited with the soul. If body and soul must interpret the dream together, how then does the soul even partially dream without the agency of the body?

The exact opposite of Ephrem's interpretation obtains in Bahā'ī anthropology. As Bahā'u'llāh states in the *Seven Valleys*: "Indeed, O Brother, if we ponder each created thing, we shall witness a myriad perfect wisdoms and learn a myriad new and wondrous truths. One of the created phenomena is the dream (*nawm*, sleep). Behold how many secrets (*asrār*) are deposited therein, how many wisdoms (*ḥikmat-hā*) treasured up, how many worlds (*‘avālim*) concealed. Observe, how thou art asleep in a dwelling, and its doors are barred; on a sudden thou findest thyself in a far-off city, which thou enterest without moving thy feet or wearying thy body; without using thine eyes, thou seest; without taxing thine ears, thou hearest; without a tongue, thou speakest. And perchance when ten years are gone, thou wilt witness in the outer world the very things thou hast dreamed tonight. Now there are many wisdoms (*chand ḥikmat*) to ponder in the dream (*naum*), which none but the people of this Valley (*ahl-i īn vādī*) can comprehend in their true elements. First, what is this world (*ān cha ‘ālam ast*), where without eye and ear and hand and tongue, a man puts all of these to use? Second, how is it that in the outer world (*‘ālam-i ẓuhūr*) thou seest today the effect of a dream (*khwāb*), when thou didst vision it in the world of sleep some ten years past? Consider the difference between these two worlds (*du ‘ālam*) and the mysteries (*asrār*) which they conceal, that thou mayest attain to divine confirmations and heavenly discoveries (*mukāshifāt-i subḥānī*) and enter the regions of holiness (*‘ālam-i quds*). God, the Exalted, hath placed these signs (*āyāt*) in men, to the end that philosophers (*muḥaqqiqīn*) may not deny the mysteries of the life beyond (*asrār-i ma‘ād*) nor belittle that which hath been promised (*va‘da*) them” (SV 32–3, AQA III: 126). [A textual note: Unlike *naum*, *khwāb* can mean either “sleep” or “dream” (PED 478).]

Ephrem and Bahā’u’llāh each adduce the phenomenon of the dream, but for diametrically opposed purposes. This example provides fair warning that some parallels may not only be superficial, they may be deceptive. Where there is symbolic overlap by virtue of the sheer multivalence of symbols, one must always be careful to contextually nuance positive correspondences, or such parallels, while not false in themselves, will be falsely interpreted.

Suggestions for Further Study

One of the counterindications itemized in the previous section was that of “False Parallels.” This category does not include the element of alleged syncretism on the part of Bahā’ī texts, for having deliberately assimilated Christ and other prophetic figures into Bahā’ī theophanology, which could be productive of false (or true) parallels. Bahā’īs are disinclined to conceive of their religion as syncretistic (cf. Stockman 1996).

Assimilation of Christ—the central symbol in Christianity—to Bahā’u’llāh himself, accentuates a perceptually dynamic relationship between the two revealers. In a Tablet addressed to German Templar leader Georg David Hardegg some time prior to July 1872, Bahā’u’llāh remarks on the Person of Christ, to the effect that there are no essential differences between Bahā'ī and Christian beliefs with respect to Jesus. As "the Spirit" (*al-rūḥ*), Christ transcends confessional distinctions and symbolisms. Bahā'u'llāh affirms that Jesus is the Light of Oneness (*nūr al-aḥadīya*) and the Sign of the Ancient (*āyat al-qidam*) as God's supreme witness to humanity. Whoever turns to Christ turns to God. Throughout salvation history, Christlike epiphanies—which Bahā'u'llāh refers to as "Mirrors" or prophets—appear in various forms and colours, with no essential difference in spiritual reality (Lambden 1983, 56). It may be said here that, from Bahā'u'llāh's perspective, Christ's greatness and uniqueness is not diminished by the confession that God has sent other great spiritual teachers. The closest counterpart in Ephrem's hymns to Bahā'u'llāh's doctrine of prophetic unity is the sentiment: "Look on the prophets and the apostles, / how like they are to each other!" (CNis XX.7, SCK 153). Ephrem could not have been expected to have been a pluralist.

The Bahā'ī Faith is a post-Islamic religion. It stands squarely within the Abrahamic tradition. Prophetologically, the Bahā'ī religion has incorporated the figure of Christ to its own notions of prophetic succession, and considers itself to be the "fulfillment" of biblical prophecies surrounding the return of Christ. Throughout his writings, Bahā'u'llāh asserts that Christ indeed had foreknowledge of the future. The following passage from a Tablet known as the *Sūrat al-Sulṭān* (AQA IV: 154–80) is of interest here in that it states that Jesus was spiritually aware of Bahā'u'llāh's future mission and of the living sacrifice the latter was destined to offer up. Bahā'u'llāh writes: "Say: When the Son of Mary [Jesus] went up into the Mountain of Command, the cloud of sanctity came down upon Him. Seeing, of a sudden, a sprinkling of blood upon His garb, He called out in wonderment to the cloud, questioning it concerning this appearance. Thereat the cloud made answer, and recounted unto Him the adversities that this Youth [Bahā'u'llāh] hath suffered. Grieving inwardly to hear this tale, He renounced the world and all that is therein, and, ascending to the Court of Holiness, entered into the presence of God, His Lord and the Lord of all things, the Lord of all the worlds." (AQA IV: 156 [Arabic text provided by Dr. Nosrat Mohammadhosseini]; translation provided by the Universal House of Justice, p.c., 10 January 1990.) Jesus is presented here as having experienced a dramatic intimation of the Promethean passion of Bahā'u'llāh. This foreknowledge, this prescience predicated of Jesus, is one of the interesting features of Bahā'ī theophanology. In so saying, Bahā'u'llāh does not minimize or undervalue Christ's passion, for in the same passage, Bahā'u'llāh states that, were he to reveal the extent of Christ's suffering, the veil of greatness would be rent asunder and the pillars of heaven would tremble.

The deliberate appropriation of Christ to the Bahā'ī concept of "Progressive Revelation" begs the question of influence. This is why it is possible to hypothetically postulate some kind of symbolic transformation of Christian symbolism by the Bahā'ī "revelation." The texts themselves invite such an investigation. The question of which Christian tradition, if any, provided the quarry of symbols from which the Bahā'ī scriptures drew their Christian exemplars for apologetic purposes, and which symbols the Bahā'ī religion stood to inherit by virtue of its Abrahamic heritage mediated by Islam, is complex and cannot be easily resolved. It is clearly a topic for further research, but if and only if the question is admitted. Notions of revelation and divine inspiration religiously tend to preclude such a secular inquiry, which perhaps justifies the separation of the "Church" and the state-funded academy.

Conclusion. "Faith," as described by Ephrem, serves as "a second soul" which, with love and wisdom, permits one to be joined (*metmzeg*) to divinity and to be reformed in its image (HdF LXXX.3; Stewart 1991, 196; cf. CH XVI.11). Religious paradigms are much like the "second soul" Ephrem describes. Once paradigms are understood, similarities can be better explained in terms of cogent paradigmatic differences. Syriac and Bahā'ī parallels were linked to core paradigms. Both similarities and differences between the two conceptual systems were shown to be consistent with paradigmatic structuring.

Evidence (based on coherence theory, not history) suggests a "symbolic transformation" of Mesopotamian and Jewish symbols by early Syriac Christianity (based on a paradigm of transformative purity), and of Syriac and Perso-Islamic symbols by the Bahā'ī Faith (paradigm of concentric unity). In any kind of genealogical endeavor, Bahā'ī symbolism must first be referenced to Bābī imagery, just as Syriac/Persian Christian symbolism must be indexed to Biblical/Judaic imagery. For example, in a lengthy work known as the *Kitāb-i Badī'* (p. 224), Bahā'u'llāh cites the following passage from the Bāb's *Qayyūm al-Asmā'* (Chapter LVII): "Indeed God hath created everywhere around this Gate [*al-Bāb*, the Bāb] oceans of divine elixir (*mā' al-iksīr*), tinged crimson (*muḥmar*) with the essence of existence (*bi-al-duhn al-wujūd* [lit., "oil of existence"]) and vitalized through the animating power of the desired fruit; and for them God hath provided Arks of ruby, tender, crimson-coloured (*sufun min yāqūtat al-ruṭbat al-ḥamrā'*), wherein none shall sail but the people of Bahā (*ahl al-Bahā'*), by the leave of God, the Most Exalted" (SWB 57–58, with transliteration inserted by the present writer). This striking image of what one might call the voyage of Ark-hearts (ruby symbolizing the heart) appears to be a Bābī innovation on very old Noachide imagery. The same thing can be said about Ephrem's use of Noachide imagery. When the Mariner's Ark describes its course in the shape of a Cross (HdF XLIX.3–4; see Palmer 1993, 212), here we see a specifically Christian usage of the very same imagery. Just as Ephrem transforms the image of Noah into a Christological and eccelesiastical symbol, Bahā'u'llāh has taken up the Bāb's imagery of the Ark-hearts and has transformed it into a corporate symbol of the Bahā'ī *ecclesia*: "Seek thou the shore of the Most Great Ocean, and enter, then, the Crimson Ark which God hath ordained in the *Qayyūm-i-Asmā'* for the people of Bahā'" (ESW 139, cf. 130; Lambden 1997–1998, 34–35).

What is the primary mechanism for symbolic transformations? The answer seems to reside in the world-structuring paradigms of each religion. Our hypothesis (*"Parallels" yield paradoxes of commensurability resolvable by paradigm "logics" within religious systems, resulting in symbolic transformation*) was vindicated, but not proven. Symbolic transformation is neither a predicate of history nor is it counterintuitive. We may ask, does typological likeness require genealogy, or does genealogy predispose typological likeness? This question is as refractory as it is circular. The answer may be to ask a new question.

As these two examples of Syriac and Bahā'ī Noachide symbolism show, while genealogy has something to say about the diffusion or transmission of such imagery, a more useful approach than that of Widengren and others is to ask other questions about how—not from whence—such imagery is used. The provenance of such material is not in question. Attending to symbolic transformation—as a recycled originality in which common symbolic clay is baked and glazed by the paradigmatic potter—is where the analogic enterprise is more investigatively incisive for the comparative method.

Relevance to the Study of Religion

Does comparison make a difference? Is comparison significant? Can the results be authenticated and borne out by the religions themselves? Constraints on comparison claims are made possible by interpreting similarities in terms of differences. This avoids two extremes, one speculative and the other reductive, characterized respectively by "parallelomania" and solipsism. Comparison serves as a descriptive tool with limited explanatory power. When similarities are explained in terms of differences, features in common are more soundly identified as either familial or universal. Universal features are especially useful in terms of illuminating what religion is and what religion does—a basic concern of the Study of Religion.

Comparative studies in the field of the Study of Religion are not so much propositional as they are relational. Inexact parallels may prove, for theoretical purposes, to be qualitatively precise. The results of specific comparative studies may be adjudicated at two levels: (a) at the methodological level; (b) at the interpretive level. The results of a comparative study should be meaningful. Otherwise, they are trivial and possibly false. There is a danger in that the very claims of a comparison can lead to its falsification, not necessarily the enterprise itself. This study has taken that risk.

This project has attempted a full-scale comparative analysis, based on a clear methodology. If successful, this study has demonstrated the utility of a modular approach to methodology, where several theoretical constructs have contributed to the overall research design. A decisive structural element in that design was Ninian Smart's dimensional model of religion. This model served as a control for representing both early Syriac Christianity and the Bahā'ī Faith comprehensively and holistically. Comparisons were prosecuted symmetrically and interpreted with a fairly sophisticated degree of precision, given the imprecise and polyvalent nature of the data. Whether or not this research project may serve as a model for the symbolic worldview analysis of other religious traditions, or has in any way advanced comparative phenomenology, is for others to judge. Beyond its purely methodological concerns, this study has demonstrated patterns of idealization common to both early Syriac Christianity (which established the symbolic world of Persian Christianity) and the Bahā'ī Faith.

Symbols ensoul ideas. In the Abrahamic faiths generally, the most important symbol complex is eschatological imagery, the positive focus of which is Paradise. Visions of the empyreal realm have, historically, had an extraordinary power to inspire. Paradise is iconoplastic. The beatific panorama, the symbolic landscape, the ideals and imagery that inform Paradise in the religious imagination are grounded in root metaphors and are animated by key scenarios reflecting a theology of activity, in a dynamic interplay of belief and behavior, myth and ritual, within the religious grasp of totality.

Paradise allegorizes ideals. These ideals are projected onto heaven. There, in the wish-images of the communal dream, ideals are reified and beatified. In a Bergeresque process of paradisical world building, Heaven functions as the impressionistic blueprint of the ideal faith-community. Paradise imagery is then dislocated from the speculative and refocused on Earth. When once the heart is transformed and society reformed, Paradise is realized. In the intersection of eschatology and ethics, in the interplay of ideas and imagery, and as a function of an organizing principle, an overarching paradigm, Paradise becomes utopia.

Appendix I

Abbreviations

Syriac Sources

Ephrem the Syrian: Hymns

CSCO scr. syr. — *Corpus Scriptorum Christianorum Orientalium Scriptores Syri* (Louvain), a series of critical editions (and translations) of Syriac texts. The volumes listed below were edited by Dom Edmund Beck, with translations in German (typically the second volume of each numbered pair in the series).

Abbr.	Hymn Cycle	CSCO vol.	scr. syr.
HdF	Hymns on Faith	154–55	73–74
CH	Hymns against Heresies	169–70	76–77
HdP	Hymns on Paradise	174–75	78–79
CJ	Hymns against Julian	174–75	78–79
Nat.	Hymns on the Nativity	186–87	82–83
Epiph.	Hymns on the Epiphany	186–87	82–83
Eccl.	Hymns on the Church	198–99	84–85
CNis	Hymns on Nisibis	218–19	92–93
	(= Carmina Nisibena)	240–41	102–103
Virg.	Hymns on Virginity	223–24	94–95
Ieiun.	Hymns on Fasting	246–47	106–107
Azym.	Hymns on Unleavened Bread	248–49	108–109
Cruc.	Hymns on the Crucifixion	248–49	108–109
Res.	Hymns on the Resurrection	248–49	108–109
Abr.	Hymns on Abraham Qidunaya	322–23	140–41
Ju. Sab.	Hymns on Juliana Saba	322–23	140–41

Other Abbreviations

Aph. Dem. — *Demonstrations* of Aphrahāṭ
Eph. Hypat. — Ephrem's *Letter to Hypatius*
Epiph. — *Hymns on the Epiphany*

SdF — Ephrem's *Sermons on Faith* CSCO, vol. 212
Od. Sol. — *Odes of Solomon*
BLC — Han J. W. Drijvers, trans. 1965. *The Book of the Laws of the Countries. Dialogue on Fate of Bardaisan of Edessa.* Semitic Texts with Translations, 3. Assen.

Works of Ephrem and Other Syriac Sources in English Translation

Harp — Sebastian Brock, trans. 1983. *The Harp of the Spirit: Eighteen Poems of Saint Ephrem.* Fellowship of St. Alban and St. Sergius.
HyP — Sebastian Brock, trans. 1990. *Hymns on Paradise.* Crestwood, NY: St Vladimir's Seminary Press.
LumE — Sebastian Brock, trans. 1985a. *The Luminous Eye: The Spiritual World of St Ephrem.* Kerala, India: Mar Mathews Press.
McV — Kathleen McVey, trans. 1989. *Ephrem the Syrian: Hymns.* New York: Paulist Press.
NPNF — The Nicene and Post-Nicene Fathers of the Christian Church.
SEC — Carmel McCarthy, trans. 1993. *Saint Ephrem's Commentary: An English Translation of Chester Beatty MS 709 with Introduction and Notes.* Journal of Semitic Studies Supplement, 2. Oxford University Press.
SPW — Joseph P. Amar and Edward G. Mathews, Jr., trans. 1994. *St. Ephrem the Syrian: Selected Prose Works.* Edited by Kathleen McVey. The Fathers of the Church, vol. 91. Washington, D.C.: Catholic University of America Press.

Syriac Studies

BarE — H. J. W. Drijvers. 1966. *Bardaiṣan of Edessa.* Assen, Netherlands: Van Gorcum.
HOA — Arthur Vööbus. 1988. *History of Asceticism in the Syrian Orient: A Contribution to the History of Culture in the Near East* Vol. III. CSCO 500, Subsidia 81; Louvain: Corpus Scriptorum Christianorum Orientalium.
HSC — W. Stewart McCullough. 1982. *A Short History of Syriac Christianity to the Rise of Islam.* Chico, CA: Scholars Press.
HyP — Sebastian Brock. 1990. *Hymns on Paradise.* Crestwood, NY: St Vladimir's Seminary Press.
LumE — Sebastian Brock. 1985a. *The Luminous Eye: The Spiritual World of St Ephrem.* Kerala, India: Mar Mathews Press.

McV — Kathleen McVey, trans. 1989. *Ephrem the Syrian: Hymns.* New York: Paulist Press.

Motifs — Tryggve Kronholm. 1978a. *Motifs from Genesis 1–11 in the Genuine Hymns of Ephrem the Syrian with particular reference to the influence of Jewish exegetical tradition.* Coniectanea Biblica, Old Testament Series 11. Lund, Sweden: CWK Gleerup.

SCK — Robert Murray. 1975a. *Symbols of Church and Kingdom: A Study in Early Syriac Tradition.* Cambridge: Cambridge University Press.

Aphrahāṭ the Persian Sage

Aph. Dem. — *Demonstrations*

Bahā'u'llāh: Published Works in Persian and Arabic

AMR — Bahā'u'llāh. 1968. *Alwāḥ-i nāzila khiṭāb ba mulūk va rū'asā-yi arż.* Tehran: Mu'asisa-yi Millī-yi Maṭbū'at-i Amrī, 124 Badī' (1967–68). Reprinted.

AKA — Bahā'u'llāh. 1980b. *Majmū'a-yi az Alvāḥ-i Jamāl-i Aqdas-i Abhā ka ba'd az Kitāb-i Aqdas Nāzil Shuda.* Ed. Ishrāq-Khāvarī. Hofheim-Langenhain: Bahā'ī-Verlag, 138 Badī'.

AQA I — Bahā'u'llāh. 1964a. *Kitāb-i Mubīn. Āthār-i Qalam-i A'lá,* vol. 1. Tehran: Mu'asisa-yi Millī-yi Maṭbū'at-i Amrī, 120 Badī' (1963–64).

AQA III — Bahā'u'llāh. 1973. *Āthār-i qalam-i a'lá,* vol. III. Tehran: Mu'asisa-yi Millī-yi Maṭbū'at-i Amrī, 129 Badī' (1972–73). Works revealed in the 1850s and early 1860s.

AQA IV — Bahā'u'llāh. 1977. *Āthār-i qalam-i a'lá,* vol. IV. Tehran: Mu'asisa-yi Millī-yi Maṭbū'at-i Amrī, 133 Badī' (1976–77).

AQA VI — Bahā'u'llāh. 1978c. *Āthār-i qalam-i a'lá,* vol. VI. Tehran: Mu'asisa-yi Millī-yi Maṭbū'at-i Amrī, 134 Badī' (1977–78).

DD — Bahā'u'llāh. 1985c. *Daryāy-i Dānish* [sic; Daryā-yi Dānish]*: Selected from the Tablets of Bahā'u'llāh.* 3rd Indian ed. New Delhi: Bahā'ī Publishing Trust.

HV — Bahā'u'llāh, *Haft Vādī.* In Bahā'u'llāh, *Āthār-i qalam-i a'lá,* vol. III (Tehran: 129 Badī' [1972–73]).

ISH — Bahā'u'llāh. 1893b. *Alwāḥ-i mubāraka-yi hażrat-i Bahā' Allāh shāmil-i Ishrāqāt va chand lawḥ-i dīgar.* Ed. Mishkīn-Qalam. Bombay: Nāṣirī Press, 1310 A.H. (1892–93).

IQT	Bahā'u'llāh. 1893a. *Iqtidārāt va chand lawḥ-i digar*. Ed. Mishkīn-Qalam. Bombay: Nāṣirī Press, 1310 A.H. (1892–93).
KA	Bahā'u'llāh, *al-Kitāb al-Aqdas*.
KI	Bahā'u'llāh. 1980c. *Kitāb-i-Īqān: Book of Certitude*. Hofheim-Langenhain: Bahā'ī Verlag, 136 Badī' (1980). Reprinted from the original edition, Egypt, 1934.
KM	Bahā'u'llāh. 1983. *Kalimāt-i Maknūnih:* [sic; Kalimāt-i Maknūna], *The Hidden Words*. Trans. Shoghi Effendi. Hofheim-Langenhain: Bahā'ī-Verlag.
MA	Bahā'u'llāh. 1974. *Mā'ida-yi āsmānī*. 9 vols. Ed. 'Abd al-Hamīd Ishrāq-Khāvarī; Tehran: Mu'asisa-yi Millī-yi Maṭbū'at-i Amrī, 128–29 Badī' (1972–74).
MHB	Bahā'u'llāh. 1984a. Mūntakhabātī az Āthār-i Ḥaḍrat-i Bahā'u'llāh. Hofheim-Langenhain: Bahā'ī-Verlag. Arabic/Persian edition of *Gleanings from the Writings of Bahā'u'llāh*.
MMM	Bahā'u'llāh. 1984b. *Majmū'a-yi maṭbū'a-yi alvāḥ-i mubāraka-yi ḥaẓrat-i Bahā'u'llāh*. Ed. Muḥyi al-Dīn Ṣabrī. Wilmette: Bahā'ī Publishing Trust [1978]. Reprinted from the Cairo: Sa'āda Press, 1338 A.H. [1920] edition.

Bahā'u'llāh: English Translations

BC	Bahā'u'llāh. 1974. *The Kitāb-i-Īqān: The Book of Certitude*. Trans. Shoghi Effendi. Wilmette: Bahā'ī Publishing Trust [1931].
ESW	Bahā'u'llāh. 1962. *Epistle to the Son of the Wolf*. Trans. Shoghi Effendi. Wilmette: Bahā'ī Publishing Trust [1941].
GT	Glad-Tiding, one of fifteen Glad-Tidings in the Tablet of Glad-Tidings, in Bahā'u'llāh. 1978a. *Tablets of Bahā'u'llāh revealed after the Kitāb-i-Aqdas*. Trans. Habib Taherzadeh. Haifa: Bahā'ī World Centre.
GWB	Bahā'u'llāh. 1969. *Gleanings from the Writings of Bahā'u'llāh*. Trans. Shoghi Effendi. Wilmette: Bahā'ī Publishing Trust [1939].
HW	*The Hidden Words* (English). Bahā'u'llāh. 1929. *The Hidden Words of Bahā'u'llāh*. Trans. Shoghi Effendi. Arabic, Persian, English edition. London: National Spiritual Assembly of the Bahā'īs of Great Britain and Northern Ireland. Bahā'u'llāh.
HWA	*The Hidden Words* (Arabic). References to numbered passages. Bahā'u'llāh. 1929.
HWP	*The Hidden Words* (Persian). References to numbered passages. Bahā'u'llāh. 1929.

K — *Kitāb-i Aqdas* (followed by paragraph number). Bahā'u'llāh. 1992a. *Kitāb-i Aqdas: The Most Holy Book*. Haifa: Bahā'ī World Centre.

PB — Bahā'u'llāh. 1978b. The Proclamation of Bahā'u'llāh to the Kings and Leaders of the World. Haifa: Bahā'ī World Centre [1967].

PM — Bahā'u'llāh. 1971. *Prayers and Meditations*. Trans. Shoghi Effendi. Wilmette: Bahā'ī Publishing Trust [1938].

SV — Bahā'u'llāh. 1986. *The Seven Valleys and the Four Valleys*. Trans. Marzieh Gail. Wilmette: Bahā'ī Publishing Trust [1945].

TB — Bahā'u'llāh. 1978a. *Tablets of Bahā'u'llāh revealed after the Kitāb-i-Aqdas*. Trans. Habib Taherzadeh. Haifa: Bahā'ī World Centre.

Other Bahā'ī Texts: English Translations

ADJ — Shoghi Effendi. 1971. *The Advent of Divine Justice*. 3rd ed. Wilmette: Bahā'ī Publishing Trust.

BR — 'Abdu'l-Bahā and Bahā'u'llāh. 1955. *The Bahā'ī Revelation*. London: Bahā'ī Publishing Trust.

DP — 'Abdu'l-Bahā. 1917. *'Abdu'l-Bahā on Divine Philosophy*. Compiled by Isobel F. Chamberlain. Boston: The Tudor Press.

Family — *Bahā'ī Marriage and Family Life* (compilation).

GPB — Shoghi Effendi. 1970. *God Passes By*. Wilmette: Bahā'ī Publishing Trust [1944].

London — *'Abdu'l-Bahā in London*.

PDC — Shoghi Effendi. 1980. *The Promised Day Is Come*. Wilmette: Bahā'ī Publishing Trust [1941].

PT — 'Abdu'l-Bahā. 1969. *Paris Talks: Addresses given by 'Abdu'l-Bahā in Paris in 1911–1912*. 11th ed. London: Bahā'ī Publishing Trust.

PUP — 'Abdu'l-Bahā. 1982. *The Promulgation of Universal Peace: Talks Delivered by 'Abdu'l-Bahā during His Visit to the United States and Canada in 1912*. Compiled by Howard MacNutt. 2nd edn. Wilmette: Bahā'ī Publishing Trust.

SAQ — 'Abdu'l-Bahā. 1981. *Some Answered Questions*. Trans. Laura Clifford Barney. Wilmette: Bahā'ī Publishing Trust [1930].

SDC — 'Abdu'l-Bahā. 1970. *The Secret of Divine Civilization*. Trans. Marzieh Gail. Wilmette: Bahā'ī Publishing Trust [1957].

SWAB — 'Abdu'l-Bahā. 1978. *Selections from the Writings of 'Abdu'l-Bahā*. Compiled by the Research Department of the Uni-

	versal House of Justice. Translated by Marzieh Gail et al. Haifa: Bahā'ī World Centre.
SWB	Bāb, The. 1976. *Selections from the Writings of the Bāb*. Trans. Habib Taherzadeh. Haifa: Bahā'ī World Centre.
TAB	'Abdu'l-Bahā. 1930. *Tablets of 'Abdu'l-Bahā Abbās*. New York: Bahā'ī Publishing Committee [1909–1916]: vol. 1.
TN	'Abdu'l-Bahā. 1891. *A Traveller's Narrative Written to Illustrate the Episode of the Bab (Maqāla-yi Shakhs-i Sayyāḥ)*. Ed. and trans. Edward Granville Browne. 2 vols. Cambridge University Press.
WOB	Shoghi Effendi. 1974. *The World Order of Bahā'u'llāh: Selected Letters of Shoghi Effendi*. 2d. rev. ed. Wilmette: Bahā'ī Publishing Trust.
Women	Universal House of Justice, *Women*. Wilmette: Bahā'ī Publishing Trust, 1980.

Bahā'ī Studies

BBD	Momen, Wendi, ed. 1989. *A Basic Bahā'ī Dictionary*. Oxford: George Ronald.
RB	Taherzadeh, Adib. 1974–87. *The Revelation of Bahā'u'llāh*. Oxford: George Ronald. 4. vols.

Other Abbreviations

AA	Fāżil Māzandarānī, *Asrār al-Āthār-i Khuṣūṣī*.
CB1	'Aṭṭār, Farīd al-Dīn. *The Conference of the Birds*. Trans. Afkham Darbandi and Dick Davis. Harmondsworth: Penguin, 1984.
CB2	Farīd al-Dīn 'Aṭṭār. 1974. *The Conference of the Birds: a philosophical religious poem in prose (rendered into English from the literal and complete French translation of Garcin de Tassy by C. S. Nott)*. London: Routledge and Kegan Paul [1954].
EI^2	*Encyclopaedia of Islam*. New edition. Leiden: E. J. Brill.
EIr	*Encyclopaedia Iranica*. Ed. Ehsan Yarshater. Boston: Routledge and Kegan Paul; Costa Mesa, Ca.: Mazda, 1984–.
MṬ	'Aṭṭār, Farīd al-Dīn. 1962. *Manṭiq al-Ṭayr*. Persian edition: Dr. M. J. Mashkur, ed. 1962. Matiq ut-Tair. A philosophical and mystical poem in Persian language. Edited from the oldest Manuscripts with introduction, critical notes, and appendices [*sic*, English title page]. 2nd ed. Tehran.
PED	Steingass, F. 1977 [1892]. *Persian-English Dictionary*. London: Routledge and Kegan Paul.
QS	Wansbrough, John. 1977. *Quranic Studies: Sources and*

	Methods of Scriptural Interpretation. Oxford: Oxford University Press.
SM	Wansbrough, John. 1978. The Sectarian Milieu: Content and Composition of Islamic Salvation History. Oxford: Oxford University Press.
n.	note
p.c.	personal communication

Appendix II

Syriac Transliteration Scheme

Consonants

Letter	Symbol	Alone	Final	Medial	Initial	Arabic
ʻĀlap̄	ʼ	ܐ	ܐ			ا
Bēṯ	b–bh/ḇ•	ܒ	ܒ	ܒ		ب
Gāmal	g–gh/ġ•	ܓ	ܓ	ܓ	ܓ	غ - گ
Dālaṯ	d–dh/ḏ•	ܕ	ܕ			ذ - د
Hē	h	ܗ	ܗ			ه
Wāw	w	ܘ	ܘ			و
Zay(n)	z	ܙ	ܙ	ܙ		ز
Ḥēṯ	ḥ	ܚ	ܚ	ܚ	ܚ	ح
Ṭēṯ	ṭ		ܛ	ܛ	ܛ	ط
Yō/ūḏ	y		ܝ	ܝ	ܝ	ى
Kāp̄	k–kh/ḵ•	ܟ	ܟ	ܟ	ܟ	خ - ك
Lāmaḏ	l	ܠ	ܠ	ܠ	ܠ	ل
Mīm	m		ܡ	ܡ	ܡ	م
Nūn	n	ܢ	ܢ	ܢ	ܢ	ن
Semkaṯ	s		ܣ	ܣ	ܣ	س
ʻĒ	ʻ	ܥ	ܥ	ܥ	ܥ	ع
Pē	p–ph/p̄•	ܦ	ܦ	ܦ	ܦ	ف پ
Ṣāḏē	ṣ/č	ܨ	ܨ			ص
Qōp̄	q/ḳ	ܩ	ܩ	ܩ	ܩ	ق
Rēś	r	ܪ	ܪ			ر
Šīn	š	ܫ	ܫ	ܫ	ܫ	ش
Tāw	t–th/ṯ•	ܬ	ܬ			ث - ت

Legend: •Spirantization of plosive consonants marked in Syriac by a dot below the letter (*rukkākā*). Non-spirantized *b, g, d, k, p, t* are marked by dot above (*quššāyā*). ••Indicates Persian equivalent, absent in Arabic.
Table by Christopher Buck.

Appendix III

Arabic/Persian Transliteration Scheme

Consonants	Arabic	Persian	Alternatives / Exceptions
ء	’ or ᵓ	’ or ᵓ	Except when initial, when only the vowel “carried” is written.
ب	b	b	
پ		p	
ت	t	t	
ث	th or ṯ	ś	
ج	j or ǰ	j or ǰ	
چ		ch or ċ	
ح	ḥ	ḥ	
خ	kh or ḵ	kh or ḵ	
د	d	d	
ذ	dh or ḏ	ẕ	
ر	r	r	
ز	z	z	
ژ		zh or ž	
س	s	s	
ش	sh or š	sh or š	
ص	ṣ	ṣ	
ض	ḍ	ż	
ط	ṭ	ṭ	
ظ	ẓ	ẓ	
ع	‘ or ᶜ	‘ or ᶜ	
غ	gh or ġ	gh or ġ	
ف	f	f	
ق	q	q	
ك	k	k	
گ		g	
ل	l	l	
م	m	m	
ن	n	n	Or “ṃ” when preceding ب .
ه	h	h	

Consonants	Arabic	Persian	Alternatives / Exceptions
و	w	v / u / w	Persian , equivalent to Arabic ق .
ی	y	y	Semi-vowel, as above. See vowels (below).
ة	-a		In construct state (-at).
ال	al or -'l	al or -'l	Disregards antero-palatals ("sun" letters).

Vowels Long	Arabic	Persian	
آ	ā	ā	
وُ	ū	ū	
يِ	ī	ī	

Other Vowels			
ىٰ	á	á	Alif maqṣūra ("dagger alif").

Otiose Vāv			
خو		khw̤ or v̤	

Doubled			With *tashdīd* (germination).
يّ	-iyy		Or -īy. Final form ī.
وّ	-uww		Or -ūw Final form ū.

Diphthongs			
وَ	au or aw	au or aw	
یَ	ai or ay	ai or ay	

Short Vowels			
أ or َ	a	a	
إ or ِ	i	i	
أُ or ُ	u	u	

Consonants	Arabic	Persian	Alternatives / Exceptions
Nunation			End-vowels—seldom in transliterated.
اً	an		Not represented.
اٌ	un		Not represented.
اٍ	in		Not represented.

*Adapted from the *International Journal of Middle East Studies* transliteration convention (with additions and remarks by the author).

Appendix IV

Fragments of a Lost Persian Christian Liturgy

Preserved in the literary amber of the East Syrian *Ḥūḏrā* are four fragments from a lost Persian Christian liturgy, "discovered" by F. C. Conybeare, described by Arthur John Maclean, and translated by D. S. Margoliouth (see below). The *Ḥūḏrā* ("Cycle")—traditionally but erroneously—is ascribed to Ephrem (Maclean 1905, 367–68). Conybeare discovered the Persian liturgy in a thirteenth-century manuscript of the *Ḥuḏrā*.

Macomber (1970) has made a list of known manuscripts of the *Ḥuḏrā*. The compilation of the *Ḥuḏrā* is traditionally ascribed to the Catholicós Patriarch Išoʻyahb III (649–659 C.E.) and his collaborator, the monk ʻEnanišoʻ of Adiabene (ibid., 120–21) in the year 650/651 C.E. During the last century, the original manuscript of the *Ḥuḏrā* is alleged to have been sold to Russia by a Nestorian priest, but its whereabouts are unknown (Pudichery 1972, 4, n. 12). The theological value of the *Ḥuḏrā* for the study of East Syrian spirituality is second only to the Persian Synods (ibid., 121–22). True as this is in terms of a formalized theology, the service of the *Ḥuḏrā* may in fact be a truer reflection of popular theology, as Macomber is careful to point out: "The writings of theologians may provide an intellectually better articulated and reasoned exposition of this theology, but it is one that is far removed from the living consciousness of the ordinary clergy and faithful. The liturgical chants, on the other hand, have had a direct, formative influence on all capable of understanding them and have had in some ways the same role in the Chaldean Church that catechisms have had in the West" (ibid., 122). There are both Nestorian and Chaldean (expurgated—that is, all overtly Nestorian passages having been removed) versions of the *Ḥuḏrā* (ibid., 120, n. 2).

His Grace Mar Emmanuel, Diocesan Bishop of the Holy Apostolic Catholic Assyrian Church of the East, Diocese of Canada, cites the late Chaldean bishop Jacques Eugène Manna (1982), who wrote: "He [Ephrem] is the Father and founder of all eastern and western Syrian Church rites. All hymns and *madrāshē* of the book of ʼNīdē (Funeral service book) are attributed to him. All *madrāshē* for the entire ecclesiastical year in the book of *Ḥūḏrā* belong to him, and many hymns of praise" (trans. Bishop Mar Emmanuel, p.c., 25 March 1996 [page in Manna not cited]). This honorific ascription to Ephrem notwithstanding, it is evident to any reader that the *Ḥūḏrā* itself is a compilation from a variety of named sources.

The text of the lost Persian Christian liturgy is embedded in the Feast of Epiphany, midnight office. I first learned of this text in Nov. 1992 from His Grace Mar Emmanuel, and later from Bishop Mar Bawai Soro (p.c., 1 April 1996). His Grace Mar Emmanuel provided me with this text in a letter dated 25 March 1996, as did Bishop Soro, in a letter dated 2 April 1996, Rome. Margoliouth's translation is worked into Maclean's rendering of the Syriac liturgy known as "The Night Service"—"Of the Holy Feast of the Epiphany of Our Lord," found in a Syriac *Gazza* ("Treasury"—Syriac Codex, no. I, in the Library of the Propaganda, Piazza di Spagna, Rome)—a compilation that contains excerpts from various liturgies, including the *Ḥūḏrā*. Following this night service, bearing the four Persian verses interpolated in the Syriac text, is a morning service, which contains a "Hymn of Praise, by Mar Ephraim, the Syrian doctor" (of undetermined authenticity), followed by another such hymn by "Mar Narsai" (Maclean 1905, 382–83).

Maclean gives a brief description of the four Persian fragments and then quotes Margoliouth: "The four interpolated stanzas here underlined are in an old Persian dialect in Syriac character; but the text is somewhat corrupt. Professor Margoliouth, who has translated them, writes as follows: 'I have no doubt that the verses are ancient, and that they are corrupt. The metre is apparently: *bahár suá nigāh kardám*, i.e. eight syllables; where it is violated, the sense is also unsatisfactory. There are no Arabic words in the lines, and this seems to me to be a proof of high antiquity. If they belong to the dialect of the Christians in Persia before the Mohammedan conquest they possess an almost unique interest'" (1905, 367–68, note c).

Both transliterated text and translation of this rather unique literary fossil are given below. Added to the Turfan Psalter and related texts in Middle Persian, these fragments—in a dialect of New Persian—provide further evidence of an indigenous Iranian Christian heritage, in which ethnic Persian converts comprised the most visible minority in the East Syrian Church of the East.

The following transliteration is based on my reading of the Syriac text of the *Ḥūḏrā*, Vol. 1, pp. 639–40 (Indian edition, 1960), in consultation with His Grace Bishop Mar Emmanuel, and Prof. Edward G. Mathews, who points out that there is, so far, no standard transliteration convention for Syriac (p.c., 1 May 1996). Text and translation are arranged in columns to facilitate comparison:

Transliteration	**Margoliouth's Translation**
(1)	
Ba-hār swe' nīgāh kardām.	*I looked to every side:*
Dīdāmdī 'estōrā'.	*I saw that security for ever:*
Paywastā' betarsāyī.	*is to him who holds:*
Dīnē' pāk mešīḥā'.	*the pure religion of Christ.*
(2)	
Marwārī mē'karī.	*Eat not, hand not over:*
Meprōšī zekān kōnī.	*Sell not, slander not:*
Rāhē' rast bē'gērī	*take the right way:*
Dīnē' pāk mešīḥā' rāh.	*the pure religion of Christ.*
(3)	
Mešīḥā' rāh dōstā'rām.	*Christ I take for my friend:*
Rōs meggō nīgāh dārām.	*the good I guard:*
'Azqō zendōḥ be'zārām.	*henceforth I live in God:*
Dīnē' pāk mešīḥā' rāh.	*the pure religion of Christ.*
(4)	
Bešem 'abbā' wabrā'yī	*In the name of the Father and the Son:*
Weruḥqudšā' 'mādā'yī.	*and the Holy Ghost thou art baptized** :*
Tāw qāddeš tarsā'yī	*thou, O Holy One, art a Christian***:*
Wetāwbāmā bakšā'yī.	*and thou give unto us (baptism?).*

(Trans. Margoliouth, in Maclean 1905, 367–68.)

*"or thou art come.—Our Lord seems to be addressed" (ibid., 368, note a.)
**"The ordinary Persian word for a Christian; *lit.* [God-]fearing" (ibid., note b).

This translation differs slightly from Margoliouth's previous one published two years prior in the *Journal of the Royal Asiatic Society*. There, these four fragments are interpreted as follows: "(1) I looked to every side: I saw that security is bound up with Christianity. The pure religion is Christ's. (2) Thou eatest, thou buyest, thou sellest, thou revilest, thou takest [not?] the right way. The pure religion is Christ's. (3) I am the friend of Christ. Bid me fear no-one [*sic*]. I remove trouble from the road. The pure religion is Christ's. (4) Thou art baptized in the name of the Father and the Son and the Holy Ghost: Thou art holy, a Christian: And thou dost bestow on us" (1903, 768–70).

Epiphany is a major Christian festival. It is celebrated on January 6th, the traditional date of Christmas now observed throughout the Eastern Christian traditions. On this date, Ephrem writes: "The number six is also perfect; / on the sixth of January Your birth gave joy to the six directions" (Nat. XXVII.3, McV 211). In the Eastern Church, Epiphany recalls Christ's baptism in the river Jordan. In the Western Church, however, Epiphany commemorates the revelation of Christ to the Gentiles, in the homage of the Magi. Ephrem himself speaks of the Magi: "Fire approved of Your birth to drive worship away by it. / The Magi used to worship [fire]—they worshipped You!" (Nat. XXII.13, McV 181; cf. Nat. XXIV.4–15, and CJ II.22–27). In the Syriac liturgy translated by Maclean, the Wise Men are explicitly related to Persia and to Zoroaster: "And he sent a star : to Persia, and called the Wise men : and guided them by its light : until it stood over the cave. • And the Wise men came : honoured men and chiefs : twelve sons of noble kings : who brought consecrated offerings. • Gold and myrrh : and frankincense as for the honour : of the King who was wondrously born : of a virgin whom man had not known. • They opened their treasures : and offered to him their offerings : as they were commanded by their Teacher : Zoroaster, who prophesied to them. •" (1905, 350). The earliest Christian traditions that explicitly ascribe the visit of the Magi as a response to a prophecy by Zoroaster appear to have originated in Persia. Anchoring the Epiphany service in a Persian context still does little to soften the impact of a sudden and remarkable intrusion of Persian in a Syriac liturgy.

The canon for this service is a passage from the "Song of Moses" (Deut. 32:21b–43). The scripture immediately preceding the first interpolated Persian verse is Deut. 33:40b–41a: "I said, I live for ever : I will whet the edge of my sword like lightning." Following the first Persian verse, Deut. 33:41b is cited. After the second Persian verse, Deut. 33:42a is intoned: "And I will deliver up mine adversaries : I will make mine arrows drunk with blood." At the end of the third Persian verse, Deut. 33:43a is given. Finally, after the fourth Persian verse, the final words of Moses in the "Song of Moses" are recited. The biblical context is clearly that of vengeance on enemies. This is possibly an allusion to persecutions of Christians by Zoroastrians. In any case, this Persian liturgy is obviously the product of a minority.

One possible Zoroastrian element might be inferred from references to the "Pure Religion" (NP: *dīn-i pāk*) of Christ, recalling the "Good Religion" (MP: *weh-dēn*) of Zarathuštra (Shaked 1994, 157 and 160; Williams 1996, 45). Zoroastrianism, after all, had opposed the "Good Religion" (*weh-dēn*) to the "Evil Religion" (*ag-dēn*). In exchanges of deprecations that reinforce boundaries, the designation of Persian Christianity as the "Pure Religion" would polemically imply that Zoroastrianism was seen as the "Impure Religion."

The text in stanza 2, line 3, must certainly be: "Take the right [or, true] path" (*rāh-i rāst bigīrī*). It is an attested Zoroastrian Middle Persian expression, as in the *Greater Bundahišn* XXVI:12–18: "A man in whose thinking the wisdom of Wahman resides, that wise spirit shows him the right way (*rāh-ī rāst*). Through the right way (*rāh-ī rāst*) he knows the will of the Creator. By performing the will of the Creator he increases and proclaims him who will cause the Resurrection through the goodness of the Renovation" (Shaked 1994, 66 [translation] and n. 43 [transliteration]). Stanza 3, line 3 could be of critical importance for the interpretation of these four passages, if it could be read as a formula for the abjuration of Zoroastrianism.

This interpretation, based on resonances with Zoroastrian sources, is problematic due to the dating of the text. The presence of rhyme is telling. There is, in fact, no attestation of rhyme in Middle Persian or New Persian prior to the ninth century. (For exemplars of New Persian from ninth and tenth centuries, see Lazard 1964 [in Persian], although the dating of some of these specimens is doubtful [Lynda Clarke, University of Pennsylvania, p.c. 15 April 1996].) A key piece of evidence for a later dating based on the presence of rhyme comes from the tenth-century writer Ḥamza al-Iṣfāhānī, speaking of Persian poetry, reports: "These are poems all composed in a single metre (*tajī'u 'alā baḥrin wāḥidin*) which is similar to rajaz. They resemble Arabic verse by the fact that they are composed in regular metres (*wa-hiya munāsiba li-l-aš'ār al-'arabīya bi-stiwā'i l-awzān*) but they differ from it by the fact that they have no rhyme" (Shaked 1970, 405). Such considerations cannot be reconciled with the date which the East Syrian tradition itself assigns. But the fact that the *Ḥuḏrā* is traditionally dated in the year 650/651 C.E. makes the study of these remnants of a lost Persian Christian liturgy all the more intriguing.

Works Cited

'Abdu'l-Bahā. 1984. *Khiṭābāt: Talks of 'Abdu'l-Bahā*. Reprint of 3 volumes of the original edition printed in Egypt 99 B.E. (1942–43), 1340 A.H. (1921) and Tehran 127 B.E. (1970–71). Hofheim-Langenhain: Bahā'ī-Verlag.

'Abdu'l-Bahā. 1983. *Al-Nūr al-Abhā fī Mufāwaḍāt 'Abd al-Bahā'*. New Delhi: Bahā'ī Publishing Trust of India.

'Abdu'l-Bahā. 1982. *The Promulgation of Universal Peace: Talks Delivered by 'Abdu'l-Bahā during His Visit to the United States and Canada in 1912*. Compiled by Howard MacNutt. 2d ed. Wilmette: Bahā'ī Publishing Trust.

'Abdu'l-Bahā. 1981. *Some Answered Questions*. Trans. Laura Clifford Barney. Wilmette: Bahā'ī Publishing Trust [1930].

'Abdu'l-Bahā. 1978. *Selections from the Writings of 'Abdu'l-Bahā*. Compiled by the Research Department of the Universal House of Justice. Translated by Marzieh Gail et al. Haifa: Bahā'ī World Centre.

'Abdu'l-Bahā. 1970. *The Secret of Divine Civilization*. Trans. Marzieh Gail. Wilmette: Bahā'ī Publishing Trust [1957].

'Abdu'l-Bahā. 1969. *Paris Talks: Addresses Given by 'Abdu'l-Bahā in Paris in 1911–1912*. 11th ed. London: Bahā'ī Publishing Trust.

'Abdu'l-Bahā and Bahā'u'llāh. 1955. *The Bahā'ī Revelation*. London: Bahā'ī Publishing Trust.

'Abdu'l-Bahā. 1930. *Tablets of 'Abdu'l-Bahā Abbas*. New York: Bahā'ī Publishing Committee [1909–1916]: vol. 1.

'Abdu'l-Bahā. 1917. *'Abdu'l-Bahā on Divine Philosophy*. Compiled by Isobel F. Chamberlain. Boston: Tudor Press.

'Abdu'l-Bahā. 1891. *A Traveller's Narrative Written to Illustrate the Episode of the Bab (Maqāla-yi Shakhs-i Sayyāḥ)*. Ed. and trans. Edward Granville Browne. 2 vols. Cambridge University Press.

AbouZayd, Shafiq. 1993. *Iḥidayutha: A Study in the Life of Singleness in the Syrian Orient. From Ignatius of Antioch to Chalcedon 451 A.D*. Oxford: ARAM Society for Syro-Mesopotamian Studies.

Adeney, Walter F. 1965. *The Greek and Eastern Churches*. Clifton, N.J.: Reference Book Publishers.

Alderink, Larry. 1992. "Introduction: Critique and Construction in

Jonathan Z. Smith's *Drudgery Divine*." In *Numen* 39.2: 217–19.
Algar, Hamid. 1973. *Mırzā Malkum Khān: A Study in the History of Iranian Modernism*. Berkeley: University of California Press.
Amanat, Abbas. 1989. *Resurrection and Renewal: The Making of the Babi Movement in Iran, 1844–1850*. Ithaca and London: Cornell University Press.
Amanat, Abbas. 1984. Review of Mangol Bayat, *Mysticism and Dissent. Iranian Studies* 17: 467–75.
Amar, Joseph P., and Edward G. Mathews, Jr., trans. 1994. *St. Ephrem the Syrian: Selected Prose Works*. Edited by Kathleen McVey. The Fathers of the Church, vol. 91. Washington, D.C.: Catholic University of America Press.
Andrae, Tor. 1932. *Mohammed, sein Leben und Glaube*. Göttingen.
Anonymous. 1993. "Bahā'ī Archives: Preserving and Safeguarding the Sacred Texts." *'Andalīb* [Nightingale] 12 (no. 48): 48–49.
Anonymous. 1982. "John of Deylam." *Encyclopaedia Iranica* 7: 336. Article printed on last page of fascicle 3 bears no author.
Armajani, Yahya. 1982. "Christian Missions in Persia." In *Encyclopaedia Iranica*, 5: 544–47.
Ashby, G. 1984. "The Hermeneutic Approach of Theodoret of Cyrrhus to the Old Testament." *Studia Patristica* 15: 131–35.
Asmussen, J. P. 1983. "Christians in Iran." In *The Cambridge History of Iran* (Yarshater 1983), Chapter 25, 924–48.
Asmussen, J. P. 1982. "Afrahāṭ." In *Encyclopaedia Iranica*, 1: 570.
Astour, M. 1964. "Greek Names in the Semitic World and Semitic Names in the Greek World." *Journal of Near Eastern Studies* 23 (1964).
'Aṭṭār, Farīd al-Dīn. 1984. *The Conference of the Birds*. Trans. Afkham Darbandi and Dick Davis. Harmondsworth: Penguin.
Aṭṭār, Farīd al-Dīn. 1962. Mantiq al-Ṭayr. Persian edition. Dr. M. J. Mashkur, ed. English title page: *Mantiq ut-Tair* A philosophical and mystical poem in Persian language [.] Edited from the oldest Manuscripts with introdution [,] critical notes and appendices [sic]. 2d. ed. Tehran.
Awn, Peter J. 1987. "Sufism." In Eliade 1987, 14: 104–23.
Baarda, T. 1962. "A Syriac Fragment of Mar Ephraem's Commentary on the Diatessaron." *New Testament Studies* 8: 287–300.
Bāb, The. 1976. *Selections From the Writings of the Bāb*. Trans. Habib Taherzadeh. Haifa: Bahā'ī World Centre.
Bahā'u'llāh. 1992a. *Kitāb-i-Aqdas: The Most Holy Book*. Haifa: Bahā'ī World Centre.
Bahā'u'llāh. 1992b. *Kitāb-i Badī'*. Reprinted from the facsimile edition (Tehran, n.d.) of a MS dated 26 *Badī'* [Bahā'ī Era = 1870 A.D.] in the hand of Zayn al-Muqarrabīn. Prague: Zero Palm Press.
Bahā'u'llāh. 1986–90. *La'ālī al-Ḥikma*. Edited by Vahid Behmardi.

Three vols. Sao Paulo: Editora Bahā'ī–Brasil.

Bahā'u'llāh. 1986. *The Seven Valleys and The Four Valleys*. Trans. Marzieh Gail. Wilmette: Bahā'ī Publishing Trust [1945].

Bahā'u'llāh. 1985a. "Tablet of the Holy Mariner." In *Bahā'ī Prayers: A Selection of Prayers revealed by Bahā'u'llāh, the Bāb, and 'Abdu'l-Bahā*. Wilmette: Bahā'ī Publishing Trust (1954): 221–29.

Bahā'u'llāh. 1985b. *The Fire Tablet and Tablet of the Holy Mariner*. Arabic, Persian, and English. Hofheim-Langenhain: Bahā'ī-Verlag.

Bahā'u'llāh. 1985c. *Daryāy-i-Dānish* [sic]*: Selected from the Tablets of Bahā'u'llāh*. 3d Indian ed. New Delhi: Bahā'ī Publishing Trust.

Bahā'u'llāh. 1985d. "Tablet of Aḥmad." In *Bahā'ī Prayers: A Selection of Prayers Revealed by Bahā'u'llāh, the Bāb, and 'Abdu'l-Bahā*. Wilmette: Bahā'ī Publishing Trust [1954]: 209–13.

Bahā'u'llāh. 1984a. *Mūntakhabātī az Āthār-i Ḥażrat-i Bahā'u'llāh*. Hofheim-Langenhain: Bahā'ī-Verlag.

Bahā'u'llāh. 1984b. *Majmū'a-yi maṭbū'a-yi alvāḥ-i mubāraka-yi ḥażrat-i Bahā'u'llāh*. Ed. Muḥyi al-Dīn Ṣabrī. Wilmette: Bahā'ī Publishing Trust [1978]. Reprinted from the Cairo: Sa'āda Press, 1338 A.H. [1920] edition.

Bahā'u'llāh. 1983. *Kalimāt-i-Maknūnih* [*sic*], *The Hidden Words*. Trans. Shoghi Effendi. Hofheim-Langenhain: Bahā'ī Verlag.

Bahā'u'llāh. 1981. "Tablets of the Hair." Universal House of Justice, trans. Authorized, unpublished translation.

Bahā'u'llāh. 1980a. *Ad'īyyih-i Haḍrat-i Maḥbūb: Prayers of Bahā'u'llāh*. Frankfurt: Bahā'ī Verlag, 136 Badī' (1980). Facsimile of the Egyptian 1339 A.H. edition.

Bahā'u'llāh. 1980b. *Majmū'a-yi az Alvāḥ-i Jamāl-i Aqdas-i Abhā ka ba'd az Kitāb-i Aqdas Nāzil Shuda*. Ed. Ishrāq-Khāvarī. Hofheim-Langenhain: Bahā'ī-Verlag, 138 Badī' (1980).

Bahā'u'llāh. 1980c. *Kitāb-i-Īqān: Book of Certitude*. Hofheim-Langenhain: Bahā'ī Verlag, 136 Badī' (1980). Reprinted from the original edition, Egypt, 1934.

Bahā'u'llāh. 1978a. *Tablets of Bahā'u'llāh Revealed after the Kitāb-i-Aqdas*. Trans. Habib Taherzadeh. Haifa: Bahā'ī World Centre.

Bahā'u'llāh. 1978b. *The Proclamation of Bahā'u'llāh to the Kings and Leaders of the World*. Haifa: Bahā'ī World Centre [1967].

Bahā'u'llāh. 1978c. *Āthār-i qalam-i a'lá*, vol. VI. Tehran: Mu'asisa-yi Millī-yi Maṭbū'at-i Amrī, 134 Badī' (1977–78).

Bahā'u'llāh. 1977. *Āthār-i qalam-i a'lá*, vol. IV. Tehran: Mu'asisa-yi Millī-yi Maṭbū'at-i Amrī, 133 Badī' (1976–77).

Bahā'u'llāh. 1976. *Majmū'i-yi alvāḥ-i mubāraka-yi Ḥażrat-i Bahā'u'llāh*. Tehran: Mu'asisa-yi Millī-yi Maṭbū'at-i Amrī, 132 Badī'/1304 A.H. (1976). Photo-offset of a manuscript in the hand of 'Alī Ashraf Lāhījānī, "'Andalīb."

Bahā'u'llāh. 1974. *The Kitāb-i-Īqān: The Book of Certitude*. Trans.

Shoghi Effendi. Wilmette: Bahā'ī Publishing Trust [1931].

Bahā'u'llāh. 1974. *Mā'ida-yi āsmānī*. 9 vols. Ed. 'Abd al-Hamīd Ishrāq-Khāvarī; Tehran: Mu'asisa-yi Millī-yi Maṭbū'at-i Amrī, 128–29 Badī' (1972–74).

Bahā'u'llāh. 1973. *Āthār-i qalam-i a'lá*. Vol. III. Tehran: Mu'asisa-yi Millī-yi Maṭbū'at-i Amrī, 129 Badī' (1972–73).

Bahā'u'llāh. 1971. *Prayers and Meditations*. Trans. Shoghi Effendi. Wilmette: Bahā'ī Publishing Trust [1938].

Bahā'u'llāh. 1969. *Gleanings from the Writings of Bahā'u'llāh*. Trans. Shoghi Effendi. Wilmette: Bahā'ī Publishing Trust [1939].

Bahā'u'llāh. 1968. *Alwāḥ-i nāzila khaṭāb ba mulūk va rū'asā-yi arż*. Tehran: Mu'asisa-yi Millī-yi Maṭbū'at-i Amrī, 124 Badī' (1967–68).

Bahā'u'llāh. 1964a. *Kitāb-i Mubīn. Āthār-i Qalam-i A'lā*, vol. 1. Tehran: Mu'asisa-yi Millī-yi Maṭbū'at-i Amrī, 120 Badī' (1963–64).

Bahā'u'llāh, 'Abdu'l-Bahā, Shoghi Effendi. 1964b. *Mā'ida-yi āsmānī*. Tehran: Mu'asisa-yi Millī-yi Maṭbū'at-i Amrī, 1963–64. Nine vols.

Bahā'u'llāh. 1962. *Epistle to the Son of the Wolf*. Trans. Shoghi Effendi. Wilmette: Bahā'ī Publishing Trust [1941].

Bahā'u'llāh and 'Abdu'l-Bahā. 1955. *The Bahā'ī Revelation*. London: Bahā'ī Publishing Trust.

Bahā'u'llāh. 1929. *The Hidden Words of Bahā'u'llāh*. Trans. Shoghi Effendi. Arabic, Persian, English edition. London: National Spiritual Assembly of the Bahā'īs of Great Britain and Northern Ireland.

Bahā'u'llāh. 1928a. "Tablet to the Queen." In Holley 1928, 111–15.

Bahā'u'llāh. 1928b. *Bahā'ī Scriptures: Selections from the Utterances of Bahā'u'llāh and 'Abdu'l-Bahā*. Ed. Horace Holley. New York: Bahā'ī Publishing Committee.

Bahā'u'llāh. 1922. "'Song of the Holy Mariner.' Revealed by His Holiness Baha'ullah" [sic]. Trans. Shoghi Effendi. *Star of the West* 13.4 (May 17, 1922): 75–77. Translation received in April 1922.

Bahā'u'llāh. 1904a. *The Book of Ighan*. Trans. Ali Kuli Khan, assisted by Howard MacNutt. New York: George V. Blackburne.

Bahā'u'llāh. 1904b. *Le Livre de la Certitude*. Trans. H[ippolyte] Dreyfus and Mirza Habib-Ullah Chirazi (Mīrzā Ḥabību'llāh Shīrāzī). Paris: E. Leroux.

Bahā'u'llāh. 1900. *Kitāb-i Īqān*. Cairo: Mawsū'āt Publishers.

Bahā'u'llāh. 1893a. *Iqtidārāt va chand lawḥ-i digar* Ed. Mishkīn-Qalam. Bombay: Nāṣirī Press, 1310 A.H. (1892–93).

Bahā'u'llāh. 1893b. *Alwāḥ-i mubāraka-yi hażrat-i Bahā' Allāh shāmil-i Ishrāqāt wa chand lawḥ-i dīgar*. Ed. Mishkīn-Qalam. Bombay: Nāṣirī Press, 1310 A.H. (1892–93).

Bahā'u'llāh. n.d. *Lawḥ al-ẓuhūr*. Bahā'ī World Centre. Archives MS.

under catalogue number AB 201.

Baldick, Julian. 1989. *Mystical Islam: An Introduction to Sufism*. London: I. B. Tauris and Co.

Balyuzi, Hasan M. 1980. *Bahā'u'llāh: The King of Glory*. Oxford: George Ronald.

Barnard, L. 1984. "The Authenticity of Athenagoras' *De Resurrectione*." *Studia Patristica* 15: 39–49.

Bausani, Alessandro. 1979. "Some Aspects of the Bahā'ī Expressive Style." *World Order* 13.2: 36–43.

Bausani, Alessandro. 1971. *The Persians: From the Earliest Days to the Twentieth Century*. Trans. from the Italian by J. B. Donne. London: Elek Books Ltd.

Bausani, Alessandro. 1963. "Can Monotheism Be Taught? (Further Considerations on the Typology of Monotheism)." *Numen* 10: 167–210.

Bayat, Mangol. 1982. *Mysticism and Dissent: Socioreligious Thought in Qajar Iran*. Syracuse University Press.

Beck, Edmund. 1986. "*Besrā* (*sarx*) und *pagrā* (*sōma*) bei Ephräm dem Syrer." *Oriens Christianus* 70: 1–22.

Beck, Edmund. 1982. "Zur Terminologie von Ephraems Bildtheologie." In Schmidt and Geyer 1982, 239–77.

Beck, Edmund. 1981. "Das Bild vom Weg mit Meilensteinen und Herbergen bei Ephraem." *Oriens Christianus* 65: 1–39.

Beck, Edmund. 1977. "Die zwie Paradoxa des Glaubens bei Ephräm." In Fischer 1977, 169–75.

Beck, Edmund. 1974. "Ephraems Brief an Hypatios." Übersetz und erklärt von E. Beck. *Oriens Christianus* 58: 76–120.

Beck, Edmund. 1961. "Les houris du Coran et Éphrem le Syrien." *Mélanges de l'Institut Dominicain d'Études Orientales du Caire* 6 (1959–61): 405–408. Repr. Paret 1975, 183–87.

Beck, Edmund. 1958. "Symbolum-Mysterium bei Aphraat und Ephräm." *Oriens Christianus* 42: 19–40.

Beck, Edmund. 1953. "Das Bild vom Spiegel bei Ephräm." *Orientalia Christiana Periodica* 19: 5–24.

Beck, Edmund. 1951. *Ephraems Hymnen über das Paradies: Übersetzung und Kommentar*. Studia Anselmiana 26. Rome.

Beck, Edmund. 1948. "Eine christliche Parallele zu den Paradiesesjungfrauen des Korans?" *Orientalia Christiana Periodica* 14: 398–405.

Beggiani, Seely. 1983. *Early Syriac Theology, With Special Reference to the Maronite Tradition*. Lanham: University Press of America.

Behmardi, Vahid, ed. 1986–90. *La'ālī al-Ḥikma*. Three vols. Sao Paulo: Editora Bahā'ī–Brasil.

Berardino, Angelo Di, ed. 1992. *Encyclopedia of the Early Church*. Oxford University Press.

Bevan, E. A., and F. C. Burkitt, eds. and trans. 1921. *S. Ephraim's Prose Refutations of Mānī, Marcion, and Bardaisan*. Vol. 2. London: Text and Translation Society.

Beyer, Peter. 1994. *Religion and Globalization*. London: Sage.

Bianchi, U. et al., eds. 1972. *Problems and Methods of the History of Religions*. Leiden: E. J. Brill.

Bishop, Peter, and Michael Darton, eds. 1990. *The Encyclopedia of World Faiths: An Illustrated Survey of the World's Living Religions*. Facts on File Publications.

Black, Max. 1962. *Models and Metaphors: Studies in Language and Philosophy*. Ithaca: Cornell University Press.

Bleeker, C. J. 1979. "Commentary." In Honko 1979, 173–77.

Bleeker, C. J. 1972. "The Contribution of the Phenomenology of Religion to the Study of the History of Religions." In Bianchi 1972, 35–54.

Bloch, M. 1970. "Two Strategies of Comparison." In *Comparative Perspectives: Theories and Methods*. Edited by A. Etzioni and F. Dubow. Boston.

Bock, K. 1966. "The Comparative Method of Anthropology." *Comparative Studies in Society and History* 8 (1965/66): 269–80.

Bondi, R. 1985. "The Spirituality of Syriac-speaking Christians." In McGinn 1985, 152–61.

Botha, P. 1989. "Christology and Apology in Ephrem the Syrian." *Hervormde Teologiese Studies* 45.1: 19–29.

Botha, P. 1988. "Antithesis and Argument in the Hymns of Ephrem the Syrian." *Hervormde Teologiese Studies* 44 : 581–95.

Bou Mansour, T. 1988. *La Pensée symbolique de saint Éphrem le Syrien*. Bibliothèque de l'Université Saint-Esprit, 14. Kaslik, Lebanon: Université Saint-Esprit.

Bou Mansour 1984. "La défense éphrémienne de la liberté contre les doctrines marcionite, bardesanite et manichéenne." *Orientalia Christiana Periodica* 50: 331–46.

Bowman, J. 1974. "The Sassanian Church in the Khārg Island." *Acta Iranica* 1: 217–20.

Boyce, Mary. 1983. "Iranian Festivals." In Yarshater 1983, 792–815.

Boyce, Mary. 1975. *Reader in Manichaean Middle Persian and Parthian. Acta Iranica*, 9. Tehran and Liege.

Boyce, Mary, and Ilya Gershevitch, eds. 1970. *W. B. Henning Memorial Volume*. London: Lund Humphries.

Boyce, Mary. 1968. "The Manichaean Literature in Middle Iranian." *Handbuch der Orientalistik* 2, Literatur, Lfg. 1. Leiden: E. J. Brill.

Boyd, Richard. 1979. "Metaphor and Theory Change: What is 'Metaphor' a Metaphor for?" In Ortony 1979, 356–408.

Braun, O. 1900. *Das Buch der Synhados oder Synodicon Orientale*.

Stuttgart/Wien. Repr. Amsterdam, 1975.

Brock, Sebastian. 1996. "The 'Nestorian' Church: A Lamentable Misnomer." *Bulletin of the John Rylands University Library of Manchester* 78.3: 23–35.

Brock, Sebastian. 1994. "The Church of the East in the Sasanian Empire Up to the Sixth Century and Its Absence from the Councils in the Roman Empire." In Stirnemann and Wilflinger 1994, 69–85.

Brock, Sebastian. 1992. *Studies in Syriac Christianity: History, Literature and Theology*. Aldershot, Hampshire: Variorum.

Brock, Sebastian, trans. 1990. *Hymns on Paradise*. Crestwood, N.Y.: St Vladimir's Seminary Press.

Brock, Sebastian. 1987. *The Syriac Fathers on Prayer and the Spiritual Life*. Kalamazoo, Michigan: Cistercian Publications.

Brock, Sebastian. 1985a. *The Luminous Eye: The Spiritual World of St Ephrem*. Kerala, India: Mar Mathews Press.

Brock, Sebastian. 1985b. "Syriac and Greek Hymnography: Problems of Origins." *Studia Patristica* 16: 77–81.

Brock, Sebastian. 1985c. "The Christology of the Church of the East in the Synods of the Fifth to Early Seventh Centuries: Preliminary Considerations and Materials." In Dragas 1985, 125–42. Reprinted in Brock 1992, XII.

Brock, Sebastian. 1984. *Syriac Perspectives on Late Antiquity*. London: Variorum Reprints.

Brock, Sebastian. 1983. *The Harp of the Spirit: Eighteen Poems of Saint Ephrem*. Fellowship of St. Alban and St. Sergius.

Brock, Sebastian. 1982a. "Christians in the Sasanian Empire: A Case of Divided Loyalties." *Studies in Church History* 18: 1–19. Reprinted in Brock 1984, VI.

Brock, Sebastian. 1982b. "Clothing Metaphors as a Means of Theological Expression in Syriac Tradition." In M. Schmidt and C. Geyer 1982, 11–40. Reprinted in Brock 1992, XI.

Brock, Sebastian. 1982c. "A Syriac Life of John of Dailam." *Parole de l'Orient* 10: 123–90.

Brock, Sebastian. 1982d. "The Prayer of the Heart in Syriac Tradition." *Sobornost* 4: 131–42.

Brock, Sebastian. 1981. "Jacob of Serugh on the Veil of Moses." *Sobornost* 3: 70–85.

Brock, Sebastian. 1979a. "Jewish Traditions in Syriac Sources." *Journal of Jewish Studies* 30: 212–32. Reprinted in idem, *Studies in Syriac Christianity*, IV.

Brock, Sebastian. 1979b. *The Holy Spirit in the Syrian Baptismal Tradition*. The Syrian Churches Series 9; Poona: Anita Printers.

Brock, Sebastian. 1976. "Ephrem's Letter to Publius." *Le Muséon* 89: 216–305.

Brock, Sebastian. 1973. "Early Syrian Asceticism." *Numen* 20: 1–19.

Brown, Lesley, ed. 1993. *The New Shorter Oxford English Dictionary*. Oxford: Clarendon Press.

Brown, Peter. 1997. *The Rise of Western Christendom: Triumph and Diversity* A.D. *200–100*. Oxford/Malden, Mass.: Blackwell Publishers [1996].

Brown, Peter. 1988. *Virginity and Society: Sexuality and Its Renunciation in Late Antiquity*.

Brown, Peter. 1971. "The Rise and Function of the Holy Man in Late Antiquity." *Journal of Religious Studies* 61: 80–101.

Browne, Edward Granville. 1987. *Selections from the Writings of E. G. Browne*. Edited by Moojan Momen. Oxford: George Ronald.

Browne, Edward Granville. 1893. *The New History of Mīrzā 'Alī Muḥammed, the Bāb*. Cambridge University Press, 1893/ Amsterdam: Philo Press, 1975.

Browne, Edward Granville. 1892. "Catalogue and Description of 27 Bābī Manuscripts." *Journal of the Royal Asiatic Society* 24: 433–99 and 637–710.

Browne, Edward Granville, ed. and trans. 1891. *A Traveller's Narrative Written to Illustrate the Episode of the Bab*, 2 vols. Cambridge University Press.

Bruning, B. et al., eds. 1990. *Collectanea Augustiniana: Mèlanges T. J. Van Bavel*. Leuven University Press.

Brunner, Christopher. 1983. "Geographical and Administrative Divisions: Settlements and Economy." In Yarshater 1983, 747–77.

Bruns, Peter. 1990. *Das Christusbild Aphrahats des Persischen Weisen*. Hereditas. Studien zur Alten Kirchengeschichte, Band 4. Bonn: Verlag Borengässer.

Bruns, Peter. 1989. "Arius hellenizans?—Ephräm der Syrer und die neoarianischen Kontroversen seiner Zeit." *Zeitschrift für Kirchengeschichte* 101: 283–316.

Buck, Christopher. 1998. "A Symbolic Profile of the Bahā'ī Faith." *Journal of Bahā'ī Studies* 8.4: 1–48.

Buck, Christopher. 1996a. "The Universality of the Church of the East: How Persian was Persian Christianity?" *Journal of the Assyrian Academic Society* 10.1: 54–95.

Buck, Christopher. 1996b. Review of *Rituals in Babism and Baha'ism* by Denis MacEoin. *International Journal of Middle East Studies* 28.3: 418–22.

Buck, Christopher. 1996c. "Native Messengers of God in Canada?: A Test Case for Bahā'ī Universalism." *Bahā'ī Studies Review* 6.

Buck, Christopher. 1995a. *Symbol and Secret: Qur'an Commentary in Bahā'u'llāh's Kitāb-i Īqān*. Studies in the Bābī and Bahā'ī Religions, 7. Los Angeles: Kalimát Press.

Buck, Christopher. 1995b. "Sapiential *Theōsis:* A New Reading of Ephrem the Syrian's *Hymns on Paradise*." *Journal of the*

Assyrian Academic Society 9.2: 80–125.

Buck, Christopher. 1991. "Bahā'u'llāh as 'World Reformer'." *Journal of Bahā'ī Studies* 3.4: 23–70.

Bullinger, E. 1968. *Figures of Speech Used in the Bible: Explained and Illustrated*. London: Messrs. Eyre and Spottiswoode, 1898. Reprinted, Grand Rapids: Baker Book House.

Bundy, David. 1991. "Jacob of Nisibis as a Model for the Episcopacy." *Le Muséon* 104: 235–49.

Bundy, David. 1990. "The Anti-Marcionite Commentary on the Lucan Parables (*Pseudo-Ephrem A*): Images in Tension." *Le Muséon* 103: 111–23.

Bundy, David. 1988a. "Language and the Knowledge of God in Ephrem Syrus." Reprinted in *Dialogue and Alliance* 1 (1988): 56–64.

Bundy, David. 1988b. "Marcion and the Marcionites in Early Syrian Apologetics." *Le Muséon* 101: 21–32.

Bundy, David. 1986. "Language and the Knowledge of God in Ephrem Syrus." *Patristic and Byzantine Review* 5 (1986): 91–103.

Bundy, David. 1985. "Criteria for Being *In Communione* in the Early Syrian Church." *Augustinianum* 25: 597–608.

Cain, Seymour H. 1979. "Commentary." In Honko 1979, 339–45.

Cameron, R., and Arthur J. Dewey, trans. 1979. *The Cologne Mānī Codex: "Concerning the Origin of His Body."* Missoula, Montana: Scholars Press.

Capps, W. 1979. "Commentary." In Honko 1979, 177–85.

Castelli, E. 1986. "Virginity and Its Meaning for Women's Sexuality in Early Christianity." *Journal of Feminist Studies in Religion* 2: 61–88.

Chabot, Jean Baptiste, ed. and trans. 1902. *Synodicon Orientale ou Recueil de Synodes Nestoriens*. Paris: Imprimerie Nationale.

Chediath, Geevarghese. 1996. "The Theological Contribution of Mar Babai the Great." In Stirnemann and Wilflinger 1994, 155–67.

Clines, D., ed. 1990. *The Bible in Three Dimensions*. Sheffield Academic Press.

Cole, Juan R. I. 1998. *Modernity and the Millennium: The Genesis of the Bahā'ī Faith in the Nineteenth-Century Middle East*. New York: Columbia University Press.

Cole, Juan R. I. 1992. "Iranian Millenarianism and Democratic Thought in the Nineteenth Century." *International Journal of Middle East Studies* 24.1: 1–26.

Colless, B. E. 1986. "The Nestorian Province of Samarkand." *Abr Nahrayn* 24: 51–57.

Colpe, C. 1979. "Symbol Theory and Copy Theory as Basic Epistemological and Conceptual Alternatives in Religious Studies." In Honko 1979, 161–73.

Conybeare, F. C., and Arthur John Maclean. 1905. *Rituale*

Armenorum: Being the Administration of the Sacraments and the Breviary Rites of the Armenian Church Together with the Greek Rites of Baptism and Epiphany, edited from the Oldest MSS. by F. C. Conybeare, M.A., F.B.A., and *The East Syrian Epiphany Rites*, translated by the Rev. A. J. Maclean. Oxford: Clarendon Press.

Cooke, B. 1990. *The Distancing of God: The Ambiguity of Symbol in History and Theology*. Minneapolis: Fortress Press.

Corbett, John. 1987. "The Pauline Tradition in Aphrahat." In Drijvers 1987, 13–32.

Corbin, Henri. 1981. *The Concept of Comparative Philosophy*. Translated by P. Russell. Ipswich: Golgonooza Press.

Coyle, J. Kevin. 1979. "The Cologne Mānī-Codex and Mānī's Christian Connections." *Église et Théologie* 10: 179–93.

Crehan, J., ed. 1967. *Catholic Dictionary of Theology*. London.

Darbandi, Afkham and Dick Davis, trans. 1984. *The Conference of the Birds* by Farīd al-Dīn 'Aṭṭār. Harmondsworth: Penguin.

Darling, D. 1987. "The 'Church from the Nations' in the Exegesis of Ephrem." In Drijvers 1987, 111–21.

Davids, Adelbert. 1994. "Is the Theology of the Assyrian Church Nestorian?" In Stirnemann and Wilflinger 1994, 134–42.

Dechow, J. 1975. *Dogma and Mysticism in Early Christianity: Epiphanius of Cyprus and the Legacy of Origen*. Ph.D. diss., University of Pennsylvania.

de Halleux, André. 1983. "Saint Ephrem le Syrien." *Revue Théologique de Louvain* 14: 328–55.

de Halleux, André. 1978. "Autonomy and Centralization in the Ancient Syriac Churches, Edessa and Seleucia-Ctesiphon." In *Wort und Wahrheit*, Supplement 4, 59–67. Vienna.

DeLoach, B. 1983. "On First Looking into Ricoeur's Interpretation Theory: A Beginner's Guide." *Pre/Text: A Journal of Rhetorical Theory* 4: 225–36.

Den Boeft, J., and A. Hilhorst, eds. 1993. *Early Christian Poetry: A Collection of Essays*. Supplements to *Vigiliae Christianae* 22. Leiden: E. J. Brill.

Dilworth, D. 1989. *Philosophy in World Perspective: A Comparative Hermeneutic of the Major Theories*. Yale University Press.

Dragas, G., ed. 1985. *Aksum-Thyateira: A Festschrift for Archbishop Methodios of Thyateira and Great Britain*. Athens.

Drijvers, Han J. W. 1996. "Early Syriac Christianity: Some Recent Publications." *Vigiliae Christianae* 50, 159–77.

Drijvers, Han J. W. et al., eds. 1987. *IV Symposium Syriacum: Literary Genres in Syriac Literature*. Series: *Orientalia Christiana Analecta* Vol. 229: Rome: Pontifical Institute of Oriental Studies.

Drijvers, Han J. W. 1982. "A Tomb for the Life of a King: A Recently

Discovered Edessene Mosaic with a Portrait of King Abgar the Great." *Le Muséon* 95: 167–89.

Drijvers, Han J. W. 1967. "Quq and the Quqites: An unknown sect in Edessa in the second century A.D." *Numen* 14: 104–29.

Drijvers, Han J. W. 1966. *Bardaiṣan of Edessa*. Assen, Netherlands: Van Gorcum.

Drijvers, Han J. W. 1965. *The Book of the Laws of the Countries. Dialogue on Fate of Bardaisan of Edessa*. Semitic Texts with Translations, 3. Assen.

Dupriez, B. 1991. *A Dictionary of Literary Devices: Gradus, A–Z*. Translated by A. Halsall. University of Toronto Press.

Edakalathur, Louis. 1994. *The Theology of Marriage in the East Syrian Literature*. Rome.

Eggan, F. 1964. "Social Anthropology and the Method of Controlled Comparison." *American Anthropologist* 56: 743–63.

Eilberg-Schwartz, Howard. 1993. Review of *Drudgery Divine* by Jonathan Z. Smith. *History of Religions* 32.3: 301–303.

Eilers, Wilhelm. 1983. "Iran and Mesopotamia." In Yarshater 1983, 3.1: 481–504.

Eilers, Wilhelm, ed. 1971. *Festgabe deutscher Iranisten zur 2500 Feier Irano*. Stuttgart.

El-Batanouny, Goudah M. 1991. "Syntactic and Semantic Classification of Paradox and Their Relation to Readers' Interpretation." *Journal of Literary Semantics* 20.3: 129–62.

Eliade, Mircea, ed. 1987. *Encyclopedia of Religion*. New York: Macmillan.

Eliade, Mircea. 1969. "Methodological Remarks on the Study of Religious Symbolism." In Kitigawa and Eliade 1969, 86–107.

El-Khoury, N. 1987. "Hermeneutics in the Works of Ephraim the Syrian." In Drijvers et al., 1987, 93–100.

El-Khoury, N. 1982. "Anthropological Concepts in the School of Antioch." *Studia Patristica* 13: 1359–65.

Ephrem the Syrian. 1989. *Ephrem the Syrian: Hymns*. Kathleen McVey, trans. New York: Paulist Press.

Ephrem the Syrian. 1993. *Saint Ephrem's Commentary: An English Translation of Chester Beatty MS 709 with Introduction and Notes*. Edited and translated by Carmel McCarthy. Journal of Semitic Studies Supplement, 2. Oxford University Press.

Ephrem the Syrian. 1994. *St. Ephrem the Syrian: Selected Prose Works*. Translated by Edward G. Mathews and Joseph P. Amar. Edited by Kathleen McVey. The Fathers of the Church, vol. 91. Washington, D.C.: Catholic University of America Press.

Ephrem the Syrian. 1912 and 1921. *S. Ephraim's Prose Refutations of Mānī, Marcion, and Bardaisan*. London: Text and Translation Society. Vol. 1 edited and translated by C. W. Mitchell. Vol. 2 edited and translated by E. A. Bevan and F. C. Burkitt.

Ernst, Carl. 1992. "The Symbolism of Birds and Flight in the Writings of Rūzbiyān Baqlī." Lewisohn 1992, 353–66.

Fāḍil-i Māzandarānī. 1923. "Seven Cities in the Spiritual Journey to God." *Star of the West* 13.11 (Feb. 1923): 301ff.

Fawcett, T. 1970. *The Symbolic Language of Religion*. London: SCM Press.

Ferguson, E. et al., eds. 1990. *Encyclopedia of Early Christianity*. New York and London: Garland.

Fiey, Jean Maurice. 1996. "The Spread of the Persian Church." In Stirnemann and Wilflinger 1994, 97–107.

Fischer, R., ed. 1977. *A Tribute to Arthur Vööbus: Studies in Early Christian Literature and Its Environment, Primarily in the Syrian East*. Chicago: Lutheran School of Theology.

Flanagan, K. 1991. *Sociology and Liturgy: Representations of the Holy*. Houndsmill, England: Macmillan Academic.

Froehlich, K. 1984. *Biblical Interpretation in the Early Church*. Philadelphia: Fortress Press.

Frye, Richard N. 1962. *The Heritage of Persia*. London: Weidenfeld and Nicolson.

Gail, Marzieh, trans. 1982. *My Memories of Bahā'u'llāh by Ustād Muḥammad-'Alīy-i Salmānī, the Barber, with a Selection of His Poems*. Los Angeles: Kalimát Press.

Garsoïan, Nina, Thomas Mathews, and Robert Thompson, eds. 1982. *East of Byzantium: Syria and Armenia in the Formative Period*. Washington, D.C.: Dumbarton Oaks, 3–16.

Gavin, F. 1920. "The Sleep of the Soul in the Early Syriac Church." *Journal of the American Oriental Society* 40: 103–20.

Geertz, A., and J. Jensen, eds. 1991. *Religion, Tradition and Renewal*. Denmark: Aarhus University Press.

Geertz, Clifford. 1965. "Religion as a Cultural System." In *Anthropological Approaches to the Study of Religion*. Edited by Michael Banton. London: Tavistock Publications.

Geertz, Clifford. 1979. "Religion as a Cultural System" (slightly abridged). In *Reader in Comparative Religion*. Edited by W. Lessa and E. Vogt, 67–178. New York: Harper and Row.

Geertz, Clifford. 1973. "Religion as a Cultural System." In idem, *The Interpretation of Cultures: Selected Essays*, 87–112. New York.

Gerö, Stephen. 1987. "Only a Change of Masters?: The Christians of Iran and the Muslim Conquest." In *Transition Periods in Iranian History*. Studia Iranica, 5: 43–48. Paris: Association pour l'avancement des études iraniennes.

Gerö, Stephen. 1982. "The See of Peter in Babylon: Western Influences on the Ecclesiology of Early Persian Christianity." In *East of Byzantium: Syria and Armenia in the formative Period*. Edited by

Nina Garsoïan. Washington, D.C.: Dumbarton Oaks, 45–51.

Gerö, Stephen. 1981. *Barṣauma of Nisibis and Persian Christianity in the Fifth Century*. CSCO 426. Louvain: Peeters.

Gervers, Michael and Ramzi Jibran Bikhazi, eds. 1990. *Conversion and Continuity: Indigenous Christian Communities in Islamic Lands, Eighth to Eighteenth Centuries*. Toronto: Pontifical Institute of Medieval Studies.

Giese, Alma, and J. Christoph Bürgel, eds. 1994. *God Is Beautiful and He Loves Beauty: Festschrift in Honour of Annemarie Schimmel*. Berne: Peter Lang.

Goedendorp, P. 1991. "Diffusion of the Concept of al-Qā'im in the Middle East in Antiquity." In Geertz and Jensen 1991, 101–18.

Goldschmidt, W. 1966. *Comparative Functionalism*. Berkeley.

Goodenough, E. R. 1951. "The Evaluation of Symbols Recurrent in Time." *Eranos Jahrbuch* 20: 285–319.

Graffin, F., and A.-M. Malingrey. 1972. "La Tradition syriaque des homélies de Jean Chrysostome sur l'incompréhensibilité de Dieu." In *Epektasis*, 603–609. Mélanges Jean Daniélou. Paris.

Greenspahn, F., ed. 1991. *Essential Papers on Israel and the Ancient Near East*. New York University.

Greer, R. 1973. *The Captain of Our Salvation: A Study in the Patristic Exegesis of Hebrews*. Beiträge zur Geschichte der biblischen Exegese, 15. Tübingen.

Gregg, R., and D. Groh. 1981. *Early Arianism: A View of Salvation*. Philadelphia: Fortress Press.

Gregorios, Paulos. 1987. "Syrian Orthodox Church of Antioch." In Eliade 1987, 14: 227–30.

Griffith, Sidney. 1990. "Images of Ephraem: The Syrian Holy Man and His Church." *Traditio* 45 (1989/90): 7–33.

Griffith, Sidney. 1987. "Ephraem the Syrian's Hymns 'Against Julian': Meditations on History and Imperial Power." *Vigiliae Christianae* 41: 238–66.

Gwynn, J. 1898. "Introductory Dissertation: Ephraim the Syrian and Aphrahat the Persian Sage." In *A Select Library of Nicene and Post Nicene Fathers of the Christian Church*, 13: 119–52. New York: The Christian Literature Company.

Hage, Wolfgang. 1988. *Syriac Christianity in the East*. Mōrā 'Eth'ō series, 1. Kottayam, India: St. Ephrem Ecumenical Research Institute.

Haloun, G., and W. B. Henning. 1952. "The Compendium of the Doctrines and Styles of the Teaching of Mānī, the Buddha of Light." *Asia Major*, n.s., 3.2: 184–212.

Hambye, E. 1970. "The Symbol of the 'Coming to the Harbour' in the Syriac Tradition." *Orientalia Christiana Analecta* 197: 401–11.

Hartman, G., and S. Budick, eds. 1986. *Midrash and Literature*. New

Haven: Yale University Press.

Harvey, Susan Ashbrook. 1996. "Sacred Bonding: Mothers and Daughters in Early Syriac Hagiography." *Journal of Early Christian Studies* 4.1: 27–56.

Harvey, Susan Ashbrook. 1993. "Feminine Imagery for the Divine: The Holy Spirit, the Odes of Solomon, and Early Syriac Tradition." *St Vladimir's Theological Quarterly* 37.2–3: 111–40.

Harvey, Susan Ashbrook. 1990. "The Edessan Martyrs and the Ascetic Tradition." In Lavenant 1990, 195–206.

Hatcher, John. 1997. *The Ocean of His Words: A Reader's Guide to the Art of Bahā'u'llāh*. Wilmette: Bahā'ī Publishing Trust.

Hatcher, John. 1994a. *The Arc of Ascent: The Purpose of Physical Reality II*. Wilmette: Bahā'ī Publishing Trust.

Hatcher, John S. 1994b. "Unsealing the Choice Wine." *Journal of Bahā'ī Studies* 6.3: 28–38.

Hawkes, T. 1972. *Metaphor*. London: Methuen.

Heath, Peter. 1994. "Ibn Sīnā's Journey of the Soul." In *Annemarie Schimmel Festschrift*. Edited by Maria Eva Subtelny. *Journal of Turkish Studies* 18: 91–102.

Heath, Peter. 1992a. *Allegory and Philosophy in Avicenna*. Philadelphia: University of Pennsylvania Press.

Heath, Peter. 1992b. "Disorientation and Reorientation in Ibn Sīnā's *Epistle of the Bird*: A Reading." In Mazzaoui and Moreen 1992.

Henning, W. B. 1946. "The Book of the Giants." *Bulletin of the School of Oriental and African Studies* 2 (1943–46): 52–74.

Hewitt, Marsha A. 1996. "How New Is the 'New Comparativism'?: Difference, Dialectics, and World-Making." *Method and Theory in the Study of Religion* 8.1: 15–20.

High, D., ed. 1969. *New Essays on Religious Language*. Oxford University Press.

Holley, Horace, ed. 1928. *Bahā'ī Scriptures*. New York: Brentano's, 1923; repr. New York: Bahā'ī Publishing Committee.

Holy Transfiguration Manastery. 1984. *The Ascetical Homilies of Saint Isaac the Syrian*. Boston: Holy Transfiguration Monastery.

Honko, Lauri, ed. 1979. *Science of Religion: Studies in Methodology*. Religion and Reason, 13. The Hague: Mouton.

Ibn al-'Arabī. 1992. *What the Seeker Needs*. Threshold.

Jensen, Jeppe Sinding. 1992."The Future of the Phenomenology of Religion?" Colloquium paper, March 1992. Centre for the Study of Religion, University of Toronto. Subsequently published as Jensen 1994.

Jensen, Jeppe. 1994. "Is a Phenomenology of Religion Possible? On the Ideas of a Human and Social Science of Religion." *Method and Theory in the Study of Religion* 5: 109–34.

King, Archdale A. 1948. *The Rites of Eastern Christendom*. Rome:

Catholic Book Agency.

Kippenberg, H. 1985. "Religionssoziologie ohne Säkularisierungsthese: É. Durkheim und M. Weber aus der Sicht der Symboltheorie." *Neue Zeitschrift für Systematische Theologie und Religionsphilosophie* 27: 177–93.

Kitigawa, J., and Mircea Eliade, eds. 1969. *The History of Religions: Essays in Methodology*; University of Chicago.

Klein, W. 1994. "A Syriac-Christian Fragment from Dunhuang, China." *Zeitschrift der Deutschen Morgenländischen Gesellschaft* 144.1: 1–13.

Knight, L., and B. Cottle, eds. 1960. *Metaphor and Symbol*. London: Butterworth Scientific Publications.

Köbben, A. 1970. "Comparativists and Non-Comparativists in Anthropology." In *A Handbook of Method in Cultural Anthropology*. Edited by R. Naroll and R. Cohen, 581–96. New York.

Koester, Helmut. 1990. *Ancient Christian Gospels: The History and Development*, Philadelphia: Trinity Press International.

Kollaparambil, Jacob. 1994. "The Persian Crosses in India are Christian, not Manichaean." *Christian Orient* 15.1: 24–35.

Koltun-Fromm, Naomi. 1996. "A Jewish–Christian Conversation in Fourth-Century Persian Mesopotamia." *Journal of Jewish Studies* 47.1: 45–63.

Koonammakkal, Thomas. 1994. "St. Ephrem and 'Greek Wisdom'." In Lavenant 1994, 169–76.

Kronholm, Tryggve. 1978a. *Motifs from Genesis 1–11 in the Genuine Hymns of Ephrem the Syrian with Particular Reference to the Influence of Jewish Exegetical Tradition*. Coniectanea Biblica, Old Testament Series 11; Lund, Sweden: CWK Gleerup.

Kugel, J. "Two Introductions to Midrash." In Hartman and Budick 1986, 77–103.

Jansma, T. 1974. "Aphraates' *Demonstration* VII. §§ 18 and 20. Some Observations on the Discourse of Penance." *Parole de l'Orient* 5.1: 21–48

Jansma, T. 1973. "Ephraem on Exodus II, 5: Reflections on the Interplay of Free-Will and Divine Providence." *Orientalia Christiana Periodica* 39: 5–28.

Jansma, T. 1970. "Narsai and Ephraem." *Parole de l'Orient* 1: 49–68.

Jasion, Jan T. 1994. "Queen Marie of Romania: A Preliminary Bibliography." *Journal of Bahā'ī Studies* 6.2: 15–25.

Jensen, Jane Richardson.1994. "Father, Son, and Holy Spirit as Mothers in Early Syrian Literature." *Continuum* 21.2–3: 27–49.

Jones, A. Duncan. 1904. "A Homily of St. Ephrem." *Journal of Theological Studies* 5: 546–52.

Justi, F. 1895. *Iranisches Namenbuch*. Marburg.

Kermode, Frank. 1979. *The Genesis of Secrecy: On the Interpretation of*

Narrative. Cambridge: Harvard University Press.

Koenen, Ludwig. 1981. "From Baptism to the Gnosis of Manichaeism." In Layton 1981, 734–56.

Labourt, J. 1904. *Le Christianisme dans l'Empire perse sous la dynastie des Sassanides*. Paris: Lecoffre. 2d ed.

Lambden, Stephen. 1997–98. "The Word Bahā': Quintessence of the Greatest Name of God." *Journal of Bahā'ī Studies* 8.2: 13–45.

Lambden, Stephen. 1991. "Some Notes on Bahā'u'llāh's Gradually Evolving Claims of the Adrianople/Edirne Period." *Bahā'ī Studies Bulletin* 5.3–6.1.

Lambden, Stephen. 1988. "The Sinaitic Mysteries: Notes on Moses/Sinai Motifs in Bābī and Bahā'ī Scripture." In Momen 1988, 64–183.

Lambden, Stephen. 1985. "At the Shore of the Black Sea: The *Lawh-i Hawdaj / Ṣāmṣūn* of Mīrzā Ḥusayn 'Alī Bahā'u'llāh." *Bahā'ī Studies Bulletin* 3.4: 84–97.

Lambden, Stephen. 1983. "A Tablet of Bahā'u'llāh to Georg David Hardegg: The *Lawḥ-i Hirtīq*." *Bahā'ī Studies Bulletin* 2.1: 32–62.

Lanciotti, Lionello, ed. 1984. *Incontro di Religioni in Asia tra il III e il X Secolo d.C.* Firenze: Leo S. Olschki Editore.

Lavenant, René, ed. 1994. *VI Symposium Syriacum 1992*. Rome: Pontificio Instituto Orientale.

Lavenant, René. 1992. "Aphraates." In Berardino 1992, 1: 54.

Lavenant, René, ed. 1990. *V Symposium Syriacum 1988*. Rome: Pontifical Institute of Oriental Studies.

Lawless, G. 1990. "Augustine and Human Embodiment." In Bruning 1990, 167–86.

Lawson, B. Todd. 1995. "Bahā' Allāh." In *The Oxford Encyclopedia of the Modern Islamic World*, 1: 176–77. Edited by John Esposito. Oxford University Press.

Lawson, E. Thomas. 1996. "Theory and the New Comparativism, Old and New." *Method and Theory in the Study of Religion* 8.1: 31–35.

Layton, Bentley, ed. 1981. *The Rediscovery of Gnosticism: Proceedings of the International Conference on Gnosticism at Yale, New Haven, Connecticut, March 28–31, 1978*. Vol. 2, *Sethian Gnosticism*. Studies in the History of Religions, 41. Leiden: E. J. Brill.

Lazard, Gilbert. 1964. *Les premiers poets Persans* (in Persian). Paris: Librairie d'Amérique et d'Orient on behalf of the Institut Franco-Iranien.

Leach, E. 1968. "The Comparative Method in Anthropology." In *International Encyclopedia of the Social Sciences*, 1: 339–45. New York, 1968.

Lerner, Judith. 1982. "Christianity. II. In Pre-Islamic Persia: Material Remains." In *Encyclopaedia Iranica*, 5: 528–30.

Lerner, Judith. 1977. *Christian Seals of the Sasanian Period*. Leiden:

E. J. Brill.

Lessa, W., and E. Vogt, eds. 1979. *Reader in Comparative Religion*. New York: Harper and Row.

Levin, S. 1988. *Metaphoric Worlds: Conceptions of a Romantic Nature*. New Haven: Yale University Press.

Levy, R. "'Urf." *Encyclopaedia of Islam* (1st ed.), 4: 1031.

Lewisohn, Leonard, ed. 1992. *The Legacy of Mediaeval Persian Sufism*, 353–66. London: Khanqah-i Nimatullahi.

Lieu, S. N. C. 1989. *The Emperor Julian: Panegyric and Polemic*. Liverpool, 2d ed.

Lieu, S. N. C. 1985. *Manichaeism in the Later Roman Empire and Medieval China: A Historical Survey*. Manchester University Press.

Lonergan, Bernard. 1972. *Method in Theology*. London: Darton, Longman and Todd; New York: Herder and Herder. 2d ed. 1973. Latest repr. University of Toronto Press, 1994 (Collected Works of Lonergan, 12).

Long, Charles H. 1986. *Significations: Signs, Symbols, and Images in the Interpretation of Religion*. Philadelphia: Fortress Press.

Louth, A. 1978. "The Hermeneutical Question Approached through the Fathers." *Sobornost* 7: 541–49.

MacEoin, Denis. 1994. *Rituals in Babism and Baha'ism*. London/New York: British Academic Press.

MacEoin, Denis. 1983. "From Babism to Baha'ism: Problems of Militancy, Quietism, and Conflation in the Construction of a Religion." *Religion* 13: 219–55.

MacGregor, G. 1973. *Philosophical Issues in Religious Thought*. Boston: Houghton Mifflin.

Maclean, A. J. 1905. "The East Syrian or Nestorian Rite: The Evening, Night, and Morning Services, with the Propria of the Liturgy, as Said on the Feast of the Epiphany, from the Gaza [*sic*] of the Library of the Propaganda Fide in Rome." In Conybeare and Maclean 1905, 298–388

Macomber, William F. 1970. "A List of the Known Manuscripts of the Chaldean Ḥuḏrā." *Orientalia Christiana Periodica* 36: 120–34.

Madey, J., and G. Kaniarakath, eds. 1984. *The Church I Love. A Tribute to Rev. Placid J. Podipara CMI*. Kottayam.

Manna, Jacques Eugène. 1982. *Morceaux choisis de littérature araméenne*. Mossoul: Imp. des Pères dominicains, 1901–1902. Reprinted: Doctinchem, Holland: Microlibrary Slangenburg Abbey.

Mardin, Şerif. 1962. *The Genesis of Young Ottoman Thought*. Princeton: Princeton University Press.

Margoliouth, D. S. 1903. "Early Documents in the Persian Language." *Journal of the Royal Asiatic Society*, 761–71.

Marsh, R. 1967. *Comparative Sociology: A Codification of Cross-Societal Analysis*. New York.

Martin, F. 1899/1900. "Memra on the Three Doctors Diodore, Theodore and Nestorius." *Journal Asiatique* 14 (1899): 446–92 (Syriac text); and 15 (1900): 469–525 (English trans.).

Martin, Luther H. 1996. "The New Comparativism in the Study of Religion. Introduction: The Post-Eliadean Study of Religion and the New Comparativism." *Method and Theory in the Study of Religion* 8.1: 1–2.

Martinez, F. 1987. "The Apocalyptic Genre in Syriac: The World of Pseudo-Methodius." In Drijvers et al. 1987, 337–52.

Mathews, Edward G., Jr., and Joseph P. Amar, trans. 1994a. *St. Ephrem the Syrian: Selected Prose Works*. Edited by Kathleen McVey. The Fathers of the Church, 91. Washington, D.C.: Catholic University of America Press.

Mathews, Edward G., Jr. 1994b. "St. Ephrem, Madrāšē on Faith, 81–85: Hymns on the Pearl, I–V." *St Vladimir's Theological Quarterly* 38.1: 45–72.

Mathews, Edward G., Jr. 1990. "'On Solitaries': Ephrem or Isaac?" *Le Muséon* 103: 91–110.

Mathews, Edward G., Jr. 1989. "The *Vita* Tradition of Ephrem the Syrian, the Deacon of Edessa." *Diakonia: Devoted to Promoting Eastern Christianity* 22 (1988–89): 15–42.

Māzandarānī, Asadu'llāh Fāżil. *Tarīkh-i Ẓuhūr al-Ḥaqq*. Vols. 4–5. Photocopy of MS in author's hands.

Mazzaoui, Michel M., and Vera B. Moreen, eds. 1992. *Intellectual Studies on Islam: Essays Written in Honor of Martin B. Dickson*. Salt Lake City: University of Utah Press.

McAuliffe, Jane Dammen. 1984. "Wines of Earth and Paradise: Qur'ānic Proscriptions and Promises." In Savoury and Agius 1984, 159–74.

McCarthy, Carmel, ed. and trans. 1993. *Saint Ephrem's Commentary: An English Translation of Chester Beatty MS 709 with Introduction and Notes*. Journal of Semitic Studies Supplement, 2. Oxford University Press.

McCullough, W. Stewart. 1982. *A Short History of Syriac Christianity to the Rise of Islam*. Chico, Calif.: Scholars Press.

McDannell, C., and B. Lang. 1988. *Heaven: A History*. New Haven: Yale University Press.

McGinn, B. et al. 1985. *Christian Spirituality: Origins to the Twelfth Century*. New York: Crossroad.

McLeod, Frederick, trans. 1979. *Narsai's Metrical Homilies on the Nativity, Epiphany, Passion, Resurrection and Ascension*. Patrologia Orientalis, tome 40, fasc. 1. Belgium: Brepols.

McVey, Kathleen, trans. 1989. *Ephrem the Syrian: Hymns*. New York: Paulist Press.

Messina, Giuseppe. *Diatessaron Persiano*. Rome: Pontificio Istituto

Biblico.

Metzger, Bruce. 1977. *Early Versions of the New Testament*. Oxford University Press.

Meyendorff, John. 1989. "Preface." In McVey 1989, 1–2.

Miller, D. 1984. "A Brief Historical and Theological Introduction to the Church of Persia to the End of the Seventh Century." In Holy Transfiguration Monastery 1984, 481–541.

Mitchell, C. W., ed. and trans. 1912. *S. Ephraim's Prose Refutations of Mānī, Marcion, and Bardaisan*. London: Text and Translation Society. Vol. 1.

Mitchell, L. 1973. "Four Fathers on Baptism: St. John Chrysostom, St. Ephrem, Theodore of Mopsuestia, Narsai." In Vellian 1973, 37–56.

Mojtabai, Fathulla. 1978. "Mānī and Shapur." *Journal of the K. R. Cama Oriental Institute* No. 46: 93–106.

Molenberg, C. 1990. "An Invincible Weapon. Names in the Christological Passages in Ephrem's 'Hymns on Faith' XLIX–LXV." In Lavenant 1990, 135–42.

Momen, Moojan, ed. 1988. *Studies in Honor of the Late Hasan M. Balyuzi*. Studies in the Bābī and Bahā'ī Religions, 5. Los Angeles: Kalimát Press.

Momen, Moojan, ed. 1987. *Selections from the Writings of E. G. Browne*. Oxford: George Ronald.

Momen, Moojan. 1981. *The Bābī and Bahā'ī Religions, 1844–1944: Some Contemporary Western Accounts*. Oxford: George Ronald.

Momen, Wendi, ed. 1989. *A Basic Bahā'ī Dictionary*. Oxford: George Ronald.

Monjazeb, Shahroakh. 1995. Provisional translation of Bahā'u'llāh's *Lawḥ-i Ittiḥād*. Unpublished,

Monjazeb, Shahroakh. 1993. "The Tablet of Bahā'u'llāh to Queen Victoria (*Lawḥ-i Malikih*): An Introductory Note and Completed Translation." *Bahā'ī Studies Bulletin* 7.3–4: 4–21.

Morony, Michael. 1990. "The Age of Conversions: A Reassessment." In Gervers and Bikhazi 1990, 135–50.

Morony, Michael. 1976. "The Effects of the Muslim Conquest on the Persian Population of Iraq." *Iran* 14.

Morony, Michael. 1974. "Religious Communities in Late Sasanian and Early Muslim Iraq." *Journal of the Economic and Social History of the Orient* 17: 113–35.

Mullen, E. 1980. *The Assembly of the Gods*. Harvard Semitic Monographs, 24. Chico: Scholars Press.

Murray, Robert. 1990. "Some Themes and Problems of Early Syriac Angelology." In Lavenant 1990, 143–53.

Murray, Robert. 1984. "The Origin of Aramaic 'ir, Angel." *Orientalia* 53: 303–17.

Murray, Robert. 1982. "The Characteristics of the Earliest Syriac Christianity." In Garsoïan et al. 1982, 3–16.

Murray, Robert. 1976. "The Theory of Symbolism in St. Ephrem's Theology." *Parole de l'Orient* 6–7 (1975–76): 1–20.

Murray, Robert. 1975b. "The Exhortation to Candidates for Ascetical Vows at Baptism in the Ancient Syriac Church." *New Testament Studies* 21 (1974–75): 59–80.

Murray, Robert. 1975a. *Symbols of Church and Kingdom: A Study in Early Syriac Tradition*. Cambridge University Press.

Murray, Robert. 1967. "Ephrem Syrus." In Crehan 1967, 220–23.

Murray, Robert. 1964. "The Rock and the House on the Rock: A Chapter in the Ecclesiological Symbolism of Aphraates and Ephrem." *Orientalia Christiana Analecta* 30: 315–62.

Murray, Robert. 1963. "St. Ephrem the Syrian on Church Unity." *Eastern Churches Quarterly* 15: 164–76.

Nagel, P. 1966. *Die Motivierung der Askese in der alten Kirche und der Ursprung des Mönchtums*. Berlin: Akademie-Verlag.

Nakhjavani, Bahiyyih. 1978. "Some Themes and Images in the Writings of Bahā'u'llāh." In *The Bahā'ī World* 16: 670–86. Haifa: Bahā'ī World Centre.

Nandrásky, K. 1980. "The Noetic Value of the Metaphoric Way of Expression in the Bible." *Communio Viatorum* 23.4: 211–27.

Nasr, Sayyid Hossein. 1972. "The Spiritual States in Sufism." In idem, *Sufi Essays*, 68–83. London: George Allen and Unwin.

National Spiritual Assembly of the Bahā'īs of Canada. 1983. *Bahā'ī Marriage and Family Life: Selections from the Writings of the Bahā'ī Faith*. Thornhill, Ontario: NSA of Canada.

Nedungatt, G. 1973. "The Covenanters of the Early Syriac-Speaking Church." *Orientalia Christiana Periodica* 39: 191–215; 419–44.

Neusner, Jacob. 1971. *Aphrahat and Judaism. The Christian-Jewish Argument in Fourth-Century Iran*. Studia Post-Biblica, 19. Leiden: E. J. Brill.

Neusner, Jacob. 1966. "The Conversion of Adiabene to Christianity." *Numen* 13: 144–50.

Nicholson, R. A., trans. 1967. *The Kashf al-Maḥjūb: The Oldest Persian Treatise on Sufiism* by al-Hujwīrī, 'Alī ibn 'Uthmān al-Jullābī. Leiden: E. J. Brill, 1911; repr. London: Luzac.

Norris, F., L. Wickham, and F. Williams. 1991. *Faith Gives Fullness to Reason: The Five Theological Orations of Gregory Nazianzen*. Supplements to *Vigiliae Christianae*, 13. Leiden: E. J. Brill.

Norris, F. 1990. "Bardesanes." In Ferguson 1990, 137.

Nurbakhsh, Javad. 1990. *Sufi Symbolism: The Nurbakhsh Encyclopedia of Sufi Terminology (Farhang-i Nurbakhsh)*. Vol. IV. *Symbolism of the Natural World*. London/New York: Khaniqahi-Nimatullahi Publications.

Olsen, G. 1977. "Allegory, Typology, and Symbol: The *Sensus Spiritalis*, Part 2: Early Church through Origen." *Communio* [US] 4: 357–84.

Ort, L. J. R. 1968. "Mānī, Manichaeism, 'Religionswissenschaft'." *Numen* 15: 191–207.

Ortiz de Urbina, I. 1955. "Le Paradis eschatologique d'après Saint Éphrem." *Orientalia Christiana Periodica* 21: 467–72.

Ortner, Sherry. 1984. "Theory in Anthropology Since the Sixties." *Comparative Studies in Society and History* 26.1: 126–66.

Ortner, Sherry. 1973. "On Key Symbols." *American Anthropologist* 75.5: 1338–46. Reprinted (slightly abridged) in Lessa and Vogt 1979, 92–98.

Ortony, Andrew, ed. 1979. *Metaphor and Thought*. Cambridge University Press.

Outtier, B. 1973. "Saint Ephrem d'après ses biographies et ses oeuvres." *Parole de l'Orient* 4: 11–33.

Oxtoby, Willard G., ed. 1996a. *World Religions: Western Traditions*. Toronto: Oxford University Press.

Oxtoby, Willard G., ed. 1996b. *World Religions: Eastern Traditions*. Toronto: Oxford University Press.

Oxtoby, Willard G. 1996c. "The Nature of Religion." In Oxtoby, 1996b, 487–506.

Oxtoby, Willard G. 1973. "Reflections on the Idea of Salvation." In Sharpe and Hinnells 1973, 17–38.

Paden, William E. 1996a. "Elements of a New Comparativism." *Method and Theory in the Study of Religion* 8.1: 5–14.

Paden, William E. 1996b. "A New Comparativism: Reply to the Panelists." *Method and Theory in the Study of Religion* 8.1: 37–49.

Paden, William. 1992. *Interpreting the Sacred: Ways of Viewing Religion*. Boston: Beacon Press.

Palmer, Andrew. 1993. "The Merchant of Nisibis: Saint Ephrem and His Faithful Quest for Union in Numbers." In Den Boeft and Hilhorst 1993, 167–233.

Paret, R. 1975. *Der Koran*. Darmstadt.

Parpola, Simo. 1993. "The Assyrian Tree of Life: Tracing the Origins of Jewish Monotheism and Greek Philosophy." *Journal of Near Eastern Studies* 52.3: 161–208.

Petersen, W. 1992. "The Christology of Aphrahat, the Persian Sage: An Excursus on the 17th Demonstration." *Vigiliae Christianae* 46: 241–56.

Pelikan, J. 1974. *The Christian Tradition*. Chicago.

Pelikan, J. 1961. *The Shape of Death*. Nashville: Abingdon Press.

Pepper, Stephen. 1984. "Metaphor in Philosophy." In *Dictionary of the History of Ideas*. Edited by Philip P. Wiener, 3: 196–201. New York: Charles Scribner's Sons.

Pepper, Stephen. 1942. *World Hypotheses*. Berkeley and Los Angeles: University of California Press.

Pierre, Marie-Joseph. 1988/1989. *Aphraates 'Les Exposés.'* 2 vols. Paris: Editions du Cerf.

Piper, Raymond Frank. 1944. "Ways to Wholeness." In *The Bahā'ī World* IX (1940–1944), 776–88.

Platvoet, J. 1982. *Comparing Religions: A Limitative Approach. An Analysis of Akan, Para-Creole, and Ifo-Sananda Rites and Prayers*. Religion and Reason, 24. The Hague: Mouton.

Poole, Fitz John Porter. 1986. "Metaphors and Maps: Towards Comparison in the Anthropology of Religion." *Journal of the American Academy of Religion* 54: 411–57.

Postlethwaite, Robert. 1994. "Queen Marie and the Bahā'ī Faith." *Journal of Bahā'ī Studies* 6.2: 55–86.

Pudichery, Sylvester. 1972. *Ramsa: An Analysis and Interpretation of the Chaldean Vespers*. India: Dharmaram College.

Puech, H.-C. 1979. *Sur le Manichéisme et autres essais*. Paris.

Pye, Michael. 1994. "Religion: Shape and Shadow." *Numen* 41: 51–75.

Ramsey, I. T. 1969. "Paradox in Religion." In High 1969.

Rice, D. and P. Schofer. 1983. *Rhetorical Poetics: Theory and Practice of Figural and Symbolic Reading in Modern French Literature*. Madison: University of Wisconsin.

Richardson, Jane E. 1990. *Feminine Imagery of the Holy Spirit in the Hymns of St. Ephrem the Syrian*. Ph.D. diss., University of Edinburgh.

Ricoeur, Paul. 1979. *The Rule of Metaphor: Multidisciplinary Studies in the Creation of Meaning in Language*. Translated by R. Czerny et al. University of Toronto Press.

Ricoeur, Paul.1960. *The Symbolism of Evil*. Boston.

Rilliet, F. 1992a. "Ephrem the Syrian." In Berardino 1992, 1: 275–77.

Rilliet, F. 1992b. "Persia." In Berardino 1992, 2: 674–75.

Rilliet, F. 1992c. "Syriac." In Berardino 1992, 2: 809–11.

Rippin, Andrew. 1993. *Muslims: Their Religious Beliefs and Practices*. Vol. 2: *The Contemporary Period*. London and New York: Routledge.

Ritter, Helmut. 1976. *Das Meer der Seele: Gott, Welt und Mensch in den Geschicten Fariduddin 'Attars*. Leiden: E. J. Brill, 1955. 2d ed.

Ritter, Helmut. 1960. "'Aṭṭār," *Encyclopedia of Islam*. New Edition, 1: 752–55. Leiden: E. J. Brill.

Rosen, Baron Viktor. 1892a. "Poslanie: 'Blagiya Vesti'" [translation of the *Lawḥ-i Bishārāt*]. *Zapiski Vostochnago Otdeleniya Imperatorskago Russkago Arkheologiches-kago Obshestva* 7: 183–192.

Rosen, Baron Viktor. 1892b. "Eschche o poslanii 'Blagiya Vesti'" [more about the translation of the *Lawḥ-i Bishārāt*]. *Zapiski*

Vostochnago Otdeleniya Imperatorskago Russkago Arkheologicheskago Obshestva 7: 311–16.

Rudolph, Kurt. 1979. "The Position of Source Research in Religious Studies (*Religionswissenschaft*)." In Honko 1979, 98–109.

Russell, James R. 1982–. "Christianity. I. In Pre-Islamic Persia." In *Encyclopaedia Iranica*, 5: 523–28.

Sa'dī. 1964. *The Gulistan or Rose Garden*. Translated by E. Rahatsek. London.

Salmānī, Ustād Muḥammad-'Alī. 1982. *My Memories of Bahā'u'llāh by Ustād Muḥammad-'Alīy-i Salmānī, the Barber, with a selection of his poems*. Trans. Marzieh Gail. Los Angeles: Kalimát Press.

al-Sarrāj, Abū Naṣr. 1914. *Kitāb al-Luma' fi't-Taṣawwuf* (Book of the Flashes on Sufism). Edited by R. A. Nicholson. Gibb Memorial Series, no. 22. Leiden/London.

Säve-Söderbergh, T. 1949. *Studies in the Coptic Manichaean Psalm Book*. Uppsala.

Savory, R. M. and D. A. Agius, eds. 1984. *Logos Islamikos*. Toronto: Pontifical Institute of Mediaeval Studies.

Schaefer, Udo. 1992. *Beyond the Clash of Religions: The Emergence of a New Paradigm*. Prague: Zero Palm Press.

Schaefer, Udo. 1983. *The Imperishable Dominion: The Bahā'ī Faith and the Future of Mankind*. Oxford: George Ronald.

Schimmel, Annemarie. 1994. *Deciphering the Signs of God: A Phenomenological Approach to Islam*. Albany: State University of New York Press.

Schimmel, Annemarie. 1992a. *A Two-Colored Brocade: The Imagery of Persian Poetry*. Chapel Hill: University of North Carolina Press.

Schimmel, Annemarie. 1992b. "Mystical and Sufi Brotherhoods." In idem, *Islam: An Introduction*. Albany: State University of New York Press.

Schimmel, Annemarie. 1982. *As Through a Veil: Mystical Poetry in Islam*. New York: Columbia University Press.

Schimmel, Annemarie. 1975. *Mystical Dimensions of Islam*. Chapel Hill: University of North Carolina Press.

Schimmel, Annemarie. 1958. "Rose und Nachtigall." *Numen* 5.2: 85–109.

Schmidt, M. 1989. "Alttestamentliche Typologien in den Paradieshymnen von Ephräm den Syrer." In *Paradeigmata: Literarische Typologie des Alten Testament*, 55–82. Berlin: Ducker und Humbolt.

Schmidt, M., and C. Geyer, eds. 1982. *Typus, Symbol, Allegorie bei den östlichen Vätern und aren Parallelen im Mittelalter*. Eichstatt: Regensburg.

Scholl, Steven, ed. 1984. *Waging Peace: Selections from the Bahā'ī Writings on Universal Peace*. Los Angeles: Kalimát Press.

Schoonenberg, P. 1967. "Presence and Eucharistic Presence." *Cross Currents* 17: 39–54.

Schütz, Edmond. 1990. "Armenia: A Christian Enclave in the Islamic Near East in the Middle Ages." In Gervers and Bikhazi 1990, 217–36.

Séd, N. 1968. "Les hymns sur le Paradise de Saint Éphrem et les traditions Juives." *Le Muséon* 81: 455–501.

Segal, J. B. 1983. "A Note on a Mosaic from Edessa." *Syria* 60: 107–10.

Segal, J. B. 1970. *Edessa, "The Blessed City."* Oxford: Oxford University Press.

Sells, Michael A. 1994. "Ibn 'Arabī's Garden Among the Flames: The Heart Receptive of Every Form." In idem, *Mystical Languages of Unsaying*, 90–115. Chicago/London: University of Chicago Press.

Shaked, Shaul. 1994. *Dualism in Transformation: Varieties of Religion in Sasanian Iran*. Jordan Lectures in Comparative Religion, XVI. London: School of Oriental and African Studies.

Shaked, Shaul. 1982. "Middle Persian Translations of the Bible." In *Encyclopaedia Iranica*, 4: 206–207.

Shaked, Shaul. 1970. "Specimens of Middle Persian Verse." In Boyce and Gershevitch 1970, 395–404.

Sharpe, E. J., and J. R. Hinnells, eds. 1973. *Man and His Salvation*. Manchester University Press.

Shoghi Effendi. 1981. *The Unfolding Destiny of the British Bahā'ī Community*. London: Bahā'ī Publishing Trust.

Shoghi Effendi. 1980. *The Promised Day Is Come*. Wilmette: Bahā'ī Publishing Trust [1941].

Shoghi Effendi. 1974. *The World Order of Bahā'u'llāh: Selected Letters of Shoghi Effendi*. 2d rev. ed. Wilmette: Bahā'ī Publishing Trust.

Shoghi Effendi. 1971. *The Advent of Divine Justice*. 3d ed. Wilmette: Bahā'ī Publishing Trust.

Shoghi Effendi. 1970. *God Passes By*. Wilmette: Bahā'ī Publishing Trust [1944].

Shoghi Effendi. 1926. *Prayer of Bahā'u'llāh. Prayers and Tablets of 'Abdu'l-Bahā*. New York: Bahā'ī Publishing Committee.

Shoghi Effendi, trans. 1922. "'Song of the Holy Mariner' Revealed by His Holiness Baha 'Ullah" [*sic*]. *Star of the West* 13.4 (May 17, 1922): 75–77. Translation received in April 1922.

Sims-Williams, Nicholas. "Sogdian Translations of the Bible." In *Encyclopaedia Iranica* 4: 207.

Sims-Williams, Nicholas. 1982. "Christian Literature in Middle Iranian Languages." In *Encyclopaedia Iranica*, 5: 534–35.

Sjöberg, G. 1955. "The Comparative Method in the Social Sciences." *Philosophy of Science* 22: 106–17.

Skalmowski, W. 1992. "The 'Seven Valleys' of 'Aṭṭār." *Orientalia Lovaniensia Periodica* 23: 281–302.

Skjaervo, P. O. 1982. "Bardesanes." In *Encyclopaedia Iranica* 3: 780–85.

Slusser, Michael. 1983. "Primitive Christian Soteriological Themes." *Theological Studies* 44: 555–69.

Smart, Ninian. 1995. *The World's Religions: Old Traditions and Modern Transformations*. Cambridge: Cambridge University Press.

Smart, Ninian. 1986a. "The Philosophy of Worldviews: The Philosophy of Religion Transformed." In Smart 1986c, 72–85. Reprinted from *Neue Zeitschrift für systematische Theologie und Religionsphilosophie* 23 (1981): 212–24.

Smart, Ninian. 1986b. "The Comparative Logical Analysis of Religious Doctrines." In Smart 1986c, 9–10. Reprinted from the proceedings of the VIIIth IAHR Congress held in Rome (April, 1955); *The Sacral Kingship*. Studies in the History of Religion, 4; Leiden: E. J. Brill, 1959.

Smart, Ninian. 1986c. *Concept and Empathy: Essays in the Study of Religion*. Edited by Donald Wiebe. London: Macmillan.

Smart, Ninian. 1985. *Worldviews: Crosscultural Explorations of Human Beliefs*. New York: Charles Scribner's Sons.

Smith, Jonathan Z. 1990. *Drudgery Divine: On Comparison of Early Christianities and the Religions of Late Antiquity*. Chicago: University of Chicago Press.

Smith, Jonathan Z. 1982a. *Imagining Religion: From Babylon to Jonestown*. Chicago: University of Chicago Press.

Smith, Jonathan Z. 1982b. "In Comparison a Magic Dwells." In Smith 1982a, 19–35.

Smith, Jonathan Z. 1982c. "The Bare Facts of Ritual." In Smith 1982a, 53–65.

Smith, Margaret. 1928. *Rābi'a the Mystic and Her Fellow Saints in Islam*. Cambridge: Cambridge University Press.

Smith, Morton. 1982. "Persian Elements in the Bible." In *Encyclopaedia Iranica* 4: 200–203.

Smith, Peter. 1987. *The Babi and Baha'i Religions: From Messianic Shi'ism to a World Religion*. Cambridge: Cambridge University Press.

Smith, Wilfred Cantwell. 1969. "Comparative Religion: Whither—and Why?" In Kitigawa and Eliade 1969, 31–58.

Snyder, G. 1985. *Ante Pacem: Archaeological Evidence of Church Life Before Constantine*. Macon, Ga.: Mercer University Press.

Špidlík, T. 1986. *The Spirituality of the Christian East: A Systematic Handbook*. Translated by A. Gythiel. Kalamazoo, Mich.: Cistercian Publications.

Spinks, B. 1991. *The Sanctus in the Eucharistic Prayer*. Cambridge: Cambridge University Press.

Sprengling, M. 1916. "Antonius Rhetor on Versification." *American*

Journal of Semitic Languages 32: 196–202

Starnes, C. 1990. *Augustine's Conversion: A Guide to the Argument of Confessions I–IX*. Waterloo: Wilfred Laurier University Press.

Steingass, F. 1977 [1892]. *Persian–English Dictionary*. London: Routledge and Kegan Paul.

Stewart, C. 1991. *'Working the Earth of the Heart': The Messalian Controversy in History, Texts, and Language to AD 431*. Oxford University Press.

Stirnemann, Alfred, and Gerhard Wilflinger, eds. 1994. *Syriac Dialogue: First Non-Official Consultation on Dialogue within the Syrian Tradition, with Focus on the Theology of the Church of the East*. Vienna: Pro Oriente.

Stockman, Robert. 1996a. "The Bahā'ī Faith and Syncretism." In Stockman 1996b, 119–21.

Stockman, Robert. 1996b. *A Curriculum Guide for the Bahā'ī Faith*. Edition 6.0. Wilmette: Research Office, Bahā'ī National Center.

Stone, Michael E. 1979. "A Persian-Armenian Manuscript in the Leeds Collection." In *Le Muséon* 92: 361–67.

Stopford, Joseph T. Sarsfield, trans. 1898. "The Nisibene Hymns." In *A Select Library of Nicene and Post-Nicene Fathers of the Christian Church*, Vol. 13: 165–219. New York: Christian Literature Company.

Strange, C. 1985. "Athanasius on Divinization." *Studia Patristica* 16: 342–46.

Stroumsa, G. 1986. "'Seal of the Prophets': The Nature of a Manichaean Metaphor." *Jerusalem Studies in Arabic and Islam* 7: 61–74.

Subtelny, Maria Eva, ed. 1994a. *Annemarie Schimmel Festschrift*. *Journal of Turkish Studies* 18.

Subtelny, Maria Eva. 1994b. "The Cult of 'Abdullāh Anṣārī under the Timurids." In Giese and Bürgel 1994, 377–406.

Sundermann, Werner. 1982a. "Bēma." In *Encyclopaedia Iranica* 4: 136–37.

Sundermann, Werner. 1982b. "Cosmogony and Cosmology III. In Manicheism." In *Encyclopaedia Iranica* 6: 310–15

Sundermann, Werner. 1982c. "Christ in Manichaeism." In *Encyclopaedia Iranica* 5: 535–39.

Sunquist, William. 1990. *Narsai and the Persians: A Study in Cultural Contact and Conflict*. Ph.D. diss., Princeton Theological Seminary. Abstracted in *Dissertations Abstracts International* 51.6 (Dec. 1990): 2055-A.

Taherzadeh, Adib. 1980. *The Revelation of Bahā'u'llāh*. Vol. 1. *Baghdād 1853–63*. Oxford: George Ronald [1974].

Taherzadeh, Adib. 1986. *The Revelation of Bahā'u'llāh*. Vol. 2. *Adrianople 1863–68*. Oxford: George Ronald [1977].

Taherzadeh, Adib. 1984. *The Revelation of Bahā'u'llāh*. Vol. 3. *'Akkā, The Early Years 1868–77*. Oxford: George Ronald [1983].

Taherzadeh, Adib. 1988. *The Revelation of Bahā'u'llāh*. Vol. 4. *Mazra'ih and Bahjī 1877–92*. Oxford: George Ronald [1987].

Talmon, S. 1991. "The 'Comparative Method' in Biblical Interpretation—Principles and Problems." In Greenspahn 1991, 381–419.

Taylor, John. 1990. "The Future of Christianity" (chapter 19). In *The Oxford Illustrated History of Christianity*. Edited by John McManners. Oxford/New York: Oxford University Press.

Terrien, S. 1978. *The Elusive Presence*. San Francisco.

Theodoret of Cyrrhus. 1985. *A History of the Monks of Syria*. Translated by R. Price. Kalamazoo, Mich.: Cisterian Publications.

Thomas, Kenneth J. 1982. "Chronology of Translations of the Bible." In *Encyclopaedia Iranica*, 4: 203–206.

Thomas, Kenneth J., and Fereydun Vahman. 1982. "Persian Translations of the Bible." In *Encyclopaedia Iranica*, 4: 209–13.

Thompson, L. 1990. "The Literary Unity of the Book of Revelation." In *Mappings of the Biblical Terrain: The Bible as Text*. Edited by V. Tollers and J. Maie, 347–63. Lewisburg: Bucknell University Press.

Torjesen, K. 1986. *Hermeneutical Procedure and Theological Method in Origen's Exegesis*.

Torrance, T. F. 1995. *Divine Meaning: Studies in Patristic Hermeneutics*. Edinburgh: Clark.

Turner, Victor. 1974. *Dramas, Fields, and Metaphors: Symbolic Action in Human Society*. Ithaca: Cornell University Press.

Underhill, Evelyn. 1961. *Mysticism: A Study on the Nature and Development of Man's Spiritual Consciousness*. London, 1911; repr. New York: E. P. Dutton.

Universal House of Justice. 1991. *Compilation of Compilations*. 2 vols. Compiled by the Research Department of the Universal House of Justice. Victoria: Bahā'ī Publications Australia.

Universal House of Justice. 1986. *Women*. Compiled by the Research Department of the Universal House of Justice. Oakham: Bahā'ī Publishing Trust.

Universal House of Justice, trans. 1981. "Tablets of the Hair." Authorized,unpublished translation of selected texts of Bahā'u'llāh.

Vellian, J., ed. 1973. *Studies on Syrian Baptismal Rites*. Kottayam: CMS Press.

Vööbus, Arthur. 1988. *History of Asceticism in the Syrian Orient: A Contribution to the History of Culture in the Near East* Vol. 3. CSCO 500, Subsidia 81; Louvain: Corpus Scriptorum Christianorum Orientalium.

Vööbus, Arthur. 1982. "Bābay the Great." In *Encyclopaedia Iranica*, 3: 308.

Vööbus, Arthur. 1965. *History of the School of Nisibis*. CSCO 266. Louvain.

Vööbus, Arthur. 1961. "The Institution of the *benai qeiama* and *benat qeiama* in the Ancient Syrian Church." *Church History* 30: 19–27.

Vööbus, Arthur. 1958. "Manichaeism and Christianity in Persia under the Sasanids: Some Notes on Manichaean Ecclesiology and Its Background." *Yearbook of the Estonian Learned Society of America* (1954–58): 2: 7–13.

Vööbus, Arthur. 1947. *A Letter of Ephrem to the Mountaineers: A Literary-Critical Contribution to Syriac Patristic Literature. Contributions of the Baltic University* 25. Hamburg-Pinneberg.

Walbridge, John. 1996. *Sacred Acts, Sacred Space, Sacred Time*. Bahā'ī Studies, 1. Oxford: George Ronald.

Warburg, M. 1991. "The Circle, the Brotherhood, and the Ecclesiastical Body: Bahā'ī in Denmark, 1925–1987." In Geertz and Jensen 1991, 201–21.

Wansbrough, John. 1977. *Quranic Studies: Sources and Methods of Scriptural Interpretation*. Oxford: Oxford University Press.

Wansbrough, John. 19 . *The Sectarian Milieu*. Oxford: Oxford University Press.

Watson, W. 1984. *Classical Hebrew Poetry: A Guide to Its Techniques*. Journal for the Study of the Old Testament Supplement Series, 26. University of Sheffield.

Weber, Max. 1950. *The Protestant Ethic and the Spirit of Capitalism*. London.

Weber, O. 1981. *Foundations of Dogmatics*. Grand Rapids: Eerdmans.

Wehr, Hans. 1973. *A Dictionary of Modern Written Arabic*. Edited by J. Milton Cowan. Ithaca: Spoken Language Services, Inc., 3d ed.

Wheelwright, P. 1962. *Metaphor and Reality*. Bloomington: Indiana University Press.

Wheelwright, P. 1960. "Semantics and Ontology." In Knight and Cottle 1960, 1–9.

Widengren, Geo. 1984. "The Nestorian Church in Sasanian and Early Post-Sasanian Iran." In Lanciotti 1984, 1–30.

Widengren, Geo. 1960. "The Fate of the Soul after Death." *Orientalia Suecana* 9: 102–106.

Widengren, Geo. 1946. *Mesopotamian Elements in Manichaeism*. Uppsala.

Widengren, Geo. 1945. "The Great Vohu Mana and the Apostle of God." In *Uppsala Universitets Arsskrift*.

Wiebe, Donald. 1996. "Is the New Comparativism Really New?" *Method and Theory in the Study of Religion* 8.1: 21–29.

Wiebe, Donald. 1989. "*Explaining Religion:* The Intellectual Ethos." *Religion* 19: 305–309.

Wiebe, Donald. 1988. "Why the Academic Study of Religion? Motive and Method in the Study of Religion." *Religious Studies* 24: 403–13.

Wiessner, Gernot. "Christlicher Heiligenkult im Umkreis eines sassanidischen Grosskönigs." In Eilers 1971, 141–55.

Wiles, Maurice. 1967. *The Making of Christian Doctrine*. Cambridge: Cambridge University Press.

Wilkinson, J. 1971. *Egeria's Travels*. London: Society for Promoting Christian Knowledge.

Williams, A. V. 1996. "Zoroastrians and Christians in Sasanian Iran." *Bulletin of the John Rylands University Library of Manchester* 78.3: 23–35.

Williams, M. 1985. *The Immovable Race: A Gnostic Designation and the Theme of Stability in Late Antiquity*. Leiden: E. J. Brill.

Winslow, David. 1984. "Soteriological 'Orthodoxy' in the Fathers." In *Studia Patristica* 15: 393–95.

Wolfson, H. A. 1956. "Immortality and Resurrection in the Philosophy of the Church Fathers." *Harvard Divinity Bulletin* 21 (1955–56): 5–36. Reprinted in Wolfson 1961, 69–103.

Wolfson, H. A. 1961. *Religious Philosophy: A Group of Essays*. Cambridge: Harvard University Press.

Wright, W. C., trans. 1923. *The Works of Emperor Julian*. London: Loeb Classical Library.

Yamauchi, Edwin. 1977. "Manichaeans." In *Eerdmans Handbook to the History of Christianity*. Grand Rapids, Mich.: Eerdmans, 48–49.

Yarshater, Ehsan, ed. 1984–. *Encyclopaedia Iranica*. Boston: Routledge and Kegan Paul; Costa Mesa, Ca.: Mazda.

Yarshater, Ehsan, ed. 1983. *The Cambridge History of Iran*, volume 3 (2): *The Seleucid, Parthian and Sasanian Periods*. Cambridge: Cambridge University Press.

Younger, K., Jr. 1990. "The Figurative Aspect and the Contextual Method in the Evaluation of the Solomonic Empire (1 Kings 1–11)." In Clines 1990, 157–75.

Yousif, P. 1984. "Approaches to Divine Realities in the Thought of St Ephrem of Nisibis." In Madey and Kaniarakath 1984, 54–69.

Yousif, P. 1978a. "St. Ephrem on Symbols in Nature: Faith, the Trinity and the Cross (Hymns on Faith, No. 18)." *Eastern Churches Review* 10 (1978): 52–60.

Yousif, P. 1978b. "Symbolisme Christologique dans la Bible et dans la Nature chez S. Ephrem de Nisibe." *Parole de l'Orient* 8 (1977–78): 5–66.

Yousif, P. 1976. "Symbol and Reality in St. Ephrem" [in Arabic]. *Bayn al-Nahrayn* 16.4: 435–48.

Index

D

T